BIOGRAPHICAL DICTIONARY
OF
AMERICAN LABOR LEADERS

Biographical Dictionary of American Labor Leaders

Editor-in-Chief
Gary M Fink

Advisory Editor
Milton Cantor

Contributing Editors
John Hevener
Merl E. Reed
Donald G. Sofchalk
Marie Tedesco

Greenwood Press
Westport, Connecticut ● London, England

Library of Congress Cataloging in Publication Data

Fink, Gary M
  Biographical dictionary of American labor leaders.

  1. Labor and laboring clases—United States—
Biography. I. Title
HD8073.A1F56   331.88′092′2 [B]   74-9322
ISBN 0-8371-7643-3

Library of Congress Catalog Card Number: 74-9322
ISBN: 0-8371-7643-3
First published in 1974

Second printing 1975

Greenwood Press, a division of Williamhouse-Regency Inc.
51 Riverside Avenue, Westport, Connecticut 06880

Manufactured in the United States of America

Consultant Editors

Maurice F. Neufeld, Professor of Industrial and Labor Relations, New York State School of Industrial and Labor Relations, Cornell University

Edward Pessen, Distinguished Professor of History, Baruch College and the Graduate Center, The City University of New York

Howard Quint, Professor of History, University of Massachusetts, Amherst

Leon Stein, Editor, *Justice*

Philip Taft, Professor Emeritus, Brown University

Leo Troy, Professor of Economics, Rutgers University

Warren R. Van Tine, Assistant Professor of History, Ohio State University

This volume is dedicated to those labor leaders who devoted their lives to the quest for social and economic justice in America.

Contents

Preface

This volume contains career biographies of approximately five hundred men and women who have had a significant impact on the American labor movement. It is made up of a diverse and interesting group. An eye-setter in a doll factory, a steelworker, and a pioneer aviator exemplify the variety of occupations of those included. Diversity also characterizes their socio-economic backgrounds and their career patterns. There are, for example, biographical sketches of a Supreme Court justice, a state governor, several cabinet officers, senators, congressmen, ambassadors, and mayors. The volume also includes those whose trade union careers ended in disgrace or in prison, and a few who lived out their final days as destitute residents of skid row. Some of the individuals included are well-known, but many others are unknown to all but the most dedicated students of the American labor movement.

The first major task in writing this *Biographical Dictionary* was selecting the five hundred figures to be included from the thousands of men and women who led or were closely associated with the labor movement in the United States. It was not an easy task, and the decisions that were made undoubtedly will not satisfy everyone, if indeed anyone! Nevertheless the number of leaders included had to be limited, and criteria were established to guide and facilitate the selection process. It was determined that each individual included in the *Biographical Dictionary* should have had a substantial impact on the American labor movement in one way or another. However, labor leaders whose significance was limited to local, state, or regional organizations were included as well as leaders of national or international unions. It was also considered important to include a broad sampling of leaders from different eras, from as many different industries, crafts, and trades as possible, and from among those women, Afro-Americans, and Chicanos whose contributions to the labor movement were largely ignored until recently. Although the emphasis was on leaders of the trade-union movement, an effort was made to include a representative group of labor-oriented radicals, politicians, editors, staff members, lawyers, reformers, and intellectuals.

In some cases those originally selected for inclusion had to be dropped because sufficient biographical information was lacking. Biographies of persons like Alfred Phelps, Homer Call, and Michael Casey certainly qualified for inclusion, but they were deleted because basic biographical information was unavailable and other comparable leaders could be substituted in their place. But in some instances, most of them concerning early-19th-century leaders, such substitutions were not possible or advisable.

Without the availability of *Who's Who in Labor*, published in cooperation with the American Federation of Labor in 1946, and Solon DeLeon's *The American Labor Who's Who*, published in 1925, the task of collecting basic biographical information would have been enormously more difficult. Many labor leaders were reticent individuals who shunned publicity. Few of them made a major effort to save personal papers or to record the significant events in their lives for posterity. Moreover, in our efforts to acquire biographical information, only a few of the many international unions responded to our correspondence. In some instances, the individuals themselves were uncertain about specific details of their lives. For example, after several conflicting birthdates were discovered for one leader, it was learned that he himself was unsure of the precise date. Samuel Gompers, who was uncertain as to whether he had 12 or 14 children, further illustrates the problem.

The Biographical Dictionary of American Labor Leaders is the second in a projected series of biographical dictionaries to be published by Greenwood Press. The first was Robert Sobel's *Biographical Directory of the United States Executive Branch, 1774-1971*.

The general format and style used in the Sobel *Directory* were followed in this volume. The biographies include significant dates in the subject's life; relevant family information, including father's occupation; religious and political preferences when known; trade-union affiliations; and offices held, both public and private. Each biography also includes bibliographical references to guide the reader who desires more detailed information. The vast majority of references cited contain additional information on the subject of the biography; in the few cases where published material dealing with the subject does not exist, sources were given that provide useful background information. In writing the sketches, an effort was made to maintain a uniform length, but, owing to the availability of information, some variance inevitably occurred. In no case should the length of the sketch be taken as an indication of relative importance. Some of the individuals included in the *Dictionary* were involved in a great variety of different union, reform, and political movements. Although this lengthened their biographies, it does not necessarily increase their significance.

Numerous individuals contributed in a variety of ways to the completion of this volume. With only minor changes, the sketches of James Davis, William Doak, Martin Durkin, Arthur Goldberg, and William Wilson were taken from the Sobel *Directory*. The scholars listed on the Consultant Editors page reviewed preliminary lists of labor leaders in their areas of specialized interest and read the finished sketches. C.L. Coburn, UAW; Stanley L. Johnson, Illinois AFL-CIO; David Selden, AFT; Al Shipka, Greater Youngstown AFL-CIO; Lazare Teper, ILGWU; Catharine B. Williams, ACWA; and Elmer T. Kehrer, John Wright, and Charles C. Mathias, Atlanta AFL-CIO, all responded generously to requests for assistance.

The following individuals either reviewed preliminary lists, previewed selected sketches, or contributed information: Louis Cantor, Jules Chametsky, Helen Elwell, Wayne Flint, Harvey Friedman, Ernesto Galarza, George Green, Alice Kessler Harris, Mark Kahn, Daniel Leab, David B. Lipsky, Garth Mangum, F. Ray Marshall, Mark Perlman, James R. Prickett, Ronald Radosh, Mark Reisler, Stephen Vladeck, and Merle W. Wells. Those of us in Atlanta owe a special thanks to Jane Hobson and her reference department staff at the Georgia State University Library. The Georgia State University School of Arts and Science and Joseph O. Baylen, Chairman of the Department of History, assisted the editor by providing release time from teaching and research assistance. Mary B. Fink read and revised many of the sketches, did much of the proofreading, and aided in drawing up the appendices. Finally, Robert Hagelstein of the Greenwood Press provided valuable ideas and advice, useful criticism, and timely encouragement.

Gary M Fink
  Atlanta, Ga.

January, 1974

Milton Cantor
  Amherst, Mass.

BIOGRAPHICAL DICTIONARY
OF
AMERICAN LABOR LEADERS

Biographies

ABEL, Iorwith Wilber. Born in Magnolia, Ohio, August 11, 1908; son of John, a blacksmith, and Mary Ann (Jones) Abel; Lutheran; married Bernice N. Joseph on June 27, 1930; three children; graduated from Magnolia (Ohio) High School and Canton Actual Business College; went to work as a molder in 1925; helped organize the first Congress of Industrial Organizations (CIO) local at Canton Timkin Roller Bearing in 1936 and served as its president; participated in the "Little Steel" strike of 1937; after serving as a union staff representative, elected director of the Canton District of the United Steelworkers of America (USWA) in 1942; served as a panel member on the War Labor Board during World War II; was an active member of the CIO Political Action Committee and the Ohio CIO Council; after the death of Philip Murray (q.v.) in 1952, elected secretary-treasurer of the USWA, succeeding David J. McDonald (q.v.) who became president; after loyally supporting McDonald for the next decade, became disturbed by his soft bargaining approach to the steel industry; aware of members' dissatisfaction with recent contracts that substituted fringe benefits for wage increases and ignored local issues, decided to challenge McDonald for the USWA presidency in 1965; unpretentious, a former steelworker who had moved up through the union hierarchy, was an excellent candidate to run against an incumbent under fire for allegedly losing sight of rank-and-file interests; promising to revive militant bargaining, to seek a general wage increase, and to restore rank-and-file control over basic union policy, and with the backing of several key USWA district directors, won by a 10,000-vote margin; elected an American Federation of Labor (AFL)-CIO vice-president and executive council member in 1965; was chosen president of the AFL-CIO industrial union department in 1968; as USWA president, tolerated dissent by staff and unfettered debate of controversial issues at conventions; encouraged greater participation by nonwhites in union affairs and in leadership positions, and acted to eliminate racial job discrimination in steel industry; presided over mergers of the International Union of Mine, Mill and Smelter Workers with District 50, Allied and Technical Workers; working through the USWA executive board beginning in 1967, sought a means of ending the boom-bust cycle created by stockpiling of steel in anticipation of steel strikes; instrumental in signing in March, 1973, by the USWA and the basic steel firms of a milestone experimental negotiating agreement providing for binding arbitration of unresolved national contract issues, thus precluding industry-wide strikes for the life of the four-year agreement; appointed an alternate representative of the U.S. delegation to the United Nations in 1967; served on the National Advisory Commission on Civil Disorders; appointed to the pay board of the National Stabilization Program in 1971, but resigned in 1972 in protest against board policy; participated in several international labor conferences; a fervent Democrat; was close to the Lyndon B. Johnson administration and helped nominate Hubert H. Humphrey as Democratic presidential candidate in 1968, but refused to support Democratic presidential candidate Sen. George S. McGovern in 1972; Lloyd Ulman, *The Government of the Steelworkers Union* (1962); John Herling, *Right to Challenge: People and Power in the Steelworkers Union* (1972); *Who's Who in Labor* (1946); *Current Biography* (1965).

(D.G.S.)

ADDES, George P.   Born in LaCrosse, Wis., August 26, 1910; son of Nicholas, a maintenance worker, and Mary Addes; Roman Catholic; married Victoria Rose Joseph on September 16, 1933; completed two years of high school; secured employment with the Willys-Overland Company in Toledo, Ohio, in 1923; later completed one year at the Wayne University Law School; joined an American Federation of Labor federal labor union in Toledo in 1933, which shortly thereafter became a local of the United Automobile, Aircraft, and Agricultural Implement Workers of America (UAW) and soon elected financial secretary of the local; involved in the 1934 Auto-Lite strike and the 1935 Chevrolet strike in Toledo; elected secretary-treasurer of the UAW in 1936 and served in that capacity until 1947; served on the Congress of Industrial Organizations (CIO) executive board and was a member of the CIO Political Action Committee; during World War II, served as a special labor mediator for the National War Labor Board; was one of the principal leaders of the left-wing, Addes-Rolland J. Thomas (q.v.)-Richard Leonard (q.v.) faction of the UAW that was defeated by Walter P. Reuther's (q.v.) faction in the union elections of 1947; defeated for reelection as secretary-treasurer in 1947; left trade union activities and became a tavern operator; supported the Democratic party; Jack Stieber, *Governing the UAW* (1962); Frank Cormier and William J. Eaton, *Reuther* (1970); Jean Gould and Lorena Hickok, *Walter Reuther: Labor's Rugged Individualist* (1972); Sidney Fine, *The Automobile Under the Blue Eagle: Labor, Management, and the Automobile Manufacturing Code* (1963).

ALLEN, William L.   Born in Comnock, Ontario, Canada, April 17, 1896; son of Gerard, a teamster, and Mary (Cripps) Allen; married Ruth Delilah Smithburg on July 15, 1932; one child; left school in 1908 to begin a career as a telegrapher, starting as a messenger and shortly thereafter became a Morse operator; served with Canadian forces in France and Belgium during World War I; after the war, resumed his occupation as a telegrapher and joined the Canadian branch of the Commercial Telegraphers Union (CTU), which represented all Western Union employees except those in New York City; during the 1920s, opposed efforts of those CTU members on the Canadian National General Committee to disaffiliate with the CTU and form an independent union; became chairman of the Western District of the CTU's Canadian Division No. 43 in 1928, and in this capacity served as local chairman, organizer, and international representative in Canada; also elected international secretary-treasurer of the CTU in 1928, serving until 1941, when elected international president of the CTU; attended several American Federation of Labor (AFL) conventions and served as a delegate to the Trades and Labor Congress convention in Canada in 1928; was a member of the AFL committees on education, transportation, and postwar planning; led the CTU in strikes against United Press in 1950 and Western Union in 1952; served as the editor of the *Commercial Telegraphers Journal*, 1928-1941; retired from union positions in 1963; died in Sun City Center, Fla., October 26, 1971; Vidkunn Ulriksson, *The Telegraphers: Their Craft and Their Unions* (1953); *Current Biography* (1953); *Who's Who in Labor* (1946).

ALPINE, John P.   Born in Boston, Mass., ca. 1868; Roman Catholic; married; three children; attended the public schools of Boston and served a trade apprenticeship, eventually joining Boston Gas Fitters' Union Local 175 of the United Association of Plumbers and Steamfitters of the United States and Canada (UA); after serving Local 175 in several capacities, including that of president, and after being president of the Building Trades Council of Boston and Vicinity for several years, became a member of the general executive board of the UA and, in 1904, was elected a vice-president, representing gas fitters; served as a special UA organizer, 1904-1906; in a close election, was selected as international president of the UA in 1906; as president, noted for the vigorous and effective introduction and administration of a radically new system of internal union government that had been drawn up shortly before his election, the strengthening of the union's organizing staff, and substantial gains in membership; was elected an American Federation of Labor vice-president and executive council member in 1908; was a member of the board of governors of the American Construction Council, presided over by Franklin D. Roosevelt; during World War I, served with Secretary of War Newton D. Baker on a commission that supervised labor relations at cantonments and aviation fields, with Assistant Secretary of Navy Franklin D. Roosevelt on a commission that oversaw labor relations at naval operations on shore, and with the War-Policies Board as a labor advisor; served as a labor advisor to the American delegation to the Paris Peace Conference in 1919; resigned union positions in 1919 to become an assistant to the president of the Grinell Company, Inc., a manufacturer of automatic sprinklers, and in 1920 also became chairman of the labor relations committee of the National Automatic Sprinkler and Fire Control Association; appointed as a special assistant to the Secretary of Labor in 1931 and placed in charge of the Federal Employment Service; attempted, with limited success, to find employment for the growing numbers of unemployed; politically a Republican; died in New York City, April 21, 1947; Martin Segal, *The Rise of the United Association: National Unionism in the Pipe Trades, 1884-1924* (1970); Philip Taft, *The A.F. of L. in the Time of Gompers* (1957); *The New York Times*, April 22, 1947.

ANDERSON, Mary.   Born in Lidköping, Sweden, August 27, 1872;

daughter of Magnus, a farmer, and Matilda Anderson; Lutheran; received a grammar school education in Sweden prior to emigrating to the United States in 1889; secured her first job in the United States as a dishwasher at a Michigan lumber camp; after holding various jobs, found employment around 1891 as a stitcher in a West Pullman, Ill., shoe factory; in 1894 joined the International Boot and Shoe Workers' Union (BSWU), while working for Schwab's in Chicago, Ill.; served as president of Stitchers Local 94, 1895-1910; was the only woman on the BSWU executive board for 11 years; served as the BSWU delegate to the Chicago Federation of Labor; joined the Chicago Women's Trade Union League (WTUL) about 1903; quit factory work in 1910 to become the Chicago WTUL representative to the United Garment Workers Union; during 1910-1913 served as an investigator to ensure that the agreement ending the Hart, Schaffner, and Marx strike of 1910 was carried out; while associated with the Chicago WTUL, served as a delegate to the Union Label League; was an organizer for the national WTUL, 1913-1920; participated in investigations of the 1913 copper miners' strike in Calumet, Mich., and the 1916 spar miners' strike in Rosiclare, Ill.; began a government career in 1916 when appointed assistant director of the Women in Industry Service of the U.S. Department of Labor and replaced Mary Van Kleeck as director in 1919; served in the Women in Industry Section of the Advisory Committee of the Council of National Defense and on the Women in Industry Section of the Ordnance Department during World War I; was director of the permanent Women's Bureau of the U.S. Department of Labor, 1920-1944; as a WTUL delegate, attended the labor conferences of the 1919 Paris Peace Conference, the 1919 First International Congress of Working Women in Washington, D.C., the 1923 Third International Congress of Working Women in Vienna, and the 1928 Pan-Pacific Union Conference in Honolulu, Hawaii; was the unofficial United States delegate to the 1931 International Labor Organization Conference in Geneva; appointed by President Franklin D. Roosevelt as an advisor to the U.S. delegation to the Technical Tripartite Conference on the Textile Industry; retired official positions in 1944; authored *Woman at Work: The Autobiography of Mary Anderson as told to Mary Winslow* (1951); died in Washington, D.C., January 30, 1964; Gladys Boone, *The Women's Trade Union Leagues in Great Britain and the United States* (1942); *AFL-CIO News*, February 8, 1964; *Current Biography* (1940).

(M.T.)

ANTONINI, Luigi.   Born in Vallata Irpina, Avellino, Italy, September

11, 1883; son of Pietro Valeriano, a school teacher, and Maria Francesca (Netta) Antonini; Roman Catholic; married Jennie Costanzo on October 24, 1909; graduated from secondary school in Tortona, Italy, then served as a sergeant in the Italian Army for four years; emigrated to the United States in 1908 and worked in a New York cigar factory for two years; worked in a piano factory, 1910-1912; became a dress presser in 1913 and joined the International Ladies' Garment Workers' Union (ILGWU); was one of the founders and initial executive board members of the Italian Chamber of Labor in 1913; became an organizer for ILGWU Local 25 in 1916; was instrumental in the organization of Italian Dressmakers Local 89, ILGWU, and served as its general secretary; one of the founders and vice-chairman of the Anti-Fascisti Alliance in 1922; during the controversy over organizing strategy in the mid-1930s, favored industrial organization and supported the efforts of ILGWU president David Dubinsky to mediate the conflict between the American Federation of Labor (AFL) and the Congress of Industrial Organizations (CIO); was elected president of the Italian-American Labor Council in 1941; served on a variety of public and private boards and agencies during World War II; following the war, served on the AFL delegation appointed to investigate the rebuilding of the Italian labor movement and to reestablish Italian-American labor relations; was first vice-president of the ILGWU, 1934-1967; was chairman of the American Labor party, 1936-1942, and was one of the founders of the Liberal party of New York in 1944; was a long-time editor of *L'Operaia*, an Italian language magazine sponsored by Local 25; retired from union activities in 1968; died in New York City, December 29, 1968; John Stuart Crawford, *Luigi Antonini, his influence on Italian American Relations* (1950); Benjamin Stolberg, *Tailor's Progress: The Story of a Famous Union and the Men Who Made It* (1944); Louis Levine, *The Women's Garment Workers: A History of the International Ladies' Garment Workers' Union* (1924); *ILGWU Report and Proceedings* (1971).

ARTHUR, Peter M.   Born in Paisley, Scotland, in 1831; emigrated to the United States in 1842; settled in New York state, working there on an uncle's farm; received little formal education; bought a horse while still a teenager and began an unsuccessful carting business in Schenectady, N.Y.; became an engine wiper in 1849 on a line which was soon incorporated into the New York Central Railroad; soon thereafter became a locomotive engineer; was a charter member of the Brotherhood of Locomotive Engineers (BLE) in 1863; elected grand chief engineer in 1874 and held this office until his death; was a conservative trade unionist who believed in the mutuality of interests between labor and capital; seldom called strikes, preferring to resolve disputes through conciliation and arbitration; while president, converted BLE from a largely benevolent and insurance society to an economic-oriented trade union; as grand chief engineer, staunchly defended the independence of the BLE and refused to affiliate with such organizations as the Knights of Labor, the American Federation of Labor, or the American Railroad Union; acquired considerable wealth through successful real-estate speculations in Cleveland; was an associate editor of *The Labor Movement: The Problem of Today* (1887); died in Winnipeg, Canada, July 17, 1903; Reed C. Richardson, *The Locomotive Engineer, 1863-1963: A Century of Railway Labor Relations and Work Rules* (1963); *Dictionary of American Biography* (Vol. I); *Encyclopedia of Social Sciences* (Vol. II).

AZPEITIA, Mario.   Born in Key West, Fla., November 22, 1899; son of Armando H. and Andrea (Esquinaldo) Azpeitia; Roman Catholic; married Rosalia Ciccarello on October 30, 1967; five children; attended San Carlos School in Key West, then eventually took a job in the cigar-making industry; joined Local 500 of the Cigarmakers' International Union (CMIU) in 1935; elected general secretary of Local 500 in 1941, serving in that capacity until 1949; elected international president of the CMIU in 1949, beginning a long and continuing term of service in that position; represented the CMIU at the annual conventions of the American Federation of Labor (AFL), 1949-1955, and the AFL-Congress of Industrial Organizations (CIO) since 1955; served on numerous AFL and AFL-CIO committees; a member of the Florida State Society in Washington, D.C., and Centro Español and Circulo Cubano in Tampa, Fla.; *Who's Who in America, 1958-1959*.

(M.E.R.)

BACON, Emery F.   Born in Indianapolis, Ind., May 1, 1909; son of Frank, an attorney, and Laura (Claason) Bacon; Presbyterian; married Helen Hotham in 1936; two children; attended Wooster College for a short time and later received a B.A. (1931) and an M.A. (1942) from the University of Pittsburgh; became a reporter for the McKeesport (Pa.) *Daily News* after receiving the B.A.; was a junior executive in business for a while during the early 1930s; became associated with the labor movement as a volunteer organizer for the Amalgamated Association of Iron, Steel, and Tin Workers during 1934-1935; became business manager and head of the classics department at a private Pennsylvania preparatory school in 1939, and saved it from bankruptcy; was a delegate at the founding convention of the United Steelworkers of America (USWA) in 1942; one of several intellectuals in the USWA and had a reputation of being a "practical realist;" was selected to head a program of worker education begun by USWA president Philip Murray (q.v.); in 1945 launched the union's pioneering Summer Labor Institutes for local union officers and rank-and-file members at regular colleges and universities; started at the Pennsylvania State University, by the 1950s the program was regularly held every summer at from 20 to 30 campuses across the United States and in Canada, offering sessions in labor history, economics, collective bargaining, and current issues like poverty and automation; guided start in 1962 of a 12-week resident program at a few state universities offering steelworkers credit courses; believed that the Institutes offered participants a means of increasing their ability to deal with "bread and butter" union matters and of participating more effectively in wider community affairs; was instrumental in initiating, in 1947, the USWA's highly successful scholarship program for the sons and daughters of steelworkers; union districts and larger locals provided an increasing number of scholarships, awarded on a competitive basis, for attendance at any accredited college or university; by 1961 a total of $700,000 in scholarships had been awarded; resigned as education director in 1964 to accept the post of assistant to the president of West Virginia University; a Democrat; ran unsuccessfully for Congress from Pennsylvania's 27th Congressional District; Lloyd Ulman, *The Government of the Steelworkers' Union* (1962); *Steel Labor*, May, 1961, April, 1965.

(D.G.S.)

BAER, Fred William.   Born in Kansas City, Mo., August 16, 1884; son of William Henry, a superintendent in a factory school, and Jenny Louise Baer; married Grace Marie Morgan on August 5, 1930; completed grammar school, then joined a fire fighters' survey group in Sonora, Calif.; joined the Kansas City Fire Department in 1907 and became a driver of the first motorized vehicle used in Kansas City; became a fire department lieutenant in 1917; retired from active service in 1919; organized Kansas City firemen into an American Federation of Labor (AFL) federal labor union in 1917 and was elected president of the federal local; participated in the organizational convention of the International Association of Fire Fighters (IAFF) called by AFL president Samuel Gompers (q.v.) in 1918; served as president of Kansas City Local 42 of the IAFF, 1918-1919; elected a vice-president in charge of the IAFF's third district in 1918;

elected international president of the IAFF in 1919, serving in that capacity until 1946; was actively involved in the organization of fire fighters in cities throughout the United States and in the campaign for an eight-hour day for firemen; was credited with building the IAFF from an infant organization in 1919 to a mature trade union with a membership of 40,000 fire fighters in 1945; politically a Democrat; edited *The Fire Fighter* for several years beginning in 1919; died in Topeka, Kan., May 15, 1946; James J. Gibbons, *The International Association of Fire Fighters* (1944); *The American Federationist* (June, 1946); *The New York Times*, May 17, 1946; *Who's Who in Labor* (1946).

BAGLEY, Sarah (fl. 1836-1847). Although little is known about her early life, including her date of birth, she is believed to have been born in Meredith, N.H.; secured employment in 1836 as an operative in a Hamilton Manufacturing Company cotton mill in Lowell, Mass.; in 1844, organized the Lowell Female Labor Reform Association (LFLRA), an auxiliary of the New England Workingmen's Association; led the campaign to collect 2,000 signatures on a petition to a Massachusetts legislative committee investigating wages, working conditions, and worker demands for a ten-hour day; appeared before the committee as a witness for the workers in 1845; actively involved in the organization of female workers in the mills of Dover, Nashua, and Manchester, N.H., and Waltham and Fall River, Mass.; criticized factory owners and the management-oriented mill-girls' magazine, the *Lowell Offering*, in a series entitled *Factory Tracts*, published in 1845; was a LFLRA delegate to three New England Workingmen's Association conventions in 1845 and served as corresponding secretary; was one of the founders of the Lowell Industrial Reform Lyceum; served on the LFLRA's publication committee; later was a frequent contributor and, for a short time, the chief editor of the *Voice of Industry* after the LFLRA acquired it from the Workingmen's Association in 1846; in 1846, was a delegate to the National Industrial Congress in Boston and the National Reform Convention in Worcester; developed an interest in utopian social philosophies, particularly those of Charles Fourier and George Ripley, and was elected vice-president of the Lowell Union of Associationists; replaced as president of the LFLRA by Mary Emerson in 1847 and appointed superintendent of the Lowell Telegraph Office, becoming the country's first female telegraph operator; disappeared from public notice shortly thereafter and little is known of her later life; John Andrews and W.D.P. Bliss, "History of Women in Trade Unions," *Report on Conditions of Woman and Child Wage-Earners in the*

United States, Vol. X (1911); *Notable American Women* (Vol. I); Madeleine B. Stern, *We the Women* (1962); Eleanor Flexnor, *Century of Struggle* (1959); Hannah Josephson, *The Golden Threads: New England's Mill Girls and Magnates* (1949).

(M.T.)

BALDANZI, George. Born in Black Diamond, Pa., January 23, 1907; son of Natale, a miner and blacksmith, and Clelia (Rutilli) Baldanzi; married Lena Parenti on February 25, 1932; one child; completed grammar school, then began working in the Pennsylvania coal fields; eventually secured employment as a textile dyer in Paterson, N.J.; organized and became the first president, 1933-1936, of the Federation of Dyers, Finishers, Printers, and Bleachers of America, a subfederation of the United Textile Workers of America (UTW); was one of the principal UTW advocates of affiliation with the Congress of Industrial Organizations (CIO); associated with the UTW-Textile Workers Organizing Committee (TWOC) campaigns in the late 1930s; became president of the UTW-TWOC in 1938; after the UTW-TWOC was reorganized into the Textile Workers Union of America (TWU) in 1939, was elected executive vice-president, serving until 1952; was a member of the CIO executive board and was the CIO representative on a five-member labor delegation visiting Italy in 1944; served as the chairman of the Committee on Constitution which, during the CIO's Eleventh Constitutional Convention, held in 1949, sponsored successful resolutions requiring officials of CIO unions to take non-Communist oaths; disillusioned with the failures of the TWU to organize the textile workers of the South; therefore, challenged President Emil Reive (q.v.) for the TWU presidency in 1952, but lost; relieved of international offices after his defeat, and eventually led a small group of textile workers back into the American Federation of Labor; served as director of organization for the UTW, 1952-1953; was a regional director of the Eastern Conference of Teamsters, International Brotherhood of Teamsters, 1953-1955; elected international president of the UTW, and a vice-president of the United Italian-American Labor Council in 1958; appointed a member of the U.S. Secretary of Commerce's Textile Advisory Committee in 1959; named chairman of the Passaic County (N.J.). Area Redevelopment Board in 1963; died in Hawthorne, N.J., April 22, 1972; Walter Galenson, *The CIO Challenge to the AFL: A History of the American Labor Movement, 1935-1941* (1960); Herbert J. Lahne, *The Cotton Mill Workers* (1944); *Who's Who in Labor* (1946).

BARKAN, Alexander Elias.   Born in Bayonne, N.J., August 8, 1909; son of Jacob and Rachel (Perelmen) Barkan; married Helen Stickno, a Textile Workers Union of America (TWU) organizer, on May 10, 1942; two children; was graduated from the University of Chicago in 1933 and then taught high school in Bayonne, N.J., until 1937; joined the Congress of Industrial Organizations' (CIO) Textile Workers Organizing Committee in 1937; became an organizer for the TWU in 1938 and served as a subregional director, 1938-1942; served with the U.S. Navy during World War II, 1942-1945; became veterans' director of the CIO Community Service Committee in 1945; elected executive director of the New Jersey CIO Council in 1946; became political action director of the TWU in 1948, serving in that capacity until 1955; appointed assistant director of the American Federation of Labor (AFL)-CIO Committee on Political Education (COPE) in 1955 and deputy director in 1957; became the director of COPE after the death of James L. McDevitt (q.v.) in 1963, and directed its highly successful efforts during the 1964 national elections; was dispatched by AFL-CIO president George Meany (q.v.) to work full-time for Hubert Humphrey's nomination as the Democratic party presidential candidate in 1968; a quiet, unostentatious administrator; created a computerized voter registration information bank during his directorship of COPE and made an effort to expand COPE's activities and influence in suburban areas; identifies himself as nonpartisan, but usually supports liberal Democratic candidates for public office; Terry Catchpole, *How to Cope with COPE: The Political Operations of Organized Labor* (1968); Joseph C. Goulden, *Meany* (1972); *The American Federationist* (April, 1957); *AFL-CIO News,* August 17, 1963.

BARNES, John Mahlon.   Born in Lancaster, Pa., June 22, 1866; the son of a bootmaker; was orphaned at an early age and resided at the Soldiers' Orphan School in Mt. Joy, Pa., 1875-1882; took Chautauqua correspondence courses, 1883-1885; joined the Knights of Labor in 1884; maintained his membership until 1887 and then joined the Cigarmakers' International Union (CMIU); served as secretary to numerous CMIU locals, 1887-1922; joined the Socialist Labor party in 1891 and in 1899 switched to the Socialist party; served as national secretary, 1906, campaign director, 1912, and wrote the Socialist party platform in 1917; favored industrial unionism, the Socialist platform, and an independent labor party and was a constant critic and antagonist of Samuel Gompers (q.v.); was instrumental in defeating Gompers' bid for reelection as president of the American Federation of Labor (AFL) in 1894; ran against Gompers at the 1896 CMIU convention for election as AFL delegate, but withdrew before election; at 1904 AFL convention introduced an unsuccessful amendment to the AFL constitution that would have prohibited a lobbying committee on the grounds that both national parties served as "tools of the capitalist class" and that lobbying produced poor results; was elected national secretary of the CMIU in 1905, serving until 1911; sponsored an unsuccessful anti-Gompers resolution at a CMIU convention that would have denied union membership to anyone holding membership in the National Civic Federation, a resolution that would have affected only Gompers; presented a resolution protesting the arrest of Mexican anarchists in Los Angeles in 1907, which led the AFL executive council to demand a congressional investigation and to appeal for justice to President William H. Taft; unsuccessfully opposed Gompers' proposed American Alliance for Labor and Democracy at the 1917 AFL convention; became the director of the American Freedom Foundation after it was organized in 1919; served as business manager of *New Day*, 1920-1921; died in Washington, D.C., in 1934; Solon DeLeon, ed., *The American Labor Who's Who* (1925); Samuel Gompers, *Seventy Years of Life and Labor: An Autobiography* (1943); Philip Taft, *The A.F. of L. in the Time of Gompers* (1957); Bernard Mandel, *Samuel Gompers: A Biography* (1963).

(M.E.R.)

BARNUM, Gertrude. Born in Chester, Ill., September 29, 1866; daughter of William J., an attorney and circuit court judge, and Clara Letitia (Hyde) Barnum; attended Chicago grammar schools and Evanston (Ill.) Township High School, then the University of Wisconsin, 1891-1892; served as a social worker in Chicago's Hull House, ca. 1889-1896; was chief social worker at Henry Booth House, Chicago, 1902-1903; joined the National Women's Trade Union League (WTUL) in 1903 and served as national secretary, 1903-1904; was a WTUL national organizer, 1903-1913; directed several strikes in 1905, including the Fall River, Mass., strike of female textile operatives, the corset workers' strike in Aurora, Ill., and the laundry workers' strike in Troy, N.Y.; served as an arbitrator and agent for the International Ladies' Garment Workers' Union (ILGWU), 1911-1916; toured the Middle West for the ILGWU during the 1911 Cleveland garment workers' strike in an unsuccessful effort to persuade wholesale and retail merchants to boycott Cleveland goods; helped direct an ILGWU strike in Boston and publicized and solicited funds for the New York white-goods workers' strike during 1913; was a special agent for President

Woodrow Wilson's United States Commission on Industrial Relations in 1914; assistant director of investigative services in the U.S. Department of Labor, 1918-1919; retired in 1919; died in Los Angeles, Calif., June 17, 1948; *Notable American Women (1971);* Louis Levine, *The Women's Garment Workers: A History of the International Ladies' Garment Workers' Union (1924);* Gladys Boone, *The Women's Trade Union Leagues in Great Britain and the United States of America* (1942).

(M.T.)

BARONDESS, Joseph. Born in Kamenets-Podolsk, Russia, July 3, 1867; son of Judah Samuel, a rabbi, and Feige (Goldman) Barondess; Jewish; married Amma Zifels in 1885; four children; acquired an orthodox Jewish education, then emigrated to England at an early age and soon became involved in the British trade union movement; emigrated to the United States in 1888 and gained employment as a kneepants-maker in New York city; attended the night school of the New York University Law School while working in the garment industry; became a union organizer during the 1890s and was involved in the organization of the Cloakmakers' Union, the Hebrew Actors' Union, the Ladies' Garment Workers' Union, and the Hebrew-American Typographical Union; led a cloakmakers' strike in 1890 that brought him to the forefront of union organizing in the New York needle trades; arrested in 1891 as a result of organizing activities and, while free on bail, fled to Canada; returned to the United States and, after spending a few weeks in jail, was granted a pardon by governor of New York; led an unsuccessful general strike of New York cloakmakers in 1895 that largely destroyed the union; was a strong, zealous, and impetuous personality, and consequently at the center of most of the divisive ideological struggles in the New York labor movement during the 1890s; participated in the founding of the International Ladies' Garment Workers' Union in 1900; became a committed Zionist in 1903 and involved in several Zionist organizations; was a founding member of the American Jewish Congress and served on its delegation to the 1919 Paris Peace Conference, which was instrumental in having a clause providing for Jewish minority rights incorporated into the treaty; appointed to the New York City Board of Education in 1910 and served two four-year terms; during his later years he became an insurance broker; politically a Socialist; translated and wrote an introduction to Frank B. Copley's *The Impeachment of President Israels* (1916); died in New York City, June 19, 1928; Benjamin Stolberg, *Tailor's Progress: The Story of a Famous Union and the Men Who Made It* (1944); Louis Levine, *The Women's Garment Workers: A History of the Interna-*

tional Ladies' Garment Workers' Union (1924); Melech Epstein, *Profiles of Eleven* (1965) and *Jewish Labor in the U.S.A., 1914-1952* (2 Vols., 1953); Aaron Antonovsky, trans., *The Early Jewish Labor Movement in the United States* (1961).

BARRY, Thomas, B.   Born in Cohoes, N.Y., July 17, 1852; received little formal education before beginning work in a knitting mill in 1860 at age eight; joined a short-lived carders' union in 1867 and shortly thereafter became an apprentice axe-polisher but was blacklisted two years later for union organizing activities; joined the Noble Order of the Knights of Labor (K of L) in the early 1880s and was appointed an organizer; elected to the Michigan state legislature on the Democratic-Greenback ticket in 1884 while residing in Saginaw County, Mich.; sponsored several pro-labor bills as a legislator, including a ten-hour bill; led a largely unsuccessful but widely publicized strike of Saginaw Valley lumber workers when mill-owners refused to institute the ten-hour day without wage reductions; as a result of activities associated with the strike, was arrested six times with total bail exceeding $20,000; elected to the executive committee of the K of L in 1885; sent to Chicago, Ill., to lead an eight-hour strike in the stock-yards in 1886, but Grand Master Workman Terence Powderly (q.v.) called the strike unauthorized and ordered it stopped; after the crushing of the strike, Barry increasingly criticized Powderly's "autocratic" leadership and sacrifice of rank-and-file interests; was therefore expelled from K of L in 1888 by Powderly's supporters; subsequently attempted to organize dissi-dent K of L unionists into a Brotherhood of United Labor, but with little success outside Barry's home state of Michigan; Norman J. Ware, *The Labor Movement in the United States, 1860-1895* (1929); Gerald N. Grob, *Workers and Utopia: A Study of Ideological Conflict in the American Labor Movement, 1865-1900* (1961); Doris B. McLaughlin, *Michigan Labor: A Brief History from 1818 to the Present* (1970); Harry J. Carman, Henry David, and Paul N. Guthrie, eds., *The Path I Trod: The Autobiography of Terence V. Powderly* (1940).

BASKIN, Joseph.   Born in Minsk, Russia, October 20, 1880; son of Nachim Mendel, a Hebrew teacher, and Rose Baskin; Jewish; married Mary Plotkin in 1918; two children; studied at various yeshivas in Russia and attended a school in Vilna, Lithuania for higher Talmudic learning; at age of 16, became active in Bund, a general union of Jewish workers; went to Geneva, Switzerland, in 1899 on a Baron de Hirsch scholarship and attended College de Genève, 1899-1900; studied electrical engineering at the University of Lausanne, 1901, and the electrical school at the University of Nancy, France, 1905; graduated with degree in electrical engineering in 1905; founded and became publisher of the Bund's Yiddish daily *Folks Zeitung* in Vilna; arrested, along with other newspaper staff members, in 1907, for antigovernment activities; emigrated to the United States later that year and took job in a Cleveland, Ohio, automobile plant; employed by the Westinghouse Electrical Company in Pittsburgh, Pa., 1908-1913; appointed assistant secretary of Workmen's Circle in 1914 and general secretary in 1916, serving until 1952; edited Workmen's Circle publication *The Friend*, 1924-1952; organized Workmen's Circle educational, medical, and social service departments during his administration; also established a home for the aged and elementary and intermediate Yiddish schools; politically a Socialist; died in New York City, June 26, 1952; Melech Epstein, *Jewish Labor in the U.S.A., 1914-1952* (2 Vols., 1953); Hyman J. Fliegel, *The Life and Times of Max Pine: A History of the Jewish Labor Movement in the U.S.A. during the Last Part of the 19th Century and the First Part of the 20th Century* (1959); *Who's Who in World Jewry* (1955); Solon DeLeon, ed., *The American Labor Who's Who* (1925); *The New York Times*, June 27, 1952.

BATES, Harry Clay.   Born in Denton, Tex., November 22, 1882; son of Jefferson Davis, a businessman, and Minnie Smith Bates; Roman Catholic; married Marguerite Roddy on July 29, 1932; shortly after graduating from high school in Denton, became an apprentice bricklayer and joined Waco, Tex., Local 9 of the Bricklayers, Masons and Plasterers International Union of America (BMPIU) in 1900; elected president of Dallas, Tex., Local 5 in 1910 and served until 1916; between 1914-1922 was president of the Texas Conference of Bricklayers, Masons and Plasterers; served as president of the Joint Labor Legislative Board of Texas, 1916-1922; was elected an international vice-president of the BMPIU in 1920 and treasurer four years later; elected the first vice-president of the BMPIU in 1928 and in 1935 became international president of the union; elected an American Federation of Labor (AFL) vice-president and member of the executive council in 1935; appointed chairman of the standing AFL housing committee that aimed to provide information and sponsor housing legislation in the United States Congress; served during World War II as labor advisor to the War Production Board and was a member of the Wage Adjustment Board; was a member of the 1942 AFL negotiating committee to discuss merger with the Congress of Industrial Organizations (CIO); was an AFL delegate to the British Trades Union

Congress in 1949; served as a member of President Harry S. Truman's Wage Stabilization Board, created during the Korean War crisis in 1950; reappointed to the Board after its 1951 reorganization; one of three AFL delegates to the AFL-CIO unity committee that reached agreement in 1955 on merger; served as a delegate to the 1958 meeting of the International Labor Organization conference in Geneva; retired from union affairs in 1967; politically a Democrat; authored *Bricklayers' Century of Craftsmanship* (1955); died in Golden Beach, Fla., April 4, 1969; Philip Taft, *The A.F. of L. From the Death of Gompers to the Merger* (1959); Walter Galenson, *The CIO Challenge to the AFL: A History of the American Labor Movement, 1935-1941* (1960); *AFL-CIO News*, April 12, 1969; *Who's Who in Labor* (1946).

BECK, Dave. Born in Stockton, Calif., June 16, 1894; son of Lemuel, a carpet cleaner, and Mary (Tierney) Beck; Presbyterian; married Dorothy E. Leschander in 1918 and remarried after her death in 1961; one child; forced by a family financial crisis to leave high school before graduation; later took extension courses from the University of Washington; secured a job as a laundry worker and joined Seattle, Wash., Local 24 of the Laundry Workers International Union; worked for a short period as an inside laundry worker, then became a driver of a company laundry wagon; became a charter member of Seattle Laundry and Dye Drivers Local 566, chartered by the International Brotherhood of Teamsters, Chauffeurs, Warehousemen and Helpers (IBT) in 1917; served with the Naval Aviation Service as a machinists' mate in England during World War I; resumed work after the war as a laundry driver and was elected to the executive board of Local 566; elected president of IBT Joint Council 28 in 1923 and secretary-treasurer of Local 566 in 1925; appointed a full-time IBT general organizer for the Pacific Northwest and elected president of Local 566 in 1927; appointed to the Washington Board of Prison Terms and Paroles in 1935; organized and became the president of the Western Conference of Teamsters in 1937; became an international vice-president in 1940 and in 1947 elected to the newly created position of executive vice-president; appointed a regent of the University of Washington in 1945; served as an American Federation of Labor (AFL) fraternal delegate to the British Trades Union Congress in 1949; elected international president of the IBT after the retirement of Daniel Tobin (q.v.) in 1952; became an AFL vice-president and executive council member in 1953; declined to seek reelection in 1957 because of his investigation by the McClellan Committee of the U.S. Senate; expelled from AFL-Congress of Industrial Organizations' executive council for refusing to answer McClellan committee questions regarding corruption and the embezzlement of union funds; served a 30-month prison term during 1962-65 after being convicted for filing a false Federal income tax return; became a successful real-estate entrepreneur in Seattle, Wash., following his retirement from union affairs; usually supported the Republican party; Donald Garnel, *The Rise of Teamster Power in the West* (1972); Sam Romer, *The International Brotherhood of Teamsters: Its Government and Structure* (1962); Robert D. Leiter, *The Teamsters Union: A Study of Its Economic Impact* (1957); *Current Biography* (1949).

BEHNCKE, David Lewis.   Born in rural Wisconsin in 1897; son of a farmer; married Gladys May Henson in 1925; two children; ended formal education in 1913 and ran away from home; joined the U.S. Army prior to World War I, hoping to become a pilot; participated in General John J. Pershing's expedition against Pancho Villa in 1916; became a pilot during World War I but failed because of the lack of formal education to become a career military flier; after World War I, joined with other former service fliers to form a flying circus that specialized in stunt flying; after a year of barnstorming, organized a short-lived air-freight express service; was forced by 1925 to sell the business, losing both his airfield and his planes; became Northwest Airlines' first pilot in 1926; served a one-year tour with the U.S. Army during 1927; became a United Air Lines pilot in 1928, and in 1930 and 1931 emerged as the spokesman for United pilots in a major wage dispute; led the formation in 1931 of a new union, the Air Line Pilots Association (ALPA), and, despite the reservations of many pilots, obtained an international union charter for ALPA from the American Federation of Labor; deliberately avoided collective bargaining for many years, successfully lobbying instead for a federal pilot pay formula based on seniority, speed, miles, and hours flown (Decision No. 83 of the National Labor Board, May 10, 1934, enacted into law in the Air Mail Act of 1934), and also for the inclusion of air transportation within the Railway Labor Act (achieved under Title II of the Act, April 10, 1936); initiated collective bargaining in 1938; signed the first ALPA contract with American Airlines on May 15, 1939, and within a few years with all other carriers; successfully led post-World War II ALPA campaign to improve and extend Decision No. 83 pay formula (including addition of "gross weight pay" in 1947) to larger four-engine aircraft; proved unable to delegate authority adequately for needs of expanding ALPA and was increasingly deaf to rank-and-file attitudes; recalled from ALPA presidency by the union's board of directors in 1951; declined an offer of president emeritus status and lifetime salary, instead waging a bitter but unsuccessful legal battle to regain control of the ALPA; politically a Democrat; died in Chicago, Ill., April 14, 1953; George E. Hopkins, *The Airline Pilots: A Study in Elite Unionization* (1971); Oscar Leiding, *A Story of the Origin and Progression of the Air Line Pilots Association and of Its Key Figure and Organizer, 1930-1944* (1945); *Who's Who in Labor* (1946); Harold M. Levinson, *et al.*, *Collective Bargaining and Technological Change in American Transportation* (1971).

BEIRNE, Joseph A.   Born in Jersey City, N. J., February 16, 1911; son of Irish immigrants Michael Joseph, a railroad engineer, and Annie T. (Giblin) Beirne; Roman Catholic; married Anne Mary Abahaze on July 2, 1933; three children; left high school after two years and went to work as an office boy; resumed high school education in the evening after gaining employment in 1928 as a utility boy in the inspection department of the Western Electric Company in Jersey City, N.J.; completed three years of college work by taking evening courses at St. Peter's College and New York University; became president of the employees association of Western Electric's New York Distribution Department in 1937 and during the same year helped establish the National Association of Telephone Equipment Workers; credited with transforming a company union into an economic-oriented trade union; elected vice-president of the National Federation of Telephone Workers in 1940, president in 1943; elected as a Democrat to the city council of Fairview, N.J., 1939-1945; served on the U.S. Board of War Communication during World War II; negotiated the first national contract with the American Telephone and Telegraph Company in 1946; became president of the reorganized Communications Workers of America (CWA) in 1947 and transformed it from a loose federation of autonomous, independent unions into a strong, centralized union; led the CWA into the Congress of Industrial Organizations (CIO) in 1949 and became a CIO vice-president; designated one of the CIO representatives on the Wage Stabilization Board in 1951; became a vice-president, executive council member, and chairman of the standing committee on community relations after the American Federation of Labor-CIO merger in 1955; appointed a Public Broadcasting Corporation Director in 1968 and a member of the National Committee on Productivity in 1970; served as member of numerous public and private boards and agencies; a Democrat; authored *New Horizons for American Labor* (1962) and *Challenge to Labor: New Roles for American Trade Unions* (1969); Jack Barbash, *Unions and Telephones: The*

Story of the Communications Workers of America (1952); *Current Biography* (1946); *Who's Who in Labor* (1946).

BELLANCA, Dorothy Jacobs. Born in Zemel, Russian Latvia (now part of the Soviet Union), August 10, 1894; daughter of Harry, a tailor, and Bernice Edith (Levinson) Jacobs; Jewish; emigrated to the United States in 1900; married August Bellanca, an Amalgamated Clothing Workers of America (ACWA) organizer, in August, 1918; attended the public schools of Baltimore, Md., until age thirteen, then hired in a Baltimore men's clothing factory as a buttonhole maker; helped to found United Garment Workers of America Local 170 and led it into the ACWA in 1914; elected a delegate and secretary to the Baltimore Joint Board, ACWA, in 1915; elected to the ACWA general executive board in 1916 and served until her marriage in 1918; headed the short-lived women's bureau of the ACWA, 1924-1926; served on the ACWA executive board, 1934-1946 and was, during this time, the ACWA's only woman vice-president; was a member of the Congress of Industrial Organizations' Textile Workers Organizing Committee, 1937-1938; served as a labor advisor to regional conferences of the International Labor Organization, 1939, 1941; participated in various organizing drives and strikes, notably the 1930 Philadelphia organizing campaign, 1932-1934, and the shirt workers' organizing drives in New York, New Jersey, Connecticut, and Pennsylvania; was appointed to the General Advisory Commission on Maternal and Child Welfare in 1938; member of the New York commissions on discrimination in employment, 1941, 1943; served on several industrial commissions responsible for establishing minimum wage rates after enactment of the Fair Labor Standards Act; was a political activist and helped organize the American Labor party (ALP) in 1936; was an unsuccessful candidate for the U.S. Congress on the ALP ticket in 1938; served as state vice-president of the ALP in 1940 and 1944; died in New York City, August 10, 1946; *Notable American Women* (1971); *Who's Who in Labor* (1946).

(M.T.)

BERGER, Victor Luitpold. Born in Nieder-Rehbach, Austria, February 28, 1860; son of Ignatz, a farmer and innkeeper, and Julia Berger; married Meta Schlichting on December 4, 1897; two children; attended the Gymnasium at Leutschau and the universities of Budapest and Vienna; emigrated to the United States in 1878 and settled near Bridgeport, Conn.; worked there variously as a metal polisher, boiler mender, and salesman;

moved to Milwaukee, Wis., in 1880 and taught German in public schools for ten years; edited the *Milwaukee Daily Vorwaerts*, 1892-1898; became editor of the *Social Democratic Herald* in 1900 and continued in that capacity after the *Herald* became a daily in 1911 and was renamed the *Milwaukee Leader*; served as its editor until his death; joined the International Typographical Union and was a delegate to several American Federation of Labor (AFL) conventions where he was one of the leading Socialist critics of established AFL leaders and policies; one of the founders of the Social Democratic party of America in 1897 and the Socialist party of America (SPA) in 1901; served as a member of the national executive board of the SPA from its founding until 1923; ran unsuccessfully for mayor of Milwaukee in 1904; elected a Milwaukee alderman-at-large in 1910 and later that year elected to the U.S. Congress, the first Socialist to be seated in Congress; reelected in 1918, but denied his seat because of his opposition to United States' involvement in World War I; reelected three more times but denied his seat each time; tried and convicted in 1921 on a number of charges growing out of an indictment for antiwar speeches and sentenced to 20 years, but the conviction was overturned by the U.S. Supreme Court; reelected to Congress in 1922 and served three consecutive terms before being defeated for reelection in 1928; died in Milwaukee, Wis., August 7, 1929; David A. Shannon, *The Socialist Party of America* (1955); James Weinstein, *The Decline of Socialism in America, 1912-1925* (1967); Sally M. Miller, *Victor Berger and the Promise of Constructive Socialism, 1910-1920* (1973); *Dictionary of Wisconsin Biography* (1960); *Dictionary of American Biography* (Vol XXI).

BERRY, George Leonard.   Born in Lee Valley, Hawkins County, Tenn., September 12, 1882; son of Thomas Jefferson, a judge and legislator, and Cornelia (Trent) Berry; Baptist; married Marie Margaret Gehres on August 6, 1907; attended the public schools of Hawkins County, Tenn., before being orphaned in 1888; ran away from a Baptist orphanage at age nine and became a newsboy for the Jackson (Miss.) *Evening News;* served with the Third Mississippi Regiment of the U.S. Army during the Spanish-American War; employed in the pressroom of the St. Louis *Globe-Democrat* after the war, and in 1899 joined the International Printing Pressmen's and Assistants' Union of North America (IPPAUNA); became involved in several successful mining ventures in Nevada during 1903-1904 and acquired a degree of financial independence; in 1907 was a San Francisco delegate to the national convention of the IPPAUNA in Brighton Beach, N.Y. and elected international president of the IP-

PAUNA; was an American Federation of Labor (AFL) delegate to the British Trades Union Congress in 1910 and two years later attended the International Printers Congress in Stuttgart, Germany, and the International Economic Conference in Zurich, Switzerland; commissioned a major in the U.S. Army Corps of Engineers during World War I and served with the American Expeditionary Force in France; appointed a labor advisor on the American Commission to the treaty negotiations ending World War I; was one of the founders of the American Legion; became a vice-president and member of the AFL executive council in 1935; was a conservative trade unionist and did not advocate militant strike activity, but preferred to resolve industrial disputes through conciliation and arbitration; was a Democrat and ran unsuccessfully for governor of Tennessee in 1914; lost the Democratic vice-presidential nomination in 1924 by a narrow margin; was chairman of the labor division during the Democratic National Convention of 1928; was a member of the National Labor Board of the National Recovery Administration, 1933-1935; was instrumental in organizing Labor's Non-Partisan League to support the reelection of Franklin D. Roosevelt in 1936; appointed a U.S. Senator from Tennessee on May 6, 1937 to fill the vacancy caused by the death of the incumbent and served until January 16, 1939; other than trade union activities, was involved in several business enterprises, including newspaper publishing, cattle raising, manufacturing cigarette wrappers, and banking; organized and led the movement creating Pressmen's Home, Tenn.; authored *Labor Conditions Abroad* (1912); died in Pressmen's Home, Tenn., December 4, 1948; Elizabeth F. Baker, *Printers and Technology: A History of the International Printing Pressmen and Assistants' Union* (1957); Philip Taft, *The A.F. of L. From the Death of Gompers to the Merger* (1959); *Current Biography* (1948); *National Cyclopaedia of American Biography* (Vol. XXXVI).

BIEMILLER, Andrew John.   Born in Sandusky, Ohio, July 23, 1906; son of Andrew Frederick and Pearl (Weber) Biemiller; Society of Friends; married Hannah Periot Morris on December 20, 1929; two children; attended public schools; received an A.B. degree from Cornell University in 1926 and did postgraduate work at the University of Pennsylvania, 1928-1931; served as an instructor in history at Syracuse University, 1926-1928, and the University of Pennsylvania, 1929-1931; moved to Milwaukee, Wis., in 1932 and became a reporter for the Milwaukee *Leader*; served as a labor-relations counselor and an organizer for the Milwaukee Federation of Trade Councils and the Wisconsin State Federation of Labor, 1932-1942; elected to the Wisconsin state assembly as a Socialist-Progressive in 1936 and served as a floor leader, 1939-1941; appointed assistant to the vice-chairman for labor production of the War Production Board in 1941, serving until 1944; elected as a Democrat to the Seventy-ninth Congress, 1945-1946, and the Eighty-first Congress, 1949-1950, but was defeated for reelection in both instances; served as a special assistant to the U.S. Secretary of Interior, 1951-1952, and thereafter became a public-relations counselor in Washington, D.C.; shortly after being defeated for election to Congress in 1952, became a legislative lobbyist for the American Federation of Labor (AFL) and in 1956 was appointed director of the AFL-Congress of Industrial Organizations' Legislative Department; considered a resourceful and effective legislative lobbyist; actively involved in the enactment of civil rights legislation and in the socio-economic reform measures passed during the 1960s; a member of numerous public and private agencies and boards; was a Socialist early in his career, but later supported Democratic candidates; Joseph C. Goulden, *Meany* (1972); Terry Catchpole, *How to Cope with COPE: The Political Operations of Organized Labor* (1968); *Fortune* (February, 1969).

BIRTHRIGHT, William Clark.   Born in Helena, Ark., May 27, 1887; son of William Conwell, a machinist, and Margaret Ellen (Linebaugh) Birthright; Presbyterian; married Birdie Lee Huss on June 29, 1910; one child; attended the public schools of Nashville, Tenn.; adopted the barber's profession in Nashville at age seventeen and joined Local 35 of the Journeymen Barbers' International Union of America (JBIUA); elected vice-president of Local 35 in 1907 and selected as a delegate to the Nashville Trades and Labor Council; served as secretary of the Tennessee State Federation of Labor, 1916-1931; appointed secretary of the Tennessee Non-Partisan Political Campaign Committee in 1920; served as an American Federation of Labor (AFL) field representative, 1918-1921, and a JBIUA field representative, 1921-1930; became a member of the JBIUA executive board in 1924; appointed along with Francis Gorman of the United Textile Workers of America and Paul Smith of the AFL to head a drive to organize southern textile workers in 1930; after serving for seven years as general secretary-treasurer of the JBIUA, elected general president in 1937; was an AFL fraternal delegate to the British Trades Union Congress in 1937; was elected a vice-president and member of the AFL executive council in 1940; elected international president of the renamed Journeymen Barbers, Hairdressers and Cosmetologists' International Union of America (JBHCIU) in 1941; frequently served as an AFL mediator in jurisdictional disputes; selected as chairman of the Marion

County (Ind.) Selective Service board and of the Indiana State Personnel Board in 1946; was one of three AFL delegates on the Wage Stabilization Board established by President Harry S. Truman during the Korean War crisis; became a member of the AFL-Congress of Industrial Organizations (CIO) executive council after the 1955 merger and served until 1965; appointed chairman of the AFL-CIO standing committee on public relations and publicity in 1955; usually supported Democratic candidates; retired from union affairs in 1963 and was named president emeritus of the JBHCIU; died in Indianapolis, Ind., April 18, 1970; W. Scott Hall, *The Journeymen Barbers' International Union of America* (1936); *National Cyclopaedia of American Biography* (1946); *AFL-CIO News*, April 25, 1970; *Who's Who in Labor* (1946).

BISNO, Abraham. Born in Belaya Tserkov, Russia, in 1866; son of Herschel, a tailor, and Malke Bisno; Jewish; married Tillie Regent in 1890 and, after that marriage ended in divorce, Sarah in 1892; six children; received little formal education; was apprenticed to a tailor at age eleven; emigrated with family to the United States in 1881, living, successively, in Atlanta, Ga., Chattanooga, Tenn., and, in 1882, Chicago, Ill.; began work as a tailor shortly after immigrating; was one of the founders of the Workingmen's Educational Society in 1888; helped organize and became the first president of the Chicago Cloak Makers' Union in 1890; served as a factory inspector under Florence Kelly during John Peter Altgeld's governorship of Illinois; was associated with John R. Commons' investigation of immigrant conditions in American industry; a vigorous critic of the conciliation method of resolving industrial disputes that was written into the "Protocol of Peace," which ended the 1910 New York garment strike, and advocated strict arbitration as an alternative; elected chief clerk of the New York Joint Board of Cloakmakers, a division of the International Ladies' Garment Workers' Union (ILGWU), in 1911 and general manager the following year; his proposed reforms encountered opposition from both garment manufacturers and the international officers of the ILGWU and therefore was forced out as chief clerk in 1913 and replaced by Dr. Isaac A. Hourwich; served as chief clerk of the Chicago Joint Board of Cloakmakers, 1915-1917; retired from union affairs after 1917 and became a Chicago realtor; authored *Abraham Bisno: Union Pioneer* (1967); died in Chicago, Ill., December 1, 1929; Benjamin Stolberg, *Tailor's Progress: The Story of a Famous Union and the Men Who Made It* (1944); Louis Levine, *The Women's Garment Workers: A History of the International Ladies' Garment Workers' Union* (1924).

BITTNER, Van Amberg.   Born in Bridgeport, Pa., March 20, 1885; son of Charles, a coal miner, and Emma Ann (Henck) Bittner; Lutheran; married Bertha Mae Walter on June 8, 1911; one child; started working in the mines at age eleven while continuing to attend school; was graduated from high school in Vanderbilt, Pa.; joined the United Mine Workers of America (UMWA) shortly after beginning to work in the mines and in 1901, at age sixteen, was elected president of his local; became a vice-president of UMWA District 5 in 1908 and three years later was elected District president; became a UMWA international representative and organized locals in Tennessee, Alabama, and West Virginia; elected president of UMWA District 17 as a result of organizing activities in West Virginia; served on the Appalachian Coal Conference between 1933-1942; associated with the organizing activities of the Steel Workers Organizing Committee (SWOC) in 1935 and assigned the task of organizing steelworkers in the Western Great Lakes area; one of the signers of the SWOC contract with the United States Steel Corporation in 1937; appointed chairman of the Packinghouse Workers Organizing Committee in 1937; involved in the successful effort to organize farm equipment workers; led the successful drive to organize the Bethlehem Steel Corporation in 1941; became an assistant to the president of the United Steelworkers of America after it was formed from the SWOC: resigned as president of UMWA District 17 in 1942 as a result of conflicts between the Congress of Industrial Organizations (CIO) and UMWA president John L. Lewis (q.v.); appointed to the West Virginia State Planning Board in 1942; during World War II, served as a labor advisor to the Offices of Emergency Management and Production Management and as a member of the National War Labor Board; served as vice-chairman of the CIO's Political Action Committee; appointed national director of the CIO Southern Organization Drive in 1946; a self-described independent in politics, but usually supported the Democratic party; died in Pittsburgh, Pa., July 19, 1949; Robert R. R. Brooks, *As Steel Goes. . . . Unionism in a Basic Industry* (1940); Lloyd Ulman, *The Government of the Steel Workers' Union* (1962); *Current Biography* (1947); *National Cyclopaedia of American Biography* (Vol. XXXVII).

BLOOR, Ella Reeve.   Born near Mariners' Harbor, Staten Island, N.Y., July 8, 1862; daughter of Charles, a drugstore owner, and Harriet Amanda (Disbrow) Reeve; married Andrew Omholt in 1932 after earlier marriages to Lucien Ware and Louis Cohen ended in divorce; attended public schools in New York City and Bridgeton, N.J., and a private school in Bridgeton until age fourteen; became associated with the labor movement for the first time around 1884-1885 by joining a mixed local of the Knights of Labor; became a member of the Prohibition party in 1887 and organized and served as president of a Women's Christian Temperance Union branch in Woodbury, N.J., participated in the Philadelphia Amalgamated Association of Street and Electric Railway Employes' strike in the early 1890s; was influenced by Eugene V. Debs (q.v.) and joined the Social Democracy of America in 1897, and was elected secretary of its Brooklyn branch; joined the Socialist Labor party (SLP) around 1900 and became a SLP organizer for Essex County, N.J.; elected to the general executive board of the Socialist Trade and Labor Alliance in 1900; became disenchanted with the SLP's theoretical approach and joined the Socialist party of America (SPA) in 1902; served as an SPA state organizer for Pennsylvania and Delaware, 1902, 1905, Connecticut, 1905-1910, and Ohio, 1910; nominated by the SPA for secretary of state of Connecticut in 1908 ; called "Mother" Bloor, worked as an organizer with Pennsylvania coal miners during the 1902 coal strike, with Ohio miners in the early 1900s and again in 1914-1915, and with Colorado miners in 1914; did relief work during the 1913 Calumet, Mich., copper strike; spent several months organizing for the United Cloth Hat and Cap Makers' Union in New York, New England, St. Louis, Mo., and Philadelphia, Pa., in 1917; was nominated for lieutenant governor of New York on the SPA ticket in 1919; worked as an organizer for the Workers' Defense Union; while an organizer in Kansas City, Mo., in 1919; quit the SPA and formed a branch of the Communist Labor party (CLP); became national organizer for the Eastern Division of the CLP in 1919; when the CLP merged with the Communist party of America (CPA) in 1922, became a CPA member; was a delegate to both the Red International of Labor Unions and the Third World Congress of the Communist International meeting in Moscow in 1921; helped form and was a field organizer for the Workers' party, Los Angeles, Calif., in 1921; was a delegate from the Central Labor Council of Minneapolis, Minn., to the Second Red International Labor Union Congress, Moscow, 1922; served as a national organizer for the International Defense, 1921-1924; was an organizer for the United Front Committee of Textile Workers in several cities, 1925-1927; worked as an organizer for the United Farmers' League in North and South Dakota and cooperated with the Farmers' Holiday Association during the Iowa dairy farmers strike in 1932; was a member of the CPA's national committee and was chairman of its Women's Commission, 1932-1948; authored *We Are Many: An Autobiography of Ella Reeve Bloor* (1940); died in Quakerstown, Pa., August 10, 1951; James Weinstein,

The Decline of Socialism in America, 1912-1925 (1969); John L. Shover, *Cornbelt Rebellion: The Farmers Holiday Association* (1965); Andrew Sinclair, *The Emancipation of the American Woman* (1965); Theodore Draper, *The Roots of American Communism* (1957).

(M.T.)

BLUMBERG, Hyman.   Born in Legum, Russian Lithuania (now part of the Soviet Union), November 25, 1885; son of Moses, a clothing worker, and Hannah (Herman) Blumberg; Jewish; married Bessie Simon on October 20, 1907; two children; emigrated with family to the United States in 1890; left school at age twelve and began work in the men's garment industry in Baltimore; began union organizing activities while employed as a pocketmaker and in 1909 was selected chairman of District Council 3 of the United Garment Workers Union of America (UGW); in 1914 helped organize the Amalgamated Clothing Workers of America (ACWA) and led members of his local out of UGW and into the new union; elected an ACWA vice-president in 1916; moved to New York City in 1922, becoming manager of the New York Joint Board and assuming responsibility for ACWA organizing activities in the eastern United States; served on the Men's Clothing Code Authority of the National Recovery Administration, 1933-1935; was a member of the Apparel Industry Committee of the Wage and Hour Division of the United States Department of Labor; served as the Congress of Industrial Organizations' labor advisor to the International Labor Organization's conference in Geneva in 1938; was manager of the Amalgamated Laundry Workers' Joint Board, 1939-1941, the Boston Joint Board, and the Shirt and Leisure-wear Joint Board of New York City; elected executive vice-president of the ACWA in 1946; was the general supervisor of the social insurance programs initiated by the ACWA; served as New York state secretary of the American Labor party (ALP) from 1944 to 1946 and then became state chairman; along with the ACWA, withdrew from the ALP in 1948 and thereafter usually supported candidates of the Democratic party; died in New York City, October 17, 1968; Harry A. Cobrin, *The Men's Clothing Industry: Colonial Through Modern Times* (1970); Hyman Bookbinder, *History of the ACWA* (1950); Matthew Josephson, *Sidney Hillman: Statesman of American Labor* (1952).

BORCHARDT, Selma Munter.   Born in Washington, D.C., December 1, 1895 (Birthdate has also been listed as December 1, 1900 and December 1, 1899); daughter of Newman and Sara (Munter) Borchardt; attended Washington, D.C., public schools; received a B.S. degree in education from Syracuse University in 1919, and an A.B. in 1922; received an LLB from Washington College of Law in 1933 and an M.A. from Catholic University in 1937; was a member of the Washington, D.C., and U.S. Supreme Court bars; joined Local 8 of the American Federation of Teachers (AFT) in 1923; served Local 8 as vice-president and legislative chairman, 1922-1924; was an AFT representative to the Women's Joint Congressional Committee, 1927-1958; served as secretary of the American Federation of Labor (AFL) committee on education, 1929-1955, and after the AFL-Congress of Industrial Organizations' (CIO) merger, served in the same capacity in the AFL-CIO; was the AFT's Washington and Congressional legislative representative; along with Florence Hanson, helped investigate Communist influence in AFT Local 5 in New York in 1935, and later in the same year recommended that Local 5's charter be withdrawn; was the director and vice-president of the World Federation of Education Associations, 1927-1947; was a member of the United States National Committee on the United Nations Educational, Scientific, and Cultural Organization; authored numerous books and articles on labor and education; retired union positions in 1962; died in Washington, D.C., January 30, 1968; Solon DeLeon, ed., *The American Labor Who's Who* (1925); *Who's Who in Labor* (1946); *AFL-CIO News*, February 3, 1968.

(M.T.)

BOWEN, William J. Born in Albany, N.Y., in 1868; son of Thomas B. and Margaret (Doran) Bowen; married; two children; after attending the grammar schools of Albany, N.Y., became an apprentice bricklayer at age thirteen; joined Albany Local 6 of the Bricklayers, Masons and Plasterers International Union (BMPIU) in 1890; served as business manager of Local 6 in 1891 and president in 1895; appointed assistant general secretary in 1900 and became first vice-president of the BMPIU a year later; was elected international president in 1904; inheriting a union that was financially insolvent; restored the financial integrity and stability of the BMPIU during the first few years of his presidency; guided the BMPIU in establishing a death benefit fund in 1910 and a relief fund in 1914; led the BMPIU into the American Federation of Labor (AFL) in 1916; served on the labor commission established by President Woodrow Wilson during World War I; was an AFL fraternal delegate to the British Trades Union Congress in 1918; was president when the BMPIU sponsored the construction of a brick plant in El Paso, Tex., to counter building contractors' efforts to constrict supplies to union contractors in the post World War I period; became president emeritus of BMPIU in 1928, but remained as chairman of the board of trustees; was a conservative trade unionist and was a vigorous critic of Communist elements in the labor movement; died in New York City, July 27, 1948; *The American Federationist* (November, 1940); Harry C. Bates, *Bricklayers' Century of Craftsmanship* (1955); *The New York Times*, July 29, 1948.

BOWER, Andrew Park.   Born in Apollo, Pa., May 14, 1869; son of Charles Columbus, a potter and itinerant school teacher, and Philippa Ann (Park) Bower; Baptist; married Maud E. Weightman on April 10, 1893; two children; left school after completing the fifth grade in the public schools of Reading, Pa.; later attended night school and a business college where he studied commercial law; joined the Cigarmakers' International Union of America (CMIU) in 1886; elected secretary-treasurer of Reading Local 286 of the CMIU in 1904 and served until his death; served as secretary-treasurer of the Federated Trades Council of Reading, 1906-1948; elected a vice-president of the Pennsylvania State Federation of Labor in 1909 and served in that capacity for nearly 40 years; during World War I, served on the judicial exemption board and on the state employment board; was a director of the Cooperative League, 1921-1925, and vice-president, 1921-1924; served as secretary-treasurer of the Cigarmakers' Co-operative Association during 1920-1948; was elected president of the CMIU in 1942 after serving as a vice-president for more than 20 years; served on several county agencies during World War II; retired union positions in 1948; politically a Socialist; edited the *Cigarmakers' Official Journal*, 1942-1948; died in Reading, Pa., October 24, 1949; *National Cyclopaedia of American Biography* (Vol. XXXVIII); Solon DeLeon, ed., *The American Labor Who's Who* (1925); *Who's Who in Labor* (1946).

BOYCE, Edward.   Born in Ireland, November 8, 1863, where he received some formal education; emigrated to the United States at age nineteen and worked for a year in Wisconsin before going to Colorado; as a hard-rock miner at Leadville, Col., joined the Knights of Labor in 1884; drifted to the Coeur d'Alene mining district of Idaho a few years later; as recording secretary of the Wardner Miners' Union, helped lead the violent Coeur d'Alene strike of 1892; was convicted of contempt of court and spent several months in jail; was then blacklisted; prospected in the Bitter Root Mountains during 1893, returning to the Coeur d'Alene mines in 1894; was a delegate from the Wardner Union to the second (1894) convention of the Western Federation of Miners (WFM) and was elected to the union's executive board; as a result of the alliance between the Populists and the

WFM, was elected on the Populist ticket to the state legislature; tried to outlaw blacklisting there; was elected president of the WFM in 1896 while still working in the Coeur d'Alene mines; concluded that the intensified class warfare between the Western miners and the mining corporations made trade unionism obsolete and vigorously debated the point with the American Federation of Labor (AFL) head Samuel Gompers (q.v.); successfully urged the WFM convention of 1897 to reject trade unionism in favor of militant industrial unionism and to disaffiliate from the AFL; was instrumental the next year in founding the Western Labor Union (later the American Labor Union) as a regional alternative to the AFL: became an associate meanwhile of Socialist leader Eugene V. Debs (q.v.); with the fusion of the Populists and Democrats in 1896, and the failure of political action to obtain the eight-hour day or curb the mining corporations in the Western states, became a Socialist, advised 1902 WFM convention to embrace "socialism without equivocation," and it adopted the platform of the Socialist party of America; led WFM, the most radically led union to that point in American history, to the apogee of its membership and influence; retired as union president in 1902 because he had become owner of a mine (which precluded him from holding union office); nevertheless was invited to conventions and endorsed the WFM initiative in founding the Industrial Workers of the World in 1905; later became a hotel manager in Portland, Ore., and lived there until his death in the late 1930s; May Arkwright Hutton, *The Coeur D'Alenes or a Tale of the Modern Inquisition in Idaho* (1900); Melvyn Dubofsky, *We Shall Be All: A History of the Industrial Workers of the World* (1969); John H. M. Laslett, *Labor and the Left: A Study of Socialist and Radical Influences in the American Labor Movement, 1881-1924* (1970).

(D.G.S.)

BOYLE, William Anthony.   Born in Bald Butte, Mont., December 1, 1904; son of James P., a miner, and Catherine (Mallin) Boyle; married Ethel V. Williams on June 3, 1928; one child; attended schools in Montana and Idaho and then began working as a coal miner; joined the United Mine Workers of America (UMWA); elected president of UMWA District 27, Montana, serving until 1948; served as regional director in four Western states for the Congress of Industrial Organizations and for UMWA District 50; represented the UMWA on several government and industry committees during World War II; was an assistant to UMWA president John L. Lewis (q.v.), 1948-1960; during this period, also served on the coal industry's Joint Review Board and Joint Industry Safety Committee;

served as an international UMWA vice-president, 1960-1963, acting president, 1962-1963, and elected international president in 1963; was a member of the executive committee and board of directors prior to his election as a vice-president of the National Coal Policy Conference; was opposed for the UMWA presidency in 1969 by Joseph A. Yablonski (q.v.), who represented Miners for Democracy, a rank-and-file insurgent group; reelected by a two-to-one margin in a bitterly contested election; shortly thereafter Yablonski, his wife, and daughter were murdered in their Clarksville, Pa., home; was defeated for reelection by Arnold Miller (q.v.) in 1972 after the U.S. Department of Labor obtained a court order invalidating the 1969 election; attempted suicide with an overdose of drugs in September, 1973; was indicted and convicted of using union funds for illegal political contributions and began serving a three-year sentence in the federal prison in Springfield, Mo., in December, 1973; in the same month, was indicted and later convicted of conspiring to murder Yablonski (see Yablonski's sketch); *United Mine Workers Journal*, February 15, 1963; *Current Biography* (1971); *Who's Who in America, 1972-1973; The New York Times*, September 7, 1973; Brit Hume, *Death and the Mines* (1971).

(J.H.)

BRENNAN, Peter Joseph.   Born in New York City, May 24, 1918; son of John, an ironworker and member of the teamsters' union, and Agnes (Moore) Brennan; Roman Catholic; married Josephine Brickley in 1940; three children; graduated from high school in New York City; received the B.S. degree in business administration from City College of New York; while in college, became an apprentice painter and joined Local 1456 of the Brotherhood of Painters, Decorators and Paperhangers of America; joined the U.S. Navy during World War II and served on a submarine in the Pacific; returned to the painting trade after the war and became the acting business agent of Local 1456; elected business agent of Local 1456 in 1947; appointed maintenance chairman of the Construction Trades Council of Greater New York in 1951, and in 1957, elected president of the Council; served as vice-president of the New York State American Federation of Labor-Congress of Industrial Organizations; was severely criticized by civil rights leaders who accused him of maintaining discriminatory hiring practices in the New York building trades; gained national publicity in 1970 when he organized New York construction workers in support of President Richard M. Nixon's Southeast Asian war policies and led them in a violent confrontation with antiwar protesters; nominated U.S. Secretary of Labor in 1972 and took office in 1973; although identified as a Democrat, has often supported Republican candidates, including Governor Nelson Rockefeller of New York and President Richard Nixon in 1968 and 1972; Joseph C. Goulden, *Meany* (1972); *Current Biography* (1973); *New York Post*, December 9, 1972; *Washington Post*, November 30, 1972.

BRESLAW, Joseph. Born in Miskifky, Russia, April 18, 1887; son of Israel, a merchant, and Marie (Burdman) Breslaw; Jewish; married Rosa Saslaw on January 3, 1908; three children; received some formal education in Russian schools; emigrated to the United States in 1907; first took employment as a shoe worker and then in 1909 hired as a cloak presser; joined Cloak, Skirt and Dress Pressers Local 35 of the International Ladies' Garment Workers' Union (ILGWU); elected to the executive board of Local 35 in 1914 and shortly thereafter became the business agent of the union; elected manager and secretary-treasurer of Local 35 in 1916; elected an ILGWU vice-president in 1922; forced out of the union as a result of a reform movement conducted by Morris Sigman (q.v.) in 1925 but regained ILGWU positions in 1929; usually considered to be on the right-wing of union politics; was a craft-conscious trade unionist who opposed the efforts to lead the ILGWU into the Congress of Industrial Organizations (CIO); attracted a large number of loyal followers within the ILGWU who provided him with considerable power within the union; served the ILGWU in a variety of capacities, including chairman of the ILGWU Union Health Center for several years and permanent treasurer of Unity House, the union's summer resort in the Poconos; was a strong advocate and supporter of the State of Israel and was chairman of the American Trade Union Council for Histadrut, the Israeli labor organization; was a member of the American Labor party and for a time served as a member of its state executive committee; authored *A Cloakmaker Looks at Stolberg's "Tailor's Progress"*; died in New York City, July 3, 1957; Louis Levine, *The Women's Garment Workers: A History of the International Ladies' Garment Workers' Union* (1924); Benjamin Stolberg, *Tailor's Progress: The Story of a Famous Union and the Men Who Made It* (1944); Melech Epstein, *Jewish Labor in the U.S.A., 1914-1952* (2 Vols., 1953); *Who's Who in Labor* (1946).

BREWER, Roy Martin. Born in Cairo, Hall County, Neb., August 9, 1909; son of Martin M., a blacksmith and mechanic, and Lottie (Woodworth) Brewer; Christian Church; married Alyce J. Auhl on July 9, 1929; two children; graduated from high school in Grand Island, Neb., in 1926 and took a job as a projectionist, continuing in that occupation until 1933; joined Local 586 of the International Alliance of Theatrical Stage Employees and Motion Picture Machine Operators of the United States and Canada (IATSE) in 1927; elected vice-president of the Nebraska State Federation of Labor (NSFL) in 1928; served as president of the NSFL, 1933-1934, 1937-1943; was president of IATSE Local 586 for 15 years and secretary of the Grand Island Central Labor Union for four years; served as Labor Compliance Officer for the National Recovery Administration in Nebraska, 1934-1935; during World War II, was a member of the Nebraska Defense Council and chief of the plant community facilities division of the Office of Labor Production, War Production Board; during 1945-1953, served as an international representative of the IATSE, assigned to resolve jurisdictional conflict in Hollywood, Calif., movie studios; became president of the American Federation of Labor's Hollywood Film Council in 1947; was a vociferous anti-Communist and strongly supported the House Committee on Un-American Activities' investigations of alleged Communist activity in the motion-picture industry; became manager of branch operations for Allied Artists Productions in 1953 and during 1966-1967 served as assistant vice-president and studio manager; was manager of production development for the IATSE in 1965; became director of industrial relations for Technicolor, Inc., in 1967; usually supported the Democratic party; *Current Biography* (1953); *International Motion Picture and Television Almanac, 1952-1953; Who's Who in Labor* (1946); *Who's Who in America, 1972-1973.*

BRIDGES, Harry Alfred Renton.   Born in Melbourne, Australia, July 28, 1901; son of Alfred Earnest, a prosperous realtor, and Julia (Dorgan) Bridges; reared as a Roman Catholic; married Noriko (Nikki) Sawada in 1956 after two previous marriages, to Agnes Brown in 1923 and to Nancy Fenton Berdecio in 1946, ended in divorce; three children; completed a secondary school education at St. Brennan's Parochial School in Melbourne in 1917, then became a clerk in a retail stationery store; quit his job after a short time and began a five-year period as a merchant seaman; emigrated to the United States in 1920 and the following year joined the Industrial Workers of the World, serving as an organizer; became a longshoreman in San Francisco in 1922; began organizing San Francisco longshoremen for the International Longshoremen's Association (ILA) in 1933 and between 1933-1935 helped edit *The Waterfront Worker*; led the longshore strike in San Francisco in 1934 that evolved into the famous San Francisco General Strike; organized the Maritime Federation of the Pacific in 1935; led most Pacific Coast locals of the ILA into the Congress of Industrial Organizations (CIO) under the auspices of the newly organized

International Longshoremen's and Warehousemen's Union (ILWU) in 1937; became CIO regional director for the Pacific Coast and a member of the national CIO executive board; began a long fight to stay in United States after Secretary of Labor Frances Perkins issued a warrant for his deportation in 1939; later, the U.S. House of Representatives voted 330 to 42 to deport him but the Senate refused to act; in 1942, was ordered deported by U.S. Attorney General Francis Biddle, but the U.S. Supreme Court invalidated the order; in 1949, was indicted and convicted of perjury for swearing during his naturalization hearing that he was not a member of the Communist party; sentenced to a prison term of five years for perjury and of two years for criminally conspiring to obstruct the naturalization laws, but the conviction was overturned by the U.S. Court of Appeals, and in 1953, the U.S. Supreme Court ruled that the statute of limitations had expired on the matter; found not guilty of a charge of a civil conspiracy to obstruct the naturalization laws by a U.S. District Court in 1955; led a long but successful strike of West Coast longshoremen in 1948; after lengthy negotiations, signed contracts with the Pacific Maritime Association in 1960 that suspended ILWU-negotiated work rules, allowing a reduced work force on the docks as called for by mechanization and automation; in return, got a multimillion dollar trust fund to be used for retirement pensions and no-layoff gurantees for registered workers; led a 135-day strike of West Coast longshoremen in 1971-1972; Charles P. Larrowe, *Harry Bridges: The Rise and Fall of Radical Labor in the U.S.* (1972), and *Shape-Up and Hiring Hall* (1955); Maud Russell, *Men Along the Shore* (1966); Charles A. Madison, *American Labor Leaders: Personalities and Forces in the Labor Movement* (1962).

BROPHY, John. Born in St. Helens, Lancashire, England, on November 6, 1883; son of Patrick, a coal miner, and Mary (Dagnall) Brophy; Roman Catholic; married Anita Anstead on August 13, 1918; two children; attended primary school in St. Helens and the public schools of Philipsburg, Pa.; later studied at Brookwood Labor College; emigrated with family to the Pennsylvania coal-mining region in 1892; at age 12, began a 21-year period working in the mines of Pennsylvania, Iowa, Michigan, and Illinois; joined the United Mine Workers of America (UMWA) in 1899 and, after serving as a local union president, was president of District 2, UMWA, Central Pennsylvania, 1916-1926; was a leading exponent of public ownership of coal mines, and from 1921 to 1923 served on the UMWA's nationalization research committee, expounding the case for nationalization in several pamphlets; when 75,000 formerly nonunion

Central Pennsylvania miners responded to the 1922 national coal strike, Brophy urged that no wage agreement be signed until operators owning both union and nonunion mines signed for both; however, on August 15, John L. Lewis (q.v.) approved the Cleveland settlement that abandoned the District 2 nonunion miners and, on January 19, 1923, called off the nonunion miners' strike; defied the international officers and continued to support the strike by soliciting funds and borrowing heavily; however, finally conceded defeat in August, 1923; for the remainder of the 1920s, criticized Lewis's "No Backward Step" policy of forcing high wages on Northern union operators while simultaneously neglecting organizing efforts in the Southern nonunion fields, thus causing operators to shift production from their Northern union mines to their Southern nonunion mines; in 1926, founded along with several other critics of Lewis the "Save the Union Committee", which sponsored Brophy's candidacy against Lewis in the UMWA elections of 1926; was defeated by a margin of 170,000 to 60,000 votes amidst charges of fraud and election abuses; supported the 1930 call for a Springfield, Ill., convention to reorganize the union, but bolted the organization when the corruption-tainted Frank Farrington (q.v.) was seated; worked as a salesman for Columbia Conserve Company, Indianapolis, Ind., 1930-1933; after a reconciliation with Lewis, served as a UMWA organizer, 1933-1935, and national director of the Congress of Industrial Organizations (CIO), 1935-1939; after participating in the effort to organize steel and auto workers, became national director of the CIO's department of industrial union councils in 1951; politically an independent; authored *A Miner's Life* (1964); retired in 1961 and died in Falls Church, Va., February 20, 1963; *United Mine Workers Journal*, March 1, 1963; Walter Galenson, *The CIO Challenge to the AFL: A History of the American Labor Movement, 1935-1941* (1960); *AFL-CIO News*, February 23, 1963.

(J. H.)

BROUN, Heywood Campbell.   Born in Brooklyn, N.Y., December 7, 1888; son of Heywood Cox, a small businessman, and Henriette (Brose) Broun; an Episcopalian early in his life, but converted to Roman Catholicism during the 1930s; married Ruth Hale on June 6, 1917, and, after a divorce in 1933, Constantina Maria Incoronata Fruscella on January 9, 1935; two children; completed his elementary and secondary education in New York City; attended Harvard University, 1906-1910, but failed to receive a degree; in 1908, while a student at Harvard, began working as a reporter on the *New York Morning Telegraph*, and continued to 1912; after traveling to China and Japan with a theatrical company, became a reporter and columnist for the *New York Tribune* in 1912; served as a correspondent with the American Expeditionary Force in France during 1917 and was replaced because of his criticism of War Department inefficiencies; switched to the New York *World* in 1921 and began a widely read column entitled, "It Seems to Me"; was highly critical of government actions during the Red Scare following World War I; became involved in the Sacco-Vanzetti controversy and was eventually fired by the New York *World* for stridently defending them; joined the Scripps-Howard newspaper chain in 1928; ran for the U.S. Congress from New York on the Socialist party ticket in 1930; was one of the founders and served as vice-president of the New York Newspaper Guild in 1933; later in 1933, was instrumental in organizing the American Newspaper Guild (ANG) and was elected its first president; led the ANG through its early formative period when it faced strong opposition from publishers, who allegedly received government aid and assistance in their efforts to crush the new union; led the ANG into the American Federation of Labor in 1936, but switched to affiliation with the Congress of Industrial Organizations in 1937; also wrote regularly for the *Nation* and the *New Republic;* founded his own literary weekly, *Connecticut Nutmeg* (later *Broun's Nutmeg*) during the 1930s; authored 12 books, including *Pieces of Hate and Other Enthusiasms* (1922), *The Boy Grew Older* (1922), and *Gandle Follows His Nose* (1926); died in New York City, December 18, 1939; Daniel J. Leab, *A Union of Individuals: The Formation of the American Newspaper Guild, 1933-1935* (1970); Bruce Minton and John Stuart, *Men Who Lead Labor* (1937); Walter Galenson, *The CIO Challenge to the AFL: A History of the American Labor Movement, 1935-1941* (1960); *Dictionary of American Biography* (Supplement II).

BROWN, Edward J.   Born in Chicago, Ill., November 20, 1893; son of John J. and Katherine (Shaughnessy) Brown; married Jean E. Duffy on October 2, 1915; no children; graduated from high school and then began an apprenticeship as an electrician in 1911, soon joining Chicago, Ill., Local 282 of the International Brotherhood of Electrical Workers (IBEW); served as chief electrician for Robert White and Company, Chicago, 1925-1929; received an LLB degree from the Chicago Law School in 1927; became an IBEW special representative in 1930, and during his ten years in that position, was especially active in organizing electricians in Milwaukee, Wis.; served as a member of the IBEW executive council, 1937-1940; was a University of Wisconsin regent, 1935-1938; appointed

IBEW president by the executive council in 1940 to replace Daniel W. Tracy (q.v.), who resigned after being appointed Assistant U.S. Secretary of Labor; elected president of the IBEW in 1941; appointed to the National Defense Mediation Board during World War II; was a member of the American Federation of Labor international labor relations committee; after being defeated for reelection in 1946 by Daniel Tracy, was expelled from the IBEW as a result of charges related to his conduct as business manager of the Milwaukee local; left the labor movement, and conducted a law practice in Wisconsin and Washington, D.C., serving as a consultant to the Fuqua Insurance Company; died in Washington, D.C., January 31, 1950; Philip Taft, *The A.F. of L. From the Death of Gompers to the Merger* (1959); Walter Galenson, *The CIO Challenge to the AFL: A History of the American Labor Movement, 1935-1941* (1960); *The New York Times*, February 2, 1950.

BROWN, Guy Linden. Born in Boone, Iowa, August 22, 1893; son of Linden Forest, a minister, and Georgia Anna (Blackburn) Brown; Methodist; married Bernice Jackson on December 17, 1908; four children; attended the public schools of Ellston, Iowa; played professional baseball for a short time; entered railroad service as a fireman on the Chicago and North Western Railroad in 1909; became an engineer in 1914 and remained active in railroad service until 1945; joined the Brotherhood of Locomotive Engineers (BLE) and was elected local chairman of Division 860, Boone, Iowa, in 1939; was BLE general chairman for the Chicago and North Western Railroad, 1945-1947; elected second alternate grand chief engineer in 1947, assistant grand chief engineer in 1949, first assistant grand chief engineer in 1950 and grand chief engineer in 1953; retired union offices in 1960; Reed C. Richardson, *The Locomotive Engineer, 1863-1963: A Century of Railway Labor Relations and Work Rules* (1963); *Who's Who in Railroading* (1959); *Who's Who in America, 1958-1959*; *Labor*, August 8, 1953, May 28, 1960.

BROWN, Harvey Winfield. Born in Dow, Pa., October 28, 1883; son of William Washington, a farmer, and Catherine Brown; Protestant; married Emma C. Abbott on December 1, 1911; one child; attended elementary school in Pottsville, Pa.; apprenticed as a machinist in 1900 and worked at the craft until 1911; joined the International Association of Machinists (IAM) in 1905; served as business agent for the Wilkes-Barre, Pa., local, 1911-1915; was an IAM international organizer, 1915-1916, and business agent for the Newark, N.J., machinists' local, 1916-1921;

served as a delegate to the American Federation of Labor (AFL) conventions in 1919 and 1921; was elected an IAM vice-president in 1921; served as acting president during the illness of President Arthur Wharton (q.v.), 1938-1939; served as IAM president, 1940-1948; was elected an AFL vice-president and executive council member in 1941; as IAM leader, responded to the challenge of the Congress of Industrial Organizations and took advantage of New Deal labor legislation, National Labor Relations Board certification machinery, and general recovery and wartime prosperity; transformed the IAM from a predominantly railroad-machinist craft orientation to an industrial union heavily concentrated in the airframe and general manufacturing industries and launched aggressive organizing drives that added hundreds of thousands of new members; was a bellicose leader and exerted strong national control over dissident autonomy-minded locals; also engaged in a bitter conflict with IAM secretary-treasurer Emmet Davison (1916-1943); embroiled in an embittered, expensive, and perhaps unnecessary jurisdictional struggle with the carpenters and operating engineers and ultimately withdrew the union's affiliation from the AFL in protest of its jurisdictional treatment of the IAM; after two adverse rulings by the National Labor Relations Board, the IAM executive council in 1948 ordered the racial exclusion clause removed from local's secret ritual, an action upheld by the national convention the following year; became a vice-president of the Union Labor Bank and Trust Company in Indianapolis, Ind., in 1924; politically nonpartisan; died in Harrisburg, Pa., September 4, 1956; Mark Perlman, *The Machinists: A New Study in American Trade Unionism* (1961), and *Democracy in the International Association of Machinists* (1962); Solon DeLeon, ed., *The American Labor Who's Who* (1925); *Who's Who in Labor* (1946).

(J.H.)

BROWN, Henry ("Hank") Stanley.   Born in Pittsburgh, Pa., October 24, 1920; son of Stanley J., a coal miner, and Sophie Brown; Roman Catholic; married Sophie E. Wigman in 1939; three children; attended the primary and secondary schools of Pennsylvania and was a student at San Antonio (Junior) College, 1950-1951, St. Mary's University, 1952, and Harvard University, 1956; joined Plumbers and Pipefitters Local 142 of the United Association of Plumbers and Steamfitters of the United States and Canada and served it as business manager, 1940-1953, 1959-1961; was educational director of the Texas State Federation of Labor (TSFL), 1953-1959; after the American Federation of Labor-Congress of Industrial Organizations' (AFL-CIO) merger in Texas, was elected president of the

Texas AFL-CIO in 1961, serving in that capacity until 1971; worked to improve conditions of Texas's low-paid Mexican and black workers, and increased their union memberships by one-third between 1961-1968; persuaded the Texas AFL-CIO Council to contribute $100,000 to support families of striking Mexican-American farm workers; as head of the Texas AFL-CIO committee on political education, promoted a liberal-labor-Mexican-black political alliance in the early 1960s and challenged the conservative wing of the Texas Democratic party with liberal candidates for state and national office; lobbied in the Texas legislature against increased auto insurance rates; increased the state AFL-CIO budget to $500,000 by raising the tax on each union member from 8¢ to 25¢; one-third of budget went to equal-opportunity activities and another large share to community service; was a frequent critic in the 1960s of Governor John Connally's conservative position on the repeal of Section 14b of the Taft-Hartley Act, medical care for the elderly, the war on poverty, bracero programs, state minimum wage laws, and minority job discrimination; served during his career as vice-president of the TSFL, president of the Texas Pipe Trades Association, executive secretary of the Texas Building and Construction Trades Council, vice-president of the San Antonio Building Trades Council, and on advisory committees for several state and national agencies and charitable organizations; politically a Democrat; *Who's Who in America, 1972-1973; Business Week,* June 22, 1968; *AFL-CIO News,* June 5, 1965.

(M.E.R.)

BROWN, Irving Joseph.   Born in New York City, November 20, 1911; son of Ralph, a Teamster union official, and Fannie (Singer) Brown; married Lillie Clara Smith on March 13, 1934; one child; received a B.A. degree in economics from New York University in 1932 and took postgraduate courses for two years at Columbia University; participated in the efforts to organize the automobile industry, 1934-1937 and was physically attacked and savagely beaten by representatives of the Ford Motor Company; became a national American Federation of Labor (AFL) organizer in 1936 and served in that capacity until 1942; after being recommended by AFL, appointed as one of the labor representatives on the War Production Board in 1942; was a member of the International Association of Machinists and elected to the executive committee of the International Metalworkers Federation in 1945; became director of the labor and management division of the branch of the United States Foreign Economic Administration designed to administer labor policy in occupied areas following World War II; resigned from the position because of his disagreement with official U.S.

policy of limiting union organization in Germany to the local and factory levels; became the AFL's European representative in October, 1945, and later was named AFL representative on the European Recovery Program trade-union advisory board; was one of the founders of the International Confederation of Free Trade Unions (ICFTU) in 1949, which seceded from the Communist-dominated World Federation of Trade Unions; served as the ICFTU representative to the 1951 labor conference in Karachi, Pakistan that created the first non-Communist regional union organization in Asia; was named ICFTU representative to the United Nations in 1962; was appointed director of the African-American Labor Center, an AFL-Congress of Industrial Organizations' agency designed to support non-Communist unions in Africa, in 1965; was a determined anti-Communist and devoted much of his trade union career to the promotion of a "free" trade union movement in Western Europe; Ronald Radosh, *American Labor and United States Foreign Policy: The Cold War in the Unions from Gompers to Lovestone* (1969); Joseph C. Goulden, *Meany* (1972); Philip Taft, *The A.F. of L. From the Death of Gompers to the Merger* (1959); *Current Biography* (1951).

BRYSON, Hugh.   Born on an Illinois farm, October 4, 1914; son of Hugh E., a farmer, and Josie W. (Gaffney) Bryson; married Abigail Alvarez on June 23, 1945; was graduated from high school and then attended a business college in 1932; joined the National Marine Cooks' and Stewards' Association (NMCSA) and served successively as assistant secretary, dispatcher, patrolman, and ship's delegate; was vice-president of the San Francisco branch of Labor's Non-Partisan League in 1939; elected to the executive board of the San Francisco Industrial Union Council, Congress of Industrial Organizations (CIO) in 1942 and vice-president in 1946; served as a vice-president of the California State Industrial Union Council, CIO, 1944-1946; elected president of the NMCSA in 1946; after the NMCSA was expelled from the CIO for alleged Communist domination in 1949, was indicted and convicted of perjury for filing a non-Communist affidavit under the provisions of the Taft-Hartley Act; the NMCSA rapidly deteriorated as a result of Bryson's imprisonment and its expulsion from the CIO and was absorbed by Harry Lundeberg's (q.v.) Sailors' Union of the Pacific; identified himself as a Democrat, but strongly supported the candidacy of Henry A. Wallace on the Progressive party ticket in 1948 and was the principal architect of the Independent Progressive party of California which was modeled after the American Labor party in New York; edited the NMCSA organ, *Voice*, 1944-1951; authored *History of the*

Marine Cooks and Stewards (1944); Joseph R. Starobin, *American Communism in Crisis, 1943-1957* (1972); David A. Shannon, *The Decline of American Communism: A History of the Communist Party of the United States since 1945* (1959); Joseph P. Goldberg, *The Maritime Story: A Study in Labor-Management Relations* (1958).

BUCHANAN, Joseph Ray.   Born in Hannibal, Mo., December 6, 1851; son of Robert Sylvester and Mary Ellen (Holt) Buchanan; married Lucy A. Clise on December 16, 1879; employed in a variety of occupations after leaving the public schools of Hannibal; obtained work on a Hannibal newspaper in 1876 and learned the typesetting trade; moved to Denver, Colo., in 1878, becoming, in turn, a typesetter and then managing editor of a daily newspaper, the proprietor of an unsuccessful printing office, and a prospector; joined the International Typographical Union (ITU) in 1878; moved to Leadville, Colo., in 1879, but threats against his life growing out of his support of striking miners forced him to return to Denver the following year; served as the Denver delegate to the national ITU convention in 1882; joined the Noble Order of the Knights of Labor (K of L) during the same year and, along with Samuel H. Laverty, began publishing the *Labor Enquirer*, a weekly labor newspaper; named Rocky Mountain representative of the International Workingmen's Association the following year; led a successful strike of Union Pacific shopmen in 1884 and later the same year won a national reputation by leading successful strikes against railroads controlled by Jay Gould; unsuccessfully attempted as a member of the general executive board of the K of L to mediate the growing differences between the K of L and the American Federation of Labor, 1884-1886; led a secessionist movement in 1886 after being expelled from the K of L as a result of differences with the Order's leader, Terence Powderly (q.v.) over the expulsion of the Cigarmakers' International Union; moved to Chicago, Ill., in 1887, and attempted to gain amnesty for the men convicted of the Haymarket Square bombings; moved to Montclair, N.J., in 1888 and failed in two attempts to be elected to the United States Congress; served as labor editor of the *New York Evening Journal*, 1904-1915; was a member of the conciliation council of the U.S. Department of Labor, 1918-1921; one of the organizers of the People's party in 1892 and served on its national committee in 1892, 1896, and 1900; was a Socialist and had at one time been a member of the Socialist Labor party; authored *The Story of a Labor Agitator* (1903); died in Montclair, N.J., September 13, 1924; Norman J. Ware, *The Labor Movement in the United States, 1860-1895* (1929); Gerald N. Grob, *Workers and Utopia: A*

Study of Ideological Conflict in the American Labor Movement, 1865-1900 (1961); *Dictionary of American Biography* (Vol. III).

BUCKLEY, Leo Jerome.   Born in Lewiston, Me., February 4, 1899; son of Michael Horace and Margaret (Moriarty) Buckley; Roman Catholic; married Elizabeth Ray on April 18, 1940; one child; completed grammar school; became an apprentice in the stereotype trade and later became an electrotyper; joined New York Local 1 of the International Stereotypers' and Electrotypers' Union of North America (SEUNA); after serving as vice-president of Local 1, 1932-1938, was elected international president of the SEUNA in 1938; served during World War II on the newspaper commission of the War Labor Board, the printing division of the War Production Board, and as a member of Industrial Division 49 of the Wage and Hour Board; served as chairman of the board of governors of the Allied Printing Trades Association and on the board of directors of the Union Labor Life Insurance Company; died in New York City, June 10, 1956; *Who Was Who in America* (Vol. III); *The New York Times*, June 11, 1956.

BUCKMASTER, Leland Stanford.   Born in Geneva, Ind., March 30, 1894; son of William Vance, a farmer and contractor, and Elizabeth (Thatcher) Buckmaster; Protestant; married Olive Beatrice Shimp on May 11, 1920; four children; was graduated from high school and then attended Tri-State College in Angola, Ind., majoring in teacher education; taught school in rural Indiana schools, 1913-1917; served with the U.S. Army during World War I; employed as a tin finisher and builder with the Firestone Tire and Rubber Company, Akron, Ohio, 1919-1937; joined American Federation of Labor (AFL) Federal Labor Union 18321 in 1933 and served as shop committeeman, member of the executive board and president; when the federal local was converted to Local 7 of the United Rubber Workers of America (URWA) (now the United Rubber, Cork, Linoleum and Plastic Workers of America), was elected president and served until 1941; became a member of the URWA general executive board in 1936 and was elected a URWA vice-president in 1941 and international president in 1945; was considered a conservative anti-Communist in the internal ideological conflicts of the union during the 1940s; removed as president in 1949 by the general executive board of the URWA for "malfeasance in office," a charge growing from his conflicts with the leadership of a Pottstown, Pa., local, but was returned to office four months later when reelected by delegates to the annual convention; was a member of the

united labor policy committee organized by the AFL, CIO, and independent unions to develop uniform policies on issues affecting labor during the
Korean War; was one of the major advocates of a merger between the AFL
and CIO; after the 1955 merger, was elected an AFL-CIO vice-president
and executive council member, serving until 1962; retired as president of
the URWA in 1960; politically a Democrat; died in Henderson, Ky.,
January 2, 1967; Harold S. Roberts, *The Rubber Workers* (1944); *Fortune*
(July, 1951); *Who's Who in Labor* (1946); *The New York Times*, January 4,
1967.

BUGNIAZET, Gustave M.   Born in New York City in 1878; Roman
Catholic; married Mary Doyle and remarried after her death in 1953; six
children (three of them stepchildren); became an apprentice electrician
after completing a grammar school education; joined Local 419 of the
International Brotherhood of Electrical Workers (IBEW) in 1902, and for
five years, served the Local as business manager; later transferred his
membership to IBEW Local 98 in Philadelphia, Pa.; was elected an IBEW
vice-president in 1911, serving until 1925; served during World War I as a
member of the adjustment board of the U.S. Railroad Administration;
appointed the IBEW's national legislative representative in Washington,
D.C., in 1918; served as an assistant to both the president and secretary of
the IBEW prior to being elected international secretary of the Brotherhood in 1925; was elected a vice-president and member of the American
Federation of Labor (AFL) executive council in 1930, serving until 1946
when a fourth vice-president; was a member of the AFL committee that in
1936-1937 attempted to resolve the differences with the Committee on
Industrial Organization (CIO); was appointed to the AFL committee on
social insurance in 1939; was appointed as an AFL alternate to the Combined War Labor Board formed by the AFL and the CIO at the request of
President Franklin D. Roosevelt in 1942; served on numerous AFL *ad hoc*
and standing committees, and as secretary of the Electrical Workers'
Benefit Fund which administreed the IBEW's insurance program; edited
The Journal of Electrical Workers and Operators, 1925-1947; retired from
union positions in 1947 and entered private business, serving for a time as
president of the American Standard Life Insurance Company; died in
Washington, D.C., March 25, 1960; Philip Taft, *The A.F. of L. From the
Death of Gompers to the Merger* (1959); Walter Galenson, *The CIO Challenge to the AFL: A History of the American Labor Movement, 1935-1941*
(1960); Solon DeLeon, ed., *The American Labor Who's Who* (1925); *Labor*,
April 2, 1960.

BURKE, John Patrick. Born in North Duxbury, Vt., January 21, 1884; son of a Vermont farmer; Roman Catholic; completed high school in Franklin, N.H., and during 1912-1913, attended the Rand School of Social Science in New York City; while completing his formal education, worked variously as a textile operative, carpenter, and paper mill worker; while working for the International Paper Company in Franklin, N.H., helped organize a local of the International Brotherhood of Pulp, Sulphite, and Paper Mill Workers (IBPSPMW); elected a vice-president of the New Hampshire State Federation of Labor in 1914; became an international vice-president of the IBPSPMW in 1914 and elected international secretary in 1916; elected international IBPSPMW president in 1918; was president until 1965 and during his time in office the IBPSPMW grew from a small, localized union into a large international organization with 700 locals in the United States and Canada and 175,000 members; during this period, the work week was reduced from 72 to 40 hours, wages were increased substantially, and paper-mill workers gained a variety of fringe benefits, including old-age pensions, hospital benefits, and paid vacations and holidays; retired from union affairs and was named president emeritus in 1965; died in Miami Beach, Fla., April 21, 1966; Harry E. Graham, *The Paper Rebellion: Development and Upheaval in Pulp and Paper Unionism* (1970); *AFL-CIO News*, January 23, 1965, April 30, 1966; Solon DeLeon, ed., *The American Labor Who's Who* (1925).

BURKE, Walter James. Born in Antioch, Ill., September 14, 1911; son of Anthony Frederick, a printer, and Margaret Luella Burke; Roman Catholic; married Aletha Phyllis Luff on August 12, 1939; five children; was graduated from Waukegan (Ill.) Township High School; taught printing in high school, 1930-1932; moved to Fond du Lac, Wis., and worked as an inspector in a metal-fabricating plant, 1932-1937; became president meanwhile of Lodge 1935, Amalgamated Association of Iron, Steel, and Tin Workers; employed on the staff of the Steelworkers Organizing Committee, 1937-1939; served as secretary-treasurer of the Wisconsin Congress of Industrial Organizations' Industrial Union Council, 1939-1941; during World War II, was a panel member of the Chicago Regional War Labor Board; was a member of the United Steelworkers of America (USWA) wage inequities committee during the 1940s and helped revise the entire wage structure in basic steel; became director of USWA District 32 (Milwaukee, Wis., area) in 1948 and was reelected to that position several times; was one of several district directors opposed to David McDonald's (q.v.) administration and managed Joseph Molony's (q.v.) 1955 campaign for international vice-president; was teamed on a slate with I.W. Abel (q.v.) and Molony in 1965 and was elected international secretary-treasurer; was reelected in 1969 and 1973; authored, and played a major role in gaining adoption of, a graduated dues increase that was accepted by a special convention in 1968 and made possible a strike fund; became a vice-president of the American Federation of Labor-CIO industrial union department in 1965; represented American unions at the 75th anniversary convention of the German Metalworkers Federation in 1966; served on numerous governmental commissions; was chairman of a special committee to direct USWA community action programs aimed at stabilizing employment and creating new jobs in communities threatened by plant shutdowns; politically a Democrat; John Herling, *People and Power in the Steelworkers Union* (1972); *Who's Who in America, 1972-1973.*

(D.G.S.)

BURNS, Matthew James.   Born in Appleton, Wis., November 6, 1887; son of Andrew Byrnes, a farmer, and Mary (Davey) Burns; Roman Catholic; married Sarah Elvira Hendricksen in 1912; four children; completed a grammar school education in Appleton and later took courses from the Funk and Wagnalls Correspondence School; began work in the pulp and paper mills of Kaukauna, Wis., in 1901; joined the Kaukauna Local 20 of the International Brotherhood of Paper Makers (IBPM) in 1902; served as an IBPM general organizer, 1920-1922; elected international secretary of the IBPM in 1922, serving in that capacity until 1928; elected international IBPM president in 1929, serving until 1940; joined the International Brotherhood of Pulp, Sulphite and Paper Mill Workers in 1940; served during World War II as a labor economist, an alternate member of the Overall Appeals Board, and assistant director, Pulp and Paper Division, of the War Production Board; reelected president of the IBPM in 1943 and served until his retirement in 1947; edited the *Paper Makers' Journal*, 1922-1928; politically a Democrat; authored *History of the International Brotherhood of Paper Makers* (1922); died in Albany, N.Y., June 15, 1967; Harry E. Graham, *The Paper Rebellion: Development and Upheaval in Pulp and Paper Unionism* (1970); *AFL-CIO News*, June 24, 1967; *Who's Who in Labor* (1946).

BURNS, Thomas F.   Born in Holyoke, Mass., June 19, 1906; son of Thomas F., a loom fixer, and Elizabeth Burns; Roman Catholic; married Maude M. Walton on July 25, 1925; three children; completed one year of high school, then left school to work full time as an employee of the Fisk

Tire and Rubber Corporation at Chicopee Falls, Mass.; was one of the principal organizers of American Federation of Labor (AFL) Federal Labor Union 18363 at the Fisk plant in 1933; became president and business agent of Fisk Local 18363; served as an AFL organizer, 1934-1935; was one of the leading critics of AFL domination of the United Rubber Workers of America (URWA), which had been chartered by the AFL in 1935, and led the movement toward autonomy; was elected a URWA vice-president in 1935 and became a member of the general executive board; was a staunch advocate of industrial unionism and supported the URWA's affiliation with the Congress of Industrial Organizations (CIO) in 1936; during World War II, was chief of the Office of Price Management's labor disputes section, a labor consultant to the National Defense Advisory Committee, and a deputy vice-chairman of the labor-products division of the War Production Board; served as an assistant to the chairman of the CIO's Political Action Committee; Harold S. Roberts, *The Rubber Workers: Labor Organization and Collective Bargaining in the Rubber Industry* (1944); *Who's Who in Labor* (1946).

BYRON, Robert.   Born in Lynwood, Scotland, ca. 1880; the son of a coal miner and active trade unionist; Protestant; married; one child; emigrated with his parents to the United States in 1888, after his father had been blacklisted in Scotland because of union organizing activities; attended the public schools of Springfield, Ill.; at age fifteen began to work in the coal mines around Springfield; in 1897 was hired in a sheet metal works, and three years later, became one of the founders of Springfield Local 84 of the Sheet Metal Workers' International Association (SMWIA); served Local 84 as recording and financial secretary; was an active participant in local and state labor organizations, serving as secretary of the Springfield Federation of Labor, business agent of the Springfield Building Trades Council, and a delegate to the Illinois State Federation of Labor; became an international representative for the SMWIA in 1908 and was assigned an organizing jurisdiction ranging from Pittsburgh, Pa., to the Pacific Coast and from Alaska to the Gulf of Mexico; was appointed international president of the SMWIA in 1939 and was subsequently reelected to the post until his death; substantially increased the membership of the SMWIA during his incumbency and helped negotiate collective bargaining agreements providing higher wages, better working conditions, and a variety of fringe benefits; was a vice-president of the American Federation of Labor (AFL) building and metal trades departments; served as a delegate to over 50 AFL and AFL-Congress of Industrial Organizations' national conventions, and represented the AFL at meetings of the International Labor Organization and the International Confederation of Free Trade Unions; died in Northbrook, Ill., May 30, 1959; *Labor*, June 6, 1959; *The New York Times*, May 31, 1959; *The American Federation of Labor Weekly News Service*, January 21, 1939.

CADDY, Samuel Hubert.   Born at Short Health, Staffordshire, England, December 9, 1883; son of Henry, a coal miner, and Amy (Davenport) Caddy; Methodist; married Dorothy Eva Johnston on September 2, 1919; two children; attended elementary school for five years and then, at age nine, began attending school six hours a day and working five hours in a mine, hand-turning a ventilation fan, then driving a mine pony, and finally, at age fifteen, becoming a full-time coal loader; emigrated to Halifax, Nova Scotia, in 1905; obtaining a series of mining jobs, worked his way across Canada, saving $1,400; used part of money to help educate his sister; dragged a supply sled 375 miles into the Alaskan gold fields with three companions and spent 23 months prospecting, making one $7,000 strike; joined the United Mine Workers of America (UMWA) in 1907 by transferring from the British Miners Union; settled near Seattle, Wash., in 1909 and worked there in coal mines; became an active union organizer; beginning in 1918, represented District 10 on the UMWA international executive board for five years, and then served as a UMWA international representative for ten years; from 1918 to 1933, organized local unions in Oklahoma, West Virginia, Indiana, Pennsylvania, and Kentucky; shortly before the passage of the National Industrial Recovery Act in June, 1933, was sent by President John L. Lewis (q.v.) to organize UMWA District 30 in Eastern Kentucky, where the UMWA had all but evaporated after World War I; solidly organized the 25,000 miners of District 30 within five weeks, in contrast to the prolonged and violent union campaign in nearby Harlan County, Ky.; in 1934, was appointed by Lewis as president of District 30 and as a member of the UMWA international executive board and served for 25 years until his death in 1959; as a result of the complicated course of the UMWA's relationship with the rival Congress of Industrial Organizations (CIO) and the American Federation of Labor (AFL), was the only man in Kentucky history to serve for two years as president of the Kentucky State Federation of Labor, AFL, and three years as president of the Kentucky Industrial Union Council, CIO; served from 1933 to 1945 on various federal government coal boards; active for a quarter of a century in Kentucky Democratic politics and served on a governor's committee to reorganize state government; fought before the state legislature and congressional committees for better mine safety laws, improved mine ventilation, rock dusting, more mine mechanization, improved hospitalization, pensions, and security benefits for miners, against the use of black powder for blasting, and for his pet project, the chain of seven UMWA hospitals in eastern Kentucky; known as "the grand old man of Kentucky labor," he died in Lexington, Ky., January 24, 1959; *United Mine Workers Journal*, February 1, 1959; *Who's Who in Labor* (1946).

(J.H.)

CAHAN, Abraham.   Born in Podberezye, Russian Lithuania (now part of the Soviet Union), July 7, 1860; son of Shachno, a storekeeper and Hebrew teacher, and Sarah C. Cahan; Jewish; married Anna Braunstein in 1887; was graduated from the Teachers' Seminary in Vilna in 1881 and became a teacher in a Jewish elementary school; participated in revolutionary activities, and therefore was forced to flee Russia in 1882 and emigrated to the United States; was a vigorous participant in the organization of immigrant Jewish workers and in the founding of a variety of Jewish trade unions; helped found the Jewish Socialist periodicals *Neue Zeit* in 1886 and *Arbeiter-Zeitung* in 1890; served as editor of the *Arbeiter-Zeitung*, 1891-1894; edited *Zukunft*, a Yiddish periodical, 1894-1897; became the first editor of the *Jewish Daily Forward* in 1897; associated with Lincoln Steffens' *Commercial Advertiser* as a police reporter, 1898-1902; was a moderate Socialist and represented the American Socialist movement at numerous international Socialist congresses; resumed editorship of the *Daily Forward* in 1902; authored numerous books and articles, including *The Rise of David Levinsky* (1917) and *Bletter von Mein Leben*, 5 vols. (1926-1931); died in New York City, August 31, 1951; Moses Rischin, *The Promised City: New York's Jews, 1870-1914* (1962); Ronald Sanders, *The Downtown Jews: Portraits of an Immigrant Generation* (1969); Melech Epstein, *Profiles of Eleven* (1965), and *Jewish Labor in the U.S.A., 1914-1952* (2 vols., 1953).

CAIRNS, Thomas Francis.   Born in Durhamshire, England, in 1875; son of John, a clerical worker, and Jane (Gibney) Cairns; Presbyterian; married Melvina Koon on June 14, 1899; two children; attended high school in England and took a mining engineering course at Scranton (Pa.) Correspondence School; emigrated to the United States, settling in Scranton; joined the United Mine Workers of America (UMWA) there; UMWA president John Mitchell (q.v.) appointed him as an international organizer in 1902; participated in the founding of the West Virginia State Federation of Labor (WVSFL) in 1903; became a member of the UMWA international executive board in 1908, representing District 17, Kanawha District of West Virginia; served as president of District 17, UMWA, 1912-1917, during the violent Kanawha Valley coal strike of 1912-1913; served as an American Federation of Labor (AFL) district representative and organizer, 1938-1949; when the officials of the WVSFL refused to execute the AFL's order to expel the UMWA and other Congress of Industrial Organizations' (CIO) affiliates in August, 1937, they were expelled from the AFL and founded the rival West Virginia State Industrial Union Council, CIO; headed, along with William Kirk, another AFL organizer, 53-delegate "loyalist" faction that reorganized the WVSFL; in December, 1937, AFL President Green (q.v.) appointed William J. Dillon as acting president of the WVSFL and he in turn appointed Cairns acting secretary-treasurer; elected president of the WVSFL during the reorganization convention in 1938, serving until 1945; transferred his local union affiliation from the UMWA to the International Brotherhood of Teamsters' Local 175, Charleston, W. Va., in 1938 and five years later affiliated with the Federal Labor Union of Enamel Workers Local 23055, Dunbar, W. Va.; provided, together with Secretary-Treasurer Volney Andrews (1938-1953), efficient and stable, but rather unimaginative, caretaker leadership of the WVSFL; as president, concentrated on adding to membership, which increased from 11,000 to 18,000, and on affiliation of craft locals, but ignored opportunities for labor legislation and public education; followed a highly controversial political policy of endorsing candidates who were anti-CIO (e.g., Republican gubernatorial candidate Chapman Revercomb in 1940 rather than Democrat Matthew M. Neely, who possessed an excellent, though pro-CIO, labor record); kept in office throughout World War II only out of deference to "Uncle Tom's" 53 years of service-to labor; finally, in 1945, was unseated by critics who, in a bitter election, bestowed the office on Eugene Carter, a reluctant, but able, Charleston teamster; Cairns was named honorary chairman for life; died in Charleston, W. Va., March 22, 1949; *Who's Who in Labor* (1946); *The New York Times*, March 23, 1949; Evelyn L. K. Harris and Frank J. Krebs, *From Humble Beginnings: West Virginia State Federation of Labor, 1903-1957* (1960).

(J.H.)

CALVIN, William Austin.   Born in St. John, New Brunswick, Canada, February 5, 1898; son of John, a boilermaker, and Agnes (Kelly) Calvin; Methodist; married Iranell Marian Jester on April 12, 1936; three children;

completed elementary school in New Brunswick; employed as a boiler-maker by the Canadian Pacific Railroad, and a Baltimore, Md., firm; joined the International Brotherhood of Boilermakers, Iron Shipbuilders, and Helpers of America (IBB) in 1914; joined the Canadian Army in 1915, not returning to civilian life until 1919 due to a combat wound; emigrated to Florida and went to work as a boilermaker for the Seaboard Airline Rail-road; elected chairman of his local shop committee in 1921 and became president of District Lodge 40 in 1924; in 1929 elected a vice-president of the IBB; served as secretary-treasurer of the American Federation of Labor (AFL) metal trades department, 1933-1940; served on several government boards during the 1930s and 1940s, including the National.Recovery Administration's Industrial Relations Committee for Shipbuilding; helped draft the Merchant Marine Act of 1936, which gave the Maritime Commission comprehensive regulatory powers; left his union position in 1951 to become a full-time labor specialist for the National Production Authority; returned to the IBB in 1953 as assistant to President Charles J. MacGowan (q.v.); replaced MacGowan as president the following year and was elected to that office in 1957 and reelected in 1961; was elected a vice-president and executive council member of the AFL in 1961; was a member of the Railway Labor Executives' Association; visited Latin America as a labor specialist on behalf of the U.S. State Department in 1958; was an AFL-Congress of Industrial Organizations' fraternal delegate to the Indian National Trade Union Congress in 1959; was an active proponent of nuclear-powered merchant vessels, serving as a director of the Fund for Peaceful Atomic Development, Inc., a nonprofit group set up in 1954 to support President Dwight D. Eisenhower's atoms-for-peace program; died in Kansas City, Kan., January 27, 1962; *The New York Times*, December 21, 1954, January 28, 1962; *Journal of the International Brotherhood of Boilermakers, Iron Shipbuilders and Blacksmiths* (March, 1962).

(D.G.S.)

CAMERON, Andrew Carr. Born in Berwick-on-Tweed, England, September 28, 1836; son of a Scots printer; worked in his father's printing shop after receiving a limited elementary education; emigrated with par-ents to the United States in 1851, settling near Chicago, Ill.; joined the International Typographical Union while working for a Chicago news-paper; as a result of a printers' strike in 1864, became the editor of the newly established *Workingman's Advocate*, which served as the official organ of the Chicago Trades Assembly and later the National Labor Union (NLU); elected president of the Chicago Trades Assembly in 1866 and served for four years; also elected president of the Grand Eight Hour League and the Illinois State Labor Association; was one of the founders of the NLU and served as an organizer and as chairman of the NLU platform committee for six years; was an NLU delegate to the Fourth Congress of the International Workingmen's Association (IWA) in Basle in 1869, but became hostile to the IWA after it moved its headquarters to the United States; was prominently identified with the cause of independent labor political action and deliberately kept himself out of the limelight in the Industrial Congress, which he helped organize; discontinued publication of the *Workingman's Advocate* in 1880 and then was editor until his death of the *Inland Printer*; died in Chicago, Ill., May 28, 1890; David Montgomery, *Beyond Equality: Labor and the Radical Republicans, 1862-1872* (1967); Norman Ware, *The Labor Movement in the United States, 1860-1895* (1929); *Dictionary of American Biography* (Vol. III); John R. Commons, *et. al., History of Labour in the United States*, Vol. II (1918).

CANNON, Joseph D.　　Born in Locust Gap, Pa., October 26, 1871; son of John, a coal miner, and Bridgid (Early) Cannon; married Laura G. Cannon on August 16, 1911; completed primary school and then began work in the mines; in 1899 joined the Western Federation of Miners (WFM); involved in the efforts to organize copper workers in Arizona in 1906-1908, 1917, and served as president of the Bisbee (Ariz.) Miners' Union and the Arizona State Federation of Labor; served as an organizer for the WFM (name changed to International Union of Mine, Mill and Smelter Workers in 1916), 1907-1920; was a member of the executive board of the WFM, 1911-1912; served as a director of the Cooperative League of the U.S.A., 1918-1920; was a member of the executive board of the American Federation of Labor mining department, 1914-1920; participated in the efforts to organize the steel industry, 1919-1920, 1936-1937, and served as an organizer and business representative for unions in the cleaning and dyeing, paper box, and doll industries; joined the Congress of Industrial Organizations (CIO) in 1937 and became a field representative; served as the chairman of the CIO's Distillery Workers' Organizing Committee; served as Kentucky regional CIO director until his retirement in 1946 from union affairs; was an active Socialist and ran for the U.S. Congress from Arizona on the Socialist party ticket in 1906 and 1908, for the U.S. Senate from New York in 1916, and for governor of New York in 1920; joined the American Labor party shortly after it was organized in New York in 1936; died in New York City, January 4, 1952; Vernon H.

Jensen, *Heritage of Conflict: Labor Relations in the Nonferrous Metals Industry up to 1930* (1950); Erma Angevine, *In League with the Future* (1959); Solon DeLeon, ed., *The American Labor Who's Who* (1925).

CAREY, James Barron.   Born in Philadelphia, Pa., August 12, 1911; son of John, a paymaster at the U.S. Mint, and Margaret (Loughery) Carey; Roman Catholic; married Margaret McCormick on January 8, 1938; two children; was graduated from high school in Glassboro, N.J.; worked in a Philco Corporation radio laboratory in Philadelphia while attending the night school of Drexel Institute; studied electrical engineering from 1929 to 1931, then attended the University of Pennsylvania's Wharton (evening) School of Finance and Commerce, 1931-1932; helped organize the workers in the Philco Corporation plant where he was employed and led a successful strike for union recognition; became a general American Federation of Labor (AFL) organizer in 1934; became president of Radio and Television Workers Federal Labor Union 18368, Philadelphia, in 1935; elected president of the National Radio and Allied Trades Council the same year and unsuccessfully sought an AFL charter; elected president of the newly organized United Electrical, Radio and Machine Workers of America (UE) in March, 1935; was an advocate of industrial unionism and led his union into the Congress of Industrial Organizations (CIO) six months later; was a staunch anti-Communist and was defeated for reelection to the UE presidency in 1941 by a left-wing coalition of delegates; elected national secretary of the CIO in 1938 and general secretary-treasurer in 1942; served during World War II as an associate member of the National Defense Mediation Board and as a member of the Production Planning Board of the Office of Production Management; attended the 1945 London and Paris conferences that resulted in the organization of the World Federation of Trade Unions; appointed to the Presidential Commission on Civil Rights in 1946; in 1949 assumed the presidency of the newly chartered International Union of Electrical, Radio, and Machine Workers (IUE) after the UE was expelled from the CIO because of alleged Communist domination; was a member of the AFL-CIO unity committee that negotiated the merger of the two organizations in 1955; became an AFL-CIO vice-president and executive council member, and was appointed secretary-general of the industrial union department; resigned as president of the IUE after his 1965 reelection was successfully challenged by Paul Jennings (q.v.); left the IUE and became a labor liaison representative of the United Nations Association; was a Democrat and a member of the national board of Americans for Democratic Action; died in Silver Spring, Md., September

1, 1973; Philip Taft, *The A.F. of L. From the Death of Gompers to the Merger* (1959); Walter Galenson, *The CIO Challenge to the AFL: A History of the American Labor Movement, 1935-1941* (1960); Max M. Kampelman, *The Communist Party vs. the C.I.O.: A Study in Power Politics* (1957); *Current Biography* (1951); *AFL-CIO News*, September 16, 1973.

CARROLL, Thomas Claude.   Born in Donalds, S.C., May 22, 1894; son of Samuel Harvey, a railroad section foreman, and Ida Mae Smith; Methodist; married Marie E. Smith in 1914 and remarried after her death; was graduated from high school and then worked in a variety of railroad jobs—clerk, brakeman, conductor, section foreman—on the Piedmont, Alabama Railroad, 1913-1919; joined the Brotherhood of Maintenance of Way Employees (BMWE) during this period; hired by the Louisville and Nashville Railroad as a section hand and yard foreman in 1919; elected general chairman for the Dixie (Southeastern) Federation of the BMWE in 1919, serving until 1925; served as president of the International Association of General Chairmen, BMWE, 1920-1922, elected secretary of the grand lodge executive board in 1922, serving until 1925; served as a grand lodge vice-president for the Southeastern region and as a member of the grand lodge executive board during the period 1925-1947; was appointed national legislative representative in Washington, D.C., in 1926, serving in that capacity for several years; elected grand lodge president in 1947; along with the leaders of other nonoperating railroad unions, negotiated shortly after taking office a 40-hour week at 48-hours' pay; also negotiated several wage increases and a variety of fringe benefits; became president emeritus in 1958, after successfully negotiating the first contract to include a national job-stabilization agreement with carriers; was a Democrat; died in Bradenton, Fla., in September, 1960; Denver Willard Hertel, *History of the Brotherhood of Maintenance of Way Employees: Its Birth and Growth, 1877-1955* (1955); Brotherhood of Maintenance of Way Employees, *Pictorial History, 1877-1951* (1952); *Who's Who in Labor* (1946); *Labor*, October 8, 1960.

CARTER, William Samuel.   Born in Austin, Tex., August 11, 1859; son of Samuel Miles and Margaret Frances (Oliphant) Carter; married Mary Evelyn Gorsuch on December 26, 1880, and, after her death in 1892, Julia I. Cross on November 27, 1902; attended the public schools of Williamson County, Tex., and then the Agricultural and Mechanical College of Texas for two years; worked for a time as a cowboy before becoming a fireman on a southwestern railroad in 1879; worked during 1879-1894 as a baggageman, fireman, and engineer on several different railroads in the United States and Mexico; joined the Brotherhood of Locomotive Firemen and Enginemen (BLFE); became editor and manager of the *Brotherhood of Locomotive Firemen and Enginemen's Magazine* in 1894 and served until 1904; elected general secretary-treasurer of the BLFE in 1904 and president in 1909; appointed director of the Division of Labor of the U.S. Railway Administration during World War I; retired from the presidency of the BLFE in 1922 and was appointed manager of the newly-organized research department; an opponent of compulsory arbitration, but was an essentially conservative trade unionist who advocated mediation and arbitration as an alternative to strikes; supported the Democratic party; died in Baltimore, Md., March 15, 1923; Brotherhood of Locomotive Firemen and Enginemen, *An Historical Sketch of the Brotherhood* (1937); *Dictionary of American Biography* (Vol. III).

CASHEN, Thomas Cecil.   Born in South Thompson, Ohio, September 15, 1879; son of John, a farmer, and Sarah (McKee) Cashen; Roman Catholic; married Marie Burhenne on September 7, 1905; one child; was graduated from high school in Cleveland, Ohio, then hired as a locomotive fireman on the Lake Shore and Michigan Southern Railroad in 1899; operated a grocery and retail meat market, 1902-1906; became a switchman on the New York Central Railroad in 1906; joined the Switchmen's Union of North America (SUNA) in 1907; served as the SUNA chairman for the Western district of the New York Central Railroad for ten years, then elected to the grand board of directors of the SUNA in 1918; elected a SUNA vice-president in 1919 and served in that capacity until elected international president in 1921; served during World War II as a member of the advisory board of the Office of War Mobilization and Reconversion; served as director of the Labor Cooperative Education and Publishing Society in Washington, D.C., a director of the Union Labor Life Insurance Company of New York, and as president of the Railway Labor Executives' Association; retired as international president of the SUNA in 1947; was a Democrat; died in Skokie, Ill., in March, 1959; Solon DeLeon, ed., *The American Labor Who's Who* (1925); *Who's Who In Labor* (1946); *Who Was Who in America* (Vol. III).

CHAPMAN, Gordon Warner.   Born in Tomah, Wis., September 5, 1907; son of Allie H. and Dora (Parshall) Chapman; Congregationalist; married Ferne Everhardt on June 28, 1935; three children; was graduated from the University of Wisconsin's School of Commerce in 1931, then became the proprietor of an advertising firm, managing it until 1934; served as an assistant director of surplus commodity distribution for the Wisconsin Public Welfare Department, 1934-1936; joined Local 1 of the American Federation of State, County and Municipal Employees (AFSCME) shortly after it was organized and appointed national accountant of the AFSCME; elected secretary-treasurer of the international union in 1937, serving in that capacity until named executive assistant to AFSCME president Arnold S. Zander (q.v.) in 1945; after the office of executive assistant was eliminated in 1948, again elected secretary-treasurer; was a member of the International Confederation of Free Trade Unions' (ICFTU) delegation that studied trade union affairs in Asia in 1950; was a member of the ICFTU committee that studied working conditions and union organization in Okinawa in 1956; resigned from his union positions in 1961 when appointed a special assistant to the Secretary of State to coordinate international labor affairs in the U.S. State Department, serving until 1962; again elected secretary-treasurer of the AFSCME in 1963; a Democrat; resigned union positions in 1966 because of failing health; Leo Kramer, *Labor's Paradox—The American Federation of State, County, and Municipal Employees, AFL-CIO* (1962); *AFL-CIO News*, July 30, 1966; *Who's Who in Labor* (1946).

CHAVEZ, Cesar Estrada. Born near Yuma, Ariz., March 31, 1927; son of Librado, a small farmer, migrant worker, and union supporter; Roman Catholic; married Helen Favila; eight children; attended more than 30 elementary schools before completing the eighth grade; worked as a field laborer from an early age; served with the U.S. Navy during World War II, 1944-1945; joined the National Agricultural Workers' Union in 1946; associated with the Community Service Organization (CSO), 1952-1962, and served as California state organizer, 1953-1960, and general director, 1960-1962; resigned from the CSO when it refused to organize farm workers; believed that people should identify and solve their problems without outside help, and was a disciple of the principle of nonviolence; in 1962 moved to Delano, Calif., and formed there the National Farm Workers Association (NFW), which in two years became self-supporting with 1,000 dues-paying members in seven counties; led minor strikes in 1965 involving rents at farm labor camps and wages in horticulture; shortly thereafter, joined Filipino workers in a strike against Coachella Valley table-grape growers, attracting nationwide support from civil rights workers, students, ministers, Walter P. Reuther (q.v.), Senator Robert F. Kennedy, and the U.S. Senate Subcommittee on Migratory

Labor headed by Senator Harrison Williams; used unconventional tactics such as "following the grapes out of the fields" to shipping terminals, consumer boycotts, and the *peregrinacion* (march) on Sacramento, Calif., in the spring of 1966; despite competition from the International Brotherhood of Teamsters (IBT), won contracts from Schenley, DiGiorgio, and others; after the merger of the NFW and the Agricultural Workers Organizing Committee, became the leader of the resulting United Farm Workers Organizing Committee (UFWOC), American Federation of Labor-Congress of Industrial Organizations (AFL-CIO); began the "great grape boycott" in August, 1967, which produced three-year contracts with major grape growers of the Coachella and San Joaquin Valleys in 1969-1970, establishing a $2 minimum wage and union hiring halls; made control of pesticides a union goal in 1968; the AFL-CIO chartered United Farm Workers' Union (UFW), which had been organized from the UFWOC, next moved against lettuce growers but with only minimal success; faced serious internal problems in administering contracts, including the unpopularity of the hiring halls with the growers and many workers, his own alleged shortcomings as an administrator, the continuing difficulty of creating a union of farm workers, and the IBT's intervention; after the grape growers and Teamsters signed contracts eliminating the union hiring hall and recognizing the IBT, the UFW, receiving substantial support from the AFL-CIO and other outraged groups and individuals, eventually negotiated a jurisdictional agreement with the IBT, but the IBT apparently failed to abide by the terms of the agreement; apparently supports the Democratic party although not a political activist; Joan London and Henry Anderson, *So Shall Ye Reap: The Story of Cesar Chavez and the Farm Workers Movement* (1970); John G. Dunne, *Delano: The Story of the California Grape Strike* (1967); George D. Horwitz, *La Causa: The California Grape Strike* (1970); *Current Biography* (1969); *New Republic*, May 19, 1973.

(M.E.R.)

CHEYFITZ, Edward Theodore. Born in Montreal, Canada, September 13, 1913; son of Joseph, a plumber, and Faye (Stephenson) Cheyfitz, national chairwoman of the Congress of Industrial Organizations' (CIO) Women's Auxiliaries; married Julia Frank Pollock on June 26, 1936; one child; spent a year in the Soviet Union; was graduated from the University of Michigan in 1934 with an A.B. in engineering and went to work for the Doehler Die Casting Company in Toledo, Ohio; joined the National Association of Die Casting Workers (NADCW), a small union affiliated with the CIO; in the late 1930s, organized automobile and other industrial workers in the Toledo area and elected secretary of the Toledo Industrial Union Council, CIO; elected national executive secretary of the NADCW in 1939, and led a difficult campaign to organize the die casters in Cleveland, Ohio, and eastern New York state; became a member of the national CIO executive board and was a protégé of John L. Lewis (q.v.); with Lewis' support, ambitiously tried to create another large mass-production industrial union alongside of steel, placing the NADCW into a large union embracing all nonferrous metal production; after Lewis broke with the CIO in 1940, Cheyfitz continued to push the proposed merger of NADCW, aluminum workers, and the International Union of Mine, Mill and Smelter Workers (IUMMSW); realized that Communists would control the union and attempted unsuccessfully to block the merger; nevertheless, became the head of the Die Casters Division within the IUMMSW in 1942; served in the U.S. Army Air Force during World War II and then returned to his IUMMSW post in 1945; sought to consolidate the conservative opposition to the growing power of the Communist faction on the union executive board; concluded that this was not possible and resigned to accept a job with Eric Johnson in the motion-picture industry; Vernon H. Jensen, *Nonferrous Metals Industry Unionism* (1954); *Who's Who in Labor* (1946).

(D.G.S.)

CHRISTMAN, Elisabeth.   Born in Chicago, Ill.; daughter of Henry, a musician, and Barbara (Guth) Christman, both German immigrants; Lutheran; attended German Lutheran schools until the age of thirteen, then was hired at the Eisendrath Glove Factory in Chicago; with Agnes Nestor (q.v.), helped form Operators Local 1 of the International Glove Workers Union (IGWU), and served as the Local's chairman of shop stewards and treasurer, 1905-1911, and president, 1912-1917; was a delegate from the ILGU to the 1916 convention of the American Federation of Labor (AFL); served as secretary-treasurer of the IGWU, 1916-1931; elected an IGWU vice-president in 1931 and served until 1937 when the glove workers affiliated with the Amalgamated Clothing Workers of America; was a member of the executive board of the Chicago Women's Trade Union League (WTUL), 1910-1929; elected to the national executive board of the WTUL in 1919; served during World War I as chief of women field representatives for the National War Labor Board; became secretary-treasurer of the WTUL in 1921; appointed to the 1921 Unemployment Conference by President Warren G. Harding; was a member of the WTUL committee that unsuccessfully attempted to persuade the AFL to grant charters to women who were not admitted to their industries' unions; was a delegate to the third meeting of the International Congress of Working Women, meeting in Vienna in 1923; served as the WTUL national representative to the International Labor Organization conference in Geneva in 1931; along with Mary Dreier (q.v.) and Ethel Smith, was a WTUL representative to a committee to work with President Herbert Hoover's Organization on Unemployment Relief in 1933; became a member of the code authority for the leather and woolen knit glove industry of the National Industrial Recovery Administration in 1934; appointed by President Franklin D. Roosevelt to the Commission on Vocational Guidance in 1936; became a member of the advisory committee of the Women's Bureau in the U.S. Department of Labor in 1940; took a WTUL leave of absence, 1942-1943, to investigate, for the Women's Bureau, the problems resulting from the employment of women in war industries; edited the WTUL publication, *Life and Labor Bulletin;* was a Democrat; Gladys Boone, *The Women's Trade Union Leagues in Great Britain and the United States* (1942); Mary Anderson, *Woman at Work* (1951); *Who's Who in Labor* (1946); *Current Biography* (1947).

(M.T.)

CHRISTOPHER, Paul Revere.   Born in Easley, S.C., February 14, 1910; son of Clarence Erasker and Mary Jane (Hemphill) Christopher; Unitarian; married Mary Elizabeth Lybrand; two children; completed an elementary school education, and then became a mill worker at age fourteen; later attended Clemson University, majoring in industrial engineering; became an organizer for the United Textile Workers of America in 1933, serving until 1937; was associated with the Textile Workers Organizing Committee created by the Congress of Industrial Organizations (CIO) in 1937; after the Textile Workers Union of America was chartered by the CIO in 1939, was elected a vice-president; served as CIO regional director for Tennessee, 1940-1955; contributed significantly to organizing activity during the CIO Southern organizing drive of the 1930s and in Tennessee during the 1940s; worked around Gaffney, S.C., during 1939-1940, making speeches and preparing affidavits on violations of textile mills' civil liberties for presentation to the U.S. Justice Department and the National Labor Relations Board; began organizing in Tennessee in 1940, when there were only 12,000 union members in the state; through his persistent organization of paper-mill workers at Harriman, iron-smelter workers at Rockwell, and the Oak Ridge atomic energy facility and Aluminum Company of

America plants after 1946, increased union membership in Tennessee to 100,000 by 1950; after the 1955 merger of the American Federation of Labor (AFL) and the CIO, appointed AFL-CIO director of Region VIII (Tennessee); led the union racial integration movement, holding mixed meetings in Nashville, Tenn.; was credited with being "the most powerful single force in bringing Tennessee industrial unions to their considerable proportions, thereby increasing their political importance"; was a Democrat, especially active in Estes Kefauver's successful campaign for the U.S. Senate in 1948; died in Knoxville, Tenn., February 27, 1974; Lucy Randolph Mason, *To Win These Rights: A Personal Story of the CIO in the South* (1952); *Who's Who in Labor* (1946).

(M.E.R.)

CLARK, Jesse. Born in Terre Haute, Ind., November 21, 1901; son of Stephen, a farmer, and Carrie (Towell) Clark; Methodist; married Mary Rosalie Ring on December 24, 1937; completed elementary school in 1915, then held various jobs before becoming a foreman in a Terre Haute spoke factory when only fifteen years of age; after a short strike in the plant, left for a job with the Standard Wheel Works and Columbia Enameling and Stamping Mill in Terre Haute, and worked there until 1918; attended night schools, taking courses in business English and typing; employed by the Pennsylvania Railroad (PRR) in 1918 and worked in its car shops and signal department until 1921, when fired for "contrariness"; employed by the Cleveland, Cincinnati, Chicago and St. Louis Railway, 1921 to 1923; employed again in the signal department of the PRR during 1924-1935; meanwhile, had joined Terre Haute Lodge 142 of the Brotherhood of Railroad Signalmen of America (BRS) in 1919, and served as recording secretary during 1924-1928; was a member of the local grievance committee of Lodge 142, 1926-1928, and local chairman, 1928-1935; served as a member of the PRR joint reviewing board, 1930-1935; was BRS vice-general chairman for the PRR, 1932-1935, and general chairman, 1935-1939; served as assistant to the grand president of the BRS, 1939-1941; was elected vice-president of the BRS in 1941, secretary-treasurer in 1943, and president in 1945; while president, extended BRS organization throughout the United States and Canada and was an effective proponent of railroad safety, especially among signal workers; became president emeritus in 1967; was a self-professed independent, but usually supported Republican candidates for public office; Brotherhood of Railroad Signalmen of America, *50 Years of Railroad Signaling: A History of the*

Brotherhood of Railroad Signalmen of America (n.d.); *Who's Who in Railroading* (1959); *Labor,* October 7, 1967.

CLARK, John.   Born in Sheffield, England, in 1888; married; emigrated to British Columbia, Canada, and in 1908 joined the Western Federation of Miners there; entered the United States; drove stagecoach in Arizona, ranched in Washington; settled during the 1920s in Great Falls, Mont., and worked there in a zinc refinery; in the early 1930s, tried panning gold for a living; became a United States citizen in 1936, and in same year elected secretary of Great Falls Local 16 of the International Union of Mine, Mill and Smelter Workers (IUMMSW); in the next decade played an increasingly important role at conventions of the IUMMSW; as a result of a shake-up in the union leadership in 1947, became vice-president, succeeding Maurice Travis (q.v.), who became president; opposed by the IUMMSW right-wing, Travis resigned at the 1947 convention and Clark was elected as a compromise candidate; was appointed a member of the executive board of the Congress of Industrial Organizations (CIO) in 1948; although not a left-winger, as president was allegedly under the influence of the Communist faction of the IUMMSW; during his presidency the union faced several crises: 14 of its top leaders (though not Clark) were tried for conspiring to falsify the Taft-Hartley Act non-Communist affidavit; more serious was the estrangement of the IUMMSW from the CIO; on good terms with CIO president Philip Murray (q.v.), but chose to defy the CIO demand that the IUMMSW purge its Communist leaders; the IUMMSW was expelled from CIO in 1950 and thus exposed to raiding by several rival unions; sought to end IUMMSW's isolation by initiating merger talks with various unions in the 1950s, including the United Steelworkers of America (USWA); was unsuccessful, but helped prepare the ground for the 1967 merger of the IUMMSW and the USWA; retired in 1963 and was named honorary president; died in Tucson, Ariz., February 26, 1967; Vernon H. Jensen, *Nonferrous Metals Industry Unionism, 1932-1954* (1954); *Mine-Mill Union* (March, April, 1967); F.S. O'Brien, "The 'Communist Dominated' Unions in the U.S. since 1950," *Labor History* (Spring, 1968).

(D.G.S.)

CLARK, Lewis J.   Born in Centerville, Iowa, April 23, 1902; son of Thomas William Grant, a farmer, and Minerva (Taylor) Clark; married Alice Wilma Ruka on June 30, 1921; was graduated from high school and eventually was hired in the Wilson and Company meat packing plant in Cedar Rapids, Iowa; helped organize the employees of the Wilson plant into a union that affiliated with the Amalgamated Meat Cutters and Butcher Workmen of North America (AMCBWNA) in 1933; elected business manager of the Cedar Rapids local; after the Wilson local in Cedar Rapids seceded from the AMCBWNA in 1935, organized the Midwest Union of All Packing House Workers, which affiliated with the Packinghouse Workers Organizing Commitee (PWOC) created by the Congress of Industrial Organizations (CIO) in 1937; served as an assistant CIO director for Iowa and Nebraska; appointed to the staff of the PWOC in 1940 and shortly thereafter named director of PWOC District 3; appointed vice-chairman of the PWOC in 1941; served for a period as PWOC secretary-treasurer and then elected president of the United Packinghouse Workers of America (UPWA), which replaced the PWOC in 1943; became secretary-treasurer of the UPWA after Ralph Helstein (q.v.) became president of the union in 1946; association with the UPWA ended when defeated for reelection in the union elections of 1950; a Democrat; David Brody, *The Butcher Workmen: A Study of Unionization* (1964); *Who's Who in Labor* (1946).

COEFIELD, John.   Born in Petroleum Center, Pa., June 18, 1869; son of John and Isabella (Wright) Coefield; married Ethel B. McKinnon; two children; was graduated from high school in Franklin, Pa. and then became a plumbers' apprentice, joining the United Association of Plumbers and Steam Fitters of the United States and Canada (UA); worked in various cities before settling in San Francisco, Calif., in 1903; became a leader in UA Local 442 and later served as business agent of the San Francisco Building Trades Council; elected first vice-president and a member of the UA executive board in 1911; elected president of the UA in 1919 and retained that position until his death; was able, while president, to unify the UA, which had become seriously divided during the administration of his predecessor, John Alpine (q.v.); was an American Federation of Labor (AFL) fraternal delegate to the British Trades Union Congress in 1927; elected an AFL vice-president and executive council member in 1929 and served as a vice-president of the AFL metal trades department; during the conflict between the craft union leaders and the Committee on Industrial Organization (CIO), was a strong critic of industrial organization and supported the suspension of the CIO unions; was a member of the AFL housing committee that cooperated with Congressman Henry Ellenbogen and Senator Robert F. Wagner in developing legislation creating the U.S.

Housing Authority; died in Washington, D.C., February 8, 1940; Philip Taft, *The A.F. of L. From the Death of Gompers to the Merger* (1959); Martin Segal, *The Rise of the United Association: National Unionsim in the Pipe Trades, 1884-1924* (1970); *Who's Who in America, 1938-1939.*

COHN, Fannia.   (Considerable disagreement exists among standard biographical sources on several of the dates used in this sketch. The dates listed here generally conform to those used in *Who's Who in Labor* (1946).) Born in Minsk, Russia, April 5, 1888; daughter of Hyman Rozofsky and Anna Cohn; Jewish; received a private school education in Russia; was a member of the Social Revolutionary party in Russia, 1901-1904; emigrated to the United States in 1904 and a year later began work in a New York garment factory; joined the International Ladies' Garment Workers' Union (ILGWU) in 1909; served as a member of the executive board of Kimona, Wrappers and Housedress Workers Local 41, 1909-1914; was chairman of the executive board of Local 41, 1911-1914; moved to Chicago, Ill., in 1915 to organize and assist garment workers striking against the Herzog Garment Company; the strike resulted in the organization of ILGWU Local 59, and she served as president during 1915; was influential in the 1919 Chicago corset makers strike that gained a 40-hour week and increased wages; served as a general ILGWU organizer in Chicago, 1915-1916; elected the ILGWU's first woman vice-president in 1916 and served until 1925; became the executive secretary of the ILGWU's education department in 1918 and served in that capacity until 1961; was one of the co-founders of the Workers' Education Bureau and the Brookwood Labor College in 1921; served on the board of directors of the Labor Publication Society of Brookwood Labor College, 1926-1928; was vice-president of Brookwood Labor College, 1932-1937; retired from union affairs in 1961; died in New York City, December 24, 1962; Benjamin Stolberg, *Tailor's Progress: The Story of a Famous Union and the Men Who Made It* (1944); Louis Levine, *The Women's Garment Workers: A History of the International Ladies' Garment Workers' Union* (1924); James Morris, *Conflict Within the A.F.L.: A Study of Craft Versus Industrial Unionism, 1901-1938* (1958); *ILGWU Report and Proceedings* (1965).

(M.T.)

COLLINS, Jennie.   Born in Amoskeag. N.H., in 1828; orphaned as a child and brought up by a grandmother; as a young girl, worked as a mill hand in Lowell and Lawrence, Mass.; later worked as a vest maker and organized a soldiers' relief fund in Boston, Mass., in 1861; after 1865, became a labor agitator and was associated with the New England Labor

Reform League; advocated the eight-hour day and better working conditions for women; supported woman's suffrage and in 1870 lectured to the Women's Suffrage Association in Washington, D.C.; established a center in Boston in 1870 that distributed food and clothing to impoverished working women; authored *Nature's Aristocracy, or Battles and Wounds in Time of Peace;* died in Brookline, Mass., July 20, 1887; David Montgomery, *Beyond Equality: Labor and the Radical Republicans, 1862-1872* (1967); *The Twentieth Century Biographical Dictionary of Notable Americans,* Vol. II (1968); *Notable American Women* (1971).

(M.T.)

COMMERFORD, John (fl. 1830-1874). Reared in Brooklyn, N.Y.; while a young man, learned and practiced the chairmakers' trade there; supported the Robert Owen (q.v.) and George Henry Evans (q.v.) faction of the New York Working Men's party in 1830; shortly thereafter, became actively involved in the labor movement and elected president of the New York Chairmakers' and Gilders' Union Society; committed to antibanking and antipaper money reform and represented the fifteenth ward of New York City on the general committee of the "New York Workingmen Opposed to Paper Money and Banking and to all Licensed Monopolies," ca. 1832; chosen by the Chairmakers' and Gilders' Society as its delegate to the National Trades' Union in 1834; elected secretary of the National Trades' Union in 1834 and in subsequent sessions served as recording secretary and treasurer; was a leader in the agitation for prison labor reform and in 1834 headed the United Working Men's Association, an ephemeral organization concerned with the prison labor issue; in 1841, chaired a meeting of Albany, N.Y., workingmen advocating prison labor reform; became active in Democratic reform politics during the mid-1830s, and advocated Locofoco separation from the Democratic party; supported the Boston, Mass., and Philadelphia, Pa., ten-hour strikes of 1835; succeeded Ely Moore (q.v.) in 1835 as president of the General Trades' Union of New York, which under his leadership became a vigorous organization that stimulated the organization of journeymen societies; was instrumental in the founding of the General Trades' organ, the *Union,* and was its editor; increasingly turned to reformist activities after 1837; served in 1842 as president of the Free Trade Association, a John C. Calhoun-inspired organization; however, devoted most of his time and energy to the land-reform principles of George Henry Evans, and espoused them for the remainder of his life; became the proprietor of a chairmaking shop in 1842; was one of the founders, along with Evans, of the National Reform Association in 1844 and was nominated for Congress by the group; was a delegate to the New York City Industrial Congress in 1850; in 1859, attracted by the free homestead plank, switched from Democratic to the Republican party and became a Republican candidate for the New York Assembly; was a Republican candidate for Congress in 1860; as late as 1874, was still involved in the land reform movement; Walter Hugins, *Jacksonian Democracy and the Working Class: A Study of the New York Workingmen's Movement, 1829-1837* (1960); Edward Pessen, *Most Uncommon Jacksonians: The Radical Leaders of the Early Labor Movement* (1967); Philip S. Foner, *History of the Labor Movement in the United States*, Vol. I (1947); Helene S. Zahler, *Eastern Workingmen and National Land Policy, 1829-1862* (1941).

CONLON, Peter J.   Born in Brooklyn, N.Y., September 23, 1869; son of a locomotive engineer; Roman Catholic; married; seven children; moved with family to Springfield, Ill.; attended elementary school there and later took Speakers' Service Bureau correspondence courses; at age fourteen, began work as a plumber, and during 1885-1889 was apprenticed as a machinist in the Cotton Belt Railroad shops, Pine Bluff, Ark.; moved to Kansas City, Kan., and in 1899 began working there for the Union Pacific Railroad; joined the Knights of Labor and for several years traveled around the West in boxcars, working and organizing local unions in every state west of the Mississippi River and in Mexico; nine months after the founding of the International Association of Machinists (IAM) in 1889, joined IAM Local Lodge 27 in Kansas City; helped form District Lodge 1 in 1894 and was elected District master machinist (president); was a delegate to the IAM's 1895 national convention and elected to the general executive board, serving until 1901; served as first vice-president of the IAM, 1901-1916; handled some of the IAM's most important strikes, and, during the Cincinnati, Ohio, eight-hour strike of 1916, arrested four times in three months for violating an antipicketing ordinance; served during World War I as an assistant to Bert M. Jewell (q.v.), president of the American Federation of Labor's Railway Employees' Department; served as an IAM general organizer, 1917-1921; was one of the IAM's eight general vice-presidents, 1921-1931; throughout his career, contributed regularly to the *Machinists' Monthly Journal*, particularly the popular "Memories of the Past" column; was an early supporter of the Populist party, but, after it collapsed in 1898, turned to Eugene V. Debs and the Socialist party and advocated a national referendum on congressional legislation and municipal ownership of public utilities; precluded because of deep Catholic faith from accepting Marxist doctrine of class conflict, but espoused "social consciousness," acknowledging the fatherhood of God but promulgating a radical interpretation of the brotherhood of man; served as chairman of the Progressive party in Virginia and vice-president of the Non-Partisan Voters' League of Arlington County, Va., during the 1920s; died in Washington, D.C., April 1, 1931; *Machinists' Monthly Journal* (May, 1903, May, 1931); Solon DeLeon, ed., *The American Labor Who's Who* (1925); Mark Perlman, *The Machinists: A New Study in American Trade Unionism* (1961); John H. M. Laslett, *Labor and the Left: A Study of Socialism and Radical Influences in the American Labor Movement, 1881-1924* (1970).

(J.H.)

COOK, Harry Herman. Born in Wheeling, W. Va., February 28, 1883; son of a glass blower; married; left school in 1892 and began working in the glass industry; joined Wheeling Local 99 of the American Flint Glass Workers Union (AFGW) in 1901; moved to Bellaire, Ohio, and affiliated with AFGW Local 13 in 1903, serving it as an organizer, secretary, and president; was an official of the Ohio Valley Trade Council, 1906-1907; elected to the AFGW national executive board in 1912, serving until 1916; became national assistant secretary of the AFGW in 1916; after serving as first vice-president and executive board member for several years, elected national president of the AFGW in 1940; frequently represented the AFGW in American Federation of Labor (AFL) conventions and served on several committees, including the auditing committee in 1923; both before and after the merger of the AFL and the Congress of Industrial Organizations in 1955, resisted suggestions of mergers between the AFGW and other unions in the glass industry; retired union positions in 1957 and was named president emeritus of AFGW; politically identified himself as an independent; died in Toledo, Ohio, May 28, 1972; Solon DeLeon, ed., *The American Labor Who's Who* (1925); *Who's Who in Labor* (1946); *AFL-CIO News*, June 15, 1957, June 3, 1972.

COPE, Elmer F. Born in Elwood, Ind., July 24, 1903; son of Gilbert, a steelworker, and Nora (Hall) Cope; Society of Friends; married Corrine Snyder on January 13, 1940; two children; shortly after going to work at age 16 in a Warren, Ohio, tin mill, joined the Amalgamated Association of Iron, Steel, and Tin Workers and became a grievance committeeman; later studied economics at Swarthmore College and received an A.B.; joined the Steel Workers Organizing Committee in 1936 and was given the task of trying to organize Weirton Steel Company plants in West Virginia; served for a short time as director of District 27 (Canton, Ohio) of the United Steelworkers of America (USWA); served during World War II on the Fifth Regional National War Labor Board; meanwhile, received an M.A. degree from Western Reserve University; participated actively in the Congress of Industrial Organizations' (CIO) Political Action Committee; was a CIO delegate to the World Federation of Trade Unions (WFTU) in 1947, at time of the rift between the Communist and non-Communist affiliates of the WFTU; became one of three CIO representatives who withdrew the CIO from the WFTU and helped form the International Confederation of Free Trade Unions in 1949; subsequently, became director of economic and international affairs for the USWA; elected as the first secretary-treasurer of the newly formed Ohio American Federation of Labor (AFL)-CIO in 1958; played a key role in the state labor movement's defeat of a powerful effort, organized by Chambers of Commerce and smaller employers, to obtain an Ohio right-to-work law along lines of law enacted in Indiana the previous year; opposed group called "Ohioans for Right-to-Work," which sought to amend the state constitution by referendum vote during the general election; by undertaking intensive voter registration and public relations campaigns, the Ohio AFL-CIO and municipal labor bodies defeated the amendment by almost 2 to 1 and also helped to defeat Republican Senator John W. Bricker, a foe of unions; due to ill health, stepped down as Ohio AFL-CIO secretary in 1963, and took a position as an educational consultant with the USWA; was a Democrat; died in Pittsburgh, Pa., May 26, 1965; *Who's Who in Labor* (1946); Glen W. Miller and S.T. Ware, "Organized Labor in the Political Process: A Case Study of the Right-To-Work Campaign in Ohio," *Labor History* (Winter, 1963).

(D.G.S.)

COSGROVE, John Tam.   Born in Elizabeth, N.J., September 11, 1873; son of Patrick, a steamboat captain, and Dora (Toner) Cosgrove; Roman Catholic; married Katherine V. Hennessy on October 21, 1901; five children; graduated from St. Patrick's High School in Elizabeth, then began work as a carpenter and joined Local 167 of the United Brotherhood of Carpenters and Joiners of America (UBC) in 1892; helped to found both the Union County (N.J.) Central Trades and the New Jersey State Federation of Labor, and served as president of both central bodies; elected business agent of Local 167 in 1899 and served until 1915; was a principal organizer of the New Jersey Building and Construction Trades Council and served as its president from 1904 to 1915; became an unofficial labor adviser to Woodrow Wilson during his governorship of New Jersey and presidency of the United States; was influential in the passage of the federal workmen's compensation act; elected first general vice-president of the UBC in 1915, serving until 1929; forced by progressive blindness to cut short his union activities during the last ten years of his life; was a Democrat; died in Elizabeth, N.J., November 3, 1948; Robert A. Christie, *Empire In Wood: A History of the Carpenters' Union* (1956); *The New York Times*, November 4, 1948; *Who's Who in Labor* (1946).

COULTER, Clarence Castrow. Born in Venango County, Pa., June 4, 1882; son of William Harry, a farmer, and Sarah J. (Brown) Coulter; Protestant; married Sarah Fowler on April 9, 1930; two children; graduated from high school, then secured employment as a clerk in Washington, D.C., and joined Local 262 of the Retail Clerks International Protective Association (RCIA) in 1901; between 1901-1926, served as business agent and financial secretary of Local 262, financial secretary and vice-president of the Washington, D.C. Central Labor Union, vice-president of the District of Columbia Federation of Labor, and vice-president of the RCIA; was elected general secretary-treasurer (then the chief administrative officer) of the RCIA in 1926; strongly supported the American Federation of Labor's traditional craft-oriented organizing tactics, and suspended a number of New York RCIA locals opposing this policy; saw the suspended locals organize the rival United Retail, Wholesale, and Department Store Employees of America, which affiliated with the Congress of Industrial Organizations in 1937; retired union positions in 1947 and was named secretary-treasurer emeritus; edited the RCIA organ, *Advocate*, 1926-1947; was a Democrat; died in Lafayette, Ind., in August, 1948; George G. Kirstein, *Stores and Unions: A Study of the Growth of Unionism in Dry Goods and Department Stores* (1950); Michael Harrington, *The Retail Clerks* (1962); *Who's Who in Labor* (1946).

CROSSWAITH, Frank Rudolph. Born in Frederiksted, St. Croix, Virgin Islands, July 16, 1892; son of William Ignatius, a painter, and Ann Eliza Crosswaith; Roman Catholic; married Alma E. Besard in January, 1915; four children; Afro-American; emigrated to the United States while still in his teens and worked as an elevator operator while attending the Rand School of Social Science; after graduation began a long term of service as an organizer for the International Ladies' Garment Workers' Union; was a Socialist early in his career, and often ran for public office on the Socialist party ticket in New York; also served as a lecturer for the party and for the League for Industrial Democracy; actively involved in the organization of black workers in such occupations as elevator operators, elevator constructors, mechanics, laundry workers, and retail clerks; served as a special organizer for the Brotherhood of Sleeping Car Porters; was appointed by Mayor Fiorello LaGuardia to the New York City Housing Authority in 1942; joined the American Labor party during the 1930s and became a member of the state executive board of the Liberal party, which was organized in 1944; served as the editor of the Negro Labor News Service for 12 years; was one of the organizers and became the chairman of the Negro Labor Committee, an association of unions with a predominantly black membership; authored *True Freedom for Negro and White Workers* and *Discrimination, Incorporated*; died in New York City, June 17, 1965; Benjamin Stolberg, *Tailor's Progress: The Story of a Famous Union and the Men Who Made It* (1944); *AFL-CIO News*, June 19, 1965; *The New York Times*, June 18, 1965.

CRULL, John L.   Born in Geneosea, Ill., August 4, 1901; son of William Albert, a carpenter, and Anna Pearl (Duncan) Crull; Christian Church; married Lydia C. Stahlheber on August 8, 1923; two children; completed a high school education, then secured work as a carpenter and joined the United Brotherhood of Carpenters and Joiners of America; began working for the Southwestern Bell Telephone Company in Wichita, Kan., in 1936; was one of the organizers of the Southwestern Telephone Workers Union, which became Wichita Local 1261 of the National Federation of Telephone Workers (NFTW) in 1937; served as a special representative for Local 1261 during 1937-1943; became Southern Regional Director of the NFTW and a member of the national executive board in 1943, serving until 1947; chosen first vice-president in 1947 of the Communications Workers of America (CWA), which had absorbed the NFTW; placed in charge of internal organization, and given responsibility for organizing non-CWA telephone workers who were represented by CWA representative units; became one of the seminal figures in the CWA; was a persistent, thorough, and conscientious union leader, and loyally carried out CWA policies even when in disagreement with them; served on the board of directors of the Council for Cooperative Development; was a Republican; retired union positions in 1967; Jack Barbash, *Unions and Telephones: The Story of the Communications Workers of America* (1952); *Who's Who in Labor* (1946); *AFL-CIO News*, February 18, 1967.

CURRAN, Joseph Edwin.   Born in New York City, March 1, 1906; son of Eugene, a cook, and Ida (Cohan) Curran; Roman Catholic; married Retta

Toblé on October 19, 1939, and, after her death in 1963, married Florence B. Stetler on April 1, 1965; one child; after being expelled from Westfield, N.J., parochial school in the seventh grade for irregular attendance, became, in turn, a caddy and a "factory monkey"; moved to New York City in 1921 and took a job as an office boy with the Gold Medal Flour Company; the following year, at age sixteen, began a 17-year period as a seaman; joined the International Seamen's Union (ISU) in 1935; led a wildcat strike of the S.S. *California's* crew, whose eventual discharge led to a long East Coast strike and the organization of the National Maritime Union of America (NMU) as a rival to the ISU; was elected president of the NMU after its establishment in 1937; elected president of the Greater New York Industrial Union Council, Congress of Industrial Organizations (CIO) in 1940; elected a CIO vice-president in 1941; ran for Congress on the American Labor party ticket in 1940; served during World War II as a member of the advisory committee for the New York area of the War Manpower Commission; after the war, was a CIO delegate to the conferences in London and Paris that resulted in the organization of the World Federation of Trade Unions; became a vice-president and executive council member of the newly merged American Federation of Labor and CIO; retired as president of the NMU in 1973; was accused of Communist leanings during his early trade union career, but eventually assumed a conservative position in the NMU's ideological conflicts; Joseph P. Goldberg, *The Maritime Story: A Study in Labor Management Relations* (1958); Walter Galenson, *The CIO Challenge to the AFL: A History of the American Labor Movement, 1935-1941* (1960); Charles P. Larrowe, *Harry Bridges: The Rise and Fall of Radical Labor in the U.S.* (1972); *Current Biography* (1945).

DALRYMPLE, Sherman Harrison.   Born in Walton, W. Va., April 4, 1889; son of Herbert Clarence and Eliza Eleanor (Atkinson) Dalrymple; married Esta Robinson on January 3, 1914, and, after her death, Grace Moomaw on October 2, 1928; one child; completed a grammar school education in the public schools of Mt. Lebanon, W. Va., then began working in the rubber industry in 1909; was an oilfield worker, 1911-1914, before returning to employment in the rubber industry, 1914-1917; served successively during World War I as a private, corporal, sergeant, and 2nd Lieutenant in the U.S. Marine Corps and received the *Fourragers* and *Croix d'Guerre* decorations; after the war, resumed work in the rubber industry; joined American Federation of Labor Federal Labor Union 18319 of Goodrich Rubber Company workers and served as its president,

1934-1935; was elected president of the newly organized United Rubber Workers of America (URWA) in 1935; led the URWA into the Congress of Industrial Organizations (CIO) in 1936 and became a CIO vice-president; led an anti-Communist campaign in the CIO in 1939; served during World War II on the Labor Policy Advisory Committee of the National Defense Advisory Commission; was a member of the CIO social security committee, the legislative committee, and the Utility and Construction Workers Organizing Committee; retired as president of URWA in 1945 as a result of his opposition to a strike against the Firestone Tire and Rubber Company and the Goodyear Tire and Rubber Company; edited the *United Rubber Worker* until his retirement; usually supported the Democratic party; died in Downey, Calif., March 16, 1962; Harold S. Roberts, *The Rubber Workers* (1944); Walter Galenson, *The CIO Challenge to the AFL: A History of the American Labor Movement, 1935-1941* (1960); *The New York Times*, March 19, 1962.

DAMINO, Harry. Born in Italy, ca. 1893; Roman Catholic; married; four children; attended primary schools in Italy; emigrated to the United States in 1914, settling in New York City; secured employment in the New York toy industry as an eye-setter in a doll factory; participated in the 1933 general strike of toy industry employees in New York City to protest deplorable working conditions and low wages; affiliated with New York Local 223 of the Doll and Toy Workers of the United States and Canada (DTW); later served as manager of Local 223, the DTW's largest affiliate, with more than 15,000 members, for several years; was elected international president of the DTW in 1953; became a member of the general board of the newly merged American Federation of Labor and Congress of Industrial Organizations (AFL-CIO) in 1955; became a vice-president and executive council member of the AFL-CIO maritime trades department in 1965; after several new affiliates were added, DTW's name was changed to the International Union of Dolls, Toys, Playthings, Novelties, and Allied Products Workers of the United States in 1965; was a trustee of Parkway Hospital in New York City and a member of the executive board of the Italian-American Labor Council; died in New York City, June 17, 1968; *AFL-CIO News*, June 22, 1968; *The New York Times*, June 19, 1968.

DAVIDSON, Roy Elton. Born in Fairmount, Ill., July 4, 1901; son of Frank A., a coal miner and farmer, and Sarah L. (Foster) Davidson; Presbyterian; married Cecil May Rinehart on October 31, 1920; four children; was graduated from Oakwood (Ill.) Township High School in

1917, then took courses at the University of Illinois and the University of Chicago and also became a fireman on the Illinois Division of the New York Central Railroad; joined the Brotherhood of Locomotive Firemen and Enginemen (BLFE) in the summer of 1918; was appointed general chairman of the New York Central's Illinois Division-Indiana Harbor Belt Railroad, BLFE, in 1922; although eligible for membership in the Brotherhood of Locomotive Engineers (BLE) after being promoted to engineer in 1921, remained active instead in the BLFE and did not join the BLE until 1937; became a member of the BLE Division 682, Hammond, Ind., in 1937 and was appointed general chairman for the engineers of the Illinois Division-Indiana Harbor Belt Railroad in 1941; was made assistant grand chief engineer for the Chicago area in 1947; was elected first assistant grand chief engineer in 1953 and, after the retirement of Guy L. Brown (q.v.) in 1960, was chosen BLE grand chief engineer; primarily involved during his incumbency with railroad management demands that unnecessary personnel be eliminated from train crews and that work rules be adjusted in response to the poor financial position of the nation's railroads; supported the Democratic party; died in Cleveland, Ohio, July 7, 1964; Reed C. Richardson, *The Locomotive Engineer, 1863-1963: A Century of Railway Labor Relations and Work Rules* (1963); *Current Biography* (1963); *Who's Who in Railroading* (1959).

DAVIS, James John.   Born in Thedegar, South Wales, England, October 27, 1873; son of David James and Esther Ford (Nichols) Davis; Baptist; married Jean Rodenbaugh on November 26, 1914; five children; emigrated to the United States with parents in 1881, living first in Pittsburgh, Pa., and moving later to Sharon, Pa.; attended the public schools there and Sharon Business College; apprenticed as a puddler in the steel industry at age eleven, and worked in Sharon, Pittsburgh, and Birmingham, Ala.; moved to Elwood, Ind., in 1893 and worked in steel and tin-plate mills; joined the Amalgamated Association of Iron, Steel, and Tin Workers of America and for a short time served as international president of the union; was elected city clerk of Elwood in 1898, serving until 1902; was recorder of Madison County, Ind., 1903-1907; moved to Pittsburgh in 1907; was elected general director of the Loyal Order of Moose in 1907, and, as chairman of its War Relief Commission, visited camps in the United States, Canada, and Europe in 1918; appointed U.S. Secretary of Labor by President Warren Harding in 1921 and reappointed by Presidents Calvin Coolidge in 1925 and Herbert Hoover in 1929; made his most important contributions in the areas of increasing public works construction to provide employment, settling labor disputes, supplying low-cost housing for tenant workers, providing machinery for securing restrictions on immigration in accordance with the 1921 quota law, creating an Immigration Board of Review, and initiating studies of mothers' pension, child dependency, and juvenile delinquency laws; resigned from office on December 9, 1930, following his election to the U.S. Senate as a Republican from Pennsylvania to fill the vacancy caused by Senate refusal to seat William S. Vare; was reelected in 1932 and 1938, but ran unsuccessfully for reelection in 1944; was appointed by Vice-President John N. Garner to serve on a special Senate committee investigating the Tennessee Valley Authority; coauthored *You and Your Job* (1927), and authored *The Iron Puddler* (1922) and *Selective Immigration* (1926); died in Tacoma Park, Md., November 22, 1947; Andrew Sinclair, *The Available Man* (1965); Francis Russell, *The Shadow of Blooming Grove: Warren G. Harding and His Times* (1968); *The American Federationist* (December, 1947).

DAVIS, Richard L.   Born in Roanoke, Va., December 24, 1864; married; number of children unknown; Afro-American; received a "very fair education" in the Roanoke public schools becoming a "good reader" and a "good writer"; at age eight, began work in Roanoke tobacco factory for nine years; worked as a coal miner in the Kanawha and New River fields of West Virginia; moved to Rendville, a coal mining village in southeastern Ohio, in 1882, and worked intermittently as a miner and union organizer until his death; participated actively in the labor movement from age eighteen, first joining the Knights of Labor and then the United Mine Workers of America (UMWA); was chosen as a delegate to the UMWA's founding convention in 1890 and as a member of the executive board of District 6, UMWA, Ohio, serving until 1896; finished seventh in a field of 28 candidates for one of six vacancies on the international executive board, UMWA, in 1895; a year later, received the highest vote among 14 candidates for a position on the international executive board, the highest UMWA office yet held by a black; reelected with the second highest vote in 1897, but lost his bid for reelection in 1898; concentrated his organizing efforts on southeastern Ohio and was most responsible for bringing Ohio's black miners into the union; participated in organizing campaigns in the New River field of West Virginia and in McDonnell, Pa., in 1892, in the Pocahontas field of West Virginia in 1894, and in West Virginia and Alabama in 1897-1898; died in Rendville, Ohio, January 24, 1900; Herbert G. Gutman, "The Negro and the United Mine Workers of America: The Career and Letters of Richard L. Davis and Something of Their Meaning," in Julius Jacobson, ed., *The Negro and the American Labor Movement* (1968).

(J.H.)

DEBS, Eugene Victor. Born in Terre Haute, Ind., November 5, 1855; son of Jean Daniel, a small businessman, and Marguerite Marie Debs; married Katherine Metzel in 1885; left school at age fifteen to work in a railroad enginehouse and two years later became a locomotive fireman; served for three years as secretary of the Terre Haute, Ind., local of the Brotherhood of Locomotive Firemen (BLF), then became associate.editor of the *Firemen's Magazine* in 1878; elected grand secretary and treasurer of the BLF (renamed the Brotherhood of Locomotive Firemen and Enginemen in 1906) and editor-in-chief of the *Firemen's Magazine* in 1880; resigned his offices in the BLF in 1892 and began organizing the American Railway Union (ARU), designed to represent all railroad laborers in one industrial union; successfully led an ARU strike against the Great Northern Railroad in 1894, but saw the union crushed in a strike against the Pullman Palace Car Company later that year; arrested for his activities during the Pullman strike, charged with conspiring to obstruct the delivery of federal mail, and sentenced to six months in prison; incarcerated in the McHenry County Jail in Woodstock, Ill.; became a Socialist shortly after serving his six-month prison term and in 1897 was instrumental in the formation of the Social Democratic party; led his new party into a 1901 merger with the "Rochester Faction" of the Socialist Labor party, led by Morris Hillquit (q.v.), and Victor Berger's (q.v.) Wisconsin party organization, resulting in the formation of the Socialist Party of America; joined with other radicals to form the Industrial Workers of the World in 1905; resigned three years later over differences concerning political action; opposed American involvement in World War I and was convicted for violating the Espionage Act; sentenced to ten years in prison on September 14, 1918, and incarcerated in the Federal Penitentiary in Atlanta, Ga.; pardoned by the executive order of President Warren G. Harding in 1921; despite his identification with the Socialist party during most of his life, first ran for political office as a Democrat and was elected to the Indiana legislature in 1885, serving one term; endorsed William Jennings Bryan in 1896; ran for president of the United States under the Socialist banner in 1900, 1904, 1908, 1912, and 1920; endorsed Robert M. LaFollette's Progressive party candidacy in 1924; authored *Walls and Bars* (1927); writings and speeches collected in

Bruce Rogers, ed., *Debs: His Life, Writings, and Speeches* (1908), Joseph M. Bernstein, ed., *Writings and Speeches of Eugene V. Debs* (1948), and Gene Tussey, ed., *Eugene V. Debs Speaks* (1970); died at Lindlahr Sanitarium, Ill., October 20, 1926; Ray Ginger, *The Bending Cross: A Biography of Eugene Victor Debs* (1949); H. Wayne Morgan, *Eugene V. Debs: Socialist for President* (1962); David Herreshoff, *American Disciples of Marx: From the Age of Jackson to the Progressive Era* (1967).

DELANEY, George Philip.   Born in Washington, D.C., February 20, 1909; son of George Patrick and Agnes E. (Connery) Delaney; Roman Catholic; married Margaret D. Mulholland in July, 1947; four children; completed a secondary education, then attended St. Mary's College, and, during 1945-1946, Harvard University; became an apprentice molder at the U.S. Navy Yard in Washington, D.C., in 1928; joined the International Molders and Foundry Workers Union of North America (IMFWU) in 1928; served as an international representative for the IMFWU, 1938-1942; joined the U.S. Navy during World War II, 1942-1945; resumed his duties after the war as an IMFWU international representative, serving until 1948; served as a labor specialist for the Civilian Production Administration, 1946-1947; became an international affairs representative for the American Federation of Labor in 1948, serving until 1958; beginning in 1948, served as a United States worker delegate and a member of the governing board of the International Labor Organization (ILO); participated actively in the formation of the International Conference of Free Trade Unions in 1949; became director of organization for the International Union of Operating Engineers, but resigned upon appointment as special assistant for international labor affairs in the U.S. Department of Labor; served on the U.S. delegation to the ILO, 1963-1970; became the first director of the Office of Labor Affairs in the Agency for International Development; following his retirement from government service in 1970, served as the Washington representative of the International Longshoremen's Association; was a Democrat; died in Washington, D.C., February 9, 1972; *AFL-CIO News*, August 1, 1964, July 19, 1972; *Who's Who in America, 1972-1973*; Philip Taft, *The A.F. of L. From the Death of Gompers to the Merger* (1959).

DeLEON, Daniel.   Born in Curaçao, Venezuela, December 14, 1852; son of Salomon, a surgeon in the Dutch colonial army, and Sara (Jesurun) DeLeon (DeLeon apparently fabricated much of the factual information concerning his youth. For this reason, the material presented here may not be entirely accurate); Jewish; married Sara Lobo on August 2, 1882, and, after her death, Bertha Canary on June 10, 1892; one child; educated in German gymnasiums; emigrated to the United States in 1874, settling in New York City; while teaching school in Westchester County, N.Y., attended classes in law and political science at Columbia University and in 1878 received the LLB degree; practiced law in Texas for a time and then returned to New York in 1883; won a prize lectureship in Latin American diplomacy at Columbia and held it for six years; supported Henry George's candidacy for mayor of New York City in 1886; joined the Knights of Labor (K of L) in 1888; became a member of the Socialist Labor Party (SLP) in 1890 and was its candidate for governor of New York in 1891 and 1902; became editor of the SLP organ, *The People,* in 1892; led a secessionist movement from the K of L in 1895 and founded the Socialist Trade and Labor Alliance; involved in the organization of the Industrial Workers of the World (IWW) in 1905 and immediately merged his Socialist Trade and Labor Alliance with it; failed to obtain a seat at the IWW's 1908 convention because of his disruptive tactics and emphasis on political action, and thus organized the rival Workers' International Industrial Union; with his doctrinaire, domineering, and egotistical manner, was one of the most controversial and divisive figures in the radical union movement; was known as an implacable opponent of the American Federation of Labor, and was a dual unionist with a strong commitment to radical politics: authored *Two Pages from Roman History* (1903), *What Means This Strike?* (1898), *Socialist Reconstruction of Society* (1905), and other tracts; died in New York City, May 11, 1914; *Daniel DeLeon, The Man and His Work, a Symposium* (1919); Charles A. Madison, *Critics and Crusaders: A Century of American Protest* (1947); Melvyn Dubofsky, *We Shall Be All: A History of the Industrial Workers of the World* (1969); *Dictionary of American Biography* (Vol. V).

DENNIS, Eugene (Francis Eugene Waldron).   Born in Seattle, Wash., August 10, 1905; son of Francis X. and Nora (Vieg) Waldron; married Reggie Schneiderman; two children; after graduation from Franklin High School in Seattle, went to work as a salesman to earn enough money to enter the University of Washington; forced to leave the university after one term because of his father's illness; worked as an electrician, teamster, carpenter, lumberjack, and longshoreman; joined the Industrial Workers of the World and participated in the general strike in Seattle in 1919; joined the Communist party of America (CPA) in 1926 and became regular party employee assigned to teach economics at a Communist camp in Woodland, Wash.; spent several years in Europe and South Africa, and attended the Lenin Institute in the Soviet Union; returned to the United States in 1935 and resumed Communist organizing in Wisconsin; was elected to the Communist National Committee from Wisconsin in 1939; served for a short period as an organizer for the National Maritime Union during the late 1930s; was appointed general secretary of the CPA in 1945; convicted for contempt of Congress after failing to respond to a subpoena issued by the House Committee on Un-American Activities in 1947 and sentenced to one year in prison; later indicted and convicted of "teaching and advocating the overthrow of the Government by force and violence," and was imprisoned during 1951-1955; modified his ideological stance after the 1956 Russian invasion of Hungary, and thus increasingly came into conflict with hardline Communist William Z. Foster (q.v.); became national chairman of the CPA in 1959 and served until his death; died in New York City, January 31, 1961; Joseph R. Starobin, *American Communism in Crisis, 1943-1957* (1972); David A. Shannon, *The Decline of American Communism* (1959); Max M. Kampelman, *The Communist Party vs. the C.I.O.: A Study in Power Politics* (1957); *Current Biography* (1949).

DERWENT, Clarence. Born in London, England, March 23, 1884; son of Charles, an actor, and Alice (Falk) Derwent; Society for Ethical Culture; attended St. Paul's School in London and the Birbeck Institute for instruction in acting; made his first stage appearance on September 1, 1902 at the Theatre Royal in Weymouth, England; performed minor roles in Shakespearean plays with the Frank Benson Company, 1902-1907; was associated with Horniman's Manchester Repertory Company, 1907-1909; made his London debut as Abergavenny in *Henry VIII* at His Majesty's Theatre in 1910; traveled to the United States in 1915, and, although remaining a British citizen, devoted most of his professional career to acting, directing, and producing in the United States; joined Actor's Equity Association (AEA) in 1925 and was chosen president in 1946, serving until 1952; served as AEA delegate to the meeting of the International Theatre Institute in Paris in 1947; was elected chairman of Experimental Theatre, Inc., in 1947; was also a member of the New York City Center of Music and Drama and the American Federation of Radio Artists; during his administration, brought about the AEA vote to boycott any performance in Washington, D.C. that denied admission to Americans of African descent; became president of the American National Theatre and Academy in 1952, serving until his death; authored *The Derwent Story: My First Fifty Years in the Theatre in England and America* (1953); died in New

York City, August 6, 1959; *Current Biography* (1947); *Who's Who in the Theater* (1947); *Who's Who in Labor* (1946); *The New York Times*, August 7, 1959.

DEVYR, Thomas Ainge.   Born in County Donegal, Ireland, in 1805; married; had several children, one of whom belonged to the Shaker community of New Lebanon, N.Y.; acquired a limited formal education, then worked as a peddler, writer, constable, and journalist; became an early convert to Chartist reform; served as assistant editor, 1839-1840, of the *Northern Liberator* published in Newcastle-on-Tyne; named corresponding secretary of the Northern Political Union; after organizing a secret, armed band of Chartist guerillas in 1840, was forced to flee Great Britain; emigrated to the United States, settling in New York; became editor of the *Williamsburg* (N.Y.) *Democrat*, a Democratic party newspaper, in 1840, but offended the party leaders with his radical principles and thus saw them withdraw vital support from the newspaper; became an organizer for the Anti-Rent party in upstate New York shortly thereafter; repeating the same paramilitary, guerilla tactics used in Newcastle, successfully exposed the feudal conditions especially prevalent in the Hudson River Valley; allied himself with George Henry Evans (q.v.) in the effort to revive the workingmen's movement in the form of the National Reform Association and the National Reform party, which was organized in New York in 1844; attended the New England ten-hour convention held in Faneuil Hall, Boston, in 1844, and addressed the delegates regarding the advantages of land reform; was an Albany, N.Y., delegate to the Industrial Congress in 1845; partly because of his indiscretion, vanity, ungovernable temper, and dictatorial manner, caused the dilution of the radical free soil principles that he advocated (termed Devyrism) and their preemption by dissident Whigs and Democrats who organized the Republican party; after exhausting his financial reserves in the Anti-Rent movement, accumulated a sizeable fortune through successful real estate speculations and developments in New York and used most of that money to endow various radical newspapers; supported the Republican party in 1860 because of its homestead plank; served as editor of the Fenian newspaper, *The Irish People*, 1865-1866, and joined the editorial staff of the *Irish World* in 1877; remained a spokesman and agitator for land reform until his death in Brooklyn, N.Y., in 1877; edited the New York periodicals *The National Reformer* and *The Anti-Renter*; authored *Our Natural Rights* (1836) and *The Odd Book, or Chivalry in Modern Days* (1882); Ray Boston, *British Chartists in America, 1839-1900* (1971); Helene S. Zahler, *Eastern Workingmen and*

National Land Policy, 1829-1962 (1941); Henry Christman, *Tin Horns and Calico* (1945).

DOAK, William Nuckles.   Born near Rural Retreat, Va., December 12, 1882; son of Canaro Drayton and Elizabeth (Dutton) Doak; married Emma Maria Cricher in 1908; after attending the public schools of the area, studied at a business college at Bristol, Va.; worked for the Norfolk and Western Railroad at Bluefield, W. Va., in 1900; joined the Brotherhood of Railroad Trainmen (BRT) in 1904; served as secretary-treasurer of the southern association of general committees of the Order of Railroad Conductors and the BRT, 1909-1916; was general chairman for the Norfolk and Western systems, 1912-1916; after his election as a BRT vice-president in 1916, became the BRT's national legislative representative in Washington, D.C.; was appointed a member of the Railway Board of Adjustment Number One in 1918; served on the train service board of adjustment for southern and eastern territories, 1921-1928; was elected first vice-president of the BRT in 1922; ran unsuccessfully for the U.S. Senate from Virginia on the Republican party ticket in 1924; became assistant BRT president in 1927; was elected managing editor of *The Railroad Trainmen* and national legislative representative in 1928; was appointed U.S. Secretary of Labor by President Herbert Hoover in 1930, serving until 1933; devoted much attention during his incumbency to immigration laws and opposed labor reforms advocated by the labor movement; was politically a Republican; died in McLean, Va., October 23, 1933; Walter F. McCaleb, *Brotherhood of Railroad Trainmen: With Special Reference to the Life of Alexander F. Whitney* (1936); Irving Bernstein, *The Lean Years: A History of the American Worker, 1920-1933* (1966); Eugene Lyons, *Herbert Hoover: A Biography* (1964).

DOBBS, Farrel.   Born in Queen City, Mo., July 25, 1907; son of a mechanical superintendent in a coal firm; married Marvel Scholl in April, 1927; three children; graduated from high school in Minneapolis, Minn., in 1925; worked during the next several years for Western Electric, rising from a blue-collar job to a supervisory position; failed in an attempt to start a small business in 1932; secured a job as a truck driver and joined General Drivers Local 574 of the International Brotherhood of Teamsters, Chauffeurs, Warehousemen, and Helpers of America (IBT); saw a small group of Trotskyists, led by Vincent R. Dunne (q.v.) and Carl Skoglund, use Local 574 to organize the coal yards, planning to make them the opening wedge for unionization of all general trucking, including helpers and inside workers; was influenced by Dunne and Skoglund to become a full-time organizer for Local 574; meanwhile, joined the Communist League, precursor of the Socialist Workers party (SWP); emerged as a brilliant unionist during Local 574's famous strikes of 1934 by displaying the keen sense of tactics he would soon apply to unionize highway drivers; was elected secretary-treasurer of Local 574 and in 1936 began organizing highway truckers throughout the Upper Midwest; sought to establish an area-wide agreement providing uniform wages and working conditions; founded the North Central District Drivers' Council in 1937; by "leapfrogging" from organized terminal cities such as Minneapolis and Chicago to other key trucking centers, was able to secure a contract in 1938 covering 250,000 over-the-road drivers; resigned from the IBT after renewing the agreement in 1939; devoted most of his time to SWP activity after 1940; was convicted of violating the Smith Act, a 1940 sedition statute, in 1941; served as editor of *The Militant*, 1943-1948; ran as the SWP candidate for president of the United States in 1948; served as SWP national chairman, 1949-1953, and as national secretary until 1972; authored *Teamster Rebellion* (1972) and *Teamster Power* (1973); Ralph C. James and Estelle D. James, *Hoffa and the Teamsters: A Study of Union Power* (1965); Irving Bernstein, *Turbulent Years: A History of the American Worker* (1969).

(D.G.S.)

DOHERTY, William Charles.   Born in Glendale, Ohio, February 23, 1902; son of Lawrence Michael, a railroader, and Catherine (Ryan) Doherty; Roman Catholic; married Gertrude Helen Dacey on February 23, 1925; nine children; was forced to leave school because of family illness and to begin work at an early age; while working as a telegraph messenger, attended the Cincinnati, Ohio, School of Telegraphy and graduated at age sixteen; appointed manager of the Postal Telegraph Office in Cincinnati in 1918; joined the Commercial Telegraphers Union in 1919; enlisted in the U.S. Army in 1919, after a telegraphers strike began in Cincinnati; participated in the occupation of Siberia following World War I; was blacklisted in the telegraph industry as a result of his union activities; eventually took the civil service examination as a letter carrier and began work with the Cincinnati Post Office in 1923; joined the National Association of Letter Carriers (NALC) in 1923; was elected financial secretary of NALC Branch 43 in 1926 and president in 1928; was chosen president of the Ohio State Letter Carriers Association in 1932; became an executive board member of the NALC in 1935 and was elected president in 1941; was chosen a vice-president and member of the executive council of the American

Federation of Labor (AFL) in 1943; served as the AFL fraternal delegate to the British Trades Union Congress in 1945 and 1957; served as a vice-president and executive council member of the newly merged AFL-Congress of Industrial Organizations (CIO) in 1955; retired from union affairs in 1962, after leading the NALC in a successful U.S. Post Office Department national representation election; associated himself with many AFL and AFL-CIO foreign policy endeavors; was appointed U.S. Ambassador to Jamaica in 1962; was politically a Democrat; authored *Mailman U.S.A.* (1960); Philip Taft, *The A. F. of L. From the Death of Gompers to the Merger* (1959); *Who's Who in Labor* (1946); *Who's Who in America, 1964-1965.*

DONNELLY, Michael (fl. 1898-1916). Married; learned the butchers' trade and joined Sheep Butchers' Local 36 in South Omaha, Neb.; was elected the first international president of the Amalgamated Meat Cutters and Butcher Workmen of North America (AMCBWNA) in 1897; was a gifted organizer; along with Homer D. Call, was largely responsible for the early growth of the AMCBWNA; was an advocate of inclusive organization and attempted to organize packinghouse workers on an industrial basis; forced by undisciplined local leaders and rank-and-file pressures into a general strike of packinghouse workers in 1904 that nearly destroyed the AMCBWNA; led a bitter but somewhat more successful strike against the Cudahy Packing Company in Louisville, Ky., in 1905; unfairly became the scapegoat for the AMCBWNA's failures, but was nevertheless able to win reelection in 1906; severely beaten twice as a result of his reform activities in the Chicago (Ill.) Federation of Labor and this, along with a growing alcohol addiction, apparently caused increasingly serious mental disorders; resigned as AMCBWNA president in 1907 and for several years disappeared from union activities; worked for a short time on several jobs, then in 1916 employed by the AMCBWNA as an organizer; succeeded in organizing a local in Fort Worth, Tex., and commissioned as an American Federation of Labor organizer assigned to the Chicago area; however, disappeared before the commission was delivered, was never heard from again; in 1950 the AMCBWNA, which had voted him a $3,000 annual pension, attempted without success to locate him; advocated an independent labor party during his trade union career; David Brody, *The Butcher Workmen: A Study of Unionization* (1964); *The American Federation of Labor Weekly News Service*, April 11, 1950.

DONNELLY, Samuel Bratton. Born in Concord, Pa., November 7,

1866; son of James M. and Hannah M. (Bratton) Donnelly; married; one child; graduated from high school in Lewistown, Pa. and attended the State Normal School at Shippensburg, Pa.; taught in rural Pennsylvania schools, 1883-1886; learned the printers' trade and became associated with various New Jersey and New York newspapers between 1886-1901; joined New York Typographical Union No. 6 and during 1895-1898 served as its president; was elected president of the International Typographical Union in 1898, but failed to win reelection in 1900; was appointed secretary of the National Civic Federation in 1901 and served for two years; became a member of the joint arbitration board of the New York Building Trades Employers Association in 1903, serving until 1908; was named to the New York Board of Education in 1901 by Mayor Seth Low and served until 1908; served as Public Printer in the administrations of Theodore Roosevelt and William Howard Taft, 1908-1913; was secretary of the New York Building Trades Employers Association, 1913-1923, and chairman of the board of control of the Allied Building Metal Industries, 1923-1931; retired in 1931 to a Monmouth County, N.J., farm; was a Republican; died in Neptune, N.J., January 26, 1946; George A. Stevens, *New York Typographical Union No. 6: A Study of a Modern Trade Union and Its Predecessors* (1913); Seymour Martin Lipset, *et al.*, *Union Democracy: What Makes Democracy Work in Labor Unions and Other Organizations?* (1956); *Encyclopedia Americana* (Vol. 9).

DOUGLAS, Dr. Charles (fl. 1831-1850). Born in New London, Conn., around the turn of the 19th century; traveled extensively throughout the world as a young man, and, although not himself a laborer, identified with the workingmen's cause at an early age; during 1831, established the *New England Artisan*, which was published in Pawtucket, R.I., and the New London *Political Observer and Workingman's Friend*, both of which championed the cause of labor; was elected first president of the New England Association of Farmers, Mechanics, and other Workingmen in 1832; favored an independent labor party, but usually supported the reform-wing of the Democratic party and ran in 1832 as the Democratic nominee for state senator from Connecticut's Seventh District; was one of the principal founders of the Boston Trades' Union, presiding over its initial meeting, helping to draft its constitution, and delivering a major address at its organizational convention in the spring of 1834; made his *New England Artisan* the official organ of the Boston Trades' Union; served as a Boston delegate to the formative meeting of the National Trades' Union (NTU) meeting in New York in 1834; despite the failure of the Boston

Trades' Union, was elected as a special delegate to represent the women and child workers of Boston cotton factories at the NTU conference in Philadelphia, Pa., in 1836; after the decline of the labor movement and start of the depression in the wake of the Panic of 1837, continued to advocate labor reforms; addressed the state convention of the Friends of Industrial Reform in Boston; fervently supported public education throughout his career; Edward Pessen, *Most Uncommon Jacksonians: The Radical Leaders of the Early Labor Movement* (1967); John R. Commons, *et al.*, eds., *A Documentary History of American Industrial Society*, Vol. VI (1910) and *History of Labour in the United States*, Vol. I (1918); Philip S. Foner, *History of the Labor Movement in the United States*, Vol. I (1947).

DRISCOLL, John J.   Born in Waterbury, Conn., December 11, 1911; son of William J., a clerk, and Mary Ellen Driscoll; Roman Catholic; attended the elementary and secondary schools of Waterbury, then matriculated at the Massachusetts Institute of Technology, 1929-1930; received the B.A. (1933) and M.A. (1934) degrees from Wesleyan University, and did graduate study at Brown University, 1934-1935; attended Harvard University Law School, 1935-1936; joined Local 251 of the International Union of Mine, Mill and Smelter Workers of America (IUMMSW) and served during the period 1937-1942 as secretary of Local 251; was a founder of the Connecticut State Industrial Union Council, and was elected its secretary-treasurer, serving until the merger of the American Federation of Labor (AFL) and Congress of Industrial Organizations (CIO) in Connecticut; proved an influential leader of IUMMSW's brass district in Connecticut, but ran unsuccessfully for the post of secretary-treasurer of IUMMSW in 1940; despite early support of IUMMSW president Reid Robinson (q.v.), grew increasingly critical of Robinson for allegedly coming under the influence of the Communist element in the international union; opposed Robinson unsuccessfully for the IUMMSW presidency in a bitterly contested election in 1942; helped to lead Connecticut-centered secessionist movement in 1947 that created the Provisional Metalworkers Council (PMC) as a rival organization; was elected chairman of the PMC and hoped to affiliate it with the International Union of Marine and Shipbuilders Workers of America; after the IUMMSW's expulsion from the CIO as a Communist-dominated union in 1950, affiliated PMC with the United Automobile, Aircraft, and Agricultural Implement Workers of America; was elected president of the newly merged Connecticut AFL-CIO, and remains in that post; devoted much of his time as leader of the Connecticut labor movement to political affairs, especially to lobbying for favorable legislation in the state legislature; was politically a Democrat; Vernon H. Jensen, *Nonferrous Metals Industry Unionism, 1932-1954* (1954); *Who's Who in Labor* (1946).

DUBINSKY, David. Born in Brest Litovsk, Russian Poland (now a part of the Soviet Union), February 22, 1892; son of Bezallel, a bakery owner, and Shaine (Wishinggrad) Dubnievski; Jewish; married Emma Goldberg in 1915; one child; ended formal schooling at age eleven and became a baker's apprentice, advancing to master baker four years later; after joining bakers' union in Lodz, Poland, participated in a successful strike against the city's Jewish bakeries, including his father's; was arrested as a labor agitator shortly thereafter, and spent 18 months in prison; was exiled to Chelyabinsk, Siberia, but escaped en route and lived under an assumed name until given amnesty in 1910; emigrated to the United States in 1911 and became a citizen the same year; learned the cloak cutting trade and joined Local 10 of the International Ladies' Garment Workers' Union (ILGWU); was elected successively between 1918 and 1920 to the executive board, vice-chairmanship, and chairmanship of Local 10; became a vice-president and member of the ILGWU executive board in 1922; was elected secretary-treasurer in 1929, at the time of ILGWU effort to rebuild itself after a disastrous Communist-led strike; was chosen president in 1932; served as a labor adviser to the National Recovery Administration, 1933-1935; became a vice-president of the American Federation of Labor (AFL) and a member of its executive council in 1935; was a delegate to the International Labor Organization conference in Geneva in 1935; served as a member of the AFL Committee for Industrial Organization (CIO); resigned from the AFL executive council after the suspension of CIO unions in 1937; opposed the establishment of a permanent CIO, and thus kept his union independent for a year-and-a-half before reaffiliating with the AFL in 1940; regained the AFL vice-presidency and membership on the executive council in 1945; participated in the founding of the International Confederation of Free Trade Unions; was a co-founder of the American Labor party, a vice-chairman of the Liberal party of New York, and a board member of Americans for Democratic Action; served on a large number of public and private boards and agencies, including the Labor League for Human Rights, the Jewish Labor Committee, and the Post-War Planning Committee; after retiring the positions of secretary-treasurer in 1959 and president in 1966, served as director of the ILGWU retiree service department; Max D. Danish, *The World of David Dubinsky* (1957); "David Dubinsky, The I.L.G.W.U. and the American Labor Movement," Special

Supplement, *Labor History* (Spring, 1968); Charles A. Madison, *American Labor Leaders: Personalities and Forces in the Labor Movement* (1962); John Dewey, *David Dubinsky: A Pictorial Review* (1951).

DUFFY, Frank.   Born in County Monaghan, Ireland, in 1861; Roman Catholic; married; at least three children; received a limited formal education in Ireland, then emigrated to the United States in 1881, settling in New York City; secured employment as a carpenter and soon became actively involved in trade union affairs; joined the Greater New York United Order of American Carpenters and Joiners and was elected the first president of its executive council; after the merger of the United Order and the United Brotherhood of Carpenters and Joiners of America (UBC) in 1888, became a member of UBC Local 478; served variously as Local 478's representative to the New York District Council, as financial secretary, and as president of the executive council of the UBC's New York District Council, 1888-1901; served as business manager of Local 478, 1896-1898; was elected to the UBC executive council in 1900, and helped to effect the removal from office of UBC founder Peter J. McGuire (q.v.) in 1901; became secretary-general in 1901, and was destined to hold that position for 48 years; was elected an American Federation of Labor (AFL) vice-president and executive council member in 1918, serving until 1940; was a member of the United States labor delegation to the 1919 Paris Peace Conference; was a conservative unionist, and a staunch ally of William Hutcheson (q.v.) who, during the 1930s and 1940s, established nearly total control of the UBC; usually supported the Republican party; retired union positions in 1950; died in Indianapolis, Ind., July 11, 1955; Robert A. Christie, *Empire in Wood: A History of the Carpenters' Union* (1956); Morris A. Horowitz, *The Structure and Government of the Carpenters' Union* (1962); *The American Federationist* (August, 1955).

DUFFY, James Michael.   Born in Wheeling, W. Va., June 28, 1889; son of Michael, a potter, and Mary (McGarry) Duffy; Roman Catholic; married Kathryn Geon on September 6, 1916; five children; after completing his formal education in the parochial schools of East Liverpool, Ohio, became an apprentice potter; joined Local 31 of the National Brotherhood of Operative Potters (NBOP) in 1909; served as a labor adviser on the Workmen's Compensation Committee for the State of Ohio; held a variety of offices in Local 31 and Buffalo Local 76 of the NBOP prior to being elected international president in 1927; was a member of the National Labor Advisory Board of the National Industrial Recovery Administration,

1933-1935; served as an American Federation of Labor (AFL) delegate to the International Labor Conference in Geneva in 1937 and later as an AFL representative on a Labor League of Human Rights visit to China; was appointed a labor representative on the Labor-Management Conference Committee established by President Harry S. Truman in 1945; served as an AFL delegate to the Inter-American Labor Conference held in Lima, Peru, in 1948; served as a vice-president of the AFL union label trades department, a member of the executive council of America's Wage Earners' Protective Conference, and a director of the Union Labor Life Insurance Company; also maintained membership in numerous public and private boards and agencies; retired union positions in 1953; died in East Liverpool, Ohio, in March, 1963; *Who's Who in Labor* (1946); *AFL-CIO News*, March 9, 1963.

DULLZELL, Paul.   Born in Boston, Mass., June 15, 1879; son of Paul, an artist, and Alice (O'Neill) Dullzell; married Vivian Korwalski in August, 1914; beginning as a child actor with little formal education, appeared in dramas, vaudeville, musical comedies, and motion pictures between 1879-1919; joined Actors' Equity Association (AEA) in 1913; after an actors' strike against the United Managers Protective Association in New York in 1919, devoted most of his time to union organizing activities; became assistant executive secretary of AEA in 1920; was named international executive secretary of Associated Actors and Artists of America (AAAA) in 1923; was elected executive secretary of AEA in 1928 and treasurer shortly thereafter; served during World War II as the director of United Theatrical War Activities; retired as executive secretary of AEA in 1948 because of poor health but remained treasurer until 1960; served as president of AAAA until 1961; also served as chairman of the executive committee of the Chorus Equity Association, president of the Theater Authority, and vice-president of the American Theatrical Wing; died in New York City, December 21, 1961; *Who's Who in Labor* (1946); *Who Was Who in America* (Vol. III); *The New York Times*, December 22, 1961.

DUNCAN, James.   Born in Kincardine County, Scotland, May 5, 1857; son of David, a farmer, and Mary (Forbes) Duncan; Presbyterian; married Lillian M. Holman in January, 1887; one child; after attending the common schools of Aberdeen, Scotland, for a short time, began serving an apprenticeship as a granite cutter; emigrated to the United States at the age of twenty-three in 1880; joined the New York Local of the Granite Cutters' National Union, precursor of the Granite Cutters International Association

(GCIA), in 1881; moved to Baltimore in 1885 and was elected secretary of the local union of granite cutters; attended the 1886 national trades' union convention, in which the American Federation of Labor (AFL) was organized to replace the Federation of Organized Trades and Labor Unions; was elected second vice-president of the AFL in 1894 and served on its executive council until his death; assumed the presidency of the GCIA in 1885; was later to become a close personal friend and confidant of Samuel Gompers (q.v.), but nominated John McBride (q.v.) for the AFL presidency in 1895; was a fraternal delegate to the British Trades Union Congress in 1898; became the first vice-president of the AFL in 1900; successfully led granite cutters in strike for an eight-hour day in 1900; represented the AFL at the 1911 International Secretariat Conference in Budapest; was named to the United States Commission to study workmen's compensation legislation in 1913; was appointed envoy extraordinary to Russia in 1917; was a member of the American labor mission to the Paris Peace Conference in 1919; nominated for the AFL presidency after the death of Samuel Gompers, but was defeated by William Green (q.v.); edited the *Granite Cutters' Journal*, 1895-1928; was an independent in politics; died in Quincy, Mass., September 14, 1928; Philip Taft, *The A. F. of L. in the Time of Gompers* (1957); *Dictionary of American Biography* (Vol. V); *Who's Who in America, 1928-1929; Granite Cutters' Journal*, October, 1928.

DUNNE, Vincent Raymond. Born in Kansas City, Kan., April 17, 1889; son of an Irish Catholic immigrant and a French Canadian; married Jennie Holm in 1914; two children; moved with family to Little Falls, Minn., and attended grade school there for a few years; beginning at age fourteen, roamed the West and South as a lumberjack and harvest worker; joined the Industrial Workers of the World; settled in Minneapolis, Minn., in 1910; drove a team, and later worked as a coal yard laborer and a weighmaster; under influence of a Swedish immigrant, Carl Skoglund, joined the Communist party in 1920; was meanwhile elected a delegate from a local American Federation of Labor union to the Minneapolis Central Labor Union; helped to found the Trotskyist Communist League of America in 1929; by 1934, along with brothers Miles and Grant and with Skoglund, led a small but dynamic Trotskyist group in Minneapolis-St. Paul; led this group to promote radical unionism by working through General Drivers 574, a local of the International Brotherhood of Teamsters, Chauffeurs, Warehousemen, and Helpers of America (IBT) that had a vague jurisdiction; won a mid-winter strike in the coal yards, then joined his colleagues, along with Farrel Dobbs (q.v.), in seeking to force recognition of Local 574 throughout general trucking, including helpers and inside workers; during the summer of 1934, led what was probably the most ingeniously conceived and effectively executed walkout of the early thirties; disrupted the powerful open-shop Citizens Alliance, as well as establishing a militant industrial type union as a new force in teamster unionism; was elected a trustee of Local 574 (now Local 544) and used the local to spark organization of general drivers throughout the state, to extend jurisdiction to warehouse and other jobs related to trucking, and to begin to unionize over-the-road drivers, a project carried through by Farrel Dobbs' Central States Drivers Council; saw IBT president Daniel Tobin (q.v.) alternately placate and harrass Local 574, and thus decided in 1941 to affiliate the local with the Congress of Industrial Organizations; shortly thereafter, allegedly at Tobin's instigation, was indicted by the Roosevelt Administration, as were the other Minneapolis Trotskyists, under the Smith Act, a 1940 sedition law; lost his appeal in 1943 and spent more than a year in a federal penitentiary; devoted himself subsequently to the affairs of the Socialist Workers party and to the study of Greek history and philosophy; died in Minneapolis, Minn., February 17, 1970; Irving Bernstein, *Turbulent Years: A History of the American Worker, 1933-1941* (1970); Farrel Dobbs, *Teamster Rebellion* (1972); *Minneapolis Daily Tribune*, February 20, 1970; Walter Galenson, *The CIO Challenge to the AFL: A History of the American Labor Movement, 1935-1941* (1960).

(D.G.S.)

DUNWODY, Thomas Edgar.   Born in Lafayette, Ga., August 1, 1887; son of Thomas Jefferson, an architect, and Elizabeth (Massey) Dunwody; Presbyterian; married Norma Backus on September 3, 1914; no children; completed high school and one year of a college education; was publisher and editor of the St. Matthews (S.C.) *Recorder*, 1905-1907; became an apprentice printing pressman in 1907 and joined Atlanta Local 6 of the International Printing Pressmen's and Assistants' Union of North America (IPPAUNA); received his journeyman's card shortly thereafter, and moved to Chattanooga, Tenn.; became a pressroom foreman there and president of the IPPAUNA Chattanooga Local 165; became an instructor in the IPPAUNA Technical Trade School in Pressmen's Home, Tenn., in 1913; was appointed editor and manager of the IPPAUNA organ, *American Pressman*, in 1916, and continued in that capacity for 35 years; was named director of the IPPAUNA Technical Trade School in 1916, serving until 1951; served as assistant president during the illness of IPPAUNA president J. Herbert de la Rosa, 1951-1952; was elected president in 1952, serving until his death; was an authority on many technological aspects of printing and wrote numerous articles on various facets of the printing industry; was a Democrat; died in Knoxville, Tenn., May 2, 1959; Elizabeth F. Baker, *Printers and Technology: A History of the International Printing Pressmen and Assistants' Union* (1957); *American Pressman*, January, 1953; *Who's Who in Labor* (1946).

DURKIN, Martin Patrick.   Born in Chicago, Ill., March 18, 1894; son of James J., an Irish immigrant and stationary fireman, and Mary Catherine (Higgins) Durkin; Roman Catholic; married Anna H. McNicholas on August 29, 1921; three children; received a grammar school education in parochial schools and for three years took evening courses in heating and ventilation at a technical school; became an apprentice steam fitter in Chicago Local 597 of the United Association of Journeymen and Apprentices of the Plumbing and Pipe Fitting Industry of the United States and Canada (UA) in 1911; became a journeyman plumber in 1915; served in France for two years in the Sixth Cavalry Corps during World War I; became a business manager of UA Local 597 in 1921; was elected a vice-president of the Chicago Building Trades Council in 1927; was appointed Illinois State Director of Labor in 1933, serving until 1941; contributed most importantly to the establishment of a state unemployment compensation system, to the formation of a state mediation and conciliation service, to the regulation of minimum wage and maximum hours for women and children, and to the enactment of safety legislation; became president of the International Association of Government Labor Officials in 1933 and served until 1955; became secretary-treasurer of the UA in 1941 and president in 1943; served during World War II as a member of the National War Labor Board; was appointed to the Defense Mobilization Board and to the National Security Resources Board in 1951; was named U.S. Secretary of Labor in the Administration of Dwight D. Eisenhower in 1953, but resigned eight months later because of Eisenhower's refusal to support his suggestions for amending the Taft-Hartley Act; resumed UA presidency in 1953, serving until his death; served as a director of the Union Labor Life Insurance Company and the National Safety Council and was vice-president of the Catholic Conference on Industrial Problems; was politically a Democrat; died in Washington, D.C., November 13, 1955; Joseph C. Goulden, *Meany* (1972); David A. Frier, *Conflict of Interest in the Eisenhower Administration* (1969); *The National Cyclopaedia of American Biography* (1962); *The American Federationist* (December, 1952).

DYCHE, John Alexander. Born in Kovno, Russian Lithuania (now part of the Soviet Union) in 1867; Jewish; married; emigrated to England in 1887 and participated for 14 years in the British trade union movement; emigrated to the United States in 1901 and secured employment in the New York garment industry as a skirt maker; joined the newly organized International Ladies' Garment Workers' Union (ILGWU) and in 1904 was elected its international secretary-treasurer, serving until 1914; regarded, along with Abraham Rosenberg, as the dominant figure in the international union during this period; was a staunchly conservative business unionist and preferred arbitration and conciliation to militant strike activity; also emphasized the sanctity of contractual relations between employers and employees; strongly supported the "Protocol of Peace" signed in September, 1910, and providing for arbitration of labor-management disputes in the garment industry; because of his conservative trade union policies, aroused great opposition among the ILGWU's left-wing, Socialist factions that finally took control of the union in 1914; left the labor movement shortly after his defeat and became a small businessman in the garment industry; authored *Bolshevism in American Labor Unions* (1926); died in New York City in October, 1938; Benjamin Stolberg, *Tailor's Progress: The Story of a Famous Union and the Men Who Made It* (1944); Louis Levine, *The Women's Garment Workers: A History of the International Ladies' Garment Workers' Union* (1924); L.P. Gartner, *Jewish Immigrant in England, 1870-1914* (1960); Julius H. Cohen, *They Builded Better Then They Knew* (1946).

EAMES, Thomas B. Born in Williamstown, N.J., November 20, 1882; son of James, a painter and paperhanger, and Ellen (Vanaman) Eames; Baptist; married Estella Charlesworth on August 5, 1908; two children; attended the grammar schools of Millville, N.J.; served an apprenticeship as a glass bottle blower and in 1906 joined the Glass Bottle Blowers Association of the United States and Canada (GBBA); served the local union in various capacities and was then elected to the GBBA international executive board in 1922, serving until 1949; was chosen somewhat later as international secretary of the GBBA, and held that post until his death; proved an influential figure in the New Jersey labor movement; served briefly during the early 1930s as president of the New Jersey State Federation of Labor after having been a vice-president for several years; was appointed to the National Recovery Administration (NRA) board for New Jersey in 1933, serving until the NRA was declared unconstitutional in 1935; served as a delegate to several American Federation of Labor conventions; was politically nonpartisan; died in Philadelphia, Pa., September 6, 1949; Leo Troy, *Organized Labor in New Jersey* (1965); *The American Federationist* (October, 1949); *The New York Times*, September 7, 1949; *Who's Who in Labor* (1946).

EASTON, John Bertham.   Born in Allegheny County, Pa., September 26, 1880; son of William, a mine foreman and lumber calculator, and Anna Easton; Congregationalist; married Jane Elizabeth Thomas in 1902; two children; attended public school and evening school; started work as a flint glass worker in 1893; joined the American Flint Glass Workers' Union of North America (AFGW) in 1897, and maintained that affiliation until joining the United Steelworkers of America in 1941; settled permanently at Williamstown (near Parkersburg), W. Va.; became a member of the AFGW international executive board; was elected president of the Parkersburg Trades and Labor Council in 1920, serving in that capacity for several years; served as vice-president of the West Virginia State Federation of Labor (WVSFL), 1922-1924, and as president, 1924-1937; symbolized by his 1924 election the effort by craft affiliates to curb the WVSFL's growing domination by locals of the United Mine Workers of America (UMWA); defeated C. Frank Keeney (q.v.), president of UMWA District 17, on the second ballot; retained the loyalty of the northern miners while the southern faction, led by Keeney and William Blizzard, bolted the WVSFL in 1925, only to return in 1927; met the challenge of dual unionism by condemning the rival "Save the Union" campaign of John Brophy (q.v.) in 1926 and the Reorganized United Mine Workers and West Virginia Miners Union led by Frank Keeney in 1930-1931; found the WVSFL $3,575 in debt in 1924, but freed it from debt by 1929; served as a Republican member of the West Virginia House of Delegates, 1926-1928; entered the Republican primary election for Congressman from the Fourth Congressional District in 1928 and 1930, but was defeated on both occasions; led the WVSFL in helping to elect Democrat Matthew Neely, an anti-injunction candidate, to the U.S. Senate in 1930 over James E. Jones, a coal operator favoring yellow-dog contracts; saw the WVSFL reach a nadir in terms of membership, finances, and influence in 1933, as a result of the Great Depression and the disintegration of the UMWA, but also witnessed its rebirth by 1934, as a result of the National Industrial Recovery Act and the revival of the UMWA; having met the challenge to the WVSFL posed by the depression and unemployment, came to experience the rivalry after 1935 of the American Federation of Labor (AFL)-Congress of Industrial Organizations (CIO); refused to obey the AFL order to the

WVSFL to expel all CIO affiliates, and also refused to appear before the AFL executive council to explain this disobedience; after ensuing revocation of the charter of the WVSFL by the AFL executive council, obtained a CIO charter for it as the West Virginia State Industrial Union Council (WVAIUC); despite withdrawal of many craft locals by August, 1938, to organize an AFL state organization, led the CIO body to add 112 locals with 21,602 members, a net gain of 15,988; remained president of the WVAIUC and regional CIO director until his retirement in 1952; died in Williamstown, W. Va., December 20, 1961; *Who's Who in Labor* (1946); Evelyn L. K. Harris and Frank J. Krebs, *From Humble Beginnings: West Virginia State Federation of Labor, 1903-1957* (1960); *Charleston* (W. Va.) *Gazette*, December 22, 1961.

(J.H.)

EKLUND, John Manly. Born in Burlington, Iowa, September 14, 1909; son of Carl Petrus, a Swedish immigrant and minister, and Laura Alvira (Malnburg) Eklund; Methodist; married Zara Frances Zerbst on September 9, 1934; three children; after graduating from high school in 1927, entered Bethany College in Lindsborg, Kan., and received a B.A. degree in 1931; coached athletics and taught English in Burdick (Kan.) High School, 1931-1933; took postgraduate courses at the University of Denver and studied at the Iliff School of Theology, 1933-1934; was pastor of the Methodist Episcopal Church at Oak Creek, Colo., in 1934-1935 and of the Lakewood (Colo.) Methodist Episcopal Church in 1936; received a Master of Theology degree from the Iliff School of Theology and an M.A. degree in education from the University of Denver in 1936; was an English teacher and vocational guidance instructor in the Denver public school system, 1937-1946; became an appraiser in the Veterans Administration Guidance Center at the Opportunity School in Denver in 1946; was a founder of the Denver Federation of Teachers, and became its president and a vice-president of the American Federation of Teachers (AFT) in 1946; served on the executive board of the Colorado Federation of Teachers, 1946-1953; was elected national president of the AFT in 1948, serving in that capacity until 1952; served as an American Federation of Labor (AFL) delegate to the United Nations Educational, Scientific, and Cultural Organization (UNESCO) conferences in 1947, 1949, and 1951; served as a member of the labor advisory committee to UNESCO in 1949 and of the U.S. National Committee for UNESCO for several years beginning in 1951; belonged to the AFL committee on vocational education; was a member of the national board of Americans for Democratic Action,

1949-1954; served as a delegate to the White House Conference on Education in 1955; became, successively, director of adult education, director of organization and education, and assistant to the president of the National Farmers Union during the period 1954-1964; was named executive vice-president of the Farmers Union International Assistance Corporation; a Democrat; authored *Tools for Peace* (1960); *Current Biography* (1949); *Who's Who in America, 1968-1969*.

ENGLISH, John Francis.   Born in Boston, Mass., April 14, 1889; son of James Patrick and Mary (Holland) English; Roman Catholic; married Gertrude Ann Kurvin and, after her death in 1930, Katherine E. Noonan on December 8, 1948; one child; ended formal schooling at age fifteen and secured a job driving a horse-drawn coal wagon; joined Boston Local 68 of the International Brotherhood of Teamsters, Chauffeurs, Warehousemen, and Helpers of America (IBT) in 1904; was elected business manager of Local 68 in 1910, serving until 1935; belonged to the Coast Artillery during World War I; after serving the Boston Teamsters' Joint Council for several years in a variety of capacities, was elected an international IBT vice-president in 1927; was an IBT auditor and general organizer, 1936-1946; after serving as acting general secretary-treasurer of the IBT for a year, was elected to that post in 1947 and served until his death; was chosen an American Federation of Labor-Congress of Industrial Organizations (AFL-CIO) vice-president and executive council member in 1957, but served only a short time before the IBT was expelled from the AFL-CIO; adamantly opposed Dave Beck (q.v.) during his ascendancy in the IBT, but became a loyal ally of Beck's successor, James R. Hoffa (q.v.); died in Miami Beach, Fla., February 3, 1969; Sam Romer, *The International Brotherhood of Teamsters: Its Government and Structure* (1962); Robert D. Leiter, *The Teamsters Union: A Study of Its Economic Impact* (1957); Ralph C. James and Estelle D. James, *Hoffa and the Teamsters: A Study of Union Power* (1965).

ENGLISH, William (fl. 1828-1836).   Self-described as a "mechanic, born to toil from early childhood [who] never . . . entered a school by the light of day"; became a journeyman shoemaker in Philadelphia, Pa.; was actively involved by the late 1820s in the Philadelphia Mechanics' Union of Trade Associations, a short-lived, ineffective union organization formed as a result of a house carpenters' strike in 1827; organized district meetings of the Philadelphia Working Men's party in 1828 to nominate candidates for the city council and state legislature; served during the same year as vice-president of the Mechanics' Library Company of Philadelphia, which published the *Mechanics' Free Press*; emerged as one of the principal leaders of the Working Men's party, 1829-1831; was elected recording secretary of the Philadelphia Trades' Union in 1834; was a Philadelphia delegate to the founding convention of the National Trades' Union (NTU), and served on committees responsible for drafting a constitution for a "National Union of Trades"; declined the nomination for NTU president, but was elected recording secretary; was chosen president of the Philadelphia Trades' Union in 1835 and again in 1836; ran unsuccessfully for the Pennsylvania state senate on a workingmen's ticket in 1835; at the founding convention of the short-lived national association of cordwainers' meeting in New York City in the spring of 1836, was appointed to committees to draft rules of order for governing the convention and to draw up a plan of cooperation for the various cordwainer societies in the United States; used his talent as an orator to speak often in favor of the ten-hour day; was elected to the Pennsylvania house of representatives as a "progressive" Democrat in 1836, thus ending his formal association with the labor movement, but attended the 1836 convention of the NTU as a special delegate; while serving in the state legislature, offended many of his supporters by voting in favor of a Pennsylvania charter for the Second Bank of the United States; William A. Sullivan, *The Industrial Workers in Pennsylvania, 1800-1840* (1955); Edward Pessen, *Most Uncommon Jacksonians: The Radical Leaders of the Early Labor Movement* (1967); John R. Commons, *et al.*, eds., *A Documentary History of American Industrial Society*, Vol. V, VI (1910), and *History of Labour in the United States*, Vol. I (1918); Philip S. Foner, *History of the Labor Movement in the United States*, Vol. I (1947).

ERNST, Hugo. Born in Varasdin, Austria-Hungary (now part of Yugoslavia), December 11, 1876; son of Dr. Ignatz, a rabbi, and Henriette (Schey) Ernst; Jewish; never married; left high school in 1892, at age sixteen, and took a job as a clerk and bookkeeper for a grain merchant; a year later, began a period of European travel meagerly financed by articles written for a hometown newspaper; after becoming involved in a nationalist movement, emigrated to the United States in 1900; worked for a short time as a reporter for a Croatian-language nationalist weekly newspaper; became a bus boy at the St. George Hotel in Brooklyn, N.Y., in 1902 and worked as a waiter in St. Louis, Mo., during the 1904 Lewis and Clark Exposition; after moving to San Francisco, joined Local 30 of the Hotel and Restaurant Employees' International Alliance and Bartenders' International League of America (HREIABIL) in 1906; was elected secretary of Local 30 in 1910 and thereafter, under the provisions of the Local's constitution, rotated in office between president and secretary every six months; was chosen an international HREIABIL vice-president for the Pacific Coast in 1927; was elected general secretary-treasurer of the HREIABIL in 1939 and succeeded Edward Flore (q.v.) as international president in 1945; served as a delegate to the San Francisco Labor Council, 1910-1939; was a frequent delegate to the conventions of the California State Federation of Labor, and represented it at the American Federation of Labor (AFL) conventions of 1915 and 1935; was an AFL fraternal delegate to the British Trades Union Congress in 1944; named a vice-president of Americans for Democratic Action and the AFL Labor League for Political Education; was a Democrat; died in Cincinnati, Ohio, July 22, 1954; Matthew Josephson, *Union House, Union Bar: The History of the Hotel and Restaurant Employees and Bartenders International Union, AFL-CIO* (1956); Jay Rubin and M.J. Obermeier, *Growth of a Union: The Life and Times of Edward Flore* (1943); *Who's Who in Labor* (1946).

ERVIN, Charles W.   Born in Philadelphia, Pa., November 22, 1865; son of Alexander, a manufacturer and banker, and Elizabeth (McBride) Ervin; married Mary McKee on November 22, 1888; three children; received a grammar school education in the public schools of Philadelphia and later took reading courses in literature; worked as a youth in the wholesale grocery and coffee business; became an editorial writer for the Philadelphia *Daily News-Post;* joined the Socialist Party of America in 1906, and in 1917 became editor-in-chief of the Socialist *New York Daily* and *Sunday Call,* serving until 1922; after running unsuccessfully on the Socialist party ticket for the U.S. House of Representatives and the Senate from Pennsylvania, became the Socialist candidate for governor of New York in 1918; was actively involved in the organization of needle trades workers from 1907 to his death; was appointed public relations adviser to the Amalgamated Clothing Workers of America (ACWA) in 1924; became an active member of the newly organized American Newspaper Guild; became associate editor of the ACWA organ, *The Advance,* in 1944; authored *The Story of the Constitution of the United States* (1946), and *Homegrown Liberal, Autobiography* (1954); died in Yonkers, N.Y., February 5, 1953; *Nation,* February 14, 1953; *Wilson Library Bulletin* (April, 1953); *Who's Who in Labor* (1946).

ETTOR, Joseph James.   Born in Brooklyn, N.Y., October 6, 1885; son of a laborer; was of Italian descent; moved with his family to Chicago, Ill., and attended grade school there until starting work as a newsboy at age twelve; worked at several other manual jobs, then went to San Francisco, Calif., ca. 1900 and became a skilled shipbuilder there; joined the Socialist party and became associated with the radical labor movement; became a West Coast organizer for the Industrial Workers of the World (IWW) in 1906; helped to organize and lead an Oregon lumberworkers' strike in 1907; because of fluency in several languages, proved especially effective in organizing Southern European immigrant workers; elected a member of the IWW general executive board in 1909 and went East to organize steelworkers, coal miners, and textile workers; made his mark as one of the most able IWW leaders during the great Lawrence, Mass., textile strike of 1912; along with his colleague Arturo Giovannitti (q.v.), called in by local Wobblies and took command of the situation; engendered solidarity among the strikers through his ebullient personality and enthusiastic oratory; also made tactical innovations—a strike committee composed of representatives of ethnic groups and nonviolent demonstrations—that were crucial in the strike's success; although a dedicated syndicalist, kept the strike focused on the immediate goals of higher wages and nondiscriminatory rehiring of all strikers; midway in the strike, imprisoned without bail along with Giovannitti for allegedly plotting the shooting death of a woman striker; after spending a year in jail, acquitted of the murder charge, largely because of an IWW protest and legel-defense campaign, conducted nationwide, that helped turn public opinion against the employers, who conceded to the strikers' demands; elected to the IWW's second highest post—general organizer—in 1915; during the Minnesota iron miners' strike of 1916, went to the ranges to help organize a legal-defense fund for IWW leaders indicted for murder; served meanwhile as one of several prominent Wobbly leaders who broke with General Secretary William Haywood (q.v.) over his policy of centralizing administration and authority in the Chicago, Ill., headquarters; was among the 166 IWW leaders indicted in 1917 under the Espionage Act, but saw his case dropped for insufficient evidence; subsequently left the labor movement and ran a small vineyard at Cucamonga, Calif.; died there on Feburary 19, 1948; Solon DeLeon, ed., *The American Labor Who's Who* (1925); *The Industrial Worker*, February 28, 1948; Melvyn Dubofsky, *We Shall Be All: A History of the Industrial Workers of the World* (1969).

(D.G.S.)

EVANS, George Henry.   Born in Bromyard, Herefordshire, England.

March 25, 1805; son of George and Sara (White) Evans; atheist; emigrated to the United States with his family in 1820; became a printer's apprentice in Ithaca, N.Y.; became the editor of *The Man*, published in Ithaca, in 1822; edited the *Working Man's Advocate*, published in New York City at various times from 1829 to 1845 and the *Daily Sentinel* and *Young America* during 1837-1853; participated in and editorially supported the various workingmen's parties developed in Philadelphia, New York, and New England; retired to a farm in New Jersey in 1837 and developed his principles of agrarianism, a social philosophy emphasizing natural rights and individualism; was a doctrinaire land reformer, firmly believing in everyone's inalienable right to a homestead of 160 acres; also opposed monopolies, chattel slavery, imprisonment for debt, and sex discrimination; organized the National Reform Association in 1844 to promulgate his land reform ideas and was instrumental in convening a series of Industrial Congresses that met in various cities from 1846 to 1856 and brought together most of the country's influential reformers; served as secretary of the Boston Industrial Congress of 1846; authored *History of the Origin and Progress of the Working Men's Party* (1840); died in Granville, N.J., February 2, 1856; Norman Ware, *The Industrial Workers, 1840-1860* (1924); John R. Commons, *et al.*, *History of Labour in the United States*, Vol. I (1918); Walter Hugins, *Jacksonian Democracy and the Working Class: A Study of the New York Workingmen's Movement, 1829-1837* (1960); Edward Pessen, *Most Uncommon Jacksonians: The Radical Leaders of the Early Labor Movement* (1967); *Dictionary of American Biography* (Vol. VI).

FARQUHAR, John McCreath.   Born near Ayr, Scotland, April 17, 1832; son of John and Marion (McCreath) Farquhar; Presbyterian; married Jane Wood on September 11, 1862; attended Ayr Academy; emigrated to the United States while still a boy and settled in Buffalo, N.Y.; learned the printing trade; during the 1850s, studied law, ventured into publishing, and did organizational work for the National Typographical Union (NTU); elected president of the NTU in 1860 and served for three years; enlisted as a private in the U.S. Army and advanced to the rank of major; served as judge advocate and inspector in the Fourth Army Corps; awarded the Congressional Medal of Honor for bravery at the battle of Stone River, Tenn.; returned to Buffalo after the war and, while maintaining his union ties, opened a successful law practice; elected as a Republican to the United States Congress in 1884, serving three terms; declined renomination in 1890; served as a member of the United States Industrial Commission, 1898-1902; shortly after retiring from public life and his private law practice, died in Buffalo, N.Y., April 24, 1918; was a Republican; David Montgomery, *Beyond Equality: Labor and the Radical Republicans, 1862-1872* (1967); *Biographical Directory of the American Congress, 1774-1971* (1971); *Who Was Who in America* (Vol. I).

FARRINGTON, Frank.   Born in Fairburg, Ill., in 1873; son of a coal miner; married; three children; had no formal education; began working at age nine in the mines at Streater, Ill.; joined the Knights of Labor in 1886 and later the United Mine Workers of America (UMWA); held several minor union offices before being elected president of District 12, UMWA, Illinois; served in that post from 1914 to August 30, 1926, when his three-year contract as a labor consultant with the Peabody Coal Company at a salary of $25,000 per year was disclosed; served on the UMWA international executive board for six years; was a conservative opponent of the Socialists in the Illinois UMWA prior to World War I, but supported the 1920 campaign of John H. Walker (q.v.), president of the Illinois State Federation of Labor, for governor of Illinois on the National Farmer-Labor party ticket; was an able contract negotiator, invariably winning greater benefits for Illinois miners than surrounding districts won; was president of the most powerful autonomous union district and a personal enemy of John L. Lewis (q.v.); engaged in a continuing feud with Lewis throughout the first 11 years of Lewis's presidency; in 1917, along with John H. Walker, opposed the confirmation of Lewis as an international vice-president by the international executive board; revoked the charters of 24 local unions when between 25,000 and 75,000 Illinois miners revolted against his refusal to convene a wage scale convention in August 1919; was upheld in this action by Lewis and the international convention; made a national martyr of Alexander Howat (q.v.), president of the Kansas district, who got no support from Lewis in his imprisonment for violating the Kansas anti-strike law; was one of three UMWA delegates who supported Samuel Gompers (q.v.) in his 1921 contest with John L. Lewis for the American Federation of Labor presidency; employed Oscar Ameringer, the famed "Adam Coaldigger," to edit the *Illinois Miner*, an anti-Lewis organ, in 1922; supported Howat's nearly successful fight at the 1924 UMWA convention to destroy the Lewis machine by instituting rank-and-file election of international organizers; after supporting John Brophy's (q.v.) "Save the Union" campaign for the UMWA presidency in 1926, was discredited by Lewis's revelation of the Peabody Coal Company contract; involved in the 1930 convention of the Reorganized United Mine Workers; died in Steator, Ill.,

March 30, 1939; Solon DeLeon, ed., *The American Labor Who's Who* (1925); *The New York Times*, March 31, 1939; Selig Perlman and Philip Taft, *History of Labor in the United States, 1896-1932*, Vol. IV (1935); Irving Bernstein, *The Lean Years: A History of the American Worker, 1920-1933* (1960); John H. M. Laslett, *Labor and the Left: A Study of Socialism and Radical Influences in the American Labor Movement, 1881-1924* (1970); McAlister Coleman, *Men and Coal* (1943); John Brophy, *A Miner's Life* (1964).

(J.H.)

FEENEY, Frank.   Born in New York City, April 22, 1870; son of a bricklayer; Roman Catholic; married; two children; completed grammar school in New York City before moving to Philadelphia, Pa.; acquired work as an elevator constructor, and became actively involved in the Philadelphia labor movement; beginning in 1896, served as a delegate to the annual conventions of the American Federation of Labor (AFL) until his death in 1938; was a founder of the International Union of Elevator Constructors (IUEC) in 1901, and served as its international president until his death; was an active and influential figure in the Philadelphia labor movement, serving as president of the Philadelphia Central Labor Union for seven years and also as president of the Philadelphia Building Trades Council for seven years; was an AFL fraternal delegate to the Canadian Trades and Labor Congress in 1905; participated actively in Republican party affairs in Philadelphia, and credited with organizing the labor movement in support of Boies Penrose's Senatorial campaigns; served as chief of the Philadelphia Bureau of Elevator Inspection, 1908-1911, and as a supervising referee for the Pennsylvania Workmen's Compensation Bureau, 1919-1922; was a member of the Council of National Defense during World War I; served for many years as an official in the AFL building trades department; saw his son, Frank Jr., serve as secretary-treasurer of the IUEC; died in Atlantic City, N.J., May 28, 1938, during son's tenure; Solon DeLeon, ed., *The American Labor Who's Who* (1925); *The American Federation of Labor Weekly News Service*, June 4, 1938.

FEINBERG, Israel.   Born in Berdichev, Russia, December 25, 1887; son of Hyman, a prosperous tailor, and Bertha Feinberg; Jewish; married Nellie Weissman in 1910; two children; acquired the equivalent of a high school education before beginning an apprenticeship in the tailor's trade at age sixteen; emigrated to England at the turn of the century and settled in Manchester; became an active participant in the British labor movement and organized a Jewish tailors' union in Manchester; emigrated to the United States in 1912 and, after finding employment as a cloak operator, joined Local 1 of the International Ladies' Garment Workers' Union (ILGWU); elected an official and executive board member of Local 1; became chairman of the New York Cloak Joint Board in 1919 and two years later elected general manager, serving until 1925; was a member of the New York Central Labor Council, 1918-1920; served as an ILGWU vice-president, 1922-1925 and 1928-1952; was an ILGWU general organizer in Canada, 1928-1931, and during 1931-1933 served as a supervisor of the ILGWU locals in Boston, Mass.; became West Coast regional director of the ILGWU in 1933 and assumed responsibility for the organization of garment workers in Los Angeles, Calif., San Francisco, Calif., Portland, Ore., and Vancouver, Wash.; became general manager of the New York Joint Board of Cloak, Suit, Skirt and Reefer Makers Unions in 1934; took the initiative in establishing the ILGWU's first retirement fund in 1943; was a member of the board of directors of the Yiddish Science Institute and served as treasurer of the Central Yiddish Culture Organization; retired from union affairs in 1952; was a member of the Liberal party of New York; died in Los Angeles, Calif., September 16, 1952; Benjamin Stolberg, *Tailor's Progress: The Story of a Famous Union and the Men Who Made It* (1944); Louis Levine, *The Women's Garment Workers: A History of the International Ladies' Garment Workers' Union* (1924); *ILGWU Report and Proceedings* (1953).

FEINSTONE, Morris.   Born in Warsaw, Russian Poland, in 1878; Jewish; married; two children; studied at the Warsaw Art School, and became a skilled carver, designer, and master draftsman; after imprisonment in Warsaw for participating in revolutionary activities, emigrated to Germany; moved somewhat later to England and secured employment as a woodcarver; joined the Woodcarver's union in London and in 1895 elected its president; actively involved in the early organizing activities of the British Labour party in Birmingham; emigrated to the United States in 1910; secured employment in the New York umbrella industry and became a leader of the Umbrella Handle and Stick Makers' Union, as well as an active participant in the affairs of the United Hebrew Trades (UHT); became assistant secretary of the UHT in 1915 and, after the retirement of Max Pine (q.v.) in 1926, became executive secretary; represented the UHT on the executive board of the Central Trades and Labor Council of Greater New York for several years; strongly supported the movement to create a Jewish state in Palestine; was a member of the board of directors of the

Hebrew Immigrant Sheltering Aid Society, chairman of the administrative committee of the National Labor Committee for Palestine, vice-chairman of the Jewish Labor Committee, and a member of the Forward Association, publisher of the *Jewish Labor Forward*; served as a member of the governing board of the Rand School of Social Science and of the *New Leader*, a Social-Democratic weekly labor newspaper; served during World War II as a panel member of the Regional War Labor Board and on the labor advisory board of the Office of Price Administration in New York City; as a Socialist and a long-time advocate of an independent labor party, became a leading proponent of the American Labor party; died in New York City, April 28, 1943; Hyman J. Fliegel, *The Life and Times of Max Pine: A History of the Jewish Labor Movement in the U.S.A. during the Last Part of the 19th Century and the First Part of the 20th Century* (1959); Melech Epstein, *Jewish Labor in the U.S.A., 1914-1952* (2 vols., 1953).

FELLER, Karl Franz. Born in Dayton, Ohio, August 6, 1914; son of Karl John and Marie (Koch) Feller; Roman Catholic; married Virginia K. Snyder on October 9, 1937; five children; completed secondary public school in Dayton, then became an apprentice brewer and joined Local 50 of the International Union of United Brewery, Flour, Cereal, and Soft Drink Workers of America (UBFCSDW) (Now the International Union of United Brewery, Flour, Cereal, Soft Drink and Distillery Workers of America); worked as a brewer in Cincinnati, Ohio, Detroit, Mich., and Milan, Ohio, prior to returning to Dayton; elected president of Local 50, in Dayton, in 1939; elected business manager of Local 50 in 1940 and served as an organizer and trouble-shooter for the UBFCSDW in Ohio; founded the Ohio-Kentucky State Council of Brewery Syrup and Soft Drink Workers; served as a special UBFCSDW organizer, 1943-1945; became corresponding secretary of the UBFCSDW in 1945; as a result of a referendum vote in 1948, elected to the newly created office of international president, assuming office on January 1, 1949; was a member of the executive board of the Congress of Industrial Organizations (CIO) and, after the American Federation of Labor (AFL)-CIO merger, became a vice-president of the AFL-CIO industrial union department; named an AFL-CIO vice-president and executive council member in 1957, but expelled from the executive council in 1973 as a result of his holding merger discussions with the International Brotherhood of Teamsters, Chauffeurs, Warehousemen and Helpers; had been a consistent supporter of Walter P. Reuther (q.v.) on the AFL-CIO executive council, but his freedom of action was reduced by the weakness of his own union and the UBFCSDW's constant fear of encroachment by the powerful Teamsters; was politically a Democrat; Fleisher Maurer, *et al.*, *Union with a Heart: International Union of United Brewery, Flour, Cereal, Soft Drink, and Distillery Workers of America: 75 Years of a Great Union, 1886-1961* (1961); *Who's Who in America, 1972-1973.*

FENTON, Francis Patrick.   Born in Boston, Mass., March 11, 1895; son of John J., a union leader, and Catherine (Delaney) Fenton; Roman Catholic; married Christine Wilhelmina Tucker in 1923; five children; attended grammar school in Boston, then became a coal driver and joined Boston Local 68 of the International Brotherhood of Teamsters, Chauffeurs, Warehousemen, and Helpers of America; later received an LLB degree from the Suffolk Law School; active during 1926-1939 in the Boston and Massachusetts labor movement, serving as an executive board member, vice-president, and president of the Boston Central Labor Union; also served during that period as president of the Workers Credit Union Bank, chairman of the resolutions committee of the Massachusetts State Federation of Labor, and president of the Board of Control of the Boston Trade Union College; was instrumental in gaining ratification in Massachusetts of the child-labor amendment to the U.S. Constitution; after serving as an American Federation of Labor (AFL) organizer for the New England district, became director of organization for the AFL in 1939; served during World War II on a number of boards and agencies, including the National War Labor Board, the War Production Board, and the Office of Price Administration; was named international representative and permanent AFL representative to the International Labor Organization after the death of Robert J. Watt (q.v.) in 1947; served as a consultant on vocational education with the U.S. Department of Education; supported the Democratic party; died in Washington, D.C., August 9, 1948; *The American Federationist* (December, 1947, September, 1948); *Who's Who in Labor* (1946).

FERRAL, John (fl. 1833-1850).   Was a handloom weaver during the 1830s and became the most influential figure in the Philadelphia, Pa., labor movement, as well as a prominent figure in the national trade-union movement; was the only non-New England delegate to the 1833 convention of the New England Association of Farmers, Mechanics and Other Working Men; attended the convention in order to study the New England labor movement; returned to Philadelphia and attempted to organize factory workers and farmers in the area around the city, hoping to effect a union (the Trades' Union of Pennsylvania) between city artisans, mechanics, and factory workers; became one of the principal figures in the Philadelphia Trades' Union and was a leader of the successful 1835 strike for the ten-hour day in Philadelphia; elected second vice-president of the National Trades' Union (NTU) at its inaugural convention in 1834 and, among other duties, served on a committee to prepare a statement regarding wages and hours; elected president of the NTU in 1835, serving until 1836; became corresponding secretary of the Philadelphia Trades' Union in 1837; believed in the inevitability of class conflict, and thus not only advocated militant trade-union activity but also supported labor's involvement in politics; during the 1840s and 1850s, supported the land-reform principles of George Henry Evans (q.v.); participated actively in the Pittsburgh Workingmen's Congress; was a delegate to the New York City Industrial Congress in 1850; Edward Pessen, *Most Uncommon Jacksonians: The Radical Leaders of the Early Labor Movement* (1967); William A. Sullivan, *The Industrial Workers in Pennsylvania, 1800-1840* (1955); John R. Commons, *et al.*, *A Documentary History of the American Industrial Society*, Vols. V, VI, VIII (1910-1911); Philip S. Foner, *History of the Labor Movement in the United States*, Vol. I (1947).

FINCHER, Jonathan C. (fl. 1858-1876).   Born in Philadelphia, Pa., in 1830; worked as a machinist in Philadelphia; along with 13 fellow machinists, founded the first International Union of Machinists' and Blacksmiths' local unions in 1858; was among 21 delegates from 12 local unions in five cities and three states who convened in Philadelphia in the spring of 1859 to establish the national union that encompassed 57 locals and 2,828 members by late 1860; served as the union's national secretary-treasurer for several years, and established its monthly publication, the *Machinists' and Blacksmiths' International Journal*, in 1862; founded *Fincher's Trade Review* in 1863 and issued it weekly for the next three years; included Ira Steward (q.v.), Richard Trevellick (q.v.), and William H. Sylvis (q.v.) among its contributors, thus making *Fincher's Review* the most influential trade-union publication of the era and one of the finest ever published in the United States; saw its circulation reach 11,000 in 31 of 36 states and in five English cities by 1865; helped found the Philadelphia Trades' Assembly in 1863 and elected to its board of trustees; attending the National Labor Congresses in Baltimore in 1866 and in New York City in 1868, opposed currency reform and favored strong trade unions and eight-hour legislation attained by pressure on the two traditional parties; opposed labor's independent political action because it resulted in neglect of trade unions and fostered a new alliance of employers and employees; bolted the

National Labor Union when it endorsed independent political action; established another Philadelphia labor paper, the *Welcome Workman*; published the Wilkes Barre, Pa., *Anthracite Monitor* in 1869; elected from Hazelton, Luzerne County, to the Pennsylvania legislature in 1876; with the support of John W. Morgan, a St. Clair miner-legislator, and John Siney (q.v.), a member of the Miners' National Association, helped exempt labor organizations from prosecution under Pennsylvania's conspiracy law; John R. Commons, *et al.*, *History of Labour in the United States*, Vol. II (1918); Edward Pinkowski, *John Siney: Miners' Martyr* (1963); David Montgomery, *Beyond Equality: Labor and the Radical Republicans, 1862-1872* (1967).

(J.H.)

FISHER, Joseph A.   Born in New York City, May 1, 1896; son of Joseph, a plumber, and Rose (Peters) Fisher; Roman Catholic; married Agnes B. Cosgrove on November 24, 1920; two children; was graduated from Holy Cross High School in Queens, New York, then attended the College of the City of New York; worked as an electrician in the New York City construction industry during 1912-1934; joined New York City Local 830 of the International Brotherhood of Electrical Workers in 1912; hired as an electrician with the Consolidated Edison Corporation in 1935; served as president of Local 830, 1937-1940; elected national president of the independent Utility Unions of America in 1941, serving until 1945; served as chairman of the joint council of the Brotherhood of Consolidated Edison Employees, 1941-1945; elected the first national president of the Utility Workers Union of America (UWUA), a new union chartered by the Congress of Industrial Organizations (CIO) in 1945; served on the executive board of the CIO, 1945-1955, and on the general board of the American Federation of Labor-CIO, 1955-1960; was largely responsible for building the UWUA into a well-organized, effective trade union and guiding it through its early formative years; retired as national president of the UWUA in 1960; *Who's Who in America, 1958-1959; Who's Who in Labor* (1946).

FITZGERALD, Albert J.   Born in Lynn, Mass., in 1906; son of Irish immigrants; Roman Catholic; married; one child; after graduation from high school, became a lathe-turner in the motor department of the General Electric plant in Lynn; supported efforts to organize the plant, and appointed shop steward; later elected president of Lynn Local 201, United

Electrical, Radio and Machine Workers of America (UE); elected district vice-president, district president, and secretary of the Massachusetts State Industrial Union Council, Congress of Industrial Organizations (CIO); elected general president of UE in 1941; denied any Communist affiliation, but usually allied with the left wing of the UE and of the labor movement nationally; became a CIO vice-president and member of the executive council; was a member of the CIO's Political Action Committee in 1943; led his union in a series of strikes in the immediate postwar period; supported Henry Wallace for president of the United States in 1948 and served as co-chairman of the Wallace for President Committee and chairman of the Wallace Labor Committee; served also as co-chairman of the Progressive party's national convention in 1948; during presidency the UE expelled from the CIO in 1949 because of alleged Communist domination; the CIO chartered the International Union of Electrical, Radio and Machine Workers which soon became the largest union in the electrical industry; nevertheless, kept the UE a viable and effective trade union; along with other unions in the electrical industry, led the UE in a successful 95-day strike against General Electric in 1970; Max M. Kampelman, *The Communist Party vs. The C.I.O.: A Study in Power Politics* (1957); *Current Biography* (1948); *Who's Who in Labor* (1946); F.S. O'Brien, "The 'Communist Dominated' Unions in the U.S. Since 1950," *Labor History* (Spring, 1968).

FITZGERALD, Frank A.   Born in New York City, September 5, 1885; son of John, an operating engineer, and Catherine (Van Ness) Fitzgerald; Roman Catholic; married Mae Gardner on September 5, 1917; after graduating from high school, served an apprenticeship as a machinist; joined New Haven, Conn., Local 478 of the International Union of Operating Engineers (IUOE) in 1910; elected shortly thereafter as business agent of Local 478 and continued in that capacity for 20 years; elected to the IUOE board of trustees in 1916 and later served as board chairman; elected an IUOE vice-president in 1931, and later that same year filled the newly vacant office of general secretary-treasurer; during the depression of the 1930s, developed an elaborate listing service to inform unemployed engineers of government building projects and other employment opportunities; while serving as general secretary-treasurer, reorganized the various departments of the IUOE and established an efficient administrative governance system for the union that became a model for many other international unions; edited *The International Engineer*, 1931-1951; died in Washington, D.C., March 29, 1951; Garth L. Mangum, *The Operating Engineers: The Economic History of a Trade Union* (1964); *The American Federationist* (April, 1951); *Who's Who in Labor* (1946).

FITZPATRICK, John. Born in Ireland, April 21, 1871; Roman Catholic; married; one child; attended grammar school in Ireland; emigrated to the United States in 1882, settling in Chicago, Ill.; became a journeyman horseshoer in 1886 and joined Local 4 of the International Journeymen Horseshoers' Union; elected president of the Chicago Federation of Labor (CFL) in 1901 and served one term; became a full-time CFL paid organizer in 1902; again elected president of the CFL in 1906, and served in that position for more than 40 years; led a movement to create a labor party in Illinois, and ran as its candidate for mayor of Chicago in 1918; headed a successful organizing drive in Chicago during World War I; was one of the leaders, along with William Z. Foster (q.v.), of the historic 1919 steel strike; assisted in the organization of Chicago packinghouse workers, garment workers, and teachers; belonged to the Regional Labor Board of the National Recovery Administration, 1933-1935; proved to be a vigorous and resourceful trade union leader and a diligent foe of racketeering and corruption in the Chicago labor movement; was a militant unionist, but opposed Communist efforts to infiltrate the labor movement during the 1920s and 1930s; long advocated an independent labor party, but usually supported Democratic candidates and served as vice-president of the Alfred E. Smith-for-President Union Labor League in 1928; enthusiastically admired President Franklin D. Roosevelt during the 1930s; died in Chicago, Ill., September 27, 1946; Barbara Warne Newell, *Chicago and the Labor Movement: Metropolitan Unionism in the 1930s* (1961); Eugene Staley, *History of the Illinois State Federation of Labor* (1930); David Brody, *Labor in Crisis: The Steel Strike of 1919* (1965); James Weinstein, *The Decline of Socialism in America, 1912-1925;* (1967).

FITZSIMMONS, Frank Edward. Born in Jeannette, Pa., April 7, 1908; son of Frank, a brewery worker, and Ida May (Stahley) Fitzsimmons; after the death of his first wife, married Mary Patricia in 1952; two children; left school at age seventeen because of his father's incapacitating illness; worked for a short while as a time clerk before securing employment as a bus driver for the Detroit Motor Company; later worked as a truck driver for the National Transit Corporation and the 3-C Highway Company; joined Detroit Local 299 of the International Brotherhood of Teamsters, Chauffeurs, Warehousemen, and Helpers of America (IBT) in 1934; appointed business manager of Local 299 by the local's president, James R. Hoffa (q.v.), in 1937; elected vice-president of Local 299 in 1940 and three years later was appointed secretary-treasurer of the IBT's Michigan Conference; became an IBT executive board member and vice-president in 1961; elected in 1966 to the newly created office of general vice-president, a position created to provide a method of filling any vacancy that might occur in the union presidency; became president in 1967 when IBT president James R. Hoffa was imprisoned in the Lewisburg, Penn., Federal Penitentiary for jury tampering, conspiracy, and fraud; along with Walter P. Reuther (q.v.), helped organize the Alliance for Labor Action in 1969; appointed a member of President Richard M. Nixon's "Phase Two" pay board in 1971, and continued serving on the board after other labor leaders, led by American Federation of Labor-Congress of Industrial Organizations' president George Meany (q.v.) resigned to protest the Administration's economic policies; elected president of the IBT in 1971; usually supported the Republican party; Walter Sheridan, *The Fall and Rise of Jimmy Hoffa* (1972); Joseph C. Goulden, *Meany* (1972); *Current Biography* (1971).

FLJOZDAL, Frederick Herman.   Born in Iceland, December 19, 1868; son of Arni Brynjolfson, a farmer and laborer, and Christine (Johnson) Fljozdal; Presbyterian; married Christina Nygren on August 24, 1893; six children; after receiving a grammar school education, emigrated to the United States in 1876; later took correspondence courses in common law and public speaking; began work as a laborer in 1888; was a farmer and justice of the peace, 1892-1898; served as a railroad construction foreman, 1898-1901; was a railroad section foreman during 1901-1915; joined the Brotherhood of Maintenance of Way Employees (BMWE) in 1902; served as secretary of BMWE Lodge 322 during 1902 and the following year elected president and local chairman; elected BMWE general chairman for the Canadian National Railway in 1905, serving until 1918; served as chairman of the BMWE's General Chairman's Association for the United States and Canada, 1910-1914; was secretary of the international executive board, 1915-1916, and chairman, 1916-1918; served as legislative representative in Washington, D.C., in 1918; elected a BMWE vice-president and member of the national committee in 1918; elected international president in 1922 and served until his retirement as president emeritus in 1940; served as a member of the executive committee of the Railroad Labor Executives' Association and as a member of the editorial committee of the railroad newspaper, *Labor*; was an independent in politics; died in Detroit, Mich., December 16, 1954; Denver W. Hertel, *History of the Brotherhood of Maintenance of Way Employees: Its Birth and Growth, 1877-1955* (1955); Brotherhood of Maintenance of Way Employees, *Pictorial History, 1877-1951* (1952); *Who's Who in Labor* (1946).

FLORE, Edward.   Born in Buffalo, N.Y., December 5, 1877; son of George, a German immigrant and saloon owner, and Catherine (Hassenfratz) Flore; Roman Catholic; married Mary Katherine Schneider on September 27, 1911; one child (died in infancy); left the public schools of Buffalo, N.Y., at age sixteen and went to work as a bartender in his father's saloon; joined Bartenders' League Local 175 in 1900 and later the same year was elected recording secretary of the Buffalo local; elected a delegate to the Buffalo Central Labor Union in 1903; became a vice-president and member of the general executive board of the Hotel and Restaurant Employees' International Alliance and Bartenders' International League of America (HREIABIL) in 1905; elected international president of the HREIABIL in 1911 and held position for the remainder of his life; elected to the Erie County Board of Supervisors in 1908, serving until 1920; was an American Federation of Labor (AFL) fraternal delegate to the British Trades Union Congress in 1934; became an AFL vice-president and executive council member in 1937; remained loyal to the AFL, but supported the concept of industrial unionism and opposed the expulsion of the Committee on Industrial Organization unions from the AFL; served as an AFL delegate to the International Labor Organization's conference in Geneva in 1936; during his incumbency, saw the HREIABIL become one of the largest unions affiliated with the AFL; confronted as the major challenges during his presidency the long period of enforced prohibition and the recurring problems of graft and corruption, especially in locals in the New York and Chicago areas; was a Democrat; died in Buffalo, N.Y., September 27, 1945; Jay Rubin and M.J. Obermeier, *Growth of a Union: The Life and Times of Edward Flore* (1943); Matthew Josephson, *Union House: Union Bar: The History of the Hotel and Restaurant Employees and Bartenders International Union, AFL-CIO* (1956); *Current Biography* (1945); *Who's Who in Labor* (1946).

FLYNN, Elizabeth Gurley.   Born in Concord, N.H., August 7, 1890; daughter of immigrant Irish revolutionaries Thomas, a civil engineer, and Annie (Gurley) Flynn; married John A. Jones in January, 1908; one child; joined the Industrial Workers of the World (IWW) in 1906 and a year later quit high school to devote full time to IWW activities; participated in the

IWW free speech and assembly struggles in Missoula, Mont., and Spokane, Wash., 1908-1910; was an active participant in the Lawrence, Mass., textile strike of 1912, the Paterson, N.J., silk strike of 1913, the Mesabi Range miners' strike of 1916, and the Passaic, N.J., textile strike of 1926; after World War I, became a mediator between the IWW and the National Civil Liberties Bureau; was one of the founders of the Workers' Liberty Defense Union in 1918; involved during the next four years in defending those political and industrial prisoners arrested during the 1919-1920 Red Scare; was a founding member of the national committee of the American Civil Liberties Union in 1920; served as chairman of the International Labor Defense Committee, 1927-1930; joined the. Communist party in 1937 and became a columnist for the party's organ, the *Daily Worker*; expelled from the American Civil Liberties Union national committee in 1940 because of her Communist party membership; convicted of teaching and advocating the overthrow of the government by force and violence and served a three-year prison sentence, 1955-1957; became the first woman to chair the Communist party's National Committee in 1961; authored *I Speak My Piece: Autobiography of the Rebel Girl* (1955); died in Moscow, USSR, September 5, 1964; Joseph R. Starobin, *American Communism in Crisis, 1943-1957* (1972); David A. Shannon, *The Decline of American Communism* (1959); Melvyn Dubofsky, *We Shall Be All: A History of the Industrial Workers of the World* (1969); *Current Biography* (1961).

(M.T.)

FORAN, Martin Ambrose.   Born in Choconut, Susquehanna County, Pa., November 11, 1844; son of James, a farmer and cooper, and Catherine (O'Donnell) Foran; married Kate Kavanaugh on December 29, 1868, and, after her death in 1893, Emma Kenny on December 20, 1893; two children; while in public school, learned the cooper's trade from his father; attended St. Joseph's College (Meadville, Pa.) for one year and then taught school for two years; served during the Civil War as a private in the Fourth Regiment, Pennsylvania Volunteer Cavalry, 1864-1865; resumed his apprenticeship as a cooper in Meadville after the war; moved to Cleveland, Ohio, in 1868 and quickly became leader of the local coopers' union; was one of the founders of the Coopers' International Union and served as its president for three years; edited the *Cooper's Journal* between 1870-1874; was a delegate to the Ohio Constitutional Convention of 1873; attended law school and admitted to the bar in 1874; served as prosecuting attorney for the city of Cleveland, 1875-1877; elected as a Democrat to the U.S.

Congress in 1882 and served until 1889; as a Congressman, authored legislation preventing the importation of contract labor; became a judge in the Cleveland Court of Common Pleas in 1911 and served in that capacity until his death; was a Democrat; authored *The Other Side* (1886); died in Cleveland, Ohio, June 28, 1921; David Montgomery, *Beyond Equality: Labor and the Radical Republicans, 1862-1872* (1967); *National Cyclopaedia of American Biography* (Vol. XIC); *Biographical Directory of the American Congress, 1774-1971* (1971).

FOSTER, William Zebulon.   Born in Taunton, Mass., February 25, 1881; son of James, an Irish railroad car washer, and Elizabeth (McLaughlin) Foster; married Esther Abramovitch on March 23, 1918; apprenticed to an artist in 1891 and learned the art crafts of modeling and stonecutting; quit art work in 1894 and for the next several years was employed as an industrial worker in a variety of occupations, including sailor, railroader, and homesteader; joined the Socialist party in 1900 but expelled nine years later for ideological reasons and joined the Industrial Workers of the World (IWW); traveled to Europe in 1910 as an IWW delegate to the Budapest meeting of the Trades Union Secretariat, but not seated and instead spent his time studying the labor movements of France and Germany; wrote the pamphlet *Syndicalism* in 1912, outlining the principles and programs of the Syndicalist League of North America; served as the league's national secretary; served as the business agent of a Chicago railway union in 1915; was a founder of the International Trade Union Educational League in 1917; served as secretary of the organizing committees that unionized packinghouse workers and steelworkers in the period 1917-1919; led the historic steel strike of 1919; founded the Trade Union Educational League in 1920 and served as its national secretary; along with Earl Browder, attended the congresses of the Communist International and Red International of Labor Unions in Moscow in 1921 and joined the Communist party of America (CPA)* shortly thereafter; was indicted but not convicted of criminal syndicalism in 1922; ran as the CPA candidate for president of the United States in 1924, 1928, and 1932; became national secretary of the CPA in 1930, and two years later was named national chairman, a position he held until 1957; ran for governor of New York as a CPA candidate in 1930; as a result of changes in ideological principles, replaced Earl Browder

---

*Over the years the name of the party was continually changing, and for short periods of time it simply ceased to exist. For the sake of conserving space and preserving clarity, this title is used throughout the sketch.

as the head of the CPA after a three-day policy conference in New York in 1945; retired as CPA national chairman emeritus in 1957; authored *The Great Steel Strike and Its Lessons* (1920); *The Russian Revolution* (1921); *Misleaders of Labor* (1927); *Towards Soviet America* (1932); *From Bryan to Stalin* (1937); and *Pages From a Worker's Life* (1939); died in Moscow, USSR, September 1, 1961; Theodore Draper, *American Communism and Soviet Russia* (1960), and *The Roots of American Communism* (1957); Joseph R. Starobin, *American Communism in Crisis, 1943-1957* (1972); David A. Shannon, *The Decline of American Communism* (1957); David Brody, *Labor in Crisis: The Steel Strike of 1919* (1965); *Current Biography* (1945).

FOX, Martin.   Born in Cincinnati, Ohio, August 22, 1848; attended the Cincinnati public schools for several years, then became an apprentice molder at age fourteen; in 1864 as a journeyman, joined Local 3 of the International Molders Union of North America (IMUNA); elected a national trustee by the IMUNA convention of 1878 and became increasingly influential in trade union circles; appointed assistant to the president of the IMUNA in 1880 and elected secretary by the 1886 convention; upon reaching IMUNA headquarters, found a union beset by antagonistic employers and weakened by strike-prone locals; after his election as union president in 1890, began to impose a centralized authority on locals, enforcing it by executive board threats to withdraw the charters of recalcitrant locals; having created a disciplined union, with a strike fund, proceeded to negotiate an agreement with the Stove Founders' National Defense Association to provide for "arbitration" of unresolved disputes by conferences composed of union and employer representatives; saw this first pact between a national union and a national trade association work surprisingly well for many years although it was not really a mechanism for arbitration; encouraged the machine founders to form a trade association, and in 1899 led the IMUNA to negotiate an agreement with the National Founders' Association, although a less satisfactory accord than the Stove Founders' agreement; refused, despite pressure from many members, to oppose the introduction of labor-saving technology; led the IMUNA executive board to condemn the exclusion of black molders from Southern locals, and in 1900 created a separate Chattanooga local in order to organize blacks; was an American Federation of Labor (AFL) fraternal delegate to the British Trades Union Congress in 1897; was a member of the Division of Conciliation and Mediation of the National Civic Federation, and had a hand in the organization of the AFL metal trades department; forced by ill health to resign as president in 1903; died in Cincinnati, Ohio, September 28, 1907; commemorated a few years later by a massive granite monument erected by the IMUNA; *Iron Molders' Journal* (October, 1907; August, 1912) Frank T. Stockton, *The International Molders Union of North America* (1921); Philip Taft, *Organized Labor in American History* (1964).

(D.G.S.)

FRANKENSTEEN, Richard Truman.   Born in Detroit, Mich., March 6, 1907; son of Harold L., a singer and composer, and Grace (Smith) Frankensteen; Episcopalian; married Grace Thelma Callahan on April 30, 1932; three children; graduated from the University of Dayton, Ohio, in 1932; after failing to secure employment as a high school teacher and coach, took a job on a Dodge assembly line in Detroit while attending law school at the University of Detroit; elected employee representative and then president of a company union that was reorganized in 1935 into the independent Automotive Industrial Workers Association and eventually amalgamated with the United Automobile, Aircraft, Agricultural Implement Workers of America (UAW); was elected a UAW vice-president in 1937; negotiated the first national contract with the Chrysler Corporation; gained national publicity after being severely beaten, along with Walter Reuther (q.v.), by Ford servicemen in the "Battle of the Overpass" at Ford's River Rouge plant; ran unsuccessfully for the Detroit Common Council in 1937; served on the Michigan Emergency Relief Committee, 1937-1938; became the national director of aircraft organization for the Congress of Industrial Organizations in 1941; appointed director of the UAW's political action and legislative activities; during World War II, served on the War Production Board and National War Labor Board; acted as chairman of the Michigan delegation to the 1944 Democratic National Convention; ran unsuccessfully for mayor of Detroit in 1945; aligned himself with the George Addes (q.v.)-Richard Leonard (q.v.)-Rolland J. Thomas (q.v.) faction in the internal politics of the UAW; retired from union affairs after the Reuther faction consolidated its control of the UAW; became the assistant general manager and labor relations consultant for Allen Industries, Inc., Detroit, in 1950; was a Democrat; authored several pamphlets on labor in the aircraft industry and co-authored the operetta, *Gypsy Moon:* Jack Stieber, *Governing the UAW* (1962); Sidney Fine, *Sit-Down: The General Motors Strike of 1936-1937* (1969), and *The Automobile Under the Blue Eagle: Labor, Management, and the Automobile Manufacturing Code* (1963); Frank Cormier and William J. Eaton, *Reuther* (1970).

FRASER, Harry Wilson.　　Born in Topeka, Kan., June 7, 1884; son of Lewis Peter, a salesman, and Lavara Virginia (Weltner) Fraser; Baptist; married Lillian Elizabeth Spane on September 8, 1905; after attending the public schools of Topeka, served as a clerk in the general offices of several different railroads headquartered either in Topeka or in Pueblo, Colo., 1900-1907; promoted to conductor in 1909; joined Local 300 of the Order of Railway Conductors of America (ORC) and served as the local's chairman of adjustment and as secretary of the general committee on adjustment for the Atchison, Topeka, and Santa Fe Railway; appointed secretary to the ORC president in 1929; became chief clerk in 1932, deputy president in 1934, vice-president in 1938, and president of the ORC in 1941; named a railroad labor member of the War Manpower Commission in 1943; became a trustee and secretary of the National Planning Association in 1945; elected chairman of the Railway Labor Executives' Association in 1947; served as a delegate-adviser to the 1944 International Labor Organization conference in Philadelphia and was a delegate to the 1947 and 1948 meetings of the Inland Transport Committee held in Geneva, Switzerland, and San Francisco, Calif., respectively; died in Chicago, Ill., May 13, 1950; *National Cyclopaedia of American Biography* (Vol. XXXIX); *Railway Age* (Vol. 128); *Who's Who in Labor* (1946); *Labor*, May 20, 1950.

FRAYNE, Hugh.　　Born in Scranton, Pa., November 8, 1869; son of Michael, an Irish immigrant, and Grace (Decon) Frayne; married Mary E. Cawley on November 8, 1888; three children; became a breaker boy in the anthracite mine fields of Pennsylvania at age eight and continued in that employment for four years; apprenticed to a sheet-metal worker in 1882 and became a journeyman working at the trade until 1900; joined the Knights of Labor during the 1880s; became a charter member of the Amalgamated Sheet Metal Workers International Alliance in 1892 and served as a general vice-president from 1900 to 1904; appointed a general organizer of the American Federation of Labor (AFL) in 1901; placed in charge of the AFL's Philadelphia, Pa., office from 1907 to 1910, and of the New York office from 1910 until his death; served as the AFL fraternal delegate to the Canadian Trades and Labor Congress in 1908; became a vice-president and director of the National Committee on Prisons and Prison Labor and was an officer in various other public boards and agencies; was a close associate of AFL president Samuel Gompers (q.v.), and identified with the more conservative wing of the American labor movement; appointed chairman of the labor division of the War Industries Board during World War I and, as a result of his service, awarded the Distinguished Service Medal by Congress in 1923; was a nonpartisan in politics; authored several pamphlets on trade union subjects; died in New York City, July 13, 1934; Philip Taft, *The A. F. of L. in the Time of Gompers* (1957), and *The A. F. of L. From the Death of Gompers to the Merger* (1959); *Dictionary of American Biography* (Supplement I); *Who's Who in America, 1934-1935.*

FREY, John Philip.   Born in Mankato, Minn., February 24, 1871; son of Leopold, a manufacturer, and Julia Philomen (Beaudry) Frey; married Nellie Josephine Higgins on June 10, 1891; three children; received his education in the public schools of Mankato, Minn.; secured employment as an iron molder in Worcester, Mass., in 1887; elected president of the Worcester local of the International Molders and Foundry Workers Union of North America (IMFWU) in 1893 and served until 1898; elected treasurer of the New England conference board of the IMFWU in 1898; elected a vice-president of the Massachusetts State Federation of Labor in 1899; became a vice-president of the IMFWU in 1900; served as an American Federation of Labor (AFL) fraternal delegate to the British Trades Union Congress in 1909, the Inter-Allied Labor and Socialist Conference in London in 1918, and the Pan-American Federation of Labor in 1921; served as president of the Norwood, Ohio, Board of Education, 1918-1922; elected president of the Ohio State Federation of Labor in 1924 and secretary-treasurer in 1927; served as chairman of the board of the National Bureau of Economic Research, 1918-1927, and as an executive board member of the Workers Education Bureau, 1923-1928; appointed to several government boards and agencies, including the Federal Commission to Investigate Scientific Management in 1927, the labor advisory board of the National Recovery Administration in 1933, and the Federal Commission on Apprentice Training and the shipbuilding stabilization committee of the War Production Board during World War II; served as a labor expert on the U.S. delegation to the 1927 International Economic Conference in Geneva; elected president of the metal trades department of the AFL in 1934, serving in that capacity until his retirement in 1950; served as a lieutenant colonel in the U.S. Army Specialist Reserve during World War II; was a conservative trade unionist, strongly supporting the apolitical, craft-conscious policies of the AFL; edited the *Iron Molders' Journal*, 1903-1927; was a Republican; authored several books, including *An American Molder in Europe* (1911), *The Labor Injunction* (1922), *Calamity of Prosperity* (1930), *Bakers Domination* (1933), *Calamity of Recovery* (1934), and *Craft Unions of Ancient and Modern Times* (1944); retired from union affairs in 1950; died in Washington, D.C., November 29, 1957; Philip Taft, *The A. F. of L. From the Death of Gompers to the Merger* (1959); Frank T. Stockton, *The International Molders Union of North America* (1921); Walter Galenson, *The CIO Challenge to the AFL: A History of the American Labor Movement, 1935-1941* (1960); *The National Cyclopaedia of American Biography* (Vol. XLVII).

FURUSETH, Andrew (Anders Andreassen Nilsen). Born in Romedal, Hedmarken, Norway, March 12, 1854; son of Andreas, a farmer, and Marthe (Jensdatter) Nilsen; Protestant; never married; forced by the impoverished condition of his family to leave home at age eight; supported himself by working as a farm laborer while continuing his education; began working full-time in 1870 and, three years later, became a merchant seaman; after 1880, shipped out primarily from ports along the West Coast of the United States; joined and in 1887 became secretary of the Sailors' Union of the Pacific; became the legislative representative of seamen's unions in Washington, D.C., in 1894 and also served as a legislative representative of the American Federation of Labor (AFL); was an AFL fraternal delegate to the British Trades Union Congress in 1908; conducted a 21-year struggle to change the legal status of sailors, and saw enactment of the LaFollette Seamen's Act of 1915 as the product of this struggle; became president of the International Seamen's Union in 1908 and served until his death in 1938; helped negotiate an end to the San Francisco, Calif., General Strike of 1934; refused to support a wildcat strike of West Coast seamen led by Joseph Curran (q.v.), thus leading to the organization of the secessionist National Maritime Union of America in 1937; died in Washington, D.C., January 22, 1938; Silas B. Axtell, ed., *A Symposium on Andrew Furuseth* (1945); Paul S. Taylor, *The Sailors' Union of the Pacific* (1923); *Dictionary of American Biography* (Supplement II); Hyman G. Weintraub, *Andrew Furuseth: Emancipator of the Seamen* (1959); Library of Congress, *Andrew Furuseth, A Bibliographical List* (1942).

GAINOR, Edward Joseph. Born in Greencastle, Ind., August 1, 1870; son of a railroad roadmaster; Roman Catholic; married; one child; after graduating from high school, secured work as a puddler and heater in an iron rolling mill in 1889; joined Muncie, Ind., Lodge 4 of the Amalgamated Association of Iron, Steel, and Tin Workers and served as secretary of the Lodge during 1890-1892; became a U.S. Postal Service letter carrier in 1897 and joined Muncie Branch 98 of the National Association of Letter

Carriers (NALC); served on the national executive board of the NALC, 1901-1902; elected a vice-president of the NALC in 1905 and served until his election as president in 1914; acted as an American Federation of Labor (AFL) fraternal delegate to the British Trades Union Congress in 1924; elected an AFL vice-president and member of the executive council in 1935; served as NALC delegate to the annual conventions of the AFL, 1917-1943; retired NALC presidency in 1941; regarded legislation providing for reduced working hours, improved retirement benefits, and large increases in the NALC's membership as his major contributions; was a Democrat; served as a delegate to the National Democratic Convention of 1920; edited *The Postal Record* for several years; retired all union positions in 1943; died in Washington, D.C., November 10, 1947; William C. Doherty, *Mailman U.S.A.* (1960); *The American Federationist* (June, 1941; December, 1947); Solon DeLeon, ed., *The American Labor Who's Who* (1925); *The American Federation of Labor Weekly News-Service*, August 26, 1941.

GALARZA, Ernesto.   Born in Jalcocotan, Nayarit, Mexico, August 15, 1905; son of migrant-worker parents; emigrated with his family to the United States at age six; married Mae Taylor, a teacher, in December, 1929; two children; after completing his primary and secondary school education in Sacramento, Calif., received the A.B. degree from Occidental College in 1927, the M.A. from Stanford University in 1929, and the Ph.D. from Columbia University in 1944; served as coprincipal of Gardner School, Jamaica, Long Island, N.Y., 1932-1936; as a result of employment during his youth as a farm worker, cannery worker, and packingshed laborer, evidenced an early interest in the organization of agricultural laborers; served as specialist in education for the Pan-American Union, 1936-1946, and as chief of its division of Labor and Social Information, 1940-1946; was director of research and education and a field organizer for the National Farm Labor Union in Florida, Louisiana, Texas, Arizona, and California, 1947-1955; served in a similar capacity for the National Agricultural Workers Union (NAWU), 1955-1960; led the strikes of San Joaquin tomato pickers in 1950 and Imperial Valley canteloupe pickers in 1951, exposing the evils of the wetback system; helped organize Louisiana sugar-cane workers and strawberry pickers, 1953-1954; waged a vigorous but fruitless campaign against the government functionaries, agricultural employers, and labor unions that supported or acquiesced in the passage of right-to-work laws restricting agricultural workers and that tolerated abuses of the *bracero* system; used a research grant from the Fund for the

Republic to investigate the *bracero* program in 1955, and wrote *Strangers in our Fields*, described as "one of the outstanding successes of Galarza's career"; after serving, in 1960, as an organizer for the Amalgamated Meat-cutters and Butcher Workmen of North America, which had absorbed the NAWU into its newly created agricultural department, withdrew from the labor movement; led the San Jose Mexican-American community in demanding a Congressional investigation of the Chualar disaster (an accident in which 32 *braceros* were killed in a truck-train collision) in 1963; was a counsel to the House of Representatives' Committee on Education and Labor and in that capacity wrote a report on the *bracero* program that was later published as *Merchants of Labor*; served as program analyst of the Economic and Youth Opportunity Agency, Office of Economic Opportunity, in Los Angeles, Calif.; acted as a consultant to the government of Bolivia, the Ford Foundation, the Whitney Foundation, the U.S. Civil Rights Commission, and other bodies; chaired the National Committee of "La Raza Unida"; held research and visiting professorships at Notre Dame University and San Jose State College; was appointed Regents Professor at the University of California, San Diego; authored *Spiders in the House and Workers in the Field* (1970), *Barrio Boy* (1971), and other works; Joan London and Henry Anderson, *So Shall Ye Reap: The Story of Cesar Chavez and the Farm Workers' Movement* (1970); *Who's Who in America, 1950-1951*.

(M.E.R.)

GARRETSON, Austin Bruce.   Born in Winterset, Iowa, September 14, 1856; son of Nathan, a lawyer, and Hannah (Garretson) Garretson; Society of Friends; married Marie Ream on September 2, 1878; three children; graduated from high school in Osceloa, Iowa, then apprenticed to a wheelwright; obtained employment as a brakeman on a spur line of the Chicago, Burlington, and Quincy Railroad; promoted to conductor somewhat later and moved to Denison, Tex.; employed there by several railroads as a conductor; joined Division 53 of the Order of Railway Conductors (ORC) in 1884; elected grand senior conductor in 1887; elected grand chief conductor and president in 1906, serving until 1919; helped convert the ORC from a benevolent and fraternal organization into an economic-oriented trade union; chaired the committee of four operating railroad brotherhoods whose negotiations with management representatives eventually led to the enactment of the Adamson Act in 1917, establishing the eight-hour day for railroad workers; served on the Federal Commission on Industrial Relations, 1912-1915; after World War I, strongly advocated the

Plumb Plan of government ownership of railroads; retired in 1919, but continued serving as an adviser to the organization until his death; edited the *Railway Conductor* for several years before his 1919 retirement; died in Cedar Rapids, Iowa, February 27, 1931; Edwin C. Robbins, *Railway Conductors: A Study in Organized Labor* (1914); *Dictionary of American Biography* (Supplement 1); *Encyclopedia of Social Sciences* (Vol. VI).

GEORGE, Leo E.   Born in Medford, Wis., January 3, 1888; son of James, a farmer, and Mary H. (Atkins) George; Christian Church; married Edith Simmons; three children; completed high school in Westfield, Pa., and later took courses at a teachers college; after entering the U.S. Postal Service in 1906, joined Local 1 of the National Federation of Post Office Clerks (NFPOC), formerly the Chicago Post Office Clerks' Union, a division of the United National Association of Post Office Clerks; elected financial secretary and a member of the executive board of Local 1 in 1918, serving until 1921; discharged from the postal service in 1920 for union activities and for publishing critical accounts of the postal service; later reinstated, but retired to work full time at union activities; served as a delegate to the Chicago Federation of Labor and the Illinois State Federation of Labor; elected vice-president of the NFPOC in 1921 and acting international president in 1923; elected general NFPOC president in 1923 and served in that capacity until 1956; served as president of the American Federation of Labor Government Employees Council; retired from union activities in 1956; died in Mount Rainier, Md., in November, 1967; Karl Baarslag, *History of the National Federation of Post Office Clerks* (1945); *Who's Who in Labor* (1946); *AFL-CIO News*, November 18, 1967.

GERMANO, Joseph Samuel.   Born in Chicago, Ill., February 12, 1904; son of Samuel Joseph, a railroad maintenance worker, and Maria (Albano) Germano; Roman Catholic; married Mary E. Alesia on April 15, 1923; two children; graduated from high school; employed as a steelworker for the Youngstown Sheet and Tube Company in South Chicago during the 1930s; helped organize and became president of Lodge 56, Amalgamated Association of Iron, Steel, and Tin Workers (AA); was a member of the AA rank-and-file faction preparing the way at the union's 1936 convention for cooperation with the Steel Workers Organizing Committee (SWOC) to unionize the industry; served as an organizer, 1936-1938, and as subdistrict director, 1938-1940, for the SWOC in the Chicago area; appointed director of United Steelworkers of America (USWA) District 31 in 1940; elected to that office in 1942 and reelected from 1945 through 1969; as director of the largest USWA district, became a powerful member of the international executive board; through his support, was instrumental in I.W. Abel's (q.v.) decision to run against President David J. McDonald (q.v.) in 1965; managed the Abel campaign that unseated McDonald; has been one of the most influential labor leaders in Illinois and has been a member of the Cook County Industrial Union Council and a vice-president of the state's American Federation of Labor-Congress of Industrial Organizations' Council; has actively involved himself in political affairs, promoting USWA subdistricts as organizational bases for committees on political education activity in Chicago; has worked closely with Democratic party organizations in Cook County and Springfield, Ill., and has frequently supported liberal candidates, such as Paul Douglas, and liberal causes, such as preservation of the Indiana Dunes lakeshore; was a founding member of the USWA national civil rights committee, and has worked for the implementation of civil rights programs in Chicago; retired as director of District 31 in 1973; J. David Greenstone, *Labor in American Politics* (1969); John Herling, *Right to Challenge: People and Power in the Steelworkers Union* (1972); *Who's Who in Labor* (1946); *Who's Who in the Midwest, 1972-1973.*

(D.G.S.)

GERMER, Adolph F.   Born in Welan, Germany, January 15, 1881; son of a coal miner; Lutheran; married Vivian Marks; no children; attended public and Lutheran parochial schools in Braceville, Ill., and studied with the International Correspondence School and LaSalle Extension University; emigrated to the United States in 1888, settling in Illinois; began working at age eleven as a coal miner at Staunton, Ill.; joined the United Mine Workers of America (UMWA) in 1894; elected secretary-treasurer of UMWA Local 728 in 1906 and state legislative committeeman and vice-president, Belleville Subdistrict of District 12, UMWA, Illinois, in 1907; served as secretary-treasurer of Belleville Subdistrict, 1908-1912; was a UMWA international representative in the Colorado coal strike of 1913-1914; elected vice-president of District 12 in 1915, but expelled from the union a year later; joined the Socialist party in 1900, and served as national secretary of the party, 1916-1919; was the only prominent Socialist among the Illinois miners to sign the party's antiwar declaration; convicted along with four party colleagues under the Espionage Act for obstructing the draft and sentenced to 20 years imprisonment in 1919; but saw the U.S. Supreme Court reverse the decision two years later on a technicality; served as a national organizer for the Socialist party, 1919-1920, and as secretary of the Massachusetts Socialist party in 1922; while working in the

California oilfields, joined and served as international organizer for the Oil Field, Gas Well, and Refinery Workers Union, 1923-1925; was a Socialist party organizer in 1925; signed the February 15, 1930, call for the Springfield convention of the Reorganized United Mine Workers of America and elected vice-president of the organization; did most of the work for the new union, speaking in Indiana, Ohio, West Virginia, and Illinois because of President Alexander Howat's (q.v.) alcoholism; was physically attacked by John L. Lewis's (q.v.) supporters at Royalton, Ill., on April 18, 1930; edited the *Rockford* (Ill.) *Labor News*, 1931-1935; through the intervention of John L. Lewis, was appointed labor representative on the National Recovery Administration's Regional Compliance Board in Chicago, Ill., in 1934; named by Lewis as the Congress of Industrial Organizations' (CIO) first field representative in November, 1935; between then and March, 1937, helped organize auto workers, rubber workers, and oil workers; helped establish the United Rubber Workers' journal, *The Rubber Worker*; served as regional director of the Michigan CIO, 1937-1939; founded Michigan labor's Non-Partisan League, the CIO's political arm; founded the Michigan Industrial Union Council, the CIO's state labor federation, in 1938 and twice elected its president; established the *Michigan CIO News*; appointed regional director of the New York CIO in 1939 and later served as regional director for the CIO in the Rocky Mountain and Pacific states; died in Rockford, Ill., May 26, 1966; Lorin Lee Cary, "Institutionalized Conservatism in the Early C.I.O.; Adolph Germer, A Case Study," *Labor History* (Fall, 1972); John H.M. Laslett, *Labor and the Left: A Study of Socialism and Radical Influences in the American Labor Movement, 1881-1924* (1970); Irving Bernstein, *The Lean Years: A History of the American Worker, 1920-1933* (1960); *United Mine Workers Journal*, June 15, 1966; Solon DeLeon, ed., *The American Labor Who's Who* (1925); *The New York Times*, May 28, 1966.

(J.H.)

GIBBONS, Harold J. Born in Taylor, Pa., April 10, 1910; son of an Irish immigrant, Patrick Thomas, a coal miner, and Bridget Gibbons; married Ann Cutler on September 8, 1938; two children; quit school before finishing high school but later took correspondence courses; after the death of his father in 1926, moved with his family (he was the youngest of 23 children) to Chicago, Ill.; worked there during the next five years as a cook, a warehouseman, and a construction laborer; won a summer scholarship to the University of Wisconsin's School for Workers in 1933; returned to Chicago later that year as a teacher in one of the workers' education projects sponsored by the Works Progress Administration (WPA); after joining the American Federation of Teachers (AFT), organized WPA teachers in Chicago into an AFT local; was elected an AFT vice-president in 1934; became a Congress of Industrial Organizations' (CIO) organizer in 1936 and was instrumental in efforts to organize Chicago taxicab drivers; joined the CIO Textile Workers Organizing Committee in 1938 and became a Midwest organizer; joined St. Louis Local 543 of the United Retail, Wholesale and Department Store Employees of America (URWDSE) in 1940 and a year later became its secretary-treasurer; served the URWDSE as an international representative, as a director of the St. Louis Joint Council, and as a member of the international executive board; was a member of the Region 7 panel of the War Labor Board during World War II; was discontented with the national administration of the URWDSE; thus, having built Local 543 into a large and influential St. Louis union, merged it with Local 688 of the International Brotherhood of Teamsters, Chauffeurs, Warehousemen, and Helpers of America (IBT) in 1949; was elected secretary-treasurer of Local 688 and president of Teamsters' Joint Council 13; became secretary-treasurer of the newly organized Central Conference of Teamsters in 1954; elected an IBT vice-president and became an executive assistant to IBT president James R. Hoffa (q.v.) in 1957; became director of the Central Conference of Teamsters in 1971; as a liberal, reform-minded union leader, has often antagonized the more conservative members of the IBT executive board, especially through his endorsement of the candidacy of George McGovern on the Democratic party ticket in 1972; was relieved of his directorship of the Central Conference of Teamsters in 1972 as a consequence of this antagonism; was a Socialist early in his career, but later described himself as an independent, although usually supporting liberal Democratic candidates; Arnold Rose, *Union Solidarity: The Internal Cohesion of a Labor Union* (1952); Walter Sheridan, *The Fall and Rise of Jimmy Hoffa* (1972); Ralph and Estelle James, *Hoffa and the Teamsters* (1965); *The Nation*, March 23, 1957.

GIBSON, Everett G.   Born in Wallingford, Conn., December 28, 1903; son of George Gluster, a laundryman, and Clara (Stearns) Gibson; Reformed Episcopalian; married Katherine Lewis on June 10, 1928; one child; completed public grammar school in Huntington, N.Y.; secured employment with the U.S. Postal Service, then joined Local 2 of the National Federation of Post Office Motor Vehicle Employees (NFPOMVE) in 1925; served as Local 2's president for eight years and as president of the Greater New York Joint Conference of Affiliated Postal

Employees for three years; served as national NFPOMVE vice-president and secretary prior to his election as national president in 1945; became the NFPOMVE legislative representative in Washington, D.C., in 1945; a Republican; Karl Baarslag, *History of the National Federation of Post Office Clerks* (1945); William C. Doherty, *Mailman U.S.A.* (1960); *Who's Who in Labor* (1946).

GIBSON, John Willard. Born in Harrisburg., Ill., August 23, 1910; son of John Joseph, an English immigrant coal miner, and Nellie (Guard) Gibson; Methodist; married Jennie Pacotti on May 12, 1934; two children; after attending public schools in several cities, entered the coal mines of Taylorville, Ill., at age sixteen; worked alternately during the next several years in the Detroit, Mich., automobile shops and the Taylorville mines; joined the United Mine Workers of America in 1926; became a salesman for a Detroit dairy company in 1934 and soon began organizing Local 83 of the United Dairy Workers; joined the United Retail, Wholesale and Department Store Employees of America in 1937; attended Wayne State University during 1936-1937; served as vice-president of the Michigan State Industrial Union Council (IUC), Congress of Industrial Organizations (CIO), and assistant CIO director for the state of Michigan, 1937-1938; elected secretary-treasurer of the Michigan IUC in 1939, serving until 1941; appointed chairman of the Michigan Department of Labor and Industry in 1941, serving until his election as president of the Michigan IUC in 1943; served during World War II on the Michigan division of the War Production Board, the Office of Price Administration, and the War Manpower Commission; was a member of the Michigan Committee for Fair Employment Practices; appointed a special assistant to U.S. Secretary of Labor Louis B. Schwellenbach in 1945, thus beginning a career in government service; became one of three assistant secretaries of labor in the reorganized Department of Labor in 1946; appointed chairman of the Displaced Persons Commission in 1950; authored two handbooks, *Workmen's Compensation* and *Industrial Safety*, besides a number of pamphlets; politically a Democrat; *Current Biography* (1947); *Who's Who in Labor* (1946); *Who's Who in America, 1950-1951*.

GILBERT, Henry E. Born in Ethel, Mo., October 5, 1906; son of Henry H., a farmer and delivery wagon operator, and Irene R. (Windle) Gilbert; Presbyterian; married Alice Marie Iman on December 26, 1925; one child; graduated from high school in 1925 and attended Cleveland College in 1943; secured employment in the signal department of the

Atchison, Topeka, and Santa Fe Railroad in 1925; became a locomotive fireman in 1926 and served in that capacity on the Alton Railroad during 1926-1935; joined Chicago, Ill., Lodge 707 of the Brotherhood of Locomotive Firemen and Enginemen (BLFE) in 1927 and served successively as secretary-treasurer, as a member of the grievance committee, as a general organizer, and, in 1931, as president of Lodge 707; became a locomotive engineman in 1935; was a member of the executive board of the BLFE legislative board for the state of Illinois; served as an assistant in the office of the BLFE president, 1942-1946; became a member of the BLFE executive board in 1944 and three years later elected vice-president; elected BLFE president in 1953; during his incumbency, led a long struggle to prevent the elimination of firemen in diesel locomotives; became assistant president of the newly organized United Transportation Union in 1969; retired union positions in 1972; Brotherhood of Locomotive Firemen and Enginemen, "Historical Sketch, 1873-1947," *Brotherhood of Locomotive Firemen and Enginemen's Magazine* (1947); *Time*, July 26, 1963; *Who's Who in Railroading* (1959).

GILLMORE, Frank.   Born in New York City, May 14, 1867; son of Parker, an author and naturalist, and Emily (Thorne) Gillmore; Episcopalian; married Laura MacGillivray on July 30, 1896; two children; educated in England at the Chiswick Collegiate School; launched an acting career in 1879 and played for three years in the provinces of England; performed on the London stage for five years; returned to the United States in 1892 after having acquired a reputation as an excellent leading man; participated in the 1912 organizational meetings resulting in the creation of Actors' Equity Association (AEA); became a member of the board of governors and chairman of the contract committee of AEA in 1913; elected to the newly created office of AEA executive secretary in 1918; as a proponent of affiliation with the American Federation of Labor, actively involved in chartering the Associated Actors and Artists of America (AAAA) in 1919; led a successful 30-day strike of actors in 1919; elected president of AAAA, AEA, and Chorus Equity in 1928; retired as president of AEA and Chorus Equity in 1937 to devote full time to the affairs of AAAA; was one of the principal architects of unionization among actors and artists in the United States and is credited with having achieved significant improvements in the wage scales and working conditions of performers; was a Democrat; died in New York City, March 29, 1943; Murray Ross, *Stars and Strikes: Unionization of Hollywood* (1941); Alfred Harding, *The Revolt of the Actors* (1929); *The American Federationist* (April, 1943).

GIOVANNITTI, Arturo.   Born in Campobasso, Italy, January 7, 1884; son of a physician; married; three children; after attending college, emigrated to the United States at age sixteen; worked at various manual and clerical jobs until 1905; rejected his Roman Catholic heritage and attended a Protestant seminary; went to New York City ca. 1908 and became secretary of the Italian Socialist Federation and editor of its newspaper, *Il Proletario*; began to write poetry during this period; concerned about the fate of Italian workers; became an advocate of revolutionary syndicalism and joined the Industrial Workers of the World (IWW) in 1912 to help in the great Lawrence, Mass., textile strike; was a brilliant orator with a romantic air, and proved very effective as a leader of the immigrant strikers; jailed on charges of plotting the murder of a striker; while in jail, penned "The Walker", a brilliant piece of verse that made him famous as the workers' poet; eventually acquitted of the murder charge along with his colleague, Joseph Ettor (q.v.), after an international defense campaign elicited the support of even American Federation of Labor unionists; helped lead the ill-fated Akron tire strike of 1913; involved with several top Wobbly organizers in protest against William Haywood's (q.v.) centralizing policy, and thus resigned from the IWW in 1916; indicted the next year as part of a U.S. Government crackdown on the IWW, but saw his case dropped in 1919; continued to work for the welfare of immigrant workers during the 1920s as an organizer for the International Ladies' Garment Workers' Union and as foreign language editor of *Advance*, the Amalgamated Clothing Workers' journal; was a founder, in 1923, of the Anti-Fascist Alliance of America that exposed and denounced Mussolini's regime; continued as an active Socialist party leader and unionist, often speaking at labor rallies, until his health failed in the 1940s; died in New York City, December 31, 1959; see *The Collected Poems of Arturo Giovannitti* (1962); Solon DeLeon, ed., *The American Labor Who's Who* (1925); Joyce L. Kornbluh, *Rebel Voices: An I.W.W. Anthology* (1964); Luciana J. Iorizzo and Salvatore Mondello, *The Italian-Americans* (1971).

(D.G.S.)

GIVENS, Paul A.   Born in Indianapolis, Ind., October 11, 1891; son of Albert S. and Anna E. Givens; married Martha C. Prather on September 11, 1911; one child; after completing a high school education, became an apprentice stone cutter and in 1909 joined the Indianapolis local of the Journeymen Stone Cutters Association of North America (JSCA); served his local union in several capacities and also actively involved in the Indianapolis Central Labor Union and Building Trades Council; elected

JSCA secretary and general president in 1937, serving in that capacity until 1957; was a JSCA delegate to the national conventions of the American Federation of Labor, 1937-1957, and served as a member of several AFL committees; served during World War II as a member of the Sixth Regional Panel of the War Labor Board; retired union positions in 1957; died in Indianapolis, Ind., in September, 1968; *Who's Who in Labor* (1946); *AFL-CIO News*, September 21, 1968.

GLEASON, Thomas William.   Born in New York City, November 8, 1900; son of Thomas W., a dockworker, and Mary Ann (Quinn) Gleason; Roman Catholic; married Emma Martin in 1923; three children; quit school in the seventh grade at age fifteen to begin work on the New York docks; joined the International Longshoremen's Association (ILA) in 1919; after having risen to the position of dock superintendent, discharged in 1932 for honoring a union picket line and returned to the waterfront as a longshoreman and checker; appointed business manager of ILA Checkers' Local 1 in 1934 and later elected president of the local; appointed a full-time ILA organizer in 1947; often found himself in opposition to the policies and decisions of ILA president Joseph P. Ryan (q.v.); was thus fired frequently from his union positions, only to be rehired because of rank-and-file pressures; participated in the 1951 strike that tied up the Port of New York and precipitated a governmental investigation of waterfront racketeering; as a result of the corruption revealed by these investigations the ILA was expelled from the American Federation of Labor (AFL) and ILA president Ryan resigned; after William V. Bradley, who he had supported, replaced Ryan, he was appointed to the newly created office of general organizer; became an ILA vice-president and elected president of the ILA's Atlantic Coast District in 1961; elected ILA president in 1963; appointed to the Maritime Advisory Committee in 1964; led a successful strike of longshoremen on the Atlantic and Gulf Port docks in 1965; served as a member of the Joint Maritime Committee and the New York City Council of Port Direction and Promotion; became an AFL-Congress of Industrial Organizations' vice-president and executive council member in 1969; a Democrat; Maud Russell, *Men Along the Shore* (1966); Charles P. Larrowe, *Harry Bridges: The Rise and Fall of Radical Labor in the U.S.* (1972); *Current Biography* (1966).

GOLD, Ben.   Born in Bessarabia, Russia, September 8, 1898; son of Israel, a watchmaker and jeweler, and Sarah (Droll) Gold; Jewish; married Sadie Algus in 1929; emigrated to the United States in 1910 and, after working for a short time at a variety of occupations, was employed as an operator in a fur shop; joined the International Fur Workers Union of the United States and Canada (IFWU) (Organized in New York City in 1913. Gold originally joined the Furriers Union of the United States and Canada) in 1912 and later the same year became an assistant shop chairman during a furrier's strike; while working as an operator, attended the Manhattan Preparatory School at night in order to pursue a frustrated ambition to enter law school; joined the Socialist party in 1916; elected to the New York Furriers' Joint Board in 1919; affiliated with the Communist faction after the 1919 split in the Socialist party; was a leader of IFWU's left-wing and was suspended from the union in 1924; reinstated later in the year in a unity effort; served as the manager of the New York Furriers' Joint Board, 1925-1929; was one of the leaders of a largely unsuccessful general strike of New York fur workers in 1926; along with other members of the New York Joint Board, was expelled from the IFWU as a Communist after the general strike; elected secretary of the Communist-organized Needle Trades Workers Industrial Union in 1928; in 1935 reinstated in IFWU after it and the Fur Workers Industrial Union division of the Needle Trades Workers Industrial Union merged; elected manager of the New York Fur Workers Joint Council in 1935 and served until 1937 when he was elected president of the IFWU; led IFWU into the CIO in 1937; in 1939 became the president of the International Fur and Leather Workers Union of the United States and Canada (IFLWU), created by the merger of the National Leather Workers Association and the IFWU; supported the candidacy of Henry A. Wallace for president of United States in 1948; after the IFLWU was expelled from the CIO as a Communist-dominated union, announced his resignation from the Communist party in 1950 in order to comply with the non-Communist provisions of the Taft-Hartley Act; indicted for perjury in 1954 in connection with his non-Communist affidavit; gave up his leadership position when the IFLWU merged with the Amalgamated Meat Cutters and Butcher Workmen of North America in 1955; ran for the New York State Assembly in 1931 and 1936 and for president of the New York Board of Aldermen in 1933 on the Communist party ticket; Philip S. Foner, *The Fur and Leather Workers Union* (1950); Max M. Kampelman, *The Communist Party vs. the C.I.O.: A Study in Power Politics* (1957); *Who's Who in Labor* (1946).

GOLDBERG, Arthur Joseph.   Born in Chicago, Ill., August 8, 1908; son of Joseph and Rebecca (Perlstein) Goldberg; Jewish; married Dorothy Kurgans on July 18, 1931; two children; attended the public schools of

Chicago and studied at Crane Junior College of City College of Chicago, 1924-1926; while attending school, worked as a delivery boy for a Chicago shoe factory and labored with construction gangs; received the B.S.L. degree from Northwestern University in 1929, and during the same year was admitted to the Illinois bar; served as editor-in-chief of the *Illinois Law Review*, 1929-1930; was associated with the firm of Kamfner, Horowitz, Halligan, and Daniels, 1929-1931; earned the J.D. degree from Northwestern University in 1930; was an associate lawyer with Pritzker and Pritzker of Chicago, 1931-1933; opened his own law office in 1933; was a professor of law at the John Marshall Law School, 1939-1948; served as a special assistant in the Office of Strategic Services in 1942, and the following year was commissioned a captain in the U.S. Army, serving until 1945, when discharged with the rank of major; was a partner in the law office of Goldberg and Devoe, 1945-1947, and in 1947, became a senior partner in the law firm of Goldberg, Devoe, Shadur, and Mikva; became general counsel for the Congress of Industrial Organizations (CIO) and the United Steelworkers of America (USWA) in 1948; devoted considerable time and energy to the legal ramifications growing out of the Taft-Hartley Act; was one of the principal figures involved in the unity negotiations leading to the American Federation of Labor (AFL)-CIO merger in 1955; after the merger, served as a special counsel for the AFL-CIO; during David McDonald's (q.v.) USWA presidency, Goldberg assumed more and more of the basic decision-making power within the international union; was appointed U.S. Secretary of Labor by President John F. Kennedy in 1961; most important contributions were the fight against unemployment, creation of the Area Redevelopment Act of 1961, increasing the minimum wage, reorganization of the Office of Manpower Administration, formation of the President's Advisory Committee on Labor Management Policies, and work to eliminate racial discrimination in employment; appointed to the U.S. Supreme Court in 1962, serving until 1965 when appointed U.S. Ambassador to the United Nations; returned to private law practice in 1968 and ran unsuccessfully for governor of New York in 1970; authored *AFL-CIO: Labor United* (1956); John Herling, *Right to Challenge: People and Power in the Steelworkers Union* (1972); Joseph C. Goulden, *Meany* (1972); *Current Biography* (1949).

GOLDEN, Clinton Strong.   Born in Pottsville, Pa., November 16, 1888; son of Lazarus, a Baptist minister, and Lucy (Strong) Golden; married Dorothy Cleve on April 23, 1923; one child; when his father died in 1900, went to work in an iron mine and thus his formal education was ended; apprenticed as a machinist, but later worked several years as a railroad fireman and became active in the Brotherhood of Locomotive Firemen and Engineers; was a full-time representative for the International Association of Machinists, 1919-1922; served on the board of directors of Brookwood Labor College, 1923-1930, and as its field representative and business manager; helped found the Conference for Progressive Labor Action to promote industrial unionization; was an Amalgamated Clothing Workers of America organizer during 1933; served as senior mediator with the Pennsylvania Department of Labor and Industry in 1934; was appointed as regional director for the National Labor Relations Board in 1935 and prepared the unfair labor charge that culminated in the U.S. Supreme Court's historic *Jones and Laughlin* decision; was appointed director of the important Northeastern region of the Steel Workers Organizing Committee (SWOC) in 1936; was the only major SWOC leader who had not been affiliated with the United Mine Workers of America, but was close to SWOC chairman Philip Murray (q.v.) and directed SWOC during Murray's illness in 1941; at the founding convention of the United Steelworkers of America (USWA) in 1942, was influential in the creation of an international executive board of regionally elected members; elected by the convention as an assistant to the international president (later vice-president); served as vice-chairman of both the War Production Board and the War Manpower Commission during World War II; was one of the few labor intellectuals with real influence in the trade union movement; believed that unions should play a greater role in socio-economic affairs and tried to persuade management and organized labor that unions should share responsibility for maximizing productivity and participate in the distribution of profits; resigned as USWA vice-president in 1946; named chief labor advisor to the U.S. Mission to Aid Greece in 1947; served as consultant on European labor to the Economic Cooperation Administration; appointed executive director of the Harvard University trade union program and continued to lecture at Harvard and at many labor education institutes until his retirement in 1959; avoided intraunion factionalism and was an independent in politics; coauthored *The Dynamics of Industrial Democracy* (1942), and numerous articles; died in Philadelphia, Pa., June 12, 1961; Robert R. R. Brooks, *As Steel Goes, . . . Unionism in a Basic Industry* (1940); *Current Biography* (1948); Lloyd Ulman, *The Government of the Steelworkers' Union* (1962).

(D.G.S.)

GOMPERS, Samuel.   Born in London, England, January 27, 1850;

son of Solomon, a cigarmaker, and Sara (Rood) Gompers; Jewish; married Sophia Julian on January 28, 1866, and after her death, Gertrude Gleaves Neuscheler in 1921; 12 or 14 children; attended a Jewish free school in London; emigrated with his family to the United States in 1863, settling in New York City; furthered a limited formal education by attending night classes; while working as a cigarmaker, joined Cigarmakers Local 15 in 1864 and in 1875 was elected president of Local 144 of the Cigarmakers' International Union (CMIU), serving until 1878; served as president of Local 144 again during the period 1880-1886; served as second vice-president of the CMIU, 1886-1896, and first vice-president, 1896-1924; helped organize the Federation of Organized Trades and Labor Unions and was its vice-presdient, 1881-1886; was one of the founders of the American Federation of Labor (AFL) and the seminal figure in its early years; served as president of the AFL during 1886-1895 and 1896-1924; was a man of great personal integrity and brilliance and for 37 years provided the AFL with strong and stable leadership, stressing business unionism, craft autonomy, and voluntarism; was hostile to Eugene V. Debs (q.v.) and the American Railway Union, which he believed to be a dual union; claimed he lacked authority to order supporting strikes during the Pullman strike which ended in the destruction of Debs' union; distrusting industrial unionism, joined with the AFL executive council in proposing a settlement between the United Brewery Workers and two AFL craft unions in a manner which would have virtually transformed the former into a craft union; however, in 1906, fought moves to expel the United Brewery Workers from the AFL; in the 1901 steel strike, was rightly suspicious of industrial union tendencies in the Amalgamated Association of Iron, Steel and Tin Workers, and although providing several AFL organizers, failed to negotiate with J.P. Morgan along the lines favored by the Amalgamated Association, refused to summon the executive council to aid the strike, and unsuccessfully urged steelworker president T.J. Shaffer to accept a company offer compromising the main strike issue, the union's demand for recognition; followed the philosophy of the AFL crafts and usually ignored unskilled workers to guarantee continued benefits for craft unionists; fearing failure, his support of the steel strike of 1919 was considered cautious by many strikers who had looked for greater encouragement; pursued a policy of voluntarism, opposing government-sponsored workmen's compensation and old-age pensions except for government employees, eight hour laws, unemployment compensation, comprehensive health insurance, independent political action, and compulsory arbitration; however, favored child labor laws, immigration restriction, and legislative lobbying, supported an 1897 AFL resolution against discrimination against blacks over Southern opposition and privately opposed discrimination, but by 1900 began countenancing Jim Crow unionism and refused blacks charters as federated locals when their affiliated unions would not grant jurisdiction; achieved significant political accomplishments by 1917 with Congressional passage of the final proposals embodied in labor's Bill of Grievances, originally proposed in 1906; protected labor's interests as a member of the Advisory Commission to the Council of National Defense during World War I and founded the American Alliance for Labor and Democracy to counter antiwar sentiments in the labor movement; appointed to the American delegation at the Paris Peace Conference in 1919; after the war, opposed sedition laws and pleaded for amnesty for political prisoners, also espoused a philosophy of business-labor cooperation for industrial self-government; authored *Seventy Years of Life and Labor*, 2 vols. (1925), *American Labor and the War* (1919), and numerous essays and pamphlets; died in San Antonio, Tex., December 3, 1924, while returning from the inauguration of Mexican president Plutarco Calles; Bernard Mandel, *Samuel Gompers: A Biography* (1963); Philip Taft, *The A. F. of L. in the Time of Gompers* (1957); Stuart B. Kaufman, *Samuel Gompers and the Origins of the American Federation of Labor, 1848-1896* (1973); Philip S. Foner, *History of the American Labor Movement in the United States*, Vol. III (1964); Rowland H. Harvey, *Samuel Gompers: Champion of the Toiling Masses* (1935).

(M.E.R.)

GOOGE, George Logan.   Born in Palaky, Ga., July 25, 1900; son of Joseph George and Elizabeth (Youmans) Googe; Baptist; married Evelyn Elliott on December 4, 1928; two children; was graduated from high school in Waterboro, S.C., in 1921, and then attended the Printing Pressman Trade School in Pressmen's Home, Tenn.; shortly after his graduation in 1922, joined the International Printing Pressmen's and Assistants' Union of North America (IPPAUNA); became a vice-president of the Georgia State Federation of Labor in 1925 and was elected president of the Trades and Labor Assembly of Savannah, Ga., in 1928; appointed Southern representative of the American Federation of Labor (AFL) in 1928 and served in that capacity until 1949; served during World War II on the National Defense Labor Board, the President's Special Commission on Education, and the War Labor Board; appointed director of the AFL's 1946 Southern organizing campaign; elected a vice-president of the IPPAUNA in 1948 and became secretary-treasurer in 1953; after the AFL-Congress of Industrial

Organizations' merger in 1955, became a vice-president of the new labor federation's union label and service trades department; elected vice-president of the International Allied Printing Trades Association in 1956; was a Democrat; died in Pressmen's Home, Tenn., September 29, 1961; Elizabeth Faulkner Baker, *Printers and Technology: A History of the International Printing Pressmen and Assistants' Union* (1957); F. Ray Marshall, *Labor in the South* (1967); *The American Federationist* (May, 1952); *Current Biography* (1947).

GORMAN, Patrick Emmet.   Born in Louisville, Ky., November 27, 1892; son of Maurice, a butcher and tanner, and Mary Ellen (Dwyer) Gorman; Roman Catholic; married Hattie Lee Dove on June 1, 1914; completed a high school education, and then began working as a butcher; joined Louisville Local 227 of the Amalgamated Meat Cutters and Butcher Workmen of North America (AMCBWNA) in 1911; served as business manager of Local 227, 1912-1920; was appointed a special AMCBWNA international organizer, 1917-1920; was graduated from the University of Louisville Law School, and then maintained a private law practice in Louisville, 1917-1920; elected president of the Louisville Union Trades and Labor Assembly in 1917, serving until 1919; served as a vice-president of the Kentucky Federation of Labor, 1918-1919; elected vice-president of the AMCBWNA in 1920 and served until becoming president in 1923; resigned as president in 1942 and became AMCBWNA secretary-treasurer (the chief administrative officer of the AMCBWNA); strongly supported industrial unionism, but opposed affiliation with the Congress of Industrial Organizations; was an American Federation of Labor fraternal delegate to the British Trades Union Congress in 1948; negotiated mergers between the AMCBWNA and the Fur and Leather Workers Union in 1955 and the United Packinghouse Workers of America in 1968; was an active participant in civic affairs, serving as a trustee of Roosevelt University, president of the Eugene V. Debs Foundation, and as an official of numerous other public and private organizations; has been the recipient of numerous honors and awards; identified himself politically as an independent; edited the *Butcher Workman* for several years; David Brody, *The Butcher Workmen: A Study of Unionization* (1964); *Who's Who in Labor* (1946); *Who's Who in America, 1972-1973.*

GOSSER, Richard Thomas.   Born in Toledo, Ohio, December 13, 1900; son of James, a railroader, and Maizie Gosser; Roman Catholic; married Ruth Marie Bonnell on January 7, 1923; one child; completed grammar school and took courses in electrical engineering for three years; after an unstable childhood that included nearly two years in a Michigan reformatory, became an electrician's apprentice at the Willys-Overland Company in Toledo; joined Local 12, United Automobile, Aircraft, Agricultural Implement Workers of America (UAW) in 1935; served as chairman of the Willys-Overland unit of Local 12, 1937-1940; elected president of Local 12 in 1938 and served until 1942; appointed director of UAW Region 2B in 1942 and became a member of the international executive board; during World War II, was a member of the War Manpower Commission for the Toledo area and served on the Office of Price Administration's committee for civic advancement; served on the Congress of Industrial Organizations' Political Action Committee; elected one of two UAW vice-presidents in 1947 (later increased to four) and placed in charge of the skilled trades department; exonerated of charges of misusing union funds by the UAW executive board in 1950; relieved of many of his duties as a UAW vice-president in 1959 after a bitter dispute with UAW president Walter P. Reuther (q.v.) over the reorganization of the competitive shop department, which he headed and which supervised UAW organizing activities; became one of the foci of the Senate Crime Investigating Committee's (McClellan Committee) investigation of the UAW in 1959; convicted of conspiring to defraud the government in a tax case in 1965 and sentenced to a three-year prison term; died in Toledo, Ohio, December 1, 1969; Jack Stieber, *Governing the UAW* (1962); Jean Gould and Lorena Hickok, *Walter Reuther: Labor's Rugged Individualist* (1972); Frank Cormier and William J. Eaton, *Reuther* (1970).

GRAHAM, Sylvester.   Born in Sheridan, Mont., September 1, 1899; son of Thomas L., a rancher and miner, and Margaret Graham; Methodist; married Edith Miller on December 7, 1926; shortly after graduating from high school in Sheridan, Mont., joined the U.S. Army during World War I; began working in the mines around Butte, Mont., after the war; joined Butte Miners' Union No. 1 of the International Union of Mine, Mill and Smelter Workers (IUMMSW) in 1933; became an international organizer for the IUMMSW in 1936; elected secretary-treasurer of the Montana State Industrial Union Council, Congress of Industrial Organizations (CIO) in 1937, and a year later, elected president, serving until 1942; became CIO sub-regional director for Montana and Wyoming in 1942; served as a member of the Montana State Apprenticeship Committee and the State Salvage Committee; served with the U.S. Army during World War II and then resumed his position with the CIO, continuing in that capacity until the American Federation of Labor (AFL)-CIO merger in 1955; became an AFL-CIO field representative in 1955, serving until 1964; died in Butte, Mont., December 25, 1970; *Who's Who in Labor* (1946); *AFL-CIO News*, January 10, 1970.

GRAY, Richard J.   Born in Albany, N.Y., December 6, 1887; son of William J., a bricklayer, and Hanora (Leahy) Gray; Roman Catholic; married Elizabeth Archambault in January, 1911; three children; after attending the public schools of Albany, began work as a bricklayer; joined Local 6 of the Bricklayers, Masons and Plasterers International Union of America (BMPIU) in 1903; worked on the construction of the Panama Canal; served as president and then elected business manager of Local 6 in 1927; was an examiner for the New York State Education Department in 1927; served as international treasurer of the BMPIU, 1928-1936, and international secretary, 1936-1946; was a director of the Union Life Insurance Company, 1928-1937, and treasurer, 1937-1946; was a staunch craft unionist and his vocal criticism of industrial unionism exacerbated relations between the American Federation of Labor (AFL) and the Committee on Industrial Organization (CIO) during the 1930s; served on the War Labor Board during World War II; elected president of the building and construction trades union department of the AFL in 1946; served as an AFL fraternal delegate to the British Trades Union Congress in 1951; his abrasive personality and conservative political, economic, and organizing policies alienated many of the union leaders affiliated with the AFL-CIO building and construction trades union department; was forced to resign as president in 1960; was a Republican and supported Dwight D. Eisenhower in 1952 and 1956; praised the work of Sen. Joseph R. McCarthy during the early 1950s; died in Washington, D.C., May 1, 1966; Harry C. Bates, *Bricklayers' Century of Craftsmanship* (1955); Philip Taft, *The A. F. of L. From the Death of Gompers to the Merger* (1959); *The New York Times*, May 3, 1966.

GREEN, John.   Born in Clydebank, Dumbartonshire, Scotland, November 15, 1896; son of Patrick and Mary Green; married Annie Allison Sievewright; four children; educated in Scotland; emigrated to the United States in 1923; hired as a sheet-metal worker at the New York Shipbuilding Corporation's yard in Camden, N.J.; helped organize a union in the Camden yard in 1933 and two years later was elected president of the newly organized Industrial Union of Marine and Shipbuilding Workers of America (IUMSWA); elected an international vice-president of the Congress of Industrial Organizations (CIO) in 1937; served as chairman of the CIO's United Railroad Workers of America; was a labor representative on the National Defense Advisory Committee in 1940; appointed to the management-labor policy committee of the War Manpower Commission in 1942; served as a CIO delegate to the World Trade Union Conference that met in 1945; retired as president of the IUMSWA in 1951; after the American Federation of Labor-CIO (AFL-CIO) merger in 1955, was appointed an AFL-CIO national representative for New Jersey; supported the Democratic party and was one of the founding members of Americans for Democratic Action; died in Audubon Park, N.J., February 19, 1957; Max M. Kampelman, *The Communist Party vs. the C.I.O.: A Study in Power Politics* (1957); *Who's Who in Labor* (1946); *The New York Times,* February 21, 1957.

GREEN, William. Born in Coshocton, Ohio, March 3, 1873; son of Hugh and Jane (Oram) Green; Baptist; married Jennie Mobley on April 14, 1892; six children; received eight years of formal education; descended from English and Welsh coal-mining families; followed his father into the coal mines of Ohio at age sixteen; in 1891, became secretary of the Coshocton Progressive Miners Union, which later became a local of the United Mine Workers Union (UMWA); became a subdistrict president of the UMWA in 1900; became president of the Ohio District Mine Workers' Union in 1906; from 1910 to 1913, served two terms in the Ohio senate where he wrote the state's workmen's compensation act, passed in 1911; served as Democratic floor leader during the second session; campaigned unsuccessfully for the presidency of the UMWA in 1910; began in 1912 a ten-year tenure as UMWA international secretary-treasurer; became a fourth vice-president and member of the executive council of the American Federation of Labor (AFL) in 1914; appointed by the AFL executive council to a five-man committee to represent labor at the international labor conferences held in connection with the Paris Peace Conference in 1919; following the death of Samuel Gompers (q.v.) in 1924, became president of the AFL and held that office until his death; during the early years of Franklin D. Roosevelt's administration, served on the advisory council of the President's Committee on Economic Security, was a member of the Labor Advisory Council of the National Recovery Administration, and served on the National Labor Board in 1934; elected to the governing board of the International Labor Organization in 1935 and served until 1937; broke with his former benefactor, John L. Lewis (q.v.), in 1935 over the issue of industrial unionism, and, acting in response to an executive council decision, ordered the expulsion of Committee on Industrial Organization (CIO) unions from the AFL in 1937; resigned from the UMWA the following year when threatened with expulsion; was a self-proclaimed advocate of labor unity, but was sometimes overwhelmed by stronger personalities on both the AFL executive council and among the leaders of the CIO; supported the mobilization effort during World War II in a variety of ways, and during the Korean War was a member of President Harry S. Truman's National Advisory Committee on Mobilization; was a member of numerous national and international boards and agencies and was associated with a variety of social and fraternal organizations; edited the *American Federationist* for many years and authored *Labor and Democracy* (1939); died in Coshocton, Ohio, November 21, 1952; Philip Taft, *The A. F. of L. From the Death of Gompers to the Merger* (1959); Max Danish, *William Green* (1952); Charles A. Madison, *American Labor Leaders: Personalities and Forces in the Labor Movement* (1950); *National Cyclopaedia of American Biography* (Vol. XLI).

GREENBERG, Max.   Born in New York City, August 6, 1907; son of Isaac and Mollie (Biegel) Greenberg; Jewish; married Billie Garfinkle on September 21, 1929; two children; completed a secondary education, then became a retail clerk and in 1929 joined a retail men's furnishings union; was one of the principal organizers of New Jersey Local 108 of the Retail Clerks International Protective Association in 1936 and elected its first president, serving until 1954; led Local 108 into the newly organized United Retail, Wholesale and Department Store Employees of America (URWDSE) in 1937; served as a labor member of the New York regional panel of the War Labor Board, 1942-1946; elected an international vice-president of the URWDSE in 1946; was a member of the New Jersey Board of Mediation, 1949-1954; elected international president of the URWDSE in 1954 and during the same year became a member of the executive board of the Congress of Industrial Organizations (CIO); after the merger between the CIO and the American Federation of Labor (AFL) in 1955, became a member of the AFL-CIO general board; appointed to the labor advisory council of the President's Committee on Equal Opportunity in 1964; named to the labor advisory council of the Office of Economic Opportunity in 1965; served as vice-president of the AFL-CIO industrial union department and on the administrative committee of the Committee on Political Education; elected an AFL-CIO vice-president and executive council member in 1967; a Democrat; *AFL-CIO News*, May 13, 1967; *Who's Who in America, 1972-1973.*

GREENE, Michael F.   Born in Kilclohor, County Clare, Ireland, January 1, 1884; son of a Roman Catholic hatter; married Mary Daly; no children; emigrated with family to the United States in 1887 and settled in Danbury, Conn., and attended St. Peter's Parochial School there; left school and went to sea at age thirteen and for the next four years worked at various occupations; became a hat makers' apprentice in 1901; joined the United Hatters of North America (UH) and in 1910 was elected president of UH Local 17 in Orange, N.J.; served as secretary-treasurer of Local 17, 1912-1918; elected international president of UH in 1918; was an American Federation of Labor (AFL) fraternal delegate to the British Trades Union Congress in 1925 and during the same year was a labor delegate to the International Labor Organization conference in Bern, Switzerland; was a member of the United States labor delegation to Italy in 1918; after negotiating a merger with Max Zaritsky (q.v.) of the United Cloth Hat and Cap Makers of North America, became the president of the amalgamated United Hatters, Cap and Millinery Workers' International Union in 1934 and served until 1936, when elected general secretary; during the conflict between the AFL and the Committee on Industrial Organization in the 1930s, supported the craft organization principle; died in Clearwater, N.J., October 20, 1951; Donald B. Robinson, *Spotlight on a Union* (1948); Charles H. Green, *The Headwear Workers* (1944); Solon DeLeon, ed., *The American Labor Who's Who* (1925).

GREENE, Prince W. (fl. 1897-1901).   Early origins unknown; a weaver from Columbus, Ga., became a vice-president of the National Union of Textile Workers (NUTW) in 1897; was a strong supporter of Samuel Gompers' (q.v.) expulsion of Socialist and New England craft locals from the NUTW over the issue of industrial unionism; elected NUTW president in 1897 and reelected in 1898 and 1900; served as NUTW secretary-treasurer, 1900-1901, when the NUTW merged with the United Textile Workers of America (UTWA); served as the editor of the *Southern Unionist* and the *Phenix Gerard News*, the latter the official organ of the NUTW; in 1899, appointed as one of three special organizers for the South covering the Carolinas, Georgia, and Alabama by the American Federation of Labor (AFL) executive council; participated in the Augusta, Ga., textile strike of 1898-1899, achieving a six percent wage increase that placed Augusta mills above the competitive district wage rate; was a tireless organizer and formed AFL locals all over his territory during 1899—organizing textile workers in Macon, Ga., and Langley, Spartanburg, and Bath, S.C., a federated union in Macon, and a federation of trades in Augusta; along with Gompers, played an important personal role in the Danville, Va., strike of 1901; with the main issue the ten-hour day, correctly believed the Danville strike to be the key to organizing the mills of the southeastern Piedmont; was "determined to strike a blow for our women and children" while in Virginia and visited the commissioner of labor in May to complain about the textile millowners' violations of Virginia's ten-hour law; later, sent the commissioner documentary evidence of violations in the Danville mills; the NUTW lost the Danville strike because of rifts among local union leaders and their failure to follow policies outlined by Gompers and Greene; in Phenix City, Ala., Greene organized furniture employees (beamers and slashers), painters and decorators, retail clerks, ladies textile workers, carpenters, and a federal labor union; had as his main goal while NUTW president the establishment of national textile-workers union; and therefore met with representatives of Northern locals in 1899 seeking their reaffiliation with the NUTW; realized the Southern union movement would fail without strong national support and hence requested that the AFL executive council persuade Northern unions of mule spinners, weavers, the National Federation of Trade Unions, the carders, and the National Loom Fixers Association to unite with the NUTW into one big union; at the NUTW convention in 1900 persuaded delegates to pass resolutions favoring one international textile workers union although realized that Southern dominance and his own leadership would end with such a merger; partly through Greene's efforts, the UTWA was formed in November, 1901; *The American Federationist* (1899-1900); Melton A. McLaurin, *Paternalism and Protest: Southern Cotton Mill Workers and Organized Labor, 1875-1905* (1971).

(M.E.R.)

GRINER, John F.   Born in Camilla, Ga., August 7, 1907; son of Will and Dollier (Shiver) Griner; Baptist; married Claranell Nicholson on November 27, 1936; two children; was graduated from high school, then worked for several different railroads during 1925-1936, joining both the Order of Railroad Telegraphers and the American Train Dispatchers Association; during this period, attended and received the LLB degree from Columbus University, Washington, D.C.; served variously as the adjudicator, liaison officer, and labor relations officer for the U.S. Railroad Retirement Board, 1936-1962; elected national president of the American Federation of Government Employees (AFGE) in 1962; is credited with building the AFGE into a strong, stable trade union organization; was elected an American Federation of Labor-Congress of Industrial Organizations' (AFL-CIO) vice-president and executive council member in 1967; served as an AFL-CIO fraternal delegate to the British Trades Union Congress in 1971; retired union positions in 1973; supports the Democratic party; *Who's Who in America, 1972-1973; AFL-CIO News.*

GROGAN, John Joseph. Born in Hoboken, N.J., March 26, 1914; son of Irish immigrants, James J., a carpenter, and Catherine (May) Grogan; Roman Catholic; married Eileen McNulty on June 5, 1937; two children; graduated from high school in Jersey City, N.J., in 1932 and later attended Columbia University for one year; after high school, became a pipefitter's helper and joined the United Association of Journeymen and Apprentices of the Plumbing and Pipefitting Industry of the United States and Canada (UA); at age nineteen, became a UA shop steward; joined Local 15 of the newly organized Industrial Union of Marine and Shipbuilding Workers of America (IUMSWA) in 1936 and, later in the same year, elected secretary of Local 15; served as executive secretary of Local 15, 1937-1943, and as financial secretary, 1938-1939; became a member of the IUMSWA general executive board in 1941 and during the period, 1941-1943, was national vice-president of the union; served on the national executive board of the Congress of Industrial Organizations (CIO), 1943-1955; elected president of the Hudson County (N.J.) Industrial Union Council, CIO, in 1943; served with the U.S. Army during World War II; served on a variety of federal and state governmental boards and agencies, including the U.S. Shipbuilding Stabilization Committee, the Labor-Management Advisory Committee, the U.S. Shipbuilding Commission, the War Labor Boards of New York and New Jersey and the Conciliation Service of the U.S. Department of Labor; served as an assemblyman in the New Jersey state legislature, 1943-1947; became a city commissioner in Hoboken, N.J., and was appointed director of the city's Parks and Public Buildings Department in 1947; elected international president of the IUMSWA in 1951; elected mayor of Hoboken in 1953 and served until 1965; elected a vice-president and member of the executive council of the American Federation of Labor (AFL)-CIO in 1963; elected Hudson County Clerk in 1963; was a member of the Democratic party; died in Jersey City, N.J., September 16, 1968; *Current Biography* (1951); *Who's Who in Labor* (1946); *AFL-CIO News,* October 12, 1963, September 21, 1968.

HAGERTY, Thomas J. (fl. 1895-1920). Born ca. 1862; little is known of his life prior to finishing seminary training in the Roman Catholic faith in

1895; appointed assistant to the rector at St. Agatha's Church, Chicago, Ill., in 1895; assigned to St. Joseph's Church, Cleburne, Tex., in 1897, and appointed rector of Our Lady of Victory Church in Paris, Tex., in 1901; became a socialist ca. 1892 and attempted to rationalize the apparent contradictions in Marxist and Catholic dogma; while a pastor in Texas, was closely associated with exploited Mexican railroad workers; found little Socialist literature available in Spanish and therefore translated several Socialist tracts from German, French, and English; transferred to Our Lady of Sorrows Church, Las Vegas, N.M., in 1901; shortly after arriving in New Mexico, became associated with the Western Federation of Miners and the American Labor Union (ALU) (originally, the Western Labor Union); during the summer of 1902, toured the mining camps of Colorado with Eugene V. Debs (q.v.), recruiting members for both the ALU and the Socialist party; suspended from his priestly duties in 1902, because of his radical views and his long absence from the Las Vegas parish; as a Catholic priest, was especially valuable to Socialists, whose appeal to Catholic workers was undermined by the Church's anti-Socialist stance; was a skillful orator and served as a Socialist party lecturer during 1903, traversing much of the country arguing that the Church should not interfere with the political convictions of its members; after the tour, wrote a series of pamphlets dealing with much the same subject; during 1903-1904, became increasingly radical and criticized in more and more vitriolic terms those right-wing Socialists who advocated boring-from-within the American Federation of Labor, gradualism, and revolution through the ballot box; as a result of his strident criticism of Socialist party leaders, his influence in the party declined precipitantly; helped draft the Industrial Union Manifesto which led to the founding of the Industrial Workers of the World (IWW); became editor of the *Voice of Labor*, a new publication of the ALU, in 1905, and used the columns of the short-lived monthly to champion industrial unionism; was an important participant in the inaugural convention of the IWW and served as secretary of the constitution committee and wrote the highly influential preamble to the IWW constitution; shortly after the IWW convention, unexplainedly dropped out of the radical union movement; lived under the name Ricardo Moreno and dissolved his connections with both the Church and the IWW and for a time earned a living teaching Spanish and maintaining a small practice as an oculist; from 1920 to his death, apparently lived as a derelict on Chicago's skid row; Robert E. Doherty, "Thomas J. Hagerty, The Church, and Socialism," *Labor History* (Winter, 1962); Melvyn Dubofsky, *We Shall Be All: A History of the Industrial Workers of the World* (1969).

HAGGERTY, Cornelius Joseph.   Born in Boston, Mass., January 10, 1894; son of Daniel, a freight handler, and Nora (Driscoll) Haggerty; Roman Catholic; married Margaret Killeher on June 30, 1920; two children; completed elementary school in Boston and then began a short-lived singing career; became a lathers' apprentice in 1913 and two years later, after becoming a journeyman, joined Local 72 of the International Union of Wood, Wire and Metal Lathers (IUWWML); served with the U.S. Navy during World War I; moved to Los Angeles, Calif., in 1921 and affiliated with IUWWML Local 42; served as a West Coast organizer for the IUWWML and president of Local 42; elected secretary of the Los Angeles Building and Construction Trades Council in 1933; served as president of the California State Federation of Labor 1937-1943, and secretary, 1943-1960; served during World War II on a variety of state and regional panels, including the War Manpower Commission, the Office of Price Administration, and the Civilian Defense Council; was a long-time vice-president of the IUWWML; became president of the American Federation of Labor-Congress of Industrial Organizations' (AFL-CIO) building and construction trades department in 1960; in the inner councils of the AFL-CIO, often opposed the proposals and policies of the president of the industrial union department, Walter P. Reuther (q.v.); served on the California State Board of Education and as a regent of the University of California; retired from union affairs in 1970; usually supported the Democratic party; died in Palm Springs, Calif., October 10, 1971; Philip Taft, *Labor Politics American Style: The California State Federation of Labor* (1968); Louis B. Perry and Richard S. Perry, *A History of the Los Angeles Labor Movement, 1911-1941* (1963); *Who's Who in Labor* (1946).

HAGGERTY, John B.   Born in St. Louis, Mo., in 1884; son of William R., an auditor, and Mary Haggerty; Roman Catholic; never married; completed a secondary school in St. Louis, then became an apprentice in the printing industry; joined St. Louis Local 18 of the International Brotherhood of Bookbinders (IBB) and eventually served as its president; served as an international representative, international vice-president, and a member of the IBB executive council during the period, 1916-1926; was an American Federation of Labor (AFL) fraternal delegate to the Trades and Labor Conference of Canada in 1929; elected international president of the IBB in 1926; served as a printing trades labor advisor to the National Recovery Administration, 1933-1935; was an AFL fraternal delegate to the British Trades Union Congress in 1937; during World War II, was a member of the labor advisory committee of the War Production

Board; served for several years prior to his death as chairman of the board of governors of the International Allied Printing Trades Association; was a Democrat and a member of the Democratic National Committee's labor committee; died in Miami, Fla., March 4, 1953; *The American Federationist* (March, 1953); *The New York Times*, March 5, 1953; *Who's Who in Labor* (1946).

HALEY, Margaret Angela.   Born in Joliet, Ill., November 15, 1861; daughter of Michael, a stone-quarry and construction firm operator, and Elizabeth (Tiernan) Haley; Roman Catholic; attended grammar school at Channahon, Ill., and high school at St. Angela's Convent, Morris, Ill.; worked as a teacher in Dresden Heights, Joliet, and Lake, Ill., before securing a position at Henricks Elementary School, Chicago, Ill.; was an organizer of the Chicago Federation of Teachers (CFT) in 1897; was elected a CFT district vice-president in 1900; served as a full-time business agent of the CFT, 1901-1939; as a result of her persuasive arguments, the CFT affiliated with the Chicago Federation of Labor (CFL) in 1902; reorganized the National Federation of Teachers in 1901 and served as its president, 1901-ca. 1906; after the CFT was chartered as Local 1 of the American Federation of Teachers (AFT) in 1916, became the first national organizer of the AFT; withdrew the CFT from the AFT in 1917, after the Illinois Supreme Court upheld the Loeb rule that gave local school boards the right to refuse to hire, or to dismiss, teachers because of union membership; was instrumental in securing the state tenure law for teachers in 1917; served on the executive committee of the Labor party which ran John Fitzpatrick (q.v.) of the CFL for mayor of Chicago in 1919; was a constant agitator throughout career for the right of teachers to engage in union activities, and was a constant critic of corporations that failed to pay taxes on school lands they used; died in Chicago, Ill., January 5, 1939; *Notable American Women* (1971); Robert J. Braun, *Teachers and Power: The Story of the American Federation of Teachers* (1972).

(M.T.)

HALL, Paul.   Born in Alabama, August 21, 1914; married Rose Hall; two children; attended the public schools of Alabama, then went to sea as an engine wiper in the early 1930s; was one of the founding members of the Seafarers International Union of North America (SIU) in 1938; served as an oiler on merchant ships during World War II; became a port patrolman after the war and elected the SIU's port agent in New York; elected first vice-president of the SIU in 1948 and became the SIU's chief officer for the

Atlantic, Gulf, Great Lakes, and Inland Waters District; continuing to serve as secretary-treasurer for the Atlantic and Gulf District, became president of the SIU and president of the American Federation of Labor-Congress of Industrial Organizations' (AFL-CIO) maritime trades department in 1957; served as chief organizer of the International Brotherhood of Longshoremen, a newly chartered AFL international union that unsuccessfully attempted to supplant the International Longshoremen's Association after its expulsion from the AFL in 1953; elected an AFL-CIO vice-president and executive council member in 1962; along with Joseph Curran (q.v.), president of the National Maritime Union, established the short-lived International Maritime Workers Union to represent seamen working on American-owned ships flying the flags of Liberia, Panama, and Honduras; devoted much of his time and energy to eliminating Communist influence in maritime unions; usually supported Democratic candidates, but was a strong supporter of Republican president Richard M. Nixon; Joseph P. Goldberg, *The Maritime Story: A Study in Labor-Management Relations* (1958); Maud Russell, *Men Along the Shore* (1966); *Current Biography* (1966).

HALLBECK, Elroy Charles.   Born in Chicago, Ill., May 15, 1902: son of Charles August and Anna Marie (Hansen) Hallbeck; Unitarian; married Myrtle Elizabeth Montgomery on August 30, 1957; one child by a previous marriage; received a secondary education in the public schools of Chicago, then hired by the U.S. Postal Service in Chicago as a clerk in 1921; joined Local 1 of the National Federation of Postal Clerks (NFPC); elected president of Local 1 in 1934 after having served as secretary since 1926; elected a national vice-president of the NFPC in 1940 and served in that capacity until 1944 when he was appointed assistant national legislative director in Washington, D.C.; became national legislative director in 1946 and served in that capacity until his death; elected national president of the NFPC in 1960; negotiated a merger of the National Postal Transport Association, the United National Association of Post Office Craftsmen, and the NFPC in 1961 that created the United Federation of Postal Clerks (UFPC); elected chairman of the Government Employees Council, American Federation of Labor-Congress of Industrial Organizations in 1961; was a member of the board of directors of the Union Life Insurance Company, New York City, and the Washington Arthritis and Rheumatism Foundation; attempting to negotiate the reunification of the UFPC and the National Postal Union at the time of his death; was a Democrat; died in

Washington, D.C., January 14, 1969; *Who's Who in America, 1968-1969;* *AFL-CIO News,* January 18, 1964.

HAPGOOD, Powers.　Born in Chicago, Ill., December 28, 1899; son of William Powers, president of Columbia Conserve Company, a producers' cooperative canning firm in Indianapolis, Ind., and Eleanor (Page) Hapgood; married Mary Donovan, national secretary of the Sacco-Vanzetti Defense Committee and frequent Socialist party candidate for vice-president of the United States, on December 28, 1927; two children; attended grammar school and Shortridge High School in Indianapolis and was graduated from Phillips Academy, Andover, Mass., in 1917, and Harvard University in 1921; after graduation, worked in a Hibbing, Minn., iron mine, for the Northern Pacific Railroad, in a Montana sugar beet factory, and in the coal mines of Montana, Colorado, and Pennsylvania; joined the United Mine Workers of America (UMWA) in 1921 and served as an organizer in John Brophy's (q.v.) District 2, Central Pennsylvania, 1922-1924; became an opponent of John L. Lewis (q.v.) after he abandoned the Somerset County miners following the national coal strike of 1922; worked during 1924-1926 in coal mines in Wales, France, Germany, and Siberia while studying mining conditions, the British Labour party, and the Communist system; returned to the United States in 1926 and worked in the Pennsylvania mines, joined the Socialist party, and managed John Brophy's "Save the Union" campaign against Lewis; joined and spoke for the Sacco-Vanzetti Defense Committee in Chicago, Ill., and the Pennsylvania coal fields in 1927; expelled from the UMWA and was unable to take a miner's job in Josephine Roche's unionized Colorado mine, but worked for her as assistant mining engineer until 1930; joined Brophy, Adolph Germer (q.v.), and Alexander Howat (q.v.) in 1930 in creating the Reorganized UMWA, which was destroyed by a court injunction; ran for governor of Illinois on the Socialist party ticket in 1932, receiving 18,735 votes; with John Brophy and his brother-in-law, Dan Donovan, worked from late 1930 until January, 1933 for his father's Columbia Conserve Company; when his father fired the latter two unionists for partially disrupting the cooperative experiment, Powers also quit; served as an organizer for the Amalgamated Clothing Workers and the Textile Workers in Kentucky, for the Socialist party in Massachusetts, for the Southern Tenant Farmers' Union in Arkansas, and for the UMWA in Illinois, 1933-1935; was convinced of Lewis's sincerity in organizing industrial unions and served as a Congress of Industrial Organizations' (CIO) organizer, helping to organize the United Rubber Workers, the United Auto Workers, the United Steelworkers, the United Shoe Workers, the Marine and Shipbuilding Workers, and the Farm Equipment Workers, 1936-1941; formed and served as regional director of the New England CIO in 1937; served as regional director of the New England CIO in 1937; served as regional director of the Indiana CIO and chairman of the Indiana CIO's political action committee, 1941-1949; authored *In Non-union Mines: The Diary of a Coal Digger in Central Pennsylvania, August-September, 1921* (1922); and several articles for *New Republic, Nation,* and the labor press; died in automobile accident near Indianapolis, Ind., February 4, 1949; John Bartlow Martin, *Indiana* (1947); John Brophy, *A Miner's Life* (1964); *Who's Who in Labor* (1946); *The New York Times,* February 5, 1949.

(J.H.)

HARRISON, George MacGregor. Born in Lois, Mo., July 19, 1895; son of Louis Harvey, a merchant, and Mary Loga (Coppedge) Harrison; Baptist; married Averil Mayo Hughes on October 16, 1912; three children; completed grammar school at age fourteen, then took a job on the Missouri Pacific Railroad; worked during 1909-1917 at various times as a yard clerk, distribution clerk, storekeeper, and mechanical valuation clerk; elected chairman of the St. Louis local of the Brotherhood of Railway and Steamship Clerks, Freight Handlers, Express and Station Employees (BRC) in 1917, serving until 1922; served as a vice-president of the BRC, 1922-1928; elected grand president of the BRC in 1928; elected an American Federation of Labor (AFL) vice-president and executive council member in 1934; served as chairman of the Railway Labor Executives' Association, 1935-1940; served on the United States delegation of the American National Committee to the Third World Power Conference and as an American labor delegate to the International Labor Organization conference in Geneva in 1936 and Cuba in 1939; helped draft both the Railroad Retirement Act and the Social Security Act; chaired the AFL executive council subcommittee which attempted to mediate differences with the Committee for Industrial Organization (CIO) in 1935; not particularly sympathetic to the CIO, but opposed the AFL executive council's suspension of CIO affiliates as an unconstitutional exercise of authority; served on the advisory board of the National Youth Administration; served during World War II on the Joint Railroad Labor-Management Committee and the National Defense Mediation Board; served after the war on the President's Labor-Management Committee and was an advisor to the Council of Economic Advisors; served for many years as a director of the Workers' Education

League of America and in 1948 became its president; became a vice-president and executive council member of the merged AFL-CIO in 1955; was appointed a member of the United States delegation to the United Nations in 1958; appointed to the President's Advisory Committee on Labor-Management Policy in 1961; was a member of numerous private and public boards and agencies, including the American Institute for Free Labor Development, the Afro-Asian Institute in Israel, and the Afro-American Labor Center; served as a trustee of both the Harry S. Truman and John F. Kennedy Library foundations; retired BRC presidency in 1963 and became chief executive officer; became president emeritus in 1965; was a Democrat; died in Cincinnati, Ohio, November 30, 1968; Harry Henig, *The Brotherhood of Railway Clerks* (1937); Philip Taft, *The A. F. of L. From the Death of Gompers to the Merger* (1959); *Current Biography* (1949); *The American Federationist* (May, 1941); *AFL-CIO News*, December 7, 1968.

HARTUNG, Albert Ferdinand. Born in Catract, Wis., June 18, 1897; son of Ernest and Minnie Hartung; married Farris Chapman on August 5, 1922 and Nina Calhoun on September 5, 1953; four children; attended the public schools of Catract and eventually became a logger in the Pacific Northwest; in 1915 joined the Industrial Workers of the World; eventually joined an American Federation of Labor local union organized in Vernonia, Ore., and in 1933 was elected president of the local; was a delegate to the founding convention of the International Woodworkers of America (IWA) in 1937, and served as president of Columbia River District Council 5, 1937-1941; was assistant director of organization for the IWA, 1941-1942; served during World War II with the lumber division of the War Production Board and the Office of Price Administration; also served on the West Coast Lumber Committee of the War Labor Board; became the Congress of Industrial Organizations' regional director for Oregon in 1942, serving until 1947; was first vice-president of the IWA during 1947-1951, then became international president; was a persistent critic of the Eisenhower administration's alleged antilabor positions, and also refused to cooperate with the Kennedy administration's Committee on Equal Employment Opportunity by providing racial breakdowns of union membership; was a Democrat; retired IWA presidency in 1967; died in Portland, Ore., in July, 1973; *Who's Who in America, 1958-1959, 1972-1973; Who's Who in Labor* (1946); *CIO News*, October 15, 1951; *AFL-CIO News*, July 28, 1973.

(M.E.R.)

HAYES, Albert John.　　Born in Milwaukee, Wis., February 14, 1900; son of Albert and Augusta (Wolter) Hayes; Lutheran; married Lillian M. Fink on February 25, 1921; one child; attended the public schools of Milwaukee, then began work in the railroad shops of Milwaukee as an apprentice machinist; joined the International Association of Machinists (IAM) in 1917; served during 1917-1934 as a local committeeman, local union officer, and as president of IAM District 7; appointed Grand Lodge representative in 1934, serving in that capacity until 1944; served on the War Labor Board during World War II; became an international vice-president in 1945 and was elected IAM president in 1949; led the IAM back into the American Federation of Labor (AFL) from which it had withdrawn in 1943 over a jurisdiction dispute with the United Brotherhood of Carpenters; served during 1950-1951 as a labor member of the National Security Board, the Advisory Committee to the Economic Stabilization Agency, and the Labor-Management Advisory Committee; became a special assistant to the Assistant Secretary of Defense in 1951; appointed chairman of the President's Commission on the Health Needs of the Nation in 1951; elected a vice-president and executive council member of the AFL in 1953; created much controversy in labor circles by advocating a plan of compulsory-arbitration during testimony before the Senate Labor Committee in 1953; after the AFL-Congress of Industrial Organizations merger, he became a vice-president and executive council member of the new federation; retired union positions in 1965; Mark Perlman, *The Machinists: A New Study in American Trade Unionism* (1961), and *Democracy in the International Association of Machinists* (1962); *Current Biography* (1953).

HAYES, Frank J.　　Born in What Cheer, Iowa, in 1882; son of a coal miner; Roman Catholic; unmarried; moved with family to Illinois in his youth; attended the public schools of Collinsville and Mt. Olive, Ill.; at age thirteen, began working as a coal miner; joined the United Mine Workers of America (UMWA) and held several local union offices; elected secretary-treasurer of the Belleville subdistrict of District 12, UMWA, Illinois, in 1904, when Adolph Germer (q.v.) served as subdistrict vice-president; with Germer, was among the most active Socialist leaders in the Illinois miners' movement; appointed to the executive board of District 12 in 1908; elected and served as international vice-president of the UMWA, 1910-1917; during his incumbency, directed the West Virginia coal strike of 1912-1913 and the violent Colorado coal strike of 1913-1914, which culminated in the Ludlow Massacre; after John P. White (q.v.) resigned as president to serve as labor consultant to the National Fuel Administration in 1917, elected as UMWA international president, serving until 1920; as president, had neither the taste nor talent for administration and, troubled by illness, turned most of his duties of office over to vice-president and acting president John L. Lewis (q.v.); resigned in 1920 and moved to Colorado, allegedly to seek a cure for alcoholism, meanwhile continuing as an UMWA international representative until his death; ran unsuccessfully for governor of Illinois on the Socialist party ticket in 1912, and in 1937-1938, after the Colorado miners were organized, elected for one term as lieutenant governor of Colorado on the Democratic ticket; was a labor poet and wrote strike songs and poems about Ludlow; died in Denver, Colo., June 10, 1948; George S. McGovern and Leonard F. Guttridge, *Great Coalfield War* (1972); *United Mine Workers Journal*, July 1, 1948.

(J.H.)

HAYES, Maximilian Sebastian.   Born in Havana, Ohio, May 25, 1866; son of Joseph Maximilian Sebastian, a farmer, and Elizabeth (Borer) Hayes; reared a Roman Catholic; married Dora Schneider on December 11, 1900; one child; gained a grammar school education in the public schools of Ohio; became a printer's apprentice at age thirteen; joined the International Typographical Union (ITU) in 1884; was one of the founders of the *Cleveland Citizen*, which in 1892 became the official organ of the Cleveland Central Labor Union; served as the editor of the *Cleveland Citizen*, 1892-1939; was an influential figure in the Cleveland labor movement and served as a general organizer in the area for 15 years; was an American Federation of Labor (AFL) fraternal delegate to the British Trades Union Congress in 1903; was a long-time ITU delegate to the annual conventions of the AFL and was one of the leaders of the Socialist opposition to the AFL leadership; authored the Ohio Workmen's Compensation Law of 1911; unsuccessfully contested Samuel Gompers (q.v.) re-election to the AFL presidency in 1912; was a member of the Ohio State Adjustment Board of the National Recovery Administration, 1933-1935; was a charter member of the Cleveland Metropolitan Housing Authority organized in 1933; spent much of his lifetime trying unsuccessfully to find a mutal basis of accord between Socialist principles and the American labor movement; identified with the Populist party until 1896, then the Socialist Labor party, 1896-1899, and finally the Socialist party of America after 1899; was a Socialist candidate for the U. S. Congress from Ohio in 1900, for secretary of state of Ohio in 1902, and for vice-president of the United States on the Farmer-Labor ticket in 1920; died in Cleveland, Ohio, October 11, 1945;

Philip Taft, *The A. F. of L. in the Time of Gompers* (1957); Lewis L. Lorwin, *The American Federation of Labor: History, Policies, and Prospects* (1933); James Weinstein, *The Decline of Socialism in America, 1912-1925* (1967); *Dictionary of American Biography* (Supplement III).

HAYWOOD, William Dudley.   Born in Salt Lake City, Utah, February 4, 1869; son of William Dudley, a pioneer and miner, who died in 1872; his mother was remarried to a miner; although his family was Episcopalian, he renounced the church; married Nevada Jane Minor in 1889; his formal education was interrupted by the necessity to hold odd jobs; subsequently read widely; at fifteen, went to work full-time as a miner, and for the next decade employed at several mines in Nevada and Utah; in 1894, moved his family to the mining town of Silver City, Idaho, and there joined and became an officer of a local of the recently formed Western Federation of Miners (WFM); elected a delegate to the 1898 WFM convention and came to the attention of President Edward Boyce (q.v.); elected in 1899 to the WFM executive board; in 1900, elected secretary-treasurer of the WFM and moved to Denver, Colo.; had a major role in directing the bitter strikes at Telluride and Cripple Creek, Colo.; reacting to the exploitative policies of the mining corporations and to their adamant opposition to unions, evolved from a militant trade unionist into an advocate of revolutionary industrial unionism; in 1905, helped organize and chaired the founding convention of the Industrial Workers of the World (IWW); jailed in 1906 along with WFM president Charles Moyer (q.v.) for the murder of a former Idaho governor, but acquitted in 1907; the case became a cause célèbre and Haywood became nationally known in labor and radical circles; purged by the moderates who dominated the WFM in 1908 and disgusted by the bickering of IWW factions, from 1908 to 1912 traveled throughout the country as an organizer and speaker for the Socialist party; became disillusioned with political socialism and rejoined the IWW as an active leader of the successful Lawrence, Mass., textile strike of 1912; elected general secretary (i.e., chief officer) of the IWW in 1915 and presided over Walter Nef's (q.v.) highly effective organizing drive of the Agricultural Workers Organization (AWO); taking advantage of the impetus and funds provided by the AWO, centralized authority in his office over organizing and altered the IWW's loose structure along the lines of separate industrial unions directly responsible to the Chicago, Ill., headquarters; his large stature, rugged features, and gruff manner seemed to personify the violent frontier milieu; but also concerned with all kinds of exploited workers; his obvious sincerity, courage, and commanding presence made him one of the most effective labor orators and agitators of the era; convicted in 1917 for violating the Espionage Act and, along with many other Wobblies, imprisoned; released in 1919 pending an appeal and agitated on behalf of his imprisoned colleagues; beguiled by the Bolshevik Revolution, jumped bail in 1921 to go to the Soviet Union and there reportedly managed a mining complex and later helped set up the International Labor Defense to aid jailed radicals and unionists; died in Moscow, USSR, May 18, 1928; *Bill Haywood's Book: The Autobiography of William D. Haywood* (1929); Joseph H. Conlin, *Big Bill Haywood and the Radical Union Movement* (1969); *Dictionary of American Biography* (Vol. VIII).

(D.G.S.)

HEIGHTON, William (fl. 1827-1830). Born in Oundle, Northamptonshire, England in 1800; emigrated to the United States as a youth and settled in Philadelphia, Pa.; received little formal education; hired as a cordwainer in Southwark, near Philadelphia; was a Ricardian Socialist who anticipated the labor theory of value popularized by the Marxists; wrote an influential pamphlet in 1827 that provided the organizational and theoretical inspiration for the Workingmen's movement in Philadelphia; was the principal founder of the Mechanics' Union of Trade Associations in November, 1827, conceiving it as a medium for political activity; became the chief editor of the Mechanics' Union newspaper, the *Mechanics Free Press*; after its candidates were defeated in the local elections of 1828, the Mechanics' Union, which had been instrumental in the founding of at least 15 new trade union societies, disbanded; was a vigorous advocate of public education and served as secretary of the Joint Committee of the City and County of Philadelphia that investigated public education in Philadelphia, 1829-1830; in 1830 ended his active association with the labor movement; authored "An ADDRESS to the Members of Trade Societies, and to the WORKING CLASSES GENERALLY" (1827), and "The Principles of Aristocratic Legislation" (1828); died in 1873; Louis H. Arky, "The Mechanics' Union of Trade Associations and the Formation of the Philadelphia Workingmen's Movement," *The Pennsylvania Magazine of History and Biography* (April, 1952); Edward Pessen, *Most Uncommon Jacksonians: The Radical Leaders of the Early Labor Movement* (1967); John R. Commons, *et al.*, *History of Labour in the United States*, Vol. 1 (1918).

HELFGOTT, Simon. Born in New York City, November 15, 1894; son of Louis Solomon and Sarah Hannah Helfgott; Jewish; married Esther Feinzig on June 10, 1922; two children; was graduated from high school, then became a debit insurance agent for the Metropolitan Life Insurance Company; joined New York Insurance Workers Local 30 of the United Office and Professional Workers of America (UOPWA); was chairman of the organizing committee and served on the executive board of Local 30; was a member of the executive board of the UOPWA and in 1949 elected president of Local 30; after the UOPWA was expelled from the Congress of Industrial Organizations (CIO) for alleged Communist domination, founded and became the first president of New York Industrial Insurance Employees Union Local 1706, which affiliated with the Insurance Workers of America International Union (IWAIU), chartered by the CIO in 1952; served as the vice-chairman of the Insurance and Allied Workers Organizing Committee and first vice-president of the IWAIU; retired because of ill-health during the summer of 1957; a member of the American Labor party and later the Liberal party of New York; died in New York City, September 8, 1957; Harvey J. Clermont, *Organizing the Insurance Worker: A History of Labor Unions of Insurance Employees* (1966); *The New York Times*, September 9, 1957; *Who's Who in Labor* (1946).

HELLER, George. Born in New York City, November 20, 1905; son of David and Frances Heller; Jewish; married Clara Mahr on June 3, 1934; two children; completed high school, then studied at the City College of New York, 1923-1925; began appearing in stage productions in 1926, performing as an actor, ballet dancer, and singer; was also a composer, director, and producer; shortly after its formation in 1937, joined the New York local of the American Federation of Radio Artists (AFRA); elected executive secretary of AFRA's New York local shortly after joining; elected national executive secretary of AFRA in 1946; was a founder and the first national executive secretary of the Television Authority (TVA) in 1949; after the 1952 merger of the TVA and AFRA that created the American Federation of Radio and Television Artists (AFTRA), became the national executive secretary of the new union; negotiated the first successful union pension and welfare plan with the major television networks in 1954; served as first vice-president of the Association of Actors and Artists of America and fifth vice-president of the American Theatre Wing; was a member of the advisory council of the United Service Organization Camp Shows, Incorporated; was a Democrat; died in New York City, May 30, 1955; Allen E. Koenig, ed., *Broadcasting and Bargaining: Labor Relations in Radio and Television* (1970); *Fortune* (January, 1951); *The New York Times*, May 31, 1955; *Who Was Who in America* (Vol. III).

HELLER, Jacob J. Born in Russia, August 21, 1889; son of Mendel and Gutte Heller; Jewish; married Rose Ackerman on June 27, 1915; one child; studied at a yeshiva for the rabbinate before emigrating to the United States in 1906; shortly after entering United States, hired as a children's cloakmaker and joined Local 17 of the International Ladies' Garment Workers' Union (ILGWU); became manager of Local 17, ILGWU, in 1916; elected an ILGWU vice-president in 1920; was graduated from New York University's School of Commerce in 1923; was removed from union positions as a result of reforms instituted by ILGWU president Morris Sigman (q.v.) in 1925, and then opened an office in New York as an accountant and served as a business advisor to several unions; regained his union positions after Sigman's resignation in 1929; had an expansive view of the jurisdiction of Local 17, which kept him constantly embroiled in jurisdictional conflicts with other cloakmakers' locals; after the amalgamation of the reefermakers and cloakmakers in 1936, became the manager of the reefermakers' department of the New York Cloak Joint Board; was a conservative in the ILGWU's ideological conflicts and strongly supported the principle of craft organization, opposing efforts of the union's leadership to support the Congress of Industrial Organizations; became manager of newly chartered Snow-Suit Workers' Local 105 in 1942; affiliated with the Liberal party of New York; authored *My Union My Life* and *Moment of Gloom*; died in New York City, September 25, 1948; Benjamin Stolberg, *Tailor's Progress: The Story of a Famous Union and the Men Who Made It* (1944); Louis Levine, *The Women's Garment Workers: A History of the International Ladies' Garment Workers' Union* (1924); *ILGWU Report and Proceedings* (1950).

HELSTEIN, Ralph. Born in Duluth, Minn., December 11, 1908; son of Henry, a manufacturer, and Lena (Litman) Helstein; married Rachel Brin on January 2, 1939; two children; received the B.A. (1929) and LLB (1934) degrees from the University of Minnesota and then was admitted to the Minnesota bar in 1936; appointed labor compliance officer for the National Recovery Administration in Minnesota in 1934; conducted a private law practice in Minneapolis, Minn., 1936-1943; became general counsel for the Minnesota Industrial Union Council, Congress of Industrial Organizations (CIO), in 1939, serving until 1943; appointed general counsel for the United Packinghouse Workers of America (UPWA) in 1942; elected international president of the UPWA in 1946; became a member of the CIO executive board in 1946, serving until 1955; led a largely unsuccessful 82-day strike against the Swift, Wilson, Armour, and Cudahy meat-packing companies in 1948; as president, was credited with successfully negotiating a guaranteed work week, maintaining membership, and improving working conditions for UPWA members; elected an American Federation of Labor-CIO vice-president and executive council member in 1965, serving until 1969; after the merger of the UPWA and the Amalgamated Meat Cutters and Butcher Workmen of North America (AMCBWNA) in 1968, became a vice-president and special counsel of the new union; retired union positions in 1968-1969; elected president emeritus of the AMCBWNA after his retirement; a Democrat; David Brody, *The Butcher Workmen: A Study of Unionization* (1964); *Current Biography* (1948); *Who's Who in America, 1960-1961; Who's Who in Labor* (1946); *AFL-CIO News*, December 9, 1972.

HELT, Daniel Webster.   Born in Shamokin, Pa., September 24, 1883; son of Jeremiah M., a railroad worker, and Amanda E. (Hoover) Helt; Methodist; married Kate Peart Gilham on September 25, 1907; six children; attended public schools, beginning work as a slate picker at age nine; enlisted in the U. S. Marine Corps in 1901 and served with the Caribbean Squad until 1905; worked as a coal miner and carpenter prior to becoming a mechanic in the signal department of the Reading Railroad in 1910; joined Reading Lodge 26 of the Brotherhood of Railroad Signalmen (BRS) in 1910; elected as a Republican to the Pennsylvania House of Representatives in 1917 and served two terms; elected grand president of the BRS in 1917 shortly after becoming a railroad fireman; was one of the founders of both the Railway Labor Executives' Association and the railroad labor newspaper, *Labor*; as president of BRS, led a major organizing campaign in which the BRS unionized 95 percent of the workers in its jurisdiction; received a leave of absence from the BRS in 1934 shortly after being appointed a member of the National Railroad Adjustment Board; resigned as BRS president in 1936 and named grand vice-president; in 1948, resigned from the National Railroad Adjustment Board and named president emeritus after resigning his BRS positions; edited the *Signalman's Journal*, 1917-1934; authored *The Signalman and His Work* (1921); was a Republican early in his career, but later became disillusioned with the party and identified himself as an independent-progressive; died in Arlington Heights, Ill., October 21, 1961; Brotherhood of Railroad Signalmen of America, *50 Years of Railroad Signaling: A History of the Brotherhood of Railroad Signalmen of America* (n.d.); *Who's Who in Labor* (1946); *Labor*, August 14, 1948, October 28, 1961.

HENDERSON, Donald James.   Born in New York City, February 4, 1902; son of Daniel, a dairy farmer, and Jean (Crawford) Henderson; married Florence McGee Thomas (second marriage) on October 10, 1943; three children; received the B.A. and M.A. degrees from Columbia University, and during the summer of 1925, attended the Geneva School of International Relations; joined the Railroad Telegraph Operators' Union in 1919, maintaining his membership until 1922; hired as a teacher at Columbia University and joined the American Federation of Teachers in 1926; dismissed by Columbia University in 1933 because his Communist party affiliation allegedly interferred with his teaching responsibilities; published the *Rural Worker* during the 1930s, and in 1935, organized the National Committee for Unity of Agricultural and Rural Workers; after the United Cannery, Agricultural, Packers and Allied Workers of America (UCAPAWA) was chartered by the Congress of Industrial Organizations (CIO) in 1937, elected its first president and built it into one of the largest CIO affiliates; negotiated a merger with the Southern Tenant Farmers' Union (STFU) in 1937, but conflicts with STFU leader H. L. Mitchell (q.v.) over local autonomy and communism led to a split in 1939 that weakened both unions; under his guidance, the UCAPAWA made its greatest advances in California, where in cooperation with Harry Bridges' (q.v.) International Longshoremen and Warehousemen's Union, seasonal workers were organized around a nucleus of permanently-employed cannery workers; in 1946 the UCAPAWA was reorganized and renamed the Food, Tobacco, Agricultural and Allied Workers Union (FTA), symbolic of the growing emphasis upon the organization of processing workers, who were easier to organize; elected president of the FTA in 1946; his career in the postwar era was intimately affected by domestic Cold War passions; FTA membership declined to 22,590 by 1949; challenged CIO leaders by endorsing Henry Wallace for president of the United States in 1948, and by attending the World Federation of Trade Unions meeting after CIO withdrew from it; in order to avoid signing a non-Communist affidavit as required under the Taft-Hartley Act, resigned as president of the FTA in 1949 and became FTA national administrative director; however, the National Labor Relations Board refused to accept this change as a legitimate tactic; after an investigation conducted by the CIO's committee on Communism, he and the FTA were expelled from the CIO in 1950; ended his association with the trade union movement shortly thereafter; U. S. Department of Labor (Stuart M. Jamieson), *Labor Unionism in American Agriculture* (1945); Donald H. Grubbs, *Cry from the Cotton* (1971); Louis

Cantor, *A Prologue to the Protest Movement: The Missouri Sharecropper Roadside Demonstration of 1939* (1969); Max M. Kampelman, *The Communist Party vs. the C.I.O.: A Study in Power Politics* (1957); *Who's Who in Labor* (1946).

(M.E.R.)

HENRY, Alice.   Born in Richmond, Australia, March 21, 1857; daughter of Charles Ferguson, an accountant, and Margaret (Walker) Henry, a seamstress; Unitarian; attended various public and private schools in Melbourne, Australia; was a feature writer for the *Melbourne Argus* and its weekly, the *Australasian*, 1884-1904; journeyed to London in 1905 as the Melbourne representative to an English conference of charity organizations; emigrated to the United States in 1906; shortly after her arrival, at the invitation of Margaret Dreier Robins (q.v.), became the secretary of the Chicago, Ill., Women's Trade Union League (WTUL); headed the women's department of the Chicago-based *Union Labor Advocate*, 1908-1911; participated in an investigation of conditions among women brewery workers in Milwaukee, Wis., in 1910; edited the WTUL's monthly, *Life and Labor*, 1911-1915; served as a national WTUL organizer, 1918-1920; was an instructor at Bryn Mawr College summer school for women workers in 1921; headed the WTUL education department, 1920-1922, attended the International Workers' Education Conference held at Ruskin College, Oxford, England, in 1924; retired to Santa Barbara, Calif., in 1928 and returned to Melbourne in 1933; authored *The Trade Union Movement* (1915), *Women and the Labor Movement* (1923), and *Memoirs of Alice Henry* (1944); died in Melbourne, February 14, 1943; *Notable American Women* (1971); Mary E. Dreier, *Margaret Dreier Robins: Her Life, Letters and Work* (1950); Gladys Boone, *The Women's Trade Union Leagues in Great Britain and the United States of America* (1942).

(M.T.)

HICKEY, Thomas L.   Born in New York City in 1893; Roman Catholic; married; one child; began working after completing only a few years of formal education; during World War I, joined the U.S. Army and served in France; after being discharged, hired as a coal-truck driver in New York City and in 1919 joined Local 807 of the International Brotherhood of Teamsters, Chauffeurs, Warehousemen and Helpers of America (IBT); after several unsuccessful campaigns for union office, elected secretary-treasurer of local 807 in 1936; became an IBT general organizer for New

York City, a position that gave him great influence in the New York area; was appointed a vice-president and member of the IBT executive board in 1951 and was elected to that position with the support of James R. Hoffa (q.v.) a year later; acquired a reputation for unswerving honesty during the public scandals concerning IBT officials during the 1950s; became one of the major antagonists of James Hoffa in his attempts to consolidate his power in the IBT during the 1950s and was a cooperative witness before John L. McClellan's Senate Select Committee on Improper Practices in the Labor or Management Field in 1957; opposed Hoffa's election to the IBT presidency in 1957 and defeated for reelection as an IBT vice-president by Hoffa's supporters; dismissed as general IBT organizer for the New York area in 1958, but continued to serve as secretary-treasurer of Local 807; retired from union affairs in 1962; died in New York City, July 2, 1963; Sam Romer, *The International Brotherhood of Teamsters: Its Government and Structure* (1962); Robert D. Leiter, *The Teamsters Union: A Study of Its Economic Impact* (1957); Walter Sheridan, *The Fall and Rise of Jimmy Hoffa* (1972); Ralph and Estelle James, *Hoffa and the Teamsters* (1965); *Fortune* (October, 1957).

HILL, Joe (Hagglund, Joel Emmanuel).   Born in Gavle, Sweden, October 7, 1879; son of Olaf, a railroad conductor, and Margareta Katarina Hagglund; raised in a conservative Lutheran family, all of whom played musical instruments in the home; became an accomplished amateur musician; was forced by his father's death to go to work in a rope factory at age ten; after his mother's death and the consequent disintegration of the family, emigrated to the United States in 1902; drifted around the country for several years working at various unskilled jobs and sporadically acting as a union organizer; in 1910, joined the San Pedro, Calif., local of the Industrial Workers of the World (IWW), soon becoming its secretary; was probably among a handful of Wobblies who in 1911 attempted to capture Baja California in support of Mexican revolutionaries; took name Joe Hill (sometimes Hillstrom) and participated in the San Pedro dockworker's strike of 1912, during which the police arrested and tried to deport him; had no home, like most Western Wobblies, and spent much time at the San Pedro Sailors' Rest Mission; there and while traveling, wrote the sardonic lyrics for the songs that made him famous; beginning in 1911, with "The Preacher and the Slave," his songs appeared in the IWW "Little Red Song Book"; although his lyrics best expressed the alienation of the homeless, migratory workers of the West, his songs dealt also with all major IWW groups, such as railway shopcraft workers, "Casey Jones—the Union

Scab," and immigrant workers in the East, "John Golden and the Lawrence Strike"; in 1914, while living with a Swedish family in Salt Lake City, Utah, indicted for the murder of a grocer and his son; although the circumstantial evidence indicated his guilt, the prosecution was unable to obtain a positive identification of him as the murderer; although there was no specific evidence to prove that either the trial court or the Utah Supreme Court were influenced by Hill's IWW associations, the IWW charged that he had been framed by Utah authorities and the Mormons because he was a Wobbly; Hill's attorneys asked the Utah Pardon Board to commute his death sentence to life, but he only demanded a new trial; despite mass protest demonstrations and appeals on his behalf by the Swedish Minister to the United States and President Woodrow Wilson, Hill was executed by firing squad on November 19, 1915; one of his last requests was that his remains be taken out-of-state, because "I don't want to be found dead in Utah"; at his funeral in Chicago, Ill., attended by thousands of workers, Wobbly orators claimed Hill as a martyr to the IWW cause; almost overnight he became a legendary labor hero; his songs continued to inspire rank-and-file union radicals, and some of them came to be recognized as folklore transcending their IWW origins; Vernon H. Jensen, "The Legend of Joe Hill," *Industrial and Labor Relations Review* (April, 1951); Philip S. Foner, *The Case of Joe Hill* (1965); Gibbs M. Smith, *Joe Hill* (1969).

(D.G.S.)

HILLMAN, Sidney.   Born in Zagare, Russian Lithuania (now part of the Soviet Union), March 23, 1887; son of Schmuel Gilman, a merchant, and Judith (Paikin) Hillman; Jewish; married Bessie Abramowitz in 1916; two children; studied to be a rabbi until age fifteen, then moved to Kovno, Russia, where he worked in a chemical laboratory and studied economics; spent eight months in prison after becoming involved in labor agitation; upon release, fled to England and in 1907 emigrated to the United States, settling in Chicago, Ill.; was a clerk for two years, then hired as a garment cutter and joined the United Garment Workers Union of America (UGW); participated in the 1910 strike against Hart, Schaffner and Marx in Chicago, beginning as a picket and becoming the leader of the strike; became chief clerk of the New York Cloakmakers' Union in 1914; led a group of unionists opposed to the leadership of the UGW and became president of the newly organized Amalgamated Clothing Workers of America (ACWA); was a member of the National Recovery Administration's Labor Advisory Board in 1933 and the National Industrial

Recovery Board in 1935; served on the National Advisory Board of the National Youth Administration and the Textile Committee of the Fair Labor Standards Board; was one of the original leaders of the Congress of Industrial Organizations (CIO) and was elected first vice-president in 1937; served as chairman of the Textile Workers Organizing Committee; associated during World War II with the National Defense Advisory Committee in 1940, the Office of Production Management in 1941, and the War Production Board in 1942; served as labor advisor to President Franklin D. Roosevelt in 1943; appointed chairman of the CIO's Political Action Committee in 1943; had an essentially conservative trade union philosophy and was a strong advocate of labor-management cooperation; associated with the American Labor party and the Democratic party; died at his summer home in Point Lookout, Long Island, N.Y., July 10, 1946; Matthew Josephson, *Sidney Hillman, Statesman of American Labor* (1952); George Soule, *Sidney Hillman—Labor Statesman* (1948); Jean Gould, *Sidney Hillman, Great American* (1952); Melech Epstein, *Profiles of Eleven* (1965), and *Jewish Labor in the U.S.A., 1914-1952* (2 vols., 1953).

HILLQUIT, Morris.   Born in Riga, Russian Latvia (now part of the Soviet Union), August 1, 1869; son of Benjamin, a school teacher, and Rebecca (Levene) Hillkowitz; Jewish; married Vera Levene on December 31, 1893; two children; attended the elementary and secondary schools of Russia and the United States, and was graduated from the New York Law School with an LLB degree in 1893; shortly after emigrating to the United States in 1886, began working in a New York City shirt factory; joined the Socialist Labor party (SLP) in 1890 and shortly thereafter joined the staff of the *Arbeiter Zeitung*, a Yiddish-language newspaper; broke with SLP leader Daniel DeLeon (q.v.) over ideological and tactical questions in 1899 and became the leader of the "Rochester" faction of the SLP, which fused with the Social Democratic party in 1901 to form the Socialist party of America; was a member of the United Hebrew Trades and was involved in organizing garment workers in New York City during the 1890s; became a member of the International Socialist Bureau in 1904 and the following year was appointed a trustee of the Rand School of Social Science; was a member of the negotiating committee that secured a settlement in the 1910 cloak-makers' strike and led to the "Protocol of Peace", which provided for conciliation machinery in labor disputes in the garment industry; became the International Ladies' Garment Workers' Union (ILGWU) general counsel in 1913, serving until 1933; involved in several significant legal cases involving left-wing activities, including the defense of Morris Sigman (q.v.) and other ILGWU leaders charged with murder in connection with the 1910 garment strike, and efforts to regain the seats of five Socialist assemblymen expelled from the New York state legislature in 1920; was an opponent of American involvement in World War I and founded the American Conference for Democracy and Terms of Peace in 1917; served as a legal advisor to the Soviet Government Bureau in the United States, 1918-1919; supported the Progressive party candidacy of Robert M. LaFollette in 1924; was one of the leaders of the Socialist party, serving as a national committeeman from New York, 1901-1906, chairman of the national committee, 1913-1933, a member of the national executive committee, 1907-1912, 1916-1933, and national chairman in 1921; served as an American delegate to several international Socialist congresses from 1904 to 1931; authored *History of Socialism in the United States* (1903), *From Marx to Lenin* (1921), *Loose Leaves From a Busy Life* (1934), and other books and pamphlets; died in New York City, October 7, 1933; David A. Shannon, *The Socialist Party of America* (1955); James Weinstein, *The Decline of Socialism in America, 1912-1925* (1967); Julius H. Cohen, *They Builded Better than They Knew* (1946); *National Cyclopaedia of American Biography* (Vol. XLIV); Melech Epstein, *Profiles of Eleven* (1965), and *Jewish Labor in the U.S.A., 1914-1952* (2 vols., 1953); Aaron Antonovsky, trans., *The Early Jewish Labor Movement in the United States* (1961).

HINCHCLIFFE, John.   Born in Bradford, Yorkshire, England, in 1822; served an apprenticeship as a tailor and eventually became the proprietor of a small tailor shop; was an active participant in the Chartist movement before emigrating to the United States in 1847; worked for short periods as a tailor in New York City, Philadelphia, Pa., and St. Louis, Mo.; settled in Bellville, Ill. and admitted to the bar, quickly becoming prominent as editor of two Democratic newspapers; not a miner, but became one of the most prominent figures in the early efforts to organize miners; presided over the founding convention of the American Miners' Association in 1860 and became the editor of the Association's journal, the *Weekly Miner*, in 1863; was an unsuccessful candidate for Congress on the Democratic ticket in 1862; lost the editorship of the *Weekly Miner* in 1865 as a result of a factional conflict that ultimately split the national union; represented the Railroad Men's Protective Union, the Printers' Union, the Machinery Molders' Union of St. Louis and the Miners' Lodge of Illinois at the Baltimore, Md., Labor Congress of 1866 that resulted in the organization of the National Labor Union (NLU); was appointed spokesman of the NLU committee assigned to petition President Andrew Johnson for the eight-hour day; served as treasurer of the NLU, then elected a delegate to the Illinois Constitutional Convention in 1870, and there was able to secure a clause in the new constitution requiring the Illinois state legislature to enact a mine-safety code; elected to the Illinois state senate in 1872, and led the efforts there to enact mine-safety legislation; nominally a Democrat, but was a fervent anti-monopolist and very susceptible to third-party movements; died in St. Louis, Mo., in 1878; David Montgomery, *Beyond Equality: Labor and the Radical Republicans, 1862-1872* (1967); John R. Commons, *et al.*, *History of Labour in the United States*, Vol. II (1918); George E. McNeill, *The Labor Movement: The Problem of To-Day* (1887); Ray Boston, *British Chartists in America, 1839-1900* (1971); Clifton K. Yearley, Jr., *Britons in American Labor: A History of the Influence of the United Kingdom Immigrants on American Labor, 1820-1914* (1957).

HOCHMAN, Julius. Born in Bessarabia, January 12, 1892; son of Samuel, a tailor, and Frieda Hochman; Jewish; married Celia Morris on October 1, 1916; one child; did not receive any formal education before being apprenticed to a tailor at age eleven; emigrated with his family to the United States in 1907 and gained employment in the New York garment industry; earned his high school diploma by attending evening school and taking courses at the Rand School of Social Science while employed in the garment industry; joined Shirtmakers' Local 23 of the International Ladies' Garment Workers' Union (ILGWU) in 1910 and in 1913 transferred his membership to Waistmakers' Local 25; became assistant organizer of Local 25 in 1916; during the next several years, served as an ILGWU organizer in Chicago, Ill., Boston, Mass., Toronto and Montreal, Canada; became department manager for the Dressmakers' Union in 1921 and the following year was named general manager of the New York Dress Joint Board; resigned in 1923 because of his opposition to the amalgamation of the dressmakers' and cloakmakers' joint boards; attended Brookwood Labor College, 1923-1924; elected an ILGWU vice-president in 1925; became manager of the Joint Board of Waist and Dressmakers Unions in 1929; served as chairman of the ILGWU educational committee, as a vice-president of the Jewish Labor Committee and the New York Dress Institute, and as a director of the Organization for Rehabilitation Through Training; after leading a dressmakers' strike in 1958, left the Dress Joint Board and became the director of the ILGWU label department; retired from union affairs in 1962; was a member of the Liberal party of New York; authored *Why This Strike* (1936), *Industry Planning Through Collective Bargaining* (1941), and *The Retirement Myth* (1950); died in New York

City, March 17, 1970; Benjamin Stolberg, *Tailor's Progress: The Story of a Famous Union and the Men Who Made It* (1944); Louis Levine, *The Women's Garment Workers: A History of the International Ladies' Garment Workers' Union* (1924); "Remarkable Union—and Union Leader," *Readers Digest* (April, 1946); Jesse T. Carpenter, *Competition and Collective Bargaining in the Needle Trades, 1910-1967* (1972).

HOFFA, James Riddle.   Born in Brazil, Ind., February 14, 1913; son of John Cleveland, a coal driller, and Viola (Riddle) Hoffa; reared in the Christian Church; married Josephine Poszywak on September 25, 1936; two children; completed the ninth grade in the public schools of Detroit, Mich., then took a full-time job as a department store stockboy; became a freight handler at a Kroger Grocery warehouse in 1930; along with four co-workers, organized American Federation of Labor Federal Labor Union 19341 in 1931; joined the International Brotherhood of Teamsters, Chauffeurs, Warehousemen and Helpers of America (IBT) in 1934 and took the membership of Federal Local 19341 into IBT Local 299; during the same year, became a full-time organizer for IBT Joint Council 43; became business agent and in 1937 elected president of Local 299; along with Farrel Dobbs (q.v.), a Trotskyist teamster from Minneapolis, organized the Central States Drivers Council in 1937; became, successively, chairman and vice-president of the Central States Drivers Council, president of the Michigan Conference of Teamsters, examiner of IBT books, and in 1940, president of Teamsters Joint Council 43, Detroit, serving until 1946; elected an IBT vice-president in 1952 and president of the Central Conference of Teamsters in 1953; charged with attempting to bribe a U. S. Senate committee investigator in 1957, but acquitted; elected international president of the IBT in 1957; accelerated as president a centralization process within the IBT that permitted him to negotiate and sign the first national contract in the trucking industry in 1964; convicted, on separate charges, of jury tampering, fraud, and conspiracy in the disposition of union benefit funds in 1964; after exhausting appeals, entered Lewisburg, Pa., Federal Penitentiary in 1967 to begin serving a 13-year prison term; retired his IBT positions in 1971 and was named president emeritus and awarded $1,700,000 in lieu of a pension; sentence commuted by President Richard M. Nixon in 1971 with the provision that he refrain from participating in union affairs until 1980; usually supports Republican candidates; authored *The Trial of Jimmy Hoffa* (1970); Walter Sheridan, *The Fall and Rise of Jimmy Hoffa* (1972); Ralph and Estelle James, *Hoffa and the*

Teamsters (1965); Robert D. Leiter, *The Teamsters Union: A Study of Its Economic Impact* (1957); *Current Biography* (1972).

HOFFMANN, Sal B. Born in Aversa, Italy, April 5, 1899; son of Leopoldo, an upholsterer, and Anna (Tornicaso) Hoffmann; Roman Catholic; married Frances Zeichner on June 2, 1920; three children; graduated from high school, then employed by the Bell Telephone Company and the Western Electric Company, 1917-1918; gained employment as an upholsterer and joined Philadelphia, Pa., Wholesale Uphosterers' Local 77 of the Upholsterers' International Union of North America (UIU) in 1919; served Local 77 as recording secretary and as an executive board member, 1920-1924, and business agent and business manager, 1924-1937; while serving as an UIU general organizer, 1929-1931, organized UIU Local 20 in Birmingham, Ala., in 1930; served as executive secretary of the Philadelphia Regional District Council, UIU, which he had been instrumental in founding, 1935-1937; elected international president of the UIU in 1937, a position he still held in 1974; during World War II, was a hearing officer for the National War Labor Board and a labor member of the War Production Board's advisory committee for the furniture industry; served on several American Federation of Labor (AFL) and AFL-Congress of Industrial Organizations' committees; was a vice-chairman of the Workers Defense League and a member of the national board of directors of Americans for Democratic Action; was a delegate to the White House Conference on Aging in 1961, chairman of the board of trustees of the Health and Welfare Fund, 1944-1971, and chairman of the board of governors of the National Pension Plan, 1953-1971; a Democrat; authored two pamphlets, *Work of a Business Agent* (1942), and *Trade Unions Under War Conditions* (1943); *Who's Who in America, 1972-1973; Who's Who in Labor* (1946).

HOLDERMAN, Carl. Born in Hornell, N.Y., January 15, 1894; son of Matthias, a railroad worker, and Anna Marie Holderman; Episcopalian; married Beatrice Pauline on September 17, 1943; four children; completed two years of high school, then left school and took employment as a messenger and shop employee of the Erie Railroad; joined the American Federation of Hosiery Workers (AFHW) in 1918 after securing employment in the textile industry; became during subsequent years a national organizer and vice-president of the AFHW; was named by Sidney Hillman (q.v.) as a regional director of the Textile Workers Organizing Committee in 1937 and shortly thereafter became a vice-president of the Textile Workers Union of America; was one of the organizers of the Joint Board (of textile unions) for New Jersey in 1937, and served as its manager until 1940, when the Joint Board was divided into three regional groups; became the manager of the North Jersey Joint Board in 1940; was one of the organizers of the New Jersey Industrial Union Council, Congress of Industrial Organizations, and served as its treasurer, 1939-1940, secretary-treasurer, 1940-1945, director of the political action committee, 1944-1954, and, between 1945-1954, its president; served during World War II as a regional member of the Manpower Mobilization Committee, Alien Enemy Board, and War Labor Board; was appointed New Jersey Commissioner of Labor and Industry in 1954; died in Newark, N.J., April 20, 1959; Leo Troy, *Organized Labor in New Jersey* (1965); *Who's Who in Labor* (1946).

HOLLANDER, Louis.   Born in Wadowice, Russian Poland, February 5, 1893; son of Hyman and Hannah Hollander; Jewish; married Mollie Bernstein on April 22, 1922; emigrated to the United States in 1903, settling in New York City; attended grammar school, then began working in a tailor shop in 1906 at age thirteen; later completed high school by taking evening courses; joined the United Garment Workers of America in 1908 and became a union organizer in 1912; was one of the founders of the Amalgamated Clothing Workers of America (ACWA) in 1914; held a variety of offices in the ACWA prior to beginning a long term of service as manager of the New York Joint Board, ACWA, in 1932; elected an ACWA vice-president in 1934; elected a city councilman from Brooklyn in 1937 and served a two year term; was the chairman of the Kings County American Labor party, 1936-1942; elected president of the New York State Congress of Industrial Organizations' (CIO) Industrial Union Council in 1943 and served until the New York American Federation of Labor (AFL)-CIO merger in 1958; during World War II was a member of the New York area War Manpower Commission and the New York State War Council; after the AFL-CIO merger in New York, became the chairman of the executive council of the New York State AFL-CIO; elected secretary-treasurer of the New York State AFL-CIO in 1962; was a co-chairman of the Jewish Labor Committee, a member of the advisory council of the New York State School of Industrial Relations, and a trustee of Cornell University; usually supported Democratic candidates; Matthew Josephson, *Sidney Hillman, Statesman of American Labor* (1952); Harry A. Cobrin, *The Men's Clothing Industry: Colonial Through Modern Times* (1970); *Who's Who in Labor* (1946).

HORN, Roy.   Born in Warsaw, Ill., March 10, 1872; son of John Henry, a carriage maker, and Leah Josephine (Shaw) Horn; Protestant; married; three children; completed grammer school, then went to work at age fourteen; joined the International Brotherhood of Blacksmiths, Drop Forgers and Helpers of America (IBBDFH) in 1901; by 1907, was business agent for the IBBDFH's St. Louis District Council 31; two years later, became general vice-president of the IBBDFH; was a leader of the movement to federate the railway shop crafts for joint bargaining, which was vigorously resisted by some railroads; in 1912, was a delegate to the founding meeting of the Federation of Federations, which shortly thereafter became the railway employees' department of the American Federation of Labor (AFL); subsequently helped organize shop craftworkers in various parts of the country; in 1926, elected international president of the IBBDFH, thereby becoming a member of the recently established Railway Labor Executives' Association, which functioned as a policy-making body for legislative matters affecting railroad workers; during the controversy over the Committee for Industrial Organizations' (CIO) industrial organizing campaigns, was a spokesman for the craft unionists and a staunch defender of their jurisdictions; at the 1936 AFL convention, spoke in favor of the suspension of the CIO and denied its contention that mass production workers could only be organized along industrial lines; by the 1940s, was second vice-president of the railway employees' department and first vice-president of the metal trades department of the AFL; was an independent in politics; widely respected among AFL leaders and employers; retired in 1947; died in St. Louis, Mo., November 22, 1947; Solon DeLeon, ed., *The American Labor Who's Who* (1925); *Who's Who in Labor* (1946); Walter Galenson, *The CIO Challenge to the AFL: A History of the American Labor Movement* (1960); *The American Federationist* (December, 1947).

(D.G.S.)

HOWARD, Charles Perry.   Born in Harvel, Ill., September 14, 1879; son of Lewis Pontius, a lawyer, and Mary M. (Williamson) Howard; married Margaret McPhail; no children; completed grammar school at age thirteen, then employed as a railroad worker, 1897-1899, and a miner, 1900-1903, prior to entering the printing trade; joined the Tacoma, Wash., local of the International Typographical Union (ITU) in 1907; transferred his membership to the Multnomah Typographical Union in Portland, Ore., and became its president in 1914; served as president of the Portland Central Labor Council, 1916-1918; was commissioner of conciliation in the

U. S. Department of Labor, 1918-1919; served as an ITU delegate to the American Federation of Labor (AFL), 1920-1922; edited the Railway Maintenance of Way Employees' Journal, 1919-1922; joined the Progressive party faction of the ITU's two-party system and was elected vice-president on that ticket in 1922; became ITU president when the incumbent, John McParland, died in 1923, but was defeated in the elections of 1924; elected ITU president in 1926 and served in that capacity for the remainder of his life, although defeated in the elections of 1938; was a proponent of industrial unionism and authored and sponsored two plans for industrial organization at AFL conventions in 1933 and 1934; joined other advocates of industrial unionism on the Committee for Industrial Organization (CIO) and became its secretary; although the ITU never affiliated with the CIO, it left the AFL after refusing to pay a special tax levied to fight the rival CIO; defeated for reelection in 1938, primarily because of his opposition to demands for additional local autonomy to deal with the problems of the depression; was a Republican; died in Colorado Springs, Colo., July 21, 1938; Seymour M. Lipset, *et al.*, *Union Democracy: The Internal Politics of the International Typographical Union* (1956); Walter Galenson, *The CIO Challenge to the AFL: A History of the American Labor Movement, 1935-1941* (1960); *Dictionary of American Biography* (Supplement II).

HOWAT, Alexander.   Born in Glasgow, Scotland, in 1876; married; emigrated to the United States; settled in Braidwood, Ill., growing up there with John Mitchell (q.v.), who admired the bellicose and impetuous youth; moved to Pittsburgh, Kan., and joined the United Mine Workers of America (UMWA); served as president of District 14, UMWA, Kansas, 1906-1921; was a member of the Socialist party, and in 1914, the District 14 convention called for the establishment of a Socialist government "as the strong right arm of labor"; supported the National Farmer-Labor party in 1920; in the summer of 1921, organized Kansas miners' support for a Republican state administration to repeal the anti-strike legislation; provided a militant, strike-prone leadership that caused Kansans to complain that local "miners did far more picketing than mining"; sporadically defied both national union officials and Kansas state law; led two brief strikes during World War I and the immediate postwar period, which led the Kansas legislature to pass the 1920 Kansas Industrial Relations Act, which empowered a three-man Industrial Court to decide all labor disputes in industries affected with a public interest and to abolish strikes, picketing, and boycotts and the deduction of union dues; the 1920 and 1921 American Federation of Labor conventions and the 1920 District 14 convention encouraged defiance of the law, but when he led a 1921 strike and was arrested for refusing to testify before the Industrial Court, President John L. Lewis (q.v.) revoked the charters of District 14 and 81 local unions, half the district's locals, and appointed a provisional president to replace Howat; as a result, became a hero and martyr to Kansas miners, the Kansas State Federation of Labor, and many city central unions; after a district leadership purge, the national UMWA convention restored the district's autonomy and toward the close of the 1920s, he was reelected president; along with Robert Harlin, District 10, Washington, opposed the incumbents for reelection to the UMWA presidency and vice-presidency; participated in the Communist-tinged Progressive International Committee of Miners in 1923; along with his Kansas followers, supported John Brophy's (q.v.) 1926 "Save the Union" campaign for the union presidency and stumped the anthracite region for the ticket; while again serving as District 14 president in 1930, elected president of the Reorganized United Mine Workers and campaigned for support in Missouri; became increasingly unstable and suffered from alcoholism, and turned over most of his duties to Vice-President Adolph Germer (q.v.); refused to appear before the international executive board and was expelled from the union after Lewis revoked the District 14 charter and appointed a provisional president; his union career destroyed, worked from 1930 to 1945 at various jobs including a state border guard, editor of a Kansas labor paper, and a Pittsburgh, Kan., city employee; died in Pittsburgh, Kan., December 10, 1945; *United Mine Workers Journal*, January 1, 1946; *The New York Times*, December 11, 1945; Irving Bernstein, *The Lean Years: A History of the American Worker, 1920-1933* (1960); Marc Karson, "Trade Unions in Kansas" in *Kansas: The First Century*, edited by John D. Bright (1956); Selig Perlman and Philip Taft, *History of Labour in the United States, 1896-1932*, Vol. IV (1935); John H. M. Laslett, *Labor and the Left: A Study of Socialism and Radical Influences in the American Labor Movement, 1881-1924* (1970).

(J.H.)

HUBER, William (fl. 1900-1912). A leader of the United Brotherhood of Carpenters and Joiners (UBC) in New York City; elected general president of the UBC in 1900; was one of the principal figures in the coterie of UBC leaders who sought to depose the union's founder and executive leader, Peter J. McGuire (q.v.); was assigned by the general executive board in 1901 to assist McGuire in the administration of his duties as general secretary-treasurer, but found it impossible to work with the "brooding and recalcitrant McGuire"; presented the charges of corruption that led to McGuire's dismissal from the UBC; allied with Frank Duffy (q.v.) and using the cadre of paid organizers that he had appointed, was able to build a powerful political machine within the UBC; his power was limited by the institutional structure of the Brotherhood and by the local autonomy that had long existed within the union's structure; while president, was able to expand gradually the jurisdictional claims of the UBC to include "all that's made of wood" and to have that jurisdiction recognized by the American Federation of Labor (AFL); led the UBC campaign against the American Wood Workers Union and drew up the merger proposal that was accepted in 1912; organized the UBC-dominated Structural Building Trades Alliance in 1902, a forerunner of the AFL building trades department; retired from the UBC presidency in 1912 after nearly a decade of internecine conflicts with various members of the general executive board; while president, was a severe critic of racial discrimination within the UBC; also created the constitutional framework that converted the UBC from a confederation to a federation; the resulting centralization of power in the hands on the general officers of the UBC was used by William Hutcheson (q.v.) to establish near total control of the Brotherhood; Robert A. Christie, *Empire in Wood: A History of the Carpenters Union* (1956); Philip Taft, *The A. F. of L. in the Time of Gompers* (1957).

HUDDELL, Arthur McIntire.   Born in Danvers, Mass., June 15, 1869; son of John, a shoemaker, and Caroline (McIntire) Huddell; Protestant; married Eliza Chase Dow on September 26, 1888; five children; completed grammar school in Salem, Mass., then went to work at age thirteen; worked as a coal-hoisting engineer during 1822-1896, then employed in the building trades; joined Boston, Mass., Local 4 of the International Union of Steam and Operating Engineers (IUSOE) (Now the International Union of Operating Engineers) in 1898; elected president of Local 4 in 1902 and business agent in 1904; was an IUSOE vice-president during 1905-1910, and in 1910 ran unsuccessfully for the union presidency; served as an IUSOE organizer, 1907-1908; elected first vice-president of the IUSOE in 1916 and became international president in 1921 after the death of the incumbent, Milton Snellings; was a member of the Massachusetts Civil Service Commission, 1919-1922; was a strong advocate of international collective bargaining agreements negotiated directly between interstate businesses and international union officers; was the victim of an unsuccessful assassination attempt in Washington, D. C., in 1931; died five days later from the trauma of the blow while still hospitalized in Washington, D.C., on June 1, 1931; Garth L. Mangum, *The Operating Engineers, Fifty Years of Progress, 1896-1946* (1946); Solon DeLeon, ed., *The American Labor Who's Who* (1925).

HUERTA, Dolores.   Born in New Mexico; spent most of her early life in Stockton, Calif.; married; seven children; Roman Catholic; in the early 1950s, met Fred Ross of the Community Service Organization (CSO) in Stockton and assisted him in setting up CSO chapters; met Cesar Chavez (q.v.) in 1955 while working for the CSO and eventually became one of his most dedicated and effective associates in organizing farm workers; became a CSO lobbyist in 1962; later that year quit the CSO and moved to Delano, Calif., to assist Chavez in organizing farm workers for the Farm Workers' Association; helped organize migrant workers in Stockton and Modesto, Calif., in 1964; joined the United Farm Workers' Organizing Committee (UFWOC) in 1964; helped the UFWOC negotiate a contract with the Delano grape growers in July, 1970; participated in the 1970 lettuce boycott against Bud Antle Co. and Dow Chemical Co.; helped the United Farm Workers' Union (UFW) negotiate a contract with the lettuce growers in California; in 1970 and again in 1973, elected a vice-president of the UFW; Mark Day, *Forty Acres: Cesar Chavez and the Farm Workers* (1971); Joan London and Henry Anderson, *So Shall Ye Reap: The Story of Cesar Chavez and the Farm Workers Movement* (1970).

(M.T.)

HUGHES, Roy Orlo.   Born in Portland, N.D., September 24, 1887; son of Elijah, a blacksmith, and Maria Madeline (Olson) Hughes; Presbyterian; married Mary Ellen Penrod on November 26, 1912; three children; left school during his senior year at Mora High School, Mora, Minn., and hired as a machinist's helper on the Great Northern Railway in 1906; raised purebred Guernsey dairy cattle while continuing employment as a railroad worker, 1907-1928; joined the Northern Pacific Railroad as a brakeman in 1912, eventually becoming a conductor; joined Duluth, Minn., Division 336 of the Order of Railway Conductors (ORC) in 1916, and served successively as the Division's legislative chairman, adjustment chairman, local chairman, and as a member of the general committee for the Northern Pacific; took employment as a conductor on the Chicago, Milwaukee, St. Paul and Pacific in 1925; gave up farming venture when transferred from Duluth to St. Paul, Minn., in 1928; elected secretary of the general committee Milwaukee Railroad in 1929 and three years later was named general chairman of the committee of adjustment elected a vice-president and appointed grand trustee of the ORC in 1940; elected to the presidency of the ORC in 1950; acquired a reputation during the wage controversies of the 1940s and 1950s as a tough and effective bargainer; was an independent in politics; retired in 1958; *Current Biography* (1950); *Who's Who in Labor* (1946); *Labor,* June 14, 1958.

HUTCHESON, Maurice Albert.   Born in Saginaw County, Mich., May 7, 1897; son of William L., a union president, and Bessie Mae (King) Hutcheson; Methodist; married Ethel Hyatt on October 23, 1926; received a grammar school education in the public schools of Michigan; became a carpenter's apprentice in 1914 and joined the United Brotherhood of Carpenters and Joiners of America (UBC); served as a carpenter's mate in the U. S. Navy during World War I; worked as a journeyman carpenter, 1918-1928; appointed a UBC auditor in 1928, serving in that capacity until 1938; elected first general vice-president of the UBC in 1938; after the resignation of his father, William L. (q.v.), in 1952, became general president of the UBC; shortly after assuming the presidency of the UBC, took the Carpenters out of the American Federation of Labor (AFL) because displeased with the no-raiding agreement negotiated with the Congress of Industrial Organizations (CIO), but reaffiliated three weeks later; became an AFL vice-president and executive council member in 1953 and retained that position after the AFL-CIO merger in 1955; cited for contempt of Congress for refusing to answer questions before the McClellan Special Senate Committee in 1957, but was later pardoned by President Lyndon B. Johnson; convicted of bribing an Indiana state official to obtain advance information on highway routes in 1960 and sentenced to two-to-fourteen years in prison, but the conviction was overturned on appeal; as president of UBC, initiated multi-union agreements for union-label factory-built housing and restructured the UBC apprenticeship program in response to minority-group pressures; a Republican; retired union positions in 1972; Maxwell C. Raddock, *Portrait of an American Labor Leader: William L. Hutcheson* (1955); Robert A. Christie, *Empire in Wood: A History of the Carpenters' Union* (1956); Joseph C. Goulden, *Meany* (1972).

HUTCHESON, William Levi.   Born in Saginaw County, Mich., February 7, l874; son of David Oliver, a Scottish immigrant, farmer, and ship carpenter, and Elizabeth (Culver) Hutcheson; Methodist; married Bessie May King on October 10, 1893; four children, apprenticed to his father as a carpenter in 1890; joined the United Brotherhood of Carpenters and Joiners of America (UBC) in 1902; four years later, became business agent for his local union; elected second vice-president of the UBC in 1913 and became president two years later; served during World War I on the War Labor Conference Committee appointed by President Woodrow Wilson to seek a way of eliminating labor-management conflicts during the war and was appointed to the War Labor Board that resulted from the committee's recommendations; elected to the American Federation of Labor (AFL) executive council in 1935 as tenth vice-president; was an AFL delegate to the International Labor Organization's conference in Chile in 1935; was an AFL fraternal delegate to the British Trades Union Congress in 1919 and 1926; resigned from the AFL executive council in 1936 over objections to the council's endorsement of New Deal legislation; returned to the executive council in 1940 and named first vice-president; was an opponent of the industrial unionism advocated by the Congress of Industrial Organizations, but favored craft-industrial unionism and was constantly embroiled in jurisdictional disputes by aggressively seeking to assume jurisdiction over any union member who had any connection with the wood-working industry; under his leadership, the UBC never conducted intensive organizing drives but instead preferred to let others organize the unorganized and then claim jurisdiction; resulting from these tactics, the membership of the UBC grew substantially during his incumbency; expanded and consolidated his near dictatorial control over a union that was increasingly plagued by unethical and corrupt activities; was a Republican and was placed in charge of the labor division of the national Republican party in 1932 and 1936; retired in December, 1951, and was succeeded as UBC president by his son, Maurice (q.v.); died in Indianapolis, Ind., October 20, 1953; Maxwell C. Raddock, *Portrait of an American Labor Leader: William L. Hutcheson* (1955); Robert A. Christie, *Empire in Wood: A History of the Carpenters' Union* (1956); Morris A. Horowitz, *The Structure and Government of the Carpenters' Union* (1962); Charles A. Madison, *American Labor Leaders: Personalities and Forces in the Labor Movement* (1962); *National Cyclopaedia of American Biography* (1946).

HYMAN, Louis. Born in Witebask, Russia, June 17, 1884; son of Max, a storekeeper, and Ida (Ades) Hyman; Jewish; married Bella Press on May 20, 1925; one child; attended Hebrew schools in Russia and night schools in Great Britain and the United States; emigrated to Manchester, England, in 1903 and began work in a men's clothing factory; joined the British Socialist movement and became an influential figure in the Manchester trade-union movement; emigrated to the United States in 1911 and a short time later joined Cloak and Suit Tailors Local 9 of the International Ladies' Garment

Workers' Union (ILGWU); served as business agent, an executive board member, and president of Local 9; appointed a director of the ILGWU Union Health Centre in 1919; elected to the general executive board of the New York Joint Board in 1925; shortly thereafter, suspended, along with several other left-wing leaders, by ILGWU international officers; became chairman of the rival Joint Action Committee and led the unsuccessful garment strike of 1925-1926; became president of the Communist-controlled Needle Trades Workers Industrial Union; broke with the Communists after the Nazi-Soviet pact of 1939 and was readmitted to the ILGWU; elected manager of ILGWU Local 9 in 1942; became an ILGWU vice-president in 1949; died in New York City, October 12, 1963; Benjamin Stolberg, *Tailor's Progress: The Story of a Famous Union and the Men Who Made It* (1944); Harry Haskel, *A Leader of the Garment Workers: The Biography of Isidore Nagler* (1950); Louis Levine, *The Women's Garment Workers: A History of the International Ladies' Garment Workers' Union* (1924); *ILGWU Report and Proceedings* (1965).

IGLESIAS, Santiago.   Born in La Coruña, Spain, February 22, 1872; son of Manuel, a carpenter, and Joseta Pantin; Roman Catholic; married Justa Bocanegra in 1902; 11 children; left school at age twelve after the death of his father and was apprenticed to a carpenter; led a walkout of workers in 1884 protesting their employers' refusal to allow them to attend a Sunday protest meeting against sales taxes, then joined the Spanish section of the Socialist party; emigrated to Cuba in 1887 and, after gaining employment in a furniture factory, began organizing workers against the 12-hour day; after the outbreak of the Cuban war of independence in 1895, the workers' movement with which he was associated was suppressed and the following year he fled to Puerto Rico; served a prison sentence as a labor agitator, but avoided deportation to Spain; became a guide and interpreter to Gen. John R. Brooke, who was in charge of the U. S. occupation of Puerto Rico; presided over the founding convention of the Puerto Rican Federation of Labor on October 20, 1898; convicted of conspiracy in 1900 and sentenced to four years in prison, but due to the intercession of American Federation of Labor (AFL) president Samuel Gompers (q.v.), who he had met a year earlier, served only seven months; along with Gompers, was granted an interview with President Theodore Roosevelt in 1902 and as a result the U. S. administration in Puerto Rico was liberalized somewhat; served during 1900-1935 as president of the AFL-affiliated Federacion Libre de Trabajadores de Puerto Rico and was an AFL organizer; organized the Puerto Rican Socialist party in 1915 and elected to the Puerto Rican senate two years later, serving until 1933, served as secretary of the Pan-American Federation of Labor, 1925-1939; elected the Puerto Rican representative to the United States Congress in 1933 and served until his death; was an advocate of statehood for Puerto Rico and he was shot and superficially wounded by a Puerto Rican nationalist in 1936; edited *Ensayo Obrero*, 1897-1899, *Porvenir Social*, 1899-1900, *Union Obrera*, 1903-1906, and *Justicia*, 1914-1925; authored *Quienes Somos* (1910), *¿Gobierno Proprio Para Quien?* (1914), *Luchas Emancipadoras* (1929); died in Washington, D. C., December 5, 1939; Lewis Lorwin, *Labor and Internationalism* (1929); Rafael Alonso Torres, *Cuarenta Anos de Lucha Proletaria* (1939); *Dictionary of American Biography* (Supplement II); William G. Whittaker, "The Santiago Iglesias Case, 1901-1902: Origins of American Trade Union Involvements in Puerto Rico," *The Americas* (April, 1968).

IRONS, Martin.   Born in Dundee, Scotland, March 1, 1833; the son of moderately prosperous Scottish parents; married Mary Brown, from whom he was separated after she bore him seven children; emigrated to the United States in 1847; became a machinist's apprentice shortly after arriving in New York City; moved to Carrollton, La.; worked there as a machinist for several years, then opened an independent grocery, but soon was forced to sell out; moved to Lexington, Ky., and there led a successful strike of machinists for an eight-hour day; then lived in several Missouri cities including Kansas City, where he again unsuccessfully attempted to set up a business; settled in Sedalia, Mo., in 1885 and resumed work as a machinist; was one of the founders and elected master workman of Local Assembly 3476 of the Noble Order of the Knights of Labor (K of L) organized in Sedalia in 1885; was one of the founders of District Assembly 101 that brought together local assemblies of Missouri Pacific Railroad workers; led the historic (but unsuccessful) strike against the Jay Gould-controlled Missouri Pacific in 1886; after the strike, business and government leaders identified him as its sole perpetrator and the leaders of the K of L branded him as the sole cause of its failure; spent the last 15 years of his life living in poverty, blacklisted and unable to practice his trade, hounded by insensitive and myopic defenders of the established order, and slandered by an official Congressional investigating committee; died in Bruceville, Tex., November 17, 1900; Ruth A. Allen, *The Great Southwest Strike* (1942); Gerald N. Grob, *Workers and Utopia: A Study of Ideological*

Conflict in the American Labor Movement, 1865-1900 (1961); Norman J. Ware, *The Labor Movement in the United States, 1860-1895* (1929).

JARRETT, John.   Born in Elbow Vale, Monmouthshire, England, January 27, 1843; son of Welsh parents; Protestant; married Margaret Price in 1869; two children; orphaned at age twelve and became an iron puddler; emigrated to eastern Pennsylvania in 1862 and joined the union of his trade, the Sons of Vulcan; returned to England, ca. 1868, became active in the Amalgamated Ironworkers Association, and assimilated the cautious trade unionism of its founder, John Kane; emigrated to Pennsylvania again in 1872 and took a job at the Westerman Iron Works in Sharon; favored amalgamated unionism and participated, while serving as a vice-president of the Sons of Vulcan, in the formation of the Amalgamated Association of Iron and Steel Workers (AA) (Later the Amalgamated Association of Iron, Steel, and Tin Workers of America.) in 1875-1876; served as a trustee, then elected president of AA in 1880; chaired the 1881 convention of the Federation of Organized Trades and Labor Union, precursor of the American Federation of Labor, but withdrew the AA when the Federation refused to endorse a high tariff; under his leadership, the AA became one of the foremost American unions, but its membership was largely confined to the iron mills of Allegheny County and the Ohio Valley; keenly aware of this, sought to create a disciplined rank-and-file and strongly urged circumspect use of the strike; in order to sustain AA wage scales, which were based on iron and steel prices, advocated protective tariffs and elimination of price competition through industrial consolidation; combined along with this job-conscious approach a broad concern about workers generally, the admission of blacks into AA, and equal pay for women; displayed however the typical trade unionists' fear of "new" immigrant labor; discouraged by internal bickering and opposed to the AA strikes of 1882, resigned in 1883; unsuccessfully sought appointment as head of the new U.S. Bureau of Labor Statistics in 1884; continued to support the labor movement during the next two decades and at same time devoted energy to establishing the tin-plate industry; was a lobbyist for the Tin Plate Association and a consistent supporter of the Republican party; successfully lobbied Congress to include high duties on Welsh plate in the McKinley Tariff of 1890; was American consul in Birmingham, England, 1889-1892, and there studied the Welsh tin-plate industry; was an executive of the tin plate and sheet steel trade association, 1892-1900; subsequently, was in business in Pittsburgh; authored Chapter XI—"The Story of the Iron Workers"—in George E. McNeill, ed., *The Labor Movement: The Problem of*

To-Day (1887); see also his extensive testimony in U.S. Senate Committee on Education and Labor, *Report upon the Relations of Labor and Capital*, Vol. I, *Testimony*, 48th Congress (1885); died in Pittsburgh, Pa., December 17, 1918; The American Historical Society, *History of Pittsburgh and Environs: Biographical* (1922); John Fitch, *The Steel Workers* (1911).

(D.G.S.)

JENNINGS, Paul Joseph.   Born in Brooklyn, N.Y., March 19, 1918; married; two children; graduated from high school, then attended the Radio Corporation of America Institute and the Crown Heights Labor School; hired by the Brooklyn Edison Company and in 1938 was elected steward of the Independent Utility Workers; became an electronics technician for the Sperry-Rand Corporation in 1939; helped organize a United Electrical and Radio Workers of America (UE) local in the plant where he was employed and served at various times as shop steward, grievance chairman, shop chairman, and acting president of the local; served with the U.S. Navy during World War II; after the war, served successively as a member of his local's executive board, treasurer, and, in 1948, president; was one of the leaders of the UE conservative faction and joined James B. Carey (q.v.) in founding the International Union of Electrical, Radio and Machine Workers (IUE) after the UE was expelled from the Congress of Industrial Organizations (CIO) in 1949 for alleged Communist domination; elected executive secretary of IUE District 4 in 1950, and, after union districts were reorganized, became the executive secretary of District 3, comprising New York and New Jersey; served as a vice-president of both the New York City Industrial Union Council, CIO, and the New York State CIO Industrial Union Council; served as chairman of the American Federation of Labor-CIO (AFL-CIO) merger committees for the CIO Councils of New York City and New York State; elected president of the IUE in 1965 by the union's executive board after a U.S. Department of Labor recount of IUE election returns revealed that the incumbent, James B. Carey, had been fraudulently declared the winner; served as a labor delegate to the Organization of Economic Cooperation and Development meeting in Germany in 1967; associated with numerous private organizations, including the National Urban League, which in 1967 honored him for his contributions to civil rights causes; served as a trustee of the University of the State of New York; a supporter of the Liberal party of New York; *Who's Who in America, 1972-1973; Current Biography* (1969); *The New York Times*, April 6, 1965, October 27, 1969.

JESSUP, William J.   Born in New York City, February 7, 1827; after the death of his mother about 1835, moved to Greenwich, Conn., where he attended a rural school for seven years and thereafter taught in the same school for two years; returned to New York City and secured employment with Harper Brothers publishers; worked for the publishing house for two years, then was attracted by the high wages in the shipbuilding industry and learned the ship joiners' trade; entered the labor movement by organizing a union of ship joiners in 1863; then mobilized successful union opposition to the Folger bill, which was introduced in the New York legislature the next year to declare strikes illegal conspiracies; became the most prominent figure in the labor organizations of New York City and state during the ensuing decade; was a strong supporter of the eight-hour movement and participated in the ship joiners' strike for shorter hours in 1866 and was active in organizing the mass rallies and demonstrations that accompanied the city's general strike of 1872; was a ship joiner's delegate to the founding Baltimore Congress of the National Labor Union (NLU) in 1866 and served on the committee that drafted its constitution; elected vice-president from New York; cooperated closely with the International Workingmen's Association throughout the years of his activity; served frequently as president or secretary of both the Workingmen's Union of New York City and the state Workingmen's Assembly, and was regularly sent as a delegate from one of those bodies or the other to the congresses of the National Labor Union until 1870; supported the formation of a labor reform party for his own state and the greenback program of the NLU, but disassociated himself from the NLU after 1870 in protest against the growing prominence of middle-class reformers within it; in 1872, became both president and secretary of the ailing Carpenters' and Joiners' National Union and tried unsuccessfully to revive it; defeated for the presidency of the Workingmen's Assembly in 1873 and withdrew from the labor movement; David Montgomery, *Beyond Equality: Labor and the Radical Republicans, 1862-1872* (1967); Norman J. Ware, *The Labor Movement in the United States, 1860-1895* (1929); John R. Commons, *et al.*, *History of Labour in the United States*, Vol. II (1918); "William J. Jessup," an unidentified biographical sketch located in the Labor Collection, Biography and Papers, of the State Historical Society of Wisconsin.

JEWELL, Bert Mark.   Born in Brock, Neb., February 5, 1881; son of Charles James, a general construction contractor and farmer, and Ella Elizabeth (Adams) Jewell; Protestant; forced to leave school in 1897 before completing the eighth grade and for the next three years worked at a variety of occupations; became an apprentice boilermaker in High Springs, Fla., in 1900; completed his apprenticeship, then joined the International Brotherhood of Boiler Makers, Iron Ship Builders and Helpers of America (IBB) in 1905; traveled around the United States during 1905-1912, working as a boilermaker on various railroads and promoting trade unionism; established residence in Jacksonville, Fla., in 1912 and became IBB general chairman for the Seaboard Air Lines; was a leader of the Jacksonville Central Labor Union during 1912-1916; appointed an IBB general organizer in 1916 and organized the crews of ship yards and war activities plants during World War I; transferred to Washington, D.C., in 1918 and was assigned to represent the IBB in all war-related activities; became president of the railroad employees department of the American Federation of Labor (AFL) in 1918, and in that capacity coordinated the activities of AFL-affiliated railroad unions for the following three decades; was one of the principal negotiators for the non-operating railroad unions during his incumbency and proved to be a resourceful and effective bargainer; represented the Railway Labor Executives' Association at international conferences in Europe and was an AFL delegate to labor meetings in South America; retired from union affairs in 1946; was named in 1948 a labor advisor to the Economic Cooperation Administration, which administered the European Recovery Program, serving in both Washington, D.C., and Europe; died in Kansas City, Kan., in December, 1968; Philip Taft, *The A. F. of L. From the Death of Gompers to the Merger* (1959); *The American Federationist* (1946); *Who's Who in Labor* (1946); *Who's Who in America, 1958-1959; Labor,* December 1, 1951, December 14, 1968.

JIMERSON, Earl W.   Born in East St. Louis, Ill., September 2, 1889; son of Elijah W., a carpenter, and Mary Jimerson; Protestant; married Frances Laura Gutwald on July 4, 1911, graduated from grade school, then began working in a hide cellar at age fourteen; gained employment in the East St. Louis meat-packing industry, joining the Amalgamated Meat Cutters and Butcher Workmen of North America (AMCBWNA) in 1914; in 1914 became one of the founders of AMCBWNA Local 534, East St. Louis, Ill., serving it as secretary-treasurer and business representative, 1914-1918; served as president of the East St. Louis and St. Louis, Mo., Packing Trades Council, 1918-1920; elected vice-president of the AMCBWNA in 1920 and served in that capacity until elected international president in 1942; participated in the merger discussions between the AMCBWNA and the United Packinghouse Workers of America in 1956; represented the American Federation of Labor-Congress of Industrial

Organizations (AFL-CIO) at the meetings of the International Confederation of Free Trade Unions in 1955; was a staunch advocate of the European Recovery Program, the state of Israel, and the elimination of the poll tax; was also strongly anti-Communist and a severe critic of the Taft-Hartley Act; along with Patrick E. Gorman (q.v.), the chief executive official of the AMCBWNA, built the union from the 5,000 members who survived a strike in 1921 to 350,000 members, the 12th largest in the AFL-CIO at the time of his death; was a Democrat; edited the East St. Louis *Union News*; died in East St. Louis, Ill., October 5, 1957; David Brody, *The Butcher Workmen: A Study of Unionization* (1964); *Current Biography* (1948); *Who's Who in Labor* (1946); *The New York Times*, October 6, 1957.

JOHNS, John S.   Born in Beaver Falls, Pa., March 4, 1915; son of George and Rose (Abraham) Johns; Syrian Orthodox; married Emma Dager on June 15, 1941; two children; his family moved to Canton, Ohio, in 1925 and there attended high school and learned the shoe repair trade; went to work in the Republic Steel Corporation tin-plate mill in Canton in 1933; joined, in 1936, and soon became financial secretary of All Nations Local No. 1200 of the Steel Workers Organizing Committee (SWOC) at Republic; was very active in the "Little Steel" strike of 1937, and therefore not rehired; as a SWOC staff representative during 1940-1942, helped prepare for a crosscheck of Republic employees; served with the U.S. Army in the South Pacific, 1942-1945; resumed his position as a United Steelworkers of America (USWA) staff representative for District 27 (Canton) in 1946; served five successive terms as president of the Stark County Congress of Industrial Organizations' (CIO) Industrial Union Council; became the director of District 27 in 1952 after the resignation of I. W. Abel (q.v.), who became international secretary-treasurer; elected to that post a few months later and reelected for 20 years; helped negotiate the merger between the American Federation of Labor (AFL) and the CIO in Ohio, and was a vice-president of the Ohio AFL-CIO for nine years; was active in local and statewide Political Action Committees (CIO) and Committee on Political Education (AFL-CIO) campaigns; was a member of United Organized Labor of Ohio, a group that in 1958 thwarted a powerful effort to enact a "right-to-work" law; throughout his involvement in the labor movement, has been sensitive to the problems and needs of minorities; opposed in the 1930s and 1940s the practice of relegating immigrant steelworkers to lower-paying jobs; worked in the 1950s and 1960s to end job discrimination against black steelworkers and to open up clerical and leadership positions in the USWA to blacks; was one of several district directors dissatisfied with USWA president David J. McDonald's (q.v.) leadership and was the first director to publicly support Abel's candidacy in 1965; elected international USWA vice-president in 1973; appointed to the board of trustees of Kent State University in 1971; served on the Ohio State Democratic Executive Committee; *Who's Who in American Politics, 1971-1972*; John Herling, *Right to Challenge: People and Power in the Steelworkers Union* (1972); Oral Interview, Labor Archives, Pennsylvania State University.

(D.G.S.)

JOHNSON, William David.   Born in Brookfield, Mo., October 18, 1881; son of Elijah and Margaret E. Johnson; Methodist; married Myrtle Maude Fisher on October 7, 1908; completed grammar school in Brookfield, then hired by the Hannibal and St. Louis Railroad in 1898, a few years later, moved to Texas and worked for the Santa Fe Railroad, joining the Brotherhood of Railroad Trainmen; promoted to conductor in 1904 and joined the Order of Railway Conductors of America (ORC) in Temple, Tex.; moved to Silsbee, Tex., and became a charter member of ORC Division 480; served in various offices in his local division and in system committees, then was named to the ORC's Texas Legislative Board in 1918; served in that capacity for 23 years and during the last 13 was chairman of the Board; elected an international vice-president in 1931 and became the ORC's national legislative representative in Washington, D. C.; during more than 30 years in Washington, became acquainted with many legislators, thus facilitating his lobbying activities; during those years, played a vital role not only in the enactment of railroad labor legislation, but also in legislation of general interest to the labor movement; at the time of his retirement in 1963, was widely acclaimed as "the dean of organized labor's legislative representatives"; was a Democrat; died in Washington, D. C., in July, 1963; *Who's Who in Labor* (1946); *Labor*, August 3, 1963.

JOHNSTON, Alvanley.   Born in Seeley's Bay, Ontario, Canada, May 12, 1875; son of Scots immigrant parents, David, an educator, and Annie (Jarrell) Johnston; Episcopalian; married Maude Ethel Forsythe on June 6, 1917; two children; attended elementary schools of Seeley's Bay and at age fifteen enrolled in Brookville Business College, Ontario, attending for two years; became a railroad employee in 1892 as a call boy for the Great Northern Railway Company in Grand Forks, N.D.; transferred to the master mechanics office in Barnesville, Minn., a year later as a clerk and stenographer; worked as a locomotive engineer on the Great Northern Railroad, 1897-1909; became general chairman of the Great Northern Railroad division of the Brotherhood of Locomotive Engineers (BLE) in 1909; elected assistant grand chief engineer of the BLE in 1918 and grand chief engineer in 1925; convicted for misappropriation of BLE funds in connection with the failure of a union bank in Cleveland, Ohio, in 1933, but was acquitted by a Court of Appeals; appointed labor consultant by President Franklin D. Roosevelt when the government seized the railroads in 1943; appointed to the Combined War Labor Board in 1943 as a railroad union representative; led the BLE in the 1946 nationwide railroad strike but was forced, after two days, to end the strike because of the threat of drastic punitive legislation; acquired nearly unlimited control of the BLE during his presidency; retired and became grand chief emeritus in 1950; supported the Republican party; died in Shaker Heights, Ohio, September 17, 1951; Reed C. Richardson, *The Locomotive Engineer, 1863-1963: A Century of Railway Labor Relations and Work Rules* (1963); Arthur F. McClure, *The Truman Administration and the Problem of Postwar Labor, 1945-1948* (1969); *National Cyclopaedia of American Biography* (Vol. XL); *Current Biography* (1946).

JOHNSTON, William Hugh.   Born in Westville, Nova Scotia, Canada, December 30, 1874; son of Adam, a leader of the Shipwrights and Spar Makers' Union, and Jane (Murray) Johnston; Congregationalist; married Harriet J. Lunn on November 1, 1907; no children; emigrated with his family to the United States in 1885, settling in Providence, R.I., and there completed a grammar school education; served a machinist apprenticeship at age fourteen at the Rhode Island Locomotive Works and plied his trade at several New England machine shops; while an employee at the Jencks Manufacturing Company, Pawtucket, R.I., 1895-1897, helped perfect automatic knitting machines; worked from 1897 to 1901 on Armington and Sims high-speed engines and Greene and Rice and Sargent stationary engines; early in his career, joined the Knights of Labor, and in 1895, joined the International Association of Machinists (IAM) and helped organize Local Lodge 379 at the Jencks Manufacturing Company in Pawtucket; selected president of Local Lodge 147 at Rhode Island Locomotive Company, Providence, in 1901; was a delegate to the IAM national convention and elected president of District 19, New England in 1905; during 1906-1909, three times elected business agent for Local Lodge 147; in 1909 elected president and general organizer of District 44, comprising all machinists employed by the federal government; was backed by the

Populist-Socialist, "progressive" faction and defeated James O'Connell (q.v.) for the IAM presidency in 1911; reelected until July, 1926, resigning then because suffering from partial paralysis; opposed O'Connell and most American Federation of Labor (AFL) leaders who favored "pure and simple" trade unionism; espoused industrial unionism, independent political action, and government intervention in the economy; served during World War I as a Wilson appointee on the National War Labor Board and accompanied AFL president Samuel Gompers' (q.v.) labor mission to France and Great Britain; after the war, along with railroad brotherhood leaders, helped organize the Plumb Plan League to promote government ownership of the railroads; helped organize the National Conference for Progressive Political Action in 1921, and in 1924, chaired the Cleveland convention that nominated senators Robert M. LaFollette and Burton K. Wheeler for president and vice-president of the United States; following resignation as IAM president, served as vice-president of the Mount Vernon Savings Bank, and from 1933 to 1936, worked at the IAM's grand lodge office; died in Washington, D. C., March 26, 1937; Mark Perlman, *The Machinists: A New Study in American Trade Unionism* (1961); John H. M. Laslett, *Labor and the Left: A Study of Socialism and Radical Influences in the American Labor Movement, 1881-1924* (1970); *Dictionary of American Biography* (Supplement II); *Who Was Who in America* (Vol. I); Solon DeLeon, ed., *The American Labor Who's Who* (1925).

(J.H.)

JONES, Mary Harris ("Mother"). Born in Cork, Ireland, May 1, 1830; daughter of Richard, a railway construction worker, and Helen (Harris) Jones; emigrated with her family to the United States in 1835, and later moved to Toronto, Canada; attended normal and convent schools in Toronto, then taught at a convent school in Monroe, Mich.; left teaching to enter the dress-making business in Chicago, Ill., but returned to her former profession after settling in Memphis, Tenn.; married an Iron Molders' Union member in 1861, but after her husband and four children died in the 1867 Memphis yellow fever epidemic, returned to dress-making in Chicago; found solace at a Knights of Labor hall when the 1871 Chicago fire destroyed her dress-making business and began attending meetings regularly; first became involved in labor strikes during the 1877 Baltimore and Ohio railroad strike in Pittsburgh, Pa.; became in the 1890s an organizer for the United Mine Workers of America (UMWA), and thereafter gained fame as an agitator for coal miners, particularly in West Virginia; helped organize the Northern (Fairmont) fields and the New River camps in West

Virginia, 1902-1903, and was active in the 1903-1904 Colorado coal miners' strikes; quit the UMWA after disagreeing with President John Mitchell's (q.v.) endorsement of a Northern fields' settlement, believing it exploited the Southern miners; left Colorado and ventured farther west, working with striking Southern Pacific Railway machinists; also agitated in favor of the Western Federation of Miners' copper strikes in Arizona in 1910; rejoined the UMWA in 1911 and became active in the 1912-1913 West Virginia coal strikes; returned to Colorado when trouble again broke out in the coal fields, 1913-1914; although arrested and deported from the coal fields three times, witnessed the 1914 Ludlow Massacre and publicized it through speeches and testimony before the House Mines and Mining Committee in 1914; was involved subsequently in the New York City streetcar and garment workers' strikes, 1915-1916, and the steel strike of 1919; was a delegate to the 1921 Pan-American Federation of Labor conference in Mexico City; was active throughout her career in publicizing the evils of child labor and led a children's march from the textile mills of Kensington, Pa., to the Oyster Bay, N.Y., home of President Theodore Roosevelt in 1903; worked in textile mills in Alabama and South Carolina to observe working conditions of child laborers during 1903-1905; was rather inconsistent in her political affiliations, supporting various parties throughout her life; helped found the Social Democratic party in 1898, was an organizer of the Industrial Workers of the World in 1905, campaigned for the Democratic party in 1916, and in 1924 supported the Farmer-Labor party; authored *Autobiography of Mother Jones*, which was edited by Mary Parton in 1925; died in Silver Spring, Md., November 30, 1930; *Notable American Women* (1971); *Dictionary of American Biography* (Vol. X); Elsie Gluck, *John Mitchell, Miner* (1929); George McGovern and Leonard F. Guttridge, *The Great Coalfield War* (1972); Ralph Chaplin, *Wobbly: The Rough and Tumble Story of an American Radical* (1948).

(M.T.)

KASTEN, Frank.   Born in Dolton, Ill., January 13, 1878; son of Louis, a brickmaker, and Caroline (Gese) Kasten; Lutheran; married Margaret Morford on November 2, 1914; two children; completed public grammar school in Dolton, then at age fifteen became a brickmaker; joined Local 3 of the United Brick and Clay Workers of America (UBCW) and served as president of the local, 1907-1912; elected business manager of UBCW District 1 in Chicago, Ill., in 1912, serving until 1916; elected general president of the UBCW in 1916 and served in that capacity until his death; led a long and divisive strike of brick and clay workers at Brazil, Ind., that demonstrated his leadership qualities and the determination of the UBCW workers in its jurisdiction; served as UBCW delegate to the conventions of the American Federation of Labor (AFL), 1913-1946, and during this period served on several AFL committees; served as mayor of Blue Island, Ill., 1929-1935; was a Republican; died in Chicago, Ill., December 12, 1946; *The American Federationist* (January, 1947); Solon DeLeon, ed., *The American Labor Who's Who* (1925); *Who's Who in Labor* (1946).

KAUFMAN, Morris (David Horodok).   Born in Minsk, Russia, in September, 1884; son of a cattle and poultry slaughterer; Jewish; married; two children; self-educated; began work at age fourteen as a grocery clerk; worked as a bank clerk, 1900-1902; emigrated to the United States in 1902 and for a year worked as a cigarmaker; became a fur worker in 1904 and joined the New York Fur Workers' Union; became a member of the executive board of the Fur Workers' Union in 1905 and two years later elected secretary; served as secretary of the New York branch of The Bund, 1906-1907; joined the International Fur Workers Union of the United States and Canada (IFWU) when it was organized in 1913; served as business agent of the New York Joint Board of Fur Workers, 1916-1917, and manager, 1917-1921; elected a vice-president of the IFWU in 1917 and president the following year; defeated for the IFWU presidency by a left-wing coalition in 1925, but reelected in 1929, serving until 1932; continued working in the fur industry after the IFWU was taken over by a left-wing faction led by Ben Gold (q.v.); indicted and convicted in 1935 of conspiring with employers to raise wages, fix prices, and eliminate competition, receiving a suspended three-year sentence; became a manager of the Muskrat Division of the Fur Dressers Factor Corporation; retired from the fur business in 1953; supported the Socialist party during the early years of his trade union activity; died in New York City, July 7, 1960; Philip S. Foner, *The Fur and Leather Workers Union: A Story of Dramatic Struggles and Achievement* (1950); Solon DeLeon, ed., *The American Labor Who's Who* (1925); *The New York Times*, July 8, 1960.

KAVANAGH, William Francis.   Born in Jersey City, N.J., September 2, 1878; son of James, an operating engineer, and Mary (Ryan) Kavanagh; Roman Catholic; married Alice Josephine Woods on April 22, 1913, after the death of his first wife, Elizabeth McAuley, in 1911; eight children; attended parochial schools for four years, then was orphaned and during the next several years worked on an aunt's farm and in the textile industry; entered vaudeville in 1898 as a member of the Sheehan and Kavanagh song-and-dance team and later was a member of the Mobile Four quartet; became interested, after meeting Samuel Gompers (q.v.), in the labor movement and devoted much of the remainder of his life to that cause; organized Local 575 of the Hotel and Restaurant Employees' International Alliance and Bartenders' International League of America (HREIABIL) in 1903 and served as its president and business agent until 1945; served as an international representative and organizer for the HREIABIL, 1903-1945; served as president of the New Jersey Federation of Trades and Labor Unions prior to the organization of the New Jersey State Federation of Labor (NJSFL); was secretary of the NJSFL, 1927-1936; served as secretary-treasurer of the Union Label League of Jersey City, 1924-1945; elected president of the Central Labor Union of Hudson County, N. J., on two different occasions and served as its secretary-treasurer for more than 30 years prior to retiring from union affairs in 1945; served as a delegate to both the Federated Trades of New York and the Essex Trades Council of Essex County, N.J.; served as a civil defense worker during World War II; was for several years a delegate to the annual meetings of the Labor Institute at Rutgers University, which he had helped organize; was a member of the Non-Partisan League of New Jersey during the 1930s, but often supported Democratic candidates; died in Jersey City, N.J., October 11, 1963; *National Cyclopaedia of American Biography* (1966); *The New York Times*, October 3, 1963.

KAZAN, Abraham Eli.   Born in Kiev, Russia, December 15, 1888; the son of a Jewish businessman; married; three children; attended elementary and secondary schools in Russia; emigrated to the United States in 1903; later took courses at New York University and Brooklyn Polytechnic Institute; secured employment in the garment industry and joined cloak pressers' Local 35 of the International Ladies' Garment Workers' Union; served as bookkeeper and financial secretary of Local 35, 1912-1914, and secretary-treasurer, 1914-1919; joined the Amalgamated Clothing Workers of America (ACWA) in 1919 and became the director of its record department, serving until 1922; was secretary-treasurer of the New York Joint Board, ACWA, 1922-1923; appointed manager of the employment bureau of the New York Joint Board, ACWA, in 1924; became the president of the ACWA's Amalgamated Housing Corporation, a cooperative housing project, in 1927, and devoted much of the remainder of his life to the promotion of cooperative housing projects; served as president of the United Housing Foundation and of Community Services, both of which supplied information and technical services to cooperative housing projects and cooperative homeowners; was a director of the Cooperative League of the United States of America, 1931-1938, and elected to the same position again in 1958; died in New York City, December 21, 1971; Louis Levine, *The Women's Garment Workers: A History of the International Ladies' Garment Workers' Union* (1924); Erma Angevine, *In League with the Future* (1959); Solon DeLeon, ed., *The American Labor Who's Who* (1925).

KEATING, Edward. Born in Kansas City, Kan., July 9, 1875; son of Stephen, a farmer, and Julia (O'Connor) Keating; Roman Catholic; married Margaret Sloan Medill on September 1, 1907, and, after her death in 1939, Eleanor Mary Connolly on May 3, 1941; after the death of his father, his family moved to Pueblo, Colo., in 1880 and Denver, Colo., in 1889; attended grammar school in the public schools of Colorado; worked as a "news butcher" on passenger trains running from Denver to the Aspen, Colo., mining camps, then became a copyholder on the *Denver Republican* in 1899; served as the Denver, Colo., city auditor, 1899-1901; was city editor of the *Denver Times*, 1902-1905, and editor of the *Rocky Mountain News*, 1906-1911; elected president of the International League of Press Clubs in 1906 and 1907; was president of the Colorado State Board of Land Commissioners, 1911-1913; purchased and became the editor of the *Pueblo Leader* in 1912; elected as a Democrat to the U.S. Congress in 1912 and served until defeated for reelection in 1918; while in Congress, was especially active in sponsoring child-labor bills, minimum-wage laws for women and children in the District of Columbia, and in campaigning for the Adamson Act, which established the eight-hour day on railroads; voted against American entry into World War I; became the editor and manager of *Labor*, a newly established official weekly newspaper of the Associated Railroad Labor Organizations, in 1919; joined the International Typographical Union in 1919; retired as editor of *Labor* in 1953 and was named editor-manager emeritus; authored *The Story of Labor: The Gentleman from Colorado* (1965); was an independent Democrat; died in Washington, D.C., March 18, 1965; Philip Taft, *The A. F. of L. From the Death of Gompers to the Merger* (1959); *Biographical Directory of the American Congress, 1774-1971* (1971); *AFL-CIO News*, March 27, 1965; *Labor*, March 27, 1965; *American Federation of Labor News-Reporter*, April 10, 1953.

KEEFE, Daniel Joseph. Born in Willowsprings, Ill., September 27, 1852; son of John, a teamster, and Catherine Keefe; Roman Catholic;

married Ellen E. Conners in 1878 and, after her death, Emma L. Walker in 1904; left school at age twelve and worked as a teamster for his father; began working as a lumber handler and longshoreman in 1870; in 1882, was elected president of the Lumber Unloaders' Association, an organization of longshoremen that contracted with various shipping companies to load and unload vessels; was one of the founders in 1892 of the Lumber Handlers of the Great Lakes, whose jurisdiction was extended to all longshore work in 1893; after the name of the union had been changed to the International Longshoremen's Association (ILA), was elected its president in 1893, serving until 1908; assumed near dictatorial control of the ILA during his incumbency; served as a member of the Illinois State Board of Arbitration, 1897-1901; was a staunch supporter and active participant in the National Civic Federation organized in 1900; essentially a conservative trade unionist, but advocated the industrial method of organization for waterfront workers; served as an American Federation of Labor vice-president and executive council member, 1903-1908; campaigned for William Howard Taft in 1908 and was appointed Commissioner General of Immigration by President Theodore Roosevelt shortly before he left office, serving until 1913; served as a conciliation commissioner for the U.S. Department of Labor during World War I; employed by the United States Shipping Board Merchant Fleet Corporation as a labor disputes mediator, 1921-1925; was a Republican; retired in 1925 and died in Elmhurst, Ill., January 2, 1929; Maud Russell, *Men Along the Shore* (1966); Charles P. Larrowe, *Maritime Labor Relations on the Great Lakes* (1959); *Dictionary of American Biography* (Vol. X).

KEENAN, Joseph Daniel. Born in Chicago, Ill., November 5, 1896; son of Edward John, a teamster, and Minnie (Curtin) Kennan; Roman Catholic; married Myrtle Fietsch in 1920; two children; began working in 1914, at age eighteen, as an apprentice electrician; joined Local 134, International Brotherhood of Electrical Workers of America (IBEW) and completed his apprenticeship under its auspices in 1918; elected an IBEW Local 134 inspector in 1923 and three years later was elected recording secretary; elected secretary of the Chicago Federation of Labor, and, with the exception of government service during World War II, served in that capacity until 1948; during World War II, served as an American Federation of Labor (AFL) representative on both the National Defense Council and the Office of Production Management and was associate director of the War Production Board; appointed chief of the Manpower Division of the Allied Control Commission for Germany in 1945; was named the first director of Labor's League for Political Education after its creation by the AFL in 1948; during the campaign and election of 1948, joined with Jack Kroll of the Congress of Industrial Organizations' (CIO) Political Action Committee to coordinate informally the political campaigns of the AFL and the CIO in behalf of Harry S. Truman's reelection effort; elected secretary-treasurer of the AFL building and construction trades department in 1951, serving until 1954; became the international secretary of the IBEW in 1954; elected an AFL vice-president and executive council member in 1955 and continued in that capacity after the AFL-CIO merger; was appointed a member of the Democratic National Committee's advisory committee on economic policy in 1957; has served on numerous public and private boards and agencies, including position as assistant to director of the Office of Civil Defense Mobilization; considered one of the AFL-CIO's premier labor politicians and has developed considerable influence in the Democratic party in Chicago and in Washington, D. C.; Joseph C. Goulden, *Meany* (1972); Philip Taft, *The A. F. of L. From the Death of Gompers to the Merger* (1959); *Who's Who in Labor* (1946).

KEENEY, C. Frank.   Born in Kanawha County, W. Va.; little is known about his childhood and early adult years; along with Mother Jones (q.v.) organized in 1912 the coal miners of Cabin Creek, W. Va., an area regular United Mine Workers of America (UMWA) organizers feared to enter; along with Fred Mooney (q.v.) and Lawrence Dwyer, a UMWA international organizer, established three years later an insurgent district, District 30, in the Cabin Creek area to protest alleged corruption and inefficiency on the part of President Thomas Cairns (q.v.) and other officials of District 17, UMWA, West Virginia; after District 17 was reorganized by the international union in 1917, elected its president and served until 1924; within a year of becoming president, helped District 17 add 10,000 members, pay off a $35,000 debt, and show a treasury surplus of $25,000; in 1919, along with the governor of West Virginia, prevented a threatened union miners' march into nonunion territory that promised to result in violence; again in 1921, along with state and federal officials, prevented a second march; an attack by state policemen and Logan County deputies on a union tent colony at Sharples, W. Va., in 1922, however, ignited a march resulting in the "Battle of Blair Mountain", in which three deputies were killed and 40 miners wounded; indicted as a result of the conflict, but acquitted of treason and murder; while under indictment, elected president of the West Virginia State Federation of Labor (WVSFL); defeated for reelection by John Easton (q.v.) in a craft union movement to curb the power of the UMWA in the WVSFL; after his defeat, his UMWA supporters in southern West Virginia boycotted the WVSFL until 1927; along with Mooney, resigned his UMWA offices in 1924 to protest UMWA president John L. Lewis's (q.v.) attempt to enforce the Jacksonville scale in West Virginia, a policy they charged would destroy the union there; thereafter, the district was administered by provisional presidents Percy Tetlow (q.v.), and, later, Van A. Bittner (q.v.); moved to Illinois in 1926 to edit *The Coal Miner*, an official organ of John Brophy's (q.v.) "Save the Union" campaign; during 1927-1930, was first the proprietor of an orange drink stand and then an oil and gas speculator; in 1930, joined John H. Walker (q.v.), Frank Farrington (q.v.), Alexander Howat (q.v.), and Oscar Ameringer in the Reorganized United Mine Workers; after Walker reaffiliated with the regular UMWA and other leaders were expelled in 1931, founded his own West Virginia Miners' Union, which grew rapidly but destroyed itself with a strike during depressed conditions; became an American Federation of Labor organizer for the Progressive Mine Workers of America in 1938 and organized three West Virginia locals, all of which were destroyed by the UMWA's 1939 union shop agreement; thereafter, his career deteriorated, and his last known job was as a parking-lot attendant; according to relatives, still living in 1973; Evelyn L. K. Harris and Frank J. Krebs, *From Humble Beginnings: West Virginia State Federation of Labor, 1903-1957* (1960); J. W. Hess, ed., *Struggle in the Coal Fields: The Autobiography of Fred Mooney* (1967); Irving Bernstein, *The Lean Years: A History of the American Workers, 1920-1933* (1960).

(J.H.)

KEHRER, Elmer Thomas (Al).   Born in Brighton, Mich., January 11, 1921; son of Charles, an autoworker, and Gertrude (Miller) Kehrer; Presbyterian; married Betty Hynson on October 4, 1952; received the B.A. degree from Olivet College and the M.A. from Yale University; joined the United Automobile, Aircraft, and Agricultural Implement Workers of America in 1937 and later affiliated with the American Newspaper Guild; became a field representative for the American Federation of Labor (AFL) Workers' Education Bureau in 1948; served as the assistant director of the International Ladies' Garment Workers' Union officer-training institute, 1950-1953, and as Southern director, 1954-1964; was appointed Southern director of the AFL-Congress of Industrial Organizations' Civil Rights Department in 1965; in that capacity, directed programs to bring minority workers into the building trades of the South, including the recruiting and training of black construction workers in major southern cities in cooperation with local building trades unions and the U.S. Department of Labor; as chairman of the Georgia Democratic Party Forum, 1971-1972, successfully challenged the delegate selection process in Georgia for national conventions and promoted reforms of the state party structure; participated actively in the founding of the Southern Labor Archives at Georgia State University, Atlanta, Ga., particularly in encouraging organized labor's support of the project; is a member of several social and reform organizations, including Workmen's Circle, the Urban League, the National Association for the Advancement of Colored People, the A. Philip Randolph Institute, and the American Civil Liberties Union; is a board member of the Southern Regional Council, the Workers' Defense League, and the Georgia Council on Economic Education.

(M.E.R.)

KELSAY, Ray. Born in Marion, Ind., July 8, 1888; son of Smith and Minerva (Morgan) Kelsay; Community Church; married Martha Weaver on January 1, 1910; three children; finished elementary school, then went to work; in 1906 joined the Metal Polishers, Buffers, Platers, and Helpers International Union (MPBPHIU); shortly thereafter elected president of his local union; later elected president of the MPBPHIU's Indiana District Council; well-regarded by union's members, was elected international vice-president in 1931 and international president and secretary-treasurer in 1945; the MPBPHIU was a small union, and Kelsay worked assiduously to sustain and expand it; during his presidency membership increased substantially; also played an active role in the American Federation of Labor metal trades department and became its second vice-president; after World War II, initiated a program whereby the MPBPHIU provided occupational rehabilitation services to injured veterans, a program that was cited as "outstanding" by the U.S. Government; killed in an automobile accident in Indianapolis, Ind., September 25, 1948; *Who's Who in Labor* (1946); *The American Federationist* (October, 1948).

(D.G.S.)

KENIN, Herman David. Born in Vineland, N.J., October 26, 1901; son of Samuel Benjamin, a member of the Cigarmakers' Union, and Anna (Gordin) Kenin; Jewish; married Maxine Bennett on July 31, 1936; two children; attended Reed College, 1920-1921, and Northwestern College of Law in Portland, Ore., 1924-1926, 1930-1931; admitted to the Oregon bar in 1931; became a professional musician while attending college and joined Local 99 of the American Federation of Musicians (AFM) in 1920; during the 1920s and 1930s, headed a band that played hotel and night club dates on the West Coast; elected president of AFM Local 99 in 1936; appointed to a vacancy on the AFM's international executive board in 1943 and subsequently elected to the position; served as an American labor delegate to the advisory committee of the salaried and professional workers division of the International Labor Organization meeting in Geneva in 1949; elected international president of the AFM in 1958 after the resignation of James C. Petrillo (q.v.); was instrumental during his presidency in establishing a pension fund for musicians, gaining Congressional repeal of a 20 percent cabaret tax, and democratizing the structure of the AFM; elected an American Federation of Labor-Congress of Industrial Organizations' vice-president and executive council member in 1963; was one of the leaders in the movement to establish the National Endowment for the Arts and Humanities, served on the advisory committee of the National Cultural Center, and was a member of the National Council of the National Council of Arts; died in New York City, July 21, 1970; *Who's Who in America* (1970-1971); *The New York Times*, July 22, 1970; *AFL-CIO News*, February 23, 1963.

KENNEDY, Thomas.   Born in Lansford, Pa., November 2, 1887; son of Peter, a coal miner killed in a mine accident, and Mary (Boyle) Kennedy; Roman Catholic; married Helen Melley on July 23, 1912, and, after her death in 1953, Evelyn Summers on November 12, 1959; two children; attended Lansford public schools for six years; started work in the mines at age twelve as a breaker boy, then became a mule driver and later a miner; joined the United Mine Workers of America (UMWA) in 1900; elected secretary of UMWA Lansford Local 1738 in 1903, serving until 1910; was a delegate to the UMWA international convention in 1906; served as member of the executive board of UMWA District 7, 1908-1910, and as District president, 1910-1925; served during these 15 years on the Anthracite Board of Conciliation and as the union's chief negotiator for anthracite contracts; served as UMWA international secretary-treasurer, 1925-1947, and as international vice-president, 1947-1960; succeeded John L. Lewis (q.v.) as international president of the UMWA in 1960, but was old and ill by that time; W. A. Boyle (q.v.), chosen acting president in November, 1962, ran the union during Kennedy's three-year incumbency; was essentially an able, loyal, and personable union bureaucrat; dominated anthracite negotiations for 50 years and participated in all bituminous negotiations after 1925; served on the Advisory Committee to the National Recovery Administration, 1933; helped lead the UMWA's fight to force the

American Federation of Labor to abandon voluntarism and endorse social security and government responsibility for unemployment; was appointed to the National Defense Mediation Board in 1941, but resigned in protest to the Board's captive mines decision; appointed to the National War Labor Board in 1942, but again resigned, this time to protest its application of the Little Steel Formula; was a member of the Advisory Committee of the Bituminous Coal Division and the Solid Fuels Administration for War during World War II; served as chairman of the board of trustees of the Anthracite Health and Welfare Fund, 1945-1963; was active in Pennsylvania Democratic politics and was elected lieutenant governor of Pennsylvania in 1934; was candidate for the Democratic gubernatorial nomination in 1938, but was defeated by the state Democratic machine; was a delegate-at-large to the Democratic National Conventions in 1936 and 1940, serving on the Resolutions Committee; served on a great variety of public and private boards and agencies, including the Pennsylvania State Welfare Commission, the Pennsylvania Emergency Relief Board, and American Coal Shipping, Inc.; died at Hazelton, Pa., January 19, 1963; *United Mine Workers Journal*, February 1, 1963; *National Cyclopaedia of American Biography* (Vol. LII); *Current Biography* (1964); *Who's Who in Labor* (1946).

(J.H.)

KENNEDY, William Parker.   Born in Huttonville, Ontario, Canada, April 3, 1892; son of William James, a wool weaver, and Margaret (Parker) Kennedy; Lutheran; married Amy Hannah Berglund on January 21, 1913; four children; emigrated with parents to Chicago, Ill., in 1902 and completed elementary school there; desirous of a career in railroading, obtained a job as a "news butcher" selling papers and magazines on the Rock Island line in 1907; became a freight brakeman for the Dakota division of the Great Northern Railway in 1909; joined Wheat Sheaf Lodge 463 of the Brotherhood of Railroad Trainmen (BRT) in Grand Forks, N.D., in 1910; became a switchman in 1911 and eventually joined the Chicago, Milwaukee, and St. Paul Railroad; transferred membership to Minnehaha Lodge 625, Minneapolis, Minn., in 1913 and served as president and local chairman; elected secretary of the BRT's general grievance committee for the Chicago, Milwaukee, St. Paul, and Pacific Railroad in 1920 and a year later was elected general chairman, serving in that capacity until 1935; elected to the BRT board of trustees in 1928 and served as secretary until 1935; elected a vice-president in charge of the BRT's Northwestern territory in 1935; was placed in charge of the BRT's super-promotion department, 1944-1946; elected general secretary-treasurer in 1946 and, upon the death of Alexander F. Whitney (q.v.) in 1949, became the general president of the BRT; served as national reporting officer for the Railroad Retirement Board and secretary of the board of trustees of the Home for Aged and Disabled Railroad Employes of America, 1946-1949; retired from union affairs in 1962; was a member of the Minnesota Democratic Farmer-Labor party; died in Minneapolis, Minn., May 14, 1968; Joel Seidman, *The Brotherhood of Railroad Trainmen: The Internal Political Life of a National Union* (1962); *Current Biography* (1950); *Who's Who in Railroading* (1959); *Labor*, January 5, 1963, May 25, 1968.

KIRKLAND, Joseph Lane. Born in Camden, S.C., March 12, 1922; son of Randolph Withers and Louise (Richardson) Kirkland; married Edith Draper Hollyday on June 10, 1944; five children; attended Newberry College in South Carolina in 1940, then graduated from the U.S. Merchant Marine Academy in 1942; received a B.S. degree from Georgetown University's School of Foreign Service in 1948; joined the National Organization of Masters, Mates, and Pilots of America while serving as a U. S. Merchant Marine pilot, 1941-1946; was a nautical scientist in the U.S. Navy Department of Hydrographic Office, 1947-1948; joined the research staff of the American Federation of Labor (AFL) in 1948 and served in that capacity until becoming assistant director of the AFL social security department in 1953; retained latter position after the AFL-Congress of Industrial Organizations' (CIO) merger in 1955; served as director of research and education for the International Union of Operating Engineers, 1958-1960; became executive assistant to President George Meany (q.v.) of the AFL-CIO in 1961; elected secretary-treasurer of the AFL-CIO after the resignation of William F. Schnitzler (q.v.) in 1969; served as president of the Institute of Collective Bargaining and Group Relations, as a director of the American Foundation on Automation and Employment, as a board member of Community Health, Inc., and as a member of the advisory board of the U.S. Merchant Marine Academy; has served on a variety of public and private boards and agencies; usually supported the Democratic party; Joseph C. Goulden, *Meany* (1972); *Who's Who in America, 1972-1973; AFL-CIO News*, May 17, 1969; *Newsweek*, September 6, 1971.

KIRWAN, James (fl. 1903-1913). Born in Terry, S. D.; was a member of the Lead City Miners' Union; played a major part in founding the Western Federation of Miners (WFM); was appointed to replace resigning representative of District 5 (South Dakota) on the WFM executive board in

1903 and was elected to the office the following year; amicable and well-respected within the WFM, thus reelected several times; served as acting secretary of WFM in 1906-1908, while then Secretary-Treasurer William Haywood (q.v.) was in jail on charge of the murder of former Idaho governor Frank Steunenberg; was a WFM delegate to the disruptive 1906 convention of the Industrial Workers of the World (IWW), which split over the ouster of President Charles Sherman (q.v.); sided with the WFM moderates in opposition to revolutionary syndicalist faction of the IWW led by William Trautmann (q.v.) and Daniel DeLeon (q.v.); in showdown at 1907 WFM convention, Kirwan and Vice-President Charles Mahoney (q.v.) led the moderates against the radical supporters of the Trautmann IWW; voiced bitter objections to IWW as a detriment to the WFM and supported complete severance from the IWW; despite compromise, the WFM in reality abandoned revolutionary unionism to move toward more conventional unionism; Kirwan was a pragmatist, eschewing both revolutionary action and ideological disputation; continued to exert important influence to keep WFM on the "narrower track" of effective industrial unionism; was a member of WFM executive board until 1910, but remained active in the labor movement for several years afterwards; during the 1913 coal miners' strike against the Colorado Fuel and Iron Company, was elected to a commission established by the Colorado State Federation of Labor, at the suggestion of the governor of Colorado, to investigate state militia's role in the strike zones; *Final Report of the U.S. Commission on Industrial Relations* (1915); Vernon H. Jensen, *Heritage of Conflict: Labor Relations in the Nonferrous Metals Industry up to 1930* (1950); Melvyn Dubofsky, *We Shall Be All: A History of the Industrial Workers of the World* (1969).

(D.G.S.)

KNIGHT, Felix Harrison.   Born in Montgomery County, Mo., December 10, 1876; son of John Robert, a teacher, and Mollie (Moore) Knight; Baptist; married Rose M. Michel on June 24, 1903; after high school graduation, secured employment with the St. Louis Street Railway and joined the Amalgamated Association of Street, Electric Railway and Motor Coach Employees of America; later became a railroad carman and joined St. Louis, Mo., Local 34 of the Brotherhood of Railway Carmen of America (BRCA) in 1902; later the same year was elected financial secretary and chairman of the local protective board; was elected a delegate to the St. Louis Central Trades and Labor Union in 1903; became secretary-treasurer of the Chicago, Burlington, and Quincy Railroad joint protective board in 1903; was appointed assistant general president of the BRCA in 1913, serving until 1934; served as member of the National Railroad Adjustment Board, 1918-1920, and again in 1934; was appointed general president of the BRCA in 1935 after the death of Martin F. Ryan (q.v.) and was elected to the position the following year; became a member of the executive council of the American Federation of Labor (AFL) railway employees department in 1935; elected an AFL vice-president and executive council member in 1936, and during that year served on an AFL executive council committee appointed to mediate dispute with the members of the Committee on Industrial Organization; served as an AFL fraternal delegate to the British Trades Union Congress in 1939; was appointed an AFL alternate on the Combined War Labor Board in 1942; was chairman of an AFL committee investigating labor conditions in Argentina under Juan Peron's regime in 1946; retired his union positions in 1947; died in Kansas City, Mo., October 13, 1952; Leonard Painter, *Through 50 years with the Brotherhood of Railway Carmen of America* (1941); Philip Taft, *The A. F. of L. From the Death of Gompers to the Merger* (1959); *The American Federationist* (October, 1941); *Who's Who in Labor* (1946); *Labor*, October 18, 1952.

KNIGHT, Orie Albert. Born in New Hampton, Iowa, September 24, 1902; son of William Leonard, a livestock dealer, and Clara Mae (Ransome) Knight; Baptist; married Evelyn Luella Dokken on January 30, 1925; after high school graduation, began working in a Shell Oil Company refinery in 1926; helped organize Hammond, Ind., Local 210 of the International Association of Oil Field, Gas Well, and Refinery Workers in 1933; elected a member of the Congress of Industrial Organizations' (CIO) international executive council in 1936; served as a CIO staff organizer, 1937-1940; elected president of the Oil Workers International Union (OWIU), a CIO affiliate, in 1940; served as a labor member of the National War Labor Board during World War II; elected a CIO vice-president in 1947 and during the same year was a member of the Committee for the Marshall Plan to Aid European Recovery; became a member of the CIO's committee on Latin American affairs and often served as the CIO's fraternal delegate to the Confederation of Latin American Workers; chaired CIO committee investigating Communist influence in CIO-affiliated unions in 1950; result was the expulsion of two unions, including Harry Bridges' (q.v.) International Longshoremen's and Warehousemen's Union; appointed deputy administrator of the National Production Authority that supervised the mobilization effort during the Korean War; led the first national strike in the United States oil industry in 1952; helped negotiate a merger between the OWIU and the United Gas, Coke, and Chemical Workers International Union in 1955 and became president of the renamed Oil, Chemical and Atomic Workers International Union; after merger between the American Federation of Labor and the CIO in 1955, became a vice-president and executive council member of the new federation; was a member of the National Urban League; retired union positions in 1965; a Democrat; Melvin Rothbaum, *The Government of the Oil, Chemical and Atomic Workers Union* (1962); Harvey O'Connor, *History of Oil Workers International Union—CIO* (1950); *Who's Who in Labor* (1946); *Current Biography* (1952).

KROLL, John Jacob (Jack).   Born in London, England, June 10, 1885; son of Mark, a tailor, and Julia Kate (Blumberg) Kroll; Jewish; married Sara Sylvia Raben on January 19, 1920; one child; emigrated with family to the United States in 1886; completed two years of a high school education in Rochester, N.Y.; became a garment cutter in 1900 and in 1903 joined the Rochester Local of the United Garment Workers of America (UGW); while a member of UGW Local 61 in Chicago, Ill., was associated with Sidney Hillman (q.v.) in the 1910 strike against Hart, Schaffner and Marx that ultimately led to organization of the Amalgamated Clothing Workers of America (ACWA) in 1914; after organizing men's garment workers in Chicago for several years, was appointed an ACWA national organizer in 1919 and shortly thereafter became the manager of ACWA's Joint Board in Cincinnati, Ohio; became a vice-president and executive board member of the ACWA in 1928; served as vice-president and then president of the Ohio Industrial Union Council, Congress of Industrial Organizations (CIO), 1939-1952; was manager of the New York Laundry Workers Joint Board, 1942-1944; appointed a regional director (Ohio, Kentucky, and West Virginia) of the CIO's Political Action Committee (PAC) in 1943 and a year later became vice-chairman of PAC; served as a labor advisor to the Office of Production Management, 1943-1944; became assistant director of the CIO's Southern organizing drive in 1946 but resigned shortly after his appointment when named director of the PAC after the death of Sidney Hillman in 1946; following the American Federation of Labor-CIO merger in 1955, became co-director with James L. McDevitt (q.v.) of the Committee on Political Education (COPE); resigned as co-director of COPE in 1957; retired from union affairs in 1966; was a member of *Histadrut*, the Zionist labor organization; although a Socialist early in his career, usually supported Democratic candidates; died in Cincinnati, Ohio, May 26, 1971;

Terry Catchpole, *How to Cope with COPE: The Political Operations of Organized Labor* (1968); Fay Calkins, *The CIO and the Democratic Party* (1952); *Current Biography* (1946).

KRZYCKI, Leo. Born in Milwaukee, Wis., August 10, 1881; son of Martin, a laborer, and Kathryn Krzycki; married Anna Kadau on February 3, 1909; four children; after attending Milwaukee elementary schools, began work as a lithographer and joined the Lithographic Press Feeders Union (LPFU) in 1898; served as LPFU general vice-president, 1904-1908; elected to the Milwaukee City Council in 1912 and served until 1916; was a successful candidate for Undersheriff of Milwaukee County on the Socialist party ticket in 1918 and served a two-year term; joined the Amalgamated Clothing Workers of America (ACWA) in 1919 and the following year became a general organizer; elected an ACWA vice-president and member of the general executive board in 1922; was appointed by the president of the Congress of Industrial Organizations (CIO), John L. Lewis (q.v.), to the Steel Workers' Organizing Committee in 1936; served as a CIO organizer in the rubber industry and participated in the strike against Goodyear Tire and Rubber Company in 1936; became president of the American Slav Congress in 1941 and served as national president of the American Polish Labor Council; was a member of the CIO Political Action Committee; was a Socialist in politics; died in Milwaukee, Wis., January 22, 1966; Walter Galenson, *The CIO Challenge to the AFL: A History of the American Labor Movement, 1935-1941* (1960); *Who's Who in Labor* (1946); Thomas W. Gavett, *Development of the Labor Movement in Milwaukee* (1965).

LABADIE, Joseph Antoine. Born in Paw Paw, Mich., April 18, 1850; son of a French-Indian interpreter father and a Potawatomi Indian mother; after briefly attending a rural school, was apprenticed to a printer in Indiana in 1866; as an itinerant printer, was subsequently active in the International Typographical Union; settled in Detroit, Mich., by the 1870s; founded the first Noble Order of the Knights of Labor (K of L) local assembly in Michigan in 1878 and, as an organizer for the K of L, was instrumental in expanding state membership to 25,000; meanwhile, played a major role in establishing the Detroit Council of Trades and Labor Unions in 1880; renewed his support of trade unionism after the K of L's decline, and in 1889 helped to found the Michigan Federation of Labor (MFL), which soon affiliated with the American Federation of Labor; was elected the first president of the MFL and served for two terms; as a talented polemicist, was a pioneer of the labor press in Michigan; ran as a

Greenback-Labor candidate for mayor of Detroit in 1878, but was active in the Socialist Labor party in the 1880s, and finally embraced philosophical anarchism as the only ultimate means of eliminating the exploitation of labor; due to ill health, retired from active participation in the labor movement in 1893 and took a job with the Detroit Water Board, but continued to publicize in favor of anarchism; was revered by unionists and radicals as the "gentle anarchist"; moved with wife to a small farm in 1912 and printed anarchist tracts with her; throughout his career, carefully preserved labor and radical materials, and in 1911 presented this collection of records and literature to the University of Michigan as the original basis for the University's Labadie Collection of Labor Materials, later one of the most important archives of its kind in the United States; especially strong in anarchist literature and manuscripts, but also contains the only large body of Industrial Workers of the World records and a wide variety of trade union sources; died in Detroit, Mich., October 7, 1933; Doris B. McLaughlin, *Michigan Labor* (1970); R. C. Stewart, "The Labadie Labor Collection," *The Michigan Alumnus Quarterly Review* (May, 1947).

(D.G.S.)

LANE, Dennis.   Born in Chicago, Ill., in 1881; son of Irish immigrant parents; Roman Catholic; after a few years of formal education, began working in the Chicago stockyards; shortly after becoming a cattle butcher, participated actively in the trade union movement and joined Cattle Butchers' Local 87 of the Amalgamated Meat Cutters and Butcher Workmen of North America (AMCBWNA); discharged as a result of his involvement in the 1904 AMCBWNA strike in Chicago but later reinstated; shortly after returning to work, was blacklisted as a result of spokesmanship for a group of workers presenting a formal grievance to a plant superintendent; worked as a truck salesman and door-to-door vegetable peddler; became an AMCBWNA international organizer; was elected an AMCBWNA vice-president and executive board member in 1913; joined an internal reform group that forced Secretary-Treasurer Homer Call's resignation in 1917 for unpopular policies; replaced Call as international secretary-treasurer, the chief AMCBWNA executive officer; as a tough, dedicated, and resourceful trade unionist, was destined to dominate the international office of the AMCBWNA for the next 25 years; led an organizing campaign among packing-house workers in the Chicago stockyards and other packing centers that achieved considerable success during World War I; but the organizing effort among packing-house workers was shattered after the war by employer resistance and the unsuccessful strike of

1921-1922; worked during the lean years of the 1920s and early 1930s to consolidate the AMCBWNA's strength among retail butchers; despite long-time support of the concept of industrial organization in meat processing and sympathy to the cause championed by the Congress of Industrial Organizations, was opposed to secession and kept the AMCBWNA loyal to the American Federation of Labor (AFL); served as an AFL fraternal delegate to the British Trades Union Congress in 1935; died in Chicago, Ill., August 10, 1942; David Brody, *The Butcher Workmen: A Study of Unionization* (1964); *The Butcher Workman*, September 1, 1942.

LAWRENSON, Jack.   Born in Dublin, Ireland, October 22, 1906; son of Robert, a farmer, and Johanna (Fogerty) Lawrenson; Roman Catholic; married Helen Strough Brown on June 28, 1939; two children; attended the public schools of Ireland and Great Britain, then began a career as a merchant seaman; emigrated to the United States and in 1937 was one of the principal founders of the National Maritime Union of America (NMU); was elected an NMU vice-president and for a short time was placed in charge of the Great Lakes Division of the NMU; became a leader of the opposition to the administration of NMU president Joseph Curran (q.v.); was defeated for reelection to an NMU vice-presidency in 1949 during a bitterly contested election amid charges of being "soft" on communism; began a moving and trucking business after his defeat and operated it until his death; authored numerous articles and pamphlets on union affairs; was a member of the American Labor party; died in New York City, October 31, 1957; Joseph P. Goldberg, *The Maritime Story: A Study in Labor-Management Relations* (1958); *Who's Who in Labor* (1946).

LAWSON, George W.   Born in Chicago, Ill., July 4, 1876; son of Louis, a clerk, and Hannah (Nelson) Lawson; Roman Catholic; married Eleanor Payer on June 8, 1904; one child; attended one year of high school in St. Paul, Minn., then worked for several years as an office clerk; entered a shoe factory ca. 1900 and shortly thereafter became a charter member of the St. Paul local of the Boot and Shoe Workers' International Union; served as the union's financial secretary for many years; was secretary of the St. Paul Trades and Labor Assembly, 1912-1919; became secretary-treasurer of the Minnesota State Federation of Labor (MSFL) in 1914; lobbied successfully in the legislature for improvement of workmen's compensation and for other labor laws; helped coordinate the 1918 political effort to unseat the administration of Governor Joseph Burnquist because of its anti-union policies; played a key role in 1919 in organizing the

Working People's Non-Partisan Political League, which, along with the Farmers' Non-Partisan League, laid the basis for the Minnesota Farmer-Labor party; meanwhile, managed to reconcile this kind of union political activism with the established American Federation of Labor (AFL) policy of political nonpartisanship by insuring that the city central bodies and the MSFL remained structurally distinct from the Farmer-Labor campaign organizations; during the rift between the AFL and the Congress of Industrial Organizations (CIO) in the 1930s, was consistently loyal to the AFL, and in Minnesota promptly executed orders of the AFL executive council to state federations to expel their CIO affiliates; cooperated simultaneously with the radical leadership of the powerful Minneapolis, Minn., Teamsters; was centrally involved in the MSFL's formal endorsement of Hubert Humphrey's candidacy for the U. S. Senate in 1948; was on the Board of Regents of the University of Minnesota, 1933-1959; after retiring as secretary of the MSFL in 1954, wrote *History of Labor in Minnesota* (1955); died in St. Paul, Minn., September 23, 1959; Solon DeLeon, ed., *The American Labor Who's Who* (1925); Theodore Christianson, *Minnesota: A History*, IV (1935).

(D.G.S.)

LAWSON, John Cummings.   Born in Aberdeen, Scotland, September 3, 1900; son of Alfred J., a quarry foreman, and Agnes (Walker) Lawson; Presbyterian; married Lillian Hasall on December 28, 1922; two children; emigrated to the United States as a child and settled in Vermont; acquired a grammar school education prior to beginning work in the quarries of Graniteville, Vt.; joined Branch 4 (Graniteville) of the United Stone and Allied Products Workers of America (USAPWA) in 1918; was elected president of Branch 4 and served in that capacity for 15 years; became a member of the USAPWA international executive board in 1930, serving until 1945; was appointed a USAPWA international organizer in 1934 and shortly thereafter was elected international secretary-treasurer, a position he still holds; was later elected secretary-treasurer of the Vermont State Industrial Union Council (IUC) and held that position until election as IUC president in 1946; was an influential figure in Vermont political affairs and served as member of the State Selective Service Appeals Board, the Vermont Vocational Training Committee, the Vermont Apprenticeship Council, and the executive committee of the National Religion and Labor Federation; retired as president of the Vermont IUC in 1950 to devote full time to his duties as secretary-treasurer of the USAPWA; was a delegate to most of the annual conventions of the Congress of Industrial

Organizations (CIO) and the biennial conventions of the American Federation of Labor-CIO; *Who's Who in Labor* (1946); *CIO News*, September 4, 1950.

LEE, William Granville.   Born in La Prairie, Ill., November 29, 1859; son of James W., a carpenter and contractor, and Sylvestra Jane (Tracy) Lee; Congregationalist; married Mary R. Rice on October 15, 1901; worked for his father as a carpenter after completing grammar school; became a brakeman on the Atchison, Topeka, and Santa Fe Railroad in 1879; was later transferred to the Rayton-New Mexico Division and was promoted to conductor in 1880; served as deputy recorder of deeds, Ford County, Kansas, 1884-1888; became a brakeman and switchman on the Wabash Railroad in 1888 and shortly thereafter joined the Missouri Pacific in a similar capacity; joined the Brotherhood of Railroad Trainmen (BRT) in 1890; secured employment on the Union Pacific Railroad as a brakeman and then a freight conductor; organized a BRT lodge in Kansas City and served it as master, chairman of the local committee, and member of the general committee of the Union Pacific; became vice grand master of the BRT in 1895; was elected BRT president in 1909; led the union through its long struggle for an eight-hour day, finally achieved through federal legislation after the threat of a nationwide strike in 1917; staunchly believed in the sanctity of contracts and thus expelled nearly one-sixth of the BRT's general membership in 1920 for unauthorized strikes; was defeated for reelection in 1928, primarily because of old-age and ill-health, but was chosen general secretary-treasurer; politically, was a Republican; refused to cooperate with presidents of other railroad brotherhoods who supported the Progressive party candidacy of Robert M. LaFollette in 1924; died in Cleveland, Ohio, November 2, 1929; Joel Seidman, *The Brotherhood of Railroad Trainmen: The Internal Political Life of a National Union* (1962); Walter F. McCaleb, *Brotherhood of Railroad Trainmen, with Special Reference to the Life of Alexander F. Whitney* (1936); *Dictionary of American Biography* (Vol. XI).

LEIGHTY, George Earle.   Born in Phillips, Wis., August 16, 1897; son of George W. and Anna B. (Klein) Leighty; Presbyterian; married Marie E. McDonald on June 15, 1917, and, after a divorce in 1923, Florence L. Gates on August 8, 1953; three children; graduating from the public schools of Phillips, Wis., worked as an agent-telegrapher and in various other capacities for the Chicago, Milwaukee, St. Paul, and Pacific Railroad, 1917-1937; joined the Order of Railroad Telegraphers (ORT) in

1917 and shortly thereafter was elected local chairman, serving until 1942; was chosen deputy president of the ORT in 1937 and general chairman of the Chicago, Milwaukee, St. Paul, and Pacific in 1942; served as vice-president of the ORT, 1942-1946 and was elected president in 1946; elected chairman of the National Employees Negotiating Committee of the 16 non-operating railway labor organizations in 1947, serving until 1965; was a member and for a time chairman of the united labor policy committee set up by the American Federation of Labor, the Congress of Industrial Organizations, and the independent railroad brotherhoods to coordinate union labor policies during the Korean War; served as chairman of the Railway Labor Executives' Association, 1950-1965; retired union positions in 1965; edited the *Railroad Telegrapher* for several years; supported the Democratic party; died in Washington, D. C., July 17, 1973; Archibald M. McIsaac, *The Order of Railroad Telegraphers: A Study in Trade Unionism and Collective Bargaining* (1933); *AFL-CIO News*, July 21, 1973; *Who's Who in Railroading* (1959).

LENNON, John Brown. Born in Lafayette County, Wis., October 12, 1850; son of John Alexander, a tailor, and Elizabeth Fletcher (Brown) Lennon; Presbyterian; married Juna J. Allen on April 5, 1871; attended the public schools of Hannibal, Mo., then served a four-year apprenticeship in his father's tailor shop; moved to Denver, Colo., in 1869 and became a merchant tailor; helped organize a Denver tailors' union in 1883 and became its secretary; in 1884 served as president of the Denver local that affiliated with the Journeymen Tailors' Union of America (JTU); while attending the JTU national convention as a delegate from Denver, was elected national president; elected vice-president in 1885 and served as general secretary, 1886-1910; elected treasurer of the American Federation of Labor (AFL) in 1890, serving until 1917; appointed to the Commission on Industrial Relations by President Woodrow T. Wilson in 1913; became a member of the U.S. Department of Labor's Board of Mediators in 1917; was a conservative trade unionist and usually supported the policies of AFL president Samuel Gompers; edited *The Tailors*, 1886-1910; politically was a Democrat; died in Bloomington, Ill., January 17, 1923; Philip Taft, *The A. F. of L. in the Time of Gompers* (1957); Charles J. Stowell, *The Journeymen Tailors' Union of America: A Study in Trade Union Policy* (1918); *Dictionary of American Biography* (Vol. XI).

LEONARD, Richard. Born in New Straitsville, Ohio, February 22, 1902; son of Bryan, a coal miner, and Anna (Thomas) Leonard; Roman

Catholic; married Mary Price on July 20, 1922; two children; secured employment in a Chrysler Corporation DeSoto plant, then helped organize the plant workers and was elected president of DeSoto Local 227 of the United Automobile, Aircraft, Agricultural Implement Workers of America (UAW); became UAW welfare director in 1937 and was elected secretary of the Michigan Congress of Industrial Organizations' (CIO) Industrial Union Council in 1938; served as a member of the UAW executive board, 1939-1943, and was director of the UAW's Ford department, 1941-1947; ran unsuccessfully for UAW secretary-treasurer in 1941 and 1943 and for a vice-presidency in 1944, but was elected a UAW vice-president in 1946; defeated for reelection in 1947 by John W. Livingston (q.v.) in a UAW election in which Walter P. Reuther (q.v.) consolidated his control of the union; returned to plant work after his defeat and was again elected president of DeSoto Local 227; attempted for a time to build an anti-administration faction in the local; joined the CIO staff in 1948 and was appointed CIO director for Arizona; became an assistant to President Philip Murray (q.v.) of the CIO in 1950 and served as assistant to Walter P. Reuther during his CIO presidency, 1951-1955; after the merger of the CIO and American Federation of Labor (AFL), was appointed assistant to the president of the AFL-CIO industrial union department and served in that capacity until his retirement in 1972; supported the Democratic party; Jack Stieber, *Governing the UAW* (1962); Frank Cormier and William J. Eaton, *Reuther* (1970); Jean Gould and Lorena Hickok, *Walter Reuther: Labor's Rugged Individualist* (1972).

LEWIS, Alma Dennie.   Born in Colfax, Iowa, January 23, 1889; son of Thomas, a coal miner, and Ann Louisa (Watkins) Lewis; Episcopalian; married Irene (Lindig) Perkins on August 30, 1934; attended the public schools of Lucas, Iowa, then began working in nearby coal mines; served overseas with the 27th Engineers, U.S. Army, during World War I; appointed director of mines and minerals for the state of Illinois in 1924, serving until 1930; served as assistant director general of the U.S. Employment Service, 1930-1934; became assistant to his brother, John L. Lewis (q.v.), president of the United Mine Workers of America (UMWA), in 1934 and served in that capacity for five years; in 1939, was appointed chairman of the newly formed United Construction Workers Organizing Committee, Congress of Industrial Organizations (CIO), which attempted to unionize unorganized construction workers; after the UMWA disaffiliated with the CIO in 1941, transferred his Construction Workers Organizing Committee into UMWA District 50; led an unsuccessful effort to organize New York City taxicab drivers in 1949; was elected president of controversial UMWA District 50 in 1954 and served in that capacity until his death in Washington, D. C., January 24, 1962; was a Republican; Saul Alinsky, *John L. Lewis: An Unauthorized Biography* (1949); *National Cyclopaedia of American Biography* (Vol. L); *Who's Who in Labor* (1946).

LEWIS, John Llewellyn.   Born in Lucas, Iowa, February 12, 1880; son of Thomas H., a coal miner, and Ann Louisa (Watkins) Lewis; Protestant; married Myrta Edith Bell on June 5, 1907; three children; completed three and one-half years of high school in Lucas; at age sixteen, started work as a coal miner in Lucas and then spent ten years in coal and metal mining in the Western states; mined coal in Lucas and Panama, Ill. from 1907 to 1909; was elected in Panama as president of the United Mine Workers of America (UMWA) local union; elected by District 12, UMWA, Illinois, as a lobbyist for state mine safety legislation in 1909; served as American Federation of Labor (AFL) field representative, 1910-1916; was appointed UMWA chief statistician and business manager of the *United Mine Workers Journal* in 1917, and later the same year was named UMWA international vice-president; served as acting UMWA president in 1919 and became international president in 1920, serving until his retirement in 1960; between 1919-1933, while overproduction caused depression of the industry, falling prices and wages, and severe unemployment, won a 27 per cent wage increase from the U.S. Coal Commission in 1919 and the shortlived Jacksonville Agreement in 1924; engaged in bitter internecine struggles to centralize administrative and bargaining power at the expense of district autonomy, particularly in Illinois and Kansas; defeated John Brophy's (q.v.) bid for the union presidency in 1926 by a vote of 173,323 to 60,661 amid charges of fraud; expelled many of his opponents, including Brophy, Alexander Howat (q.v.), Frank Farrington (q.v.), Adolph Germer (q.v.), and Powers Hapgood (q.v.), from the UMWA, and survived challenges from successive rival unions such as the National Miners Union, the Reorganized UMWA, and the West Virginia Mine Workers; meanwhile, union membership dwindled from approximately 500,000 to 75,000; in 1933, played an important role with UMWA economist W. Jett Lavek in the enactment of Section 7 (a) of the National Industrial Recovery Act, and within 90 days of its passage, 92 percent of U. S. coal miners were organized; in December, 1935, established the Committee for Industrial Organization (CIO) to organize industrial-type unions in the unorganized mass production industries; after quickly winning contracts with the United States Steel Corporation, Goodyear Rubber Corporation, and General

Motors Corporation, CIO unions attained a larger membership than AFL affiliates by the end of 1937; CIO unions, expelled by the AFL executive council, reorganized as a rival federation, the Congress of Industrial Organizations (CIO); in 1936, Lewis, a life-long Republican, supported the reelection of President Franklin D. Roosevelt, and the CIO contributed $500,000 to his campaign; but backed Republican Wendell Willkie in 1940 because of disillusionment with Roosevelt's attitude toward the "Little Steel" strike, his failure to eliminate unemployment, and his interventionist foreign policy; resigned the presidency of the CIO after Roosevelt's reelection; UMWA withdrew from the CIO in 1942, briefly reaffiliated with the AFL in 1946-1947, and then reassumed its independent status; controversial strikes during World War II won the miners a captive mines agreement and portal-to-portal pay; UMWA strikes in 1946 and 1948 won a royalty on every ton of coal mined and thus helped to finance the UMWA welfare and retirement program, but subjected the mines to federal government seizure and Lewis and his union to fines totaling $2,120,000 for civil and criminal contempt of court; by 1956, the welfare and retirement fund had been used to construct ten hospitals in Southern Appalachia, and by 1969 more than $2,600,000 had been dispersed to five million beneficiaries in medical and retirement benefits; "open-end agreement" worked out by Lewis and the Bituminous Coal Operators Association in 1951 eliminated national strikes from the industry for several years; in 1952, led the campaign for the first Federal Mine Safety Act; resigned the UMWA presidency in 1960 and served until his death as president emeritus at an annual salary of $50,000; also served as chairman of the board of trustees and as chief executive officer of the Welfare and Retirement Fund; died in Washington, D. C., June 11, 1969; Saul D. Alinsky, *John L. Lewis: An Unauthorized Biography* (1949); James A. Wechsler, *Labor Baron: A Portrait of John L. Lewis* (1944); Robert Cairns, *John L. Lewis: Leader of Labor* (1941); Charles A. Madison, *American Labor Leaders: Personalities and Forces in the Labor Movement* (1962); Charles K. McFarland, *Roosevelt, Lewis and the New Deal* (1970); Irving Bernstein, *The Lean Years: A History of the American Worker, 1920-1933* (1960), and *Turbulent Years: A History of the American Workers, 1920-1933* (1970); Melvyn Dubofsky, "J. L. Lewis," *McGraw-Hill Encyclopedia of World Biography*, Vol. VI (1973); *United Mine Workers Journal*, June 15, 1969.

(J.H.)

LEWIS, Joseph.   Born in Centerville, Calif., October 1, 1906; son of

Manuel S., a farmer, and Mary S. (Francisco) Lewis; Roman Catholic; married Marie Narcizo in March, 1929, and, after her death, Gladys Florence Goulart on March 28, 1942; two children; graduated from high school, then began working at the Wedgewood Stove Company in Centerville, Calif. in 1924; joined the Centerville local of the Stove Mounters International Union of North America (SMIU) in 1924; was elected president of SMIU Local 61 in Newark, Calif., in 1932; became an international vice-president of the SMIU in 1935 and was placed in charge of the West Coast District; elected international president of the SMIU (now the Stove, Furnace, and Allied Appliance Workers) in 1944, serving until 1956; was elected a vice-president of the American Federation of Labor (AFL) union label department in 1952, and became secretary-treasurer of the AFL-Congress of Industrial Organizations' union label department in 1956, serving in that capacity until his death; was a Democrat; died in Inverness, Fla., December 14, 1970; *AFL-CIO News*, December 19, 1970; *Who's Who in Labor* (1946); *Who's Who in America, 1970-1971.*

LEWIS, Thomas L.   Born in Locust Gap, Pa., in 1866; was of Welsh ancestry; began work as a breaker boy in the Ohio mines at an early age; a brother, W. T. Lewis, served as master workman of District 135, Knights of Labor; was a founder of the United Mine Workers of America (UMWA); after the resignation of Michael Ratchford (q.v.) in September, 1898, opposed John Mitchell (q.v.) for the union presidency but withdrew before a vote was taken; despite Mitchell's attempts at accommodation, including appointment of Lewis's friends as international organizers and, in 1903, placement of the staff of 60 international organizers under Lewis's direction, worked consistently as international vice-president to undermine Mitchell's prestige; participated in the successful organizing campaign in District 16, Maryland, in 1903; efforts to preserve the Central Competitive Field Agreement won in 1897 led to a serious rift with Mitchell who, in 1906, sought sectional agreements to restore the 1903 scale; after Mitchell's resignation in 1908, defeated William B. Wilson (q.v.), the incumbent international secretary-treasurer who had Mitchell's support, for the UMWA presidency; during his incumbency, perfected the technique of appointing international organizers to build a personal political machine and converted the *United Mine Workers Journal* into a house organ to support his continued elections; as a result of these innovations, was able to withstand strong challenges from John H. Walker (q.v.) of Illinois in 1909 and William Green (q.v.) of Ohio in 1910, both of whom lost presidential elections marked by serious charges of fraudulent vote counts;

signed agreements over the heads of district officers in Pennsylvania in 1909 and Illinois in 1910, thus helping to create an alliance of district officers that brought about his defeat in 1911; was annoyed by John Mitchell's retention of the American Federation of Labor's second vice-presidency and allied himself with the Socialists at the 1911 convention to force Mitchell to resign from either the National Civic Federation or the UMWA; after an unsuccessful effort to regain power in the UMWA in 1912, secured employment as a labor advisor to an antiunion West Virginia's operators' association; was an unsuccessful candidate for Ohio secretary of state on the Republican party ticket in 1912; published a coal trade journal, the *Coal Mining Review*, and helped found the National Coal Association; died in Charleston, W. Va., May 1, 1939; *United Mine Workers Journal*, May 15, 1939; Elsie Gluck, *John Mitchell: Miner* (1929); George S. McGovern and Leonard F. Guttridge, *Great Coalfield War* (1972).

(J.H.)

LINDELOF, Lawrence Peter.   Born in Malmö, Skane, Sweden, May 18, 1875; son of Anders Peter, a railway superintendent for the Swedish government, and Marie (Larson) Lindelof; Presbyterian; married Marie I. Rodriquez on March 31, 1902; two children; attended the public schools of Malmo, then served a four-year apprenticeship as a painter and interior decorator; emigrated to the United States in 1893; settled in Chicago, Ill., attended night school and, in 1910, took courses in commercial law at the Marshall School of Law; failed to find employment in his trade between 1894-1901; traveled throughout the United States working at various jobs; gained employment as a painter and decorator in Aurora, Ill., in 1901 and organized Local 448 of the Brotherhood of Painters, Decorators, and Paperhangers of America (BPDPHA); transferred his membership to Local 465, Ottawa, Ill., in 1904 and served as its treasurer until 1909; accepted employment with a Chicago painting and decorating contractor in 1909 and transferred his membership there; was elected in 1910 as chairman of the board of trustees of BPDPHA's newly organized District Council 14; elected secretary-treasurer of District Council 14 in 1912 and served until 1926; during this period, was credited with instituting a model apprenticeship system; moved to Hammond, Ind., in 1927, and affiliated with Local 460; was elected a vice-president of the BPDPHA and placed in charge of the union's Southern district, comprising 13 southern states; elected general president of the BPDPHA in 1929, and in the same year, became the first vice-president of the American Federation of Labor's building and construction trades department; retired union positions in 1952;

was a Republican; died in Lafayette, Ind., in October, 1952; Philip Zausner, *Unvarnished: The Autobiography of a Union Leader* (1941); *The National Cyclopaedia of American Biography* (1946); *Who's Who in Labor* (1946).

LITCHMAN, Charles Henry. Born in Marblehead, Mass., April 8, 1849; son of William, a shoe manufacturer, and Sarah E. (Bartlett) Litchman; married Annie Shirley on February 5, 1868; attended the public schools of Marblehead and spent two years at Marblehead Academy; completed his formal schooling, then became a shoe salesman for his father; established a shoe factory with his brother and began the study of law; as a result of the depression of 1873, lost the shoe factory and had to give up the study of law; secured employment as a journeyman shoemaker; joined the Knights of Saint Crispin and served as the grand scribe of its grand lodge during 1875-1878; was a member of the Marblehead school committee, 1873-1876; joined the Noble Order of the Knights of Labor (K of L) and served as the head of the Massachusetts District Assembly; was general secretary of the K of L, 1878-1881 and 1886-1888; after running unsuccessfully as a Republican, was elected to the Massachusetts state legislature on the Greenback Labor party ticket in 1878 and served one term; campaigned for Republican presidential nominee Benjamin Harrison in 1888, and was appointed by Harrison as a special agent in the U.S. Treasury Department in 1889, serving until 1893; appointed to the U.S. Industrial Commission in 1900 and served until his death; was a Republican; died in Newark, N.J., in 1902; Don D. Descohier, *The Knights of St. Crispin, 1867-1874* (1910); Gerald N. Grob, *Workers and Utopia: A Study of Ideological Conflict in the American Labor Movement, 1865-1900* (1961); Norman J. Ware, *The Labor Movement in the United States, 1860-1895* (1929).

LITTLE, Frank H. (fl. 1900-1917). Born in 1879, son of a Cherokee Indian mother and a Quaker father; by 1900, was a member of the Western Federation of Miners (WFM); was one of the militants who left the WFM for the Industrial Workers of the World (IWW) in 1907; was jailed for participation in the famous IWW free-speech struggle in Spokane, Wash., in 1909; organized California agricultural and construction workers, including Japanese and Mexicans, into IWW Local 66 at Fresno in 1910; called for "direct action" and was arrested after Fresno officials prohibited street speeches; Wobblies, packing the jail and being brutalized and tormented by their jailers, forced the city to grant them free speech; subsequently,

Little led free-speech fights in Denver, Colo., Kansas City, Mo., and elsewhere; as a member of the IWW general executive board in 1914, persuaded IWW to plan a coordinated effort to organize migratory harvest workers, thus leading in 1915 to the founding of the Agricultural Workers Organization; was involved in the Mesabi iron miners' strike in 1916; as chairman of the general executive board, strongly supported the centralizers' plan for organization of agricultural and industrial workers into unions controlled directly by IWW head William Haywood (q.v.); was archetype of the Western Wobbly agitator in his fearlessness, bluntness, uncompromising view of the "master" class, and vehement opposition to American intervention in World War I, but failed to convince IWW general executive board to condone draft resistance; helped lead the Arizona copper strikes of 1917; went to Butte, Mont., earlier a bastion of militant unionism but then kept as open shop by the giant Anaconda Company until a serious mine disaster in June, 1917, sparked a spontaneous revival of unionism; Little tried to exploit this situation for the IWW by urging the striking miners to persist and publicly agitating against the war; was feared by the industry as a person who might prolong the strike and was branded by the press as a seditious traitor; on the night of August 1, 1917, was seized and brutally killed by six men; with several thousand people attending his funeral in Butte, soon became one of the major Wobbly martyrs; despite investigation by Montana attorney general, killers were never identified; but hysteria about seditious activity fueled by the affair led to passage of the federal Sedition Act, used paradoxically to persecute national IWW leaders in 1918; Ralph Chaplin, *Wobbly: The Rough-and-Tumble Story of an American Radical* (1948); James P. Cannon, *Notebook of an Agitator* (1958); Arnon Gutfeld, "The Murder of Frank Little," *Labor History* (Spring, 1969).

(D.G.S.)

LIVINGSTON, John William.   Born in Iberia, Mo., August 17, 1908; son of Richard Monroe, a farmer, and Mary Alice (Burks) Livingston; married Rubye Britt on May 9, 1931; attended high school for two years, then secured employment with the Fisher Body Division of the General Motors Corporation (GMC) in St. Louis, Mo.; helped organize American Federation of Labor (AFL) Federal Labor Union 18386, which later became St. Louis Local 25 of the United Automobile, Aircraft, Agricultural Implement Workers of America (UAW); elected president of Federal Labor Union 18386 in 1934; was chairman of Local 25's strike committee during the successful strikes against GMC for recognition in 1936-1937;

became a UAW international representative in 1939 and served until elected director of UAW Region 5 and member of the international Executive board in 1942; served as vice-chairman and chairman of the national UAW-GMC negotiating committee, 1939-1942; was a regional panel member of th National War Labor Board and chairman of the Kansas City Office of Price Administration Labor Advisory Committee during World War II; became co-director, along with Walter P. Reuther (q.v.), of the UAW's GMC department in 1946; elected a UAW vice-president in 1947, and, at the same time, became director of the UAW aircraft, airline, McQuay-Norris, and piston ring department; appointed director of the UAW's agricultural implement department in 1948; named to the National Wage Stabilization Board in 1951; chaired a 12-member UAW delegation to visit various European countries in 1950 as guests of the British Amalgamated Engineering Union; later in the same year, presided in Paris over initial meeting of the automotive and truck department of the International Metalworkers Federation; became sole director of the UAW's GMC department in 1952; retired his UAW vice-presidency in 1955 and became director of organization of the newly merged AFL-Congress of Industrial Organizations, serving in that capacity until retirement in 1965; appointed director of union relations of the National Alliance of Businessmen in 1968; usually supported the Democratic party; Frank Cormier and William J. Eaton, *Reuther* (1970); Jack Stieber, *Governing the UAW* (1962); *Current Biography* (1959).

LLOYD, Thomas John.   Born in Spanish Forks, Utah, November 13, 1895; son of William E. and Isabelle (Spens) Lloyd; married Ethel M. Foyer; three children; at age twelve, while still attending school, began work as a helper in a slaughterhouse in Mammoth, Utah; completed a high school education, then started working full-time as a meat cutter with the Mammoth Supply Company, continuing in that capacity until 1917; served with the U.S. Navy during World War I, 1917-1919; after the war, in 1919-1921, became head meat cutter for the Valley Supply Company in Utah; after securing employment as a retail butcher with Stanford Market Company in Salt Lake City, Utah, in 1921, joined Local 537 of the Amalgamated Meat Cutters and Butcher Workmen of America (AMCBWNA); was store manager of the Stanford Market Company, 1921-1931; elected president of Local 537 in 1924; served as its secretary (chief administrative officer), 1931-1933; became an international vice-president of the AMCBWNA in 1933; was appointed director of the AMCBWNA's packinghouse workers' department in Chicago, Ill., in 1956; after the death of Earl

W. Jimerson (q.v.), was elected international president of the AMCBWNA in 1957; helped negotiate a merger between the AMCBWNA and the United Packinghouse Workers of America in 1968; retired from union positions in 1972; David Brody, *The Butcher Workmen: A Study of Unionization* (1964); *AFL-CIO News*, November 9, 1957; *Who's Who in America, 1972-1973*.

LONDON, Meyer.   Born in Suwalki, Russia, December 29, 1871; son of Ephraim, an intellectual and social radical, and Rebecca (Berson) London; Jewish; married Anna Rosenson in 1890; one child; received both a public and private education; emigrated with his family to the United States in 1891, settling in New York City; attended law school there at night and admitted to the bar of the state of New York in 1898; joined the Socialist Labor party (SLP) and in 1896 received its nomination for the New York assembly; broke with SLP leader Daniel DeLeon (q.v.) in 1897 and became associated with the newly organized Social Democratic party; was one of the founding members of the Socialist party of America in 1901; was a leading figure in the movement to organize the needle trades and served them as legal counsel for nearly three decades; supported strikes, participated in negotiations, and was an inspiring and effective speaker in behalf of trade union causes; was a leader of the New York City garment workers' strike of 1910; elected to the U.S. Congress on the Socialist party ticket from New York's Ninth Congressional District in 1914 and served two terms before being defeated for reelection in 1918, primarily as a result of his opposition to American intervention in World War I and his vote against the declaration of war; reelected in 1920, but defeated in 1922 after his Congressional district had been radically gerrymandered; during three terms in Congress, supported a variety of labor and social reforms, including anti-lynching measures, old-age pensions, and child labor reforms; was involved in numerous Jewish organizations, notably the Workmen's Circle; died as a result of an automobile accident in New York City, June 6, 1926; Melech Epstein, *Profiles of Eleven* (1965) and *Jewish Labor in the U.S.A., 1915-1952* (2 vols., 1953); Harry Rogoff, *An East Side Epic* (1930); *Dictionary of American Biography* (Vol. XI).

LUHRSEN, Julius G.   Born in Des Plaines, Ill., April 1, 1877; son of Henry W., a hardware merchant, and Louise (Henningsmeyer) Luhrsen; Evangelical Lutheran; married Josephine Cross on December 23, 1900; two children; while attending grammar school, worked on a farm and studied telegraphy at night; became a telegrapher on the Illinois Central

Railroad at age sixteen; moved somewhat later to the Northern Pacific Railroad and was promoted to dispatcher; despite great employer resistance and blacklisting threats, organized the American Train Dispatchers Association (ATDA) in Spokane, Wash., in 1917; was elected the first president of ATDA and held that position until obtaining a leave of absence in 1938; was executive secretary of the Railway Labor Executives' Association during 1938-1945; named by President Franklin D. Roosevelt to the Railroad Retirement Board in 1945; served on a large number of government boards and agencies during World War II; retired union positions in 1950; was a Republican; died in Chicago, Ill., October 16, 1956; *Who's Who in Labor* (1946); *Labor*, October 20, 1956.

LUNA, Charles.   Born in Celeste, Tex., October 21, 1906; son of Charles and Lillie (Green) Luna; married Opal Lewis on November 29, 1929; two children; after graduating from high school, secured employment as a yardman on the Santa Fe Railroad in 1925; joined East Dallas, Tex., Local 671 of the Brotherhood of Railroad Trainmen (BRT) in 1929; was a member of the BRT grievance committee for the Santa Fe Railroad, 1936-1946, and served as chairman of the committee, 1904-1946; worked as a national BRT organizer, 1943-1946; became general BRT chairman of the Gulf, Colorado, and Santa Fe Railroad in 1947, serving until 1954; was a member of the national wage-rules committee in 1949 and 1953; served as chairman of the International Association of General Chairmen, 1951-1955; was elected a BRT vice-president in 1954; served as assistant to BRT president William P. Kennedy (q.v.), 1960-1963, and was elected president in 1963; was a founder and was elected first president of the United Transportation Union (UTU), created by the merger of the BRT, the Brotherhood of Locomotive Firemen and Enginemen, the Order of Railway Conductors, and the Switchmen's Union of North America in 1969; was elected chairman of the Congress of Railway Unions created by the UTU, the Brotherhood of Maintenance of Way Employees, the Brotherhood of Railway and Airline Clerks, the Hotel and Restaurant Employees Union, and the Seafarers International Union of North America in 1969; resigned the presidency of the UTU in 1972; after retiring, as required by the UTU constitution, named vice-president and director of transportation for the Stirling Homex Corporation; Joel Seidman, *The Brotherhood of Railroad Trainmen: The Internal Political Life of a National Union* (1962); *Who's Who in America, 1972-1973; AFL-CIO News*, January 5, 1963, August 14, 1971.

LUNDEBERG, Harry.   Born in Oslo, Norway, March 25, 1901; son of Karl, a small businessman and syndicalist, and Allette (Koffeld) Lundeberg, an official of the Norwegian Labor party; was married and had three children; after completing grammar school education, began work at age fourteen as a sailor on sailing ships; during a 19-year period at sea, joined a variety of unions, including the Norwegian and British maritime unions, a Spanish syndicalist union, and the Industrial Workers of the World; decided in 1923 to sail only from the port of Seattle, Wash., and transferred his membership from the Australian Seamen's Union to the Sailors Union of the Pacific (SUP) in 1926; rose to prominence during the West Coast waterfront strike of 1934 as an associate of Harry Bridges (q.v.), the West Coast labor leader; was elected business agent of the Seattle local of the SUP in 1935; became the president of the Maritime Federation of the Pacific in 1936, but resigned shortly because of break with Bridges over personal and ideological differences; became secretary-treasurer of the SUP in 1936; founded and became first president of the American Federation of Labor (AFL)-affiliated Seafarers International Union of North America in 1938; led his union in a series of postwar strikes that provided substantial improvements in wage scales and working conditions; served as a vice-president of the California State Federation of Labor during the 1940s; was an officer of the AFL maritime trades council and, after the merger of the AFL and the Congress of Industrial Organizations (CIO), became president of the AFL-CIO maritime trades department; was a radical anti-capitalist early in his career, but became a vitriolic anti-Communist in the late 1930s and a conservative Republican in the 1950s; edited the *West Coast Sailors* for several years; died in Burlingame, Calif., January 28, 1951; Joseph P. Goldberg, *The Maritime Story: A Study in Labor-Management Relations* (1958); Charles P. Larrowe, *Harry Bridges: The Rise and Fall of Radical Labor in the U. S.* (1972); *Current Biography* (1952).

LUTHER, Seth (fl. 1817-1846).   Born in Providence, R. I., toward the end of the 18th century; son of an American Revolutionary War veteran; received very little formal education; was probably a Baptist; after an extensive trip down the Ohio River in 1817, returned to New England and worked as a carpenter; as an early advocate of labor reform, traveled widely in support of the workingmen's cause and was a gifted orator, agitator, and publicist; in an address delivered to striking workers during a ten-hour strike in Boston, Mass., in 1832, condemned factory working conditions; after publication and reprinting of the address, won immediate recognition as a leading New England labor agitator; after addressing the second convention of the New England Association of Farmers, Mechanics, and Other Working Men in the autumn of 1832, developed a close working relationship with Dr. Charles Douglas (q.v.), a leading Boston unionist; helped organize, along with Douglas, the short-lived Boston Trades' Union in 1834; represented the house carpenters at the founding convention of the Boston Trades' Union and was elected its secretary; during the Boston ten-hour strike of 1835, coauthored the *Ten Hour Circular*, which had a profound impact on the national ten-hour movement, but despite the circular and other extensive efforts in behalf of the strike, could not prevent its failure; was a delegate to the New York meeting of the National Trades' Union in 1836; addressed the convention on factory conditions and the ten-hour day and served on the ways and means committee; was arrested and imprisoned as a result of activities on behalf of the free suffrage movement in Rhode Island in the 1840s; was still agitating for the ten-hour day, in this case in New Hampshire, as late as 1846; authored several pamphlets, including *An Address on the Right of Free Suffrage* (1833) and *An Address Delivered Before the Mechanics and Workingmen of the City of Brooklyn* (1836); Louis Hartz, "Seth Luther: The Story of a Working Class Rebel," *New England Quarterly* (September, 1940); Edward Pessen, *Most Uncommon Jacksonians: The Radical Leaders of the Early Labor Movement* (1967); John R. Commons, *et al.*, eds., *A Documentary History of American Industrial Society*, Vols. V, VI, VIII (1910-1911); *Dictionary of American Biography* (Vol. XI).

LYDEN, Michael J.   Born in Barnikelle, County Mayo, Ireland, in 1879; son of Patrick, a farmer, and Mary Lyden; Roman Catholic; married Mary Jane Burke, a precinct committeewoman, in 1911; was forced by economic necessity to leave school at age fourteen to work on the family farm; emigrated to the United States in 1899, settling in Philadelphia, Pa.; worked there as a common laborer; took a job in the Carnegie Steel works at Youngstown, Ohio, in 1903, and later that year became a streetcar operator; joined the Amalgamated Association of Street, Electric Railway and Motor Coach Employees of America and helped negotiate the Youngstown local's first contract; elected shortly thereafter as president of the local and served in that position for 30 years; elected secretary of the Youngstown Labor Congress in 1912, and a vice-president of the Ohio State Federation of Labor (OSFL) in 1924; was a pioneer labor lobbyist in Ohio for such reforms as workmen's compensation; admired Samuel Gompers (q.v.), but was a militant unionist concerned with the welfare of all workers;

during the 1930s, helped to organize steelworkers, as well as the crafts, in the Youngstown industrial area; during the bitter "Little Steel" strike of 1937, supported the Steel Workers Organizing Committee; became president of the OSFL in 1935 and served continuously in that post until 1958; in later years, was instrumental in bringing about the merger of the American Federation of Labor (AFL) and Congress of Industrial Organizations (CIO) state bodies to form the Ohio AFL-CIO, and elected its president; resigned from this post in 1960, but remained active in union affairs for another decade as a member of the Greater Youngtown AFL-CIO Council; throughout his career, deeply involved in civic affairs and political organizations; helped found and was secretary of the Federated Improvement Clubs; was an ardent promoter of public libraries and scholarship programs; was very active in local and state Democratic party affairs; revered as the "grand old man" of Ohio labor; died in Youngstown, Ohio, February 12, 1973; *AFL-CIO News*, June 18, 1960; *Steel Labor* (December, 1960).

(D.G.S.)

LYNCH, James Mathew.   Born in Manlius, N.Y., January 11, 1867; son of James and Sarah (Caulfield) Lynch; Roman Catholic; married Letitia C. McVey on June 28, 1899; nine children; after attending the public schools of Manlius, became a "printers' devil" in the offices of the Syracuse (N.Y.) *Evening Herald* in 1884; joined the Syracuse local of the International Typographical Union (ITU) in 1887 and soon became secretary and then vice-president of the local; elected president of the Syracuse local in 1889 and served two terms; was president of the Syracuse Central Trades and Labor Assembly for seven terms; elected first vice-president of the ITU in 1898 and president two years later; led ITU during a period when it won an eight-hour day, established an old-age pension system, reformed its apprentice educational system, and doubled its membership; resigned in 1914 when appointed New York Commissioner of Labor; was named one of five commissioners of the newly merged New York Department of Labor and New York Industrial Commission; served as a commissioner until 1921; after serving as president of the American Life Society, a mutual insurance company, for one year, was again chosen ITU president in 1924 and served until reelection defeat in 1926; appointed to the New York Old Age Security Commission in 1929; was a Democrat; edited the *Advocate*, a Syracuse labor newspaper, in 1930; died in Syracuse, N.Y., July 16, 1930; Seymour M. Lipset, *et al.*, *Union Democracy: The Internal Politics of the International Typographical Union* (1956); Irwin Yellowitz, *Labor and the*

Progressive Movement in New York State, 1897-1916 (1965); *Dictionary of American Biography* (Vol. XI).

LYON, Arlon Everett.　Born in Thedford, Neb., October 15, 1899; son of Alfred S. and Mable (Wright) Lyon; entered the U.S. Army in 1918 shortly after completing his formal education; after discharge in 1919, secured employment in the signal department of the Southern Pacific Railroad; joined the Brotherhood of Railroad Signalmen of America (BRS) in 1920; elected local chairman for the Southern Pacific Railroad in 1924, serving in that capacity until 1927; became assistant grand president of the BRS in 1927; elected grand president of the BRS in 1934; became a vice-president of the Railroad Labor Executives' Association in 1940; served during World War II as an alternate member of the National Labor-Manpower Policy Committee and the War Manpower Commission; was executive secretary of the Railway Labor Executives' Association, 1945-1962; appointed by President John F. Kennedy as the labor member of the tripartite Railroad Retirement Board in 1962, serving until 1969; retired from union activities in 1969; served as a member of the executive committee of the International Transport Workers Federation; *Who's Who in Railroading* (1959); *Who's Who in Labor* (1946).

LYONS, John H.　Born in Cleveland, Ohio, October 29, 1919; son of John H., international president of the International Association of Bridge, Structural, and Ornamental Iron Workers (IABSOIW), and Elizabeth M. (Sexton) Lyons; married Dorothy Ann Boyen on April 15, 1944; two children; secured employment as an iron worker while working for a B.S. degree in mechanical engineering from the University of Missouri's School of Mines; joined the IABSOIW in 1937; received the B.S. degree in 1942; joined the U.S. Air Force in 1943, serving until 1946; was employed by the General Bronze Corporation, New York City, 1946-1954; became an international representative and general organizer for the IABSOIW in 1954; elected a general IABSOIW vice-president in 1959, and in 1961 chosen international president; became a member of the internal disputes panel and a vice-president of both the American Federation of Labor-Congress of Industrial Organizations' (AFL-CIO) metal trades department and the building and construction trades department in 1961; was appointed to the citizens' advisory committee of the President's Commission on Juvenile Delinquency and to the advisory council of the Bureau of Employment Security in 1962; served as a member of the Taft-Hartley Labor-

Management Panel and of the National Advisory Manpower Committee in 1963, as chairman of the labor advisory committee of the President's Committee on Equal Employment Opportunity in 1964, and on the National Commission on Urban Problems in 1967; elected an AFL-CIO vice-president and executive council member in 1967; *AFL-CIO News*, September 16, 1967; *Who's Who in America, 1972-1973;* Joseph C. Goulden, *Meany* (1972).

McAVOY, Harold.   Born in Philadelphia, Pa., November 5, 1904; son of Thomas and Mary (Owens) McAvoy; Roman Catholic; married Jean A. Buechner on June 22, 1928; one child; after graduating from high school, attended Hefley Business School; secured employment with the U. S. Postal Service in New York City and joined the New York City branch of the National Association of Post Office and Railway Handlers (NAPORH); elected president of the New York branch shortly after NAPORH's affiliation with the American Federation of Labor (AFL) in 1937; elected NAPORH national president in 1941 and served in that capacity until his death; was a NAPORH delegate to the annual conventions of the AFL, 1942-1952, and to the biennial conventions of the AFL-Congress of Industrial Organizations, 1955-1967; led the NAPORH into a merger with the International Hod Carriers', Building, and Common Laborers' Union of America in 1968; died in New York City, December 2, 1968; *Who's Who in America, 1968-1969; AFL-CIO News*, December 7, 1968.

McBRIDE, John.   Born in Wayne County, Ohio, July 25, 1854; went to work in the coal mines at age nine; joined the Ohio Miners' Amalgamated Association in 1870, and was elected president in 1883; was elected to the Ohio legislature in 1883 and 1885, but was an unsuccessful Democratic candidate for Ohio secretary of state in 1886; organized the Amalgamated Association of Miners of the United States in 1883, but the six-month Hocking Valley, Ohio, coal strike destroyed it; was one of the founders and was elected president of the National Federation of Miners and Mine Laborers in 1885; served as temporary chairman of the American Federation of Labor's (AFL) founding convention in 1886; unsuccessfully sought the AFL's endorsement for U.S. Commissioner of Labor in 1888; was chosen president of the new National Progressive Union of Miners and Mine Laborers, formed by the National Federation of Miners' leaders and a splinter group of Knights of Labor Assembly 135; led a unity convention with John B. Rae of Assembly 135 and established the United Mine Workers of America (UMWA) in 1890, with Rae as its president; was himself elected president by 1892 convention after Rae lost strikes in 1890 and 1891 and refused to run for reelection; served until 1895, then resigned to serve a one-year term as president of the AFL; served as UMWA head during the Depression of 1893-1897, which resulted in unemployment, falling wages, and desperate straits for miners; an eight-week strike of 100,000 miners in 1894 to deplete coal stocks and raise coal prices and wages was destroyed by an influx of non-union Pennsylvania anthracite and West Virginia bituminous coal into the market; during the administrations of McBride and his successor, Phil Penna, UMWA's membership fell from 13,000 to 9,731 and its treasury from $2,600 to $600; lost to Samuel Compers (q.v.) by 18 votes in his bid for reelection to the AFL presidency in 1895; was a principal organizer of a convention of Ohio trade unionists that endorsed the People's party's Omaha platform with the addition of several labor planks and nominated a Populist-Labor state ticket that polled five percent of Ohio's vote; purchased the *Columbus* (Ohio) *Record*, a weekly newspaper, in 1896 and edited the paper until moving to Arizona in 1917 due to poor health; died in Globe, Ariz., in October, 1917; Philip Taft, *The A. F. of L. in the Time of Gompers* (1957); McAlister Coleman, *Men and Coal* (1943); Charles A. Madison, *American Labor Leaders: Personalities and Forces in the Labor Movement* (1950); John H. M. Laslett, *Labor and the Left: A Study of Socialism and Radical Influences in the American Labor Movement, 1881-1924* (1970).

(J.H.)

McCARTHY, Patrick Henry.   Born in Killoughteen, Newcastle West, County Limerick, Ireland, March 17, 1863; son of Patrick and Eileen McCarthy; Roman Catholic; married Jeanette H. Saunders on January 15, 1905; attended the national schools of Ireland and learned the carpenters' trade before emigrating to the United States in 1880; resided in Chicago, Ill., and St. Louis, Mo., for six years, then moved to San Francisco, Calif., and joined the United Brotherhood of Carpenters and Joiners of America (UBC); organized and became the president of the Building Trades Council of San Francisco in 1894 and the State Building Trades Council of California in 1901; elected a member of the UBC executive board in 1904; was one of the founders and became the first president of the Building Trades Temple Association of San Francisco in 1908; served on the Freeholders Committee that framed the charter for the city of San Francisco prior to his election as mayor in 1909 on the Union Labor party ticket; served a two-year term as mayor; acquired near-monopoly control of the construction industry of San Francisco before being deposed by a coalition of businessmen and financers in 1922; retired from union positions in 1923 and became involved in the investment banking business; identified himself as a Republican; died in San Francisco, Calif., June 30, 1933; Robert A. Christie, *Empire in Wood: A History of the Carpenters' Union* (1956); Ira Brown Cross, *History of the Labor Movement in California* (1935); Walton Bean, *Boss Ruef's San Francisco: The Story of the Union Labor Party, Big Business, and the Graft Prosecution* (1952).

McCURDY, Joseph Patrick.   Born in Baltimore, Md., March 20, 1892; son of John Andrew, superintendent of parks, and Mary Ellen McCurdy; Roman Catholic; married Genevieve Elizabeth Birrane on February 24, 1938; two children; completed grammar school and took night courses at Baltimore Business College; joined Local 15 of the United Garment Workers of America in 1910; elected business representative of Local 15 in 1925, serving until 1941; served as president of the Maryland State Federation of Labor and the District of Columbia Federation of Labor, 1932-1942; elected president of the Baltimore Federation of Labor in 1933, serving until 1942; was the American Federation of Labor (AFL) fraternal delegate to the Canadian Trades and Labor Congress in 1934; served as a member of the Maryland Unemployment Compensation Board, 1937-1951; appointed to the National Labor Relations Regional Board in 1939; helped draft the Maryland old-age pension law and served on state commissions concerned with workmen's compensation, occupational diseases, and unemployment; served as AFL fraternal delegate to the British Trades Union Congress in 1950; served as vice-president of the AFL union label trades department; elected international president of the UGW in 1950; authored "Reasons Why Labor Should Oppose Prohibition"; politically a Democrat; *Who's Who in Labor* (1946); *Who's Who in America, 1972-1973*.

McDEVITT, James Lawrence.   Born in Philadelphia, Pa., November 3, 1898; son of William Paul, a plasterer, and Sarah Margaret (Hickey) McDevitt; Roman Catholic; married Margaret Winifred Murphy on January 25, 1921, and, after her death, Margaret Mary Toole on January 3, 1953; three children; attended Catholic parochial schools for ten years prior to being apprenticed in the plasterers' trade under the direction of Local 8 of the Operative Plasterers' International Association in 1916; enlisted in the U.S. Army in 1918 and served in France during World War I; became a journeyman plasterer after the war; began a ten-year term as business manager of Local 8 in 1925; also served during this period as president of the Philadelphia, Pa., Building Trades Council and as a member of the city's Building Code Commission and Housing Authority; named area labor relations director of the Works Progress Administration in 1935 and appointed to the Philadelphia Regional Labor Board; served as president of the Pennsylvania State Federation of Labor, 1938-1954; during his incumbency, served on a variety of state agencies, including the State Unemployment Compensation Board of Review, the Philadelphia War Chest, the State Planning Commission, the Displaced Persons Commission, the Advisory Committee on Public Utility Arbitration Law, and the Advisory Council for Private Trade Schools; was appointed director of Labor's League for Political Education, American Federation of Labor (AFL), in 1951; after the AFL-Congress of Industrial Organizations' merger in 1955, became co-director with Jack Kroll (q.v.) of the Committee on Political Education (COPE); after Kroll's resignation in 1957, became sole director of COPE; was a Democrat; died in Washington, D.C., March 19, 1963; Anonymous, *Fraternally Yours, James L. McDevitt: The Portrait of a Man and a Movement* (1956); Terry Catchpole, *How to Cope with COPE: The Political Operations of Organized Labor* (1968); *Current Biography* (1959); *AFL-CIO News*, March 23, 1963.

McDONALD, David John. Born in Pittsburgh, Pa., November 22, 1902; son of David, a steelworker, and Mary (Kelly) McDonald; Roman Catholic; married Emily Price on August 4, 1937, and Rosemary C. McHugh on January 3, 1950; one child; he went to work at age fifteen in a mill office of the Jones and Laughlin Steel Corporation; completed high school in 1920, while employed as a machinist's helper in a National Tube Company plant; as a result of experience in the steel industry, became aware of worker grievances and sympathetic to the trade union movement; in 1923, at age twenty, became secretary to United Mine Workers of America (UMWA) Vice-President Philip Murray (q.v.); despite completion of the Carnegie Institute Drama program in 1932, decided to remain with the UMWA; in 1936, was named secretary-treasurer of the Congress of Industrial Organizations' (CIO) Steel Workers Organizing Committee (SWOC) by Murray, its chairman; performed adeptly in this key post; with the founding of the United Steelworkers of America (USWA) in 1942, became its secretary-treasurer; was named acting president of USWA by its executive board after Murray's death in 1952; was elected to the position the following year; subsequently became a vice-president of the American Federation of Labor-CIO executive council; gained substantial wage and fringe benefits for USWA members, notably a generous supplemental unemployment benefit program negotiated in 1956, and, after the marathon 1959 steel strike, much-improved pension payments; in order to avoid a repetition of the 1959 conflict, worked with basic steel leaders to create a human relations committee for continuous top-level union-management discussion to resolve differences—especially those arising from automation and foreign competition—in advance of actual contract negotiations; thus, contributed to situation in which there were no basic steel strikes during the 1960s; was unsuccessfully challenged in the mid-1950s by dues protestors, who tried to unseat him, and by district directors, who resented his centralization of bargaining in the presidency; also began to suffer from criticism that he was too cozy with management and out of touch with union rank-and-file members; was further damaged by results of the 1962 and 1963 contracts, which were negotiated in a slack period when steelworkers were more concerned with job security than wage hikes, and which failed to yield benefits when the industry recovered in 1963-1964; had the USWA consititution altered to permit himself two more four-year terms, but Secretary-Treasurer I. W. Abel (q.v.) successfully opposed him in 1965; usually supported Democratic candidates, but served on several governmental commissions in both Republican and Democratic administrations; coauthored *Coal and Unionism* (1939) and authored his autobiography, *Union Man* (1969); *Current Biography* (1953); John A. Orr, "The Steelworker Election of 1965," *Labor Law Journal* (February, 1969); John Herling, *Right to Challenge: People and Power in the Steelworkers Union* (1972).

(D.G.S.)

McDONALD, Joseph Donald. Born in Clatskanine, Ore., July 10, 1895; son of James William, a carpenter, and Dora (Aldridge) McDonald; married Louisa May Doucette on April 21, 1920; two children; graduated from high school; eventually became an apprentice butcher and joined Local 143 of the Amalgamated Meat Cutters and Butcher Workmen of North America; was elected secretary-treasurer of Local 143, secretary-treasurer of the Oregon Federated Butchers, and secretary-treasurer of the label trades section of the Portland (Ore.) Central Labor Council (CLC); was elected a vice-president of the Oregon State Federation of Labor (OSFL) in 1939 and became a member of the executive council of the Portland CLC; served during World War II as a labor member of the advisory committee for the Office of Price Administration in Oregon and as a labor member of the Twelfth Regional Panel of the War Labor Board; elected president of the OSFL in 1942, serving in that capacity until the merger of the American Federation of Labor-Congress of Industrial Organizations (AFL-CIO) in Oregon; after the merger, elected president of the Oregon AFL-CIO; during his years of labor leadership in Oregon, was closely associated with labor-oriented problems growing from wartime and from postwar reconversion conflicts, with the negotiation of the AFL-CIO merger in Oregon, and with successful lobbying efforts in the Oregon state legislature; was a delegate to several AFL and AFL-CIO conventions; a Democrat; retired union positions in 1967; *Who's Who in Labor* (1946); *AFL-CIO News*, September 30, 1967.

McDONNELL, J. P.   Born in Dublin, Ireland, ca. 1840; was reared in a middle-class, Roman Catholic family; became deeply committed to the Fenian movement and was often arrested and imprisoned; converted to Marxian communism in 1869, and was an Irish delegate to the Hague Congress of the International in 1872; shortly after the Hague Congress, emigrated to the United States, settling in New York City; was one of the leaders of the Trades and Labor Council of New York in 1876; after the collapse of the International, aligned himself with its American successor, the Workingmen's Party of the United States; became the editor of the New York *Labor Standard*, the official English-language organ of the Workingmen's party; broke with the American Communist movement in 1877 when the Socialist Labor party was organized and committed itself exclusively to political action; meanwhile, moved the *Labor Standard*, of which he had assumed control, to Fall River, Mass., and then to Paterson, N.J.; was one of the principal founders of the International Labor Union (ILU) in 1878, which brought together Ira Steward's (q.v.) eight-hour advocates and Socialist trade unionists in an alliance committed to the organization of the unskilled; was a member of the ILU executive board; was one of the leaders in organizing Paterson textile workers and in the textile strikes of 1878; selected as the ILU delegate to the Trades Congress of England in 1879, but prevented from attending by the collapse of the ILU; twice convicted as a result of allegedly libelous utterances in the *Labor Standard*, one of which referred to strikebreakers as "scabs" and the other exposing working conditons in a Paterson brick-making yard; was one of the major organizers of the New Jersey State Federation of Trades and Labor Unions in 1883 and served as its chairman for 15 years; organized the Paterson Trades Assembly in 1884; was given credit for the enactment of the New Jersey Labor Day law, the first such law to be enacted in the United States; joined the Anti-Poverty Association organized by Henry George (q.v.) in 1887; never rejected the class consciousness engendered by his faith in socialism, but during his career became increasingly committed to immediate and practical trade union objectives; died in Paterson, N.J., in 1906; John R. Commons, *et al.*, *History of Labour in the United States*, Vol. II (1918); Philip S. Foner, *History of the Labor Movement in the United States*, Vol. II (1955); Norman Ware, *The Labor Movement in the United States, 1860-1895* (1929).

McFETRIDGE, William Lane.   Born in Chicago, Ill., November 28, 1893; son of William F., a teamster, and Wilhelmina (Quesse) McFetridge; Roman Catholic; married Barbara A. Werner on October 22, 1923; one child; attended the public schools of Chicago, Ill., and McFarland, Wis., until 1904 when, at age thirteen, quit school and became an office boy for the Milwaukee Railroad in Chicago; with the exception of a short period during which he was employed by the American Express Company, worked for the Milwaukee Railroad from 1904 to 1923; eventually promoted to traveling claims agent; during his employment with the Milwaukee Railroad, attended night schools, graduating from high school, pre-law, and law school; accepted employment in 1923 as a confidential secretary, investigator, and trouble-shooter for his uncle, William Quesse, the president of the Chicago Flat Janitors Union, which was Local 1 of the Building Service Employees International Union (BSEIU); organized Chicago school maintenance workers and elected president of the new BSEIU local; was an officer of the Chicago Federation of Labor and served as a vice-president of the Illinois State Federation of Labor, 1939-1950; shortly after his election as a national vice-president of the BSEIU, the union president, George Scalise, was imprisoned for extortion, and he assumed the presidency of the shattered, corruption-ridden international and rebuilt it into a solid, respected union; elected an American Federation of Labor (AFL) vice-president and executive council member in 1940; was one of the committee members who drafted the AFL-CIO merger agreement in 1955; became a vice-president and member of the executive council of the new federation; was very active in community affairs in Chicago and was a member of numerous public and private organizations, including the National Conference of Christians and Jews, the National Urban League, the Israel Bond Committee, and served as a member of the fiscal advisory committee of the Chicago Board of Education; was the recipient of numerous awards and honors and in 1957 was selected one of Chicago's 100 outstanding citizens; retired and was named president emeritus of the BSEIU in 1960 and resigned as AFL-CIO vice-president in 1965; was a Republican; died in Chicago, Ill., March 15, 1969; Philip Taft, *The A. F. of L. From the Death of Gompers to the Merger* (1959); *Business*

Week, August 18, 1951; *Fortune* (November, 1946); *AFL-CIO News,* March 22, 1969; *Who's Who in America, 1966-1967.*

MacGOWAN, Charles J.   Born in Argyllshire, Scotland, in 1887; married; three children; emigrated with his father, a stonemason and trade unionist, to Canada in 1897 and gained a grammar school education prior to beginning an apprenticeship as a boilermaker on the Grand Trunk Pacific Railroad in 1909; shortly thereafter, joined the International Brotherhood of Boilermakers, Iron Ship Builders and Helpers of America (IBB); emigrated to the United States in 1913; beginning in 1917, served his union and the labor movement in various capacities, including as IBB international representative, as assistant to the president of the American Federation of Labor (AFL) railroad labor department, and as a member of the Railroad Adjustment Board; elected an international vice-president of the IBB in 1936, and served in that capacity until elected international president in 1944; served on President Harry S. Truman's Labor-Management Conference in 1945, and during the same year, served as a labor consultant at the founding conference of the United Nations in San Francisco, Calif.; elected an AFL vice-president and executive council member in 1947, and after the AFL-Congress of Industrial Organizations' (CIO) merger in 1955, retained the same position in the new labor federation until his death; was instrumental in the establishment of the AFL's League for Political Education in 1948; was a delegate to the founding convention of the International Confederation of Free Trade Unions in London in 1949; served as an AFL fraternal delegate to the British Trades Union Congress and the International Transportworkers Federation in Utrecht, Holland, in 1951; was an influential participant in the negotiations between the AFL and CIO that resulted in the 1955 merger; retired as president emeritus of the IBB in 1954; was a Democrat; died in Parkville, Mo., October 25, 1960; Philip Taft, *The A. F. of L. From the Death of Gompers to the Merger* (1959); *AFL-CIO News,* October 29, 1960; Arthur J. Goldberg, *AFL-CIO: Labor United* (1956); *Labor,* November 5, 1960; *The American Federation of Labor News-Reporter,* April 30, 1954.

McGRADY, Edward Francis.   Born in Jersey City, N.J., January 29, 1872; son of James T., an assistant foreman in the Boston, Mass., street department, and Jane (Gawley) McGrady; Roman Catholic; married Mary J. Griffin on October 11, 1897; two children; completed high school in Jersey City, N.J., then moved to Boston where he took evening courses in economics and business management; took a job with the Boston *Traveler* as a pressman in 1894 and joined the Web Pressmen local of the International Printing Pressmen's and Assistants' Union of North America (IPPAUNA); became an organizer for the Web Pressmens' local and in 1907 elected president of the local; served as state superintendent and then acting federal director of the U.S. Employment Service in Massachusetts; during 1907-1909, served variously as secretary of the IPPAUNA, president of the Boston Central Labor Union, and vice-president and president of the Massachusetts State Federation of Labor; served a two-year term on the Boston Common Council and a two-year term in the Massachusetts House of Representatives; became the American Federation of Labor (AFL) official legislative representative in Washington, D.C., in 1919 and served in that capacity until 1933; appointed deputy administrator of the National Recovery Administration in 1933; served as assistant secretary of labor in the U.S. Department of Labor, 1933-1937; retired from union activities in 1937 and became a vice-president for labor relations of the Radio Corporation of America; during World War II, was a special labor consultant to the secretary and under-secretary of war; retired from all business affairs in 1959; was a Democrat; died in Newtonville, Mass., July 17, 1960; Philip Taft, *The A. F. of L. From the Death of Gompers to the Merger* (1959); Bruce Minton and John Stuart, *Men Who Lead Labor* (1937); Elizabeth F. Baker, *Printers and Technology: A History of the International Printing Pressmen and Assistants' Union* (1957).

McGUIRE, Peter James.   Born in New York City, July 6, 1852; son of John J., a department store porter, and Catherine Hand (O'Riley) McGuire; Roman Catholic; married Christina Wolff in 1884; four children; forced by family financial circumstances to quit school at age eleven; took odd jobs while attending free night classes at Cooper Union; became an apprentice wood joiner in 1867 and joined the International Workingmen's Association; was an organizer for the Social Democratic party (later the Socialist Labor party), 1874-1879; credited with successfully sponsoring legislation in the Missouri state legislature establishing one of the first bureau of labor statistics in the United States; appointed deputy commissioner of the Missouri Bureau of Labor Statistics, but resigned after a short time to take a job as a St. Louis furniture worker; organized St. Louis carpenters; inspired the meeting of 12 carpenters' unions in Chicago, Ill., in 1881, which resulted in the organization of the United Brotherhood of Carpenters and Joiners (UBC); elected the first secretary (the chief administrative official) of the UBC and became the editor of the union's newspaper, *The Carpenter*; wrote the convention call for the Chicago conference of national labor unions that resulted in the formation of the Federation of Organized Trades and Labor Unions of the United States and Canada in 1881; moved the headquarters of the UBC to New York and became involved in the eight-hour day movement; was one of the leaders of the May Day demonstrations of 1886 and 1890; led the movement which ultimately resulted in legislation in 1894 creating a national Labor Day holiday; was one of the founders of the American Federation of Labor (AFL) in 1886 and became its first secretary; in 1889 elected a vice-president of AFL, but forced to resign in 1900 because of poor health and alcoholism; growing opposition to his leadership of the UBC resulted in a contrived charge of embezzlement of funds and his expulsion from the union in 1902; died in Camden, N.J., February 18, 1906; Robert A. Christie, *Empire in Wood: A History of the Carpenters' Union* (1956); Philip Taft, *The A. F. of L. in the Time of Gompers* (1957); Gerald Grob, *Workers and Utopia: A Study of Ideological Conflict in the American Labor Movement, 1865-1900* (1961).

McMAHON, Thomas F.   Born in Ballybay, County Monaghan, Ireland, May 2, 1870; son of James, a flax buyer, and Bridget (Shreenan) McMahon; Roman Catholic; married Catherine E. Murray on October 15, 1891; attended the national schools of Ireland before emigrating to the United States in 1887; joined the Knights of Labor in 1889; hired as a cloth folder and joined Cloth Folders' Local 505, United Textile Workers of America (UTW) in 1901; served as business agent of Local 505, 1904-1912; was a UTW national organizer, 1912-1917; elected a national vice-president of the UTW in 1917 and became president in 1921, serving until 1937; appointed a labor board member of the National Recovery Administration in 1934; was a proponent of industrial organization and a charter member of the Committee for Industrial Organization in 1935; resigned UTW presidency in 1937 and accepted an appointment as Rhode Island State Labor Director, serving until 1939; usually supported Democratic candidates; authored *United Textile Workers of America* (1926); died in Cranston, R. I., April 22, 1944; Walter Galenson, *The CIO Challenge to the AFL: A History of the American Labor Movement, 1935-1941* (1960); Philip Taft, *The A. F. of L. From the Death of Gompers to the Merger* (1959); Robert R. R. Brooks, *The United Textile Workers of America* (1935).

McNAMARA, Patrick Vincent.   Born in North Weymouth, Mass., October 4, 1894; son of Patrick Vincent, an Irish laborer and ship fitter, and Mary Jane (Thynne) McNamara; Roman Catholic; married Kathleen Kennedy, June 21, 1921, and, after her death in 1929, Mary Mattee on September 3, 1930; two children; completed high school, then attended the Fore River Apprentice School in Quincy, Mass., 1912-1916; worked as a pipe fitter and foreman for the Bethlehem Shipyard, Fore River, 1916-1919; played semiprofessional football, 1919-1920; moved to Detroit, Mich., in 1921 and there worked for various construction contractors for the next several years; joined Local 636 of the United Association of Journeymen and Apprentices of the Plumbing and Pipe Fitting Industry of the United States and Canada (UA) in 1924; elected president of UA Local 636 and served in that capacity until 1954; served as a vice-president of the Detroit Federation of Labor, 1939-1945; during World War II, was rent director for the Office of Price Administration in the Detroit area; elected as one of nine members of the Detroit Common Council in 1946; served as a member of the Detroit Board of Education, 1949-1955; elected as a Democrat to the United States Senate in 1954; was one of the co-sponsors of the Labor-Management Reporting and Disclosure Act of 1959; died in Bethesda, Md., April 30, 1966; *Biographical Directory of the American Congress, 1774-1971* (1971); *AFL-CIO News*, May 7, 1966; *The National Cyclopaedia of American Biography* (Vol. I).

McNEILL, George Edwin.   Born in Amesbury, Mass., August 4, 1837; son of John, a Scots-Irish immigrant, and Abigail Todd (Hickey) McNeill; married Adeline J. Trefethen on December 24, 1859; educated in public and private schools; began work in 1851 in the Amesbury woolen mills at age fifteen; during the next few years, attempted shoemaking and salesmanship; moved to Boston, Mass., in 1856; was an advocate of Ira Steward's (q.v.) eight-hour philosophy, serving as secretary of the Grand Eight-Hour League in 1863-1864 and as president of the Boston Eight-Hour League, 1869-1874; edited and served on the editorial staff of labor newspapers in Fall River, Mass., New York City, and Paterson, N.J.; was a founder and served as president of the Workingmen's Institute, 1867-1869; cooperated with Wendell Phillips in lobbying for the creation of the first state bureau of labor statistics, which was approved by the Massachusetts legislature in 1869; served as the deputy director of the Massachusetts Bureau of Labor Statistics, 1869-1873; wrote a charter for an 1874 labor congress in Rochester, N.Y., which was later adopted as the Declaration of Principles of the Noble Order of the Knights of Labor (K of L); became president of the International Labor Union in 1878; joined the K of L in 1883 and served as treasurer of District 30 (Mass.), 1884-1886; organized the Massachusetts Mutual Accident Insurance Company in 1883; after the rejection of his plan for American Federation of Labor (AFL)-K of L cooperation, resigned from the K of L and joined the AFL; became the editor and proprietor of the Boston *Labor Leader* in 1886, and in the same year, ran unsuccessfully for mayor of Boston on the United Labor party ticket; was an AFL fraternal delegate to the British Trades Union Congress in 1897; edited and contributed to *The Labor Movement: The Problem of Today* (1886); authored *The Philosophy of the Labor Movement* (1893), *Eight Hour Primer* (1889), *A Study of Accidents and Accident Insurance* (1900), and *Unfrequented Paths: Songs of Nature, Labor, and Men* (1903); died in Somerville, Mass., May 19, 1906; David Montgomery, *Beyond Equality: Labor and the Radical Republicans, 1862-1872* (1967); Norman Ware, *The Labor Movement in the United States, 1860-1895* (1929); John R. Commons, *et al.*, *History of Labour in the United States*, Vol. II (1918); *Dictionary of American Biography* (Vol. XII).

McNULTY, Frank Joseph.   Born in Londonderry, Ireland, August 10, 1872; son of Owen and Catherine (O'Donnell) McNulty; Roman Catholic; married Edith H. Parker in 1893; immigrated with parents to the United States in 1876; attended the public schools of New York City; adopted the electricians' trade; moved to Perth Amboy, N.J., and there helped organize a local of the International Brotherhood of Electrical Workers (IBEW); elected an international vice-president of the IBEW in 1901 and its president in 1903, serving until 1918; was a committed craft unionist and vigorously fought the efforts of a group of secessionist IBEW unionists to organize on an industrial basis and during his incumbency consolidated the IBEW's control of electrical workers; appointed to a commission established under the auspices of the National Civic Federation that studied public ownership in Great Britain in 1906; appointed acting director of public safety in Newark, N. J., in 1917 and two years later resigned his position in the IBEW to become deputy director of public safety in Newark; became president emeritus and chairman of the IBEW international board of directors in 1919, serving in this capacity until his death; served during World War I as vice-chairman of Railway Board of Adjustment No. 2; resigned in August, 1918, to accept appointment to a special commission that visited France and Italy at the request of the president of the United States; retired from the Newark City government in 1922 and ran successfully as a Democrat for Congress from the Eighth Congressional District of New Jersey and served one term; died in Newark, N.J., May 26, 1926; Michael A. Mulcaire, *The International Brotherhood of Electrical Workers* (1923); *Dictionary of American Biography* (Vol. XII); *Journal of* *the Electrical Workers and Operators* (June, 1926); *Who's Who in America, 1926-1927.*

McSORLEY, William Joseph. Born in Philadelphia, Pa., December 13, 1876; son of a lather; Roman Catholic; married; six children; attended the elementary schools of Philadelphia; began working as a lather at age fourteen; joined Philadelphia Local 53 of the Wood, Wire and Metal Lathers' International Union (WWMLIU) in 1899 and served Local 53 in a variety of capacities during the following six years; elected international president of the WWMLIU in 1904, and held that office, with the exception of a short period, for 51 years; served on the board of governors of the Structural Building Trades Alliance, 1905-1908; was an American Federation of Labor (AFL) delegate to the Canadian Trades and Labor Congress in 1913; elected a vice-president of the AFL building trades department in 1914; was a member of the labor committee of the Council of National Defense during World War I; elected to the executive committee of the American Construction Council in 1922; served as president of the AFL building trades department, 1927-1932; was an AFL fraternal delegate to the British Trades Union Congress in 1937; represented the AFL at the founding congress of the International Confederation of the Free Trade Unions (ICFTU) in 1949 and was an AFL delegate to the 1955 ICFTU congress in Vienna; retired as WWMLIU president in 1955 and named president emeritus; identified himself politically as nonpartisan; died in Cleveland, Ohio, December 15, 1962; *American Federation of Labor News-Reporter*, November 18, 1955; *AFL-CIO News*, December 20, 1962; Solon DeLeon, ed., *The American Labor Who's Who* (1925).

MAGUIRE, Matthew. Born in New York City in 1850; son of Irish immigrants, Christopher and Mary (Stafford) Maguire; Roman Catholic; married Martha McCormick in 1870; educated in public schools; began factory work at age fourteen; served an apprenticeship as a machinist and joined the Machinists' and Blacksmiths' International Union (MBIU); served as a national officer of the MBIU during the early 1870s; was an active union organizer; joined the Knights of Labor and was actively involved in its activities during the 1880s; espoused the Socialist cause and elected to the Paterson, N.J., Board of Aldermen on the Socialist Labor party (SLP) ticket; was also an unsuccessful SLP candidate for vice-president of the United States in 1896 and for governor of New Jersey in 1898; after 1893, edited the Paterson *People; Who Was Who in America*

(Vol. IV); David Montgomery, *Beyond Equality: Labor and Radical Republicans, 1862-1872* (1967).

(J.H.)

MAHON, William D.   Born in Athens County, Ohio, August 12, 1861; son of an itinerant tanner; married; four children; formal education ended at an early age with his father's death; worked as a miner in the Hocking Valley district of Ohio; entered the street-railway service in Columbus, Ohio, in 1888 and shortly thereafter assisted in organizing employees of the Columbus transit system and served the local at various times as president, secretary, and business agent; served two terms as president of the Columbus Trades and Labor Council; attended the organizing convention of the Amalgamated Association of Street, Electric Railway and Motor Coach Employees of America (AASERCME) in 1892 and shortly thereafter became an assistant organizer for the new union in Indianapolis, Ind.; elected general president of the AASERCME in 1893 and led the organization into the American Federation of Labor (AFL); appointed presiding judge of the Michigan State Court of Arbitration in 1898, serving until 1900; served on the executive committee of the National Civic Federation; appointed to the first municipal ownership committee after Detroit, Mich., assumed control of its transit system in 1914; appointed by the AFL to investigate municipal ownership and operation in Europe in 1914 and two years later was an AFL fraternal delegate to the British Trades Union Congress; elected an AFL vice-president and executive council member in 1917 and served until 1922, resigning to run (unsuccessfully) for the United States Congress; appointed to the Federal Electric Railway Commission by President Woodrow Wilson in 1918 and the following year appointed to Wilson's Federal Industrial Commission; served on the National Recovery Administration's Transit Code Authority, 1933-1935; reelected to the AFL executive council in 1936, serving until his death; was an essentially conservative trade unionist who strongly advocated the voluntary arbitration of labor disputes in the street-railway industry; was a Democrat; resigned as AASERCME president, an office he had held for more than 52 years, in 1946 and was named president emeritus; edited *The Motorman, Conductor and Motor Coach Operator* for 11 years; died in Detroit, Mich., October 31, 1949; Emerson P. Schmidt, *Industrial Relations in Urban Transportation* (1937); *The American Federationist* (December, 1949); *Mass Transportation* (September, 1946); *Who's Who in Labor* (1947).

MAHONEY, Charles E. (fl. 1904-1914).   Was a member of Butte, Mont., Miner's and Smeltermen's Local 74 of the Western Federation of Miners (WFM); became a member of the WFM executive board in 1904; elected vice-president of the WFM in 1905; served as acting president when Charles Moyer (q.v.) was imprisoned during the famous Steunenberg murder case, 1906-1908; served as acting chairman of the schismatic 1906 convention of the Industrial Workers of the World (IWW) and elected by convention to the IWW general executive board; when the radical faction of the IWW, led by William Trautmann (q.v.) and Daniel DeLeon (q.v.), succeeded in having IWW president Charles Sherman (q.v.) deposed in disregard of the IWW constitution, Mahoney led the WFM moderates out of the convention; was determined to prevent the IWW split from tearing the WFM apart and therefore persuaded the executive board to withdraw from the IWW; when the issue was raised at the 1907 convention, the most decisive in the WFM's history, Mahoney rallied the moderates to thwart the radical attempt to continue affiliation of the WFM with the IWW (then led by William Trautmann); called a reactionary by his IWW detractors, but was a capable, militant unionist who supported the radical, direct-action preamble adopted by the WFM in 1907; involved in the Michigan copper-miners' strike of 1913, one of the bitterest strikes of the period; along with Moyer, went to Upper Michigan seeking to open negotiations with the operators; persuaded the governor of Michigan to propose arbitration of the strikers' grievances, but the industry's persistent refusal to deal with the WFM in any way defeated Mahoney's repeated efforts to arrange a peaceful settlement; reelected WFM vice-president in every election from 1906 to 1914; Vernon H. Jensen, *Heritage of Conflict: Labor Relations in the Nonferrous Metals Industry up to 1930* (1950); Emma F. Langdon, *Labor's Greatest Conflicts* (1908); U. S. Department of Labor, Bureau of Labor Statistics, *Michigan Cooper District Strike, Bulletin 139* (1914).

MAHONEY, William.   Born in Chicago, Ill., January 13, 1869; son of a railroader and farmer; married; one child; completed grammar school in Kansas, then apprenticed as a printer and joined the International Typographical Union in 1887; transferred to the International Printing Pressmen's and Assistants' Union of North America in 1893; became a Socialist ca. 1896; attended the Indianapolis College of Law and was admitted to the bar, but after moving to St. Paul, Minn., in 1905 continued to work in his trade; elected president of the St. Paul Trades and Labor Assembly in 1919; was instrumental in founding the Minnesota *Union*

Advocate and edited it until 1932; left the Socialist party believing it to be an inadequate political vehicle, but continued to call for gradual replacement of industrial capitalism by government ownership and production for use; in 1918 began promoting independent political action by organized labor and played the key role in involving labor in the Minnesota Farmer Labor party; with the backing of the State Federation of Labor, organized the Working People's Nonpartisan Political League in 1919; it cooperated with the farmer's Nonpartisan League in fielding Farmer Labor candidates; after impressive electoral victories in 1922, initiated along with Nonpartisan League secretary Henry Teigan the merger of the two leagues into a permanent Farmer Labor party, planning to use the Minnesota party as the nucleus for a national Farmer Labor party in 1924; this movement failed when Senator Robert LaFollette repudiated it and Communists gained control of its St. Paul convention, but Mahoney continued to play a prominent role in the state party; meanwhile, expounded as editor of the *Union Advocate* Farmer Labor ideology and rallied union members behind its candidates; still favored a national third party, but in 1928 warned Farmer Laborites against trying to launch one until they had created more state movements; by 1931, condemned the major parties for offering only "palliatives" and advocated a new national third party to effect "radical" economic change; in 1932, elected mayor of St. Paul; promised municipal ownership, but was only able to impose regulation on the utility firms; defeated for reelection in 1934, then served for a year as regional member of the National Labor Board; in 1942 entered as a candidate for Congress but withdrew before the election; retired in 1944; died in St. Paul, August 16, 1952; Solon DeLeon, ed., *The American Labor Who's Who* (1925); James Weinstein, *The Decline of Socialism in America, 1912-1925* (1967); Carl H. Chrislock, *The Progressive Era in Minnesota* (1971).

(D.G.S.)

MALONEY, James.   Born In Scranton, Pa., September 11, 1870; son of P. W., a salesman, and Mary A. (Duleau) Maloney; Roman Catholic; completed grammar school in Scranton, Pa., then began an apprenticeship as a glass-bottle blower; joined the Glass Bottle Blowers' Association of the United States and Canada (GBBA) in 1890; served his local union in several capacities and in 1909 elected a member of the GBBA general executive board; elected a GBBA international vice-president in 1917, and in 1925, elected to succeed John A. Voll as international president of the union; as a result of prohibition, by 1924 the GBBA had nearly ceased to exist; inspired a joint legislative lobbying effort of the distilling and brewing industries along with the glass container industry to help win repeal of prohibition; during his incumbency, the GBBA grew from 2,000 members to 34,000 and the glass blowing industry in the United States and Canada was effectively organized; was an American Federation of Labor fraternal delegate to the Canadian Trades and Labor Congress in 1935 and to the British Trades Union Congress in 1939; retired as president emeritus in 1946 and succeeded by Lee W. Minton (q.v.); was one of the founders of the Union Labor Life Insurance Company and served as its treasurer for several years; died in Scranton, Pa., January 28, 1960; *The American Federationist* (August, 1946); *Who's Who in Labor* (1946).

MALONEY, William E.   Born in Detroit, Mich., June 17, 1884; son of James and Mary (Connelly) Maloney; Roman Catholic; married Helen Goodrich on June 7, 1938; acquired a grammar school education, then began working as an itinerant railroad machinist; moved to Chicago, Ill., about 1907 and gained employment with the Rock Island Railroad; employed by the Southern Pacific Railroad as a machinist, 1908-1912; secured a civil service job as a hoisting engineer in Chicago and in 1919 joined Local 459 of the International Union of Operating Engineers (IUOE); served as a marine engineer with the U.S. Government Merchant Marine, 1917-1919; while serving as business manager of Local 569, it merged with Local 42, thus creating IUOE Local 150 in 1929; served Local 150 as an international supervisor; elected to the IUOE board of trustees in 1931 and the following year became an international vice-president; elected a vice-president of the Chicago Federation of Labor in 1932, beginning a long term of service in that capacity; during the 1930s, led a vigorous drive to organize workers within the IUOE's jurisdiction in Chicago and the surrounding area; successfully resisted the efforts of underworld figures to gain influence in Local 150 during Chicago's turbulent 1930s, but the moderate wealth gained from real estate investments and his later actions in taking into receivership local unions, moves which violated IUOE policies, led to unproven charges of corruption; elected international president of the IUOE in 1940; as president, greatly expanded the use of international agreements and restored the financial stability of the IUOE, while the membership increased from 58,000 to 294,000; retired as IUOE president in 1958 and named president emeritus; died in Chicago, Ill., January 2, 1964; Garth L. Mangum, *The Operating Engineers: The Economic History of a Trade Union* (1964); *Who's Who in America, 1958-1959; AFL-CIO News,* January 11, 1964.

MALOY, Elmer J.   Born in Pittsburgh, Pa., March 22, 1896; son of William Patrick, a stationary engineer, and Bridget Jane (Tighe) Maloy; Roman Catholic; married Ruth Gilfoyle on April 19, 1922; left high school in 1913 and went to work in the Duquesne Works of the Carnegie Steel Company; served in the U.S. Army in World War I, then returned to the Duquesne Works and, failing to land a job as a millwright, worked as a crane operator in the open hearth; when the U.S. Steel Corporation instituted employee representation plans (ERP) to comply with the National Industrial Recovery Act of 1933, Maloy was elected as open hearth representative; was aggressive and persistent and used the local ERP to extract concessions from management on wages and job classifications; by 1936 the Carnegie-Illinois ERPs had become self-assertive; trying to hold the loyalty of the ERPs in the face of increasing Congress of Industrial Organizations' activity, U.S. Steel agreed to the creation of a central joint committee of ERPs for the Pittsburgh district of the Carnegie-Illinois subsidiaries; now secretly working with the Steel Workers Organizing Committee (SWOC) chairman, Philip Murray (q.v.), Maloy engineered his own election as chairman of the Pittsburgh ERP District Council in late 1936; then went to Washington, D.C., where, after meeting with John L. Lewis (q.v.) and Secretary of Labor Frances Perkins, launched a publicity campaign that discredited the ERP as a bargaining agent; was the first president of SWOC Local 1256; elected mayor of Duquesne, Pa., in 1937, running as a Democrat, and twice reelected; was an international representative of the United Steelworkers of America (USWA) during World War II, serving on the labor division of the War Production Board, organizing in central Pennsylvania, and helping to settle the Canadian steel strike of 1943; beginning in 1947, worked out of Pittsburgh as the USWA's expert on job evaluation; in this capacity, worked to eliminate wage discrimination against black steelworkers in Alabama, and helped end the sectional wage differential in basic steel; retired as director of the USWA Wage Division in 1963; died in Tampa, Fla., April 16, 1970; Labor Archives, Pennsylvania State University; Robert R. R. Brooks, *As Steel Goes, . . . Unionism in a Basic Industry* (1940); Irving Bernstein, *Turbulent Years: A History of the American Worker* (1970); *Who's Who in Labor* (1946).

(D.G.S.)

MARCIANTE, Louis Paul.   Born in Lutcher, La., August 2, 1898; son of Benjamin, a woodworker, and Marie (Di Maria) Marciante; married Anna Louise Smith on June 30, 1922, four children; before completing high school, became at age sixteen an apprentice in the electrical industry; joined Local 269 of the International Brotherhood of Electrical Workers of America in 1915; elected business agent of Local 269 in 1917 and thereafter served as its president for four years; served with the U.S. Marine Corps during World War I; after the war, elected secretary of the Mercer County (Trenton, N.J.) Building Trades Council and served for five years; served as president of the Mercer County Central Labor Union for several years prior to being elected president of the New Jersey State Federation of Labor in 1934, a position he held for the remainder of his life; appointed to the regional labor board organized under the National Recovery Administration in 1933; was an implacable foe of Communist influence in the labor movement, especially in the Congress of Industrial Organizations, and successfully fought the reunification of the labor movement in New Jersey until his death; served as a member of the Trenton Board of Education, 1936-1948; was considered a powerful figure in state Democratic politics and was sometimes allied with Frank Hague's Jersey City organization; died in Atlantic City, N.J., March 30, 1961; Leo Troy, *Organized Labor in New Jersey* (1965); *The New York Times*, March 31, 1961; *Who's Who in Labor* (1946).

MAROT, Helen.   Born in Philadelphia, Pa., June 9, 1865; daughter of Charles Henry, a bookseller and publisher, and Hannah (Griscom) Marot; Society of Friends; educated at Society of Friends schools in Philadelphia; employed by the University Extension Society, Philadelphia, 1893-1895; became a librarian for the Wilmington, Delaware, Public Library in 1896; one of the organizers, in 1897, of the Library of Economic and Political Science, Philadelphia, which became a center for radical thought; investigated, along with Caroline Pratt, the Philadelphia custom tailoring trades for the United States Industrial Commission in 1899; did investigative work for the Association of Neighborhood Workers of New York City, and as a result the New York Child Labor Commission was formed in 1902; served as secretary of the Pennsylvania Child Labor Commission, 1904-1905; joined the New York Women's Trade Union League (WTUL) in 1906 and became its executive secretary, a position she held from 1906 until 1913; was a delegate to the first national convention of the WTUL in 1907 and served as the chairman of the WTUL finance committee; helped organize the WTUL strike committee for the 1909-1910 New York garment workers' strike; resigned from the WTUL, then pursued a full-time writing career; served on the editorial board of the *Masses*, 1916-1917; was a staff member of *Dial*, 1917-1919; retired in 1920; authored *Handbook of Labor Literature* (1898), *American Trade Unions* (1913), and *Creative Impulse in Industry* (1918); died in New York City, June 3, 1940; Gladys Boone, *The Women's Trade Union Leagues in Great Britain and the United States* (1942); *Notable American Women* (1970); *Who's Who in America* (Vol. I).

(M.T.)

MARTIN, Harry Leland, Jr.   Born in Hollandale, Miss., October 28, 1908; son of Dr. Harry Leland, a pastor, and Beatrice Mae (Cockcroft) Martin; Baptist; married Montez Weeks on June 1, 1930, and was divorced in 1940; one child; served as the editor of his high school newspaper and associate editor of the *Mississippi Collegian*, the student newspaper of Mississippi College in Clinton, Miss., from which he graduated *cum laude*, majoring in English, in 1928; served as assistant principal and coach in both Moorhead City School, Moorhead, Miss., 1928-1929, and Hickory Flat Consolidated High School, 1929-1930; joined the staff of the Memphis, Tenn., *Evening Appeal* in 1930; became amusements editor of the Memphis *Commerical Appeal* in 1936, serving in that position until 1948; was the founder and first president of the Newspaper Guild of Memphis and elected an international vice-president and member of the executive board of the American Newspaper Guild (ANG) in 1938; served as the founding president of the Newspaper Film Critics of America in 1939; was a vice-president of the Tennessee State Industrial Union Council, Congress of Industrial Organizations (CIO), and was a member of the executive board of the Memphis Industrial Union Council, CIO; served during World War II as a petty officer in the U. S. Navy, 1942-1945; elected as an anti-Communist candidate to the presidency of the ANG in 1947, serving until 1953; was appointed by President Harry S. Truman to the United Nations' Freedom of Information Conference in Geneva in 1948; served as an official consultant to the United Nations' subcommittee on freedom of information in 1948; during the same year, appointed a special labor advisor and information specialist to the European Recovery Program; served as vice-president of the International Organization of Journalists, 1948-1949, but resigned from the organization in 1949, because of its alleged Communist domination; was an active participant in the organization of the International Federation of Journalists and during 1952-1954 served as its alternate president and North American vice-president; was a member of the CIO executive board, 1950-1953; became director of public information for the American Red Cross in 1955, serving until his death;

was a Democrat and member of Americans for Democratic Action; died in Washington, D. C., December 23, 1958; *Current Biography* (1948); *Who's Who in Labor* (1946); *Who's Who in America, 1958-1959.*

MARTIN, Warren Homer.   Born in Marion, Ill., August 16, 1902; son of an Illinois school teacher; Baptist; married twice; four children; graduated from William Jewell College, Mo., in 1928 and attended Kansas City Baptist Theological Seminary; named to the United States Olympic team in 1924 as the national hop, step, and jump champion but failed to make the trip because of financial difficulties; assumed a Baptist pastorate in Leeds, Mo., in 1931 but after pro-labor comments antagonized some members of his congregation, left the ministry and took a job in a General Motors Corporation Chevrolet plant in 1932; when an American Federation of Labor (AFL) federal local was organized in the plant (later Local 93 of the United Automobile, Aircraft, Agricultural Implement Workers of America [UAW]), he joined and a short time later became its president; was discharged in 1934 and moved to Detroit, Mich., devoting his energies there to organizing automobile workers; after the UAW was chartered by the AFL in 1935 elected its vice-president; elected UAW president in 1936, reflecting the UAW's growing independence of the AFL; led the UAW into the Congress of Industrial Organizations in 1936; during three years as UAW president, was constantly embroiled in bitter and divisive factional conflicts at the same time that the UAW was making significant organizational gains; was a gifted orator with considerable rank-and-file support, but his impulsive and temperamental personality along with serious administrative deficiencies resulted in his downfall in 1939; led a small group of UAW unions back into the AFL but after losing several representation elections resigned as the president of the UAW-AFL; left the labor movement and became a farmer; actively involved in Michigan politics; led a movement in 1958 to reduce UAW influence in the Michigan Democratic party; moved to Los Angeles, Calif., in 1961 and became labor counselor for the Tulare and Kings County Employers Council; died in Los Angeles, Calif., January 22, 1968; Sidney Fine, *Sit-Down: The General Motors Strike of 1936-1937* (1969), and *The Automobile Under the Blue Eagle: Labor, Management, and the Automobile Manufacturing Code* (1963); Jack Stieber, *Governing the UAW* (1962); Frank Cormier and William J. Eaton, *Reuther* (1970).

MASHBURN, Lloyd Abner.   Born in Greeley, Colo., October 10, 1897; son of William James, a farmer, and Susan (Southard) Mashburn;

married Luella Carroll on January 22, 1922; four children; completed high
school through correspondence courses and then spent two years in a
vocational trade school and one year in a manual arts school; served with
the U.S. Marine Corps during World War I; joined Los Angeles, Calif.,
Local 42 of the International Union of Wood, Wire and Metal Lathers
(WWMLIU) in 1922; elected business agent in 1933, serving until 1939;
during 1939-1950, served in a variety of positions in the Los Angeles labor
movement, including assistant secretary and later secretary-treasurer of
the Los Angeles Building and Construction Trades Council, secretary of
the Southern California District Council of Lathers, president of the Los
Angeles Labor Temple Association, president of the Los Angeles Labor
Council, and vice-chairman of the United American Federation Political
Committee; served during World War II on the Los Angeles division of the
Selective Service board and the War Finance Committee of the War
Manpower Commission; was on variety of other public committees, serv-
ing as vice-chairman of the Los Angeles City Housing Authority and as a
member of the personnel board of the Los Angeles Board of Education; was
Labor Commissioner of the State of California, 1951-1953; served as Un-
dersecretary of Labor in the U.S. Department of Labor, 1953-1954, then
became an assistant to the president of the WWMLIU in 1954 and elected
international president in 1955; was a Republican; died in Chicago, Ill.,
December 7, 1963; *Who's Who in America, 1960-1961; Who's Who in
Labor* (1946); *The New York Times,* December 10, 1963.

MASO, Sal.   Born in New York City, July 25, 1900; son of Salvatore, a
merchant, and Amelia (Margiotta) Maso; Episcopalian; married Agnes
Calvacca on June 15, 1924; one child; completed high school by taking
night classes, then attended a teachers' college for two years; became a
metal lather and joined the Albany, N.Y., local of the International Union
of Wood, Wire and Metal Lathers (WWMLIU) in 1926; transferred to
WWMLIU Local 143 in Paterson, N.J., and served the local in various
capacities; was an influential figure in the Paterson and New Jersey labor
movements, and served as vice-president and then president of the New
Jersey State Building and Construction Trades Council, president of the
United Building and Construction Trades Council of Paterson, and president of the Passaic County Central Labor Union; elected a vice-president
of the WWMLIU in 1939; was active in civic and governmental affairs in
New Jersey, serving as a member of the New Jersey State Board of
Mediation, the Paterson Housing Authority, the Appeals Board of the
Passaic County Selective Service, and as a commissioner of the Paterson

Board of Education; also served on the New Jersey Governor's Committee on Equal Employment Opportunity; after the death of Lloyd A. Mashburn (q.v.) in 1964, elected international president of the WWMLIU, serving until his retirement in 1970; was nonpartisan in politics, died in Paterson, N.J., January 21, 1971; *AFL-CIO News*, January 30, 1971; *Who's Who in Labor* (1946).

MASON, Lucy Randolph.   Born in Clarens, Va., July 26, 1882; daughter of Rev. Landon Randolph, an Episcopalian minister, and Lucy (Ambler) Mason; Episcopalian; completed her formal education, then worked as a stenographer, 1904-1914; employed by the Richmond, Va., Young Women's Christian Association (YWCA), 1914-1918; did volunteer work for various service organizations, 1918-1923, and was president of the Richmond Equal Suffrage League and the Richmond League of Women Voters; during World War I, appointed by Samuel Gompers (q.v.) as Virginia chairman of the Committee on Women in Industry of the National Advisory Commission; returned to the YWCA as general secretary in 1923; joined the Union Label League in Richmond in 1923 and later became a member of the International Ladies' Garment Workers' Union Label League; left the YWCA in the spring of 1932 and replaced Florence Kelley as general secretary of the National Consumers' League; helped organize the Friedman-Harry Marks plant in Richmond for the Amalgamated Clothing Workers of America (ACWA) in 1935; began her Congress of Industrial Organizations' (CIO) career in 1937 as Southern director of organization for textiles and clothing, working for Stephen Nance (q.v.) out of the Atlanta, Ga., Textile Workers Organizing Committee office; her work with the CIO mainly involved traveling throughout the South as a "troubleshooter", helping to establish unions in particularly difficult areas; helped organize numerous textile and clothing plants throughout the South, including Cluett, Peabody, and Company of Atlanta, organized for the ACWA in 1941; was also involved in the organization of miners in Ducktown, Tenn., for the International Union of Mine, Mill and Smelter Workers in 1938, and in Port Gibson, Minn., for the International Woodworkers in 1944, and in Cuthbert, Ga., in 1947; was instrumental in convincing the 1938 Southern Baptist Convention to adopt a resolution favoring collective bargaining; worked in 1944 with Sidney Hillman (q.v.) and Paul Christopher (q.v.) for the CIO Political Action Committee in the Carolinas, Georgia, Alabama, and Tennessee; hired by the Southern Organizing Committee to contact local authorities in areas where the CIO was active or expected to be active in 1946; retired from active union work in

1951; authored *To Win These Rights: A Personal Story of the CIO in the South* (1952); died in Atlanta, Ga., May 6, 1959; Ray Marshall, *Labor in the South* (1967); *AFL-CIO News*, May, 1959.

(M.T.)

MATHIAS, Charles G.   Born in Baltimore County, Md., August 17, 1913; son of William T., a steel-mill electrician, and Elizabeth R. Berger; Roman Catholic; married Evelyn Mathias on September 11, 1940; two children; attended the public schools of Baltimore and night classes at Maryland Institute and Baltimore Tech; was the organizer and president of the Soap and Glycerine Workers' Union at the Gold Dust Corporation in Baltimore, 1935-1937; served as president of Local 1224 of the Steel Workers Organizing Committee, Bethlehem Steel Company, Sparrows Point, Md., and grievance chairman in several departments, 1937-1941; became the Georgia director for the United Textile Workers of America in 1941; during 1941-1943, served on the plant grievance and bargaining committee of the Atlantic Steel Company in Atlanta, Ga., and as a staff member of the Congress of Industrial Organizations' (CIO) shipyard workers in South Georgia and Florida; served with the U.S. Army during World War II; after the war, became a staff representative and subdistrict director, District 35, for the United Steelworkers of America and still held position in 1974; during 1947-1956, served as secretary, vice-president, and president of the Atlanta Industrial Union Council, CIO, and after the American Federation of Labor-CIO merger in Georgia, served as treasurer of the Georgia AFL-CIO, 1956-1964; was involved during his years of service to the state labor movement in legislative lobbying against right-to-work laws and for unemployment compensation legislation, welfare legislation, and the fluoridation of water; involved in civil rights activities since 1946, opposing pension discrimination against blacks at the Atlantic Steel Company and supporting voter registration and cooperation with the Southern Regional Council; served on the federal Rent Control Board, 1947-1950, and as chairman of the Fulton County (Ga.) Board of Public Welfare; a Democrat; Ray Marshall, *Labor in the South* (1967).

(M.E.R.)

MAURER, James Hudson.   Born in Reading, Pa., April 15, 1864; son of James D., a shoemaker and policeman, and Sarah (Lorah) Maurer; married Mary J. Missmer on April 15, 1886; two children; acquired only 13 months of formal education in the public schools of Reading; at age six began working as a newsboy, then worked as a farm laborer and a factory worker; at age fifteen served a machinist apprenticeship; joined the Knights of Labor in 1880 and served as an organizer; joined the United Association of Plumbers and Steamfitters of the United States and Canada in 1901; entered political life as a Populist and edited a party paper, *The Reading Kicker,* in 1898; joined the Socialist Labor party in 1899, and three years later, the Socialist Party of America, serving on its national executive committee for ten years; was an unsuccessful Socialist party candidate for governor of Pennsylvania in 1906; during 1911-1918, served three terms as a Socialist member of the Pennsylvania House of Representatives, successfully sponsoring workmen's compensation, old-age, and mothers' pension legislation; served as president of the Pennsylvania State Federation of Labor, 1912-1928, during which the organization grew from 267 to 1,400 affiliates representing 400,000 members, the largest and most powerful state labor body in the United States; was the Socialist party candidate for vice-president of the United States in 1928 and 1932; ran for the U.S. Senate on the Socialist ticket in 1934, but two years later resigned from the party because of its "trend toward Communism"; served on the City Council, Reading, Pa., 1928-1932, and later served as finance commissioner; after 1917, served as chairman of the Pennsylvania Old Age Assistance Commission; became president of the Workers' Educational Bureau of America and a member of the board of directors of Brookwood Labor College in 1921; after 1922, served on the national committee of the Conference for Progressive Political Action and as president of the Labor Age Publishing Company, publisher of *Labor Age Monthly*; authored *The Far East* (1910), *It Can Be Done* (1938), and *The American Cossack*, the latter denouncing the Pennsylvania constabulary's strike-breaking activities; died in Reading, Pa., March 16, 1944; *National Cyclopaedia of American Biography* (Vol. C); *Dictionary of American Biography* (Supplement III); Solon DeLeon, ed., *The American Labor Who's Who* (1925); *The New York Times*, March 17, 1944.

(J.H.)

MAZEY, Emil.   Born in Regina, Saskatchewan, Canada, August 2, 1913; son of Lawrence, an auto worker, and Wilma Mazey; married Charlotte Marshall in 1938; one child; moved with family to the United States in 1915, settling in Detroit, Mich.; graduated from Cass Technical High School, Detroit, in 1931; shortly after graduating became an organizer of unemployed workers for the Detroit Unemployed Citizens League; during 1933, attempted to organize workers in the Briggs Manufacturing Company and the following year was discharged from the Gulf Refining Company after organizing workers in the plant where he was employed; organized workers at the Rotary Electric Steel Company, then returned to the Briggs Manufacturing Company in 1936 but was soon discharged for union organizing activities; then became an international representative for the United Automobile, Aircraft, Agricultural Implement Workers of America (UWA) and was assigned to organize the Briggs plant in Detroit; organized Briggs Local 212 in 1937 and served as its president until 1941; involved in the organization of the Ford Motor Company River Rouge Plant in 1941 and directed the negotiations in the UAW's first national labor agreement with the Ford Motor Company; returned as president of Briggs Local 212 in 1943 and remained there until inducted into the U.S. Armed Forces in 1944; served with the U.S. Army in the Philippines but was transferred to Ie Shima, a small island west of Okinawa, after leading a series of demonstrations protesting the shipping and demobilization program of the U.S. Army; elected to the UAW international executive board in 1946 and made co-director of UAW Region 1, comprising Detroit's east side; elected to the office of secretary-treasurer in 1947, beginning a long and continuing term of service in that capacity; served as acting president of the UAW in 1948 when Walter P. Reuther (q.v.) was disabled due to an assassination attempt; led the UAW in the 1948 strike against the Chrysler Corporation; long an advocate of independent political action; usually supports Democratic candidates after 1960; Jack Stieber, *Governing the UAW* (1962); Jean Gould and Lorena Hickok, *Walter Reuther: Labor's Rugged Individualist* (1972); Frank Cormier and William J. Eaton, *Reuther* (1970).

MEANY, George.   Born in New York City, August 16, 1894; son of Michael Joseph, a plumber, and Anne (Cullen) Meany; Roman Catholic; married Eugenia A. McMahon on November 26, 1919; three children; graduated from public school in New York City, then became an apprentice plumber in 1910; became a journeyman plumber in 1915 and joined the United Association of Plumbers and Steam Fitters of the United States and Canada (UA); elected business agent of the New York Local 463, UA, in 1922; served as a delegate to the New York City Central Trades and Labor Assembly and in 1932 was elected a vice-president of the New York State Federation of Labor (NYSFL); while serving as president of the NYSFL, 1934-1939, devoted much of his time and energy to highly successful lobbying efforts before the New York State legislature, to dealing with the varied circumstances related to the initiation of federal work-relief and other labor-oriented programs, and to restoring the membership and finances of the state federation during the depression; served on the New York State Industrial Council and on the State Advisory Council on Unemployment Insurance; elected secretary-treasurer of the American Federation of Labor (AFL) in 1939; somewhat frustrated during the early years of his tenure by the conservative, uninnovative policies of AFL president William Green (q.v.), but after 1948 assumed more and more of the decision-making power from the old and ill Green; during World War II, served as a labor delegate to the National Defense Mediation Board and the National War Labor Board; served as AFL fraternal delegate to the British Trades Union Congress in 1945; became the first director of Labor's League for Political Education in 1948; was a member of the executive board of the International Confederation of Free Trade Unions in 1951; appointed to the National Advisory Board on Mobilization Policy in 1951 and to the Contract Compliance Committee in 1952; after the death of William Green in 1952, appointed by the AFL executive council as acting president and subsequently elected president; devoted considerable time during his first years as president to negotiating a merger with the rival Congress of Industrial Organizations (CIO); after the AFL-CIO merger in 1955, elected president of the new federation; served as a delegate to the General Assembly of the United Nations in 1957 and 1959; was a vociferous anti-Communist and devoted much of his own time and influence as well as that of the AFL-CIO to the crusade against Communism; during the 1960s, established firm control over the AFL-CIO, beating down all opposition to his policies, including that of the former president of the CIO, Walter Reuther (q.v.); was a Democrat and exerted considerable influence in the councils of the Democratic party; worked closely with the Democratic administrations of the 1960s; broke a tradition dating back to the AFL-CIO merger by refusing to endorse the Democratic presidential nominee in 1972, George S. McGovern; Joseph C. Goulden, *Meany* (1972); Philip Taft, *The A. F. of L. From the Death of Gompers to the Merger* (1959); Ronald Radosh, *American Labor and United States Foreign Policy: The Cold War in the Unions from Gompers to Lovestone* (1969); *The National Cyclopaedia of American Biography* (1964); *Current Biography* (1954).

MEGEL, Carl J.   Born in Hayden, Ind., December 3, 1899; son of Peter and Lena (Kirsch) Megel; married Marion Stewart in April, 1925, and after a divorce in 1947, Beverly Falk in October, 1962; two children; received A.B. degree from Franklin College in 1923, then attended the graduate schools of the University of Illinois and DePaul University; served as athletic director in a number of schools, 1924-1935, and then became a teacher in Chicago's Lake View High School, serving in that capacity until 1965; was a trustee of the Chicago Teachers Union, 1943-1946, treasurer, 1946-1948, and vice-president, 1949-1951; served as a delegate to the Chicago Federation of Labor and the Illinois State Federation of Labor, 1948-1952; elected president of the American Federation of Teachers (AFT) in 1952, serving until 1964; was a member of the American Federation of Labor-Congress of Industrial Organizations' education committee, 1952-1964; was a delegate to United Nations Educational, Scientific, and Cultural Organization (UNESCO) conferences, 1952-1961, serving as a member of the UNESCO committee, 1953-1959; appointed a member of the White House Conference on Education in 1955; began a long and continuing term of service as the AFT's Congressional legislative representative in Washington, D. C., in 1964; Robert J. Braun, *Teachers and Power: The Story of the American Federation of Teachers* (1972); Stephen Cole, *The Unionization of Teachers: A Case Study of the UFT* (1969); *Who's Who in America, 1964-1965.*

MENDELOWITZ, Abraham.   Born in Nikolaev, Ukraine, Russia, March 5, 1894; son of Solomon, a tailor, and Leah (Rubenstein) Mendelowitz; Jewish; married Sarah Chayt on April 1, 1917; three children; received little formal education before emigrating to France; joined the French Foreign Legion during World War I and was wounded in Egypt; emigrated to the United States in 1915 and secured employment in the New York cap and millinery industry; joined Local 1 of the Cloth Hat, Cap and Millinery Workers' International Union (CHCMW) in 1916 and shortly thereafter elected an officer in the local; elected a CHCMW vice-president in 1923; became an executive board member of the influential CHCMW Local 24 in 1924 and in 1934 became a co-manager of the local; after the merger between the CHCMW and the United Hatters of North America, became a vice-president of the newly organized United Hatters, Cap and Millinery Workers' International Union (UHCMWIU) in 1934; was one of the founders in 1936 of the Millinery Stabilization Commission, which provided for labor-management cooperation in the millinery industry; was a vigorous opponent of Communist efforts to take control of CHCMW locals during the 1920s and of similar efforts by racketeers in the 1930s; was a member of the New York Central Trades and Labor Council, the Jewish Hebrew Trades, and Workmen's Circle; elected co-manager of millinery workers union Locals 2, 24, 30, 42, 90, and 92; supported the Liberal party of New York; died in New York City, November 14, 1966; Donald B. Robinson, *Spotlight on a Union: The Story of the United*

Hatters, Cap and Millinery Workers International Union (1948); Charles H. Green, *The Headwear Workers* (1944); *Who's Who in Labor* (1946).

MERRILL, Lewis Robert. Born in Toronto, Canada in 1908; son of Phillip and Esther (Kreengle) Merrill; married twice; two children; emigrated to the United States in 1929 after having attended the University of Toronto; worked as a credit and investment analyst; while employed by the New York Credit Clearing House, joined the American Federation of Labor (AFL) Bookkeepers, Stenographers and Accountants' Union Federal Local 12646 in 1930; became an office employee of Local 281 of the New York City Sheet Metal Workers' Union in 1931; elected president of Federal Local 12646 in 1936 and in that capacity led the campaign for an international charter from the AFL; began a campaign to organize insurance workers in 1936; after the repeated failure of the AFL to grant an international charter to organize banking, social service, and insurance workers, led much of the membership of Federal Local 12646 into the Congress of Industrial Organizations (CIO) in 1937 and served as general secretary of the convention sponsoring committee that led to the creation of the United Office and Professional Workers of America (UPPW); elected the first president of the UPPW in 1937; was a member of the CIO executive board and was a member of the CIO health and welfare committee; negotiated one of the then largest white-collar worker union labor contracts with the Prudential Insurance Company in 1943; often denied Communist party membership, but was a contributing editor to the *New Masses* and a trustee of the Jefferson School of Social Science; ended his association with the *New Masses* and the Jefferson School of Social Science in 1946 and became a critic of Communist influence in the UPPW; resigned as president of the UPPW in 1947, a move apparently prompted by the increased Communist influence in the UPPW; after his resignation, became involved in the distribution of magazines, comic books, and paperback books through supermarket chains, and later became a consultant to publishing firms and an investment and financial advisor to various corporations; was affiliated with the American Labor party until 1946; authored several pamphlets relating to the organization of white-collar workers; died in New York City, June 18, 1965; Harvey J. Clermont, *Organizing the Insurance Worker: A History of Labor Unions of Insurance Employees* (1966); Max Kampelman, *The Communist Party vs. the C.I.O.: A Study in Power Politics* (1957); *Who's Who in Labor* (1946).

MILLER, Edward S. Born in Cameron, Mo., June 24, 1901; son of

John K., a cigarmaker, and Maxine (Stout) Miller; Christian Church; married Blanche Spurgeon on January 9, 1938; graduated from high school, then served with the U.S. armed services during World War I; following the war, eventually secured work as a bartender and joined Kansas City, Mo., Local 420 of the Hotel and Restaurant Employees' International Alliance and Bartenders' International League of America (HREIABIL); was elected secretary-treasurer of Local 420 and quickly regenerated the moribund local; elected president of the Kansas City local joint executive board of the HREIABIL and reinvigorated the union's organizing efforts in Kansas City; began a major drive to organize Kansas City hotels in 1937, and after a divisive 19-day strike, succeeded; was a protégé of HREIABIL president Edward Flore (q.v.); in 1938 successfully opposed the reelection of the corruption-tainted vice-president from the union's Fifth District; led a major organizing drive in Chicago, Ill., during the early 1940s, which resulted in large membership gains; appointed secretary-treasurer by the HREIABIL executive board in 1946 and elected to the same position a year later; elected international president after the death of Hugo Ernst (q.v.) in 1954; during his incumbency, the HREIABIL began an expensive but successful effort to organize the hotels and restaurants of Miami Beach, Fla.; was a friend of Kansas City political leader Tom Pendergast and Harry S. Truman and usually supports the Democratic party; retired union positions because of failing health in 1973; Matthew Josephson, *Union House: Union Bar: The History of the Hotel and Restaurant Employees and Bartenders International Union, AFL-CIO* (1956); *Who's Who in Labor* (1946); *AFL-CIO News*, February 10, 1973.

MILLER, Marvin Julian.   Born in New York City, April 14, 1917; son of Alexander, a salesman, and Gertrude (Wald), a school teacher, Miller; Jewish; married Theresa Morgenstern on December 24, 1939; two children; while attending the public schools of Brooklyn, worked as a newspaper delivery boy, a Wall Street runner, and a clerk at a soda fountain; received a B.S. degree in economics from New York University in 1938 and later took graduate courses at the New School for Social Research; worked briefly as a clerk in the U.S. Department of the Treasury and as an investigator for the New York City Department of Welfare; served with the Wage Stabilization Division of the War Labor Board during World War II; after the war was associated with the U.S. Conciliation Service until 1947; then joined the staff of the International Association of Machinists; became the associate director of research for the United Steelworkers of America (USWA) in 1950, serving in that capacity until 1960; appointed assistant to

USWA president David J. McDonald (q.v.) in 1960; replaced Arthur Goldberg (q.v.) in 1961 on the tripartite committee created by the USWA and the Kaiser Steel Corporation to manage and improve industrial relations; was a member of the National Labor-Management Panel, 1963-1967; elected executive director of the Major League Baseball Players Association in 1966; quickly became a controversial figure in the sports industry; won important concessions from major league baseball club owners and led players in a 13-day strike in the spring of 1972; a Democrat; *Current Biography* (1973); *Sports Illustrated*, February 24, 1969; *Sport* (October, 1972).

MILLIMAN, Elmer Edward. Born in Mount Morris, N.Y., November 22, 1890; son of John, a hotel keeper, and Mary (Ward) Milliman; Roman Catholic; married Esther D. Gumaer on June 7, 1919; two children; graduated from high school, then attended Rochester Institute of Technology until family financial problems forced him out of school; secured work on a section gang of the Delaware, Lackawana and Western Railroad in 1909; served as the foreman of a construction and maintenance crew, 1910-1919; joined the Brotherhood of Maintenance of Way Employees (BMWE) in 1918; elected general chairman of the Delaware, Lackawana and Western system division of the BMWE in 1919; served as secretary-treasurer of the national General Chairmen's Association and president of the Eastern District General Chairmen's Association, 1919-1922; elected international secretary-treasurer of the BMWE in 1922, serving until 1940; was an American Federation of Labor (AFL) fraternal delegate to the British Trades Union Congress in 1932; elected a member of the AFL committee on education in 1938; served as chairman of the Association of National Reporting Officers established under the railroad Retirement Act, 1938-1944; elected international president of the BMWE in 1940; during World War II, was a member of the War Production Board's Railway Labor Executives' Association Committee and a member of the Office of Defense Transportation Advisory Board; served on the Railway Labor Executives' Association, 1940-1946; was a member of the AFL committee on international labor relations; was an official in several voluntary organizations, including vice-president of the Catholic Conference on Industrial Problems, chairman of the Committee on Consumer Cooperatives, and president of the Workers Education Bureau of America; was a member of the national advisory board of the Labor League for Human Rights; died in Detroit, Mich., January 1, 1946; Denver W.

Hertel, *History of the Brotherhood of Maintenance of Way Employees: Its Birth and Growth, 1877-1955* (1955); Brotherhood of Maintenance of Way Employees, *Pictorial History, 1877-1951* (1952); *Who's Who in Labor* (1946).

MILNE, J. Scott. Born in Vancouver, British Columbia, Canada, January 21, 1898; son of Robert and Martha (Steele) Milne; married Doris M. Ford on June 20, 1923; two children; completed his formal education in Canada, then served in the Canadian Army during World War I; after the war, emigrated to the United States, settling in Portland, Ore.; became an electrical lineman and joined Local 125 of the International Brotherhood of Electrical Workers (IBEW); elected financial secretary and business manager of Local 125 in 1923, serving until 1929; appointed an IBEW international representative in 1929; elected an international vice-president representing the IBEW's Ninth District West Coast Division in 1936; served as international secretary of the IBEW, 1947-1954; was an American Federation of Labor (AFL) fraternal delegate to the British Trades Union Congress in 1953; elected international president succeeding Daniel W. Tracy (q.v.) in 1954; became an AFL vice-president and executive council member in 1954; elected president of the International Labor Press of America in 1953; edited the *Electrical Workers Journal*, 1947-1954; died in Portland, Ore., July 20, 1955; *The American Federation of Labor News-Reporter*, March 25, 1954, July 22, 1955; *The New York Times*, July 21, 1955; *Who's Who in America, 1954-1955*.

MINTON, Lee Webb. Born in Washington, Pa., November 17, 1911; son of Romney, a restaurateur, and Lulu (Bayne) Minton; Christian Scientist; married Helen Irene Thompson on July 31, 1938; two children; completed three years of high school, then attended a business college for a short time; learned the glass-blowing trade and in 1934 joined a Pennsylvania local of the Glass Bottle Blowers' Association of the United States and Canada (GBBA); served as a local representative and a tri-state representative, then elected to the GBBA executive board in 1938; elected GBBA international treasurer in 1945, vice-president in 1946, and president later in 1946; served as a delegate to the Philadelphia Central Labor Union and the Pennsylvania State Federation of Labor; was an American Federation of Labor (AFL) fraternal delegate to the Canadian Trades and Labor Congress in 1951; elected an AFL-Congress of Industrial Organizations' (AFL-CIO) vice-president and executive council member in 1956; was an

AFL-CIO delegate to the International Confederation of Free Trade Unions in 1966; appointed a member of the President's Task Force on Economic Growth for the 70s and served on the board of directors of CARE; retired as president emeritus of the GBBA in 1971; Republican, served as chairman of National Labor for Rockefeller Committee in 1964 and 1968; *Who's Who in Labor* (1946); *Who's Who in America, 1972-1973.*

MITCH, William A.   Born in Minersville, Ohio, April 10, 1881; son of Fredrick, a coal miner, and Matilda (Jones) Mitch; Methodist; married Mary Evans on April 9, 1909; three children; went to work in the coal mines and joined the United Mine Workers of America (UMWA) in 1894; served as international traveling auditor of the UMWA, 1913-1914, and as secretary-treasurer of District 11, UMWA, Indiana, 1915-1931; played a leading role in the independent labor party movement in Indiana in 1919; served with John Brophy (q.v.) and Cris Golden on the UMWA's Nationalization Research Committee to investigate the feasibility of public ownership of coal mines in 1912-1923; attended the International Mining Congress at Frankfurt, Germany, in 1922; as president of UMWA District 11 in 1932, conducted a violent strike to resist a 25 percent wage reduction, but was forced to accept a reduction from $6.10 to $4.75; along with William Dalrymple and Walter Jones, an Alabama black miner who had been forced by blacklist to move to Ohio, in early June, 1933 reorganized District 20, Alabama, which had two locals with 225 members; by July 23, they had organized 18,000 members into 85 locals; in February and March, 1934, 11,000 miners struck for union recognition and the dues check-off; on March 14, they signed an Alabama Agreement covering 90 percent of the state's operators and 85 percent of its tonnage, granting the check-off and raising wages from $3.40 to $3.60; served as president of District 20, UMWA, Alabama, from 1933 until at least 1946, and president of the Alabama State Federation of Labor from 1933 until 1937; during the 1936 convention of the State Federation, John W. Altman, the Federation's general counsel, attacked "Mitch of Indiana" for organizing racially integrated locals, with blacks occasionally serving as officers with authority over white miners; appointed director of the Southern Region of the Steel Workers' Organizing Committee by Philip Murray (q.v.) in 1936; after the American Federation of Labor-Congress of Industrial Organizations (CIO) split, served as president of the Alabama State Industrial Union Council, CIO; *Who's Who in Labor* (1946); Solon DeLeon, ed., *The American Labor Who's Who* (1925); F. Ray Marshall, *Labor in the South* (1967); John Brophy, *A Miner's Life* (1964); John H. M. Laslett, *Labor and the Left: A*

Study of Socialism and Radical Influences in the American Labor Movement, 1881-1924 (1970).

(J.H.)

MITCHELL, Harry Leland.   Born near Halls, Tenn., June 14, 1906; son of James Y., a barber, tenant farmer, and Baptist preacher, and Maude Ella (Stanfield) Mitchell, reared a Baptist; married Lyndell Carmack, a teacher, on December 26, 1926, and in October, 1951, Dorothy Dowe, a social worker who had been associated with the Works Progress Administration, the National Youth Administration, and in 1943 became secretary-treasurer of the Southern Tenant Farmers Union (STFU); three children; graduated from Halls High School in 1924 and shortly thereafter became a sharecropper near Riply, Tenn.; operated a dry-cleaning business in Tyronza, Ark., 1927-1934; along with 17 others, founded the STFU in 1934 and served as its executive secretary, 1934-1939, 1941-1944; conducted aggressive organizing drives during 1934 when the initial Agricultural Adjustments Administration cotton program provided no guarantees to tenant farmers; led strikes in Arkansas and Tennessee during the spring of 1935, which brought local repression of tenants' civil liberties but national publicity to the STFU; by 1937, 30,000 tenant farmers and sharecroppers, organized interracially, had been enrolled in the STFU; frequently testified before public and private agencies on agricultural problems in an effort to enlist the aid of federal agencies and national organizations for tenants' and sharecroppers' cause; gradually lost faith in orthodox union tactics after the failure of several strikes and instead emphasized the role of the STFU as a pressure group advocating publicity, new legislation, and law enforcement; however, the STFU executive council favored the union approach, and hence he sought affiliation with the Congress of Industrial Organizations and merged, reluctantly, with the Communist-led United Cannery, Agricultural, Packing and Allied Workers of America (UCAPAWA) in 1937; after numerous quarrels with UCAPAWA president Donald J. Henderson (q.v.) over STFU autonomy, dues, communism, and alleged dual union tactics, withdrew from the UCAPAWA following the Missouri sharecroppers demonstration in 1939; elected president of the STFU in 1944 and led the union into the American Federation of Labor (AFL) under the newly chartered National Farm Labor Union (NFLU); served as president of the NFLU, 1945-1955, and its successor, the National Agricultural Workers Union-AFL-CIO (NAWU), 1955-1960; despite the general failures to achieve the STFU's union-oriented goals during the 1930s, he and others exhibited considerable personal courage, stood up to the power of local planters, gained national publicity for sharecroppers and tenants, and won occasional economic victories; after the NAWU merged with the Amalgamated Meat Cutters and Butcher Workmen of North America in 1960, served his new union as an agricultural specialist and was involved in organizing dairy farm and plant workers, rice mill, sugar plantation, and seasonal sugar mill workers, and menhaden fishermen on the Gulf of Mexico; during his career, also served as a special assistant to the National Youth Administration, as an International Ladies' Garment Workers' Union organizer, and as a consultant to the U.S. Department of Labor and the International Labor Organization; was a Socialist until 1936, then supported the Democratic party; Donald H. Grubbs, *Cry from the Cotton* (1971); Louis Cantor, *A Prologue to the Protest Movement: The Missouri Sharecropper Roadside Demonstration of 1939* (1969); Joan London and Henry Anderson, *So Shall Ye Reap: The Story of Cesar Chavez and the Farm Workers Movement* (1970); David E. Conrad, *The Forgotten Farmers: The Story of Sharecroppers in the New Deal* (1965); *Current Biography* (1947); *Who's Who in Labor* (1946).

(M.E.R.)

MITCHELL, James J.   Born in Carfin, Lanarkshire, Scotland, November 25, 1896; son of Lawrence, a coal miner, and Rose (Tummons) Mitchell; Roman Catholic; married Mrs. Catherine Hallinan Parker on May 21, 1944; three children (adopted); received a grammar school education in Scotland, then began working in the Lanarkshire mines and joined the Lanarkshire Miners and Boilermakers Union; emigrated to the United States as a youth and settled in Lynn, Mass., there gaining employment in the shoe industry; joined the Lasters Shoe local in Lynn in 1932; served as a member of the Lasters Shoe local executive board and negotiating agreement committee, 1933-1936; served as secretary of the Lynn Joint Council of Shoe Workers, 1933-1936; was one of the organizers of the independent United Shoe and Leather Workers Union (USLWU) in 1935 and elected its secretary; following the amalgamation of the USLWU, the Shoe Workers Protective Association, and several other independent local unions creating the United Shoe Workers of America (USWA), which was chartered by the Congress of Industrial Organizations in 1937, elected secretary-treasurer of the new national union and served in that capacity until his death; considered one of the seminal figures in the USWA, was instrumental in its founding, growth, and development; died in Washington, D.C., November 11, 1957; *AFL-CIO News*, November 16, 1957; *Who's Who in Labor* (1946).

MITCHELL, John. Born in Braidwood, Ill., February 4, 1870; son of Robert, a coal miner and farmer, and Martha (Halley) Mitchell; Roman Catholic; married Katherine O'Rourke on June 1, 1891; six children; attended Braidwood public schools for five years and later studied in evening school; studied law for one year; worked in the coal mines of Illinois, Colorado, New Mexico, and elsewhere, 1882-1890; joined the Knights of Labor in 1885, and the United Mine Workers of America (UMWA) at its founding in 1890; elected secretary-treasurer of District 12, UMWA, Illinois, in 1895; appointed international organizer in 1897 and worked with John H. Walker (q.v.) and Mother Jones (q.v.) in southern Illinois and West Virginia; elected UMWA international vice-president in 1897 and appointed acting international president in September, 1898, when President Michael Ratchford (q.v.) resigned; elected and served as UMWA international president, 1899-1908; during his administration, the UMWA increased its membership from 34,000 to 300,000 and its treasury from $12,000 to $900,000; due to his skillful direction of the 147,000 man Pennsylvania anthracite strike in 1902, public opinion swung to the miners' side and the Anthracite Coal Strike Commission, appointed by President Theodore Roosevelt, awarded the miners a 14 percent wage increase and the eight- or nine-hour day; served as fourth vice-president of the American Federation of Labor (AFL), 1898-1900, and as second vice-president, 1900-1914, much to the chagrin of the ambitious Thomas L. Lewis (q.v.), who succeeded him as UMWA international president in 1908; along with AFL president Samuel Gompers (q.v.) and Secretary-Treasurer Frank Morrison (q.v.), was convicted and sentenced to prison for violating a federal court injunction during a strike at Buck's Stove and Range Company of St. Louis, Mo.; on appeal, the U. S. Supreme Court relieved them of prison sentences; assisted in organizing the National Civic Federation in 1900 and retained his membership until a resolution adopted by a combination of Socialists and followers of retiring President Thomas Lewis forced him to resign from the Federation or the UMWA; was chairman of the trades agreement department of the National Civic Federation, 1908-1911; served as a member of the New York State Workmen's Compensation Commission, 1914-1915, and chairman of the New York State Industrial Commission from 1915 until his death; served during World War I on several city, state, and regional bodies; died in New York City, September 9, 1919, and was buried at Scranton, Pa., where in 1924, the UMWA erected a statue designed by Philip Sheridan; miners still celebrate the second Monday in April as Mitchell Day; Elsie Gluck, *John Mitchell, Miner* (1929); Charles A. Madison, *American Labor Leaders: Personalities* *and Forces in the Labor Movement* (1962); *Dictionary of American Biography* (Vol. VII); *National Cyclopaedia of American Biography* (Vol. XXIV); *Who Was Who in America* (Vol. I).

(J.H.)

MITCHELL, Walter L.   Born in Florence, Ala., January 30, 1915; son of Goodlow S. and Exel T. (Hendon) Mitchell; married Ruby A. Jenkins on April 8, 1936, and after that marriage ended in divorce in 1954, Lucille Snowden on December 24, 1955; two children; received the LLB degree from the Atlanta, Ga., Law School in 1950 and the LLM degree in 1951; attended the University of Georgia, 1951-1952; graduated from high school, then began work as a laborer at the Tennessee Valley Authority (TVA) chemical, phosphates, and nitrates plant in 1933 and eventually was promoted to a position as laboratory analyst; organized TVA laboratory workers into an American Federation of Labor (AFL) federal labor union in 1941 and became the first president of the TVA Council of Office, Technical and Service Unions; served as an AFL organizer, 1942-1944, 1946; elected a vice-president and Southern regional director of the newly organized International Chemical Workers Union (ICWU) in 1946, serving in that capacity until 1956; elected international president of the ICWU in 1956 and served in that position until his death; became a vice-president of the industrial union department of the AFL-Congress of Industrial Organizations (CIO) and a member of the executive board of the maritime trades department in 1962; was a delegate to the International Labor Organization's chemical industries committee meeting in Geneva in 1962; served on the national board of Americans for Democratic Action and Citizens' Crusade Against Poverty; was a Democrat; died in New Orleans, La., September 19, 1968; Melvin Rothbaum, *The Government of the Oil, Chemical, and Atomic Workers Union* (1962); *Who's Who in America, 1968-1969; AFL-CIO News,* September 28, 1968.

MOFFETT, Elwood Stewart.   Born in Williamstown, Pa., April 30, 1908; son of Alfred, a coal miner, and Jennie A. (Showers) Moffett; Methodist; married Hannah P. Ely on January 31, 1931; four children; completed high school, then went to work as an anthracite miner in 1924 and joined the United Mine Workers of America (UMWA); elected president of his local at age twenty-seven and reelected several times; when John L. Lewis (q.v.) reorganized District 50, a small UMWA affiliate in the coal and coke by-products field, into a catch-all union for raiding purposes, Moffett was hired as an organizer in 1942; held various staff posts until appointed assistant to the president of District 50, A. D. Lewis (q.v.), in 1948; became a vice-president, in 1958 and president after the death of Lewis in 1962; as president, asserted himself on behalf of District 50, reducing per capita payment to the UMWA and building membership in the chemical industry; his relations with the UMWA became increasingly strained; in 1968 the District 50 executive board acclaimed nuclear generation of power and announced it would organize atomic energy workers; within a month UMWA president W. A. Boyle (q.v.) expelled District 50, denouncing its officers for betraying the parent union and jeopardizing coal miners' jobs; expulsion had little effect on District 50 as it was already in fact an independent union whose membership exceeded that of the UMWA; as a result of a UMWA suit, the union changed its name to District 50, Allied and Technical Workers; instituted staff training conferences, worker-education programs, and union-management conferences; concerned about his union's financial standing and seeking to establish coordinated bargaining in chemicals and utilities, began merger talks with the United Steelworkers of America (USWA) in 1969; defeated vice-president Angelo Cafalo in a race for the presidency in 1970; won a legal battle to prevent a District 50 referendum on merger, then gained members' approval of the merger of his 200,000 member union with the USWA in 1972; became a special assistant to the USWA president after the merger; was a Democrat; died in Washington, D. C., February 22, 1973; *Who's Who in America* (1972); *Wall Street Journal,* March 7, 1968; *Steel Labor* (March, 1973).

(D.G.S.)

MOHN, Einar Oliver. Born in Atwater, Minn., August 27, 1906; son of Christopher, a minister, and Hattie (Hansen) Mohn; Lutheran; married Margaret Flockoi on January 1, 1930; three children; graduated from high school, then studied bacteriology at Augsburg College, ·Minneapolis, Minn., 1925-1927, and the University of Washington, 1927-1928; worked as a bacteriologist for the Whatcom County Dairyman's Association, Bellingham, Wash., 1928-1933; joined Milk Drivers and Dairy Employees Local 93 of the International Brotherhood of Teamsters, Chauffeurs, Warehousemen and Helpers of America (IBT) in 1933; elected secretary of the Billingham Central Labor Council and served as the Chief administrative officer of IBT Local 231, 1934-1937; was one of the principal founders of the Western States Dairy Employees Council and its IBT international representative in 1936; became an IBT international organizer in 1941 and was placed in charge of the Southern California district; was a founder of the Western Line Drivers Council in 1944 and was its first vice-chairman; elected president of IBT Joint Council 42 and of Warehouse and Produce Council 846; elected an IBT vice-president in 1952; served as an executive assistant to IBT president Dave Beck (q.v.), 1952-1957; began a long term of service as chairman of the powerful Western Conference of Teamsters in 1957; served on numerous commissions and boards in California, including the Citizen's Advisory Commission of Revision and Updating the California Constitution, 1964-1968, the Governor's Commission on Automation and Technological Developments, 1963-1967, the California Commission on Manpower, 1963-1967, and the Stanford Mid-Peninsula Urban Coalition; was a member of the University of California Board of Regents, 1965-1967; usually supported Democrats in state elections; Donald Garnel, *The Rise of Teamster Power in the West* (1972); Sam Romer, *The International Brotherhood of Teamsters: Its Government and Structure* (1962); Robert D. Leiter, *The Teamsters Union: A Study of Its Economic Impact* (1957); *Who's Who in Labor* (1946).

MOLONY, Joseph Patrick.   Born in Ennis, County Clare, Ireland, November 6, 1906; Roman Catholic; married Marguerite Bouchard in 1938; one child; attended school for ten years in Ireland, then emigrated to the United States in 1926; worked in various blue-collar jobs before being employed by Republic Steel at its Buffalo works in 1936; became an organizer for the Steel Workers Organizing Committee during the "Little Steel" strike of 1937; elected director of United Steelworkers of America (USWA) District 4, New York State, in 1942; headed the USWA's Bethlehem Steel negotiating committee for many years; was an unsuccessful "rank-and-file candidate" for a USWA vice-presidency in 1955, which was the first real contest for an elective international office in the union's history and was an indirect challenge to USWA president David J. McDonald (q.v.); supported McDonald a year later when a group opposed to increased dues attempted to unseat him; helped launch and manage I. W. Abel's (q.v.) successful bid for the USWA presidency in 1965; elected an international vice-president in 1965 and reelected in 1969; as chairman of the USWA civil rights committee, worked to speed implementation of equal-rights policy; presided over changes in the wage policy committee that dispersed authority to ratify wage settlements among conferences composed of local union representatives in basic steel, aluminum, can, and nonferrous mining industries; after the merger of the International Union of Mine, Mill and Smelter Workers and the USWA, became the chief negotiator for several unions with jurisdictions in the copper industry; led a nine-month copper strike, 1967-1968, which established company-wide coalition bargaining; as chairman of the USWA constitution committee, helped marshal support for a dues increase and for the creation of a strike fund by special convention in 1968; is knowledgeable and articulate and is widely respected in labor circles as a self-taught intellectual; frequently lectures at colleges and universities; a fervent believer that union leaders should participate in civic affairs, served on numerous public and private boards and agencies; before retiring as USWA vice-president in 1973, was chairman of the nonferrous industry coordinating committee; received the Negro Trade Union Council's award for outstanding work on behalf of civil rights in 1974; a Democrat; Lloyd Ulman, *The Government of the Steelworkers Union* (1962); John Herling, *Right to Challenge: People and Power in the Steelworkers Union* (1972); *Wall Street Journal*, February 28, 1973.

(D.G.S.)

MONTGOMERY, Robert (Henry Jr.).   Born in Beacon, N.Y., May 21, 1904; son of Henry, a rubber corporation executive, and Mary Weed (Bernard) Montgomery; married Elizabeth Bryan Allen on April 14, 1928 and after that marriage ended in divorce, Elisabeth Grant on December 9, 1950; two children; attended exclusive boys' schools until age sixteen but then was forced by his father's death to work as a mechanic on the New York, New Haven, and Hartford Railroad; somewhat later, was an oiler on a Standard Oil tanker; briefly tried to become a writer, then made stage debut in 1924; appeared in a silent film in 1926 and made first sound film in 1929; joined the Screen Actors Guild (SAG) in 1933 and the following year served on the National Recovery Administration committee concerned with the film industry; elected a vice-president of the SAG in 1934 and a year later elected president, serving until 1940; during his incumbency the SAG became a strong organization capable of maintaining a closed shop in Hollywood studios; enlisted in the American Field Service in London in 1940 and a year later was commissioned a Lieutenant (junior grade) in the U. S. Navy; discharged from the Navy in 1945 and reelected president of the SAG, serving until his resignation in 1947; was also a member of the Directors Guild of America and Actors Equity Association; was a cooperative witness before the House Committee on Un-American Activities concerning Communist influence in the film industry; began directing films in 1946 and later became a producer and ended his association with the labor movement; was a Democrat early in his career, but usually supported Republican candidates after 1940; Murray Ross, *Stars and Strikes: Unionization of Hollywood* (1941); *Current Biography* (1948); *Who's Who in America, 1972-1973.*

MOONEY, Thomas Joseph.   Born in Chicago, Ill., December 8, 1882; son of Bryan, a coal miner, and Mary (Heffernan or Hefferon) Mooney; reared a Roman Catholic; married Rena Ellen (Brink) Hermann on July 3, 1911; attended the parochial and public schools of Holyoke, Mass., until age fourteen, then quit school and began working in a Holyoke factory; became an apprentice iron molder in 1898 and shortly thereafter joined the International Molders Union; while traveling in Europe in 1907, was converted to socialism and upon his return to the United States, took an active role in the distribution of Socialist literature; attended the International Socialist Congress meeting in Copenhagen in 1910; was an unsuccessful candidate for superior court judge in San Francisco, Calif., in 1910 and the following year ran unsuccessfully for sheriff on the Socialist ticket; joined the Industrial Workers of the World and in 1910 was involved in the publication of *Revolt*, a Socialist newspaper; became an organizer somewhat later for William Z. Foster's (q.v.) Syndicalist League of North America and a member of the International Workers Defense League; charged with illegal possession of high explosives during a strike of electrical workers against the Pacific Gas and Electric Company in 1913, and a year later, after two trials resulted in hung juries, was acquitted; convicted of murder and sentenced to be hung as a result of a bombing that killed ten persons during a San Francisco Preparedness Day parade in July, 1916; after it became increasingly obvious that he had been convicted on false and perjured testimony, his case became an international cause célèbre; largely as a result of potential international repercusions, his sentence was commuted to life imprisonment by the governor of California in November, 1918; pardoned by the governor of California in 1939 after over two decades of agitation and legal maneuvers on his behalf; died in San Francisco, Calif., March 6, 1942; Richard H. Frost, *The Mooney Case* (1968); Curt Gentry, *Frame-up: The Incredible Case of Tom Mooney and Warren Billings* (1967); *Dictionary of American Biography* (Supplement III).

MOORE, Ely.   Born near Belvidere, N. J., July 4, 1798; son of Moses and Mary (Coryell) Moore; married Emma Conant, who bore him six children, and after her death, Mrs. Clara Baker; attended the public schools of Belvidere, then served an apprenticeship as a printer; later studied medicine in New York City, but, after practicing medicine for a few years, resumed the printer's trade and eventually became a land speculator and political activist; elected the first president of the New York General Trades' Union, a federation of craft unions, in 1833, and became the editor of its organ, the *National Trades' Union*; elected chairman of the National Trades' Union, a federation of labor unions from six Eastern cities, in 1834, and served through 1835; was a popular orator and was able to maintain his influence in the labor movement despite his failure to become actively involved in labor conflicts and his equivocal stand on the important prison-labor issue; elected as a Democrat to the U.S. Congress in 1834 and served until 1839; became the political editor of the *New York Evening Post* in 1838; was president of the board of trade and surveyor of the Port of New York City, 1839-1845; appointed as a U.S. marshal for the Southern district of New York in 1845; became the publisher and editor of the *Warren Journal*, Belvidere, N.J.; after declining appointments as minister to England and governor of the Territory of Kansas, appointed agent for the Miami and other Kansas Indian tribes in 1853; appointed register of the United States land office in Lecompton, Kan., in 1855 and served until 1860; was a Democrat; died in Lecompton, Kan., January 27, 1861; Walter E. Hugins, "Ely Moore: The Case History of a Jacksonian Labor Leader," *Political Science Quarterly* (March, 1950), and *Jacksonian Democracy and the Working Class: A Study of the New York Workingmen's Movement, 1829-1837* (1960); Edward Pessen, *Most Uncommon Jacksonians: The Radical Leaders of the Early Labor Movement* (1967); John R. Commons, *et al.*, *History of Labour in the United States*, Vol. I (1918); *Dictionary of American Biography* (Vol. XIII).

MORAN, John J.   Born in Cecil, Pa., February 26, 1897; son of Thomas, a miner, and Sara A. (Beagan) Moran; married Martha R. Schwartz on July 9, 1923; one child; graduated from high school, then began working in the coal mines and joined the United Mine Workers of America; learned the telegrapher's trade, and became a member of the Order of Railroad Telegraphers; joined the Federation of Long Lines Telephone Workers (FLLTW) in 1938 and the following year elected FLLTW president; after the FLLTW affiliated with the National Federation of Telephone Workers (NFTW) in 1941, became a member of the executive board of the NFTW; elected a vice-president of the NFTW in 1943; during World War II, was a labor member of the telephone committee and the review and appeals committees of the National War Labor Board, and a labor representative on the Board of War Communications; was a staunch advocate of a strong national union and of affiliation with a national labor federation and was a constant critic of the NFTW's independent status and its allegedly excessive provisions for local autonomy; helped lead the bitter and largely unsuccessful strike of telephone workers in 1947, then left the NFTW and became vice-chairman of the Congress of Industrial Organizations' (CIO) rival Telephone Workers' Organizing Committee; following the NFTW's reorganization into the Communications Workers of America (CWA) and its affiliation with the CIO in 1949, became a vice-president of the CWA and was placed in charge of external organization; became a member of the CIO executive board in 1949; resigned the positions of CWA vice-president and director of organization in 1956 because of ill health; died in Boca Raton, Fla., in September, 1968; Jack Barbash, *Unions and Telephones: The Story of the Communications Workers of America* (1952); *Who's Who in Labor* (1946).

MORESCHI, Joseph.   Born in Italy in 1884; Roman Catholic; married; at least two children; emigrated with parents to the United States in 1892 and settled in Chicago, Ill.; gained work as a laborer and joined Chicago Local 1 of the International Hod Carriers', Building and Common Laborers' Union of America (IHCBCLU) in 1912; served Local 1 in several capacities, including as president, and also served as president of the Laborers District Council in Chicago; served as a vice-president and executive board member during 1921-1926, then elected president of the IHCBCLU in 1926, holding position for 42 years; served as an American Federation of Labor (AFL) fraternal delegate to the British Trades Union Congress in 1931; negotiated mergers with the Tunnel and Subway Constructors' International Union in 1929 and the International Union of Pavers, Rammermen, Flag Layers, Bridge and Stone Curb Setters and Sheet Asphalt Pavers in 1937; introduced several innovations during his incumbency, including the institution of a system of regional offices in 1935 to facilitate governing the union, the establishment of a legal department, the creation of a death benefit fund, and the publication of *The Laborer*, a monthly IHCBCLU organ founded in 1947; became the editor of *The Laborer* in 1947; as international president, the IHCBCLU increased its membership from less than 20,000 to more than 500,000; retired union positions and named president emeritus in 1968; died in Hot Springs, Ark., March 11, 1970; Arch A. Mercey, *The Laborers' Story, 1903-1953: The First Fifty Years of the International Hod Carriers', Building and Common Laborers' Union of America (AFL)* (1954); *AFL-CIO News*, March 14, 1970.

MORGAN, Thomas John.   Born in Birmingham, England, October 27, 1847; son of Thomas John and Hannah (Simcox) Morgan, both impoverished nail-makers who labored 17 hours a day; married Elizabeth Chambers on January 26, 1868; attended a paupers' school until age nine;

learned writing and arithmetic at a Unitarian Sunday school, studied mechanical drawing at the Athenaeum night school, and while employed on the Illinois Central Railroad carshops during 1875-1895, read law and was graduated from Chicago Law College; worked, beginning at age nine, as a nail-maker, a printer, a molder in an iron foundry, worker in a thimble factory, and as a machinist and brass finisher; unable to escape poverty, even though wife also worked; emigrated to the United States in 1869; settling in Chicago, Ill.; during the Panic of 1873, experienced along with his wife 15 months of unemployment; became active in 1871 in the labor movement and was elected president of his local union of machinists; in the late 1870s, was a prime mover in the creation of the Chicago Trade and Labor Assembly; when it split in 1884, formed along with other radicals the Chicago Central Labor Union, which endured to 1896; in 1879, guided a special committee of the Illinois General Assembly on a tour of Chicago factories that resulted in the creation of a State Bureau of Labor Statistics; also in 1879, drafted city ordinances patterned after the English factory acts that were adopted by the Chicago Board of Aldermen; in the early 1890s, wrote a program for labor's political action, the heart of which, Plank 10, espoused collective ownership of all means of production and distribution; in 1894, the Springfield, Ill., Populist convention and two Illinois State Federation of Labor conventions adopted most of his program, but rejected Plank 10; was a political radical as early as 1875; joined the Socialist Labor party and was its unsuccessful candidate for mayor of Chicago in 1891; was an unsuccessful candidate on the Social Democratic party ticket for Chicago City Attorney, 1903, Superior Court Judge, Cook County, 1903, 1907, and for U.S. Senator, 1909; from 1900 until his death, served on numerous Socialist party city, county, state, and national executive and campaign committees; was the editor and publisher of *The Provoker*, 1909-1912; died on December 10, 1912; *Who Was Who in America* (Vol. I); Eugene Staley, *History of the Illinois State Federation of Labor* (1930).

(J.H.)

MORREALE, Vincent F.   Born in New York City, July 29, 1902; son of Michele, a builder and contractor, and Angela Maria Morreale; Roman Catholic; married Marie Sambuchelli on June 21, 1934; two children; attended Fordham Preparatory School and Fordham College; received an LLB from Fordham Law School; then served as attorney for the New York City Compressed Air Workers Union, 1930-1934; became the attorney for the International Hod Carriers', Building and Common Laborers' Union of America (IHCBCLU) in 1934; associated during World War II with the government war-construction and ship-building program as a labor advisor and public-relations official; assumed the title of general counsel after the position was created by the IHCBCLU in 1946 and became the head of the international's legal department; served frequently as an IHCBCLU delegate to the national conventions of the American Federation of Labor (AFL) and the AFL-Congress of Industrial Organizations; actively involved in numerous civic, political, and religious organizations; supported the Democratic party; authored numerous pamphlets and frequently contributed to the IHCBCLU organ, *The Laborer*; Arch A. Mercey, *The Laborers' Story, 1903-1953: The First Fifty Years of the International Hod Carriers', Building and Common Laborers' Union of America* (1954); U. S. Department of Labor, *The Workers' Story, 1913-1953* (1953); *Who's Who in Labor* (1946).

MORRISON, Frank.   Born in Franktown, Ontario, Canada, November 23, 1859; son of Christopher, a Scots-Irish immigrant, farmer, and sawyer, and Elizabeth (Nesbitt) Morrison; Church of Christ; married Josephine Curtis on June 11, 1891, and Alice S. Boswell on August 11, 1908; two children; completed one year of high school, then left school to learn the printing trade; soon thereafter emigrated to the United States and in 1873 secured employment on the Madison, Wis., *Journal*; while working as a compositor on a Chicago newspaper in 1886, joined Local 16 of the International Typographical Union (ITU); admitted to the Illinois bar after attending Lake Forest University Law School, 1893-1894; elected a delegate to the ITU national convention in 1896 and selected to represent the ITU at the national American Federation of Labor (AFL) convention meeting in Colorado later in the same year; elected AFL secretary in 1897, and served in that capacity for more than 40 years; became secretary of the AFL labor representation committee that was organized in 1906 to coordinate political activities; sentenced to six months in prison in 1907 as a result of contempt charges growing out of violations of the injunction issued in the Buck's Stove and Range Company case, but the conviction was later reversed by the U.S. Supreme Court; was a close associate and collaborator of AFL presidents Samuel Gompers (q.v.) and William Green (q.v.) and was one of the leading architects of the American labor movement; was a skillful administrator who efficiently managed the routine affairs of the AFL; retired union positions in 1939 and named AFL secretary emeritus; was a nonpartisan in political affairs; died in Washington, D.C., March 12, 1949; Philip Taft, *The A. F. of L. in the Time of Gompers* (1957); Louis L.

Lorwin, *The American Federation of Labor: History, Policies, and Prospects* (1933); *The American Federationist* (April, 1949).

MORTIMER, Wyndham.   Born in Karthaus, Clearfield County, Pa., March 11, 1884; son of Thomas George, a miner and Knights of Labor member, and Rachel (Jenkins) Mortimer; reared a Protestant; married Margaret Hunter on December 24, 1907; two children; left school at age twelve and went to work in the Pennsylvania coal fields as a "trapper boy"; joined the United Mine Workers of America in 1900; spent several years in the mines, then worked at a variety of occupations prior to taking employment with the White Motor Company in Cleveland, Ohio; organized the employees of the White Motor Company into American Federation of Labor (AFL) Federal Local 18463; became president of the Cleveland Auto Council in 1934; led organizing efforts in Flint, Mich., prior to the successful United Automobile, Aircraft, Agricultural Implement Workers of America (UAW) strike against the Fisher Body Company in 1936; considered one of the most effective UAW organizers and strike leaders; was a vocal critic of the AFL leadership's control of the UAW; elected a UAW vice-president in 1936, serving until 1939; was a leader of the union's left-wing "Unity Caucus" and strongly supported affiliation with the Congress of Industrial Organizations (CIO); led the opposition to UAW president Warren Homer Martin (q.v.) in 1937-1938; moved to Los Angeles, Calif., in 1940 as a UAW organizer assigned to the California aircraft industry; was one of the principal leaders of the 1941 strike against the North American Aviation Company; became a CIO organizer in 1942 but resigned after a short time; returned to Los Angeles and there held a number of minor union positions until his retirement in 1945 from union affairs; authored *Organize! My Life as a Union Man* (1971); was a Socialist, but stoutly denied charges of being a member of the Communist party; died in Los Angeles, Calif., August 25, 1966; Jack Stieber, *Governing the UAW* (1962); Sidney Fine, *Sit-Down: The General Motors Strike of 1936-1937* (1969), and *The Automobile under the Blue Eagle: Labor, Management, and the Automobile Manufacturing Code* (1953); Frank Cormier and William J. Eaton, *Reuther* (1970).

MOYER, Charles H. (fl. 1893-1929).   Little known about his early years prior to 1893; as a smelter worker for the Homestake Mining Company at Lead, S.D., in the 1880s, was active in the Lead City Miners' Union, which played a major role in the founding of the Western Federation of Miners (WFM) in 1893; was a member by 1900 of the executive board of WFM District 5, South Dakota; elected president after the resignation of WFM president Edward Boyce (q.v.) in 1902; was a thoroughgoing industrial unionist and influenced the WFM to push for the organization of all types of mine employees; as a result of this policy, the WFM became involved in the bitter Cripple Creek and Telluride, Colo., strikes of 1903-1904; during these strikes, was jailed and denied habeus corpus; was convinced by the use of the state militia to crush the strikes of the futility of isolated unionism and the need for a broader, more militant, radical unionism; during this period, became a supporter of the Socialist party; along with his union colleagues William Haywood (q.v.) and John O'Neill (q.v.), participated in January, 1905, in the Chicago conference that laid the groundwork for the establishment of the Industrial Workers of the World (IWW) and was offered but declined its presidency; WFM affiliation provided the IWW its only substantial initial membership; involved in one of the most famous and bizarre labor conspiracy trials in 1906-1907, when, along with William Haywood and George Pettibone, he was alleged to be a part of a WFM 'inner circle', which was accused of murdering former Idaho governor Frank Steunenberg; kidnapped along with his WFM colleagues by Colorado officials and turned over to Idaho authorities; indicted for conspiracy to murder; after Haywood and Pettibone were acquitted, the charge against Moyer was dropped; angered by the revolutionaries among IWW leaders and by their tactics and opposition to union endorsement of political parties, therefore led the WFM out of the IWW in 1908; was convinced that the union's reputation for revolutionary agitation made dealing effectively with employers more difficult, hence in 1911 helped reaffiliate the WFM with the American Federation of Labor (AFL) and adopted the trade union goal of time contracts; under his guidance, the WFM substituted a commitment to trade union goals for its radical program; within the AFL, tended to veer away from the Socialists, who supported independent political action, advocating instead AFL nonpartisanship; meanwhile, beset by the IWW policy of destroying locals it could not capture and continued employer hostility, the WFM, which changed its name in 1916 to the International Union of Mine, Mill and Smelter Workers, experienced a steady decline in membership; was unable to revive union strength, especially in the crucial copper industry, and hence along with his executive board was forced to resign in 1926; died in Pomona, Calif., June 2, 1929; Vernon H. Jensen, *Heritage of Conflict: Labor Relations in the Nonferrous Metals Industry up to 1930* (1950); John

H. M. Laslett, *Labor and the Left: A Study of Socialist and Radical Influences in the American Labor Movement, 1881-1924* (1970).

(D.G.S.)

MULLANEY, Joseph A.   Born in New York City, June 11, 1872; Roman Catholic; married; four children; completed grammar school, then at age fifteen began an apprenticeship as an asbestos worker at the Asbestos Felting Works in New York City in 1888; joined the New York Salamander Association of Boiler and Pipe Coverers in 1888; became the business agent of the Salamander Association in 1902 and led the Association out of the Knights of Labor and into the newly organized International Association of Heat and Frost Insulators and Asbestos Workers (IAHFIAW), which affiliated with the American Federation of Labor in 1904; elected international president of the IAHFIAW in 1912; became a vice-president of the New York State Federation of Labor (NYSFL) in 1912 and served in that capacity until 1954; served for many years as chairman of the resolutions committee of the NYSFL but three times refused to assume the presidency of the NYSFL; served as manager of George Meany's (q.v.) successful campaign to win election as president of the NYSFL in 1934; was the seminal figure in the organization of asbestos workers and was popularly known as "Mr. Asbestos"; in 1937, elected president of the IAHFIAW for life; appointed to the New York State Committee on Employment of the Physically Handicapped in 1951; was an active participant in New York State Democratic politics; involved in successful efforts to achieve protective legislation for industrial workers; was instrumental in the NYSFL's decision to endorse Alfred E. Smith for president of the United States in 1928; died in Flushing, Queens, N.Y., December 25, 1954; *The American Federationist* (February, 1955); *The New York Times*, December 25, 1954.

MURPHY, Vincent.   Born in Newark, N.J., August 1, 1893; son of Thomas Francis, a leather worker, and Sarah (Gaskin) Murphy; Roman Catholic; married Marie K. McConnell on May 30, 1917; two children; attended parochial schools in Newark and Newark Business College; became an apprentice plumber and in 1913 joined Local 24 of the United Association of Plumbers and Steam Fitters of the United States and Canada (UA); elected secretary-treasurer of UA Local 24 in 1920, serving until 1938; began a long tenure as secretary-treasurer of the New Jersey State Federation of Labor (NJSFL) in 1932; served during the 1930s as a labor representative on the New Jersey Security Advisory Board and as a member of the State Unemployment Compensation Committee; elected to the Newark City Council in 1937 and served as director of the Department of Revenue and Finance and as commander of the Newark Defense Council; elected mayor of Newark on a labor party ticket in 1941, serving in that position until 1949; won the Democratic nomination for governor of New Jersey in 1943, but lost the general election; was one of the principal figures in the difficult merger negotiations between the American Federation of Labor (AFL) and Congress of Industrial Organizations (CIO) in New Jersey which did not reach fruition until 1961; elected the first president of the New Jersey AFL-CIO in 1961; is a member of the board of trustees of the Newark College of Engineering and the Essex County Medical Foundation, chairman of the joint committee for the annual labor institutes sponsored by the NJSFL and Rutgers University, an honorary vice-chairman of the American-Jewish Trade Union Committee for Palestine, and a member of the National Association for the Advancement of Colored People; a Democrat; retired union positions in 1970; Leo Troy, *Organized Labor in New Jersey* (1965); *Who's Who in Labor* (1946); *AFL-CIO News*, February 28, 1970.

MURRAY, Philip.   Born in Blantyre, Scotland, on May 25, 1886; son of William, a coal miner and for a time president of a local of the Scottish miners' union, and Rose Ann (Layden) Murray; Roman Catholic; married Elizabeth Lavery on September 7, 1910; one son; began working in the mines at age ten after a few years of public education; emigrated with family to the United States in 1902; settled in western Pennsylvania and there began working in the mines; elected president of a local miners' union in 1904 after a dispute with management that cost him his job; became a citizen of the United States in 1911; elected to the executive board of the United Mine Workers of America (UMWA) in 1912; became president of UMWA District 5, Western Pennsylvania, in 1916 and three years later elected a vice-president of the UMWA; during World War I, appointed to the Pennsylvania regional panel of the War Labor Board and served on the National Bituminous Coal Production Committee, 1917-1918; appointed to the Labor and Industrial Advisory Board of the National Recovery Administration in 1933; assisted in the writing and enactment of the Guffy-Snyder Coal Stabilization Act of 1935; participated in the establishment of the Congress of Industrial Organizations (CIO) in 1938; appointed chairman of the Steel Workers Organizing Committee in 1936 and served in that capacity until it was reorganized into the United Steelworkers of America (USWA) in 1942; elected president of the CIO in 1940 after the resignation of John L. Lewis (q.v.); elected international president of the USWA in 1942; expelled from the UMWA in 1942, because of differences with the temperamental UMWA president John L. Lewis; was critical of many administration policies and programs, but generally supported President Franklin D. Roosevelt and the various productivity programs initiated during World War II; served on the National Defense Mediation Board and several other government boards and agencies during World War II; led major strikes against the steel industry in 1946, 1949, and 1952; was a vigorous critic of the Taft-Hartley Act and was indicted by a Federal Grand Jury on charges of violating its provisions barring political expenditures by unions, but after hearing the case the Supreme Court dismissed the indictment; was an opponent of Communist influence in the labor movement and generally assumed a conservative position in the ideological conflicts within the CIO; was actively involved in public affairs and served on the Pittsburgh, Pa., Board of Education from 1918 until his death; was a member of the executive committee of the National Association for the Advancement of Colored People and a member of the Board of directors of the National Red Cross; was a Democrat; coauthored *Organized Labor and Production* (1940); died in San Francisco, Calif., November 9, 1952; Lloyd Ulman, *The Government of the Steel Workers' Union* (1962); Charles A. Madison, *American Labor Leaders: Personalities and Forces in the Labor Movement* (1962); John Herling, *Right to Challenge: People and Power in the Steelworkers Union* (1972); Walter Galenson, *The CIO Challenge to the AFL: A History of the American Labor Movement, 1935-1941* (1960); Irving Bernstein, *Turbulent Years: A History of the American Worker, 1933-1941* (1970).

MURRAY, Thomas A.   Born in New York City in 1885; Roman Catholic; married Elizabeth Jane O'Keefe; four children; attended grammar school, then became an apprentice bricklayer at age fourteen; joined the Bricklayers, Masons and Plasterers International Union (BMPIU) after completing his apprenticeship; while working as a bricklayer, took courses at Cooper Union for the Advancement of Science and Art; served as a foreman bricklayer and general superintendent for the Kenwell Construction Company, New York City, 1909-1933; elected chairman of the New York Bricklayers' executive committee for Manhattan and the Bronx in 1933; served as president of the Building and Construction Trades Council of Greater New York, 1936-1943; elected a vice-president of the New York State Federation of Labor (NYSFL) in 1940 and three years later appointed president of the organization after the death of the incumbent, Thomas J.

Lyons; served as president of the NYSFL from 1943 to 1958; considered an adept conciliator and was one of the principal leaders in the effort to affect a merger between the American Federation of Labor (AFL) and Congress of Industrial Organizations' (CIO) unions in New York State; was scheduled to become president of the New York State AFL-CIO after the 1958 merger, but died in Albany, N.Y., May 2, 1958; was a Democrat; *The American Federationist* (June, 1958); *The New York Times*, May 1, 1958.

MUSTE, Abraham Johannes. Born in Zierikzee, the Netherlands, January 8, 1885; son of Martin, a coachman, and Adriana (Jonker) Muste; Dutch Reformed; married Anna Huizenga on June 21, 1909; three children; emigrated with his family to the United States in 1891, settling in Grand Rapids, Mich.; attended a Dutch Reformed parochial school and the public schools of Grand Rapids before entering Hope College in Holland, Mich., to prepare for the ministry; received the B.A. degree in 1905; after a year of teaching Latin and Greek, entered the theological seminary of the Dutch Reformed Church in New Brunswick, N.J.; was ordained in the Reformed Church of America in 1909 and during the same year received the M.A. degree from Hope College; while serving pastorates in New York City and Boston, Mass., gradually grew more critical of Calvinist dogma and increasingly susceptible to Quaker thought and Christian pacifism; joined the pacifist Fellowship of Reconciliation (FOR) in 1916; as his opposition to American intervention in World War I became more controversial, left the ministry and became a volunteer worker for the newly organized American Civil Liberties Union; was one of the principal leaders of the Lawrence, Mass., textile strike of 1919, and elected executive secretary of the strike committee; elected executive secretary of the newly organized Amalgamated Textile Workers of America (ATWA) after the strike was resolved; resigned from the ATWA in 1921, when appointed education director and a member of the faculty of Brookwood Labor College; joined the American Federation of Teachers and in 1923 elected an international vice-president; served on the executive committee of the American Federation of Labor's Workers Education Bureau; was national chairman of FOR, 1926-1929; during 1929-1936, temporarily abandoned pacifism and, associated with the effort to organize mass-production workers, participated in the activities of the Conference for Progressive Labor Action and its successor, the American Workers party; resigned from the faculty of Brookwood Labor College after an ideological schism developed in 1933; after 1936, returned to his advocacy of Christian pacifism, hoping to combine radicalism and direct action through nonviolent civil disobedience; became the director of the Presbyterian Labor Temple in 1936; appointed industrial secretary of FOR in 1936 and executive secretary in 1940, serving until 1953; after the late 1930s, ended his close association with the labor movement and devoted his time and attention almost exclusively to the peace movement; authored *Non-Violence in an Aggressive World* (1940), *War is the Enemy* (1942), *Wage Peace Now* (1942), *Not by Might* (1947), and *The Camp of Liberation* (1954); died in New York City, February 11, 1967; Nat Hentoff, *Peace Agitator: The Story of A. J. Muste* (1963); Lawrence S. Wither, *Rebels against War: The American Peace Movement, 1941-1960* (1969), and "Muste", *The McGraw-Hill Encyclopedia of World Biography* (1973); *Current Biography* (1965).

MYRUP, Andrew A.   Born in Copenhagen, Denmark, March 13, 1880; married; three children; attended the common schools of Copenhagen, then emigrated with his family to the United States in 1893, settling in Racine, Wis.; shortly after arriving, served an apprenticeship as a baker and by 1897 had become a journeyman baker; during the period 1897-1901, traveled around the country working at his trade; after a lengthy stay in California, moved to Chicago, Ill., in 1901 and joined Local 62 of the Bakery and Confectionary Workers' International Union of America (BCWIU); elected business agent of Local 62 in 1904 and a year later became a member of the BCWIU executive board; in 1907, elected international secretary-treasurer (chief administrative officer) of the BCWIU; elected international president when the office was created in the early 1940s; during his long leadership tenure in the BCWIU, was able to gain general application of the 40-hour week, substantial increases in wage scales, and improvement of the intolerable working conditions that had characterized the bakery trade at the turn of the century; was a devoted advocate of the union label and made the label an important instrument in organizing the bakery and confectionery trade; was a delegate to the annual conventions of the American Federation of Labor (AFL), 1907-1943, served on numerous AFL committees, and was a vice-president of its union label trades department; served as a vice president of the Union Labor Life Insurance Company; died in Boston, Mass., October 1, 1943; *The American Federationist* (July, 1941); *The American Federation of Labor Weekly News Service*, October 10, 1943.

NAGLER, Isidore.   Born in Uscie Biscupie, Austria-Hungary (now part of Austria), February 25, 1895; son of Lasser, a businessman, and Bertha (Pohoriles) Nagler; Jewish; married Pauline Lefkowitz on

November 23, 1919; emigrated to the United States in 1909; employed as a cutter in the garment industry and joined Local 10 of the International Ladies' Garment Workers' Union (ILGWU) in 1911; elected business agent of Local 10 in 1920; served as general manager of the New York Cloak Joint Board, 1928-1939; became an ILGWU vice-president in 1929; served as an ILGWU delegate to the International Clothing Workers' Congress in London in 1934; resumed leadership of the seriously divided Local 10 in 1939 at the request of the international officers of the ILGWU; elected a vice-president and executive board member of the New York State Federation of Labor in 1942; served as an American Federation of Labor fraternal delegate to the British Trades Union Congress in 1943; served on the state executive committee of the American Labor party (ALP), 1936-1944; ran unsuccessfully as the ALP candidate for borough president of the Bronx in 1937 and for the U. S. Congress a year later; served as a member of the state executive and administrative committee of the Liberal party of New York and as the secretary of the regional appeals' panel of the War Manpower Commission; became general manager of the New York Joint Board of the Cloak, Shirt, Skirt and Reefer Makers' Union in 1952; served as labor advisor to the United States delegation to the International Labor Organization conference in Geneva in 1958; was a vice-chairman of the Jewish Labor Committee; died in New York City, September 21, 1959; Harry Haskel, *Leader of the Garment Workers: The Biography of Isidore Nagler* (1950); Benjamin Stolberg, *Tailor's Progress: The Story of a Famous Union and the Men Who Made It* (1944); Max D. Danish, *The World of David Dubinsky* (1957); *ILGWU Report and Proceedings* (1962).

NANCE, Alexander Stephens.   Born in Bowman, Ga., May 19, 1895; son of John L. and Victoria (Bond) Nance; Baptist; married Frances K. McMurtrey; four children; attended grammar school, then moved to Atlanta, Ga., at age fifteen and began working in various newspaper mailrooms; was a charter member of Atlanta Mailers' Union Local 34, organized in 1911; elected president of Local 34 in 1919; led a mailroom workers' strike against Atlanta newspapers in 1922; was circulation manager of the *Southern Ruralist* in 1924 and served as vice-president and director of the Ruralist Press, Inc., in 1926; elected vice-president of the Georgia State Federation of Labor (GSFL) in 1927, serving until his resignation in 1929; served as the GSFL's legislative representative, 1930-1935; elected president of the Atlanta Federation of Trades in 1930, serving until 1935; during 1933, served on the compliance board of the National Recovery Administration and was a member of the National Labor Board; was an active participant in the textile strike of 1934; served as president of the GSFL from 1935 until 1937, when American Federation of Labor president William Green (q.v.) ordered the GSFL divided; appointed director of the Congress of Industrial Organizations' Textile Workers Organizing Committee (TWOC) in the Southeast, which attempted to organize textile, hosiery, and clothing industry workers; was credited with organizing 25,000 workers during the TWOC's first year of activity and, after his death at the end of that year, was described by Sidney Hillman (q.v.) as a martyr to the campaign; was a prominent community and political figure in Atlanta and Georgia; refused a presidential appointment as postmaster of Atlanta; served as a regional director of the Social Security Board and was instrumental in getting Works Progress Administration funds for the consolidated school at Baconton, Ga., which was named in his honor in 1936; also served with the Community Chest, the Family Welfare Society, the Salvation Army, the Georgia Conference on Social Work, and the Christian Council; was a Democrat; died April 3, 1938; Anonymous, *A. Steve Nance, Labor Statesman and Citizen* (n.d.); Lucy Randolph Mason, *To Win These Rights: A Personal Story of the CIO in the South* (1952); Matthew Josephson, *Sidney Hillman, Statesman of American Labor* (1952).

(M.E.R.)

NEF, Walter T. (fl. 1909-1920). Born in Europe of German-Swiss parents; was a member by 1909 of the Industrial Workers of the World (IWW) and organized for them while moving from job to job as a construction worker and logger in Oregon; took part in the Spokane, Wash., free speech fight, but was generally not a "soapboxer," rather a tough, practical Wobbly; in 1910 organized Minnesota timber workers and represented them as a delegate to the 1912 IWW convention; also attempted to unionize the harvest hands of the Great Plains, which the IWW had not attempted in any systematic way; in the spring of 1915, met with several Wobblies from the Midwest and the Far West in Kansas City, Mo., to establish the Agricultural Workers Organization (AWO) and elected its secretary-treasurer (i.e., chief officer); concentrating on the migratories who rode the freight trains to the grain fields, the AWO sought higher pay, a ten-hour day, and decent food and bedding for its members; after initial AWO efforts in Oklahoma and Kansas were very successful, moved AWO headquarters to Minneapolis, Minn., and sent his organizers into the northern grain fields; in accord with AWO policy and his own experience, rejected the practice of propagandizing harvesters in the cities where they congregated between jobs; instead, recruited job delegates to organize on the trains and in the fields; thus the AWO solved the problem of organizing a very mobile labor force; insisted on a high initiation fee and as membership grew AWO not only maintained solvency but also helped the IWW to build a larger national headquarters in Chicago, Ill.; reelected secretary-treasurer of AWO in May, 1916, leader of the IWW's most impressive branch, whose control of the main source of harvesters forced high wages and improved living conditions; by the end of the 1916 season, AWO membership reached 20,000, the largest ever attained by a single IWW union; the AWO had enlisted some nonagricultural workers, including loggers and railroad laborers; as the result of a dispute over this with William Haywood (q.v.), Nef resigned in late 1916; became secretary of the Philadelphia, Pa., Marine Transport Workers, an IWW local with a large black membership, which controlled the docks until 1920; convicted in Chicago trial of Wobblies, 1919; died in the 1930s; see his "The Militant Harvest Workers," *International Socialist Review* (October, 1916); Philip S. Foner, *History of the Labor Movement in the United States*, Vol. IV (1965); John S. Gamba, *The Decline of the I.W.W.* (1962).

(D.G.S.)

NELSON, Oscar Fred.   Born in Chicago, Ill., September 29, 1884; son of Nels and Johanna (Nelson) Nelson; Lutheran; married Helen Hoyer on April 21, 1909; three children; attended the public schools of Chicago; secured employment in a Chicago department store in 1897 and five years later joined the U.S. Postal Service as a clerk; organized a Chicago Local of the United National Association of Post Office Clerks (UNAPOC) in 1903 and elected its president; in 1910, elected president of the National Federation of Post Office Clerks (NFPOC), which had been organized in 1906 by a group of Chicago locals that had seceded from the UNAPOC; served as a vice-president of the Chicago Federation of Labor, 1910-1935; was instrumental as the Washington, D. C., representative of the NFPOC in passage of law fixing eight-hour day for postal clerks; served as chief factory inspector for the Illinois State Labor Department, 1913-1917; appointed commissioner of conciliation in the U. S. Department of Labor in 1917, serving until 1929; attended Webster Night School of Law in Chicago and admitted to the Illinois bar in 1922; elected as a Democrat to the Chicago City Council in 1923, but switched to the Republican party in 1927 and served as a city councilman until 1935; served as chairman of the Republican Central Committee of Chicago, 1934-1936; elected a judge of the Chicago superior court in 1935; died in Chicago, Ill., July 14, 1943; Karl Baarslag,

History of the National Federation of Post Office Clerks (1945); *National Cyclopaedia of American Biography* (Vol. XXXIII).

NESTOR, Agnes. Born in Grand Rapids, Mich., June 24, 1880; daughter of Irish immigrant, Thomas, a machinist, and Anna (McEwen) Nestor; Roman Catholic; acquired a grammar school education in public and parochial schools, then employed by the Eisendrath Glove Factory, Chicago, Ill., in 1897; led a successful ten-day strike against the Eisendrath Company in 1902 and became president of the newly organized Local 2 of the International Glove Workers Union (IGWU); served as vice-president of the IGWU, 1903-1906; joined the Chicago Women's Trade Union League (WTUL) in 1904 and three years later became a member of the executive board of the national WTUL, serving until 1948; elected secretary-treasurer of the IGWU in 1906 and served until 1913 when elected to a two-year term as president; along with Elizabeth Maloney, lobbied the ten-hour bill through the Illinois legislature in 1909; actively involved in the WTUL publicity campaigns in support of striking garment workers in Philadelphia, Pa., in 1909 and Chicago, 1910-1911; elected president of the Chicago WTUL in 1913 and vice-president of the IGWU in 1915, serving in both positions until 1948; appointed to the Commission on Federal Aid to Vocational Education by President Woodrow Wilson in 1914; served on the Department of Labor Advisory committee established by Secretary of Labor William B. Wilson (q.v.) in 1917; during the same year, appointed to the Industrial Survey Commission by the governor of Illinois; was instrumental in the passage of the eight-hour bill in Illinois in 1937; served as the IGWU's director of education and research, 1938-1948; was a Democrat; authored *Brief History of the International Glove Workers Union of America* (1942), and *Woman's Labor Leader: Autobiography of Agnes Nestor* (1954); died in Chicago, Ill., December 20, 1948; Gladys Boone, *The Women's Trade Union Leagues in Great Britain and the United States* (1942); Mary Dreier, *Margaret Dreier Robins: Her Life, Letters and Work* (1950); Mary Anderson, *Woman at Work: The Autobiography of Mary Anderson as Told to Mary N. Winslow* (1951).

(M.T.)

NEWMAN, Pauline. Born in Russia, October 18, 1891 (Birthdate has also been listed as 1887 and 1889); daughter of Meyer and Tillie Newman; Jewish; emigrated to the United States in 1901; served as a general organizer and lecturer for the International Ladies' Garment Workers' Union

(ILGWU), 1909-1913; was educational director and inspector for the Joint Board of Sanitary Control for the women's garment industry in New York, 1912-1918; served as an organizer and president of the Philadelphia, Pa., Women's Trade Union League (WTUL), 1918-1923; appointed director of the ILGWU Health Center in New York City in 1923, beginning a long and continuing term of service in that capacity; served as a vice-president of the New York branch of the WTUL and was a member of the national executive board of the WTUL; served as a WTUL delegate to the International Congress of Working Women in Vienna in 1923; appointed to the minimum wage board of New York City in 1933; was characterized as a woman of great tact and efficiency; served as a liaison between the ILGWU Health Center medical staff and local unions during much of her career; was a Socialist in her political sympathies and was a Socialist party organizer and lecturer for the northeastern section of the United States, 1913-1915; later supported the American Labor party and the Liberal party of New York; was a member of the organizing committee to oppose the Equal Rights Amendment in 1938; was a frequent contributor to journals such as *Justice*, the *Cleveland Federationist*, and the *Jewish Daily Forward*; Benjamin Stolberg, *Tailor's Progress: The Story of a Famous Union and the Men Who Made It* (1944); Solon DeLeon, ed., *The American Labor Who's Who* (1925); Louis Levine, *The Women's Garment Workers: A History of the International Ladies' Garment Workers' Union* (1924).

(M.T.)

NINFO, Salvatore. Born in Santo Stefano, Camastra, Messina, Italy, May 13, 1883; son of Guiseppe, a tailor, and Raffaella (Martino) Ninfo; Roman Catholic; married Maria Consentino on June 1, 1904: four children; attended grammar school for five years in Italy; emigrated to the United States at age sixteen; in 1900, led a New York City strike of diggers on the Lexington Avenue subway, the first Italian-American strike; gained employment in the New York garment district and in 1902 joined Cloak Finishers' Local 9 of the International Ladies' Garment Workers' Union (ILGWU); during 1903-1906, served as an American Federation of Labor organizer with the assignment of organizing Italian workers in various crafts in New York, Philadelphia, Pa., and Boston, Mass.; became a member of the executive board of Local 9 in 1906; elected a delegate to the New York Cloak Joint Board in 1908 and the following year appointed a general ILGWU organizer; elected business agent of the New York Cloak Joint Board in 1910; became an ILGWU vice-president in 1916 and served as first vice-president from 1922 to 1934; elected manager of Italian Cloakmakers' Union Local 48 in 1917; served briefly as acting president of the ILGWU after the resignation of Benjamin Schlesinger (q.v.) in 1923; served as treasurer of the Italian Labor Center, the Italian Chamber of Labor, and the Anti-Fascisti Alliance of North America; became manager of ILGWU Local 145, Passaic, N.J., in 1936; elected to the New York City Council in 1937 on the American Labor party ticket and served until 1943; joined the newly organized Liberal party in 1944; retired as ILGWU vice-president in 1956 and three years later retired from all union activities; contributed many articles on industrial and trade union subjects to *Giustizia*, the official Italian language organ of the ILGWU; died in New York City, January 1, 1960; Benjamin Stolberg, *Tailor's Progress: The Story of a Famous Union and the Men Who Made It* (1944); Louis Levine, *The Women's Garment Workers: A History of the International Ladies' Garment Workers' Union* (1924); *ILGWU Report and Proceedings* (1962).

NOCKLES, Edward N. Born in Dubuque, Iowa, September 21, 1869; married; attended the public schools of St. Paul, Minn.; moved to Chicago, Ill., by 1900; became an electrician and joined the International Brotherhood of Electrical Workers Local 134; elected secretary of the Chicago Federation of Labor (CFL) in 1901 and retained office until his death; joined with John Fitzpatrick (q.v.), an ally for more than 30 years, to wrest control of the CFL from the corrupt unionists who had dominated it for years; under their leadership, the Chicago labor movement became one of the nation's most dynamic, succeeding after 1905 in organizing many of the city's clothing, meatpacking, and steel workers; was a close friend of Frank P. Walsh, the noted labor lawyer, and served as Walsh's assistant on the National War Labor Board during World War I; coauthored, with Walsh and Fitzpatrick, "Labor's Fourteen Points;" demanding a governmental guarantee of the right to organize and bargain collectively, an eight-hour day, and nationalization of utilities, the Fourteen Points became the basis for the American Federation of Labor's postwar "Reconstruction Program;" was a key participant in the formation of the Labor party of Illinois in 1919 and the attempt to launch a national Farmer-Labor party, 1919-1923; was a pioneer in the use of radio broadcasting by organized labor and was instrumental in 1926 in founding station WCFL, "The Voice of Labor," serving it as general manager; was disillusioned by his earlier foray into third-party activity and exerted influence against it in the 1930s, supporting Democrat Mayor Edward Kelly and President Franklin D. Roosevelt; was opposed to domination of the airwaves by powerful network stations and was pressing the Federation Communications Commission to grant more transmitting power to WCFL when he died in Chicago, Ill., February 27, 1937; Illinois State Federation of Labor, *Proceedings* (1937); Barbara W. Newell, *Chicago and the Labor Movement: Metropolitan Unionism in the 1930s* (1961); Eugene Staley, *History of the Illinois State Federation of Labor* (1930).

(D.G.S.)

NOONAN, James Patrick.   Born in St. Louis, Mo., December 15, 1878; son of Irish immigrants, Thomas P., a farmer, and Bridget (Kemmey) Noonan; Roman Catholic; married Inez M. Mitchell, June 26, 1901; two children; orphaned at an early age; quit school at age thirteen and held various manual-labor jobs; enlisted as a private during the Spanish-American War and after being discharged from the army, became an electric lineman in St. Louis, Mo.; joined the International Brotherhood of Electrical Workers (IBEW) in 1901; a year later, elected president of his local union; elected president of the Missouri and Illinois District Council in 1903, and the following year, an international vice-president of the IBEW; became acting president in 1917 when the incumbent, Frank J. McNulty (q.v.), took a leave of absence and elected president two years later; elected a vice-president of the American Federation of Labor (AFL) building trades department in 1922; appointed to the National Board of Jurisdictional Awards for the Building Trades; became an AFL vice-president and executive council member in 1924; during 1921-1924, served on a committee of the President's Conference on Unemployment that was concerned with seasonal fluctuations in the construction industry; appointed the American labor delegate to the World Power Conference in London in 1924; appointed by Governor Gifford Pinchot to Pennsylvania's Giant Power Board and to the St. Lawrence .Waterway Commission by Secretary of Commerce Herbert Hoover; died in Washington, D.C., December 4, 1929; M. A. Mulcaire, *The International Brotherhood of Electrical Workers* (1923); *Dictionary of American Biography* (Vol. VIII); Solon DeLeon, ed., *The American Labor Who's Who* (1925).

OAKES, Grant Wilson.   Born in Westfield, N.Y., April 18, 1905; son of Fred J., a railroad electrician, and Ellen (Lawson) Oakes; Protestant; married Hazel A. Bacon on February 14, 1931; three children; completed high school; studied electrical engineering for three years in a General Electric Company industrial college, then worked for General Electric for seven years; after moving to Chicago, Ill., in 1928, employed by the International Harvester Company as a skilled experimental mechanic; was one of the Congress of Industrial Organizations' (CIO) organizers of Tractor Local 101 of the Steel Workers Organizing Committee at International Harvester's Chicago works in 1936; became secretary, chairman of the grievance committee, and president of Local 101; headed the Farm Equipment Workers Organizing Committee after it was founded in 1938; elected first president of the CIO-chartered United Farm Equipment and Metal Workers of America (FE) in 1942; maintained a strict no-strike policy during World War II, but led his union in major strikes against International Harvester, Allis-Chalmers, and other farm implement manufacturers immediately before and after the war; was a member of the executive board of the CIO, but often opposed CIO policies and was involved in numerous jurisdictional conflicts with the larger United Automobile, Aircraft, and Agricultural Implement Workers Union (UAW); defied a CIO order to merge his union with the UAW in 1949 and the FE's charter was revoked; led the FE into a merger with the United Electrical, Radio and Machine Workers Union (UE), which was expelled from the CIO in 1949 for alleged Communist domination; a disastrous 1952 strike against International Harvester and successful UAW raids resulted in the absorption of the remaining UE-FE membership by the UAW in 1954; was purged, whereas many former FE officials were transferred to the UAW; self-identified as a Democrat; supported Henry Wallace's Progressive party candidacy in 1948 and in the same year ran unsuccessfully on the Progressive party ticket for governor of Illinois; *Current Biography* (1950); *Who's Who in Labor* (1946); Robert Ozanne, *A Century of Labor-Management Relations at McCormick and International Harvester* (1967).

(D.G.S.)

OBERGFELL, Joseph F.   Born in Germany, July 26, 1881; son of Robert, a carpenter, and Martha (Strobel) Obergfell; married Erna C. Weier on August 20, 1919; emigrated to the United States while still an infant; attended the public elementary schools of Indianapolis, Ind., then secured employment as a bottler in the brewery industry; joined the International Union of United Brewery, Flour, Cereal and Soft Drink Workers (UBFCSDW) in 1898; served as the business representative of several Indianapolis UBFCSDW locals, 1901-1914; was an officer in the Indianapolis Central Labor Union, 1900-1914, and during the same period served as a delegate to the Indiana State Federation of Labor; elected secretary-treasurer of the UBFCSDW in 1914 and continued in that capacity after being elected international president in 1924; was a member of the Trades Union Liberty League and Labor's Joint Legislative Committee for Modification of the Volstead Law, 1919-1933; elected a vice-president of the American Federation of Labor (AFL) union label trades department in 1922, serving until 1942; represented workers in the bakery and brewing industries on the U. S. Minimum Wage Board; led the UBFCSDW through a long jurisdictional dispute with the International Brotherhood of Teamsters, Chauffeurs, Warehousemen and Helpers of America during the 1930s, which resulted in the UBFCSDW affiliating with the Congress of Industrial Organizations (CIO) in 1942 after the failure of the AFL to resolve the dispute satisfactorily; became a member of the CIO executive council in 1942; died in Cincinnati, Ohio, November 3, 1945; Fleisher Maurer, *et al.*, *Union with a Heart: International Union of United Brewery, Flour, Cereal, Soft Drink and Distillery Workers of America, 75 years of a Great Union, 1886-1961* (1961); Philip Taft, *The A. F. of L. From the Death of Gompers to the Merger* (1959); *Who's Who in Labor* (1946).

O'CONNELL, James P.   Born in Minersville, Pa., August 22, 1858; son of James, a machinist, and Margaret (Donough) O'Connell; Roman Catholic; married Ellen Gallagher on June 12, 1886; four children; graduated from high school in Oil City, Pa., then began, at age sixteen, a machinist apprenticeship at the W. J. Innis Engine Works in Oil City; during the following eight years, worked as a machinist in Pennsylvania and Michigan; left the shops in 1882 for two years and enjoyed brief success in the oil business; worked for Fall Brook Coal Company, Corning, N.Y., 1884-1887, before returning to Oil City and working in a railroad round-house; joined the Knights of Labor and organized and joined an International Association of Machinists' (IAM) local, Lodge 113, Oil City; served as an American Federation of Labor (AFL) fraternal delegate to the British Trades Union Congress in 1889; elected to the IAM general executive board in 1891, and became grand master machinist (president) in 1893, serving through 1911; was a close associate of AFL president Samuel Gompers (q.v.) and was an AFL vice-president and executive council member, 1895-1918; served as president of the AFL's metal trades department, 1911-1934; was a rallying point in the AFL for the conservative, pure and simple trade unionists who opposed the Populist-Socialist faction led by his successor as IAM president, William H. Johnston (q.v.); appointed to the Commission on Industrial Relations by President Woodrow Wilson in 1913, and received a similar appointment to the Executive Committee on Labor of the Council of National Defense in 1917; was an opponent of industrial unionism, but expanded the jurisdiction of the IAM and reduced skill requirements; during his presidency, the IAM's

Populist-Socialist faction became increasingly powerful and was able to democratize the internal governance structure and endorse the government ownership of railroads and telegraph and telephone companies over his opposition; the crowning success of his career was the Murray Hill Agreement, negotiated in 1900 after a prolonged strike, which provided for a nationwide agreement, the closed shop, the nine-hour day, and other reforms; when employers initiated the nine-hour day in 1901, they maintained the same hourly rates thus reducing machinists' wages by ten percent; as a result, 50,000 IAM unionists went on strike, but employers pooled their financial resources, organized a strikebreaking service, and defeated the strike; the conflict led to a long war against the IAM by employers striving to maintain the open shop; was a Democrat; died in Washington, D. C., October 30, 1936; *Machinists' Monthly Journal* (December, 1936); Mark Perlman, *The Machinists: A New Study in American Trade Unionism* (1961) and *Democracy in the International Association of Machinists* (1962); John H. M. Laslett, *Labor and the Left: A Study of Socialism and Radical Influences in the American Labor Movement, 1881-1924* (1970); *Who Was Who in America* (Vol. I).   (J.H.)

O'CONNOR, Harvey.   Born in Minneapolis, Minn., March 29, 1898; son of James J., a railroad cook, and Jessie (Kenney) O'Connor; Unitarian; married Jessie Bross Lloyd in 1930; two children; completed public high school in St. Paul, Minn., and Tacoma, Wash.; employed as a lumber worker prior to becoming the managing editor of the *Seattle Daily Call*, 1917-1918; became editor of the *International Weekly of Seattle* in 1919; indicted for criminal anarchy in 1919 as a result of his activities associated with the Seattle, Wash., general strike but charges were later dropped; became a reporter, city-news editor, and labor editor of the *Seattle Union Record* in 1921, serving until 1924 when named assistant editor of the *Locomotive Engineers Journal*; served during 1927-30 as New York Bureau manager for the Federated Press, a leftist news agency; was the managing editor of the *People's Press*, 1936-1937; became the editor of the *International Oil Worker* in 1937; served as publicity director of the Oil Workers International Union, 1945-1948; refused to testify before Joseph R. McCarthy's Senate Permanent Investigating Committee in 1954 and was convicted of contempt-of-Congress; his conviction was reversed on appeal; indicted for contempt-of-Congress again in 1959 after refusing to obey a subpoena to appear before the House Committee on Un-American Activities, but the indictment was later dismissed; authored *Steel-Dictator* (1935), *History of Oil Workers International Union—CIO* (1950), *The*

Empire of Oil (1955), *World Crisis in Oil* (1962), and other books and articles; Melvin Rothbaum, *The Government of the Oil, Chemical and Atomic Workers Union* (1962); *Who's Who in Labor* (1946); Solon DeLeon, ed., *The American Labor Who's Who* (1925).

O'CONNOR, Thomas Ventry.   Born in Toronto, Canada, in 1870; son of Stephen, an Irish immigrant and brush maker, and Eileen O'Connor; Roman Catholic; married Bridget Gertrude Carney; six children; moved with parents to Buffalo, N.Y., in 1872; became a marine engineer and tugboat captain and was actively involved in trade union activities; served as president of the Licensed Tugmen's Association of the Great Lakes, 1906-1908; elected president of the International Longshoremen's Association (ILA) in 1908; was an American Federation of Labor fraternal delegate to the British Trades Union Congress in 1910; during his ILA incumbency, ruthlessly crushed unauthorized strikes and prided himself in never having sanctioned a longshoremen's strike; assumed the title of honorary president after resigning from the ILA to become a member of the New York State Industrial Board; appointed vice-chairman of the U. S. Shipping Board in 1921 and became chairman in 1924; although no legal improprieties were ever proven, was often accused as president of the U. S. Shipping Board of being overly solicitous of private shipping interests; served as a member of the advisory council of Lincoln Memorial University; was a Republican; died in Buffalo, N.Y., October 17, 1935; Maud Russell, *Men Along the Shore* (1966); Charles P. Larrowe, *Shape-Up and Hiring Hall: A Comparison of Hiring Methods on the New York and Seattle Waterfronts* (1955), and *Maritime Labor Relations on the Great Lakes* (1959).

O'HARE, John.   Born in Armadale, West Lothian, Scotland, June 14, 1904; son of Owen, a coal miner, and Ellen O'Hare; Roman Catholic; married Rosella Cecilia Simonis on October 29, 1938; completed secondary school, then attended night-school classes at Toledo University while working in the tobacco industry; joined Local 196 of the Tobacco Workers International Union (TWIU) in 1935 and shortly thereafter elected recording secretary of Local 196; was a member of the committee on minimum wages for the tobacco industry in 1941; served as a general TWIU organizer prior to being elected international president of the union in 1944; represented the TWIU at national conventions of the American Federation of Labor for several years; retired from union affairs in 1968; a Democrat; *Who's Who in Labor* (1946).

OHL, Henry, Jr. Born in Milwaukee, Wis., March 16, 1873; son of Henry, a laborer, and Mary Elizabeth (Dietrich) Ohl; married Anna W. E. Fleischmann on April 7, 1894; three children; attended grammar school, then went to work in the printing trade at age thirteen; joined both Milwaukee, Wis., Local 23 of the International Typographical Union and the Socialist party in 1901; was an organizer and editor for Local 23, 1903-1909; became an organizer for the American Federation of Labor and the Wisconsin State Federation of Labor (WSFL) in 1914; when the prominent unionist, Frank J. Weber (q.v.), died in 1917, became head of the WSFL, retaining position until his death; also played an influential role in the Milwaukee Federated Trades Council; in the 1930s, helped form the Wisconsin Farmer-Labor Federation, an attempt to unify the Progressive and Socialist parties; was a major leader of the Socialist trade unionists who dominated Milwaukee politics before World War I and was deputy city clerk in Mayor Emil Seidel's administration and served in the Wisconsin Assembly, 1917-1918; his most important contribution was the promotion of worker-education; helped establish the Milwaukee Workers College in 1921 and served as a trustee; largely as a result of his efforts, worker-education classes were available in several other Wisconsin cities by 1928; was a member of the Wisconsin University Labor Joint Committee on Education for Workers, 1927-1940; not opposed to industrial unionism, but became involved in a bitter jurisdictional battle with the Congress of Industrial Organizations (CIO) over the organization of Allis-Chalmers workers in Milwaukee during the 1930s; left the Socialist party after it endorsed the CIO in 1937; died in Milwaukee, Wis., October 16, 1940; Solon DeLeon, ed., *The American Labor Who's Who* (1925); *Dictionary of Wisconsin Biography* (1960); Thomas W. Gavett, *Development of the Labor Movement in Milwaukee* (1965).

(D.G.S.)

OLANDER, Victor A. Born in Chicago, Ill., November 28, 1873; married Elizabeth Grace Cervenko on May 28, 1902; two children; before completing grammar school, began a career as a merchant sailor and for 14 years sailed primarily on the Great Lakes; joined the International Seamen's Union of America (ISU) (name changed to Seafarers International Union of North America in 1938) in 1899 and served as the business agent of the Sailor's Union of the Great Lakes (SIU-GL), 1901-1903; elected a vice-president of the ISU in 1902; served as a delegate from the ISU to both the Chicago and Illinois federations of labor; elected assistant secretary of the SIU-GL in 1903, serving until 1909 when elected general secretary; became a member of the ISU legislative committee in 1913 and participated in the lobbying efforts resulting in the enactment of the LaFollette Seamen's Act of 1914; elected secretary-treasurer of the Illinois State Federation of Labor in 1914, serving until 1949; was a member during World War I of the National War Labor Board and the Illinois State Council of Defense; lost the sight in both eyes in 1919 due to cataracts, but his vision was restored by surgery in 1924; elected secretary-treasurer of the ISU in 1925, serving until 1935; was a member of the Unemployment Compensation Advisory Board of the Illinois State Department of Labor; served as secretary of the American Federation of Labor Resolutions Committee during the conventions of 1927-1933; appointed to the National Recovery Administration District Recovery Board for Illinois and Wisconsin in 1933; died in Chicago, Ill., February 5, 1949; Barbara Warne Newell, *Chicago and the Labor Movement: Metropolitan Unionism in the 1930s* (1961); Eugene Staley, *History of the Illinois State Federation of Labor* (1930); Joseph P. Goldberg, *The Maritime Story: A Study in Labor-Management Relations* (1958).

O'NEILL, John M.   Born ca. 1857; graduated from Niagara University, Buffalo, N.Y.; lived in the Black Hills of South Dakota for a time, then worked as a journalist in various Colorado mining towns during the 1890s and elected to the state legislature; resigned as editor of the anti-union *Butte Miner* in order to support the Western Federation of Miners (WFM); participated as a WFM representative in the founding convention of the Western Labor Union successfully urging it to adopt a Socialist program; became the editor of the WFM journal, *Miners' Magazine* in 1901; was a competent journalist with an incisive mind, making the weekly journal an exponent of the radical industrial unionism espoused by WFM presidents Edward Boyce (q.v.) and Charles Moyer (q.v.); during 1901-1905, when WFM radicalism reached its peak, used his vitrolic pen to attack Samuel Gompers (q.v.) for allegedly selling out to the capitalists; used the *Miners' Magazine* to promote the proposal for a new radical labor movement, and, along with his close friend Moyer, was a delegate to the founding convention of the Industrial Workers of the World (IWW) in 1905; in the 1906 struggle for control of the IWW between President Charles Sherman (q.v.) and the left-wing DeLeon-Trautmann faction, condemned the former for deposing Sherman; supported Moyer as he moved away from the IWW toward a moderate position and denounced the IWW leadership in the pages of the *Miners' Magazine*; by 1910, pointed out that the WFM's isolation from the rest of organized labor rendered it powerless to cope with the corporations and advocated reaffiliation with the American Federation of Labor; when the *Miners' Magazine* changed from a weekly to a monthly, became editor of the UMWA Trinidad *Free Press* as a result of a friendship that he had struck up with United Mine Workers of America (UMWA) leader Adolph Germer (q.v.); died in Colorado, January 5, 1936; Vernon H. Jensen, *Heritage of Conflict: Labor Relations in the Nonferrous Metals Industry Up to 1930* (1950); John H. M. Laslett, *Labor and the Left: A Study of Socialist and Radical Influences in the American Labor Movement, 1881-1924* (1970).

(D.G.S.)

ORNBURN, Ira M.   Born in Moberly, Mo., November 28, 1889; son of Cyrus P., a farmer, and Sallie J. Ornburn; completed his formal education, then gained employment as a railroad call boy; later became a cigarmaker and joined the Cigarmakers' International Union of America (CMIU); elected secretary-treasurer of the Connecticut State Federation of Labor in 1912, serving until 1923; served as a vice-president of the CMIU during 1918-1926, then elected international president in 1926, serving until 1936; despite the objections of Senator George W. Norris of Nebraska, was appointed to the U.S. Tariff Commission in 1930 and served until 1933; was secretary of the National Labor Legislative Committee for Amendment of the Volstead Act in 1931; appointed secretary-treasurer of the American Federation of Labor's union label trades department in 1934 and continued in that capacity until his death; served during World War II on the labor policy committees of the Office of Price Administration and the U.S. Department of Agriculture; during his association with the union label trades department, created labor-management exhibitions and organized the American Federation of Women's Auxiliaries of Labor; died in Washington, D.C., December 17, 1950; *Who's Who in Labor* (1946); *The American Federationist* (January, 1950).

(M.E.R.)

OWEN, Robert Dale.   Born in Glasgow, Scotland, November 9, 1801; son of Robert, an industrialist and social reformer, and Ann Caroline (Dale) Owen; married Mary Jane Robinson on April 12, 1832, and, after her death in 1871, Lottie Walton Kellogg on June 23, 1876; instructed by private tutors before attending the Philipp Emanuel von Fellenberg School at Hofwyl, Switzerland, 1820-1823; traveled to the United States with his father in 1825 and shortly thereafter proceeded to New Harmony, Ind., where the elder Owen began his cooperative colony; was unable to perform physical labor and taught school and edited the *New Harmony Gazette*; after the failure of the New Harmony experiment, accompanied Frances Wright to the Nashoba Community near Memphis, Tenn., which she had founded in 1825; as the Nashoba colony was also failing, returned to Europe in 1827 for further study; returned to the United States and became a naturalized citizen; founded and edited, 1828-1832, the *Free Enquirer* and, in association with Frances Wright, opposed organized religion and supported liberal divorce laws, industrial education, and a redistribution of wealth; participated in the organization of the "Association for the Protection of Industry and for the Promotion of National Education," which in 1829 succeeded in replacing the influence of Thomas Skidmore (q.v.) and his agrarians in the New York Working Men's Party, but soon its own program emphasizing public education and redistribution of wealth was repudiated by the workers; elected to the Indiana legislature for three terms, 1832-1838; defeated in 1838 and 1840, but elected to the United States Congress as a Democrat in 1842 and served two terms; major contributions were a resolution that became the basis for resolving the Oregon boundary dispute and a bill leading to the creation of the Smithsonian Institute; served as a delegate to the Indiana Constitutional Convention in 1850; was a member of the Indiana legislature in 1851; appointed chargé d'affaires in Naples by President Franklin Pierce in 1853 and a year later became minister resident, serving until 1858; authored *Threading My Way* (1874); following a period of mental illness, died in Lake George, N.Y., June 24, 1877; Frank Podmore, *Robert Owen: A Biography* (1906); Edward Pessen, *Most Uncommon Jacksonians: The Radical Leaders of the Early Labor Movement* (1967); Richard W. Leopold, *Robert Dale Owen, A Biography* (1940); *Dictionary of American Biography* (Vol. XIV).

PACHLER, William J.   Born in Thornwood, N.Y., August 20, 1904; son of John A. and Mary (Reilly) Pachler; Roman Catholic; married Gunhild Swanson on June 17, 1928; four children; graduated from high school and attended a business college for one year, majoring in accounting and business law; secured employment with the New York Edison Company and in 1933 became the spokesman for the Tremont Building employees; after the firm became Consolidated Edison Company, joined Local 829 of the International Brotherhood of Electrical Workers (IBEW) and in 1936 became the local's first chairman for the Rider Avenue plant committee; elected president of Local 829 in 1939 and retained that position in 1940 when the local disaffiliated with the IBEW and became Local 12 of the independent Brotherhood of Consolidated Edison Employees; led Local 12 into the Congress of Industrial Organizations (CIO) in 1945, and when the Utility Workers Union of America (UWUA) was chartered later that year, elected its first secretary-treasurer; was one of the organizers of the National Conference of Secretary-Treasurers and served as its chairman until 1960; elected national president of the UWUA in 1960, serving in that capacity until his death; was a member of the American Federation of Labor (AFL)-CIO ethical practices committee and was one of the authors of the AFL-CIO Ethical Practices Code; served as a mediator under the AFL-CIO internal disputes plan, was a member of the administrative committee of the Committee on Political Education, and was a member of the executive board of the industrial union department; was a United States delegate to the International Labor Organization conference in Geneva in 1963; was a Democrat; died in Washington, D.C., May 25, 1970; *AFL-CIO News*, June 6, 1970; *Who's Who in Labor* (1946); *The New York Times*, May 29, 1970.

PADWAY, Joseph Arthur. Born in Leeds, Yorkshire, England, July 25, 1891; son of Morris and Rose Padway; married Lydia Rose Paetow on March 9, 1912; one child; acquired an elementary and secondary education in England before emigrating to the United States in 1905; graduated from Marquette University Law School with an LLB degree in 1912 and admitted to the Wisconsin bar the same year; became the general counsel for the Wisconsin State Federation of Labor in 1915 and in that capacity was responsible for writing numerous labor and social-welfare bills enacted by the state legislature; served as a senator in the Wisconsin state legislature in 1925; appointed judge of the Milwaukee County Civil Court in 1925 and elected to a full-term the following year, resigning in 1927 to resume his labor-law practice; served as a regent of the state teachers colleges of Wisconsin, 1933-1938; became the legal counsel for the American Federation of Labor (AFL) in 1938; was a professor of labor law at Columbus University, Washington, D. C., 1938-1942; as the legal counsel for the AFL and several international unions affiliated with the AFL, was involved in the antitrust suit brought against the American Federation of Musicians' president James C. Petrillo (q.v.) in 1942 and the contempt charges brought against United Mine Workers of America president John L. Lewis (q.v.) for violating an injunction issued during the 1946 coal strike; was a severe critic of the Taft-Hartley Labor Act; was associated most of his life with the Progressive party of Wisconsin; died in San Francisco, Calif.,

October 9, 1947; Thomas W. Gavett, *Development of the Labor Movement in Milwaukee* (1965); *The American Federationist* (November, 1947); *The New York Times*, October 9, 1947.

PARSONS, Albert Ross.   Born in Montgomery, Ala., June 24, 1848; son of Samuel and Elizabeth (Tompkins) Parsons; married Lucy Eldine Gonzalez on June 10, 1871; two children; was orphaned at age five and was reared by a brother in Texas; at age thirteen, joined the Confederate forces during the Civil War and served for four years; apprenticed to a printer after returning to Texas and in 1868 founded the Waco *Spectator*, a weekly Republican periodical; served with the U.S. Internal Revenue Bureau, 1869-1871; moved to Chicago, Ill., in 1871 and worked as a printer during the depression of 1873-1878 and during this time joined the International Typographical Union, helped organize a branch of the Knights of Labor, and became a member of the Socialist party; ran for public office as a Socialist in Cook County, Ill., in 1877 but was defeated; during the railroad strikes of 1877, gained prominence as a Socialist orator and agitator; became secretary of the Chicago Eight Hour League in 1870; joined the Anarchist, or "Black", International after the ideological fissure in the Socialist party in 1881; became the editor of the *Alarm* in 1884 and was one of the leaders of the eight-hour demonstration held on May 1, 1886; although out of the city when the *Alarm* published a call for a demonstration at Chicago's Haymarket Square on May 4, 1886, to protest the killing of strikers at the McCormick Harvester Works, was convicted along with seven other innocent anarchists for the murder of seven policemen by a bomb thrown during the demonstration; authored *Anarchism: Its Philosophy and Scientific Basis as Defined by Some of Its Opposites* (1887); executed on November 11, 1887; Lucy E. Parsons, *Life of Albert R. Parsons with Brief History of the Labor Movement in America* (1903); Alan Calmer, *Labor Agitator, the Story of Albert R. Parsons* (1937); Norman J. Ware, *The Labor Movement in the United States, 1860-1895* (1929); *Encyclopedia of Social Sciences* (Vol. XI).

PERKINS, George W.   Early origins unknown; began working at an early age as a cigarmaker and became involved in the trade union movement; was a dedicated craft unionist and was a constant foe of the Knights of Labor and industrial unionism; closely identified with Samuel Gompers (q.v.) during the formative years of the American Federation of Labor (AFL) being referred to by Gompers as one of the "local (Chicago, Ill.) shock troops of labor," and by others as a member of "Sam's gang"; elected international president of the Cigarmakers' International Union of America (CMIU) in 1891 and served in that capacity until 1926; worked hard for the reelection of Gompers as AFL president after his defeat by John McBride (q.v.) in 1894; opposed AFL support of a general strike during the Pullman controversy; in 1918, appointed by the AFL executive council to its Commission of Reconstruction, which planned the postwar recovery program approved by the 1919 AFL convention and called for industrial democracy; represented United States labor at the International Federation of Trade Unions conference meeting in Zurich in 1918; believed that American labor should stop neglecting the world movement, but distrusted European revolutionary slogans and emphasis on politics; along with others, appointed by the AFL executive council to investigate the Federated Press, a news agency serving labor leftist and radical publications, which was banned by the committee from use by AFL publications; during his incumbency as president of the CMIU, charged by critics with pursuing shortsighted policies with regard to mechanization, leading to a decline of union membership from 51,500 to 12,900 between 1909 and 1929; believed the union had "nothing to fear from machines;" ignored unskilled and women workers and the rise of the large-scale factories; in 1912 the CMIU enrolled only about two-fifths of the total number of cigarmakers and none of the 19,000 machine workers or 25,000 team workers; along with Gompers, opposed at the 1912 CMIU convention Socialist-sponsored resolutions to organize women workers and refused to implement a resolution to this effect that was passed; his restrictive membership policy was not abandoned until he left the union presidency; with Gompers' support, the CMIU under his leadership held only infrequent conventions; served during 1926-1934 as president of the AFL union label trades department; died in Washington, D. C., February 5, 1934; Philip S. Foner, *History of the Labor Movement in the United States*, Vol. II (1955); Samuel Gompers, *Seventy Years of Life and Labor, an Autobiography* (1943); Bernard Mandel, *Samuel Gompers: A Biography* (1963); Philip Taft, *The A. F. of L. in the Time of Gompers* (1957); Rowland H. Harvey, *Samuel Gompers, Champion of the Toiling Masses* (1935).

(M.E.R.)

PERLSTEIN, Meyer. Born in Cartyz Bereza, Grodno, Russia, September 15, 1884; son of a tailor; Jewish; married; three children; attended grammar schools in Russia and night school in the United States; emigrated with his family to London in 1905 and the following year to the United States; became a shirtmaker in the New York City garment industry; joined

Shirtmakers Local 23 of the International Ladies' Garment Workers' Union (ILGWU) in 1909; elected recording secretary of the New York Cloak Joint Board in 1910, serving until 1913; forced to resign from the Cloak Joint Board in 1913 because of internal conflicts and assigned to Philadelphia, Pa., as a general organizer; elected an international ILGWU vice-president in 1916; transferred to Cleveland, Ohio, in 1918 and there headed the union until 1923 and initiated early experiments in production engineering; placed in charge of the ILGWU in Chicago in 1923 and led the fight against William Z. Foster (q.v.) and the Trade Union Educational League's efforts to take over the union there; was a staunch supporter of Morris Sigman (q.v.) administration's opposition to the Communists; returned to New York in 1925 and joined the general staff of the Cloak Joint Board; was disillusioned by efforts to accommodate Communist dissidents in the union and resigned from the ILGWU in 1925; rejoined the union and regained union positions in 1934; appointed director of the Southwestern region of the ILGWU with headquarters in St. Louis, Mo., in 1934, and served in that capacity until his death; usually supported Democratic candidates, but opposed President Franklin D. Roosevelt's third term candidacy in 1940 and endorsed Republican Wendell L. Willkie; died in St. Louis, Mo., September 11, 1958; Benjamin Stolberg, *Tailor's Progress: The Story of a Famous Union and the Men Who Made It* (1944); Louis Levine, *The Women's Garment Workers: A History of the International Ladies' Garment Workers' Union* (1924); *Who's Who in Labor* (1946); *ILGWU Report and Proceedings* (1959); Sumner H. Shichter, *Union Policies and Industrial Management* (1941).

PETERSON, Eric. Born in Dalarne, Sweden, September 3, 1894; son of Daniel, a village shoemaker, and Karen Amanda Peterson; Protestant; married Theresa T. on June 1, 1916; three children; at age eight emigrated with his family to Rawlins, Wyo., a booming railroad center; began work as a bell boy at a boarding house for railroad employees and served a machinist apprenticeship in Rawlins; joined the International Association of Machinists (IAM) during a strike in 1913; held local lodge offices at Rawlins and at Deer Lodge, Mont., working in the latter town for the Milwaukee Road; appointed an international organizer in 1929 and assigned to organize the machinists on the Pennsylvania Railroad, a task that required 20 years; elected a general vice-president in 1940, and elected and served as general IAM secretary-treasurer, 1945-1959; cooperated closely with President Harvey Brown (q.v.), with whom others had personal difficulty, and his successor, President Albert J. Hayes (q.v.); computerized union records and trained and supervised the grand lodge's 24-man financial auditing staff; served in 1957 as a member of a special American Federation of Labor-Congress of Industrial Organizations' (AFL-CIO) committee to draft a code for Minimum Accounting and Financial Controls for Unions that was incorporated into the AFL-CIO's Ethical Practices Code on Financial Practices; retired to Bradenton, Fla., in 1959; represented the AFL-CIO at the White House Conference on Problems of the Aging in 1961; was an independent in politics; died in Tampa, Fla., March 3, 1961; *The Machinist*, March 16, 1961; *Who's Who in Labor* (1946); Mark Perlman, *The Machinists: A New Study in American Trade Unionism* (1961).

(J.H.)

PETERSON, Esther.   Born in Provo, Utah, December 9, 1906; daughter of Lars, a school superintendent, and Annie (Nielson) Eggertson; Church of Jesus Christ of Latter-Day Saints; educated in the public schools of Provo; received a B.A. degree from Brigham Young University, Provo, 1927, and an M.A. from Columbia University, N.Y., 1930; married Oliver A. Peterson in 1932; taught physical education at Branch Agricultural College, Cedar City, Utah, 1927-1929, and Windsor School, Boston, Mass., 1930-1936; began teaching in the industrial section of the Boston Young Women's Christian Association in 1930; taught economics at Byrn Mawr Summer School for Women Workers and the Hudson Shore Labor School, 1932-1939; served as an organizer for the American Federation of Teachers, 1936; served for a short time as the New England educational director for the International Ladies' Garment Workers' Union before becoming the director of education for the Amalgamated Clothing Workers of America (ACWA) in 1939, serving until 1945; during World War II, was the ACWA's director of war activities; became the ACWA legislative representative in Washington, D. C., in 1945; accompanied her husband, a foreign service officer, to Europe in 1948 and from 1948 to 1952 worked with the women's committee of the Swedish Confederation of Trade Unions; was a United States delegate to the founding conference of the International Confederation of Free Trade Unions (ICFTU) in London in 1949; associated with the women's committee of the ICFTU, 1952-1957; was a founder and later an instructor in the ICFTU's International School for Working Women in Paris; appointed to head the U.S. Department of Labor's Women's Bureau in 1961 and later the same year became First Assistant Secretary of Labor; served as vice-chairman of the President's Commission on the Status of Women, 1961; appointed the first Special

Presidential Assistant on Consumer Affairs in 1964; a Democrat; Rose Pesotta, *Bread Upon the Waters* (1945); *Current Biography* (1961); *National Cyclopaedia of American Biography* (Vol. I).

(M.T.)

PETRILLO, James Caesar.   Born in Chicago, Ill., March 16, 1892; son of an Italian immigrant, who was a city-sewer digger; Roman Catholic; married Marie Frullate in 1916; four children; attended the Dante Elementary School in Chicago for nine years but never progressed beyond the fourth grade; began playing the trumpet in 1900 and took free lessons at Chicago's Hull House; organized a four-piece band at age fourteen and in 1906 joined the American Musicians' Union (AMU) in Chicago; elected president of the AMU in 1914, serving until 1917, when defeated for reelection; after this defeat, resigned from the AMU and joined Chicago Federation of Musicians Local 10 of the American Federation of Musicians (AFM); elected a vice-president of Local 10 in 1919 and president in 1922; elected to the national executive board of the AFM in 1932, and in 1940, elected national president; shortly after being elected led the AFM in a 27-month strike against the recording industry that resulted in an agreement whereby the companies paid royalties directly into the AFM treasury on all recordings; was an aggressive, sometimes overly suspicious union leader and often offended the public when attempting to protect musicians from the effects of new technological innovations; elected an American Federation of Labor (AFL) vice-president and executive council member in 1951 and retained the position after the AFL-Congress of Industrial Organizations' merger in 1955; resigned all union positions except for the presidency of AFM Local 10 in Chicago, in 1958; defeated for reelection to the presidency of Local 10 in 1962; a Democrat with considerable political influence in Chicago; Robert D. Leiter, *The Musicians and Petrillo* (1953); Paul S. Carpenter, *Music, an Art and a Business* (1950); J. Gould, "Portrait of the Unpredictable Petrillo," *The New York Times Magazine*, December 28, 1947.

PHILLIPS, James Andrew.   Born in Clay County, Ill., September 10, 1873; son of John Jiles, a farmer, and Nancy (Bouseman) Phillips; Christian Scientist; married Inez Richey on February 22, 1902; and after her death in 1906, Cecil Black on September 5, 1924; two children; completed public grammar school in Louisville, Ill.; began working as a messenger for the Ohio and Mississippi Railroad at age fifteen; became successively a brakeman, a switchman, and a conductor on the Illinois Central Railroad; placed in charge of a work train that in 1901 helped build a railroad line through Indian territory, which later became a part of the state of Oklahoma; joined Division 3 of the Order of Railway Conductors (ORC) in 1902; placed in charge of the first passenger train to make the run between St. Louis and Kansas City during the Louisiana Purchase Exposition in 1904; served as the legislative representative of the ORC during the 1911 and 1913 sessions of the Missouri General Assembly; became ORC general chairman of the Chicago, Rock Island and Pacific Railway in 1918; elected an ORC vice-president in 1919 and senior vice-president in 1931; assumed the ORC presidency in 1934; served as a United States delegate to the preparatory technical conference on rail transportation to the International Labor Organization in 1939; served as chairman of the Railway Labor Executives' Association, 1939-1941; retired in 1941 and became ORC president emeritus; earlier in his career identified with the Socialist and Progressive parties, but later usually supported the Democratic party: died in Cedar Rapids, Iowa, December 4, 1949; *National Cyclopaedia of American Biography* (Vol. XXXVIII); Solon DeLeon, ed., *The American Labor Who's Who* (1925).

PHILLIPS, Paul L.   Born in Strong, Ark., August 10, 1904; son of H.E. and Coma (Laughlin) Phillips; Methodist; married Fannie S. Simmons on August 29, 1940, and, after her death in 1963, Kathleen G. Canby on June 14, 1964; two children; attended Louisiana Polytechnic Institute during 1928-1930, then secured employment in the paper-making industry; helped organize a local of the International Brotherhood of Paper Makers (IBPM) at an International Paper Company mill in Camden, Ark., in 1932 and became its first president; served as an international representative of the IBPM, 1937-1941; elected a vice-president of the IBPM in 1942 and international president in 1948; during World War II, represented labor on the New York area division of the War Manpower Commission; elected first president of the United Paper Makers and Paper Workers, formed in 1957 by the merger of the IBPM and the United Paperworkers of America, Congress of Industrial Organizations (CIO); elected an American Federation of Labor (AFL)-CIO vice-president and executive council member in 1957, serving until 1968; served as vice-president of the AFL-CIO industrial union department, 1957-1968; was a member of the advisory boards of the New York State Committee on Atomic Energy and the National Park Service of the U.S. Department of Interior; was a trustee of the College of Forestry, State University of New York; a Democrat and a member of Americans for Democratic Action;

retired union positions in 1968 because of ill health; Harry E. Graham, *The Paper Rebellion: Development and Upheaval in Pulp and Paper Unionism* (1970); *Who's Who in Labor* (1946); *AFL-CIO News*, January 20, 1968.

PHILLIPS, Thomas.　　　Born in Whitson, Yorkshire, England, March 22, 1833; son of a farmer; christened in the Church of England, but later became a fervent Methodist; acquired a common-school education, then was apprenticed at age thirteen to his brother-in-law, an active Chartist, as a bootmaker; joined the Rotherham Union of Bootmakers in 1849, and later the same year, became a member of the Chartist Association; emigrated to the United States in 1852, settling in New York City, there working as a shoemaker; moved to Philadelphia, Pa., later in the same year and soon became actively involved in the antislavery movement and in labor-organizing activities among shoemakers; became a naturalized citizen of the United States in 1862; was a vigorous advocate of both producer cooperatives and the Rochdale principle of consumers' cooperation; participated in the organization of the very influential Union Co-operative Association, which failed in 1866 after two years of operation because of undercapitalization and overexpansion; helped organize the Philadelphia Lodge of the Knights of St. Crispin (K of SC) in 1869 and devoted considerable time and effort to building up the organization; involved in the organization of a second K of SC lodge in Philadelphia, Friendship Lodge, and served it as Sir Knight; in 1870, elected Grand Sir Knight of the five Philadelphia lodges; served as an organizer for the Sovereigns of Industry during the early 1870s; joined Section 26 of the International Workingmen's Association and represented it at the 1872 convention of anti-Marxist sections in Philadelphia; was a delegate to the K of SC convention in Boston, Mass., in 1871, and served on the committee on cooperation; joined Local Assembly 2, of the Knights of Labor (K of L) in 1873 and eventually participated in the organization of Shoemakers Local Assembly 64; elected as Local Assembly 64's delegate to K of L District Assembly 1 and served a three-year term; wrote a K of L column for the Philadelphia *Public Record* for fourteen months, ca. 1874-1875; actively involved during 1876 in the Greenback Movement and traveled throughout Pennsylvania organizing Greenback Labor Clubs; was an unsuccessful Greenback and Single-tax candidate for mayor of Philadelphia in 1887; as a result of his growing disenchantment with Terence Powderly's (q.v.) leadership, broke with the K of L and organized the Boot and Shoe Workers' International Union and elected its general president in 1889; under his leadership, the new union affiliated with the American Federation of Labor; died in 1916;

David Montgomery, *Beyond Equality: Labor and the Radical Republicans, 1862-1872*; John R. Commons, *et al., History of Labour in the United States*, Vol. II (1918); Norman J. Ware, *The Labor Movement in the United States, 1860-1895* (1929); autobiographical sketch in the Thomas Phillips Papers, Labor Collection, Biography and Papers, State Historical Society of Wisconsin.

PINE, Max.   Born in 1866 in Liubavitch, Russia; Jewish; married; four children; after his father died in 1869, went to live with an aunt in Wielitch, Russia, and there eventually learned the typesetters trade; emigrated to the United States in 1890 and secured employment as a knee-pants' operator; became an official in the New York Knee-Pants Makers' Union; joined the staff of the *Jewish Labor Forward* in 1897 as a reporter and in other capacities; was the proprietor of a print shop, 1901-1906; ran for the New York State Assembly in 1903 on the Socialist party ticket; served as secretary and executive director of the United Hebrew Trades (UHT), 1906-1909; again operated a print shop during 1909-1916; again became secretary of the UHT in 1916, serving until 1926; served as an organizer during the successful efforts to organize New York City tailors, 1912-1913; was one of the principal organizers of the People's Relief Committee, created to assist in the efforts to provide relief to European Jews after World War I; sent to Poland by the Committee in 1919 to assist Jewish war victims and in 1921 sent to the Soviet Union to negotiate assistance for Jewish victims of pogroms; in 1923, was instrumental in the founding of the Geverkshaften Campaign for Palestine, which endeavored to create a bond of friendship between the Jewish labor movement in the United States and Jewish workers in Palestine in the interests of the creation of a Jewish State of Palestine; died in Maywood, N.J., March 2, 1928; Hyman J. Fliegel, *The Life and Times of Max Pine: A History of the Jewish Labor Movement in the U.S.A. during the Last Part of the 19th Century and the First Part of the 20th Century* (1959); *Universal Jewish Encyclopedia* (Vol. 8).

PIZER, Morris.   Born in Russian Poland on February 12, 1904; son of David, a tailor, and Dorothy (Gostinsky) Pizer; Jewish; married Florence Werlinsky in February, 1942; one child; acquired a high school education by attending night schools and then attended Jewish Teachers' Seminary for two years; emigrated to the United States in 1921 and worked at a variety of occupations before securing a job as an upholsterer in 1922; joined Local 73 of the United Furniture Workers of America (UFWA) and in 1936 elected secretary-treasurer of Local 73; served as president of the UFWA's Metropolitan District Council 3 and executive secretary of the North Atlantic Council, then elected vice-president of the UFWA in 1943, and three years later elected international president; became a member of the Congress of Industrial Organizations' (CIO) executive board in 1946, serving until the American Federation of Labor-CIO merger in 1955; as UFWA president, stressed the importance of coordinated organizing drives in cooperation with other unions, particularly in the Southeast; retired as UFWA president in 1970; edited the *Furniture Workers Press*, 1946-1970; supported the American Labor party during the 1930s and early 1940s; *Who's Who in Labor* (1946); *Who's Who in World Jewry* (1955); *AFL-CIO News*, May 30, 1970.

(M.E.R.)

POLLOCK, William.   Born in Philadelphia, Pa., November 12, 1899; son of Louis, a weaver, and Agnes (Garner) Pollock; Congregationalist; married Anna Mae Keen on February 3, 1919; two children; left high school in 1914 and began working in various capacities in the Philadelphia shipbuilding industry; later completed high school by taking night school courses; after several of the Philadelphia shipyards were closed following World War I, secured employment as a weaver in a textile mill and in 1920 joined Local 25 of the United Textile Workers of America; elected business agent of Local 25 in 1931, serving until 1937; served as the Pennsylvania labor representative for the National Recovery Administration and was a member of the Philadelphia Labor Board, 1933-1935; joined the staff of the Textile Workers Organizing Committee as a general organizer in 1937, serving until 1939; was one of the organizers and became the first manager of the Philadelphia Joint Board of Textile Workers in 1937; elected secretary-treasurer of the newly organized Textile Workers of America (TWUA) in 1939; was a member of the Federal Textile Commission during World War II; was a delegate to the Inter-American Conference of Free Trade Unions in Mexico City in 1951; served as executive vice-president of the TWUA, 1953-1956; elected national president in 1956; became a member of the executive committee of the American Federation of Labor-Congress of Industrial Organizations (AFL-CIO) industrial union department and a member of the AFL-CIO general board in 1956; elected an AFL-CIO vice-president and executive council member in 1967; served on the executive committee of the International Federation of Textile, Garment and Leather Workers and was treasurer of the Inter-American Textile and Garment Workers Federation, 1967-1970; retired as TWUA president in 1972; authored *Textiles: A National Crisis* (1956), *No Rights at All* (1957), and *An Industry That's Sick* (1958); *AFL-CIO News*, March 4, 1972.

POSSEHL, John.   Born in Chicago, Ill., in 1886; son of a chemical engineer; married; one child; at age four moved with his family to Savannah, Ga., and there completed public grammar school; completed his formal education, then secured employment as a marine fireman and engineer and later as a piledriver operator: prior to World War I, organized a mixed local of the International Union of Operating Engineers (IUOE) (then called the International Union of Steam and Operating Engineers) in Savannah and was elected its secretary; was an influential figure in the Savannah labor movement and served as president of the Savannah Central Labor Union, 1914-1919; during World War I, served as a government mediator in the sugar industry; became an international IUOE organizer in 1919, concentrating on organizing activities in Texas, Louisiana, Tennessee, and other parts of the South; elected an IUOE vice-president in 1922 and somewhat later became international secretary-treasurer; elected international IUOE president after the death of Arthur M. Huddell (q.v.) in 1931; as president, reorganized the structure of the IUOE by dividing the IUOE into administrative districts, converted organizers into international representatives, revived the IUOE stationary jurisdiction that had been neglected by Huddell, rewrote the international constitution, held regular conventions, reached an important accord with the Associated General Contractors, and generally guided the IUOE successfully through the difficult depression period of the 1930s; served as first vice-president of the American Federation of Labor's building and construction trades department; was a Democrat; died in Washington, D.C., September 14, 1940; Garth L. Mangum, *The Operating Engineers: The Economic History of a Trade Union* (1964); *The American Federationist* (October, 1940); *The American Federation of Labor Weekly News Service*, September 17, 1940.

POTOFSKY, Jacob Samuel.   Born in Radomisl, Ukraine, Russia, November 16, 1894; son of Simon, a businessman in Russia and later a clothing worker in Chicago, and Rebecca Potofsky; married Callie Taylor in 1934, and, after her death, Blanche Lydia Zetland on May 18, 1951; three children; emigrated with family to the United States in 1905; attended the grammar schools in Russia and Chicago and high school in Chicago; became a "floor boy" in a Chicago men's clothing factory in 1908 and joined Pantsmakers' Local 144 of the United Garment Workers of America; took part in the historic 1910 strike against Hart, Schaffner and Marx that eventually led to the organization of the Amalgamated Clothing Workers of America (ACWA); became a shop secretary after the strike and during 1912-1913 served as treasurer of Local 144; became secretary-treasurer of the Chicago Joint Board, ACWA, in 1914; moved to New York City in 1916 to assist in establishing a national office and for the next 18 years was assistant general secretary-treasurer of the ACWA; during the 1930s, devoted his energies to organizing cotton-garment workers in Pennsylvania, New Jersey, Connecticut, upstate New York, and Missouri; became ACWA assistant president in 1934; was an original member of the Congress of Industrial Organizations' (CIO) executive board; served as general secretary-treasurer of the ACWA, 1940-1946; served on the CIO Latin-American Affairs Committee and the Political Action Committee; led the CIO delegation attending the inauguration in 1946 of Miguel Alemán, president of Mexico, at the invitation of the Mexico Federation of Labor; elected president of the ACWA in 1946 after the death of Sidney Hillman (q.v.); after the merger of the American Federation of Labor (AFL) and the CIO in 1955, became a vice-president and executive council member of the AFL-CIO; was a member of a large number of public and private boards and agencies, including the Jewish Labor Committee, the Labor Management and Manpower Policy Committee of the Office of Defense Mobilization, and the New York City Temporary Commission on City Finances, 1965; voted Socialist until 1932 and thereafter supported the American Labor party, the Liberal party of New York, and the Democratic party; retired as ACWA president in 1972; authored "John E. Williams, Arbitrator"; Louis Finkelstein, *American Spiritual Autobiographies, Fifteen Self-Portraits* (1948); Jesse T. Carpenter, *Competition and Collective Bargaining in the Needle Trades, 1910-1967* (1972); Harry A. Cobrin, *The Men's Clothing Industry: Colonial Through Modern Times* (1970); *Current Biography* (1946).

POWDERLY, Terence Vincent.   Born in Carbondale, Pa., January 22, 1849; son of Terence, an Irish immigrant and teamster, and Margery (Walsh) Powderly; married Hannah Deyer on September 19, 1872, and after her death, Emma Fickenscher on March 31, 1919; attended the schools of Carbondale until age thirteen and then took employment as a railroad worker; apprenticed as a machinist in 1866 and worked at that trade until 1877; joined the Machinists' and Blacksmiths' Union in 1871, becoming an organizer for Western Pennsylvania three years later; initiated into the Noble Order of the Knights of Labor (K of L) in Philadelphia, Pa., on September 6, 1876; elected master workman of the Scranton, Pa., assembly and then corresponding secretary of the reorganized district assembly in 1877; elected on the Greenback Labor party ticket to the first of three two-year terms as mayor of Scranton in 1878; believed that skilled workers should assist in organizing of the unskilled and opposed the craft or trade union form of organization; was a critic of the wage system and hoped to see it replaced by the organization of producer cooperatives; served on the Committee on Constitution of the K of L national convention in 1878; became grand worthy foreman in 1879, and, later the same year, grand master workman, holding the latter until 1893; during his incumbency, usually opposed militant trade union activity and advocated conciliation and mediation; was removed from office in 1893; admitted to the bar of Pennsylvania in 1894; supported the candidacy of William McKinley in 1896 and was appointed U.S. Commissioner General of Immigration, 1897, serving until 1902; in the following years held several positions in the U.S. Department of Labor; was a life-long advocate of temperance and land reform; consistently supported the Republican party in his later years; contributed to George E. McNeill, ed., *The Labor Movement: The Problem of Today* (1887); authored several pamphlets and wrote *Thirty Years of Labor, a History of the Organization of Labor since 1860* (1889); died in Washington, D.C., June 24, 1924; Harry J. Carman, Henry David, and Paul N. Guthrie, eds., *The Path I Trod: The Autobiography of Terence V. Powderly* (1940); Norman J. Ware, *The Labor Movement in the United States, 1860-1895* (1929); Gerald N. Grob, *Workers and Utopia: A Study of Ideological Conflict in the American Labor Movement, 1865-1900* (1961); Charles A. Madison, *American Labor Leaders: Personalities and Forces in the Labor Movement* (1962); *Dictionary of American Biography* (Vol. XV).

POWERS, Frank Bernard. Born in Clear Lake, Minn., May 13, 1888; son of Bernard, a railroad station agent and telegrapher, and Katherine (Donovan) Powers; Roman Catholic; married Laura Knapp on November 9, 1910, and, after her death, Lillian S. Dewey on July 3, 1941; three children; completed two years of high school in Morris, Minn., then quit school at age fifteen and became a telegrapher; later completed high school through night school courses and attended the University of Minnesota's School of Journalism; joined the Commercial Telegraphers' Union (CTU) in 1905 and the Order of Railroad Telegraphers in 1909; became circuit chairman of the CTU's United Press Division 47 in 1912 and three years later elected general chairman, serving until 1919; served as the general chairman of the CTU's Universal Service Division 97, 1919-1921; elected international secretary-treasurer of the CTU in 1921; elected international president in 1928 and served until 1941; was vice-president of the International Labor Press Association of America in 1925 and vice-president of the Eastern Labor Press Conference in 1942; served as the American Federation of Labor fraternal delegate to the Trades and Labor Congress of Canada in 1932; became the CTU's editor and statistician in 1941; a Democrat; Vidkunn Ulriksson, *The Telegraphers: Their Craft and Their Unions* (1953); *Who's Who in Labor* (1946).

PRESSMAN, Lee.   Born in New York City, July 1, 1906; son of Harry, a Russian immigrant, and Clara (Rich) Pressman; married Sophia Patnick on June 28, 1931; two children; graduated from high school in New York City, then attended Cornell University, earning a B.A. degree and becoming a member of Phi Beta Kappa; received an LLB degree from Harvard Law School; admitted to the New York bar in 1929; was an associate in a New York law firm specializing in cases involving corporations, receiverships, and labor, 1929-1933; campaigned for the Democratic ticket in 1932, then appointed assistant general counsel for the Agricultural Adjustment Administration of the Department of Agriculture; served as general counsel for the Works Progress Administration and the Resettlement Administration during 1935-1936; joined the Steel Workers Organizing Committee in 1936 and later became general counsel for the United Steelworkers of America (USWA), the Congress of Industrial Organizations (CIO), and the National Marine Engineers Beneficial Association; supported the Roosevelt administration's mobilization effort during World War II; was a member of the CIO delegation that visited the Soviet Union in 1945; assisted USWA president Philip Murray (q.v.) in negotiating a new contract with the United States Steel Corporation in 1947; directed the efforts of the CIO legal staff to analyze and consider ways of circumventing the Taft-Hartley Act; a left-winger during the period after World War II, he was forced to resign as general counsel of the CIO and the USWA in 1948; supported Henry Wallace's candidacy for president of the United States on the Progressive party ticket and himself ran for Congress from a New York district in 1948; appearing before the House Committee on Un-American Activities in 1950, admitted membership in the Communist party; resigned from and repudiated the American Labor party in 1950; left the labor movement and resumed a private law practice, 1948; Lloyd Ulman, *The Government of the Steel Workers' Union* (1962); John Herling, *Right to Challenge: People and Power in the Steelworkers Union* (1972); Max M.

Kampelman, *The Communist Party vs. the C.I.O.: A Study in Power Politics* (1957); *Current Biography* (1947).

PRESTON, George.   Born in Lincolnshire, England, November 3, 1864; Methodist; completed a grammar school education at an early age; went to sea for three years; settled in Nottingham, England, and served a machinist's apprenticeship; as soon as age permitted, joined a trade union; was a member of a citizen's committee that secured John Burns' nomination as a Labour party candidate for Parliament from Nottingham in 1885; emigrated to the United States in 1886, settling in Detroit, Mich.; joined the Knights of Labor Assembly 7750 of Machinists and Blacksmiths; joined the International Association of Machinists (IAM) Local Lodge 82 in Detroit in 1890; was a delegate to the 1895 national IAM convention, which elected him grand (national) secretary-treasurer; reelected to office until July, 1917; afterward, held several responsible positions and retired to Bay View, near Elkton, Md., a few years before his death; died in Elkton, Md., February 18, 1933; *Machinists' Monthly Journal* (March, 1933); Mark Perlman, *The Machinists: A New Study in American Trade Unionism* (1961).

(J. H.)

PRICE, George Moses.   Born in Poltava, Russia, May 21, 1864; Jewish; married Anna Kopkin on July 22, 1891; two children; educated in the Real Gymnasium (high school) of Poltava; emigrated to the United States, settling in New York City; shortly after arriving in the United States, became a sanitary inspector for the Tenth Ward of New York City, holding position while attending the Medical College of New York University; received the M.D. degree in 1895; worked as an inspector in the Tenement Commission for a year, then joined the New York City Department of Health in 1895; chosen to head the Joint Board of Sanitary Control provided for by the "Protocol of Peace" that ended the historic 1910 garment strike; served in that capacity for 15 years; under his direction, the Joint Board initiated regular shop inspections, fire drills, and educational campaigns in sanitation and public health; headed the New York Factory Commission's investigation of the tragic Triangle Waist Company fire of 1911 that resulted in 142 deaths; gained the support of several International Ladies' Garment Workers' Union (ILGWU) locals in 1913 and founded the Union Health Center, the first medical clinic organized to serve the workers of a particular industry; under his direction, the Union

Health Center, which emphasized clinical services and outpatient care, quickly became a popular and valuable institution; the Union Health Center was officially taken over by the ILGWU in 1930 and had a large, well-trained staff, which by the time of Price's death had treated well in excess of 50,000 patients; authored *A Handbook on Sanitation* (1901), *Tenement Inspection* (1904), *Hygiene and Public Health* (1910), and several other pamphlets; died in New York City, July 30, 1942, succeeded as director of the Health Center by his son, Dr. Leo Price; Benjamin Stolberg, *Tailor's Progress: The Story of a Famous Union and the Men Who Made It* (1944); Louis Levine, *The Women's Garment Workers: A History of the International Ladies' Garment Workers' Union* (1924); Leon Stein, *The Triangle Fire* (1962); *Who Was Who in America* (Vol. III); *The New York Times*, July 31, 1942.

QUILL, Michael Joseph.   Born in Gourtloughera, Kilgarvan, County Kerry, Ireland, September 18, 1905; son of John Daniel, a farmer, and Margaret (Lynch) Quill; Roman Catholic; married Maria Theresa O'Neill on December 26, 1937, and after her death in 1959, Shirley Garry in 1962; one child; attended the schools of Ireland during 1910-1916, then volunteered for the Irish Republican Army and served during the Irish Rebellion of 1919-1923; emigrated to the United States in 1926 and, after working at various jobs, joined the Interborough Rapid Transit Company of New York City as a gateman; was one of the founders of the Transport Workers Union of America (TWUA) in 1934; elected president of the TWUA and full time organizer in 1935; after the previously independent TWUA affiliated with the Congress of Industrial Organizations (CIO) in 1937 and was given an international charter, elected president of the new international union and joined the national executive board of the CIO; elected to the New York City Council from the Bronx in 1937 on the American Labor party (ALP) ticket; served one term, then refused to support the ALP's condemnation of the Russo-German peace pact of 1939 and ran unsuccessfully for a council seat as an independent; elected to the New York City Council in 1943 as an independent and, returning to the ALP, reelected in 1945; after serving as a vice-president for several years, elected president of the Greater New York CIO Industrial Union Council in 1947, but resigned a year later (also resigning from the ALP) and led a reorganization designed to eliminate Communist influence; elected president of the reorganized New York CIO Council in 1949; became a CIO vice-president in 1950; served on the CIO delegation to the International Confederation of Free Trade Unions in 1949 and 1950; served as the chairman of the Confederation's committee on resolutions in 1951; led a 12-day strike against the New York City subways and bus lines in 1965 that paralyzed public transportation in the city; arrested for refusing to obey a court order to end the strike and suffered a heart attack shortly after being imprisoned; was a volatile trade union leader whose rhetoric was often more militant than his actions; usually followed the Communist line early in his career, but in the 1940s became a militant anti-Communist; died in New York City, January 28, 1966; L. H. Whittemore, *Man Who Ran the Subways, The Story of Mike Quill* (1968); *Current Biography* (1953); *Newsweek*, January 17, 1966; *Who's Who in Labor* (1946).

RAFTERY, Lawrence M. Born in St. Louis, Mo., February 27, 1895; son of Sylvester T., a painting contractor, and Rosa (Winterbauer) Raftery; Roman Catholic; married Enid Veil King on October 19, 1916; nine children; graduated from high school after attending both public and parochial schools; attended Christian Brothers College School of Art and Interior Decorating; worked as a paperhanger and painter and joined St. Louis Local 115 of the Brotherhood of Painters, Decorators and Paperhangers of America (BPDPA) in 1913; served as a trustee and business agent of Local 115, 1919-1923; became secretary and business agent of the St. Louis Painters' District Council in 1925; was a member of the executive board of the Missouri State Federation of Labor, a member of the advisory board of the Missouri Unemployment Bureau in 1929, and a member of the St. Louis Grand Jury in 1936; elected a vice-president of the BPDPA in 1937 and in 1942 became general secretary-treasurer, serving until 1952; elected BPDPA general president in 1952; after the merger of the American Federation of Labor (AFL) and the Congress of Industrial Organizations (CIO), became a vice-president and member of the executive council of the building and construction trades department, AFL-CIO, serving until 1968; elected a vice-president and member of the AFL-CIO executive council in 1958; became BPDPA president emeritus in 1964 and was replaced as president by his son, S. Frank Raftery; a Democrat; Philip Zausner, *Unvarnished: The Autobiography of a Union Leader* (1941); *Who's Who in Labor* (1946); *AFL-CIO News*, August 29, 1964; *Who's Who in America, 1960-1961.*

RAMSAY, Claude E. Born in Ocean Springs, Miss., December 18, 1916; son of C. A. and Blanche (Bilbo) Ramsay; married Mae Helen Hillman on June 16, 1941; six children; attended the public schools of Jackson County, Miss., and Perkinston Junior College; completed his formal education, then secured employment with the International Paper Company, working for that firm for 24 years; joined the United Paperworkers of America (UPA) in 1939 and in 1951 elected president of UPA Local 203, serving in that capacity until 1959; served as president of the Jackson County Central Labor Union, 1952-1959; was a participant in the merger discussions between the American Federation of Labor and Congress of Industrial Organizations (AFL-CIO) in Mississippi, and elected president of the Mississippi AFL-CIO in 1959, a position he still held in 1974; possessed dynamic leadership qualities and oratorical ability, and had considerable success in the areas of state legislation, political education, public relations, and race relations; was a persistent critic of Mississippi's "Balance Agriculture with Industry" program for attracting low-paying, low-profit, garment-type industries; was also critical of the Mississippi press (characterizing it as "the worst in the nation"), Governor Ross Barnett (who "almost ruined our state"), the Ku Klux Klan, and Jackson, Miss., television station WLBI (which was "dominated by the Citizen's Council and other 'Right Wing' influences"); under his leadership, the Mississippi AFL-CIO became an effective foe of extremist groups including white racists, the John Birch Society, and others; served on the board of directors of the AFL-CIO Appalachian Council, as chairman of the AFL-CIO southern advisory committee on civil rights, and on numerous other civic boards and agencies; a Democrat; Richard A. McLemore, ed., *A History of Mississippi*, Vol. II (1973); Address by Claude Ramsay to the NDEA Institute in History, University of Mississippi (1966).

(M.E.R.)

RANDOLPH, Asa Philip.   Born in Crescent City, Fla., April 15, 1889; son of James William, a minister, and Elizabeth (Robinson) Randolph; Methodist; married Lucille E. Green in 1914; Afro-American; completed a high school education at Cookman Institute in Jacksonville, Fla., then moved to New York City and worked there as an elevator operator, porter, and railroad waiter while continuing his education at the College of the City of New York; was a cofounder of the *Messenger*, a militant, Socialist monthly in 1917; served as an instructor in the New York Rand School of Social Science; ran unsuccessfully as a Socialist for New York Secretary of State in 1921; acquired considerable experience in labor organization, then founded and served as organizer and first president of the Brotherhood of Sleeping Car Porters (BSCP) in 1925; after ten years of agitation and strife, negotiated a collective bargaining contract with the Pullman Palace Car Company in 1935; served as a member of Mayor Fiorello LaGuardia's New

York City Commission on Race in 1935; organized the March on Washington Movement in 1941, which led to the creation of the Fair Employment Practices Committee (FEPC); became co-chairman of the National Council for a Permanent FEPC; appointed to the New York Housing Authority in 1942; was a founder of the League for Nonviolent Civil Disobedience Against Military Segregation in 1947; served as a delegate to the International Confederation of Free Trade Unions in 1951; elected a vice-president and executive council member of the American Federation of Labor-Congress of Industrial Organizations (AFL-CIO) at its merger convention in 1955; was one of the leaders of the 1963 March on Washington; was one of the founders of the Negro American Labor Council and served as its president from 1960 to 1966; as one of the principal black spokesman within the AFL-CIO executive council, often clashed with President George Meany (q.v.) and the conservative leaders of numerous AFL-CIO affiliates over the discriminatory activities of some international unions, but always remained loyal to the AFL-CIO; a Socialist early in his career, but later supported the Liberal party of New York; retired from union activities in 1968; Brailsford R. Brazeal, *The Brotherhood of Sleeping Car Porters: Its Origin and Development* (1946); Jervis Anderson, *A. Philip Randolph: A Biographical Portrait* (1972); Joseph C. Goulden, *Meany* (1972); *The New Yorker*, December 2, 9, 16, 1972; *Current Biography* (1951).

RANDOLPH, Woodruff.   Born in Warrenton, Mo., January 31, 1892; son of Joseph Freeman, a carpenter, and Mary Tracy (Busekrus) Randolph; married Agnes M. Johnson on July 1, 1916, and after her death in 1947, Helen M. Grist-McKenzie on November 6, 1948; four children; entered the printing trade after graduation from high school and became a typesetter; joined the International Typographical Union (ITU) in 1912; received an LLB degree from the Webster College of Law, Chicago, Ill., and admitted to the bar of Illinois in 1921; elected president of Chicago ITU Local 16 in 1927; became secretary-treasurer of both the ITU and the International Allied Printing Trades Association in 1928, serving in that capacity until 1944; served as a delegate to the International Labor Organization conference in Geneva in 1936; elected international president of the ITU in 1944 on the Progressive party ticket of the ITU's two-party system and served until 1958; was vigorous opponent of the Taft-Hartley Labor Act, especially its prohibition of the closed shop contract, and devoted much of his time and his union's resources to combating the provisions of the law; edited the ITU's monthly organ, the *Typographical Journal*,

1928-1944; retired from union affairs in 1958 because of ill health; died in Colorado Springs, Colo., October 24, 1966; Elizabeth F. Baker, *Printers and Technology: A History of the International Printing Pressmen and Assistants' Union* (1957); Seymour M. Lipset, *et al.*, *Union Democracy: The Internal Politics of the International Typographical Union* (1956); *Current Biography* (1948); *Who's Who in Labor* (1946).

RARICK, Donald C.   Born in 1919; Roman Catholic; married Eunice Morrison; one child; served in the U.S. Army during World War II, then took a job in the steel industry of western Pennsylvania and joined the United Steelworkers of America (USWA); was an ordinary steelworker in the United States Steel Corporation's Irvin works at McKeesport, Pa., in 1956 and was a local grievance committeeman and a delegate to the USWA convention; voiced opposition at the convention to a dues increase that was coupled with a raise in the salaries of USWA officers and unsuccessfully demanded a roll-call vote; a few months later, formed along with other local USWA leaders from the Pittsburgh-McKeesport area the Dues Protest Committee; failed to force a special convention to reconsider the dues issue and decided to challenge USWA president David J. McDonald (q.v.) in the international elections of 1957; the first contest for the USWA presidency, his bid reflected dissatisfaction not only with the dues increase but with the gap between the "union aristocracy," led by McDonald, and the rank-and-file; running without the support of any major USWA official, polled an imposing 223,000 votes to McDonald's 404,000; elected president of his local at the Irvin works in 1958; along with his backers, ordered tried for dual unionism and actions detrimental to the union by the 1959 convention, which was dominated by the McDonald forces; was acquitted of the charges brought against him and tried to revive the protest movement for a larger rank-and-file voice in the USWA in 1961 but was unable to obtain the necessary local union nominations to get on the presidential ballot; supported I. W. Abel's (q.v.) successful campaign for the USWA presidency in 1965, but three years later announced his intention to run against Abel in 1969; was an unsuccessful candidate for the Democratic nomination in the 20th Congressional District of Pennsylvania; died in McKeesport, Pa., September 17, 1968; Dan Wakefield, "Steelworkers at the Polls," *The Nation*, February 23, 1957; Lloyd Ulman, *The Government of the Steel Workers Union* (1962); John Herling, *Right to Challenge: People and Power in the Steelworkers Union* (1972).

(D.G.S.)

RATCHFORD, Michael D.   Born in County Clare, Ireland, in August, 1860; married Deborah Jordan in December, 1884; attended public and evening school; emigrated with his parents to the United States in 1872, settling in Stark County, Ohio; began working in the coal mines at age twelve and became an active trade unionist at age twenty; elected president of a United Mine Workers of America (UMWA) local at Massillon, Ohio, in 1890, serving until 1892; served as a general organizer, 1893-1894; served as president of District 6, UMWA, 1895-1896, and as international president of the UMWA, 1897-1898; due to unemployment, wage reductions, and an unsuccessful strike in 1894, union membership had fallen to 10,000 and the treasury contained less than $600, insufficient to pay the American Federation of Labor (AFL) per-capita tax; under his leadership, the UMWA called a 12-week strike in July, 1897, involving 100,000 miners, which paralyzed all bituminous coal fields except those in West Virginia; as a result of the strike, which was supported by AFL organizers and strike funds, he signed the Central Competitive Field Agreement, covering all important coal-producing states except West Virginia; under the terms of the agreement, the eight-hour day was established throughout the bituminous fields, and coal loading-rates were based on the 65¢ per ton rate current in the Pittsburgh district; during his short incumbency, raised the union's membership to 33,000 and increased its treasury holdings to $11,000; the UMWA recovery reinvigorated the entire labor movement following the depression; resigned the UMWA presidency in 1898 to serve as labor's representative on the U.S. Industrial Commission, 1898-1900; served as Ohio's Commissioner of Labor Statistics, 1900-1908, as commissioner of the Ohio Coal Operators, 1909-1912, and as commissioner of the Illinois Coal Operators' Association after 1913; was a partisan Republican and a personal friend of Mark Hanna and William McKinley; died in Massillon, Ohio, December 12, 1927; *Who Was Who in America* (Vol. IV); Elsie Gluck, *John Mitchell: Miner* (1929); Selig Perlman and Philip Taft, *History of Labour in the United States, 1896-1932,* Vol. IV (1935); McAlister Coleman, *Men and Coal* (1943).

(J.H.)

REAGAN, Ronald.   Born in Tampico, Ill., February 6, 1911; son of John Edward, a shoe merchant, and Nellie (Wilson) Reagan; Christian Church; married Jane Wyman on January 24, 1940, and after that marriage ended in divorce in 1948, Nancy Davis on March 4, 1952; two children; attended Eureka (Ill.) College and majored in economics and sociology;

graduated with a B. A. degree in 1932, then became a radio broadcaster and soon acquired a national reputation as a sportscaster; after a successful screen test, made his film debut in 1937; joined the Screen Actors Guild (SAG) in 1941; served with the U. S. Army during World War II and rose to the rank of captain while making training films for the Air Force; became a member of the board of directors of the SAG in 1946; served as a friendly witness before the House Committee on Un-American Activities in 1947, but denied extensive Communist influence in the film making industry; elected president of the SAG in 1947 and served until 1952; organized the Labor League of Hollywood Voters to support Harry S. Truman's campaign for reelection in 1948; elected chairman of the Motion Picture Industry Council in 1949; during 1954-1962, employed by the General Electric Company as a personnel relations counselor and as host and supervisor of a weekly television program, *General Electric Theater*; reelected president of the SAG in 1959 but resigned a year later after becoming a film producer; during 1962-1965, was the host and an occasional performer in *Death Valley Days*, a weekly television program; during the 1960s, the once liberal Democrat became increasingly conservative, appearing on anti-Communist television programs, supporting the Christian Anti-Communist Crusade led by Dr. Fred Schwartz, campaigning for political candidates connected with the John Birch Society, and serving on the advisory board of Young Americans for Freedom; elected governor of California on the Republican party ticket in 1966 and reelected in 1970; *Current Biography* (1967); *The New York Times Magazine*, November 14, 1965, October 16, 1966; *Look*, November 1, 1966.

REDMOND, John P.   Born in Chicago, Ill., June 2, 1892; son of John E., a livery business operator, and Anna (Statia) Redmond; Roman Catholic; married Theresa V. Lyons on November 22, 1919; two children; was a high school graduate and completed two years of college work; after concluding his formal education, secured employment with the Chicago Fire Department; joined Chicago Local 2 of the International Association of Fire Fighters (IAFF) in 1912 and served as secretary-treasurer of the Local's credit union; while serving as an international organizer, organized more than 150 IAFF locals; elected a vice-president of the IAFF in 1930; served as a general IAFF consultant to local unions concerned with pension funds, minimum wage-maximum-hour laws, civil-service legislation, and fire prevention and control; appointed by the executive board to fill the unexpired term of IAFF president Fred W. Baer (q. v.) who died in 1946; elected international president in 1947 and served in that capacity until his death; was a member of the American Federation of Labor-Congress of Industrial Organizations' community service committee; died in Atlantic City, N.J., December 10, 1957; James J. Gibbons, *The International Association of Fire Fighters* (1944); *Who's Who in Labor* (1946); *The New York Times*, December 12, 1957.

REUTHER, Roy. Born in Wheeling, W. Va., August 29, 1909; son of Valentine, a steel and brewery worker and trade union leader, and Anna (Stoker) Reuther; reared a Lutheran; married Fania Sankin on July 8, 1944; two children; graduated from high school, then began work as an electrician's helper and joined the Wheeling local of the International Brotherhood of Electrical Workers in 1927; moved to Detroit, Mich., in 1932, and, after attending Wayne University for a year-and-a-half, joined the American Federation of Teachers while studying and teaching at Brookwood Labor College in Katonah, N.Y.; enrolled in the Federal Emergency Relief Administration's workers' education teacher-training program at the University of Wisconsin and in 1934 was assigned to the FERA's workers' education program in Flint, Mich.; joined the United Automobile, Aircraft, Agricultural Implement Workers of America (UAW) after beginning work at the General Motors Corporation's (GMC) Chevrolet gear and axle plant in Detroit; became the assistant director of UAW organizing efforts in Flint in 1936; was one of the principal strategists and leaders of the successful efforts to organize GMC plants in Flint; was a charter member and the first president of the Greater Flint Congress of Industrial Organizations' (CIO) Industrial Union Council; during World War II, was an information specialist for the labor division of the War Production Board; appointed director of the UAW citizenship department in 1947; became an administrative assistant to UAW vice-president John W. Livingston (q.v.) in 1948, and administrative assistant to UAW president Walter P. Reuther in 1949; appointed national director of the UAW citizenship-legislation department in 1949; took a leave of absence from the UAW to become chairman of the National Voters' Registration Committee during the 1960 presidential campaign; served as the director of the American Federation of Labor-CIO National Voter Registration and Get Out the Vote campaigns in 1962 and 1964; was a Democrat; died in Detroit, Mich., January 10, 1968; Sidney Fine, *Sit-Down: The General Motors Strike of 1936-1937* (1969); Jack Stieber, *Governing the UAW* (1962); Wyndham Mortimer, *Organize! My Life as a Union Man* (1971).

REUTHER, Victor George. Born in Wheeling, W. Va., January 1,

1912; son of Valentine, a steel and brewery worker and trade union leader, and Anna (Stoker) Reuther; reared a Lutheran; married Sophia Good on July 18, 1936; three children; graduated from high school in Wheeling in 1928; attended the University of West Virginia in 1929, and Wayne University, 1930-1932; joined his brother, Walter (q.v.), on a three year world tour in 1933 that included Europe, the Soviet Union, India, and Japan; became a speaker for the Emergency Peace Campaign after his return to the United States in 1935; secured employment in 1936 in the Detroit, Mich., automobile industry at the urging of his brother, Walter, who was involved in organizing automobile workers; participated in the organization of United Automobile, Aircraft, Agricultural Implement Workers of America (UAW) Local 174 in West Detroit in 1936; was one of the leaders of the 1936 sit-down strike at the Kelsey-Hayes Wheel Company plant in Detroit and participated in the General Motors Corporation (GMC) strike in Flint, Mich.; became UAW director of organization in Indiana in 1937 and later the same year became an international representative with the task of organizing the employees of the GMC in Michigan and Indiana; served as a labor member of the War Manpower Commission during World War II and was co-director of the UAW's War Policy Committee; became the UAW education director in 1946; was a Congress of Industrial Organizations (CIO) fraternal delegate to the London meetings of the Trade Union Advisory Committee of the European Recovery Program and became a co-chairman of the Anglo-American Labor Committee on Productivity in 1948; was severely wounded by an assassin in May, 1949, losing the sight in one eye; was a member of the CIO committee sent to study trade union and economic conditions in Europe, 1951; appointed in 1951 to head the CIO's European office, which was opened as a result of that study; became an administrative assistant to the president of the CIO in 1953 and the UAW in 1955; was a Socialist early in his career, but later supported Democratic candidates; retired union positions in 1971; Sidney Fine, *Sit-Down: The General Motors Strike of 1936-1937* (1969); Frank Cormier and William J. Eaton, *Reuther* (1970); Jean Gould and Lorena Hickok, *Walter Reuther: Labor's Rugged Individualist* (1972); Jack Stieber, *Governing the UAW* (1962).

REUTHER, Walter Philip.   Born in Wheeling, W. Va., September 1, 1907; son of Valentine, a steel and brewery worker and trade union leader, and Anna (Stoker) Reuther; reared a Lutheran; married May Wolf on March 13, 1936; two children; attended high school in Wheeling for three years, then became a tool and die maker apprentice at the Wheeling Steel Corporation; later completed high school and took courses at Wayne University, Detroit, Mich., for three years; moved to Detroit in 1926 after being discharged by the Wheeling Steel Corporation for union activities; employed by several Detroit companies before accepting a job with the Ford Motor Company as a tool and die worker; became a foreman in the tool and die room in 1931; discharged for union activities and unable to find other employment, embarked with his brother, Victor (q.v.), on a three year world tour, 1933-1935, that included Europe, the Soviet Union, China, and Japan; unable to find employment after his return to Detroit because of his reputation as a labor agitator, became a voluntary organizer for the United Automobile, Aircraft, Agricultural Implement Workers of America (UAW); successfully organized many automobile workers in Detroit's West Side into UAW Local 174 and became its president in 1935; elected to the international executive board of the UAW in 1936; was a leader of the important sit-down strike at the Kelsey-Hayes Wheel Company plant in Detroit in 1936; became director of the UAW's General Motors Corporation (GMC) department in 1939; elected first vice-president of the UAW in 1942; served during World War II with the Office of Production Management, the War Manpower Commission, and the War Production Board; elected president of the UAW in 1946 and the following year the so-called "Reuther Caucus" consolidated its control of the UAW after defeating the George Addes (q.v.)-Rolland J. Thomas (q.v.)-Richard Leonard (q.v.) faction in union elections; elected a vice-president of the Congress of Industrial Organizations (CIO) in 1946; led the UAW in a number of postwar strikes and in 1948 negotiated a contract with GMC that included an "escalator clause" tied to the U. S. Bureau of Labor Statistic's cost-of-living index; was the victim of an attempted assassination in April, 1948, that left him partially disabled; became president of the CIO in 1951 after the death of Philip Murray (q.v.); served on the American Federation of Labor (AFL)-CIO unity committee that negotiated the merger of the two organizations in 1955; became an AFL-CIO vice-president and executive council member and president of its industrial union department after the merger; led the UAW out of the AFL-CIO in 1968 and along with the International Brotherhood of Teamsters organized the Alliance for Labor Action in 1969; was a Socialist early in his career, but usually supported the Democratic party after 1933; died in an airplane crash near Pellston, Mich., May 10, 1970; Henry M. Christman, ed., *Walter P. Reuther, Selected Papers* (1961); Jack Stieber, *Governing the UAW* (1962); Frank

Cormier and William J. Eaton, *Reuther* (1970); Jean Gould and Lorena Hickok, *Walter Reuther: Labor's Rugged Individualist* (1972); Sidney Fine, *Sit-Down: The General Motors Strike of 1936-1937* (1969).

RICKERT, Thomas A.   Born in Chicago, Ill., April 24, 1876; son of Charles and Hannah Rickert; married; attended the public schools of Chicago and a business college; became a cutter in a garment factory; joined the United Garment Workers of America (UGW) in 1895; elected president of the UGW in 1904, beginning a life-long tenure in that position; as a result of dissatisfaction with his leadership, a secessionist movement of dissident garment workers emerged after the 1910 strike against Hart, Schaffner and Marx and culminated in the organization of the rival Amalgamated Clothing Workers of America in 1914; served during World War I on the War Labor Conference Board and its successor the War Labor Board; elected an American Federation of Labor (AFL) vice-president and executive council member in 1918; nominated William Green (q.v.) for the AFL presidency after the death of Samuel Gompers (q.v.) in 1924; was appointed to several federal committees during the early years of Franklin D. Roosevelt's administration, but soon became highly critical of New Deal policies and the Democratic administration; was a conservative trade union leader who had previously established a close personal relationship with Samuel Gompers and became a bitter opponent of the Congress of Industrial Organizations (CIO); in turn was characterized by CIO president John L. Lewis (q.v.) as being "regarded in labor circles as an official entertainer for members of the Executive Council"; served on the unsuccessful AFL-CIO unity committee in 1939; identified himself politically as nonpartisan; died in New York City, July 28, 1941; Joel Seidman, *The Needle Trades* (1942); Walter Galenson, *The CIO Challenge to the AFL: A History of the American Labor Movement, 1935-1941* (1960); Philip Taft, *The A. F. of L. From the Death of Gompers to the Merger* (1959).

RIEVE, Emil.   Born in the province of Zyradow, Russian Poland, June 8, 1892; son of Fred, a textile machinist, and Pauline (Lange) Rieve; Lutheran; married Laura Wosnack on July 1, 1916; one child; elementary school, then emigrated to the United States in 1904 and began working in a Pennsylvania hosiery mill; joined the American Federation of Hosiery Workers (AFHW) in 1907; elected a vice-president of the AFHW in 1914 and became president in 1929; was a labor advisor for the hosiery industry to the National Recovery Administration, 1933-1935; was a member of the national executive board of the United Textile Workers Union in 1934, and led an unsuccessful national strike of 500,000 textile employees; became executive director of the Congress of Industrial Organizations' (CIO) Textile Workers Organizing Committee in 1939 and left the AFHW to become president of the newly organized Textile Workers Union of America (TWU); became a CIO vice-president in 1939, serving until 1955; appointed to the national committee of the International Labor Organization in 1936; served during World War II as an alternate member of the National Mediation Board and of the National War Labor Board, and on them opposed antistrike legislation and the "Little Steel" formula of wage determination; was a U.S. Delegate to the Inter-American Conference on Social Security in Santiago, Chile, in 1942; resigned from the National War Labor Board in 1945 and released CIO textile workers from their no-strike pledge of December, 1941; visited the Soviet Union in 1945 as a member of the CIO delegation invited by the Soviet trade-union movement; was a CIO delegate to the World Federation of Trade Unions, 1945-1947; became an executive council member of the International Confederation of Free Trade Unions in 1949; appointed as a labor advisor to the National Security Resources Board in 1950 and served on the Wage Stabilization Board, 1950-1952; became a vice-president and executive council member of the American Federation of Labor-CIO after the 1955 merger; retired as TWU president in 1956, then served as chairman of the TWU executive council, 1956-1960; served as an AFL-CIO fraternal delegate to the British Trades Union Congress in 1956; became president emeritus in 1960; was an early member of the American Labor party and later supported candidates of the Liberal party of New York and the Democratic party; authored *Free Enterprise for Whom?* (1948); Walter Galenson, *The CIO Challenge to the AFL: A History of the American Labor Movement, 1935-1941* (1960); Art Preis, *Labor's Giant Step: Twenty Years of the CIO* (1964); *Current Biography* (1946).

ROBERTSON, David Brown. Born in West Austintown, Ohio, May 13, 1876; son of Robert, a merchant, and Jane (Brown) Robertson; Presbyterian; married Edna M. Hayes on September 8, 1907; two children; left the public schools at age twelve, but later continued his education through night school and correspondence courses; during 1888-1895, worked in a brick factory and a machine shop; took a job on the Pennsylvania Railroad as an engine wiper in 1895; during 1898-1913 he worked for the Erie Railroad as a hostler, fireman, and engineer; elected general chairman of the Brotherhood of Locomotive Firemen and Enginemen (BLFE) for the Erie Railroad in 1905; elected a vice-president of the BLFE in 1913; became international president in 1922; served as chairman of the Railway Labor Executives' Association, 1926-1932; was chairman of the committee that sponsored the Railway Labor Act of 1926; was strongly opposed to the elimination of firemen jobs on diesel-powered locomotives and negotiated national agreements in 1937 and 1950 providing for the employment of firemen as helpers on diesel locomotives; became BLFE president emeritus in 1953; appointed by the Chief Justice of the Supreme Court, Earl Warren, to head a commission to study and recommend salary and retirement benefits for members of Congress and the Federal judiciary; was a liberal in politics, and identified himself as an independent voter; died in Cleveland, Ohio, September 27, 1961; Robert H. Zieger, *Republicans and Labor, 1919-1929* (1969); *Current Biography* (1950); Solon DeLeon, ed., *The American Labor Who's Who* (1925).

ROBINS, Margaret Dreier. Born in Brooklyn, N.Y., September 6, 1868; daughter of Theeder, a businessman, and Dorothea Adelheid (Dreier) Dreier; German Evangelical and Congregational; married Raymond Robins, head of the Northwestern University Settlement in Chicago, on June 21, 1905; completed private secondary school in Brooklyn, then at age nineteen became secretary-treasurer of the women's auxiliary of the Brooklyn Hospital; served as chairman of the legislative committee of the Women's Municipal League, New York City, 1903-1904; joined the New York Women's Trade Union League (WTUL) in 1904; after marrying, transferred her membership to the Chicago WTUL in 1905; served as president of the Chicago WTUL, 1907-1913 and of the national WTUL, 1907-1922; was a member of the Chicago Federation of Labor's executive board, 1908-1917; during her WTUL career, often performed publicity work and raised funds for strikers, most notably during the 1909-1910 New York and Philadelphia garment workers' strikes and the 1911 International Ladies' Garment Workers' strike in Cleveland; was active in state labor and political affairs; was a member of the Vocational Education Committee of the Illinois State Federation of Labor in 1914 and chairman of the Women in Industry Committee of the Illinois State Council of Defense in 1917; was instrumental in convening the 1919 International Congress of Working Women in Washington, D. C., and at the Geneva Congress in 1921 elected president of the International Federation of Working Women, serving until 1923; supported William Jennings Bryan and the Democratic party in 1908; supported the Progressive party in 1912, and was a member of the executive committee of the Illinois Progressive party; supported the Republican party from 1916 to 1932, and thereafter supported Franklin D. Roosevelt and the Democratic party; was a member of the Republican National Committee in 1928; appointed to the planning committee of the White House Conference on Child Health and Protection by President Herbert H. Hoover in 1929; reelected to the WTUL executive board in 1934 and in 1937 became chairman of the WTUL's Southern committee; died in Brooksville, Fla., February 21, 1945; Mary Dreier, *Margaret Dreier Robins: Her Life, Letters, and Work* (1950); Agnes Nestor, *Woman's Labor Leader: An Autobiography of Agnes Nestor* (1954); Mary Anderson, *Woman at Work: The Autobiography of Mary Anderson as told to Mary N. Winslow* (1951); *Notable American Women* (1971); *Dictionary of American Biography* (Supplement III).

(M.T.)

ROBINSON, Reid. Born in Butte, Mont., June 7, 1908; son of James, a skilled mechanic and boilermaker and a member of the Western Federation of Miners; in 1914, moved to Alberta, Canada, where his family tried homesteading; returned to the United States during World War I; as a newsboy in Seattle, Wash., witnessed the general strike of 1919; in 1921, returned with his family to Butte, where his father edited a labor newspaper; attended high school in Butte, then went to work in the copper mines; during the early 1930s, along with his father, who had been recently elected secretary-treasurer of the International Union of Mine, Mill and Smelter Workers (IUMMSW), and several other organizers, revived the Butte Miners' No. 1, the key local of the IUMMSW; became financial secretary of No. 1 and in 1935 elected its president; with strong backing of a conservative faction, elected international president of the IUMMSW in 1936; although only 28 years old, was capable, a good speaker, and ambitious; the IUMMSW was one of the founding unions of the Congress of Industrial Organizations (CIO) and by virtue of being president of the IUMMSW, became a member of the CIO executive board and in 1940 a vice-president; was president of the IUMMSW for ten years and during this period the union increased its membership from about 20,000 to more than 90,000; negotiated a merger with the National Association of Die Casting Workers in 1943; in expanding the IUMMSW before and during World War II, gained Communist organizers from within the IUMMSW and from other CIO unions; Communist members alienated his original supporters, and by 1946 the union was divided into warring rightist and leftist factions; shortly after being reelected in 1946, resigned after losing majority support of the executive board; elected Eastern vice-president of the IUMMSW in 1947 and organized in Canada until deported as a

Communist agitator; resigned as vice-president and returned to Butte in 1950; later moved to California and there worked at various blue-collar jobs; was not a member of the Communist party, but was on the left ideologically; was an opponent of United States Cold War policies and supported Henry Wallace's Progressive party candidacy for president of the United States in 1948; Vernon H. Jensen, *Nonferrous Metals Industry Unionism, 1932-1954* (1954); Transcript of Reid Robinson Interview, 1969, Labor History Archives, Pennsylvania State University.

(D.G.S.)

ROLLINGS, John Isaac.   Born in St. Charles County, Mo., July 1, 1905; son of John William, a farmer and Sara Ella (Palmer) Rollings; married Fannie Ocepek on December 6, 1928; no children; completed elementary school, then learned the barber's trade in St. Louis, Mo.; joined St. Louis Local 102 of the Journeymen Barbers, Hairdressers, and Cosmetologists' International Union of America in 1925; served Local 102 in several capacities, including secretary-treasurer, business representative, and during 1931-1937, president; became the state legislative representative for the barber industry in 1928, serving in that capacity until 1953; served as president of the St. Louis Union Label Trades Section, 1935-1937; served during World War II as a member of the Seventh Regional Panel of the War Labor Board and was a member of the St. Louis Advisory Committee and the Price Panel Board of the Office of Price Administration; elected executive secretary (the chief administrative officer) of the St. Louis Central Trades and Labor Union in 1942, serving until 1953; became the president of the Missouri State Association of Barbers in 1944; elected president of the Missouri State Federation of Labor in 1953; was one of the principal negotiators of the American Federation of Labor (AFL)-Congress of Industrial Organizations' (CIO) merger in Missouri in 1956 and elected president of the resulting Missouri AFL-CIO Council; was a member of numerous public and private boards and agencies; retired from his union positions in 1969 and was named president emeritus of the Missouri AFL-CIO Council; usually supported the Democratic party; died in St. Louis, Mo., in December, 1970; Gary M Fink, *Labor's Search for Political Order: The Political Behavior of the Missouri Labor Movement, 1890-1940* (1974); *Who's Who in Labor* (1946); *AFL-CIO News*, December 26, 1970.

ROMBRO, Jacob (Philip Krantz).   Born in Zuphran, Wilna Province, Russia, October 10, 1858; son of Baruch and Bella Rosa (Uger) Rombro;

Jewish; married Eva Gordon; graduated from a rabbinical seminary in 1879, then spent two years at the Technological Institute of St. Petersburg; after the assassination of Alexander II in 1881, was forced into exile and settled in Paris; while continuing his studies at the Sorbonne, began a productive literary career with a treatise on Spinoza; one of the founders of a short-lived Socialist organization, the Jewish *Arbeiter Verein*; emigrated to London in 1883 and there wrote articles in Yiddish for a weekly Socialist journal, *Der Polischer Yidel*; became the editor of a Yiddish Socialist monthly, *Arbeiter Freund*, in 1885; represented the Jewish workers of London as a delegate to the first International Socialist Congress in Paris in 1889; emigrated to the United States in 1890 and became editor of a new Socialist weekly, the *Arbeiter Zeitung*, which, after being renamed the *Abend-Blatt*, became a daily and the official organ of the Socialist Labor party; as the editor of the first Socialist paper published in Yiddish, had an extraordinary influence during the formative years of the Jewish labor movement in the United States; at the time of his death, was associated with the *Jewish Daily Forward*; died in New York City, November 28, 1922; Melech Epstein, *Jewish Labor in the U.S.A.*, 1914-1952 (2 vols., 1950-1953); *American Jewish Year Book* (1904-1905); *Dictionary of American Biography* (Vol. XVI).

ROMUALDI, Serafino.   Born in Bastia Umbra, Italy, November 18, 1900; son of Romualdo, a shoemaker, and Emilia (Cormanni) Romualdi; Roman Catholic; married Rose Pesci Gioconda on September 4, 1928, and remarried after her death; two children; completed secondary school, then attended an Italian teachers' college; emigrated to the United States in 1923, after actively opposing the Fascist regime of Benito Mussolini; continued his opposition to fascism through the Italian language press in the United States; joined the American Newspaper Guild and served as a lecturer for the Rand School of Social Science as well as several international unions, including the Amalgamated Clothing Workers of America and the United Shoe Workers; joined the editorial and publicity staff of the International Ladies' Garment Workers' Union in 1933; served as an editor of the monthly magazine, *El Mondo*, 1939-1941, and as a labor economist in the Office of the Co-ordinator of Inter-American Affairs; as a labor advisor to the Office of Strategic Services in Italy in 1944, involved in the effort to rebuild the Italian labor movement; became the inter-American representative of the American Federation of Labor in 1948; served as assistant secretary general of the Inter-American Regional Labor Organization; became the executive director of the American Institute for Free Labor

Development after its organization in 1962; was a vigorous opponent of Communist influence in the labor movements of Latin America and devoted much of his time and energy to the promotion of anti-Communist unions and leaders; retired in 1965, then served as a special consultant on inter-American affairs to the U.S. State Department and as a lecturer at the Cuernavaca Labor College; authored *Presidents and Peons: Recollections of a Labor Ambassador in Latin America* (1967); died while attending a meeting of the Mexican Labor Federation in Mexico City, Mexico, November 11, 1967; Ronald Radosh, *American Labor and United States Foreign Policy: The Cold War in the Unions from Gompers to Lovestone* (1969); *The American Federationist* (March, 1948); *AFL-CIO News*, November 18, 1967.

RONEY, Frank. Born in Belfast, Ireland, August 13, 1841; son of a wealthy contractor; Roman Catholic; married three times; three children; as a young man, became associated with the Fenians and quickly rose to a leadership position in the revolutionary movement to overthrow British rule in Ireland; was arrested and charged with treason and emigrated to the United States to avoid imprisonment; lived in New York City and Chicago, Ill.; then moved to Omaha, Neb., and there secured employment as an iron molder with the Omaha Smelting Workers; joined Iron Molders Union 190 and elected its secretary and then its president; while residing in Nebraska, became active in the affairs of the National Labor Reform party (the political arm of the National Labor Union) and elected president of the Nebraska branch; was laid off as a foundry worker, then hired as a U.S. Government teamster and sent to Fort Sedgewich, Wyo.; returned to Omaha, again working as a molder; moved to Utah; worked in the Salt Lake City foundry and when it failed in 1875, moved to California, there securing employment as a molder with the Pacific Iron Works and then with the Union Iron Works of San Francisco; became a U.S. citizen in 1875; joined the Workingmen's party of California in 1877 and served as the temporary chairman of the party's first state convention, held secretly in San Francisco in January, 1878; wrote the platform of the Workingmen's party; broke with the leader of the Workingmen's party, Denis Kearney, then led an opposition faction for a short time before disassociating himself from the party; converted to socialism and joined the International Workingmen's Association (IWA), a forerunner of the Socialist Labor party, but devoted more of his attention to trade-union activities; although not a sailor, organized the Seamen's Protective Union in 1880 and was its delegate to the San Francisco Representative Assembly of Trades and Labor Union in

1881, serving as president during 1881-1882; was one of the leaders of the anti-Chinese agitation and helped found the "League of Deliverance", serving as its chairman; also led a campaign to advertise the anti-Chinese labels of cigar and shoe makers, the forerunner of the American labor movement's commitment to the trade-union label; blacklisted in his trade as a labor agitator; employed as an assistant to the City Engineer of San Francisco, holding the position until a change in the city administration cost him his job; in 1885, was one of the principal organizers of the first iron trades council in the United States, the Iron Trades Council of San Francisco (origianally the Federated Iron Trades Council) and served as a member of its executive board; was one of the founders of the Representative Council of the Federated Trades and Labor Organization of the Pacific Coast, an anti-Knights of Labor federation dominated by the IWA, and served as its president, 1885-1887; worked for a short time with the U.S. Immigration Service and at other odd jobs prior to gaining steady employment in the Mare Island Navy Yard, Vallejo, Calif., as a foundry worker in 1898; involved in the organization of the Trades and Labor Council of Vallejo in 1899 and served as its president for one term; in 1909, moved to Los Angeles, Calif., and there took no part in labor activities until 1915, then serving one term as secretary-treasurer of the Iron Trades Council of Los Angeles; after 1916, lived a lonely, poverty-stricken existence; authored *Frank Roney: Irish Rebel and Labor Leader* (edited by Ira B. Cross) (1931); died in Long Beach, Calif., January 24, 1925; Ira B. Cross, *A History of the Labor Movement in California* (1935); John R. Commons, *et al.*, *History of Labour in the United States*, Vol. II (1918).

ROSE, Alex (Olesh Royz).   Born in Warsaw, Russian Poland, October 15, 1898; son of Hyman, a wealthy tanner, and Faiga (Halpern) Royz; Jewish; married Elsie Shapiro on July 7, 1920; two children; completed secondary school in Warsaw, but because of discriminations against Jews, could not pursue a higher education in Poland; emigrated to the United States in 1913 in pursuit of a medical career; after the outbreak of war in Europe in 1914, his parents could no longer finance his education and hence forced to take a job as a millinery worker; joined the Cloth Hat, Cap and Millinery Workers' International Union (CHCMW) in 1914; became recording secretary of CHCMW Local 24 in 1916; enlisted in the British Army's "Jewish Legion" in 1918, serving in Palestine, Egypt, and Syria; returned to the United States in 1920 and resumed union activities; elected secretary-treasurer of Local 24 in 1923 after a bitter campaign against a Communist-supported opponent; elected vice-president of the CHCMW in 1927 and retained that position in the United Hatters, Cap and Millinery Workers International Union (UHCMW), which was organized in 1934 after the CHCMW and the United Hatters of North America merged; appointed president of the international by the UHCMW executive board in 1950 and subsequently elected to the post; led a successful strike against the Norwalk, Conn., based Hat Corporation of America in 1953-1954; chaired the American Federation of Labor-Congress of Industrial Organizations' appeals committee that expelled the International Brotherhood of Teamsters in 1957; was a vigilant opponent of Communist as well as gangster elements in the labor movement during his long career as a labor leader; was a Socialist early in his career, but became an advocate of labor-management cooperation to insure stability of the hat, cap and millinery industry; was an active and influential political leader; helped organize the American Labor party in 1936 and served as state secretary and director of the party, 1936-1944; was one of the founders of the Liberal party of New York, becoming its vice-chairman in 1944; was a delegate to the New York State Constitutional Convention in 1966; served as a presidential elector in the national elections of 1940, 1948, 1964, and 1968; Donald B. Robinson, *Spotlight on a Union: The Story of the United Hatters, Cap and Millinery Workers International Union* (1948); J. M. Budish, *History of the Cloth Hat, Cap and Millinery Workers* (1926); *Current Biography* (1959).

ROSENBLUM, Frank.   Born in New York City, May 15, 1888; son of Louis, a clothing worker, and Annie (Karna) Rosenblum; Jewish; married Ida Beispil on September 19, 1924; three children; completed grammar school, then began work in the garment industry and eventually secured employment as a cutter in a Hart, Schaffner and Marx plant in Chicago, Ill.; joined a Chicago Local of the United Garment Workers of America in 1910; was one of the founders of the Amalgamated Clothing Workers of America (ACWA) in 1914; became an ACWA vice-president and executive-council member in 1914; appointed director of the Congress of Industrial Organizations' (CIO) Midwest Textile Workers Organizing Committee in 1937 and served in that capacity for three years; elected a CIO vice-president in 1940 and became a member of the executive board; was a member of the CIO Political Action Committee and the Union Label Committee; served as chairman of the Finance Committee; elected ACWA executive vice-president in 1940 and served until 1946, when elected general secretary-treasurer, beginning a long term of service in that capacity; was a vice-president and member of the executive bureau of the World Federation of

Trade Unions, 1948-1949; served on a large number of ACWA boards and agencies; retired in 1972; died in Chicago, Ill., February 9, 1973; Matthew Josephson, *Sidney Hillman: Statesman of American Labor* (1952); Leo H. Wolman, *The Chicago Clothing Workers* (1924); Harry A. Cobrin, *The Men's Clothing Industry: Colonial Through Modern Times* (1970).

RUTTENBERG, Harold Joseph.   Born in St. Paul, Minn., May 22, 1914; son of Charles and Fannie (Weinstein) Ruttenberg; married Katherine Monori on September 23, 1936; two children; moved with family, while still a youth, to western Pennsylvania; during the 1920s, came into contact with the rigors of the miners' lives, including a coal-mine disaster; received a B.A. in economics from the University of Pittsburgh, then worked as a newspaper reporter for a time; by 1934-1935, was deeply involved in advising the "rank-and-file" militants within the Amalgamated Association of Iron, Steel and Tin Workers who prepared the way for the takeover of that union by the Congress of Industrial Organizations (CIO); was one of several intellectuals recruited by Philip Murray (q.v.) for the CIO's Steel Workers Organizing Committee (SWOC) and became its research director in 1936; in addition to serving as an idea man, acted as an organizer and troubleshooter for SWOC; helped subvert the steel industry's employee representation plans and participated in the "Little Steel" strike of 1937; served during World War II as assistant director of the Steel Division of the War Production Board; in *The Dynamics of Industrial Democracy*, coauthored with Clinton Golden (q.v.) in 1942, called for union-management cooperation to lower costs and maximize productivity, to be achieved through substitution of an annual system of pay for the established system of hourly wage rates and job classification; resigned from the United Steelworkers of America (USWA) to become vice-president of the Portsmouth Steel Corporation in 1946; established his own steel-fabricating firm in 1951; in order to eliminate the periodic unemployment and unstable annual income resulting from the recurrent steel strikes of the 1950s, urged the USWA to accept a two-year wage freeze in return for a guarantee of annual employment coupled with a reduction in basic steel prices; his concern about strike-induced unemployment was ultimately accepted by the USWA leadership in the Experimental Negotiation Agreement of 1973; authored numerous articles on labor-management policies which appeared in various periodicals; *Harper's* (December, 1955); Robert R. R. Brooks, *As Steel Goes, . . . Unionism in a Basic Industry* (1940); *Who's Who in Labor* (1946).

(D.G.S.)

RYAN, Joseph Patrick.   Born in Babylon, N.Y., May 11, 1884; son of James F., a landscape gardener, and Mary (Shanahan) Ryan; Roman Catholic; married Margaret Ann Conners on December 31, 1908; two children; attended St. Xavier's school in the Chelsea district of New York City, completing the sixth grade; worked, beginning at age twelve, as a stock boy, clerk, and streetcar conductor; began work on the New York docks in 1912; joined Local 791 of the International Longshoremen's Association (ILA) in 1912 and a year later was elected financial secretary of the local; became a full-time, professional union leader in 1916; elected president of the Atlantic Coast District of the ILA in 1918; during the same year, elected vice-president of the ILA; elected president of the international union in 1927; served as a vice-president of the New York State Federation of Labor for more than 20 years prior to 1946 and served as president of the Central Labor Council of Greater New York and Vicinity, 1928-1938; as a result of conflicts with West Coast ILA locals led by Harry R. Bridges (q.v.), the rival International Longshoremen's and Warehousemen's Union was organized in 1937 and gained control of Pacific ports; headed an American Federation of Labor (AFL) investigation of corruption in the International Seamen's Union (ISU); as a result of the investigation and the AFL-Congress of Industrial Organizations split, the ISU was reorganized into the Seafarers International Union of North American in 1938; elected ILA president for life in 1943; retired after the ILA was expelled from the AFL for corruption in 1953 and named president emeritus with a life-long pension; convicted of violating the Taft-Hartley Act in 1955 by accepting $2,500 from a company employing longshoremen and given a six-month suspended sentence and fined $2,500; the conviction was later overturned on appeal; often brought into conflict with left-wing unions and unionists because of his obsessive anti-Communism and determined opposition to industrial unionism on the waterfront; during his ILA incumbency, little militant trade union activity occurred and the ILA became increasingly dominated by gangsters and racketeers; was a Democrat; died in New York City, June 26, 1963; Charles P. Larrowe, *Shape-Up and Hiring Hall: A Comparison of Hiring Methods and Labor Relations on the New York and Seattle Waterfronts* (1955); Maud Russell, *Men Along the Shore* (1966); *Current Biography* (1949).

RYAN, Martin Francis.   Born in Coldwater, W. Va., October 23, 1874; son of John and Mary (Call) Ryan; Roman Catholic; married Sue Ellen Myers on April 8, 1904; four children; completed high school, then hired as a mechanic on the Southern Pacific Railroad in 1894 in Fort Worth,

Tex.; was a charter member of Fort Worth Lodge 23 of the Brotherhood of Railway Carmen of America (BRCA) in 1899; elected a member of the BRCA executive board in 1903; elected a general vice-president of the BRCA in 1905, and in 1909, elected general president, serving until his death; was a member of the American Federation of Labor (AFL) mission to England, Ireland, Scotland, Wales, and France in 1918, and, along with Samuel Gompers (q.v.), represented American labor at the Pan-American Federation of Labor conference in Mexico City in 1924; became a vice-president and member of the AFL executive council in 1923, serving until 1928, when elected AFL treasurer; elected a vice-president and member of the executive council of the AFL Railway Employees' Department in 1927; died in Kansas City, Mo., January 17, 1935; Leonard Painter, *Through 50 Years with the Brotherhood of Railway Carmen of America* (1941); Philip Taft, *The A. F. of L. in the Time of Gompers* (1957); Solon DeLeon, ed., *The American Labor Who's Who* (1925).

ST. JOHN, Vincent.   Born in Newport, Ky., July 16, 1876; son of Irish-Dutch parents; moved around the West with his family, drifting from job to job; settled in Colorado as a prospector and hard-rock miner; by 1901, was president of the Telluride Local of the Western Federation of Miners (WFM) and led the bitter strikes of 1901 and 1903 there; was blacklisted and harassed by state officials and accused of (but not tried for) being an accomplice in the murder of former Idaho governor Frank Steunenberg; was one of the WFM militants and supported the WFM in its important role in establishing the Industrial Workers of the World (IWW) in 1905; as a leader of the faction that sought to commit the IWW to revolutionary industrial unionism, helped wrest control of the national organization from President Charles Sherman (q.v.) at the 1906 convention; as a member of the IWW executive board, went to Goldfield, Nev., and there organized the entire labor force; in 1908, elected general secretary-treasurer (i.e., chief national officer) of the IWW, which was nearly broke and had less than 10,000 members; was intelligent, shrewd, and widely respected among Wobblies for his utter dedication to the cause and sustained the IWW as an industrial union dedicated to revolutionary syndicalism; at the 1908 convention, was instrumental in purging all references to political action from the constitution; rather than the renowned "Big" Bill Haywood (q.v.), led the IWW during the crucial years in which it recovered, waged free speech fights, and provided strike leadership during the Lawrence, Mass., and Paterson, N.J., textile strikes; was committed to revolution as the ultimate aim, but, as a former trade unionist, influenced the Wobblies to keep in mind the immediate needs of decent wages and working conditions; was convinced by 1915 that he could do no more for the IWW and resigned as general secretary; in 1917, while prospecting and managing a small mining venture in New Mexico, arrested in the federal government's mass roundup of IWW leaders; although not active in the union since 1915, was convicted and spent several years in federal prison; after being released, resumed his mining activities in Arizona; when his health failed, moved to San Francisco, Calif.; was at one time a member of the Socialist party, but abandoned political action after becoming a Wobbly; authored *The I.W.W.: Its History, Structure and Methods* (1917), an influential manifesto; died in San Francisco, Calif., June 21, 1929; *The Industrial Worker*, June 29, 1929; Elizabeth G. Flynn, *I Speak My Own Piece, Autobiography of "The Rebel Girl"* (1955); Melvyn Dubofsky, *We Shall Be All: A History of the Industrial Workers of the World* (1969).

(D.G.S.)

SARGENT, Frank Pierce.   Born in East Orange, Vt., November 18, 1854; son of Charles Edwin, a farmer, and Mary C. (Kinney) Sargent; married Georgia M. McCullough on October 17, 1881; one child; completed grammar school and attended Northfield Academy, Northfield, Mass., for one year; worked as a textile operative and a farm laborer, then moved to Arizona because of poor health and enlisted in the U.S. Cavalry; participated in the campaigns against the Apache Indians, 1878-1880; discharged in 1880, then hired by the Southern Pacific Railroad as an engine wiper; somewhat later, became a locomotive fireman and joined the Brotherhood of Locomotive Firemen and Enginemen (BLFE); elected vice-grand master of the BLFE in 1883 and two years later elected grand master; as grand master during 1885-1902, played a prominent role in the Chicago, Burlington and Quincy strike of 1888 and the American Railway Union strike against the Great Northern Railroad in 1894; appointed to the U.S. Industrial Commission in 1898; declined an appointment as director of the Bureau of Engraving and Printing in 1900; became U.S. Commissioner General of Immigration in 1902; was committed to restricting immigration and was especially critical of the increased immigration from southern and southeastern Europe; as a member of the National Civic Federation, was a confidant of Samuel Gompers (q.v.) and John Mitchell (q.v.) and counseled them during their conferences with President Theodore Roosevelt during the Anthracite Coal Strike of 1902; supported the Republican party; died in Washington, D.C., September 4, 1908;

Dictionary of American Biography (Vol. XVI); *Encyclopedia Americana* (Vol. XXIV).

SCHILLING, Robert.   Born in Osterburg, Saxony (now part of East Germany), October 17, 1843; Spiritualist; emigrated with his parents to the United States in 1846, settling in St. Louis, Mo.; served an enlistment in the Union Army during the Civil War, then became an apprentice cooper and in 1863 joined the first cooper's union organized in Missouri; elected first vice-president of the Coopers' International Union (CIU) in 1871; moved to Cleveland, Ohio, in 1871 and edited the German-language edition of the *Coopers' Journal*; elected president of the National Industrial Congress in 1874, and a year later, elected president of the CIU; joined the Noble Order of the Knights of Labor (K of L) in 1875; as an enthusiastic advocate of currency inflation, was one of the founders of the Greenback party and served as Ohio state chairman of the party; moved to Milwaukee in 1880 and edited two German-language newspapers, *Der Reformer* and *Volksblatt*; became a state K of L organizer for Wisconsin in 1881 and led the movement to considerable political power in 1885-1886, before ideological conflicts divided the movement; became national secretary of the Union Labor party in 1888 and in 1891 served in the same capacity for the People's (Populist) party, after helping to organize it; during 1892-1900, led the People's party in Wisconsin and several times was an unsuccessful candidate for public office; was opposed to the growing strength of the Socialist party in Milwaukee and successfully negotiated a fusion between Democrats and Populists that temporarily stalled the Socialist initiative; retired from active political participation in 1900 and entered the dairy business; died in Milwaukee, Wis., December 26, 1922; M. Small, "Biography of Robert Schilling," (M.A. thesis, 1953); Thomas W. Gavett, *Development of the Labor Movement in Milwaukee* (1965); *Dictionary of Wisconsin Biography* (1960).

SCHLESINGER, Benjamin.   Born in Krakai, Russian Lithuania (now part of the Soviet Union), December 25, 1876; son of Nechemiah, a rabbi, and Judith Schlesinger; Jewish; married Rae Schanhouse; three children; received a rabbinical education in Krakai prior to emigrating to the United States in 1891; orphaned at age twelve; settled in Chicago, Ill., and employed in the garment industry as a sewing-machine operator; served as the secretary of the Chicago Cloakmakers' Union and elected treasurer of the short-lived International Cloakmakers' Union of America in 1892-1893; was one of the founders of the International Ladies' Garment Workers'

Union (ILGWU) in 1900; served as business manager of the Chicago Cloakmakers' Union, 1902-1903; elected international president of the ILGWU in 1903, but defeated for reelection the following year; during 1904-1907, became manager of the *Jewish Daily Forward* in 1907, serving until 1912; again elected president of the ILGWU in 1914; was a member of the general executive board of the International Clothing Workers Federation, 1919-1923; served as an American Federation of Labor fraternal delegate to the British Trades Union Congress in 1922; resigned as ILGWU president in 1923 and resumed association with the *Jewish Daily Forward*; elected vice-president of the ILGWU in 1928 and upon the resignation of the incumbent, Morris Sigman (q.v.), became president for the third time; was a skilled bargainer and negotiator, but had a domineering and exacerbating personality, which reduced his ability for leadership; was a Socialist; authored several pamphlets and during 1914-1917 edited *The Ladies' Garment Worker*; died in a sanitarium in Colorado Springs, Colo., June 6, 1932; Benjamin Stolberg, *Tailor's Progress: The Story of a Famous Union and the Men Who Made It* (1944); Louis Levine, *The Women's Garment Workers; A History of the International Ladies' Garment Workers' Union* (1924); *Dictionary of American Biography* (Vol. XVI); Melech Epstein, *Profiles of Eleven* (1965), and *Jewish Labor in the U.S.A., 1914-1952* (1953).

SCHLOSSBERG, Joseph.   Born in Koidanovo (now Dzerzhinsk), Belorussia, Russia, May 1, 1875; son of Max, a tailor, and Bessie (Feldman) Schlossberg; Jewish; married Anna Grossman on September 5, 1905; two children; emigrated to the United States in 1888 and, after attending the public schools of New York City for one year, began work as a cloakmaker in the New York City garment industry; while involved in the organization of garment workers during the 1890s, joined the Socialist Labor party and edited its Yiddish language journals, *Das Abend Blatt*, 1899-1902 and *Der Arbeiter*, 1904-1911; attended the Columbia University School for Political Science, 1905-1907; supported a group of New York City tailors striking against the wishes of their parent organization, the United Garment Workers of America, in 1913, and led a secessionist movement that resulted in the organization of the United Brotherhood of Tailors (UBT); elected secretary of the New York Joint Board of the UBT; was one of the founders of the Amalgamated Clothing Workers of America (ACWA) in 1914 and elected general secretary-treasurer of the new organization; served as a fraternal delegate to the Congress for Labor Palestine, 1918, the International Congress of Clothing Workers, Copenhagen, 1920, and the Mexican

Federation of Labor, Juarez, 1924; was a charter member of the National Labor Committee for Labor Israel and elected chairman in 1934; appointed to the New York City Board of Higher Education in 1935, serving until 1963; resigned union positions in 1940 to devote further time and effort to Zionist and community affairs; after the establishment of the State of Israel, joined the Histadrut, the Israel General Federation of Labor; was a director of the American Civil Liberties Union, the American Association for Jewish Education, and the Yiddish Scientific Institute; edited the ACWA weekly, *Advance*, for several years; authored *The Workers and Their World* (1935); died in New York City, January 15, 1971; Matthew Josephson, *Sidney Hillman, Statesman of American Labor* (1952); Erma Angevine, *In League with the Future* (1959); Joel Seidman, *The Needle Trades* (1942); Melech Epstein, *Jewish Labor in the U.S.A., 1914-1952* (1953).

SCHNEIDERMAN, Rose.   Born in Savin, Russian Poland, April 6, 1884 (Birthdate is listed as 1882 in *All for One*); daughter of Samuel, a tailor, and Deborah (Rothman) Schneiderman; Jewish; emigrated to the United States in 1890; attended the public schools of New York until age thirteen, then began work in a New York department store; secured employment as a lining maker in the hat and cap industry in 1899 and four years later helped organize Local 23 of the United Cloth Hat and Cap Makers of North America (UCHCM); served as a delegate to the Central Federated Union of New York City during 1903; was the first woman elected to the general executive board of the UCHCM in 1904; joined the Women's Trade Union League (WTUL) in 1905; became vice-president of the New York WTUL in 1907 and a part-time organizer for the national WTUL in 1908; became a full-time organizer for the national WTUL in 1910 and was elected to its executive board in 1911; served as an International Ladies' Garment Workers' Union organizer, 1914-1916; resumed work with the WTUL in 1917 and was elected its president in 1918; served as a WTUL vice-president, 1919-1926, and as president, 1926-1947; was a delegate to the International Congress of Working Women meeting in Washington, D.C., in 1920; was the only woman appointed to the Labor Advisory Board of the National Industrial Recovery Administration in 1933; investigated the needle trades industry in Puerto Rico for the National Recovery Administration in 1934; was secretary of the New York State Department of Labor, 1933-1944; was a political activist and chaired the industrial section of the Women's Suffrage party of New York City, 1916-1917; ran unsuccessfully for the New York Senate on the Farmer-

Labor ticket in 1920; headed the women's division of the American Labor party; although nominally a Socialist, usually supported Democratic candidates; served on the board of trustees, Brookwood Labor College, 1924-1929; was an honorary vice-president of the United Hatters, Cap and Millinery Workers' International Union; authored, with Lucy Goldthwaite, *All for One* (1967); died in New York City, August 11, 1972; Gladys Boone, *The Women's Trade Union Leagues in Great Britain and the United States* (1942); Agnes Nestor, *Woman's Labor Leader: An Autobiography* (1944); Donald B. Robinson, *Spotlight on a Union: The Story of the United Hatters, Cap, and Millinery Workers International Union* (1948); Leon Stein, *The Triangle Fire* (1962).

(M.T.)

SCHNITZLER, William F.   Born in Newark, N.J., January 21, 1904; son of Wilhelm, a metal polisher, and Marie (Weithenwit) Schnitzler; married Edith Eckert on September 12, 1931; two children; after attending the public schools of Newark, N.J., began work at age fourteen in an ammunition factory during World War I; after working briefly in a metal grinding shop, became an apprentice baker in 1920; joined Local 84 of the Bakery and Confectionery Workers' International Union of America (BCWIU) in 1924; elected business agent of Local 84 in 1934, serving until 1937; became an international representative in 1941; elected a BCWIU vice-president and financial secretary in 1943; elected to the newly created position of secretary-treasurer in 1946; became the international president of the BCWIU in 1950; replaced George Meany (q.v.) as the secretary-treasurer of the American Federation of Labor (AFL) in 1952; was one of the three AFL delegates meeting with Congress of Industrial Organizations' (CIO) representatives to work out a merger of the two labor federations in 1955; elected secretary-treasurer of the newly merged AFL-CIO; served as a fraternal delegate from the AFL-CIO to the British Trades Union Congress in 1956; attended the International Confederation of Free Trade Unions' (ICFTU) African Regional Conference in 1956 and the Tunis conference of the ICFTU in 1957 as an AFL-CIO fraternal delegate; was appointed to the Labor Advisory Committee by the U.S. Secretary of Labor in 1955; became chairman of the reorganized AFL-CIO civil rights committee in 1961; retired union positions in 1969; usually supports the Democratic party; Joseph C. Goulden, *Meany* (1972); *Current Biography* (1965); *Fortune* (January, 1953); *The American Federationist* (November, 1952); *AFL-CIO News*, May 10, 1969; *Who's Who in America, 1968-1969*.

SCHOEMANN, Peter Theodore.   Born in Milwaukee, Wis., October 26, 1893; son of Paul, a laborer, and Mary (Bauer) Schoemann; Roman Catholic; married Mary Margaret Furey on October 21, 1925; three children; began to work full-time after finishing elementary schooling in the public schools of Milwaukee; became an apprentice in the plumbing industry and joined Local 75 of the United Association of Plumbers and Steamfitters of the United States and Canada (UA) in 1914; served sucessively as recording secretary and business representative of Local 75; was chairman of the credentials committee of UA national conventions, 1928-1932, and chairman of the laws committee in 1942; elected president of the Milwaukee Building and Construction Trades Council in 1932, serving until 1952; during World War II, was a regional labor representative on the War Manpower Commission; after serving as a UA vice-president for several years, became acting president in 1953 after appointment of the incumbent, Martin P. Durkin (q.v.), as U.S. Secretary of Labor; elected UA president after the death of Durkin in 1955; became an American Federation of Labor-Congress of Industrial Organizations' (AFL-CIO) vice-president and executive council member in 1957; appointed chairman of the AFL-CIO committee on education and also served on its committee on economic policy; was a conservative trade unionist; became one of the principal spokesmen for the building trades in the AFL-CIO; served on several public boards and agencies, including posts as vice-president of the Milwaukee Housing Authority, chairman of the Wisconsin Board of Vocational and Adult Education, a member of the Milwaukee School Board and certifying officer for Milwaukee County, and a member of the advisory committee of the Milwaukee civil works administration; a Democrat; retired UA presidency in 1971; Joseph C. Goulden, *Meany* (1972); *AFL-CIO News*, April 24, Agust 7, 1971; *Who's Who in America, 1970-1971; Who's Who in Labor* (1946).

SCHOENBERG, William.   Born in Germany in August, 1879; married; two children; after a few years of formal education, became an apprentice machinist and worked at his trade in Germany, Switzerland, and South Africa; was an active trade unionist in both Germany and Switzerland; emigrated to the United States in 1907, settling in Chicago, Ill., and joined the International Association of Machinists (IAM); elected business agent of IAM District 8 in 1913, serving until 1920; served as an IAM international representative, 1920-1933; appointed a personal representative of American Federation of Labor (AFL) president William Green (q.v.) in 1933 and placed in charge of AFL organizing activities in

Illinois, Iowa, Indiana, and Missouri; was placed in charge of AFL efforts to organize Portland cement plant employees in 1936; saw these efforts bear fruit in the chartering of the United Cement, Lime, and Gypsum Workers International Union (UCLGWU) by the AFL in 1939; elected first president of the UCLGWU in 1939; during his presidency, saw the UCLGWU successfully organize more than 90 percent of the cement plants in the United States and Canada; retired in 1955 and designated president emeritus; died in Des Plaines, Ill., August 2, 1966; *The American Federation of Labor News-Reporter*, December 31, 1954; *AFL-CIO News*, August 13, 1966.

SCHOLLE, August.   Born in Creighton, Pa., May 23, 1904; son of Henry, a glass worker, and Elizabeth (Danner) Scholle; married Kathleen B. Jones on October 23, 1942; two children; completed one year of high school, then became a glass worker; joined Toledo, Ohio, Local 9 of the Federation of Glass, Ceramic, and Silica Sand Workers of America (FGCSSW) (At the time it was the Federation of Flat Glass Workers; it assumed its current name in 1940.) in 1933; while serving as national president of the FGCSSW, 1935-1937, led the union into the Congress of Industrial Organizations (CIO); became a CIO regional director and, while based in Toledo during 1937-1940, helped organize auto and other industrial workers in Ohio and Michigan; served as president of the Michigan Industrial Union Council, CIO, from 1940 until the merger of the CIO and American Federation of Labor (AFL) state bodies in 1958; became president of the AFL-CIO Council in the latter year; headed the Michigan CIO Political Action Committee during the 1940s and the Michigan Committee on Political Education (COPE) from 1956; successfully prosecuted a "portal-to-portal" suit to the U.S. Supreme Court in 1946, resulting in millions of dollars in additional wages for affected workers; played a salient role during the 1940s and 1950s in developing a new political strategy whereby unionists involved themselves directly in the organizational structure and electoral machinery of the Democratic party; was instrumental in initiating Michigan labor's voter registration campaigns, especially among the auto workers in Wayne County; was also most responsible for creating, in the late 1940s, the labor-liberal basis of the Michigan Democratic party, thus insuring the successive electoral triumphs of Governor G. Mennen Williams, 1948-1960; lobbied, with Williams's support, for enactment of a steeply progressive state income tax, but saw the Republican legislative majority prevent its passage; initiated legal action to force redistricting on the basis of the "one man, one vote" principle, thus aiming to outlaw the rural overrepresentation in Michigan that enabled Republicans to stymie such liberal proposals; through the case of *Scholle vs. Hare* (1959-1962), ultimately brought about equal representation for Michigan cities, and also contributed materially to the U.S. Supreme Court's national application of one man, one vote; served as a delegate to all Democratic national conventions from 1948 to 1964; managed the COPE campaign in a way that was crucial in enabling Hubert H. Humphrey to carry Michigan in the presidential race of 1968; served over the years on numerous public agencies, such as the State Board of Education; was a member of several liberal and civil rights organizations, including the National Association for the Advancement of Colored People; retired from the presidency of the Michigan AFL-CIO in 1971; died in Saginaw Bay, Mich., February 15, 1972; Doris B. McLaughlin, *Michigan Labor* (1970); *AFL-CIO News*, February 19, 1972; *The New York Times*, February 17, 1972; *Who's Who in Labor* (1946); *Who's Who in the Midwest, 1969-1970.*

(D.G.S.)

SCOTT, Sam H.   Born in Orange County, N. C., March 1, 1901; son of Edward C., a farmer, and Martha J. Scott; Christian Church; married Kathryn C. on January 21, 1943; two children; after graduating from high school, attended Duke University for three years; eventually gained employment in the tobacco industry and joined Local 183 of the International Union of Tobacco Workers (IUTW) in 1933; served as president of IUTW Local 183, 1933-1935; became an IUTW general organizer in 1935, serving in that capacity until 1942; joined the United Stone and Allied Products Workers of America (USAPWA) in 1942 and was appointed its international representative in North Carolina, South Carolina, and Georgia; elected USAPWA international president in 1944; served on the Congress of Industrial Organizations' (CIO) executive board until the 1955 merger with the American Federation of Labor (AFL); represented the USAPWA at the biennial conventions of the AFL-CIO, 1955-1967; served as a vice-president of the North Carolina AFL-CIO for a long period; retired as USAPWA's representative in the Southern region, 1968; was a Democrat; died in Winston-Salem, N.C., January 30, 1969; *Who's Who in Labor* (1946); *AFL-CIO News*, February 1, 1969.

SCULLY, John James Joseph.   Born in South Amboy, N.J., February 10, 1867; son of Stephen, a hotel proprietor and coal shipper, and Mary B. (Kelly) Scully; Roman Catholic; married Mary Ann Coleman on February 8, 1888; received a public and private school education in New Jersey and later attended the U.S. Navy Reserves' Columbia Training University; after completing his formal education, became a marine pilot and in 1890 joined the American Brotherhood of Steamboat Pilots—renamed National Organization of Masters, Mates, and Pilots of America (NOMMPA) in 1916; was a member of the eight-hour day committee established in 1890 by American Federation of Labor (AFL) president Samuel Gompers (q.v.) to press for a shorter working day; served as a state and national organizer for the AFL; was an executive officer in the U.S. Navy Reserve and served as the supervisor of a minesweeper training school in New York, 1917-1921; elected secretary-treasurer of the NOMMPA after the war and served in that capacity until 1945; was a regional director of the National Labor Relations Board until 1945; served in several public positions, including two terms as Hudson County, N.J., Harbor Master, president of the New Jersey State Pilots Commission, and member of a variety of conciliation and arbitration committees; was a Democrat; edited *The Master, Mate, and Pilot* magazine until his retirement in 1945; died in Jersey City, N.J., April 5, 1947; *Who's Who in Labor* (1946); *The New York Times*, April 7, 1947.

SEFTON, Lawrence Frederick.   Born in Iroquois Falls, Ontario, Canada, March 31, 1917; son of Harry, an accountant, and Mary (McNeil) Sefton; Roman Catholic; married Elaine Marie Melhuish on July 9, 1943; two children; at age of seventeen, began working as a hard-rock miner in Northern Ontario and soon became recording secretary and organizer for Kirkland Lake local of the International Union of Mine, Mill, and Smelter Workers; blacklisted following an unsuccessful strike; moved to Toronto, obtained work in a metal plant, and, in 1942, joined Steel Workers Organizing Committee Local 1039; completed high school while living in Toronto; after serving in the Canadian Army during World War II, was appointed a staff representative of the United Steelworkers of America (USWA); led the USWA campaign to organize workers of the Steel Company of Canada's Hamilton, Ontario, works, the largest Canadian steel mill, in 1946; appointed after this success as senior USWA staff representative for Hamilton and Niagara Peninsula; was elected director of USWA District 6, comprising Ontario and all of Western Canada, in 1953; became a vice-president of the newly formed Canadian Labour Congress in 1956; belonged to a small group of district directors indirectly challenging David McDonald's (q.v.) leadership in 1955 by supporting Joseph Moloney (q.v.) for USWA vice-president; backed secretary-treasurer I.W. Abel's (q.v.) decision to run against McDonald in 1965; influenced the majority of Canadian locals to nominate Abel, thus significantly strengthening Abel's campaign; as chairman of the Congress of Industrial Organizations' committee on white collar organization, spoke and wrote widely to dispel the "myth" that white collar workers were not receptive to unionization; was a Socialist, but also became deeply involved in support of the New Democratic Party of Canada; declined to run again for director in the USWA elections of 1973; died in Toronto, Canada, May 9, 1973; commemorated through the naming of the new USWA Centre in Toronto as the "Larry Sefton Building"; John Herling, *Right to Challenge: People and Power in the Steelworkers Union* (1972); *Canadian Labor* (June, 1965); *Who's Who in Labor* (1946).

(D.G.S.)

SELDEN, David Seeley.   Born in Dearborn, Mich., June 5, 1914; son of Arthur Willis, a school administrator, and Florence Loretta (Seeley) Selden; married Bernice Cohen on March 22, 1956, after two divorces; three children; received an A.B. degree in education from Michigan State Normal College (now Eastern Michigan University) in 1936 and took a job as a social studies instructor in a Dearborn, Mich., junior high school; joined the Progressive Education Association in 1936; joined the Dearborn local of the American Federation of Teachers (AFT) in 1940 and, while serving as the president of the local, 1940-1943, led the successful efforts to build a strong teachers' union in the city; received an M.A. degree from Wayne State University in 1940; joined the U.S. Navy in 1943 and served as a crewman on a destroyer; after the war, moved to Jacksonville, Fla., and unsuccessfully attempted to pursue a literary career and to found an experimental college; shortly after returning to classroom teaching, appointed a full-time organizer by the American Federation of Labor (AFL) in 1948 and assigned to the AFT; became the AFT's special representative in New York City in 1953; along with Albert Shanker (q.v.), built United Federation of Teachers, Local 2, AFT, into a strong, militant trade union; appointed to the newly created post of assistant to the AFT president in 1964, serving until 1968; served as a delegate to the White House Conference on Education in 1965; elected president of the AFT in 1968, and during the same year became a member of the executive board of the AFL-Congress of Industrial Organizations' industrial union department; was a member of the Urban Task Force on Education in 1969; sentenced to sixty days in jail for violating an injunction during the Newark, N.J., teachers' strike of 1970; proved to be a vigorous proponent of a merger between the AFT and the National Education Association, but caused considerable divisiveness during the early years of his presidency through his efforts to reach this objective; politically a Democrat; Robert J. Braun, *Teachers and Power: The Story of the American Federation of Teachers* (1972); Stephen Cole, *The Unionization of Teachers: A Case Study of the UFT* (1969).

SHANKER, Albert.   Born in New York City, September 14, 1928; son of Morris, a Polish immigrant and newspaper deliveryman, and Mamie (Burko) Shanker, a member of the Amalgamated Clothing Workers of America; Jewish; married Edith Gerber on March 18, 1961; four children (one by a previous marriage); graduated from Stuyvesant High School after attending elementary schools in Queens; earned a B.A. degree in philosophy at the University of Illinois and became active in various Socialist groups at the university; received the M.A. degree in philosophy and mathematics from Columbia University; became a substitute teacher in an East Harlem school in 1952; after transferring to Junior High School 126 in Long Island City, joined the New York Teachers Guild (NYTG); became a member of the union's delegate assembly in 1957 and shortly thereafter elected to the executive board; became an American Federation of Teachers (AFT) vice-president and full-time organizer in 1959; became secretary of the newly founded United Federation of Teachers (UFT), Local 2, AFT, formed through merger of the NYTG with a group of high school teachers; served from 1962-1964 as an assistant to the UFT president; became editor of the *United Teacher*, the official organ of the UFT, in 1962; elected UFT president in 1964; led a two-week strike of New York City teachers in 1967, thus leading to conviction for violating a state law prohibiting strikes by public employees and imprisonment for 15 days; led another teacher's strike a year later in opposition to school decentralization believing that decentralization would transfer personnel policies, including the hiring and firing of teachers, to local authorities without safeguards for the employment rights of teachers and would negate collective bargaining provisions effecting those rights; as a result of the 1968 strike, again sentenced to 15 days in jail, this time for defying a court injunction; following merger of the UFT and the New York State Teachers' Association, became the executive vice-president of the newly organized New York State United Teachers; served as a vice-president of the New York City Central Labor Council, American Federation of Labor-Congress of Industrial Organizations (AFL-CIO), and the Jewish Labor Committee; acted as a director of the League for Industrial Democracy, and was a vice-chairman of the Liberal party's Trade Union Council; elected an AFL-CIO vice-president and executive council member in 1973; Stephen

Cole, *The Unionization of Teachers: A Case Study of the UFT* (1969); Robert J. Braun, *Teachers and Power: The Story of the American Federation of Teachers* (1972); *Current Biography* (1969).

SHELLEY, John Francis. Born in San Francisco, Calif., September 3, 1905; son of Denis, a longshoreman, and Mary (Casey) Shelley; Roman Catholic; married Genevieve Giles in September, 1932; three children; after attending both parochial and public schools in San Francisco, became a bakery wagon driver and joined Local 484 of the International Brotherhood of Teamsters, Chauffeurs, Warehousemen, and Helpers of America (IBT) in 1929; graduated from the University of San Francisco Law School in 1932; elected vice-president of IBT Local 484 in 1935; elected vice-president of the San Francisco Labor Council in 1936 and the following year became president, serving until 1948; elected to the California State Senate in 1938 and reelected in 1942; was Democratic floor leader in the California Senate, 1942-1946; during World War II, served on temporary duty with the U.S. Coast Guard; ran unsuccessfully for lieutenant governor of California on the Democratic ticket in 1946; elected president of the California State Federation of Labor in 1947 and served until his resignation in 1964; ran unsuccessfully against James R. Hoffa (q.v.) for the IBT presidency in 1957; elected mayor of San Francisco in 1963 and served until 1968; became a legislative lobbyist for the city of San Francisco in 1969; was a delegate to the Democratic party's national conventions of 1940 through 1960; Philip Taft, *Labor Politics American Style: California State Federation of Labor* (1968); *Who's Who in Labor* (1946).

SHERMAN, Charles O. (fl. 1894-1907). Blacklisted in the Pullman strike of 1894; appointed an American Federation of Labor (AFL) organizer, 1902-1903, by Samuel Gompers (q.v.); during that period, founded and served as general secretary of the United Metal Workers International Union; helped the union raid other AFL affiliates in the metal trades as soon as it was chartered by the AFL; beginning in November, 1904, participated in the secret meetings that issued a manifesto calling for the founding of the Industrial Workers of the World (IWW); was representative of the IWW group that Ben Williams (q.v.) editor of *Solidarity*, called "also-rans," craft unionists wishing to return to the union movement out of personal ambition or hope for personal profit; at the IWW's founding convention in 1905, was elected the first and only president; during his one-year administration, appointed incompetent organizers and contracted to purchase union labels and insignia from a firm in which he had a personal financial interest; at the IWW's second convention, in September, 1906, saw insurgents led by Daniel DeLeon (q.v.) take control of the convention, abolish the office of president, transfer its powers to the general organizer, and elect William Trautmann (q.v.) to that office; supported by factions within the Socialist party and the Western Federation of Miners, briefly maintained a rival IWW, seized physical control of union headquarters, expelled Trautmann from office, ruled the 1905 constitution still in force and the 1906 convention's actions null and void, published the *Industrial Worker* in Joliet, Ill., requested that all per capita payments be paid to the "legal" organization, and appealed to the courts for injunctive relief; watched his organization collapse in 1907 with the courts ruling in favor of the DeLeon-Trautmann faction and the Western Federation of Miners failing to affiliate and pay per capita tax to either organization; Melvyn Dubofsky, *We Shall Be All: A History of the Industrial Workers of the World* (1969).

(J.H.)

SHIELDS, James Percy. Born in Neoga, Ill., June 9, 1889; son of an Illinois farmer; married; one child; attended West Salem, Ill., High School prior to becoming a fireman on the Michigan Central Railroad at the age of seventeen; during the following several years worked as a fireman for several Midwestern and Southwestern railroads; became an engineer in 1916 and joined Evanston, Wyo., Division 136 of the Brotherhood of Locomotive Engineers (BLE); was elected chairman of Division 136 in 1926; became vice-chairman of the Eastern division of the Union Pacific Railroad in 1931 and chairman the following year; became acting assistant grand chief engineer in 1939, and was elected to the position in 1942; elected grand chief engineer of the BLE in 1950; condemned the government seizure of railroads during labor-management disputes, and also criticized the St. Lawrence Seaway and other competitive fields of transportation; died in Cleveland, Ohio, June 29, 1953; Reed C. Richardson, *The Locomotive Engineer: 1863-1963, A Century of Railway Labor Relations and Work Rules* (1963); *Current Biography* (1951); *Labor*, July 4, 1953.

SIEMILLER, Paul Leroy. Born in Gothenberg, Neb., September 4, 1904; son of Israel Frank, a soldier and farmer, and Lillie May (Sherman); Baptist; married Thelma Mary East on February 16, 1926; one child; attended the public schools of St. Cloud, Fla.; after completion of his formal education, traveled extensively, working at a variety of odd jobs prior to settling in Atlanta, Ga., to serve an apprenticeship as a machinist; during World War I, served with the U.S. Navy; resumed his travels after the war, working as a machinist for various railroad shops; joined International Association of Machinists (IAM) Lodge 823, Port Arthur, Tex., in 1929; laid off during the depression, but moved to Arkansas and secured employment with the Missouri and Arkansas Railroad; joined Harrison, Ark., Lodge 1093 and served it as financial secretary and then president; became a general IAM representative in 1937 and was assigned to organizing activities on the Pennsylvania Railroad; during World War II, served as a labor member of the Sixth Regional War Labor Board; was an American Federation of Labor (AFL) delegate to the International Labor Organization in 1947; was elected an international vice-president and member of the IAM executive board in 1948 and became a Midwestern supervisor; served as director of the manpower division of the Defense Transport Administration in 1951; elected international president of the renamed International Association of Machinists and Aerospace Workers in 1965; was co-chairman of the American Foundation on Automation and Unemployment in 1966; became a vice-president and executive council member of the AFL-Congress of Industrial Organizations in 1965; belonged to numerous public and private boards and agencies; was a political activist, advocating a large role for organized labor in national elections and in legislative lobbying; supported the Democratic party; retired union positions in 1969; *Current Biography* (1966); *Who's Who in America, 1972-1973.*

SIGMAN, Morris.   Born in Costesh, Bessarabia, Russia, May 15, 1881; son of Samuel, a farmer and lumberjack, and Rebecca (Sikernetsky) Sigman; Jewish; married Mathilda Sikernetsky on March 17, 1912; received little formal education; after working as a lumberjack, emigrated to London in 1902 and obtained employment in a men's clothing factory; emigrated to the United States a year later and secured employment as a presser in a New York cloak shop; organized the independent Cloak and Skirt Pressers' Union in 1904 and later affiliated it with Daniel DeLeon's (q.v.) Socialist Trade and Labor Alliance; helped it to become one of the original unions comprising the Industrial Workers of the World (IWW) a year later; became disillusioned with the dual union activities of the IWW, and thus led his union into the International Ladies' Garment Workers' Union (ILGWU) in 1908; helped organize the New York Joint Board of Cloakmakers in 1909 and served as its general manager, 1910-1913; served as a vice-president of the ILGWU during the same period; chaired the picket committee during the historic strikes of 1910 that established the ILGWU as the principal bargaining agent for New York garment makers; indicted and arrested in 1914-1915 for murder as a result of incidents occurring during the 1910 strike, but acquitted after spending several months in jail; was secretary-treasurer of the ILGWU, 1914-1915; served as business manager of the New York Joint Board of Cloakmakers, 1917-1921; became first vice-president of the ILGWU in 1920 and president in 1923; resigned in 1928 after successfully conducting a long and divisive struggle to prevent a Communist takeover of the union; retired to a small farm near Storm Lake, Iowa; died there on May 20, 1931; Louis Levine, *The Women's Garment Workers: A History of the International Ladies' Garment Workers' Union* (1924); Benjamin Stolberg, *Tailor's Progress: The Story of a Famous Union and the Men Who Made It* (1944); *Dictionary of American Biography* (Vol. XVII).

SINEY, John.　　Born in Bornos, County Queens, Ireland, July 31, 1831; son of Patrick, a small farmer, and Catherine Siney; Roman Catholic; married Mary Hennessey, and, after her death in 1862, Margaret Behan on November 6, 1876; two children; at age five, moved with his family to Wigan, Lancashire, England; began working in the cotton mills there two years later and kept working for nine years; became an apprentice bricklayer in 1849, and in his early twenties helped to organize the Bricklayers' Association of Wigan; elected president of the association seven times; emigrated to St. Clair, Schuylkill County, Pa., in 1863, and worked as an anthracite miner until 1868; participated in strikes in 1864 and 1868, the first to win a wage increase and the second to resist a wage reduction; in 1868, along with 15 other miners, founded and was elected the first president of the Workingman's Benevolent Association of St. Clair to resist wage cuts, settle grievances, provide sickness, accident, and death benefits, and improve intellectual life; chaired a convention of delegates in July, 1868, representing 20,000 anthracite miners that founded the Workingman's Benevolent Association (later the Miners' and Laborers' Benevolent Association) of Schuylkill County; served as the association's president at $1,500 per year until 1874; declined the nomination by the National Labor Union convention in 1869 to be its first vice-president; chaired the founding convention of the Labor Reform party at Columbus, Ohio, in 1872; owned and published *The Workingman* for one year, 1873-1874, at Pottsville, Pa.; chaired a Youngstown, Ohio, convention of 42 delegates from five states in 1873 that founded the first national miners' union, the Miners' National Association (MNA), which gained 35,000 members by 1875 but was destroyed by the depression; was elected president of the MNA three times; president of the Independent party in 1875 and vice-president of the Greenback party in 1878; participated in the formation of the Greenback Labor party; became a truck farmer and tavern keeper in St. Clair in 1876; died in St. Clair, Pa., April 16, 1880; Edward Pinkowski, *John Siney: The Miners Martyr* (1963); David Montgomery, *Beyond Equality: Labor and the Radical Republicans, 1862-1872* (1967); Ray Boston, *British Chartists in America, 1839-1900* (1971).

(J.H.)

SKIDMORE, Thomas. Born in Newton, Fairfield County, Conn., August 13, 1790; married in 1821; proved a gifted student and, at age thirteen, was appointed a teacher in the Newton district school; after teaching there for five years, moved to Weston, Conn., for one year and thereafter taught at Princeton and Bordentown, N.J., Richmond, Va., and Edenton and Newbern, N.C.; moved to Wilmington, Del., in 1815 and began a new career in chemical and mechanical research, concentrating on improvements in the manufacture of gunpowder, wire drawing, and paper making; after moving to New York City in 1819, secured employment as a machinist; actively supported the National Republican party and John Q. Adams in the national elections of 1828; was one of the principal founders of the New York Workingmen's party, and was a leading figure in the Committee of Fifty that formulated the platform of the new party; published *The Rights of Man to Property* in 1829, elaborating the agrarian principles upon which he hoped to build a labor reform movement; was nominated for the New York assembly by the Workingmen's party in 1829 but was narrowly defeated; after being forced out of the Workingmen's party, along with his agrarian reformers late in 1829, organized a new party but never made it successful; briefly published a newspaper, *The Friend of Equal Rights*; was a controversial reformer, often characterized as overly zealous and arrogant, but was nevertheless a legitimate radical leading the Workingmen's party at the time of its greatest power and influence; died in New York City during a cholera epidemic in the summer of 1832; Walter Hugins, *Jacksonian Democracy and the Working Class* (1960); Edward Pessen, *Most Uncommon Jacksonians: The Radical Leaders of the Early Labor Movement* (1967), and "Thomas Skidmore, Agrarian Reformer in the Early American Labor Movement," *New York History* (July, 1954); John R. Commons, *et al.*, *History of Labour in the United States*, Vol. I (1918).

SLAMM, Levi D. (fl. 1833-1850). Born in New York City, ca. 1800; although apparently serving an apprenticeship as a locksmith, was listed as a grocer during the period 1833-1837; began his association with the labor movement as a delegate from the Journeymen Locksmith's Society to the General Trades' Union of New York in 1835; besides serving the General Trades as a director of its journal and corresponding secretary, active on several committees and sponsored resolutions covering a variety of subjects; served during 1835 and 1836 as a delegate to the conventions of the National Trades' Union, acting as corresponding secretary and playing an instrumental role in the formulation of the organization's prison labor policy; was involved, despite threats of imprisonment, in the meetings organized to protest the sentencing of striking journeymen tailors in 1837; increasingly active during the second half of the 1830s in New York politics; closely identified himself with the reformist, Locofoco Equal Rights party often derisively referred to as "Slamm Bang & Co."; ran as a candidate for the state assembly on the Locofoco ticket in 1837 and shortly after the election was named recording secretary of the Equal Rights party; having seen the Panic of 1837 crush the neophyte labor movement, devoted his energies to politics and to publishing the reformist *New Era* in 1840 and the *Daily Plebeian* somewhat later; joined the Tammany Society in 1842 and thereafter fairly consistently supported the Democratic party; exercised considerable influence on the labor movement, despite some questions raised by others about the sincerity of his commitment to the labor movement and about his political opportunism; Walter Hugins, *Jacksonian Democracy and the Working Class: A Study of the New York Workingmen's Movement, 1829-1837* (1960); Edward Pessen, *Most Uncommon Jacksonians: The Radical Leaders of the Early Labor Movement* (1967); John R. Commons, *et al.*, eds., *A Documentary History of American Industrial Society*, Vol. VI (1910); Frederic Byrdsall, *History of the Loco-Foco or Equal Rights Party* (1842).

SODERSTROM, Reuben G. Born in Wright County, Minn., March 10, 1888; son of John F., a minister and shoe merchant, and Anna (Ericson) Soderstrom; married Jeanne M. Shaw on December 2, 1912; two children; after completing the seventh grade, moved to Streator, Ill., and secured work in a glass factory at age twelve; became an apprentice printer a few years later and, in 1910, joined the International Typographical Union; soon became president of his local union; was president of the Streator Trades and Labor Assembly, 1913-1920; was elected in 1916 to the Illinois Assembly as an Independent Republican; served in that capacity for 16 years and authored or promoted many bills, including the Illinois Anti-injunction Act of 1925 and measures to assist disabled and disadvantaged women and children; as chairman of the house education committee in the 1920s, advocated massive state aid for education; became president of the Illinois State Federation of Labor in 1930, a position retained until 1958; elected president in the latter year of the newly formed American Federation of Labor-Congress of Industrial Organizations' (AFL-CIO) state body; co-edited the Illinois AFL *Weekly News Letter*; was an AFL fraternal delegate to the Canadian Trades and Labor Congress in 1954; served on wartime governmental boards, sat on various AFL and AFL-CIO committees, and was active in numerous charitable and community service organizations; actively supported the War on Poverty during the 1960s; was a life-long promoter of public education, and in 1969 received a University of Illinois certificate of appreciation for his service to labor education and to the University; due to ill health, retired as president of the Illinois AFL-CIO in 1970, but received the title of president emeritus from the executive board; died in Streator, Ill., December 15, 1970; *Who's Who in Labor* (1946); Illinois AFL-CIO *Weekly News Letter*, December 19, 1970.

(D.G.S.)

SORGE, Friedrich Adolph.   Born in Bethau bei Torgau, Saxony (now part of East Germany), November 9, 1828; son of Georg Wilhelm, a clergyman, and Hedwig Klothilde (Lange) Sorge; married; two children; after private tutoring from his father, attended the Franckeschen Stiftungen at Halle; as a result of participating in revolutionary activities in 1848, incarcerated for a short period; after released from prison, moved to Geneva and taught music; forced to leave Geneva in 1851, and moved to Liège; worked there in a carpentry shop and taught German in a private school; arrived in London in 1852 after being forced to leave both Belgium and Germany; emigrated to the United States later in the same year and supported himself as a musician and music teacher in New York City; joined a New York Communist society in 1858; supported the antislavery wing of the Republican party during the Civil War; during 1868, was a member of the executive committee of the Union for German Freedom and Unity, secretary of the Secularists, and a member of the *Soziale Partei*; joined the International Workingmen's Association (IWA) in 1869; attended The Hague convention of the IWA in 1872; became general secretary of the IWA after its headquarters moved to New York; along with Otto Weydemeyer, represented the North American Federation of the IWA in 1876 at a Philadelphia conference designed to unify the American labor and socialist movements; joined with Ira Steward (q.v.) in the Boston Eight-

Hour League in 1877, and organized textile workers in New Jersey the following year; was an intimate friend of Karl Marx and Friedrich Engels, and became the most authoritative spokesman for Marx in the United States; died in Hoboken, N.J., October 26, 1906; David Montgomery, *Beyond Equality: Labor and the Radical Republicans, 1862-1872* (1967); G. M. Stekloff, *History of the First International* (1928); Morris Hillquit, *History of Socialism in the United States* (1903); *Dictionary of American Biography* (Vol. XVII).

SPRADLING, Abe L.   Born in Woodford County, Ky., June 19, 1885; son of Abe L. and Annie E. (Gilvin) Spradling; married Lula May Hutton in September, 1907, and, after her death in December, 1910, Mary A. Jones on October 3, 1931; one child; after completing his formal education in the public schools, became a motorman for the Cincinnati Traction Company in 1903; joined Division 627 of the Amalgamated Association of Street, Electric Railway and Motor Coach Employees of America (AASERMCE) in Cincinnati and in 1915 was elected secretary-treasurer of the local; became an international AASERMCE vice-president in 1927 and was elected to the international executive board in 1935; served as an assistant to international president William D. Mahon (q.v,), 1936-1944; elected international president of the AASERMCE after the resignation of Mahon in 1946; elected an American Federation of Labor-Congress of Industrial Organizations' vice-president and executive council member during the 1955 merger convention; served as a director of the Union Labor Life Insurance Company; resigned union positions because of failing health in 1959; died in Cincinnati, Ohio, May 22, 1970; Emerson P. Schmidt, *Industrial Relations in Urban Transportation* (1937); *AFL-CIO News*, May 30, 1970; *Who's Who in America, 1958-1959*.

STARR, Mark.   Born in Shoscombe, Somersetshire, England, April 27, 1894; son of William, a miner, and Susan (Padfield) Starr; reared as a Methodist; married Helen Grosvenor Norton on May 31, 1932; one child; after graduating from grammar school in 1907, began work as a hod carrier; entered the coal mines a year later working as a powder monkey, a carting boy, and a hewer; attended night school during 1913-1914, while working in the mines, and the following year was awarded a two-year scholarship to the London Labor College by the South Wales Miners' Federation; won an extension of the scholarship for two years following the end of World War I; instructed miners in economics and history for the South Wales Federation of Miners and then became a lecturer for the British National Council of

Labor Colleges; joined the faculty of Brookwood Labor College in Katonah, N.Y., in 1928 and served as its extension director during 1933-1935; joined Local 189 of the American Federation of Teachers (AFT) in 1928; appointed director of the newly organized educational department of the International Ladies' Garment Workers' Union in 1935, serving until 1960; became the focus of a public controversy when the New York Board of Education rejected the recommendation that he be appointed director of a newly established adult education program; served as a consultant to the Office of War Information during World War II; elected president of AFT Local 189, became a member of the AFT executive council, and served as an AFT vice-president, 1941-1943; ran unsuccessfully for Congress on the Liberal party ticket in 1946; appointed by President Harry S. Truman to the National Commission on Higher Education in 1946; served as an expert on workers' education for the International Labor Organization in Singapore, 1960-1961, Tanganyika, 1961-1962, and East Africa, 1962-1963; became the United Nations' representative to the New York Universala Esperanto-Asocco in 1965 and during the same year became chairman of the Esperanto Information Center in New York City; was a member of the Liberal party of New York; authored several books, including *Trade Unionism: Past, Present, and Future* (1923), *Labor in America* (1944), and *Labor Politics in the U. S.* (1949); Benjamin Stolberg, *Tailor's Progress: The Story of a Famous Union and the Men Who Made It* (1944); *Current Biography* (1946).

STEPHENS, Uriah Smith.   Born in Cape May County, N.J., August 3, 1821; Baptist; educated for the Baptist ministry, but indentured to a tailor during the 1837 depression; taught school for a short time; moved to Philadelphia, Pa., in 1846 and worked as a tailor for several years; left Philadelphia in 1853, traveling through the West Indies, Central America, and Mexico, and then spent five years in California; returned to Philadelphia in 1858 as a reformer and abolitionist; supported the Republican candidacies of John Fremont in 1856 and Abraham Lincoln in 1860; helped organize the Garment Cutters' Association in 1862; after the failure of the Garment Cutters' Association, became a cofounder of the Noble Order of the Knights of Labor (K of L) in 1869; as a member of several secret fraternal societies, became much impressed with tradition, secrecy, and ritualism and incorporated those principles into his concept of labor organization; also opposed the wage system, favoring cooperation instead, and advocated a single all-embracing organization of the "producing classes"; was elected master workman when 20 K of L assemblies organized

District Assembly 1; ran unsuccessfully for Congress on the Greenback Labor party ticket in 1878 from Pennsylvania's Fifth District; elected grand master workman of the K of L in 1878; resigned his office in the K of L the following year due to illness and to differences over the wisdom of his emphasis on secrecy; died in Philadelphia, Pa., February 13, 1882; Norman J. Ware, *The Labor Movement in the United States, 1860-1900* (1929); Gerald N. Grob, *Workers and Utopia: A Study of Ideological Conflict in the American Labor Movement, 1865-1900* (1961); David Montgomery, *Beyond Equality: Labor and the Radical Republicans, 1862-1872* (1967).

STEWARD, Ira.   Born in New London, Conn., March 10, 1831; married Jane (Steward) Henning in 1880 after the death of his first wife, Mary B. Steward, in 1878; self-educated; became a short-hours advocate while serving a 12-hour-a-day apprenticeship as a machinist in 1850; joined the Machinists' and Blacksmiths' International Union after being discharged from his machinist's job because of his agitation for shorter hours; secured a resolution at the 1863 national convention of the Machinists demanding an eight-hour-day law; organized the first independent eight-hour organization, the Workingmen's Convention (later renamed the Labor Reform Association), in Boston, Mass., in 1864; played a prominent role in the organization and affairs of the Grand Eight-Hour League and its successor, the Boston Eight-Hour League; served as titular head of numerous eight- and ten-hour leagues; successfully advocated an effective ten-hour law for women and children in the Massachusetts legislature in 1874; was a cofounder with J. P. McDonnell (q.v.) of the International Labor Union in 1878; also served as an organizer; was a pamphleteer whose theories strongly influenced his generation of labor leaders; believed that eight hours of labor was a vital first step in achieving a fundamental redistribution of wealth that would eventually result in the decline of capitalism and the inauguration of a cooperative commonwealth; emphasized the eight-hour solution and thus often came into conflict with reformers propagating more broadly conceived programs of social reform; his disciples George McNeill (q.v.) and George Guntan carried his theories into the American Federation of Labor; died in Plano, Ill., March 13, 1883; David Montgomery, *Beyond Equality: Labor and the Radical Republicans, 1862-1872* (1967); Norman Ware, *The Labor Movement in the United States, 1860-1895* (1929); John R. Commons, *et al.*, *History of Labour in the United States*, Vol. II (1918); *Science and Society* (Spring, 1956); *Dictionary of American Biography* (Vol. XVIII).

STOKES, Rose Harriet Pastor.   Born in Augustowo, Suwalki, Russian Poland, July 18, 1879; daughter of Jacob and Anna (Lewin) Wieslander; Jewish; married a millionaire, James G. P. Stokes, on July 18, 1905, and, after that marriage ended in divorce, Isaac Romaine in 1927; moved with her family to London in 1872, and there, from ages seven to nine, received her only formal education at the Bell Lane Free School; emigrated with her family to the United States, settling in Cleveland, Ohio, in 1890; shortly after began work in a Cleveland cigar factory; moved to New York City in 1903 and became a feature writer for the *Jewish Daily News*, already a publisher of some of her poems; became a member of the Socialist party of America (SPA) and active in the Intercollegiate Socialist Study Society headed by her husband from 1907 to 1917; participated in the 1912 New York restaurant and hotel workers' strike; in association with her husband, helped found the short-lived National party in Chicago, Ill., in 1912; withdrew from the SPA in July, 1917, because of its opposition to American entry into World War I; convicted in March, 1918, for violating the Espionage Act, but saw the conviction overturned on appeal in 1920; rejoined the SPA in February, 1918; became increasingly radical and aligned herself with the SPA's left wing; remained with this group when it seceded from the SPA in September, 1919, to form the Communist party of America (CPA); wrote for *Pravda* and the *Daily Worker* during the 1920s; elected an American delegate to the Fourth Congress of the Communist International in Moscow in 1922, and was elected to the central executive committee of the Workers' party; served as a reporter for the Congress's Negro Commission; authored numerous poems, an unpublished autobiography, and a feminist play, *The Woman Who Wouldn't* (1916); translated with Helena Frank the Yiddish *Songs of Labor* (1914); died in Frankfurt-am-Main, Germany, June 20, 1933; *Dictionary of American Biography* (Vol. VIII); *Notable American Women* (1971); James Weinstein, *The Decline of American Socialism, 1912-1925* (1967).

(M.T.)

STONE, Warren Stanford.   Born in Ainsworth, Iowa, February 1, 1860; son of John, a farmer, and Sarah (Stewart) Stone; married Carrie E. Newell on October 15, 1884; after completing high school, attended Western College, Iowa; began work as a fireman on the Rock Island Railway in 1879; became an engineer in 1884 and eventually joined the Brotherhood of Locomotive Engineers (BLE); served as secretary-treasurer and chairman of the adjustment committee of his local union; appointed grand chief engineer of the BLE after the death of Peter M. Arthur (q.v.) in 1903, and a year later elected to the same position by the delegates to the BLE's national convention; strongly supported the agitation that successfully led to a legislated eight-hour day for railroad workers; although an essentially conservative trade union leader, was a strong advocate of government ownership of the railroads; served as treasurer of the Conference for Progressive Political Action that sponsored the Progressive party candidacy of Robert M. LaFollette in 1924; involved the BLE during his presidency in cooperative banking and a wide variety of financial ventures, most of which failed during the early years of the Great Depression; served as a member of the Industrial Peace Committee administering the Nobel Peace Prize; became a director of the Cooperative League in 1923; died in Cleveland, Ohio, June 12, 1925; Reed C. Richardson, *The Locomotive Engineer: 1863-1963, A Century of Railway Labor Relations and Work Rules* (1963); Erma Angevine, *In League with the Future* (1959); *Encyclopedia of Social Sciences* (Vol. XIV).

STRASSER, Adolph (1871-1910).   Born in Austria-Hungary (an area now part of Hungary); emigrated to the United States in 1871 or 1872; helped organize the Social Democratic party in 1873 and the Socialist Labor party in 1877; participated in the 1872 eight-hour strikes and helped organize those New York cigarmakers excluded from membership in the Cigarmakers' International Union of America (CMIU); joined Local 15 (English-speaking), led by Samuel Gompers (q.v.), and guided a successful drive to merge that group with Local 85 (German-speaking) and the Bohemian cigarmakers; founded the United Cigarmakers, open to all regardless of sex, and fought to liberalize the CMIU constitution and to legitimize local membership policies; after the United Cigarmakers received a CMIU charter as Local 144 in 1875, became financial secretary while Gompers was elected president; was elected international president of the CMIU in 1877, serving until 1891; during the early 1880s, sided with Gompers in his refusal to turn Local 144 over to the democratically-elected Progressive (Socialist) faction and instead illegally expelled the Progressive president, Samuel Schimkowitz, and disastrously disrupted the union; meanwhile, saw the Progressive defectors joined by other secessionist Socialists to create in 1882 a new union larger than Local 144; maneuvered CMIU committees and the annual convention to maintain control of Local 144 as part of the Gompers machine; fought against the Knights of Labor (K of L) and its District Assembly 49 for giving support to the Progressives, and permitted CMIU members to scab against Progressive strikers in the early 1880s; fearing K of L encroachment, demanded that the K of L cease organizing the trades and in 1886, with four others, issued a call for the Columbus (Ohio) Convention that organized the American Federation of Labor (AFL) in December of that year; testified, in 1883, before the U.S. Senate Committee on Education and Labor against the Pacific Coast migration of Chinese who competed with cigarmakers; opposed the Gompers-inspired proposal for the use of initiative and referendum in CMIU elections, and thus resigned his CMIU presidency in 1891; later accepted the proposal after voting was made compulsory; was opposed to independent political activity and to the Socialist Plank 10 at the 1894 AFL convention; appointed to the newly created AFL legislative committee in 1895 to promote congressional action favorable to labor; named by the AFL executive council in 1904 to arbitrate jurisdictional disputes between brewery workers, who favored industrial unionism, and the craft-oriented firemen and engineers; saw his activities result in revocation of the charter of the Brewery Workers' Union in 1907; served as a CMIU organizer in Pennsylvania, 1909-1910; Philip Taft, *The A. F. of L. in the Time of Gompers* (1957); Bernard Mandel, *Samuel Gompers: A Biography* (1963); Roland H. Harvey, *Samuel Gompers: Champion of the Toiling Masses* (1935); Philip Foner, *History of the Labor Movement in the United States*, Vol. II (1955); Samuel Gompers, *Seventy Years of Life and Labor* (1925); *Cigarmakers Official Journal* (1909-1910).

(M.E.R.)

STULBERG, Louis.   Born in Bogria, Russian Poland, April 14, 1901; son of Benjamin, a coal dealer, and Jeannette Stulberg; Jewish; married Bebe Friedman on February 17, 1929; one child; after emigrating to Toronto, Canada, began work as a junior cutter in a dress shop and at age fourteen joined Local 83 of the International Ladies' Garment Workers' Union (ILGWU); graduated from Harbord Collegiate Institute in Toronto; emigrated to the United States in 1919; while working in the garment industry in Chicago, Ill., completed high school and attended the University of Chicago for one year; played professional baseball for two years with the Memphis Chicks of the Southern Association; served as an ILGWU general organizer for the Midwest, 1924-1927; after moving to New York, affiliated with ILGWU Local 10 and from 1929-1945 served as its business agent and assistant manager; became assistant general secretary of the ILGWU in 1945 and an international vice-president two years later; served as manager of New York Undergarment and Negligee Workers' Union, Local 62, ILGWU, 1947-1956; became executive vice-president after the position was created by the ILGWU executive board in 1956; served until his election as general secretary-treasurer in 1959; elected president of the ILGWU after the retirement of David Dubinsky (q.v.) in 1966; elected shortly thereafter as a vice-president and executive council member of the American Federation of Labor-Congress of Industrial Organizations (AFL-CIO); was appointed a United States delegate to the United Nations by President Lyndon B. Johnson in 1968; served as AFL-CIO fraternal delegate to the British Trades Union Congress in 1972; was appointed a fellow of Brandeis University; has usually supported the Democratic party; Max D. Danish, *The World of David Dubinsky* (1957); Benjamin Stolberg, *Tailor's Progress: The Story of a Famous Union and the Men Who Made It* (1944).

SUFFRIDGE, James Arthur.   Born in Knoxville, Tenn., February 2, 1909; son of Chester Arthur, a retail merchant, and Angie (Dodson) Suffridge; Methodist; married Georgia Nutting on November 18, 1928; two children; after graduating from high school in Oakland, Calif., worked at a variety of odd jobs, including those of wholesale-jewelry salesman in northern California and route boss for a wholesale bakery in St. Louis, Mo.; later took courses at the University of California, Berkeley; became a counter clerk for an Oakland grocery store in 1931 and later promoted to store manager; joined Oakland Food and Drug Local 870 of the Retail Clerks International Protective Association (RCIA) in 1934; was elected secretary-treasurer, the chief administrative officer, of Local 870 in 1936; served as president of the California State Council of Retail Clerks and as financial secretary of the Oakland Central Labor Union; elected international president of the RCIA in 1944 and became the chief administrative officer of the union after the retirement of Secretary-Treasurer C. C. Coulter (q.v.) in 1947 (his title was secretary-treasurer, 1947-1955, and president thereafter); during World War II, was a member of the regional board of the Office of Price Administration and a panel member of the Oakland division of the War Labor Board; created an organizational division within the RCIA in 1945 that stimulated major organizing successes; became an American Federation of Labor-Congress of Industrial Organizations' (AFL-CIO) vice-president and executive council member in 1957; served as a member of the executive board of the AFL-CIO industrial union department and was a vice-president of the union label department; retired as president emeritus of the RCIA in 1968 and became chairman of the union's executive board; a Republican; edited the RCIA organ, *Advocate*, 1947-1968; Michael Harrington, *The Retail Clerks* (1962); Albert

A. Blum, *et al.*, *White-Collar Workers* (1971); George G. Kirstein, *Stores and Unions: A Study of the Growth of Unionism in Dry Goods and Department Stores* (1950); *Saturday Evening Post*, March 16, 1957.

SULLIVAN, David. Born in Cork City, Ireland, May 7, 1904; son of Stephen and Margaret (Fouhy) O'Sullivan; Roman Catholic; married Catherine Connaire on February 12, 1930; five children; received a secondary education in Ireland before emigrating to the United States in 1925; after arriving in New York City, took a job as an elevator operator; became a naturalized citizen in 1932; was one of the founders of New York City Local 32B of the Building Service Employees International Union (BSEIU) in 1934; was elected secretary-treasurer of Local 32B in 1938 and became president in 1941, serving until 1960; during his assocaiation with Local 32B, saw it become one of the largest local unions in the United States; was elected an international vice-president of the BSEIU in 1941; elected international president of the BSEIU in 1960, serving until 1971; during his 12-year incumbency, watched the BSEIU experience a 70 percent increase in membership; was elected a vice-president and executive council member of the American Federation of Labor-Congress of Industrial Organizations in 1967; served as chairman of the labor advisory committee of the Office of Economic Opportunity, as a member of the National Advisory Council on Economic Opportunity and the advisory committee of the National Institute on Labor Education, and on numerous other public and private boards and agencies; was the recipient of the Equal Opportunity Award presented by the National Urban League in 1961; retired as president of the BSEIU in 1971 and was named president emeritus; usually supports the Democratic party; Local 32B, Building Service Employees International Union, *"Going Up!"*; *The Story of 32B* (1955); *Who's Who in America, 1972-1973; AFL-CIO News*, March 20, 1971.

SULLIVAN, James William. Born in Carlisle, Pa., March 9, 1848; son of Timothy and Elizabeth (Hagan) Sullivan; married Lillian Stewart in 1877; left high school shortly before his scheduled graduation to become a printer's apprentice; moved to New York City in 1882 and soon became foreman of the proof room of *The New York Times* and joined the International Typographical Union; during 1887-1889, edited the *Standard*, a weekly newspaper published by Henry George (q.v.) to propagate his land reform proposals; served as a member of the advisory council of the Ethical Culture Society's People's Institute in 1897; elected president of the Central Federated Union of New York City in 1913; as a close friend and adviser of American Federation of Labor (AFL) president Samuel Gompers (q.v.), accompanied Gompers on a tour of Europe in 1909, assisted in the editing of the *American Federationist*, and defended the AFL from Socialist attacks; became an active member of the National Civic Federation, serving on several of its commissions and committees and, as the head of one such commission, returning an unfavorable report on the British system of compulsory health insurance; sailed to Europe in 1916 on an AFL mission to arrange for labor representatives in the postwar peace conference; served during World War I as an assistant to Gompers on the Advisory Commission of the Council of National Defense; was one of the principal American advocates of direct legislation and was able to convince much of the labor movement of its importance; authored *Direct Legislation by the Citizenship Through the Initiative and Referendum* (1892) and *Markets for the People* (1913); died in Carlisle, Pa., September 27, 1938; Marguerite Green, *The National Civic Federation and the American Labor Movement, 1900-1925* (1956); *Dictionary of American Biography* (Supplement II); Samuel Gompers, *Seventy Years of Life and Labor* (1925).

SULLIVAN, Jere L.   Born in Williamansett, Mass., January 3, 1863; son of a civil engineer working in the paper industry; Roman Catholic; attended the public schools of Williamansett, Mass., and, for a short time, Catholic parochial schools; after completing grammar school, worked as an itinerant waiter for several years; while serving as a Knights of Labor organizer in 1885, helped to organize a local assembly of waiters in St. Louis, Mo., which was to become Local 20 of the Hotel and Restaurant Employees' International Alliance and Bartenders' International League (HREIABIL); after moving to Salt Lake City, Utah, joined Local 6 and served as its delegate to the second national convention of the HREIABIL meeting in Chicago, Ill., in 1893; after returning to St. Louis, elected an international vice-president in 1899 and later the same year became secretary-treasurer of the HREIABIL, serving in that capacity until his death; generally regarded as the dominant figure in the early history of the HREIABIL, having assumed the leadership of a union that had nearly been destroyed by bitter factional conflicts and turned it into a solid, unified international union; died in Cincinnati, Ohio, July 27, 1928; Matthew Josephson, *Union House: Union Bar: The History of the Hotel and Restaurant Employees and Bartenders International Union, AFL-CIO* (1956); Jay Rubin and M. J. Obermeier, *Growth of a Union: The Life and Times of*

Edward Flore (1943); Solon DeLeon, ed., *The American Labor Who's Who* (1925).

SWARTZ, Maud O'Farrell.   Born in County Kildare, Ireland, May 3, 1879; daughter of William J., part-owner of a flour mill, and Sarah Matilda (Grace) O'Farrell; Roman Catholic; married Lee Swartz, a printer, in 1905; after attending convent schools in Germany and France, became a governess in Italy; emigrated to the United States in 1901; became a proofreader for a printing firm in New York City in 1902; shortly after becoming a member of the national Women's Trade Union League (WTUL), joined Local 6 of the International Typographical Union in 1913; served as secretary of the New York WTUL, 1917-1921; was a WTUL delegate to numerous conferences, including the 1919 First International Congress of Working Women held in Washington, D.C., the 1919 American Federation of Labor convention, the 1921 Second International Congress of Working Women in Geneva, and the 1922 Pan-American Congress, in Baltimore, Md.; was the American vice-president of the International Federation of Working Women, 1921-1923; served as compensation adviser for the New York WTUL during 1922; succeeded Margaret Dreier Robins (q.v.) as president of the National WTUL in 1922 and served in that capacity until 1926; became the secretary of the New York State Department of Labor in 1931, serving until 1937; died in New York City, February 22, 1937; *Notable American Women* (1971); Solon DeLeon, ed., *The American Labor Who's Who* (1925); Rose Schneiderman and Lucy Goldthwaite, *All for One* (1967); Gladys Boone, *The Women's Trade Union Leagues in Great Britain and the United States of America* (1942).

(M.T.)

SWEENEY, Vincent D.   Born in Pittsburgh, Pa., March 3, 1900; son of Philip, a steelworker, and Anna Sweeney; Roman Catholic; married; graduated from Donora, Pa., High School and received a journalism degree from Notre Dame University in 1922; after editing a small Pennsylvania newspaper, worked for the International News Service, becoming editor of its New York bureau; beginning in 1925, spent a decade with the Pittsburgh *Press*; in order to cover New Deal labor policy and union activity, gave up his post as Sunday editor of the *Press* to become its labor reporter and analyst; recruited by Chairman Philip Murray (q.v.) as public relations director of the Steel Workers Organizing Committee (SWOC), set up by the Congress of Industrial Organizations (CIO); within a month started *Steel Labor,* a monthly distributed free to steelworkers as part of the initial SWOC campaign; later in 1936, began to edit *Steel Labor,* soon developing it into a very readable, informative, and balanced union journal; among the upper echelon staff personnel at United Steelworkers of America (USWA) headquarters, was one of those on whom President Murray relied most; worked closely with Murray as an adviser on USWA matters, a general troubleshooter, and a speechwriter; served in a somewhat similar capacity after David J. McDonald (q.v.) became president in 1952; as when serving Murray, again carefully avoided publicity about himself; helped to establish USWA's program of summer institutes on university campuses after USWA began to develop worker education; was a member of the American Newspaper Guild and the National Press Club; authored *The United Steelworkers of America, Twenty Years Later, 1936-1956* (1956); retired due to ill health in 1961; died in Uniontown, Pa., May 20, 1967; Robert R. R. Brooks, *As Steel Goes, . . . Unionism in a Basic Industry* (1940); *Who's Who in Labor* (1946).

(D.G.S.)

SWINTON, John.   Born in Edinburgh, Scotland, December 12, 1829; son of William and Jane Swinton; after acquiring a few years of formal education, apprenticed to a printer in 1841 at age thirteen; emigrated to Canada in 1843 and, while living in Montreal, became a journeyman printer; moved to New York City in 1850 and secured work as a printer; attended Easthampton Seminary in Massachusetts and New York Medical College, but did not receive a degree; became involved in the abolitionist movement of the 1850s, and participated in John Brown's raid at Osawatomie, Kan., in 1857; served as chief of *The New York Times* editorial staff, 1860-1870; began working for the New York *Sun* in 1870 and became chief editorial writer in 1875; as a result of the labor conflicts of the 1870s, became an ardent champion of the emerging labor movement; ran as the Socialist Labor party candidate for mayor of New York City in 1874; established in 1883 and served as the editor of *John Swinton's Paper,* described by one authority as "the best labor paper in the country's history"; ran unsuccessfully for the New York State Senate on the Progressive Labor party ticket in 1887; resumed his position as an editorial writer for the New York *Sun* after the failure of his own paper in 1887; although totally blind by 1889, continued his work as a journalist until his death; authored *John Swinton's Travels* (1880) and *Striking for Life* (1894); died in Brooklyn, N.Y., in 1901; John R. Commons, *et al., History of Labour in the United States,* Vol. II (1918); Norman J. Ware, *The Labor Movement in the*

United States, 1860-1895 (1929); Gerald N. Grob, *Workers and Utopia: A Study of Ideological Conflict in the American Labor Movement, 1865-1900* (1961); *Encyclopedia of Social Sciences* (Vol. XIV).

SWISHER, Elwood Denver.   Born in Jenningston, W. Va., March 24, 1913; son of Francis Columbus and Kate Flossie (Lantz) Swisher; Methodist; married Blanche S. Sneed on August 28, 1934, and Gladys E. Simmons on December 25, 1938; four children; received a public school education in Elkins, W. Va.; after completing high school became an overhead crane operator for a subsidiary of the Union Carbide and Carbon Company and joined Local 89 of the United Gas, Coke and Chemical Workers International Union (UGCCW); elected treasurer and vice-president of Local 89 in 1943 and served until becoming a UGCCW international representative in 1945; became a member of the executive board in 1948 and in 1952 elected UGCCW president; was a member of the Congress of Industrial Organizations' executive board and served on its community services committee and the committee on power and atomic energy and resources development; after the merger of the UGCCW and the Oil Workers International Union in 1955, creating the Oil, Chemical and Atomic International Union, became administrative vice-president of the new union; was a delegate to the International Labor Organization conference in Geneva in 1953; served as a vice-president of the American Federation of the Physically Handicapped; Melvin Rothbaum, *The Government of the Oil, Chemical and Atomic Workers Union* (1962); Harry Seligson, *Oil, Chemical and Atomic Workers: A Labor Union in Action* (1960); *Who's Who in America, 1960-1961*.

SYLVIS, William H.   Born in Armagh, Indiana County, Pa., November 26, 1828; son of Nicholas, a self-employed wagonmaker, and Maria (Mott) Sylvis; Methodist; married Amelia A. Thomas on April 11, 1852, and after her death in 1865, Florrie Hunter; five children; due to family poverty, received no formal education; apprenticed at age eighteen to a Pennsylvania founder and became a journeyman molder; failed in an effort to set up a foundry, then spent several years as an itinerant molder before finding a permanent job in Philadelphia; during a strike called by a recently established molders' local in 1857, joined the union, soon becoming its secretary; recognizing the need for a national organization to protect molders in an emergent nationwide market and against founders' trade associations, persuaded his union, then the largest of the molders' locals, to propose a national union; elected to issue the call in 1859 that resulted in the founding convention of the Iron-Molders' International Union (IMIU) in 1860; was a Douglas Democrat in 1860; helped recruit a company of molders for the Pennsylvania militia in which he served; was alarmed by the decline of the IMIU during the war and left the militia to revive the union; elected president in early 1863; traveled throughout the country on meager financial resources in 1863, reviving existing locals and forming many new ones; during the next few years made several innovations, including the issuance of union membership cards, the imposition of high dues, and the creation of a centralized administration, which transformed the IMIU into the largest and most effective trade union of the era; opposed in principle to strikes, but deftly managed those which were necessary; was a cofounder of the National Labor Union (NLU) in 1866 and conceived of it as a vehicle for the promotion of producer cooperatives, the eight-hour day, and currency reform to liberate labor from exploitation by the wage system and the "money power"; elected president of the NLU in 1868; combined a commitment to sweeping social reforms with a skill as a practical trade unionist, allowing him to exercise a remarkable influence over the labor movement during his brief career of leadership; was convinced by 1868 that neither major party had labors' interests at heart and hence advocated that the NLU function as a workingmens' party; died on July 27, 1869, in Philadelphia, Pa.; NLU, split by dissension over whether it should become a labor party, declined rapidly after his death; J. C. Sylvis, *The Life, Speeches, Labors, and Essays of William H. Sylvis* (1872); Reed C. Richardson, *Bulletin 31*, New York State School of Industrial and Labor Relations, *Labor Leader 1860's* (1955); Jonathan Grossman, *William Sylvis: Pioneer of American Labor* (1945); Charles A. Madison, *American Labor Leaders: Personalities and Forces in the Labor Movement* (1962); David Montgomery, *Beyond Equality: Labor and the Radical Republicans, 1862-1872* (1967).

(D.G.S.)

TAHNEY, James P.   Born in Chicago, Ill., in 1897; Roman Catholic; married; three children; completed secondary school, then hired by the Chicago and North Western Railroad as an air brake repairman; during 1915-1934, continued to work in the repair shops of the Chicago and North Western and eventually promoted to the position of yard foreman; after the enactment of the National Industrial Recovery Act in 1933, along with a group of like-minded railroad supervisors organized Lodge 1 of the American Railway Supervisors Association (ARSA) in 1934; elected the first president of the ARSA, and, in 1936 retired from railroad when the ARSA presidency was made a full-time, salaried position; although leading a comparatively small, independent, national union with a limited jurisdiction, was able successfully to extend the ARSA's organization to most of the nation's railroads and many of its airlines during his long incumbency, 1934-1970; was an effective negotiator as well as organizer and gained substantial increases in wage scales, improved work rules, and employment security; died in Chicago, Ill., August 26, 1970; *Chicago Tribune*, August 27, 1970; *Labor*, September 5, 1970.

TALBOT, Thomas W.   Born on a South Carolina farm, April 17, 1845; at age ten, went to work in a shoe factory; began a machinist apprenticeship in the North Carolina Railroad machine shops at Florence, S. C., in 1865, and worked as an engineer for the firm until 1874; opened his own machine shop, but later returned to Florence to work in the Wilmington, Columbia, and Augusta Railroad shops; joined the Knights of Labor, and, serving as a master workman and state organizer, organized 11 assemblies; unsuccessfully attempted to organize a machinists' union in Florence; moved to Atlanta, Ga., to work for the Eastern Tennessee, Virginia and Georgia Railroad in 1888 and established the first local union of the future International Association of Machinists; on September 10, 1888, called for the founding of a national Order of United Machinists and Mechanical Engineers of America for the purpose of resisting wage reductions, providing insurance against unemployment, illness, accident, and old age, and to identify craft skill and reputable character; at the first convention of the National Association of Machinists (NAM), held in Atlanta, Ga., in 1889, unanimously elected grand master machinist (national president) and was reelected the following year at Louisville, Ky.; guided NAM in establishing 101 local lodges, of which 41 were in the South, 40 in the Midwest, and 17 in the Far West; the union was originally confined to Southern railroad machinists, but within two years, as it organized job machinists in the North and West, economic issues superseded social ties as the unifying factor; resigning shortly after his reelection in 1890 because of "matters of personal concern;" murdered in Florence, S.C., in February, 1892, by two youths, one of whom he had recently horsewhipped for insulting a member of his family; Mark Perlman, *The Machinists: A New Study in American Trade Unionism* (1961); the Southern Labor Archives, Atlanta, Ga., has the records of Machinists Lodge No. 1.

(J.H.)

TETLOW, Percy.   Born in Leetonia, Ohio, December 16, 1875; son of

William, a miner, and Ann (Hadfield) Tetlow; Methodist; married Sadie M. Carrier on July 3, 1900; three children; completed public grammar school in Leetonia and at age twelve began working in the coal mines at Washingtonville, Ohio; later, during 1900-1901, attended Scranton (Pa.) School of Mines, taking courses in mine engineering; joined the Knights of Labor and was one of the charter members of the United Mine Workers of America (UMWA) in 1890; served as a private in the U.S. Army during the Spanish-American War; elected a subdistrict president, District 6, 1901-1911; served after 1911 at various times as an international representative, president of District 17, West Virginia, and as UMWA statistician; was a member of the Ohio Mine Commission in 1909 and the Constitutional Convention of Ohio in 1912; elected to the Ohio state legislature in 1913; during his service in these capacities, was a champion of mine-safety and workmen's compensation legislation; served with the American Expeditionary Force in France and Belgium during World War I; was the first Director of Industrial Affairs of Ohio, serving during 1921-1922; was a member of the International Mining Congress held in Paris in 1927; served by presidential appointment on the National Bituminous Coal Commission, 1935-1943, and during 1938-1943 chaired the Commission; after World War II, was instrumental in the creation of the UMWA welfare and retirement fund and as a special UMWA staff representative, helped organize and administer the program until his death; was a member of numerous veterans' organizations, becoming a charter member of the American Legion in 1919; was a Republican; died in Columbus, Ohio, November 19, 1960; J. W. Hess, ed., *Struggle in the Coal Fields: The Autobiography of Fred Mooney* (1967); Robert Cairns, *John L. Lewis: Leader of Labor* (1941); *National Cyclopaedia of American Biography* (Vol. L); *Who's Who in Labor* (1946).

THIMMES, James Garrett. Born in Hemlock, Ohio, October 4, 1896; son of Philip, a coal miner, and Cora Belle (Hayden) Thimmes; Protestant; married Thelma Rosalie Runyan on December 2, 1917; five children; was forced by family poverty to leave high school at age fifteen, gaining employment in a pottery; employed subsequently in several steel mills in the Ohio Valley; served with the U. S. Army Infantry overseas during World War I; moved to Chicago, Ill., in 1924 and became president of Lodge 59, Amalgamated Association of Iron, Steel, and Tin Workers (AA); was one of the delegates to the 1936 AA convention who pressured the union leadership into cooperating with the Congress of Industrial Organizations (CIO) in launching the Steel Workers Organizing Committee (SWOC); after two years on the SWOC staff in Chicago, was assigned to organize steelworkers in California; named director of United Steelworkers of America (USWA) District 38, California, in 1940; became president of the California Industrial Union Council, CIO; served during World War II on the California War Manpower Commission and Reemployment Commission; selected by the USWA executive board to serve the unexpired term of Clinton Golden (q.v.) as international vice-president in 1946, thus becoming the first steelworker to serve as an international USWA officer; elected vice-president by membership referendum in 1953; at the 1950 USWA convention, chaired the constitutional committee that recommended that vacancies in international offices be filled by election; was a Democrat; died in Los Angeles, Calif., January 16, 1955; Lloyd Ulman, *The Government of the Steelworkers' Union* (1962); Vincent D. Sweeney, *United Steelworkers of America: Twenty Years Later* (1956); *Who's Who in Labor* (1946).

(D.G.S.)

THOMAS, Norman Mattoon. Born in Marion, Ohio, November 20, 1884; son of Welling Evan, a minister, and Emma (Mattoon) Thomas; Presbyterian; married Frances Violet Stewart on September 1, 1910; five children; attended the public schools of Marion, Ohio, then attended Bucknell College for one year and entered Princeton Theological Seminary; after graduation, worked for two years in New York City's East Side Settlement; became an assistant pastor at Christ Church, New York, in 1910; after extensive world travel, ordained as a Presbyterian clergyman in 1911; in the same year appointed pastor of the East Harlem Church and chairman of the American Parish; joined the Socialist party and resigned his pastorate during World War I, when church elders criticized his outspoken opposition to the war; became secretary of the Fellowship of Reconciliation, an antiwar organization, in 1918 and became editor of its organ, *World Tomorrow*; was one of the founders of the American Civil Liberties Union (originally the National Civil Liberties Bureau); participated in the strike of textile workers at Passaic, N.J., in 1919; became an associate editor of the *Nation* in 1919, and resigned his editorship of *World Tomorrow*; with Harry W. Laidler, helped organize the League for Industrial Democracy; was a long-time participant in the strikes conducted by the Southern Tenant Farmers Union during the 1930s; was a pacifist and opposed American involvement in World War II, often speaking against the war under the auspices of the America First Committee and the Keep America Out of the War Congress; was a candidate on the Socialist party ticket for several New York offices, including governor and state senator, and for mayor of New York City; ran as a Socialist for president of the United States in each election during 1928-1944; was a critic of United States foreign policy following World War II and was especially vocal in his opposition to U. S. involvement in the Vietnam War; authored *The Conscientious Objector in America* (1923), *America's Way Out—A Program for Democracy* (1930), *As I see It* (1932), and several other books and pamphlets; died in New York City, December 19, 1968; Harry Fleischman, *Norman Thomas: A Biography, 1884-1968* (1969); Charles O. Gorham, *Leader at Large: The Long and Fighting Life of Norman Thomas* (1920); Bernard K. Johnpoll, *Pacifist's Progress: Norman Thomas and the Decline of American Socialism* (1970); Murray B. Seidler, *Norman Thomas: Respectable Rebel* (1961); *Current Biography* (1944).

THOMAS, Rolland Jay.   Born in East Palestine, Ohio, June 9, 1900; son of Jacob William, a railroad worker, and Mary Alice (Jackson) Thomas; married Mildred Wettergren on August 7, 1937; one child; graduated from high school in Hubbard, Ohio, then attended Wooster College in Wooster, Ohio, for two years; forced to end his college education because of financial difficulties; took a job in the engineering department of the Bell Telephone Company and then in 1923 became a metal finisher in a Detroit, Mich., Fisher Body plant; became a welder in Detroit Chrysler plant in 1929 and in 1934 joined the American Federation of Labor (AFL) federal labor union that later became Chrysler Local 7 of the United Automobile, Aircraft, Agricultural Implement Workers of America (UAW); elected president of Chrysler Local 7 in 1936 and the following year elected a UAW vice-president; appointed president of the UAW by its executive board in 1939 and a few months later formally elected to the position; served during World War II as a labor member of the National War Labor Board and as a member of the President's Labor Advisory Committee; elected a Congress of Industrial Organizations' (CIO) vice-president and served as secretary-treasurer of the CIO Political Action Committee; defeated for reelection as UAW president by Walter P. Reuther (q.v.) in 1946, but elected first vice-president; defeated for the office of vice-president in 1947, then became the assistant director of organization for the CIO; became an assistant to President George Meany (q.v.) after the 1955 merger of the American Federation of Labor (AFL) and the CIO; appointed an AFL-CIO trouble-shooter in 1963; retired from union activities in 1964 because of ill health; usually supported the Democratic party; died in Muskegon, Mich., April 18, 1967; Jack Stieber, *Governing the UAW* (1962); Jean Gould and

Lorena Hickok, *Walter Reuther: Labor's Rugged Individualist* (1972); Frank Cormier and William J. Eaton, *Reuther* (1970).

TIGHE, Michael F. Born in Boonton, N.J., March 10, 1858; son of a blast furnace worker; Roman Catholic; married Elizabeth Leonhart on August 15, 1879; one child; moved, after his father was blacklisted for union activities, with his family to West Virginia; left school at age ten, when his father's death forced him to seek employment; hired by the Wheeling Iron and Nail Company and eventually became a puddler and a member of the Sons of Vulcan; joined the newly-founded Amalgamated Association of Iron, Steel, and Tin Workers' (AA), Wheeling (W. Va.) Lodge 5 in 1877 and elected its president; was an organizer for AA and the Amalgamated Street Car Workers and was president of the Ohio Valley Trades and Labor Assembly, 1896-1899; was assistant secretary and field organizer for the AA, 1899-1911, a period during which his union was driven out of basic steel; served as secretary, then elected international president in 1918; favored an industrial approach, but was a cautious, conservative business unionist, preoccupied with protecting the interests and jurisdictional claims of the AA; during the great steel strike of 1919, ordered AA members back to work in order to protect existing AA contracts, a policy that caused resentment within the American Federation of Labor (AFL) National Committee for Organizing Iron and Steel Workers; during the 1920s, AA membership dwindled to insignificance; under the impetus of the labor provisions of the National Industrial Recovery Act of 1933, the AA made a comeback in basic steel, spearheaded by a militant rank-and-file faction that challenged his leadership; was able to subdue these insurgents, but could not sustain momentum in organizing; was under internal and external pressures to accommodate himself to an effective organizational strategy and hence faced an acute dilemma; John L. Lewis' (q.v.) proposal that the AA affiliate with the Congress of Industrial Organizations (CIO) in a joint steel-organizing drive was attractive in that Lewis promised to respect the AA's jurisdiction, but Tighe was reluctant to act independently of the AFL executive council in spite of its contempt for his leadership and unwillingness to accord AA broad industrial jurisdiction; was ill and incapable of resolving the impasse and hence authorized the AA executive board to use its own discretion; the board's acceptance of the CIO proposal gave the Steel Workers Organizing Committee (SWOC) the jurisdictional legitimacy it sought for its campaign; was named a member of the SWOC and resigned as AA president in December, 1936 and lived in retirement in Pittsburgh, Pa.; was a Democrat; died in Pittsburgh, Pa., August 5, 1940;

David Brody, *Labor in Crisis: The Steel Strike of 1919* (1965); Irving Bernstein, *Turbulent Years: A History of the American Worker, 1933-1941* (1970); *The Amalgamated Journal*, August 8, 1940.

(D.G.S.)

TOBIN, Daniel Joseph.   Born in County Clare, Ireland, in April, 1875; son of John, a general storekeeper, and Bridget (Kennelly) Tobin; Roman Catholic; married Annie Elizabeth Reagan in August, 1898 and, after her death, Irene Halloran on October 31, 1922; six children; attended the schools of Ireland before emigrating to the United States in 1890; hired by a Boston sheet-metal factory, but continued his education in a Cambridge (Mass.) night school; became a driver and motorman for a Boston street railway company in 1894; became the driver of a delivery truck for a meatpacking firm and joined Local 25 of the International Brotherhood of Teamsters, Chauffeurs, Warehousemen and Helpers of America (IBT), which had been organized in Boston in 1900; elected business representative in 1904; elected the general president of the IBT in 1907, holding position until 1952; served during World War I on President Woodrow T. Wilson's Industrial Conference; elected American Federation of Labor (AFL) treasurer in 1917 and served until 1928; served as a delegate to the International Federal Trade Union Conference in 1919 and as an AFL delegate to the Pan-American Labor Conference in 1920; elected an AFL vice-president and executive council member in 1933, serving until 1952; served as a vice-president of the AFL's building trades department, 1933-1952; served as an American delegate to the International Labor Organization in 1939 and as an AFL fraternal delegate to the British Trades Union Congress in 1911, 1938, and 1942; was an administrative assistant to President Franklin D. Roosevelt in 1940; traveled to England at the request of the President in 1942 to investigate the conditions of labor, capital, and government; was a Democrat and served as chairman of the Labor Division of the Democratic National Committee during the campaigns of 1932, 1936, 1940, and 1944; edited the *Teamsters Magazine*, 1908-1952; retired from union positions in 1952; died in Indianapolis, Ind., November 14, 1955; Sam Romer, *The International Brotherhood of Teamsters: Its Government and Structure* (1962); Robert D. Leiter, *The Teamsters Union: A Study of Its Economic Impact* (1957); *Current Biography* (1945); *National Cyclopaedia of American Biography* (1946).

TOTTEN, Ashley Leopold.   Born in St. Croix, Virgin Islands, October 11, 1884; son of Richard W. and Camilla C. Totten; Lutheran; married

Nellie Violet Victoria on March 20, 1924; two children; Afro-American; graduated from high school in the West Indies, then emigrated to the United States in 1905; eventually hired as a sleeping-car porter with the Pullman Palace Car Company; elected by the New York Central District in 1924 as a delegate to a wage conference called by the officials of Pullman under the auspices of its employee representation plan; in 1925 was one of the principal founders, along with Asa Philip Randolph (q.v.), of the Brotherhood of Sleeping Car Porters (BSCP) and was immediately discharged by Pullman, becoming an assistant organizer for the new union; elected international secretary-treasurer of the BSCP in 1930, serving in that capacity for more than 30 years; was a founder and elected first president of the American Virgin Islands Civic Association in 1932; became the national reporting officer of the Railroad Retirement Board in 1937; during World War II, was a member of the Labor Arbitration Panel of the War Manpower Commission and was chairman of Selective Service Board No. 55; appointed by President John F. Kennedy as a director of the Virgin Island Corporation in 1961; served as an executive board member of the League for Industrial Democracy, the American China Policy Association, and the Welfare Defense League; was a member of the Liberal party of New York; died in St. Croix, Virgin Islands, January 26, 1963; Brailsford R. Brazeal, *The Brotherhood of Sleeping Car Porters: Its Origin and Development* (1946); Jervis Anderson, *A. Philip Randolph: A Biographical Portrait* (1972); Ray Marshall, *The Negro and Organized Labor* (1965); Herbert R. Northrup, *Organized Labor and the Negro* (1944).

TOWNSEND, Robert, Jr. (fl. 1807-1843).   Born on the British prison ship, *Jersey*, during the American Revolution; son of Robert Townsend, Sr., a New York merchant and coffeehouse owner, who, under the alias Samuel Culper, Jr., served as a spy for General George Washington during the American Revolution; his mother died in childbirth, and hence was reared by two prominent Brooklyn ladies; listed as a member of the Tammany Society of New York City in 1807 and as a house carpenter in 1825; became actively involved in the New York Workingmen's party after the 1829 elections; elected president of the Workingmen's state convention in 1830 and two years later chosen vice-president of the Antimasonic state convention; switched political allegiance to the Whig party in 1834 and became an anti-Tammany spokesman; did not participate in the New York house-carpenters' strike of 1834, but joined and became president of the Journeymen House Carpenters of New York City; attended the preliminary meetings and helped organize the New York General Trades'

Union (GTU) and served it as treasurer; offered a resolution during the GTU convention in July, 1832, proposing the issuance of a call for a national trades' union convention; served as a carpenters' delegate to the first convention of the National Trades' Union (NTU) in 1834 and read a controversial resolution favoring political action to bring about social reform; resigned from the NTU in the fall of 1834, thus ending his short-lived formal association with the trade union movement; during the early summer of 1836, actively supported journeyman tailors convicted of conspiracy; became associated with the Locofoco movement in 1836 and presided over the state convention that created the Equal Rights party; refused the new party's nomination for lieutenant governor, but nominated for the New York Assembly by both the Locofocos and the Whigs and elected, serving one term; presided over the second Locofoco state convention in 1837 and again nominated for the Assembly, losing to the Whig candidate in the general elections; appointed city sealer in 1839 and served in that capacity until becoming city weigher of merchandise in 1843; Walter Hugins, *Jacksonian Democracy and the Working Class: A Study of the New York Workingmen's Movement, 1829-1837* (1960); John R. Commons, *et al.*, eds., *A Documentary History of American Industrial Society*, Vol. VI (1910), and *History of Labour in the United States*, Vol. I (1918); Philip S. Foner, *History of the Labor Movement in the United States*, Vol. I (1947).

TOWNSEND, Willard Saxby.   Born in Cincinnati, Ohio, December 4, 1895; son of William, a contractor, and Beatrice (Townsend) Townsend; Episcopalian; Afro-American; married Consuelo Mann on October 1, 1930; one child; graduated from high school in 1912 and somewhat later studied pre-medicine for two years at the University of Toronto; received a degree in chemistry from the Royal College of Science in Toronto and an LLB from Blackstone College of Law in Chicago, Ill.; worked as a redcap at Cincinnati's Union Depot, 1914-1916, and as a dining-car waiter on the Canadian National Railroad, 1921-1925; served as a teacher in Texas, then was a redcap on the Great Northern Railroad, 1930-1936; served during World War I as a first lieutenant in the U. S. Army in France; was a founder of the American Federation of Labor (AFL) Labor Auxiliary of Redcaps in Chicago in 1936 and became its first president; organized an independent Brotherhood of Redcaps in Chicago in 1938 and, when the organization was given an international charter by the Congress of Industrial Organizations (CIO) in 1942 as the United Transport Service Employees of America, elected its president; became a member of the CIO executive board in 1942; elected a vice-president of the National Urban League in 1940; was a member of the board of directors and executive committee of the American Council on Race Relations in 1944; served on the CIO committees on Latin American affairs and housing and community development and on the committee to abolish discrimination; served as a CIO fraternal delegate to the Cuban Federation of Labor in 1944; was a labor advisor to the International Labor Organization conference in Mexico City in 1946; served as a member of the committee of the World Federation of Trade Unions to study conditions in Japan, China, Korea, the Philippines, and the Malayan states in 1947; was a CIO delegate to the International Confederation of Free Trade Unions in 1952; elected a vice-president and executive council member of the AFL-CIO at the merger convention in 1955; was a vice-president of the National Association for the Advancement of Colored People, a trustee of Hampton Institute, and a director of the American Labor Education Service, also serving on numerous other public and private boards and agencies; coauthored *What the Negro Wants* (1944) and authored *Full Employment and the Negro Workers* (1945), *Japanese Handbook: Trade Union Practices* (1948); died in Chicago, Ill., February 3, 1957; *The American Federationist* (March, 1957); *Current Biography* (1948); *AFL-CIO News*, February 9, 1957; *Who's Who in Labor* (1946).

TRACY, Daniel William.   Born in Bloomington, Ill., April 7, 1886; married; completed his formal education and eventually moved to Houston, Tex., in 1910; adopted the electrician's trade; joined Local 716 of the International Brotherhood of Electrical Workers (IBEW) in 1913; worked as a lineman and wireman in Texas and Oklahoma, 1913-1915; elected business manager of IBEW Locals 716 and 66 in 1916; became an IBEW international vice-president in 1920; appointed international president of the IBEW in 1933 and later elected to the position; was a U.S. delegate to the International Labor Organization (ILO) conference in Geneva in 1935 and served as a labor advisor to Secretary of State Cordell Hull during the Pan-American Conference in Lima, Peru, in 1938; was a staunch critic of the Committee of Industrial Organizations (CIO) and strongly supported the suspension of the CIO unions by the American Federation of Labor (AFL) executive council in 1936; resigned as IBEW president in 1940 after being appointed Assistant Secretary of Labor, serving in that capacity until 1946; served as labor director of the ILO during 1946; became IBEW international president for the second time in 1947; during the same year, elected an AFL vice-president and executive council member and also a vice-president of the AFL metal trades department; served as an AFL delegate to the AFL-CIO United Labor Policy Committee in 1950; became

IBEW president emeritus in 1954; was a Democrat; died in Washington, D. C., March 22, 1955; Philip Taft, *The A. F. of L. From the Death of Gompers to the Merger* (1959); Walter Galenson, *The CIO Challenge to the AFL: A History of the American Labor Movement, 1935-1941* (1960); *The American Federationist* (September, 1955); *The American Federation of Labor News-Reporter*, March 25, 1955.

TRAUTMANN, William E. (fl. 1900-1917).   Born in New Zealand of German-American parents in 1869; became a radical unionist while living in Germany; emigrated to the United States in the late 1890s; and settled in Ohio; became an organizer for the Brewery Workers Union (BWU); in 1900, elected to BWU's executive board and became editor of its journal, *Brauer-Zeitung*; was a well-versed Marxist and began advocating syndicalism; meanwhile, joined the Socialist Party of America and was a national committeeman from Ohio; when the BWU clashed with the American Federation of Labor (AFL) over a jurisdictional matter in 1902, made a scathing attack on the AFL leaders, accusing them of dividing the workers and selling out to the capitalists; took the initiative in calling the secret conference of radicals that laid the groundwork for the founding of the Industrial Workers of the World (IWW) in 1905 and was influential in formulating its Industrial Union Manifesto; relieved of his posts with the BWU as a result of these activities; as general secretary-treasurer of the IWW and a member of its first general executive board, headed the faction that opposed political action; in 1906, joined with Daniel DeLeon (q.v.) to depose IWW president Charles Sherman (q.v.), which caused a split resulting in the withdrawal of the Western Federation of Miners; with Vincent St. John (q.v.), took advantage of the direct-actionists' control of the 1908 convention to oust DeLeon from the IWW and to eliminate the political clause from the constitution; was an effective polemicist and organizer, but was an indifferent administrator; in 1908, replaced by St. John as secretary-treasurer; elected as a general organizer; in 1909, led the McKees Rocks, Pa., steel strike, the IWW's first successful effort among Eastern United States immigrant workers; was aware of their plight and convinced they could be organized, and enlisted several thousand in an IWW local at McKees Rocks; called an IWW convention of the Pittsburgh district to unionize throughout the district, but his efforts failed to create permanent steelworkers' unions; subsequently tried to establish the IWW among Akron, Ohio, tire and Detroit, Mich., automobile workers, and helped direct the great Lawrence, Mass., textile strike; became disillusioned with the IWW's preoccupation with direct action and joined

Daniel DeLeon's Detroit IWW, an adjunct of the Socialist Labor party, in 1913; during World War I, became involved in the Works Council Movement; Melvyn Dubofsky, *We Shall Be All: A History of the Industrial Workers of the World* (1969); Philip S. Foner, *History of the Labor Movement in the United States*, Vol. IV (1965); Patrick Renshaw, *The Wobblies* (1967).

(D.G.S.)

TRAVIS, Maurice Eugene.   Born in Spokane, Wash., April 24, 1910; son of Charles Franklin, a salesman, and Lotus Clark; married Ursula Vinca Dexter; one child; during the 1930s and 1940s, was a business agent for a United Steelworkers of America (USWA) local in California and a member of the California State Industrial Union Council, Congress of Industrial Organizations (CIO); was purged from the USWA in 1944 and became an international representative for the International Union of Mine, Mill and Smelter Workers (IUMMSW); appointed executive assistant to the IUMMSW president, Reid Robinson (q.v.), in 1946; chosen vice-president in the 1946 election that brought the dissension between the left- and right-wing factions to a head, resulting in the secession of a large faction of Connecticut brass workers; was a member of the Communist party and with other IUMMSW officials allegedly coordinated union policies with top members of the Communist party; became international president of the IUMMSW after Robinson's resignation in 1946; urged to resign or be removed from the presidency by a CIO special committee set up to investigate the disputed 1946 election; at a special IUMMSW convention in 1947, resigned as president, nominating John Clark (q.v.); became secretary-treasurer as part of the arrangement leading to his resignation from the IUMMSW presidency; along with Clark, consolidated the left-wing control of the IUMMSW, thus off-setting the secessionist movement; helped defend the IUMMSW against the CIO's accusation of Communist domination, thus paving the way for the expulsion of the union in 1950; taking advantage of charges that he and others had run roughshod over the rank-and-file, the USWA tried unsuccessfully to capture the crucial Butte, Mont., and Anaconda, Mont., IUMMSW locals in 1954; in 1949 publicly resigned his Communist party membership, because the IUMMSW needed to avail itself of National Labor Relations Board procedures to fend off raiding; in 1956, however, indicted along with 13 other IUMMSW leaders for conspiring to falsify the non-Communist affidavits of the Taft-Hartley Act; the case, which involved two trials and several appeals, was dismissed in 1967 by a U.S. district court; left his union post in the late

1950s and lived in retirement in California; Vernon H. Jensen, *Nonferrous Metals Industry Unionism, 1932-1954* (1954); F. S. O'Brien, "Communist-Dominated Unions in the U. S. since 1950," *Labor History* (Spring, 1968); *Who's Who in Labor* (1946).

(D.G.S.)

TRAVIS, Robert Carroll.   Born in Toledo, Ohio, February 7, 1906; son of Fred F. and Esther L. Travis; Lutheran; married Sophie Beaudel on July 24, 1940; one child; graduated from high school, then took a job in a General Motors Corporation (GMC) Chevrolet plant in Toledo; was one of the founders of United Automobile, Aircraft, Agricultural Implement Workers of America (UAW) Local 14 in Toledo in 1935 and shortly therafter elected president of the local; became president of the UAW GMC Council in 1936; was director of organization for the UAW in Flint, Mich., in 1936 and led the successful sit-down strikes against GMC in 1936-1937 that helped the UAW organize the automobile industry; became an international representative of the United Farm Equipment and Metal Workers of America (FE) in 1939 and was one of the leaders of FE's strike against the International Harvester Company in Chicago, Ill., in 1941; during the early 1940s, rejoined the UAW in Illinois, affiliating with the allegedly Communist-controlled Amalgamated Local 453; served as a member of the labor advisory council of the Metropolitan Chicago division of the Office of Price Administration and a member of the Regional Labor Panel of the War Labor Board during World War II; elected president of the Cook County State Industrial Union Council, Congress of Industrial Organizations (CIO), and a vice-president of the Illinois CIO Council, serving until 1947; was a member of the policy committee of the Illinois CIO Political Action Committee; often associated with radical causes; was a member of the Board of Directors of Abraham Lincoln School, a writer for the *Chicago Star*, and a sponsor of the American Peace Mobilization; edited the *Legislative Guide*, the organ of the legislative committee of the Illinois State Industrial Union Council, CIO; identified himself as a Democrat; Sidney Fine, *Sit-Down: The General Motors Strike of 1936-1937* (1969); Frank Cormier and William J. Eaton, *Reuther* (1970); Max M. Kampelman, *The Communist Party vs. The C.I.O.: A Study in Power Politics* (1957).

TREVELLICK, Richard F.   Born on St. Mary's, one of the Scilly Isles off the coast of England, May 20, 1830 (Birthdate has also been listed as May 2, 1830.); son of peasant farmers of Cornwall; Methodist; married Victoria in 1858; five children; as a young man, worked as a ship's carpenter and as a seaman in Southampton, England; acquired a reputation as a labor agitator while advocating an eight-hour day in Auckland, New Zealand, and Melbourne, Australia, during 1852-1854; arrived in New Orleans, La., in 1857 and shortly thereafter became president of the Ship Carpenters' and Caulkers' Union and led a successful effort to win a nine-hour day; moved to Detroit, Mich., in 1861 and became the first president of the Detroit Trades' Assembly and the Michigan Grand Eight Hours League; national Union of Ship Carpenters and Caulkers in 1865; attended the Congress of the National Labor Union (NLU) in 1867 as a delegate from the Detroit Trades' Assembly and the Michigan Grand EightHours League; elected a NLU delegate to the International Workingmen's Association in 1867 but was unable to attend because of financial difficulties; served as president of the NLU in 1869 and during 1871-1872; served as an organizer and lecturer for the Knights of Labor, 1878-1895; besides his life-long agitation for eight-hour legislation, fought the blacklist, the importation of Chinese contract labor, and the racial-exclusion clauses contained in many trade-union charters; was one of the first labor lobbyists and successfully lobbied an eight-hour day act for federal mechanics and laborers through the U.S. Congress in 1868; was a founder of the Greenback Labor party, serving as temporary chairman of the national Greenback Labor party in 1878 and as chairman in 1880; died in Detroit, Mich., February 15, 1895; Obediah Hicks, *Life of Richard F. Trevellick, The Labor Orator* (1896); David Montgomery, *Beyond Equality: Labor and the Radical Republicans, 1862-1872* (1967); Doris B. McLaughlin, *Michigan Labor* (1970); *Dictionary of American Biography* (Vol. XVIII).

TROUP, Augusta Lewis. Born in New York City, ca. 1848; daughter of Charles and Elizabeth (Rowe) Lewis; Roman Catholic; married Alexander Troupe on June 12, 1874 (Date of marriage has also been listed as June 12, 1872.); seven children; attended Brooklyn Heights Seminary and Sacred Heart Convent School in Manhattanville, N.Y.; became a reporter for the New York *Sun* in 1866; served an apprenticeship as a typesetter on the *New York Era* and shortly thereafter joined the *New York World* as a typesetter; was one of the participants in the initial meeting of the Working Women's Association founded by Elizabeth Cady Stanton and Susan B. Anthony in 1868; later in the same year, became the first president of the Women's Typographical Union (WTU), which evolved from the Working Women's Association; after the WTU was recognized and granted a charter by the International Typographical Union (ITU) in 1869, attended the ITU's 1870 national convention and elected corresponding secretary; after marrying, left the WTU which, torn by dissension and discord because of the failure to win wage rates comparable to those obtained by men, eventually disbanded in 1878; moved to New Haven, Conn., in 1874 and became a reporter for her husband's newspaper, the *New Haven Union*; died in New Haven, Conn., September 14, 1920; George A. Stevens, *New York Typographical Union No. 6: Study of a Modern Trade Union and Its Predecessors* (1913); George A. Tracy, *History of the Typographical Union* (1913); *Notable American Women* (1971); Eleanor Flexner, *Century of Struggle* (1959).

(M.T.)

TURNER, Frederick. Born in England in 1846; emigrated to the United States in 1856, settling in Philadelphia, Pa.; completed public high school in Philadelphia; practiced the gold-beating trade and joined the Noble Order of the Knights of Labor (K of L); organized Local Assembly 20, consisting of gold-beaters, in 1873; shortly thereafter, organized the first K of L assembly in New York, Local Assembly 28, and, along with James L. Wright (q.v.), the first local in Scranton, Pa., Local Assembly 88, in 1875; served as secretary of District Assembly No. 1, general secretary-treasurer of the K of L, and two terms on the K of L general executive board; was a member of the "Home Club", an inner-ring that controlled New York District Assembly No. 49 and opposed many of Grand Master Workman Terence V. Powderly's (q.v.) policies; lobbied the U.S. Congress in support of the Foran bill to restrict contract labor in 1884; because of his activities in the K of L during the 1870s and 1880s, blacklisted in his trade; became an independent grocer; Norman J. Ware, *The Labor Movement in the United States, 1860-1895* (1929); Gerald N. Grob, *Workers and Utopia: A Study of Ideological Conflict in the American Labor Movement, 1865-1900* (1961); *Journal of United Labor*, Vol. IV (July, 1883).

VALENTINE, Joseph F. Born in Baltimore, Md., May 13, 1857; Roman Catholic; married; no children; became an apprentice molder at an early age, and went to San Francisco, Calif., as a journeyman in 1880; immediately joined the International Molders Union (IMU) and elected president of his local within a few months; in 1885, helped found a city central council of metal craftsmen, the first such body formed in the United States; emerged as an exceptionally capable leader in handling the bitter San Francisco molders' strike of 1890; as a result, elected first vice-president by the IMU convention of 1890; was responsible for administering the pioneering conciliation agreements of 1891 with the Stove Founders Trade Association and of 1899 with the National Founders' Association; although the latter broke down in 1904, the IMU under his guidance sustained its trade interests; became president of the IMU after the resignation of Martin Fox (q.v.) in 1903; elected a vice-president and executive council member of the American Federation of Labor in 1905 and a vice-president of the metal trades department, reorganizing it on a sounder basis in 1908; as IMU president, maintained the established policy of not opposing the introduction of labor-saving technology; was a militant craft unionist and consistently tried to avoid strikes; however, staunchly supported strikes when vital union interests were at stake; acquired a reputation for firm but fair dealings with unionists and employers; during his term, the IMU executive board tightened up its policy of prohibiting unauthorized strikes; supported the California unions' anti-Chinese agitation, but later succeeded in pressuring several Southern locals to admit black molders; under the strain of interminable years of service to the labor movement, forced to resign union positions in 1924 because of ill health; died in San Francisco, Calif., February 7, 1930; Frank T. Stockton, *The International Molders Union* (1921); Philip Taft, *Organized Labor in American History* (1964); Robert E. L. Knight, *Industrial Relations in the San Francisco Bay Area* (1960).

(D.G.S.)

VAN ARSDALE, Harry, Jr.   Born in New York City, November 23, 1905; son of a union electrician; Roman Catholic; married Mary (Molly) Casey in 1922; four children; attended an experimental high school for gifted children for two years before quitting school to take a job; worked in a variety of occupations, then, like his father, adopted the electrician's trade and joined New York City Local 3 of the International Brotherhood of Electrical Workers (IBEW); served in several minor positions in the union, then became embroiled in the efforts to frustrate the attempts of both Communists and racketeers to gain control of Local 3; as a result of the ensuing conflicts, arrested on an assault charge in 1932, but released; the following year, again charged and convicted of assault and sentenced to six to twelve years in prison; however, the conviction was reversed on appeal; became business manager of Local 3 in 1933 and held that position until 1968, when succeeded by his son; became the financial secretary of Local 3 in 1968; negotiated a seven-hour day for the members of Local 3 in 1933; in 1940 the work day was reduced to six hours and in 1962 to five hours; elected president of the Greater New York Central Trades and Labor Council in 1957 and two years later, after the American Federation of

Labor-Congress of Industrial Organizations' (AFL-CIO) merger in New York City, became president of the New York City Central Labor Council, AFL-CIO; helped organize New York City taxi drivers in 1965 and later became president of Local 3036 of the New York City Taxi Drivers Union; served as international treasurer of the IBEW and was a member of the executive board of the Building and Construction Trades Council; besides serving on numerous federal, state, and local government boards and agencies, was a director of the Lincoln Center for Performing Arts, a trustee of the Carnegie Hall Corporation, and a trustee of the National Urban League; a Democrat; *Reader's Digest* (January, 1956); *The New Yorker*, March 16, 1968; *Current Biography* (1969).

VLADECK, Baruch Charney (Baruch Nachman Charney).   Born in Dookorah, Minsk, Russia, in January, 1886; son of Wolf, a merchant, and Broche (Horowitz) Charney; Jewish; married Clara Richman in 1911; three children; received a few years of formal education in a Russian yeshivah; prior to emigrating to the United States in 1908, was active in the revolutionary movement in Russia and in 1901 was imprisoned the first of several times as an agitator; after arriving in the United States, spent four years traveling, lecturing, and studying; became the manager of the Philadelphia office of *Jewish Daily Forward* in 1912; studied the English language and American history at the University of Pennsylvania; moved to New York City in 1915 and two years later elected to the New York City Board of Aldermen on the Socialist party ticket, serving until 1921; was a moderate in the internal conflicts of the Socialist movement and usually supported the party's right wing when forced to make a choice; became the general manager of the *Jewish Daily Forward* in 1921 and served in that capacity until his death; appointed by Mayor Fiorello LaGuardia to the New York Housing Authority in 1934; was one of the original sponsors of the American Labor party (ALP) in 1936 and elected to the New York City Council on the ALP ticket in 1937; served as chairman of the Jewish Labor Committee, 1934-1938, was a director of the Hias during 1916-1938 and was a member of the executive committee of the American Civil Liberties Union; died in New York City, October 30, 1938; Melech Epstein, *Jewish Labor in the U.S.A., 1914-1952* (2 vols., 1953); Solon DeLeon, ed., *The American Labor Who's Who* (1925); *Dictionary of American Biography* (Supplement II); *American Jewish Year Book* (Vol. 41); *Universal Jewish Encyclopedia* (Vol. X).

VORSE, Mary Heaton.   Born in New York City, ca. 1882; daughter of

Hiram and Ellen Cordelia (Blackman) Heaton; married Albert White Vorse, a writer, in October, 1898, and after his death, Joseph O'Brien, a newspaper correspondent, in 1912, and after his death, Robert Minor, a radical artist and writer, in 1920; raised in Amherst, Mass., but educated in Europe; after completing her education, employed as a reporter for various magazines and served as World War I correspondent; after 1912 focused most of her writing on labor-union activities, but covered the famine in the Soviet Union for the Hearst newspapers in 1921-1922 and Hitler's rise to power in 1933; was often involved in labor strikes and took part in the 1926 Passaic, N.J., textile strike and the 1929 Gastonia, N.C., National Textile Union strike; as a result of those experiences, wrote two novels, *Passaic* (1926) and *Strike—A Novel of Gastonia* (1930); held several governmental positions throughout her career, including publicity positions during World War I and service in the Department of Interior's Bureau of Indian Affairs; most notable among her numerous labor writings are *Men and Steel* (1921) and *Labor's New Millions* (1938), the latter detailing the rise of the Congress of Industrial Organizations; also wrote *A Footnote to Folly: Reminiscenses of Mary Heaton Vorse* (1935); died in Provincetown, Mass., June 14, 1966; *Who Was Who in America* (Vol. IV); *Twentieth-Century Authors* (1942); *AFL-CIO News*, June 25, 1966.

(M.T.)

WALKER, John Hunter.   Born in Binny Hill, Stirlingshire, Scotland, April 27, 1872; married; one child; emigrated to Braidwood, Ill., with his parents in 1881; at age nine, began working in a coal mine at Coal City, Ill., and two years later enrolled in the Knights of Labor; subsequently joined the Miners' Federation, the Mine Laborers, and the United Mine Workers of America (UMWA); organized UMWA Local 505 at Central City, Ill., in 1896; assigned to work with John Mitchell (q.v.) and Mother Jones (q.v.) in organizing miners of southern Illinois and West Virginia in 1897; served as a member of the executive board, vice-president, and during 1905-1913 and 1930-1933 president of District 12, UMWA, Illinois; as district president, played a leading role in obtaining the Miners' Qualification Law and the Shot Firers' Law; also worked for a workmen's compensation law and was largely responsible for affiliating the Illinois miners with the State Federation of Labor in 1908, which, by 1911, became the nation's largest state federation; served as president of the Illinois State Federation of Labor from 1913 until 1930, when the American Federation of Labor (AFL) executive council demanded his resignation for participating in the Reorganized United Mine Workers; was an active, but moderate, member of the Socialist party in his early years and defended John Mitchell (q.v.) from Socialist attack for his membership in the National Civic Federation; supported U.S. entry into World War I and participated in the conference of the American Alliance for Labor and Democracy in 1917, which endorsed the war; participated in the founding of the National Farmer-Labor party at Chicago, Ill., in November, 1919, and elected vice-chairman; chosen national chairman in 1920 and ran unsuccessfully for governor of Illinois on the National Farmer-Labor ticket; was a consistent defender of district autonomy within the UMWA and nearly defeated Thomas Lewis (q.v.) for the international presidency in 1909; ran unsuccessfully against John White (q.v.) and Frank Hayes (q.v.) for the UMWA presidency in 1916 and 1918; along with Frank Farrington (q.v.), also a member of the international executive board, opposed confirmation of John L. Lewis (q.v.) as international vice-president; charging that Lewis had suspended the union constitution by neglecting to convene a national convention, in 1930 called, along with other opponents of Lewis, the Springfield convention to reorganize the UMWA; was designated to be president of the Reorganized UMWA, but Oscar Ameringer managed the election of Alexander Howat (q.v.) as president and Walker as secretary-treasurer; as a result of the Springfield convention and the attempted reorganization of the UMWA, forced to resign as president of the state federation by the AFL executive council; succeeded Harry Fishwick as president of District 12, UMWA in 1930; after a three-month strike in 1932, forced to sign an Illinois agreement reducing daily wages from $6.10 to $5.00, which the rank-and-file rejected four to one; at that point, the international president, John L. Lewis, took over the negotiations, signed the same agreement, destroyed the referendum ballots, and announced it ratified; in February, 1933, Lewis destroyed district autonomy in the last important bituminous district by assuming the district debt, appointing a provisional government, and naming William Sneed to replace Walker as district president; retired from active union work in 1945; died in Denver, Colo., August 28, 1955; *The New York Times*, August 29, 1955; Eugene Staley, *History of the Illinois State Federation of Labor* (1930); Irving Bernstein, *The Lean Years: A History of the American Worker, 1920-1933* (1960); John H. M. Laslett, *Labor and the Left: A Study of Socialism and Radical Influences in the American Labor Movement, 1881-1924* (1970).

(J.H.)

WALSH, Richard Francis.   Born in Brooklyn, N.Y., February 20, 1900; son of William and Catherine (O'Toole) Walsh; Roman Catholic;

attended public school in Brooklyn, then became an apprentice electrician in the Fifth Avenue Theater, Brooklyn, in 1917 and joined Local 4 of the International Alliance of Theatrical Stage Employees and Moving Picture Operators of the United States and Canada (IATSE); served as an electrician in the Metropolitan Theater, 1923-1936; elected president of the IATSE Local 4 in 1924 and served until 1926, when elected business agent, serving in that capacity until 1937; became an IATSE international vice-president in 1934; again elected president of Local 4 in 1939 and elected international president of the IATSE in 1941; served as the American Federation of Labor (AFL) fraternal delegate to the Trades and Labor Congress of Canada in 1948 and the British Trades Union Congress in 1952; became an AFL-Congress of Industrial Organizations vice-president and executive council member in 1955; served as a director of the Union Labor Life Insurance Company; a Democrat; Murray Ross, *Stars and Strikes: Unionization of Hollywood* (1941); *Who's Who In America, 1971-1972*; *Who's Who in Labor* (1946).

WATT, Robert J.   Born in Scotland, July 16, 1894; son of Alexander, a garment worker, and Helen (Robertson) Watt; Roman Catholic; married Janet Learmonth on April 28, 1917; two children; attended grammar school for six years, then served a four-year apprenticeship in the painting, paper hanging, and house decorating trade; emigrated to the United States in 1912 and took employment in a Lawrence, Mass., paper mill while continuing his education in night schools; became involved in trade union activities in 1914; served during World War I as a private with the Canadian Army in France, 1917-1919; resumed trade-union activities after the war and in 1925 elected president of the Lawrence Central Labor Union, serving until 1930; served as a vice-president of the Massachusetts State Federation of Labor (MSFL), 1926-1929; was secretary-treasurer of the MSFL, 1930-1938; was the permanent American Federation of Labor (AFL) delegate to the International Labor Organization, 1936-1947; appointed to the Massachusetts Unemployment Commission in 1936 and served for two years; appointed a labor member of the commission created by President Franklin D. Roosevelt in 1938 to study labor conditions in Great Britain and Sweden; appointed a labor member of the National Defense Mediation Board in 1942 and an alternate labor member of the National War Labor Board; was a committed anti-Communist and devoted much of his energy to the task of keeping the Soviet Union out of international labor federations with which the AFL was affiliated; was an independent in politics; died aboard the liner *Saturnia* enroute to New York City,

July 23, 1947; Philip Taft, *The A. F. of L. From the Death of Gompers to the Merger* (1959); *Current Biography* (1945); *The American Federationist* (August, 1947).

WEAVER, George Leon Paul.   Born in Pittsburgh, Pa., May 18, 1912; son of George J., a maintenance worker, and Josephine (Snell) Weaver; married Mary Frances on September 7, 1941; Afro-American; graduated from high school, then attended Roosevelt University in Chicago (then YMCA College), Columbia University, and the Howard University Law School; joined the United Transport Service Employees (UTSE) in 1940; served as chairman of the grievance committee and was a member of the executive board of UTSE Local 603; became assistant to the international president of the UTSE and a member of the general executive board in 1942; appointed director of the Congress of Industrial Organizations' (CIO) committee to abolish discrimination in 1942; appointed assistant secretary-treasurer of the CIO in 1945; named special assistant to the chairman of the National Security Resources Board in 1950; after the American Federation of Labor (AFL)-CIO merger in 1955, appointed executive secretary of the AFL-CIO civil rights committee; was a delegate to the 1957 and 1958 conferences of the International Labor Organization (ILO); served as an assistant to the President of the International Union of Electrical, Radio and Machine Workers, 1958-1961; appointed assistant secretary of labor for international affairs by President John F. Kennedy in 1961 and became the permanent United States representative to the ILO and chairman of the United States delegation; elected chairman of the ILO board of governors in 1968; appointed special assistant to Director General David A. Morse of the ILO in 1969; a Democrat; *Fortune* (February, 1951); *AFL-CIO News*, October 21, 1961, October 4, 1969; *Who's Who in Colored America* (1950); *Who's Who in Labor* (1946).

WEBER, Frank Joseph.   Born in Milwaukee, Wis., August 7, 1849; son of Joseph, a German-American coal miner, and Marie Engel (Niemeyer) Weber; married Augusta Streich on December 27, 1877; three children; educated in the Milwaukee, Wis., public schools; during the 1860s and 1870s, employed as an able seaman, teacher, and ship's carpenter; joined a seaman's union in 1868 and, within a few years of its founding, the Knights of Labor in 1869; helped organize several different trade union locals in Milwaukee and in 1887 helped found the Federated Trades Council (FTC); was instrumental in the founding of the Wisconsin State Federation of Labor in 1893 and, having declined to run for president, served it as a general organizer until 1917; during the 1890s, was an American Federation of Labor (AFL) organizer in West Virginia and in the Gulf ports; served as secretary of the Milwaukee FTC during 1902-1934 (upon his motion the office of president had been abolished in 1893); was a leading unionist and a Socialist and had a key role in creating the working coalition of the Milwaukee FTC and the Social Democratic party; elected to the state assembly five times between 1907 and 1925; worked with progressive reformers, including John R. Commons, to secure enactment of workmen's compensation and other labor legislation; also promoted vocational schools; rejected the antiwar policy of Victor Berger (q.v.) and helped swing the Milwaukee FTC to support the AFL's prowar American Alliance for Labor and Democracy in 1918; served during World War I on the Waukesha County Council of Defense; in spite of his membership in the Socialist party, was a conservative trade unionist in several respects; during the 1920s, deplored the lethargy within the labor movement; widely respected as the "grand old man" of the Wisconsin labor movement; retired in 1934; died in Milwaukee, Wis., February 4, 1943; *National Cyclopaedia of American Biography* (1950); Edwin E. Witte, "Labor in Wisconsin," *Wisconsin Magazine of History* (Winter, 1951); Thomas W. Gavett, *Development of the Labor Movement in Milwaukee* (1965).

(D.G.S.)

WEBER, Joseph N. Born in Neu Beschenowa, Hungary, June 21, 1866; son of Joseph and Katharine (Wasmer) Weber; married Gisela Liebhodt on September 22, 1891; after a few years of formal education in Hungarian normal schools and gymnasiums, toured the United States at age fourteen as a clarinetist in a boy's band; stayed in the United States at the end of the tour and secured employment as a clarinetist at the Tabor Opera House in Denver, Colo.; was one of the organizers of the Denver Musical Union and served the organization as president and secretary; later served as vice-president of the Portland (Ore.) Musical Union and as president of the Cincinnati (Ohio) Musical Union; participated in the organization of the American Federation of Musicians (AFM) in 1896 and in 1900 elected its president; elected an American Federation of Labor vice-president and executive council member in 1930, serving in that capacity until his death; was credited with building the AFM from a weak trade union with 6,000 members into a mature collective-bargaining organization with a membership in excess of 170,000; retired as AFM president in 1940 due to poor health and was named president emeritus; died in New York City, December 12, 1950; Robert D. Leiter, *The Musicians and*

Petrillo (1953); *The American Federationist* (July, 1940 and January, 1951); Solon DeLeon, ed., *The American Labor Who's Who* (1925); *Who's Who in America, 1938-1939.*

WEIHE, William. Born in Baldwin, Pa., January 21, 1845; married Philopena Ohlinger; two children; after his family moved to Pittsburgh, Pa., went to work in an iron mill at age fifteen; later, as a "boiler" on a puddling furnace, joined the union of his trade, the Sons of Vulcan, and served as an officer of his local; when the Sons of Vulcan joined with several other unions to form the Amalgamated Association of Iron and Steel Workers (AA) in 1876, became a member of its executive committee; elected a trustee of AA in 1879; became president of AA in 1884 when John Jarrett (q.v.) resigned; was conservative like most AA leaders, but tried to adjust his union to the mechanization in the emergent steel industry; as president, helped AA substantially increase its membership so that it became one of the American Federation of Labor's (AFL) largest affiliates; also was instrumental during his presidency in substituting the eight-hour day for the twelve-hour day in sheet mills; attempted to expand the base of the AA, which was concentrated in the old iron mills, and it established several lodges in the Homestead Works of the Carnegie Steel Company; unsuccessfully sought to compromise the issue when the Homestead manager, H. C. Frick, reduced the tonnage scales of the skilled in 1892; the ensuing strike, famous for its dramatic violence, not only destroyed the AA locals at Homestead but marked the beginning of a general AA decline; defended craft interests against the expanding Knights of Labor in the spring of 1886 and later in that year was one of the trade unionists who issued the call for the founding convention of the AFL; resigned as AA president in 1892, but remained active in trade-union affairs; helped organize western Pennsylvania for the United Mine Workers during its strike of 1897; elected to the Pennsylvania state legislature as a Democrat in 1882, but later became a Republican; was deputy immigration inspector and a member of the board of inquiry at Ellis Island from 1896 until his death; died in Pittsburgh, Pa., August 24, 1908; John A. Fitch, *The Steel Workers* (1911); Philip Taft, *The A. F. of L. in the Time of Gompers* (1957); *National Labor Tribune*, August 27, 1908.

(D.G.S.)

WERKAU, Carlton William. Born in Clifton, Ill., September 25, 1907; son of William, a merchant, and Jeannette Cecilia Werkau; Methodist; married Viola Cecelia Litkey on January 4, 1930; completed two years of high school, then left school to work full time; joined the Illinois Union of Telephone Workers in 1926, and, for a time, served as its president; joined the Communications Workers of America (CWA) (Then the National Federation of Telephone Workers) in 1939, and, after having served as acting secretary for several months, elected international secretary-treasurer in 1943; joined the Indiana Union of Telephone Workers in 1942; served as a trustee for the village of Bedford Park, Ill., 1941-1947; credited with transforming the CWA into an efficient, business-like organization, establishing the economic policies and practices that insured its financial solvency and stability; a Democrat; Jack Barbash, *Unions and Telephones: The Story of the Communications Workers of America* (1952); *Who's Who in Labor* (1946).

WHARTON, Arthur O.   Born on November 9, 1873; during the 1880s, served a machinist apprenticeship in the Santa Fe Railroad shops and eventually joined the International Association of Machinists (IAM); served as general chairman of District 5, Missouri Pacific Railroad, in 1903; during the early 1900s, was secretary of the IAM's Southwestern section; after signing a satisfactory joint agreement with 26 Southwestern railroads in 1910, led a successful ten-month strike against the Missouri Pacific and one or two other railroads that refused to sign the agreement; in 1911, elected president of the Federation of Federations, a combination of shop-craft unions that dominated the American Federation of Labor's (AFL) railroad employees' department; during 1918-1920, was labor advisor to the Lane Commission that dealt with railroad employees' wages and to its successor, the Railroad Administration's Board of Wages and Working Conditions, which formulated and administered wage and working condition standards for all classes of railroad employees; in 1920, appointed labor advisor to the U. S. Railroad Labor Board; upon William H. Johnston's (q.v.) resignation in 1926, appointed international president as a compromise between conflicting IAM factions; elected to the position in 1927 and served continuously until 1939; as a vice-president and executive council member of the AFL, led the campaign in the executive council to withhold AFL affiliates' support from Brookwood Labor College, believing it had fallen under Communist domination; was a moderate conservative and led a reaction to the progressive policies of Johnston and called on the membership to be less visionary and concentrate its efforts on securing immediate material benefits; reorganized and consolidated the IAM's strength in the 1920s and 1930s, while its membership declined; was an adamant foe of industrial unionism and became the AFL's "archpriest of craft exclusivism"; despite his dislike for industrial organization and the Congress of Industrial Organizations, realized that the IAM would have to expand its concept of organizing or lose its jurisdiction in the airframe industry; forced into semiretirement in Tucson, Ariz., in 1936 by acute bronchial asthma; formally resigned in 1939; died in Tucson, Ariz., December 21, 1944; *Machinists' Monthly Journal* (February, 1945); Mark Perlman, *The Machinists: A New Study in American Trade Unionism* (1961), and *Democracy in the International Association of Machinists* (1962); John H. M. Laslett, *Labor and the Left: A Study of Socialism and Radical Influences in the American Labor Movement, 1881-1924* (1970).

(J.H.)

WHITE, John P.   Born in Coal Valley, Ill., February 28, 1870; Roman Catholic; worked as a coal miner in Coal Valley; moved with his family to Iowa, working there in the coal mines; joined the United Mine Workers of America (UMWA); served UMWA District 13 as secretary-treasurer, 1899-1904, and president, 1904-1907 and 1909-1912; elected international vice-president of the UMWA in 1907, serving until 1909; elected and served as international president, UMWA, from 1912 to 1917, resigning to serve as labor consultant to Dr. Harry A. Carfield, chairman of the National Fuel Administration during World War I; after the war, took a management position with the Haynes Powder Company and thereafter occasionally served as a field agent for the UMWA; presided over the Colorado coal strike of 1913-1914, which was marred by the Ludlow Massacre; pledged to unite warring factions within the UMWA during the first two years of his administration and restored harmony and replenished the union treasury, which was later depleted by the Colorado strike; during his administration, helped revise the union constitution to call for the six-hour day, a minimum age of 16 for employment in the mines, old-age pensions, workmen's compensation, and the prohibition of membership to National Civic Federation members and Boy Scout leaders; the 1912 convention resolved that the American Federation of Labor organize industrial type unions, and the radical faction, led by Adolph Germer (q.v.), attempted to endorse the Socialist party as the political arm of the working class; was a political conservative and was accused of attempting to purge Socialists from positions of power in the Illinois district; won the eight-hour day and recognition of mine committees in the anthracite field and universal run-of-mine wage base in the bituminous field; appointed John L. Lewis (q.v.) as the union's chief statistician and business manager of the *Journal*, sinecures from which Lewis rose to the union presidency; died in Des Moines, Iowa,

September 21, 1934; *United Mine Workers Journal*, October 1, 1934; George S. McGovern and Leonard F. Guttridge, *Great Coalfield War* (1972); McAlister Coleman, *Men and Coal* (1943).

(J.H.)

WHITFIELD, Owen H. Born in Jamestown, Miss., in 1892; Protestant; married; several children; attended Okolona College in Mississippi for two years; Afro-American; worked as a railroad fireman and minstrel show tap dancer, then became a sharecropper on a plantation near Charleston in Missouri's southeastern "Bootheel" region in 1928; while sharecropping, began preaching in several rural black churches; joined the Southern Tenant Farmers Union (STFU) in 1937 and organized black and white sharecroppers in the Bootheel; was charismatic and an excellent speaker, and was an effective union organizer who followed the principle of nonviolence; organized more than 20 STFU locals with a total membership of 5,000; became a STFU vice-president in 1937; was a labor reformer who sought gains for sharecroppers beyond wage increases; favored government intervention over union-led strikes as the most effective means of ameliorating the living conditions of sharecroppers; was not a Communist sympathizer, but strongly supported the merger of the STFU with the Communist-led United Cannery, Agricultural, Packing and Allied Workers of America (UCAPAWA) (the STFU's association with the UCAPAWA was short-lived, and the two unions split in 1939), and in 1937 became a member of the UCAPAWA executive council; elected a UCAPAWA vice-president in 1938; planned in late 1938 the demonstration of Bootheel sharecroppers driven off the land by planters who kept government parity checks for themselves; led the sharecroppers' campout along U.S. Routes 60 and 61 in January, 1939, involving 330 families and 1,307 persons; forced to flee the Bootheel shortly thereafter because of lynching threats by planters; organized the St. Louis Committee for the Rehabilitation of the Sharecroppers, which raised money and purchased land for sharecropper resettlement; made a national speaking tour in January, 1939, on behalf of the sharecroppers and the STFU, but became disillusioned because of the STFU's inability to provide financial aid to campers; helped form the Missouri Agricultural Workers Council, UCAPAWA, and led the organizing drive to capture STFU locals in the belief that a union affiliated with the Congress of Industrial Organizations could achieve greater gains for the sharecropper; threatened new campout demonstrations in January, 1940, as Bootheel planters removed more sharecroppers, thus effectively halting further evictions; appointed by Missouri governor Lloyd Stark as

sharecropper-spokesman on a six-member landlord-sharecropper committee supported by the state government and Bootheel planters; went to
Washington, D.C., in early 1940 and received promises of aid from the
Farm Security Administration, Works Progress Administration, and the
U.S. Housing Authority; left the labor movement in 1944, joining the
People's Institute of Applied Religion; his goal of improving economic
conditions of Bootheel sharecroppers ultimately failed, but the campout
demonstrations changed political and social attitudes in Missouri to the
advantage of the sharecroppers; Louis Cantor, *A Prologue to the Protest
Movement: The Missouri Roadside Demonstration of 1939* (1969).

(M.E.R.)

WHITNEY, Alexander Fell.   Born in Cedar Falls, Iowa, April 12,
1873; son of Joseph Leonard, a minister, and Martha Wallin (Batcheller)
Whitney; Presbyterian; married Grace Elizabeth Marshman on September 7, 1893, and, after her death in 1923, Dorothy May Rowley on July
2, 1927; three children; left high school in 1888 and became a news agent on
the Illinois Central Railroad; served as a brakeman on several Midwestern
railroads during 1890-1901; joined G. F. Boynton Lodge 138 of the
Brotherhood of Railroad Trainmen (BRT) in 1896; elected master of the
general grievance committee of the Chicago and North Western Railway,
BRT, in 1901; elected vice-president in 1902 and secretary-treasurer in
1903 of the newly organized Western Association of General Committees
of the Order of Railway Conductors and BRT; became a member of the
BRT board of grand trustees in 1905 and two years later elected vice-
president; elected general secretary-treasurer in 1928 and later the same
year became president of the BRT; served as chairman of the Railway
Labor Executives' Association, 1932-1934; was one of the principal sponsors and advocates of the Railroad Retirement Act passed by the U.S.
Congress in 1935; appointed by President Franklin D. Roosevelt as a
delegate to the Inter-American Conference for the Maintenance of Peace
in 1936; along with Alvanley Johnston (q.v.) of the Brotherhood of Locomotive Engineers, led his union into a national railroad strike in May, 1946,
but was forced, after two days, to end the strike because of the threat of
drastic punitive legislation; was a liberal in politics and usually supported
Democratic candidates for public office; authored *Main Street, Not Wall
Street* (1938), and *Wartime Wages and Railroad Labor* (1944); died in
Cleveland, Ohio, July 16, 1949; Walter F. McCaleb, *Brotherhood of
Railroad Trainmen, with Special Reference to the Life of Alexander F.
Whitney* (1936); Joel Seidman, *The Brotherhood of Railroad Trainmen: The*

Internal Political Life of a National Union (1962); Charles A. Madison, *American Labor Leaders: Personalities and Forces in the Labor Movement* (1962); *Current Biography* (1946).

WILLIAMS, Benjamin Hayes.   Born in Monson, Me., March 15, 1877; son of Thomas Huxley, a Welsh quarry worker, and Carrie Williams; married Rose Gerhart on February 27, 1914; at age eleven was put to work in his half-brother's print shop in Nebraska; later, while working as a farm hand, completed high school; in 1900, entered Tabor College, Iowa, graduating in 1904; in 1905, went to Butte, Mont.; evolutionary theory, Bellamy's utopianism, and Marxian socialism shaped his intellectual growth; in Butte, his association with Thomas J. Hagerty (q.v.), a founder of the Industrial Workers of the World (IWW), influenced him to devote himself to union movement; agitated for the Socialist Labor party (SLP) and organized Western timber workers for the IWW, 1905-1907; was a delegate to the 1907 IWW convention and elected to its general executive board; assigned as organizer for the eastern United States; was gradually convinced that industrial action must precede political agitation and attacked the program of SLP leader Daniel DeLeon (q.v.), playing a key role in ousting him from the IWW in 1908; gave up his general executive board post in 1908 and helped publish the *Industrial Union Bulletin* until its demise in 1909; was attracted by the IWW-led steel strike and went to New Castle, Pa., where in December, 1909, along with a local Wobbly, C. H. McCarty, founded *Solidarity;* became its editor, expanding its circulation to several thousand, and began publishing Wobbly tracts; in 1913, moved *Solidarity* to Cleveland, Ohio, where it became the official organ of the IWW; for several years *Solidarity*'s press published the bulk of the pamphlets, songbooks, and leaflets that were crucial for Wobbly agitation and rank-and-file morale; was a disciple of Marx and Darwin and combined their ideas to argue that evolution was creating a working-class structure parallel to concentrated industrial capitalism; held that industrial capital was more advanced in the United States, making U.S. workers unique in their potential for great class cohesiveness; admitted that the IWW's initial appeal was its ability to improve the workers immediate lot and insisted that through participation they would achieve solidarity and recognize the need for industrial organization to usher in the cooperative commonwealth; principally advocated direct action, the strike, and the slow-down; urged that the IWW concentrate on eastern rather than western workers; favored centralization of the IWW, but when William Haywood (q.v.) insisted on moving *Solidarity* to Chicago, Ill., quit as editor in 1917;

returned as editor in 1920 and used the position to advocate IWW cooperation with other radical groups to seize control of industry; was rebuffed by the 1921 convention and left the IWW; participated during the 1930s in the Technocracy movement and continued to be active as a radical in Ohio until his death in 1965; see his "Trends Toward Industrial Freedom," *American Journal of Sociology* (March, 1915); Warren R. Van Tine, "Ben H. Williams" (M.A. Thesis, 1967); Melvyn Dubofsky, *We Shall Be All: A History of the Industrial Workers of the World* (1969).

(D.G.S.)

WILLIAMS, Elijah ("Lige") Henson. Born in Bienville Parish, La., August 16, 1895; son of William Henson, a farmer, and Martha Anne Price; Baptist; married Annie Laurie Canfield on November 26, 1946; no children; attended the public schools of Bienville Parish, then eventually learned the barber's trade and joined Shreveport, La., Local 161 of the Journeymen Barbers, Hairdressers and Cosmetologists' International Union of America; served as secretary-treasurer of Local 161, then elected president of the Louisiana State Federation of Labor in 1933 and served in that capacity until declining to run for reelection in 1956; was a regional organizer for American Federation of Labor (AFL) president William Green (q.v.) and served as director of AFL Region 16 prior to the merger of the AFL and the Congress of Industrial Organizations (CIO); appointed director of AFL-CIO Region VII in 1956 and continued in that position the remainder of his life; was an advocate of a constant labor offensive and witnessed the creation of most of Louisiana's craft unions; was instrumental in joining local groups into central bodies; as AFL-CIO regional director, helped organize New Orleans, La., hotel workers and Pascagoula, La., shipyard workers; was a Democrat and played an important role in building labor's political power in Louisiana; during the 1950s, was a member of the Louisiana State Democratic Central Committee; died in Shreveport, La., March 17, 1972; *AFL-CIO News*, March 25, 1972; E. H. Williams' Folder, Southern Labor Archives, Atlanta, Ga.

(M.E.R.)

WILSON, D. Douglas (fl. 1895-1915). Was the first regularly elected editor of the International Association of Machinists' (IAM) official organ, the *Machinists' Monthly Journal*, serving from 1895 until his death in 1915, and established its basic format; as editor of the *Journal*, solicited general discussions of political and economic philosophy, articles on technical developments in the trade, regular reports from the national vice-presidents, sporadic reports from local business agents, letters from the membership, and editorial comment on current issues; because his moderate Socialist views were frequently at odds with those of President James O'Connell (q.v.), carefully balanced the *Journal*'s function as mouthpiece for the national administration and voice of the rank-and-file; averaging 96 pages per issue and costing the union $34,000 annually, the *Journal* attained a level of, in Mark Perlman's estimate, "a machinists' version of *Harper's* or *Scribner's* magazines"; President O'Connell recommended to the 1911 convention that the union reduce expenses by limiting the *Journal* to eight pages and selling it by subscription rather than mailing it to all members; a convention committee reported that on the basis of the *Journal*'s educational, economic, and social value and the devotion of its readers, it constituted the IAM's "richest asset"; as general vice-president and editor, with President O'Connell and Hugh Doran, participated in the famous Murray Hill collective bargaining agreement between the IAM and the National Metal Trades Association; died in 1915; Mark Perlman, *The Machinists: A New Study in American Trade Unionism* (1961).

(J.H.)

WILSON, James Adair.   Born in Erie, Pa., April 23, 1876; son of Scottish immigrants, James, a blacksmith, and Mary (Adair) Wilson; Methodist; married Elsie Schaeffer on June 21, 1905; two children; attended the public schools of Erie, Pa., then became a pattern maker and joined the Pattern Makers League of North America (PMLNA); elected president of the Erie (Pa.) Central Labor Union in 1900 and appointed legislative representative of the Pennsylvania State Federation of Labor; elected president of the PMLNA in 1902; was the American Federation of Labor (AFL) fraternal delegate to the British Trades Union Congress in 1906; appointed during World War I by President Woodrow Wilson as the chairman of a U.S. delegation designed to encourage trade-union movements in allied European nations to cooperate with their governments in prosecuting the war; became an AFL vice-president in 1924 and at the same time appointed a vice-president of the AFL metal trades department; appointed by President Franklin Roosevelt as a labor advisor to the World Monetary and Economic Conference in London in 1933; served as a member of the Public Works Administration's board of labor review; resigned his trade union offices in 1934 and became labor counselor to the International Labor Office in Geneva, Switzerland; during World War II, was an AFL alternate on the Defense Mediation Board and served on a variety of War Labor Board panels; died in Washington, D.C., September

3, 1945; Solon DeLeon, ed., *The American Labor Who's Who* (1925); *National Cyclopaedia of American Biography* (Vol. XXXIII); *The American Federationist* (September, 1945).

WILSON, William Bauchop. Born in Blantyre, Scotland, April 2, 1862; son of Adam, a miner, and Helen Nelson (Bauchop) Wilson; Presbyterian; married Agnes Williamson on June 7, 1883; 11 children; emigrated with parents to the United States in 1870, settling in Arnot, Pa.; received a common school education in Scotland; began working in the Pennsylvania coal mines at age nine; elected secretary of a local miners' union in 1877 and secretary of a local Greenback club the following year; joined the Knights of Labor in 1878 and during 1888-1894 served as a district master workman; was a member of the district executive board of the American Association of Miners and Mine Laborers, 1884-1885; was an unsuccessful candidate for the Pennsylvania state legislature on the Union Labor party ticket in 1888 and shortly thereafter became a supporter of the Populist party; was one of the founding members of the United Mine Workers of America (UMWA) in 1890 and was a member of the UMWA general executive board, 1891-1894; appointed to the Pennsylvania commission that in 1891 revised state laws relating to coal mining; broke with the Knights of Labor in 1894 and helped organize and became general master workman of the Independent Order of the Knights of Labor, a short-lived attempt to reestablish the original principles of the Knights of Labor; was prominently involved in the coal strikes of 1899 and 1902; served as international secretary-treasurer of the UMWA, 1900-1908; elected as a Democrat to the United States Congress in 1906 and served as chairman of a special committee to investigate the effect of the Taylor system and other methods of scientific management; served as an American Federation of Labor fraternal delegate to the British Trades Union Congress in 1910; appointed as the first secretary of labor by President Woodrow Wilson in 1913 and served until 1921; as secretary of labor, reorganized the Bureau of Immigration and Naturalization, developed agencies to mediate industrial disputes, and organized the U.S. Employment Service to handle the problems of wartime deployment and transfer of workers; during World War I, was also a member of the Council for National Defense; served as president of the International Labor Conference of 1919; was a member of the Federation Board for Vocational Education, 1914-1921; in 1921, served on the International Joint Commission, created to prevent disputes between the United States and Canada regarding the use of the boundary waters; after 1921, engaged in mining and agricultural pursuits near Blossburg, Pa.; ran unsuccessfully as a Democratic candidate for the U.S. Senate in 1926; died on a train near Savannah, Ga., May 25, 1934; R. W. Babson, *William B. Wilson and the Department of Labor* (1919); Chris Evans, *History of the United Mine Workers of America* (2 vols., 1918, 1920); McAlister Coleman, *Men and Coal* (1943); Arthur S. Link, *Woodrow Wilson: The New Freedom* (1956).

WINDT, John (fl. 1830-1844).   Born in New York City early in the 19th century; was of German-Irish descent; became a journeyman printer and an agnostic as a young man; joined the New York Typographical Society in 1830; when the journeymen printers struck for a wage increase in 1831, organized and became an official in the Typographical Association; continued as a journeyman printer until establishing his own printing shop in 1835; became an active participant in the New York Workingmen's party in 1834 and elected secretary of the Workingmen's General Committee; shortly thereafter, however, transferred his allegiance to the Democratic party when it championed labor's cause; was an "ultra antimonopolist" and aligned himself with the anti-Tammany slate of reformers within the Democratic party and became a leader of the Locofocos; nominated for the New York Assembly by the anti-Tammany slate in 1835; during the following two years, published the reformist organ *Democrat*, participated in Locofoco affairs, and ran unsuccessfully for alderman and assemblyman; became a leader of the minority "Rump" faction of the Locofocos that opposed reunification with Tammany Democrats; played a prominent role in the unemployment demonstrations during the Panic of 1837; during the 1840s, became an advocate of the land-reform ideas of George Henry Evans (q.v.) and published the *Working Man's Advocate*, served as secretary and treasurer of the National Reform Association, and ran unsuccessfully for Congress on the Reform Association ticket; his printing shop was a center for reformist activities and publications until his death in the 1870s; Walter Hugins, *Jacksonian Democracy and the Working Class: A Study of the New York Workingmen's Movement, 1829-1837* (1960); John R. Commons, *et al., A Documentary History of American Industrial Society*, Vol. VII (1911); Helene S. Zahler, *Eastern Workingmen and National Land Policy, 1829-1862* (1941); Philip S. Foner, *History of the Labor Movement in the United States*, Vol. I (1947).

WOLCHOK, Samuel.   Born in Bobruisk, Russia, September 20, 1896; son of Moses, a carpenter, and Doba (Grazel) Wolchok; Jewish; married Bella Delman on December 31, 1917; two children; emigrated with his family to the United States in 1912; took a job in the New York garment industry as a suspender-maker and joined the International Ladies' Garment Workers' Union; attended the Manhattan Preparatory School, 1916-1917; during World War I, joined the U.S. Army and served in France with the Sixth Division's Eighteenth Machine Gun Battalion; after the war, became a clerk in a New York City dairy store and joined the New York local of the Retail Clerks International Protective Association; between 1922 and 1937, served as the New York local's financial secretary, vice-president, president, and secretary-manager; after the local was suspended in 1937 because of criticism of American Federation of Labor policies, organized a secessionist movement that eventually resulted in the formation of the United Retail, Wholesale and Department Store Employees of America (URWDSE) under the auspices of the Congress of Industrial Organizations (CIO); elected president at the first national convention of the URWDSE; became a member of the CIO executive council in 1938 and during 1938-1939 served as vice-president of the New York State Industrial Union Council, CIO; served during World War II as a labor member of the New York regional panel of the War Labor Board, the Regional War Manpower Employment Practices Committee, and the New York State Permanent Fair Employment Practices Committee; led his union in the historic strike against Montgomery Ward and Company during World War II; took an indefinite leave of absence and ultimately resigned his union offices after the provisions of the Taft-Hartley Act intensified existing divisions in the URWDSE over Communist influence; member of the executive board of the Liberal party of New York and executive board member of Americans for-Democratic Action; George G. Kirstein, *Stores and Unions* (1950); Michael Harrington, *The Retail Clerks* (1962); *Current Biography* (1948).

WOLL, Matthew. Born in Luxembourg, January 25, 1880; son of Michael and Janette (Schwartz) Woll; Roman Catholic; married Irene Kerwin in 1899, and after her death, Celenor Dugas; two children; emigrated to the United States in 1891; attended the public schools of Chicago until 1895, then apprenticed to a photo-engraver; entered the night school of Kent College of Law, Lake Forest University in 1901 and admitted to the Illinois bar three years later; elected president of the International Photo-Engravers Union of North America (IPEU) in 1906; served as an American Federation of Labor (AFL) fraternal delegate to the British Trades Union Congress in 1915 and 1916; served on the War Labor Board during World War I; became an AFL vice-president and executive council member in

1919; because of other duties, resigned as president of the IPEU in 1929 and became first vice-president; served as the president of the AFL's union label trades department, director of the AFL's Legal Bureau, and chairman of the AFL standing committees on education and social security and international relations; was an AFL delegate to the International Federation of Trade Unions meeting in Warsaw in 1937 and to the International Labor Organization's conference in Oslo in 1938; during the controversy between the AFL and the Committee on Industrial Organization (CIO), usually supported the craft organizing concept, but attempted to project himself as a conciliator; was considered one of the most conservative leaders in the U.S. labor movement and was a vitriolic anti-Communist; served on the National War Labor Board during World War II; became a vice-president and executive council member of the AFL-CIO after the 1955 merger; was president of the Union Labor Life Insurance Company from 1925 until 1955 and then became general executive chairman of the Company; at various times, edited both the *American Photo-Engraver* and *The American Federationist*; authored *Labor, Industry and Government* (1935); usually supported the Republican party; died in New York City, June 1, 1956; Philip Taft, *The A. F. of L. From the Death of Gompers to the Merger* (1959); Walter Galenson, *The CIO Challenge to the AFL: A History of the American Labor Movement, 1935-1941* (1960); *Current Biography* (1943); *The American Federationist* (July, 1956).

WOOD, Reuben Terrell.   Born in Springfield, Mo., August 7, 1884; son of Henry Nicholas Buruley, a college professor, and Martha Wood; Baptist; married Mary Ellen Eshman on December 31, 1936; no children; received six years of formal education in the public schools of Springfield, Mo., and some private tutorial instruction; apprenticed as cigarmaker in 1901 and shortly thereafter joined the Springfield local of the Cigarmakers' International Union; served in several positions in the Springfield labor movement during 1902-1912, including president of the Springfield Central Union; elected president of the Missouri State Federation of Labor (MSFL) in 1912 and served continuously until 1953; during World War I, was a member of the state advisory board of the U.S. Fuel Administration and also served on the Missouri division of the U.S. Food Administration; was national legislative representative of the Brotherhood of Maintenance of Way Employes in 1919-1920; was a Socialist during the early years of his career and served as chairman of the Missouri branch of the Conference for Progressive Political Action (CPPA) in 1922; appointed to the executive committee of the CPPA and served on credentials committee of the 1924 Progressive party convention in Cleveland, Ohio, that nominated Robert M. LaFollette for president of the United States; elected to the 73rd Congress as a Democrat in 1932, and, during four terms in the U.S. House of Representatives, consistently supported New Deal legislation; was a member of the House labor committee and played an important role in the enactment of labor legislation, especially the National Labor Relations Act and the Fair Labor Standards Act; defeated for reelection in 1940; was a member of the Missouri Constitutional Convention in 1944; was a politics-oriented, militant trade unionist and often disagreed with the apolitical, craft-conscious policies of the national American Federation of Labor leadership; retired from his union positions in 1953 and was named MSFL president emeritus; died in Springfield, Mo., July 16, 1955; Gary M Fink, *Labor's Search for Political Order: The Political Behavior of the Missouri Labor Movement, 1890-1940* (1974); *Biographical Directory of the American Congress, 1774-1971* (1971); *Who's Who in Labor* (1946).

WOODCOCK, Leonard Freel.   Born in Providence, R. I., February 15, 1911; son of Ernest, a manufacturer's representative, and Margaret (Freel) Woodcock; reared as a Roman Catholic; married Loula Martin on May 28, 1941; three children; raised in Northampton, England, after his father was interned in Germany during World War I; attended British schools including the prestigious Chipsey preparatory school; returned with family to the United States in 1926 and settled in Detroit, Mich.; attended Wayne University and the Walsh Institute of Accountancy, 1928-1930; became a machine assembler at the Detroit Gear and Machine Company and joined a plant union that in the late 1930s became a local of the United Automobile, Aircraft, Agricultural Implement Workers of America (UAW); served as educational director for the Wayne County Industrial Union Council, Congress of Industrial Organizations, for two years; became a UAW staff representative in 1940 and served in that capacity until 1944; appointed first administrative assistant to UAW president Walter P. Reuther (q.v.) in 1946; became director of UAW Region 1D in 1947; elected a UAW vice-president in 1955 and assigned the responsibility for the UAW's General Motors and aerospace departments; assumed the office of UAW president after the death of Walter P. Reuther in 1970 and elected to the office in 1972; led the UAW in a eight-week strike against the General Motor's Corporation in the autumn of 1970; is a member of several reform-oriented organizations, including the Urban League, the American Civil Liberties Union, and the National Association for the

Advancement of Colored People; became a member of the Wayne State University board of governors in 1959; is a liberal in politics and usually supports Democratic candidates for public office; Jack Stieber, *Governing the UAW* (1962); Jean Gould and Lorena Hickok, *Walter Reuther: Labor's Rugged Individualist* (1972); Frank Cormier and William J. Eaton, *Reuther* (1970).

WRIGHT, James Lendrew.   Born in County Tyrone, Ireland, April 6, 1816; Protestant; son of Scots-Irish parents; emigrated with his family to the United States in 1827, eventually settling in Philadelphia, Pa., where the family evidently prospered; graduated from the Mount Vernon Grammar School, then attended Charles Mead's private academy; served a six-year apprenticeship as a tailor; joined the Tailors' Benevolent Society of Philadelphia in 1837; opened a tailor shop in Frankfort, Pa., in 1847; served as the manager of a prosperous Philadelphia clothing store from 1854 until losing his job in the 1857 depression; along with Uriah S. Stephens (q.v.), organized the Garment Cutters' Association in 1862 and for several years served as the president of the organization; in 1863, helped organize the Philadelphia Trades Assembly and elected treasurer; was one of the seven original founders of the Noble Order of the Knights of Labor (K of L) in 1869 and was credited with naming the organization; served as the temporary chairman of the 1876 conventions that created a national labor organization; became politicized as a result of the violent strikes of the 1870s and ran unsuccessfully for Pennsylvania state treasurer on the United Workingmen ticket in 1877, and the following year ran unsuccessfully for state secretary of internal affairs on the Greenback-Labor party ticket; thereafter forsook politics; continued his activities on behalf of the K of L for the remainder of his life; led a caucus calling for a return to secrecy and other "original principles" of the Order in 1889 in opposition to the leadership of Terence V. Powderly (q.v.); died in Germantown, Pa., August 3, 1893; Norman J. Ware, *The Labor Movement of the United States, 1860-1895* (1929); David Montgomery, *Beyond Equality: Labor and the Radical Republicans, 1862-1872* (1967); John R. Commons, *et al.*, *History of Labour in the United States*, Vol. II (1918); *Dictionary of American Biography* (Vol. XX).

WURF, Jerry.   Born in New York City, April 18, 1919; son of Sigmund and Lena (Tannenbaum) Wurf; Jewish; married Mildred Kiefer on November 26, 1960; three children; attended the public schools of New York City, then earned an A.B. degree from New York University in 1940; worked in a New York City cafeteria, 1940-1943; became an organizer for

Local 448 of the New York Hotel and Restaurant Employees in 1943; appointed administrator of Local 448's welfare fund in 1947; served as an organizer in New York for the American Federation of State, County and Municipal Employees (AFSCME), 1947-1948; became executive director of AFSCME District Council 37 in 1959, serving in that capacity until 1964; defeated Arnold S. Zander (q.v.), founding president of the AFSCME, in a closely contested election in 1964; elected a vice-president and executive council member of the American Federation of Labor-Congress of Industrial Organizations (AFL-CIO) in 1969; served as a vice-president of the AFL-CIO industrial union department and as a member of the executive board of the martime trades department; served on a variety of public and private boards and agencies and was a member of the executive board of the Americans for Democratic Action, the Jewish Labor Committee, the Leadership Conference on Civil Rights, and Common Cause; a Democrat; Leo Kramer, *Labor's Paradox—The American Federation of State, County and Municipal Employees, AFL-CIO* (1962); *AFL-CIO News*, May 2, 1964; *Who's Who in America, 1972-1973.*

YABLONSKI, Joseph A.   Born in Pittsburgh, Pa., March 3, 1910; son of a coal miner who was killed in a mine accident in 1933; married Margaret Rita Wasicek; three children; at age fifteen, began work as a coal miner and joined the United Mine Workers of America (UMWA); elected a local union president in 1934; served on the executive board of District 5, UMWA, Pittsburgh, 1934-1942; served on the international executive board, UMWA, 1942-1969; elected president of District 5 in 1958, serving until 1966 when President W. A. Boyle (q.v.) forced him to resign under threat of placing the district in trusteeship; supported Boyle over insurgent Steve Kochis for the union presidency in 1964, but secretly supported an insurgent for election to the national executive board; defeated by George Titler, a Boyle supporter, when, in 1966, the international executive board filled a vacancy in the union vice-presidency; was a power in local Democratic politics and appointed by Boyle to direct Labor's Non-Partisan League, the union's political organization; without the union's support, succeeded in adding pneumoconiosis (black lung) to the list of compensated industrial diseases in Pennsylvania in 1965; challenged Boyle for the union presidency in 1969, charging the incumbent administration with neglecting miners' health and safety, collusion with coal operators, and dictatorial union administration; pledged a restoration of district autonomy and democracy, an end to nepotism, mandatory retirement of union officers at age sixty-five, an aggressive campaign to improve miners' health and safety, and an increase in royalties and benefits from the welfare and retirement fund; meanwhile, Boyle increased pensions by 30 percent and promised to double royalties to finance a further increase to woo the votes of more than 40,000 voting union pensioners; Boyle also pledged to increase wages from $33 to $50 per day, to support a stringent federal mine safety bill, and to seek a guaranteed annual wage; on December 9, defeated by Boyle by a vote of 81,056 to 45,872; along with his wife and daughter, Yablonski was murdered in his Clarksville, Pa., home on December 31, 1969, by Paul Gilly, Claude Villey, and Aubren Martin; the assassins were employed by Gilly's wife, Annette, her father, Silas Huddleston, retired president of a Tennessee UMWA local, William Prater, secretary-treasurer of District 19, and, according to an affidavit made by William Turnblazer, president of District 19, he and President Boyle; all were convicted; a federal court invalidated the 1969 election, and in December, 1972, Arnold Miller (q.v.), an insurgent, defeated Boyle; *The New York Times*, January 6, 1970; Brit Hume, *Death and the Mines* (1971).

(J.H.)

ZANDER, Arnold Scheuer. Born in Two Rivers, Wis., November 26, 1901; son of Arnold, a saw filer, and Anna (Scheuer) Zander; Protestant; married Lola Miriam Dynes on June 15, 1929; three children; graduated from the University of Wisconsin in 1923 with a B.S. degree in civil engineering, then worked as a draftsman for the Wisconsin Telephone Company, 1923-1924, a bridge draftsman for the Baltimore and Ohio Railroad, 1925-1927, and a structural steel draftsman for the Manitowoc Shipbuilding Corporation, 1927-1928; received an M.S. degree in city planning from the University of Wisconsin in 1929 and became secretary of the League of Wisconsin Municipalities; awarded the Ph.D. degree in public administration from the University of Wisconsin in 1931; became the chief examiner of the Wisconsin State Civil Service Department's Bureau of Personnel in 1930, serving until 1934; helped found the Wisconsin State Employees' Union and elected its executive secretary in 1933; was one of the founding members of the American Federation of State, County and Municipal Employees (AFSCME) and elected its first president; was a member of the Labor Advisory Board of the National Youth Administration; served during World War II as a labor consultant to the War Manpower Commission and the U.S. Civil Service Commision; served as an American Federation of Labor (AFL) fraternal delegate to the

Trades and Labor Congress of Canada in 1943 and the British Trades Union Congress in 1947; was an AFL advisor to the American delegation to the International Labor Organization conference in 1945 and was a delegate to the Tjanstemannens Centralorganisation conference in Stockholm in 1949; served as vice-president of the World Congress of Professional Employees in 1951; became a member of the AFL-Congress of Industrial Organizations' (CIO) general board after the 1955 merger; was chairman of the AFL-CIO committee on consumer cooperatives; defeated for reelection in 1964 in a closely contested election against Jerry Wurf (q.v.); served as president of United World Federalists, 1966-1967; became a lecturer at Wisconsin State University, Green Bay, Wis., in 1968; was a member of numerous public and private boards and agencies, including the American Civil Liberties Union, the National Association for the Advancement of Colored People, and the International Labor Press of America; edited *The Public Employee* for several years; a Democrat; Leo Kramer, *Labor's Paradox: The American Federation of State, County, and Municipal Employees, AFL-CIO* (1962) *Current Biography* (1947); *Who's Who in America, 1972-1973; Who's Who in Labor* (1946).

ZARITSKY, Max.   Born in Petrikov, Russia, April 15, 1885; son of Morris, a rabbi and wealthy lumberman, and Anna Zaritsky; Jewish; married Sophie Pilavin on November 21, 1909; acquired the equivalent of a high school education, then left home at age fifteen and moved to Vilna, supporting himself there by tutoring the children of wealthy families; witnessed a three-day pogrom against students, liberals, intellectuals, and Jews in Kiev in 1905, then left Russia, eventually emigrating to the United States; settled in Boston, Mass., and in 1907 joined the Cloth Hat, Cap and Millinery Workers' International Union (CHCMW); elected secretary of the Boston Cap Makers' Local in 1908 and three years later became assistant general secretary of the CHCMW and the protégé of the union's leader, Max Zuckerman; elected the first general president of the CHCMW after the office was created in 1919; served as secretary-treasurer of the Needle Trades' Workers Alliance in 1923; resigned the presidency of the CHCMW in 1925 as a result of internal conflicts between right- and left-wing forces in the union; again elected president in 1927; in 1934, elected secretary-treasurer of the United Hatters, Cap and Millinery Workers' International Union (UHCMWIU), formed by the amalgamation of the United Hatters of North America and the CHCMW; was one of the original members of the Committee for Industrial Organization (CIO) formed in 1935; elected president of the UHCMWIU in 1946; withdrew from the CIO in 1937 after unsuccessfully attempting to mediate the conflicts between the American Federation of Labor and the CIO; was an advocate of labor-management cooperation to promote the hat, cap, and millinery industry; along with David Dubinsky (q.v.) and Sidney Hillman (q.v.), was one of the principal founders of the American Labor party in 1936; joined the Liberal party of New York in 1944; retired from his union positions in 1950; died in Boston, Mass., May 10, 1959; Donald B. Robinson, *Spotlight on a Union: The Story of the United Hatters, Cap and Millinery Workers International Union* (1948); Walter Galenson, *The CIO Challenge to the AFL: A History of the American Labor Movement, 1935-1941* (1960); Marx Lewis, *Max Zaritsky at Fifty: The Story of an Aggressive Labor Leadership* (1935).

ZIMMERMAN, Charles S.   Born near Kiev, Russia, November 27, 1896; son of Ben Zion and Leah Zimmerman; Jewish; married Rose Prepstein on November 23, 1925; one child; attended Russian schools and completed the equivalent of two years of high school; emigrated to the United States in 1913; secured employment as a knee-pants worker in a New York garment factory and joined the United Garment Workers' Union; later became a member of the Amalgamated Clothing Workers' Union after its formation in 1914; took employment in a waistmaking factory in 1916 and joined the International Ladies' Garment Workers' Union (ILGWU); shortly thereafter, became secretary-manager of Dressmakers' Union Local 22 of the ILGWU; became an organizer for the Joint Board of the Dress and Waistmakers' Union in 1924; was a member of the Communist party during much of the 1920s, and therefore was expelled from the ILGWU in 1925, but was reinstated in 1931; headed the Joint Action Committee of the left-wing ILGWU locals that led the unsuccessful cloak strike of 1926; elected an ILGWU vice-president in 1934; served as head of the Trade Union Council of the American Labor party; later joined the Liberal party of New York and became a member of the administrative and state executive committees; was a member of numerous public and private boards and agencies, including Americans for Democratic Action and the National Council for a Permanent Fair Employment Practices Commission; appointed chairman of the American Federation of Labor-Congress of Industrial Organizations' civil rights committee in 1957; elected president of the Jewish Labor Committee in 1968; retired as general manager of the ILGWU Dress Joint Council and New York Dress

Joint Board in 1972; Louis Levine, *The Women's Garment Workers: A History of the International Ladies' Garment Workers' Union* (1924); Benjamin Stolberg, *Tailor's Progress: The Story of a Famous Union and the Men Who Made It* (1944); Walter Galenson, *The CIO Challenge to the AFL: A History of the American Labor Movement, 1935-1941* (1960).

Appendices

Appendix I
Union Affiliations

The alphabetic listing of unions is followed by those labor leaders affiliated or identified with each particular union. State and local unions are listed separately at the end of the Appendix. Those individuals listed in capital letters had a significant impact on the union, whereas for those listed in regular type, the union was not their most significant union affiliation. Where it did not create unnecessary confusion, the most recent title of the particular union was used.

Actors and Artists of America, The Associated
DULLZELL, PAUL   Heller, George
GILLMORE, FRANK

Actors' Equity Association
DERWENT, CLARENCE   GILLMORE, FRANK
DULLZELL, PAUL   Montgomery, Robert

Agricultural Workers' Union, National
CHAVEZ, CESAR E.   MITCHELL, HARRY L.
GALARZA, ERNESTO

Air Line Pilots Association, International
BEHNCKE, DAVID L.

Amalgamated Transit Union
   See *Street, Electric Railway and Motor Coach Employees of America, Amalgamated Association of*

American Federation of Labor
BROWN, IRVING J.   LENNON, JOHN B.
DELANEY, GEORGE P.   McBRIDE, JOHN
FENTON, FRANCIS P.   McDEVITT, JAMES L.
FRAYNE, HUGH   McQUIRE, PETER J.
FREY, JOHN P.   MEANY, GEORGE
GOMPERS, SAMUEL   MORRISON, FRANK
GOOGE, GEORGE L.   PADWAY, JOSEPH A.
GRAY, RICHARD J.   RYAN, MARTIN F.
GREEN, WILLIAM   SCHNITZLER, WILLIAM F.
JEWELL, BERT M.   TOBIN, DANIEL J.
KEENAN, JOSEPH D.   WOLL, MATTHEW

American Federation of Labor-Congress of Industrial Organizations
BARKAN, ALEXANDER E.   Green, John
BIEMILLER, ANDREW J.   HAGGERTY, CORNELIUS J.
Christopher, Paul R.   Kehrer, Elmer T.
Graham, Sylvester   KIRKLAND, JOSEPH L.
GRAY, RICHARD J.   KROLL, JOHN J.

Leonard, Richard
Livingston, John W.
McDEVITT, JAMES L.
MEANY, GEORGE

SCHNITZLER, WILLIAM F.
Thomas, Rolland J.
Williams, Elijah H.

American Labor Union (Western Labor Union)
HAGERTY, THOMAS J.
O'NEILL, JOHN M.

Automobile, Aircraft and Agricultural Implement Workers of America, United
ADDES, GEORGE P.
FRANKENSTEEN, RICHARD T.
GOSSER, RICHARD T.
LEONARD, RICHARD
LIVINGSTON, JOHN W.
Kehrer, Elmer T.
MARTIN, WARREN H.
MAZEY, EMIL

MORTIMER, WYNDHAM
REUTHER, ROY
REUTHER, VICTOR G.
REUTHER, WALTER P.
THOMAS, ROLLAND J.
TRAVIS, ROBERT C.
WOODCOCK, LEONARD F.

Bakery and Confectionery Workers' International Union of America
MYRUP, ANDREW A.
SCHNITZLER, WILLIAM F.

Barbers, Hairdressers and Cosmetologists' International Union of America, The Journeymen
BIRTHRIGHT, WILLIAM C.
Rollings, John Issac

Williams, Elijah H.

Blacksmiths, Drop Forgers and Helpers, International Brotherhood of
HORN, ROY

Boilermakers, Iron Ship Builders, Blacksmiths, Forgers and Helpers, International Brotherhood of
CALVIN, WILLIAM A.
Jewell, Bert M.

MacGOWAN, CHARLES J.

Bookbinders, International Brotherhood of
HAGGERTY, JOHN B.

Boot and Shoe Workers' International Union
PHILLIPS, THOMAS

Boot and Shoe Workers' Union
ANDERSON, MARY
Lawson, George W.

Brewery, Flour, Cereal, Soft Drink and Distillery Workers, International Union of United
FELLER, KARL F.   TRAUTMANN, WILLIAM E.
OBERGFELL, JOSEPH F.

Brick and Clay Workers of America, The United
KASTEN, FRANK

Bricklayers, Masons and Plasterers International Union of America
BATES, HARRY C.   GRAY, RICHARD J.
BOWEN, WILLIAM J.   Murray, Thomas A.

Bridge and Structural Iron Workers, International Association of
LYONS, JOHN H.

Building Service Employees' International Union
  See *Service Employees International Union, AFL-CIO*

Cannery, Agricultural, Packing and Allied Workers of America, United
HENDERSON, DONALD J.
WHITFIELD, OWEN H.

Carpenters and Joiners of America, United Brotherhood of
COSGROVE, JOHN T.   HUTCHESON, MAURICE A.
Crull, John   HUTCHESON, WILLIAM L.
DUFFY, FRANK   McCARTHY, PATRICK H.
HUBER, WILLIAM   McGUIRE, PETER J.

Cement, Lime and Gypsum Workers International Union, United
SCHOENBERG, WILLIAM

Chemical Workers Union, International
MITCHELL, WALTER L.

Cigarmakers' International Union of America

AZPEITIA, MARIO
BARNES, JOHN M.
BOWER, ANDREW P.
GOMPERS, SAMUEL

ORNBURN, IRA M.
PERKINS, GEORGE W.
STRASSER, ADOLPH
Wood, Reuben T.

Clothing Workers of America, Amalgamated

BELLANCA, DOROTHY J.
BLUMBERG, HYMAN
ERVIN, CHARLES W.
Golden, Clinton S.
HILLMAN, SIDNEY
HOLLANDER, LOUIS
KAZAN, ABRAHAM E.

KROLL, JOHN J.
KRZYCKI, LEO
PETERSON, ESTHER
POTOFSKY, JACOB S.
ROSENBLUM, FRANK
SCHLOSSBERG, JOSEPH
Zimmerman, Charles S.

Commercial Telegraphers Union

ALLEN, WILLIAM L.
Doherty, William C.

POWERS, FRANK B.

Communications Workers of America

BEIRNE, JOSEPH A.
CRULL, JOHN L.

MORAN, JOHN J.
WERKAU, CARLTON W.

Congress of Industrial Organizations

BROPHY, JOHN
Cannon, Joseph D.
CAREY, JAMES B.
Christopher, Paul R.
GERMER, ADOLPH F.
GOLDBERG, ARTHUR J.
Graham, Sylvester
HAPGOOD, POWERS

KROLL, JOHN J.
Krzycki, Leo
Leonard, Richard
LEWIS, JOHN L.
Mason, Lucy R.
MURRAY, PHILIP
Nance, Alexander S.
PRESSMAN, LEE

Reuther, Victor G.
REUTHER, WALTER P.

Weaver, George L. P.

Coopers' International Union
FORAN, MARTIN A.
SCHILLING, ROBERT

Die Casting Workers, National Association of
CHEYFITZ, EDWARD T.

Directors Guild of America
Montgomery, Robert

District 50, Allied and Technical Workers
LEWIS, ALMA D.
MOFFETT, ELWOOD S.

Dolls, Toys, Playthings, Novelties and Allied Products of the United States and Canada
DAMINO, HARRY

Electrical, Radio and Machine Workers, International Union of
CAREY, JAMES B.
JENNINGS, PAUL J.

Electrical, Radio and Machine Workers of America, United
CAREY, JAMES B.
Jennings, Paul J.

FITZGERALD, ALBERT J.
Oakes, Grant W.

Electrical Workers, International Brotherhood of
BROWN, EDWARD J.
BUGNIAZET, GUSTAVE M.
Fisher, Joseph A.
KEENAN, JOSEPH D.
McNULTY, FRANK J.
Marciante, Louis P.
MILNE, J. SCOTT

Nockles, Edward
NOONAN, JAMES P.
Pachler, William J.
Reuther, Roy
TRACY, DANIEL W.
VAN ARSDALE, HARRY, JR.

Elevator Constructors, International Union of
FEENEY, FRANK

Engineers, International Union of Operating
Delaney, George P.   Kirkland, Joseph L.
FITZGERALD, FRANK A.   MALONEY, WILLIAM E.
HUDDELL, ARTHUR M.   POSSEHL, JOHN

Farm Equipment and Metal Workers of America, United
OAKES, GRANT W.
Travis, Robert C.

Farm Labor Union, National
GALARZA, ERNESTO
MITCHELL, HARRY L.

Farm Workers' Union, United
CHAVEZ, CESAR E.
HUERTA, DOLORES

Farmers Union, Southern Tenant
MITCHELL, HARRY L.
WHITFIELD, OWEN H.

Fire Fighters, International Association of
BAER, FRED W.
REDMOND, JOHN P.

Fur and Leather Workers Union, International
GOLD, BEN
KAUFMAN, MORRIS

Furniture Workers of America, United
PIZER, MORRIS

Garment Cutters' Association
WRIGHT, JAMES L.

Garment Workers of America, United

Blumberg, Hyman
Hillman, Sidney
Kroll, John J.
McCURDY, JOSEPH P.
Potofsky, Jacob S.
RICKERT, THOMAS A.
Rosenblum, Frank
Zimmerman, Charles S.

Garment Workers' Union, International Ladies'

ANTONINI, LUIGI
BARONDESS, JOSEPH
Barnum, Gertrude
BISNO, ABRAHAM
BRESLAW, JOSEPH
COHN, FANNIA
Crosswaith, Frank R.
DUBINSKY, DAVID
DYCHE, JOHN A.
FEINBERG, ISRAEL
GIOVANNITTI, ARTURO
HELLER, JACOB J.
HILLQUIT, MORRIS
HOCHMAN, JULIUS
HYMAN, LOUIS
Kazan, Abraham E.
Mitchell, Harry L.
NAGLER, ISIDORE
NEWMAN, PAULINE
NINFO, SALVATORE
PERLSTEIN, MEYER
Peterson, Esther
PRICE, GEORGE M.
Romualdi, Serafino
SCHLESINGER, BENJAMIN
SIGMAN, MORRIS
STARR, MARK
STULBERG, LOUIS
Wolchok, Samuel
ZIMMERMAN, CHARLES S.

Gas, Coke and Chemical Workers of America, United
SWISHER, ELWOOD D.

Glass Bottle Blowers Association of the United States and Canada
Eames, Thomas B.
MALONEY, JAMES
MINTON, LEE W.

Glass, Ceramic, and Silica Sand Workers of America, Federation of*
SCHOLLE, AUGUST

Glass Workers Union, American Flint
COOK, HARRY H.
Easton, John B.

*Now the United Glass and Ceramic Workers of North America.

Gloveworkers Union of America, International
CHRISTMAN, ELISABETH
NESTOR, AGNES

Government Employees, American Federation of
GRINER, JOHN F.

Granite Cutters International Association of America
DUNCAN, JAMES

Hatters, Cap and Millinery Workers' International Union, United
GREENE, MICHAEL F.   SCHNEIDERMAN, ROSE
MENDELOWITZ, ABRAHAM   ZARITSKY, MAX
ROSE, ALEX

Heat and Frost Insulators and Asbestos Workers, International Association of
MULLANEY, JOSEPH A.

Hod Carriers' Building and Common Laborers' Union of America, International
See *Laborers' International Union of North America*

Horse Shoers of the U.S. and Canada, International Union of Journeymen
Fitzpatrick, John

Hosiery Workers, American Federation of
HOLDERMAN, CARL
RIEVE, EMIL

Hotel and Restaurant Employees' and Bartenders' International Union
ERNEST, HUGO   MILLER, EDWARD S.
FLORE, EDWARD   SULLIVAN, JERE L.
Kavanagh, William F.   Wurf, Jerry

Industrial Workers of the World
Bridges, Harry A.   Debs, Eugene V.
DeLEON, DANIEL   LITTLE, FRANK H.

Dennis, Eugene
Dunne, Vincent R.
ETTOR, JOSEPH J.
FLYNN, ELIZABETH G.
Foster, William Z.
GIOVANNITTI, ARTURO
HAGERTY, THOMAS J.
Hartung, Albert F.
HAYWOOD, WILLIAM D.
HILL, JOE
Jones, Mary H.
Kirwan, James

Lundeberg, Harry
Mahoney, Charles E.
Mooney, Thomas J.
MOYER, CHARLES H.
NEF, WALTER T.
O'NEILL, JOHN M.
ST. JOHN, VINCENT
SHERMAN, CHARLES O.
Sigman, Morris
TRAUTMANN, WILLIAM E.
WILLIAMS, BENJAMIN H.

Insurance Workers of America International Union
HELFGOTT, SIMON

International Labor Union
McDONNELL, J. P.
McNEILL, GEORGE E.

STEWARD, IRA

Iron, Steel, and Tin Workers, Amalgamated Association of
Bacon, Emery F.
Burke, Walter J.
Cope, Elmer F.
DAVIS, JAMES J.
Gainor, Edward J.

Germano, Joseph F.
JARRETT, JOHN
Thimmes, James G.
TIGHE, MICHAEL F.
WEIHE, WILLIAM

Knights of Labor, Noble Order of the
Barnes, John M.
BARRY, THOMAS B.
Boyce, Edward
BUCHANAN, JOSEPH R.
Conlon, Peter J.
Davis, Richard L.
DeLEON, DANIEL
Farrington, Frank
Frayne, Hugh

IRONS, MARTIN
Johnston, William H.
Jones, Mary H.
LABADIE, JOSEPH A.
LITCHMAN, CHARLES H.
McMahon, Thomas F.
McNEILL, GEORGE E.
Maurer, James H.
Mitchell, John

Mullaney, Joseph A.
O'Connell, James P.
Parsons, Albert R.
Phillips, Thomas
POWDERLY, TERENCE V.
Preston, George
SCHILLING, ROBERT
STEPHENS, URIAH S.

Sullivan, Jere L.
Talbot, Thomas W.
Tetlow, Percy
TREVELLICK, RICHARD F.
TURNER, FREDERICK
Walker, John H.
Weber, Frank J.
WRIGHT, JAMES L.

Knights of St. Crispin
LITCHMAN, CHARLES H.
PHILLIPS, THOMAS

Laborers International Union of North America
MORESCHI, JOSEPH
MORREALE, VINCENT F.

Laundry Workers International Union
Beck, Dave

Letter Carriers, National Association of
DOHERTY, WILLIAM C.
GAINOR, EDWARD J.

Lithographic Press Feeders Union
Krzycki, Leo

Locomotive Engineers, Brotherhood of
ARTHUR, PETER M.
BROWN, GUY L.
DAVIDSON, ROY E.

JOHNSTON, ALVANLEY
SHIELDS, JAMES P.
STONE, WARREN S.

Locomotive Firemen and Enginemen, Brotherhood of
CARTER, WILLIAM S.
DEBS, EUGENE V.
Davidson, Roy E.
GILBERT, HENRY E.

Golden, Clinton S.
ROBERTSON, DAVID B.
SARGENT, FRANK P.

Longshoremen's Association, International

Bridges, Harry A.	KEEFE, DANIEL J.
Delaney, George P.	O'CONNOR, THOMAS V.
GLEASON, THOMAS W.	RYAN, JOSEPH P.

Longshoremen's and Warehousemen's Union, International
BRIDGES, HARRY A.

Machinists and Aerospace Workers, International Association of

BROWN, HARVEY W.	PRESTON, GEORGE
Brown, Irving J.	O'CONNELL, JAMES P.
CONLON, PETER J.	Schoenberg, William
Golden, Clinton S.	SIEMILLER, PAUL L.
HAYES, ALBERT J.	TALBOT, THOMAS W.
JOHNSTON, WILLIAM H.	WHARTON, ARTHUR O.
Miller, Marvin J.	WILSON, D. DOUGLAS
PETERSON, ERIC	

Machinists' and Blacksmiths' International Union

FINCHER, JONATHAN C.	STEWARD, IRA
Powderly, Terence V.	

Maintenance of Way Employees, Brotherhood of

CARROLL, THOMAS C.	MILLIMAN, ELMER E.
FLJOZDAL, FREDERICK H.	

Major League Baseball Players Association
MILLER, MARVIN J.

Marine Cooks' and Stewards' Association, National
BRYSON, HUGH

Marine and Shipbuilding Workers of America, Industrial Union
GREEN, JOHN
GROGAN, JOHN J.

Maritime Union of American, National
CURRAN, JOSEPH E.
LAWRENSON, JACK

Masters, Mates and Pilots of America, National Organization
Kirkland, Joseph L.
SCULLY, JOHN J. J.

Meat Cutters and Butcher Workmen of North America, Amalgamated
Clark, Lewis J.
DONNELLY, MICHAEL
GORMAN, PATRICK E.
HELSTEIN, RALPH
JIMERSON, EARL W.
LANE, DENNIS
LLOYD, THOMAS J.
McDonald, Joseph D.
Mitchell, Harry L.

Metal Polishers, Buffers, Platers, and Helpers International Union
KELSAY, RAY

Metal Workers International Union, United
SHERMAN, CHARLES O.

Mine, Mill and Smelter Workers, International Union of
BOYCE, EDWARD
CANNON, JOSEPH D.
CHEYFITZ, EDWARD T.
CLARK, JOHN
DRISCOLL, JOHN J.
Graham, Sylvester
HAYWOOD, WILLIAM D.
KIRWAN, JAMES
Little, Frank H.
MAHONEY, CHARLES E.
MOYER, CHARLES H.
O'NEILL, JOHN M.
ROBINSON, REID
St. John, Vincent
Sefton, Lawrence F.
TRAVIS, MAURICE E.

Mine Workers of America, United
BITTNER, VAN A.
BOYLE, WILLIAM A.
BROPHY, JOHN
CADDY, SAMUEL H.
CAIRNS, THOMAS F.
DAVIS, RICHARD L.
FARRINGTON, FRANK
GERMER, ADOLPH F.
Gibson, John W.
GREEN, WILLIAM
HAPGOOD, POWERS
HAYES, FRANK J.
HOWAT, ALEXANDER
JONES, MARY H.
KENNEDY, THOMAS
LEWIS, ALMA D.

LEWIS, JOHN L.
LEWIS, THOMAS L.
KEENEY, C. FRANK
McBRIDE, JOHN
McDonald, David J.
MITCHELL, JOHN
MITCH, WILLIAM A.
Moffett, Elwood S.

Mortimer, Windham
MURRAY, PHILIP
RATCHFORD, MICHAEL D.
TETLOW, PERCY
WALKER, JOHN H.
WILSON, WILLIAM B.
WHITE, JOHN P.
YABLONSKI, JOSEPH A.

Miners, Western Federation of
See *Mine, Mill and Smelter Workers, International Union of*

Miners' Association, American
HINCHCLIFFE, JOHN

Miners and Mine Laborers, National Federation of
McBRIDE, JOHN

Miners' National Association
SINEY, JOHN

Molders and Foundry Workers Union of North America, International*
Delaney, George P.
FOX, MARTIN
FREY, JOHN P.
Mooney, Thomas J.

RONEY, FRANK
SYLVIS, WILLIAM H.
VALENTINE, JOSEPH F.

Musicians, American Federation of
KENIN, HERMAN D.
PETRILLO, JAMES C.

WEBER, JOSEPH N.

National Labor Union
CAMERON, ANDREW C.
Fincher, Jonathan C.
HINCHCLIFFE, JOHN
JESSUP, WILLIAM J.

Siney, John
SYLVIS, WILLIAM H.
TREVELLICK, RICHARD F.

*Now the International Molders and Allied Workers Union, AFL-CIO.

National Trades' Union
COMMERFORD, JOHN
DOUGLAS, CHARLES
ENGLISH, WILLIAM
FERRAL, JOHN

LUTHER, SETH
MOORE, ELY
SLAMM, LEVI D.
TOWNSEND, ROBERT, JR.

Needle Trades Workers Industrial Union
GOLD, BEN
HYMAN, LOUIS

Negro American Labor Council
RANDOLPH, ASA P.

Negro Labor Committee
CROSSWAITH, FRANK R.

Newspaper Guild, America
MARTIN, HARRY L.
Kehrer, Elmer T.
Romualdi, Serafino

BROUN, HEYWOOD C.
Ervin, Charles W.

Oil, Chemical and Atomic Workers International Union
KNIGHT, ORIE A.
SWISHER, ELWOOD D.

Oil Field, Gas Well and Refinery Workers, International Association of
Germer, Adolph F.
KNIGHT, ORIE A.

Oil Workers International Union
KNIGHT, ORIE A.
O'CONNOR, HARVEY

Office and Professional Workers of America, United
HELFGOTT, SIMON
MERRILL, LEWIS R.

Packinghouse Workers of America, United
CLARK, LEWIS J.
HELSTEIN, RALPH

Painters, Decorators and Paperhangers of America, Brotherhood of*
BRENNAN, PETER J.   RAFTERY, LAWRENCE M.
LINDELOF, LAWRENCE P.

Paper Makers, International Brotherhood of
BURNS, MATTHEW J.
PHILLIPS, PAUL L.

Paperworkers of America, United
PHILLIPS, PAUL L.
Ramsey, Claude E.

Pattern Makers League
WILSON, JAMES A.

Photo-Engravers' Union of North America, International
WOLL, MATTHEW

Plasterers' and Cement Masons' International Association of the United States and Canada, Operative
McDevitt, James L.

Plumbers and Steamfitters of the United States and Canada, United Association of
ALPINE, JOHN P.   McNamara, Patrick V.
Brown, Henry S.   Maurer, James H.
COEFIELD, JOHN   Meany, George
DURKIN, MARTIN P.   Murphy, Vincent
Grogan, John J.   SCHOEMANN, PETER T.

Post Office Clerks, National Federation of
GEORGE, LEO E.   NELSON, OSCAR F.
HALLBECK, ELROY C.

*Now the International Brotherhood of Painters and Allied Trades of the United States and Canada.

Post Office Clerks, United National Association of
Nelson, Oscar F.

Postal Clerks, United Federation of
HALLBECK, ELROY C.

Post Office Motor Vehicles Employees, National Federation of
GIBSON, EVERETT G.

Post Office and Railway Mail Laborers', National Association of
McAVOY, HAROLD

Potters, National Brotherhood of Operative
DUFFY, JAMES M.

Printing Pressmen's and Assistants' Union of North America, International
BERRY, GEORGE L.   McGRADY, EDWARD F.
DUNWODY, THOMAS E.   Mahoney, William
GOOGE, GEORGE L.

Pulp, Sulphite and Paper Mill Workers, International Brotherhood of
BURKE, JOHN P.
Burns, Matthew J.

Railroad Signalmen, Brotherhood of
CLARK, JESSE   LYON, ARLON E.
HELT, DANIEL W.

Railroad Telegraphers, Order of
Griner, John F.   Moran, John J.
LEIGHTY, GEORGE E.   Powers, Frank B.

Railroad Trainmen, Brotherhood of
DOAK, WILLIAM N.   LEE, WILLIAM G.
Johnson, William D.   LUNA, CHARLES
KENNEDY, WILLIAM P.   WHITNEY, ALEXANDER F.

Railway Carmen of America, Brotherhood of
HARRISON, GEORGE M.   RYAN, MARTIN F.
KNIGHT, FELIX H.

Railway Conductors of America, Order of
FRASER, HARRY W.   JOHNSON, WILLIAM D.
GARRETSON, AUSTIN B.   PHILLIPS, JAMES A.
HUGHES, ROY O.

Railway Supervisors Association, Ind., American
TAHNEY, JAMES P.

Railway Union, American
DEBS, EUGENE V.

Retail Clerks International Protective Association
COULTER, CLARENCE C.   SUFFRIDGE, JAMES A.
Greenberg, Max   Wolchok, Samuel

Retail, Wholesale and Department Store Employees of America, United
Gibbons, Harold J.   GREENBERG, MAX
Gibson, John W.   WOLCHOK, SAMUEL

Rubber, Cork, Linoleum and Plastic Workers of America, United*
BUCKMASTER, LELAND S.   DALRYMPLE, SHERMAN H.
BURNS, THOMAS F.

Screen Actors' Guild
MONTGOMERY, ROBERT
REAGAN, RONALD

Seafarers International Union of North America**
Curran, Joseph E.   LUNDEBERG, HARRY
FURUSETH, ANDREW   OLANDER, VICTOR A.
HALL, PAUL

*Formerly the United Rubber Workers of America.
**Formerly the International Seamen's Union.

Service Employees International Union, AFL-CIO
McFETRIDGE, WILLIAM L.
SULLIVAN, DAVID

Sheet Metal Workers' International Association
BYRON, ROBERT
FRAYNE, HUGH

Ship Carpenters and Caulkers, International Union of
TREVELLICK, RICHARD F.

Shoe Workers of America, United
MITCHELL, JAMES J.

Signalmen of America, Brotherhood of Railroad
CASHEN, THOMAS C.

Sleeping Car Porters, Brotherhood of
RANDOLPH, ASA P.
TOTTEN, ASHLEY L.

Stage Employees and Moving Picture Machine Operators of the United States and Canada, International Alliance of Theatrical
BREWER, ROY M.
WALSH, RICHARD F.

State, County and Municipal Employees, American Federation of
CHAPMAN, GORDON W.   ZANDER, ARNOLD S.
WURF, JERRY

Steelworkers of America, United

ABEL, IORWITH W.	GOLDBERG, ARTHUR J.
BACON, EMERY F.	GOLDEN, CLINTON S.
BITTNER, VAN A.	JOHNS, JOHN S.
BURKE, WALTER J.	McDONALD, DAVID J.
Cope, Elmer F.	MALOY, ELMER J.
Easton, John B.	Mathias, Charles G.
GERMANO, JOSEPH S.	Miller, Marvin J.

MOFFETT, ELWOOD S.
MOLONY, JOSEPH P.
MURRAY, PHILIP
PRESSMAN, LEE
RARICK, DONALD C.

RUTTENBERG, HAROLD J.
SEFTON, LAWRENCE F.
SWEENEY, VINCENT D.
THIMMES, JAMES G.
Travis, Maurice E.

Stereotypers and Electrotypers Union of North America, International
BUCKLEY, LEO J.

Stone and Allied Products Workers of America, United
LAWSON, JOHN C.
SCOTT, SAM H.

Stonecutters' Association of North America, Journeymen
GIVENS, PAUL A.

Stove, Furnace and Allied Appliance Workers' of North America*
LEWIS, JOSEPH

Street, Electric Railway and Motor Coach Employees of America, Amalgamated Association of
Knight, Felix H.
Lyden, Michael J.

MAHON, WILLIAM D.
SPRADLING, ABE L.

Tailors, United Brotherhood of
SCHLOSSBERG, JOSEPH

Tailors' Union of America, Journeymen
LENNON, JOHN B.

Teachers, American Federation of
BORCHARDT, SELMA M.
EKLUND, JOHN M.
Gibbons, Harold J.
HALEY, MARGARET A.
Henderson, Donald J.
MEGEL, CARL J.

Muste, Abraham J.
Peterson, Esther
Reuther, Roy
SELDEN, DAVID S.
SHANKER, ALBERT
STARR, MARK

*Formerly the Stove Mounters International Union of North America.

Teamsters, Chauffeurs, Warehousemen and Helpers of America, International Brotherhood of

Baldanzi, George
BECK, DAVE
Cairns, Thomas F.
DOBBS, FARREL
Dunne, Vincent R.
ENGLISH, JOHN F.
Fenton, Francis P.

FITZSIMMONS, FRANK E.
GIBBONS, HAROLD J.
HICKEY, THOMAS L.
HOFFA, JAMES R.
MOHN, EINAR O.
Shelley, John F.
TOBIN, DANIEL J.

Telephone Workers, National Federation of
See *Communication Workers of America*

Television and Radio Artists, American Federation of
Derwent, Clarence
HELLER, GEORGE

Textile Workers, National Union of
GREENE, PRINCE W.

Textile Workers of America, Amalgamated
MUSTE, ABRAHAM J.

Textile Workers of America, United
BALDANZI, GEORGE
Christopher, Paul R.
GREENE, PRINCE W.
McMAHON, THOMAS F.

Mathias, Charles G.
Pollock, William
RIEVE, EMIL

Textile Workers Union of America
BALDANZI, GEORGE
Barkan, Alexander E.
CHRISTOPHER, PAUL R.

HOLDERMAN, CARL
POLLOCK, WILLIAM
RIEVE, EMIL

Tobacco Workers International Union
O'HARE, JOHN
Scott, Sam H.

Train Dispatchers Association, America
Griner, John F.
LUHRSEN, JULIUS G.

Transport Service Employees of America, United
TOWNSEND, WILLARD S.
WEAVER, GEORGE L. P.

Transport Workers Union of America
QUILL, MICHAEL J.

Transportation Union, United
GILBERT, HENRY E.
LUNA, CHARLES

Typographical Union, International

Berger, Victor L.
Buchanan, Joseph R.
Cameron, Andrew C.
DONNELLY, SAMUEL B.
Hayes, Maximilian S.
HOWARD, CHARLES P.
Keating, Edward
Labadie, Joseph A.
LYNCH, JAMES M.

Mahoney, William
Morrison, Frank
Ohl, Henry
Parsons, Albert R.
RANDOLPH, WOODRUFF
Soderstrom, Reuben G.
Sullivan, James W.
Swartz, Maud O.
TROUP, AUGUSTA L.

Typographical Union, National
FARQUHAR, JOHN M.

United Hebrew Trades
FEINSTONE, MORRIS
Hillquit, Morris

Mendelowitz, Abraham
PINE, MAX

Upholsterers' International Union of North America
HOFFMANN, SAL B.

Utility Workers Union of America
FISHER, JOSEPH A.

PACHLER, WILLIAM J.

Vulcan, Sons of
See *Iron, Steel, and Tin Workers, Amalgamated Association of*

Women's Trade Union League

ANDERSON, MARY	NESTOR, AGNES
BARNUM, GERTRUDE	NEWMAN, PAULINE
CHRISTMAN, ELISABETH	ROBINS, MARGARET D.
HENRY, ALICE	SCHNEIDERMAN, ROSE
MAROT, HELEN	SWARTZ, MAUD O.

Wood, Wire and Metal Lathers, International Union of

Haggerty, Cornelius J.	MASHBURN, LLOYD A.
McSORLEY, WILLIAM J.	

Woodworkers of America, International
HARTUNG, ALBERT F.

STATE AND LOCAL UNIONS

ALABAMA

AFL-CIO Council
MITCH, WILLIAM A.

State Federation of Labor
MITCH, WILLIAM A.

CALIFORNIA

Los Angeles Building and Construction Trades Council
Haggerty, Cornelius J.
Mashburn, Lloyd A.

Los Angeles Iron Trades Council
RONEY, FRANK

Los Angeles Labor Council
Mashburn, Lloyd A.

Oakland Central Labor Union
Suffridge, James A.

San Francisco Building Trades Council
Coefield, John
McCARTHY, PATRICK H.

San Francisco Industrial Union Council
Bryson, Hugh

San Francisco Labor Council
Ernst, Hugo
SHELLEY, JOHN F.

San Francisco Representative Assembly of Trades and Labor Unions
RONEY, FRANK

San Francisco, Iron Trades Council of
RONEY, FRANK

State Building Trades Council
McCARTHY, PATRICK H.

State Industrial Union Council
Bryson, Hugh
Thimmes, James G.
Travis, Maurice E.

State Federation of Labor
Ernst, Hugo
HAGGERTY, CORNELIUS J.
Lundeberg, Harry
SHELLEY, JOHN F.

Vallejo Trades and Labor Council
Roney, Frank

CONNECTICUT

AFL-CIO Council
DRISCOLL, JOHN J.

State Industrial Union Council
DRISCOLL, JOHN J.

DISTRICT OF COLUMBIA

Federation of Labor
Coulter, Clarence C.
McCURDY, JOSEPH P.

Washington Central Labor Union
Coulter, Clarence C.

FLORIDA

Jacksonville Central Labor Union
Jewell, Bert M.

GEORGIA

AFL-CIO Council
MATHIAS, CHARLES G.

Atlanta Federation of Trades
Nance, Alexander S.

Atlanta Industrial Union Council
MATHIAS, CHARLES G.

Savannah Trades and Labor Assembly
GOOGE, GEORGE L.
Possehl, John

State Federation of Labor
Googe, George L.
NANCE, ALEXANDER S.

ILLINOIS

AFL-CIO Council
GERMANO, JOSEPH S.
SODERSTROM, REUBEN G.

Chicago Building Trades Council
DURKIN, MARTIN P.

Chicago Central Labor Union
MORGAN, THOMAS J.

Chicago Federation of Labor

Anderson, Mary	Maloney, William E.
Donnelly, Michael	Megel, Carl J.
FITZPATRICK, JOHN	Nelson, Oscar F.
George, Leo E.	NOCKLES, EDWARD N.
KEENAN, JOSEPH D.	Olander, Victor A.
McFetridge, William L.	ROBINS, MARGARET D.

Chicago Trade and Labor Assembly
MORGAN, THOMAS J.

Cook County Industrial Union Council
GERMANO, JOSEPH S.
TRAVIS, ROBERT C.

Springfield Building Trades Council
Byron, Robert

Springfield Federation of Labor
Byron, Robert

State Federation of Labor

Byron, Robert

George, Leo E.

McFetridge, William L.

Megel, Carl J.

OLANDER, VICTOR A.

Robins, Margaret D.

SODERSTROM, REUBEN G.

WALKER, JOHN H.

State Industrial Union Council
Travis, Robert C.

Streator Trades and Labor Assembly
SODERSTROM, REUBEN G.

INDIANA

Indianapolis Central Labor Union
Obergfell, Joseph F.

State Federation of Labor
Obergfell, Joseph F.

KENTUCKY

Louisville Union Trades and Labor Assembly
GORMAN, PATRICK E.

State Federation of Labor
CADDY, SAMUEL H.
Gorman, Patrick E.

State Industrial Union Council
CADDY, SAMUEL H.

LOUISIANA

State Federation of Labor
WILLIAMS, ELIJAH H.

MARYLAND

Baltimore Federation of Labor
McCURDY, JOSEPH P.

State Federation of Labor
McCURDY, JOSEPH P.

MASSACHUSETTS

Boston Central Labor Union
FENTON, FRANCIS P.
McGrady, Edward F.

Boston Trades' Union
DOUGLAS, CHARLES
LUTHER, SETH

Lawrence Central Labor Union
WATT, ROBERT J.

State Federation of Labor
Fenton, Francis P.   McGrady, Edward F.
Frey, John P.   WATT, ROBERT J.

State Industrial Union Council
Fitzgerald, Albert J.

MICHIGAN

AFL-CIO Council
SCHOLLE, AUGUST

Detroit Council of Trades and Labor Unions
LABADIE, JOSEPH A.

Detroit Federation of Labor
McNAMARA, PATRICK V.

Detroit Trades Assembly
TREVELLICK, RICHARD F.

Flint Industrial Union Council
REUTHER, ROY

State Federation of Labor
LABADIE, JOSEPH A.

State Industrial Union Council
GERMER, ADOLPH F.   LEONARD, RICHARD
GIBSON, JOHN W.   SCHOLLE, AUGUST

MINNESOTA

Minneapolis Central Labor Union
Dunne, Vincent R.

St. Paul Trades and Labor Assembly
Lawson, George W.
MAHONEY, WILLIAM

State Federation of Labor
LAWSON, GEORGE W.

State Industrial Union Council
Helstein, Ralph

MISSISSIPPI

AFL-CIO Council
RAMSAY, CLAUDE E.

Jackson County Central Labor Union
RAMSAY, CLAUDE E.

MISSOURI

AFL-CIO Council
ROLLINGS, JOHN I.

St. Louis Central Trades and Labor Union
Knight, Felix H.
ROLLINGS, JOHN I.

Springfield Central Labor Union
Wood, Reuben T.

State Federation of Labor
Raftery, Lawrence M.   WOOD, REUBEN T.
ROLLINGS, JOHN I.

MONTANA

State Industrial Union Council
GRAHAM, SYLVESTER

NEBRASKA

Grand Island Central Labor Union
BREWER, ROY M.

State Federation of Labor
BREWER, ROY M.

NEW HAMPSHIRE

State Federation of Labor
Burke, John P.

NEW JERSEY

AFL-CIO Council
MURPHY, VINCENT

Hudson County Central Labor Union
KAVANAGH, WILLIAM F.

Hudson County Industrial Union Council
GROGAN, JOHN J.

Mercer County Building Trades Council
Marciante, Louis P.

Mercer County Central Labor Union
Marciante, Louis P.

Paterson Trades Assembly
McDONNELL, J. P.

State Building and Construction Trades Council
COSGROVE, JOHN T.

State Federation of Labor
COSGROVE, JOHN T.   MARCIANTE, LOUIS P.
EAMES, THOMAS B.   MURPHY, VINCENT
KAVANAGH, WILLIAM F.

State Federation of Trades and Labor Unions
KAVANAGH, WILLIAM F.
McDONNELL, J. P.

State Industrial Union Council
Barkan, Alexander E.
HOLDERMAN, CARL

Union County Central Trades
COSGROVE, JOHN T.

NEW YORK

AFL-CIO Council
Brennan, Peter J.
HOLLANDER, LOUIS

General Trades' Union
COMMERFORD, JOHN
MOORE, ELY
SLAMM, LEVI D.
TOWNSEND, ROBERT, JR.

New York City Building and Construction Trades Council, Greater
MURRAY, THOMAS A.

New York City Central Labor Council, AFL-CIO
Shanker, Albert
VAN ARSDALE, HARRY, JR.

New York City Central Trades and Labor Council
Feinberg, Israel
Feinstone, Morris
Meany, George
Mendelowitz, Abraham
RYAN, JOSEPH P.
Schneiderman, Rose
Sullivan, James W.
VAN ARSDALE, HARRY, JR.

New York City, Construction Trades Council of, Greater
BRENNAN, PETER J.

New York City Industrial Union Council, Greater
CURRAN, JOSEPH E.
Jennings, Paul J.
QUILL, MICHAEL

State Federation of Labor
MEANY, GEORGE
Mullaney, Joseph A.
MURRAY, THOMAS A.
Nagler, Isidore
Ryan, Joseph P.

State Industrial Union Council
HOLLANDER, LOUIS
Jennings, Paul J.
Wolchok, Samuel

State Trades and Labor Council
McDONNELL, J. P.

State Workingmen's Assembly
JESSUP, WILLIAM J.

Syracuse Central Trades and Labor Unions
LYNCH, JAMES M.

NORTH CAROLINA

AFL-CIO Council
Scott, Sam H.

OHIO

AFL-CIO Council
COPE, ELMER F.   LYDEN, MICHAEL J.
JOHNS, JOHN S.

Stark County Industrial Union Council
JOHNS, JOHN S.

State Federation of Labor
FREY, JOHN P.
LYDEN, MICHAEL J.

State Industrial Union Council
KROLL, JOHN J.

Valley Trade Council, Ohio
Cook, Harry H.

OREGON

AFL-CIO Council
McDONALD, JOSEPH D.

Portland Central Labor Council
Howard, Charles P.
McDONALD, JOSEPH D.

State Federation of Labor
McDONALD, JOSEPH D.

PENNSYLVANIA

Erie Central Labor Union
Wilson, James A.

Philadelphia Building Trades Council
FEENEY, FRANK
McDEVITT, JAMES L.

Philadelphia Central Labor Union
FEENEY, FRANK
Minton, Lee W.

Philadelphia Mechanics' Union of Trade Associations
HEIGHTON, WILLIAM

Philadelphia Trades Assembly
FINCHER, JONATHAN C.
WRIGHT, JAMES L.

Philadelphia Trades' Union
ENGLISH, WILLIAM
FERRAL, JOHN

Reading Federated Trades Council
BOWER, ANDREW P.

State Federation of Labor
BOWER, ANDREW P.   Minton, Lee W.
McDEVITT, JAMES L.   Wilson, James A.
MAURER, JAMES H.

PUERTO RICO

Federacion Libre de Trabajadores de Puerto Rico
IGLESIAS, SANTIAGO

TENNESSEE

Memphis Industrial Union Council
Martin, Harry L.

State Federation of Labor
BIRTHRIGHT, WILLIAM C.

State Industrial Union Council
Martin, Harry L.

TEXAS

AFL-CIO Council
BROWN, HENRY S.

San Antonio Building and Construction Trades Council
Brown, Henry S.

State Building and Construction Trades Council
BROWN, HENRY S.

VERMONT

State Industrial Union Council
LAWSON, JOHN C.

WEST VIRGINIA

Parkersburg Trades and Labor Council
EASTON, JOHN B.

State Federation of Labor
CAIRNS, THOMAS F.
EASTON, JOHN B.

KEENEY, C. FRANK

State Industrial Union Council
EASTON, JOHN B.

WISCONSIN

Milwaukee Building and Construction Trades Council
SCHOEMANN, PETER T.

Milwaukee Federation of Trades Councils
Biemiller, Andrew J.
OHL, HENRY
WEBER, FRANK J.

State Federation of Labor
Biemiller, Andrew J.
OHL, HENRY

PADWAY, JOSEPH A.
WEBER, FRANK J.

State Industrial Union Council
Burke, Walter J.

Appendix II
Religious Preference

The lists in this Appendix include individuals who were identified with certain religious groups even though they may not have maintained their affiliations throughout their lives. Religious preferences were not ascertained for approximately one-third of the individuals listed in the *Biographical Dictionary*.

BAPTIST
Berry, George L.
Bower, Andrew P.
Davis, James J.
Eames, Thomas B.
Fraser, Harry W.
Googe, George L.
Green, William
Griner, John F.
Harrison, George M.
Knight, Felix H.

Knight, Orie A.
Luther, Seth
Martin, Harry L., Jr.
Martin, Warren H.
Mitchell, Harry L.
Nance, Alexander S.
Siemiller, Paul L.
Stephens, Uriah S.
Williams, Elijah H.
Wood, Reuben T.

CHRISTIAN
Brewer, Roy M.
Crull, John L.
George, Leo E.
Hoffa, James R.

Miller, Edward S.
Reagan, Ronald
Scott, Sam H.

CHRISTIAN SCIENTIST
Minton, Lee W.
Phillips, James A.

CHURCH OF CHRIST
Morrison, Frank

CHURCH OF JESUS CHRIST OF LATTER-DAY SAINTS
Peterson, Esther

CONGREGATIONALIST
Chapman, Gordon W.
Easton, John B.
Johnston, William H.

Lee, William G.
Pollock, William
Robins, Margaret D.

DUTCH REFORMED
Muste, Abraham J.

EPISCOPALIAN
Frankensteen, Richard T.

Gibson, Everett G.

Gillmore, Frank
Haywood, William D.*
Holderman, Carl
Johnston, Alvanley

Lewis, Alma D.
Maso, Sal
Mason, Lucy R.
Townsend, Willard S.

JEWISH

Barondess, Joseph
Baskin, Joseph
Bellanca, Dorothy J.
Bisno, Abraham
Blumberg, Hyman
Breslaw, Joseph
Cahan, Abraham
Cohn, Fannia
DeLeon, Daniel
Dubinsky, David
Dyche, John A.
Ernst, Hugo
Feinberg, Israel
Feinstone, Morris
Gold, Ben
Goldberg, Arthur J.
Gompers, Samuel
Greenberg, Max
Helfgott, Simon
Heller, George
Heller, Jacob J.
Hillman, Sidney
Hillquit, Morris
Hochman, Julius
Hollander, Louis
Hyman, Louis

Kaufman, Morris
Kenin, Herman D.
Kroll, John J.
London, Meyer
Mendelowitz, Abraham
Miller, Marvin J.
Nagler, Isidore
Newman, Pauline
Pine, Max
Pizer, Morris
Price, George M.
Rombro, Jacob
Rose, Alex
Rosenblum, Frank
Schlesinger, Benjamin
Schlossberg, Joseph
Schneiderman, Rose
Shanker, Albert
Sigman, Morris
Stulberg, Louis
Vladeck, Baruch C.
Wolchok, Samuel
Wurf, Jerry
Zaritsky, Max
Zimmerman, Charles S.

LUTHERAN

Abel, Iorwith W.
Anderson, Mary
Bittner, Van A.
Christman, Elisabeth

Germer, Adolph F.
Hayes, Albert J.
Hill, Joe
Kasten, Frank

*Later rejected the church.

Kennedy, William P.
Luhrsen, Julius G.
Mohn, Einar O.
Nelson, Oscar F.
Reuther, Roy

Reuther, Victor G.
Reuther, Walter P.
Rieve, Emil
Totten, Ashley L.
Travis, Robert C.

METHODIST
Brown, Guy L.
Caddy, Samuel H.
Calvin, William A.
Carroll, Thomas C.
Clark, Jesse
Eklund, John M.
Gibson, John W.
Graham, Sylvester
Helt, Daniel W.
Hutcheson, Maurice A.
Hutcheson, William L.
Johnson, William D.
Mitch, William A.

Moffett, Elwood S.
Phillips, Paul L.
Phillips, Thomas
Preston, George
Randolph, Asa P.
Starr, Mark
Suffridge, James A.
Swisher, Elwood D.
Sylvis, William H.
Tetlow, Percy
Trevellick, Richard F.
Werkau, Carlton W.
Wilson, James A.

PRESBYTERIAN
Bacon, Emery F.
Beck, Dave
Birthright, William C.
Cairns, Thomas F.
Davidson, Roy E.
Duncan, James
Dunwody, Thomas E.
Farquhar, John M.
Fljozdal, Frederick H.
Gilbert, Henry E.

Hughes, Roy O.
Kehrer, Elmer T.
Lawson, John C.
Leighty, George E.
Lennon, John B.
Lindelof, Lawrence P.
Robertson, David B.
Thomas, Norman M.
Whitney, Alexander F.
Wilson, William B.

PROTESTANT (Gen.)
Brown, Harvey W.
Buckmaster, Leland S.
Byron, Robert
Coulter, Clarence C.
Furuseth, Andrew
Giovannitti, Arturo*

Horn, Roy
Huddell, Arthur M.
Jarrett, John
Jewell, Bert M.
Jimerson, Earl W.
Kelsay, Ray

*Was reared a Roman Catholic but later attended a Protestant seminary.

Lewis, John L.
Mortimer, Wyndham
Oakes, Grant W.
Peterson, Eric

Thimmes, James G.
Whitfield, Owen H.
Wright, James L.
Zander, Arnold S.

ROMAN CATHOLIC

Addes, George P.
Alpine, John P.
Antonini, Luigi
Azpeitia, Mario
Bates, Harry C.
Beirne, Joseph A.
Brennan, Peter J.
Bridges, Harry A.*
Brophy, John
Broun, Heywood C.**
Brown, Henry S.
Buckley, Leo J.
Bugniazet, Gustave M.
Burke, John P.
Burke, Walter J.
Burns, Matthew J.
Burns, Thomas F.
Carey, James B.
Cashen, Thomas C.
Chavez, Cesar E.
Conlon, Peter J.
Cosgrove, John T.
Crosswaith, Frank R.
Curran, Joseph E.
Damino, Harry
Delaney, George P.
Doherty, William C.
Driscoll, John J.
Duffy, Frank
Duffy, James M.

Durkin, Martin P.
English, John F.
Feeney, Frank
Feller, Karl F.
Fenton, Francis P.
Fisher, Joseph A.
Fitzgerald, Albert J.
Fitzgerald, Frank A.
Fitzpatrick, John
Flore, Edward
Gainor, Edward J.
Germano, Joseph S.
Gleason, Thomas W.
Gorman, Patrick E.
Gosser, Richard T.
Gray, Richard J.
Grogan, John J.
Hagerty, Thomas J.
Haggerty, Cornelius J.
Haggerty, John B.
Haley, Margaret A.
Hayes, Frank J.
Hayes, Maximilian S.
Hickey, Thomas J.
Hoffmann, Sal B.
Huerta, Dolores
Iglesias, Santiago
Jones, Mary H.
Kavanagh, William F.
Keating, Edward

*Reared a Roman Catholic.
**Reared an Episcopalian but converted during the 1930s.

Keefe, Daniel J.
Keenan, Joseph D.
Kennedy, Thomas
Lane, Dennis
Lawrenson, Jack
Lawson, George W.
Leonard, Richard
Lewis, Joseph
Lyden, Michael J.
Lynch, James M.
McAvoy, Harold
McCarthy, Patrick H.
McCurdy, Joseph P.
McDonald, David J.
McDevitt, James L.
McDonnell, J. P.
McFetridge, William L.
McGrady, Edward F.
McGuire, Peter J.
McMahon, Thomas F.
McNamara, Patrick V.
McNulty, Frank J.
McSorley, William J.
Maguire, Matthew
Maloney, James
Maloney, William E.
Maloy, Elmer J.
Mathias, Charles G.
Meany, George
Milliman, Elmer E.
Mitchell, James J.
Mitchell, John
Molony, Joseph P.
Mooney, Thomas J.
Moreschi, Joseph
Morreale, Vincent F.
Mullaney, Joseph A.
Murphy, Vincent
Murray, Philip

Murray, Thomas A.
Nestor, Agnes
Ninfo, Salvatore
Noonan, James P.
O'Connell, James P.
O'Connor, Thomas V.
O'Hare, John
Pachler, William J.
Petrillo, James C.
Powers, Frank B.
Quill, Michael J.
Raftery, Lawrence M.
Rarick, Donald C.
Redmond, John P.
Romualdi, Serafino
Roney, Frank
Ryan, Joseph P.
Ryan, Martin F.
Schoemann, Peter T.
Scully, John J. J.
Sefton, Lawrence F.
Shelley, John F.
Siney, John
Sullivan, David
Sullivan, Jere L.
Swartz, Maud O.
Sweeney, Vincent D.
Tahney, James P.
Tighe, Michael F.
Tobin, Daniel J.
Troup, Augusta L.
Valentine, Joseph F.
Van Arsdale, Harry, Jr.
Walsh, Richard F.
Watt, Robert J.
White, John P.
Woodcock, Leonard F.
Woll, Matthew

SOCIETY FOR ETHICAL CULTURE
Derwent, Clarence
Sullivan, James W.

SOCIETY OF FRIENDS
Biemiller, Andrew J.   Garretson, Austin B.
Cope, Elmer F.   Marot, Helen

SPIRITUALIST
Schilling, Robert

SYRIAN ORTHODOX
Johns, John S.

UNITARIAN
Christopher, Paul R.   Henry, Alice
Hallbeck, Elroy C.   O'Connor, Harvey

Appendix III
Place of Birth

This appendix is divided into two groups of persons: those born in the United States and those born in other countries. Na. indicates that the date or place of birth was not ascertained.

UNITED STATES

ALABAMA

Name	Birthdate	Birthplace
Hall, Paul	August 21, 1914	Na.
Mitchell, Walter L.	January 30, 1915	Florence
Parsons, Albert R.	June 24, 1848	Montgomery

ARIZONA

Name	Birthdate	Birthplace
Chavez, Cesar E.	March 31, 1927	Yuma

ARKANSAS

Name	Birthdate	Birthplace
Birthright, William C.	May 27, 1887	Helena
Phillips, Paul L.	August 10, 1904	Strong

CALIFORNIA

Name	Birthdate	Birthplace
Beck, Dave	June 16, 1894	Stockton
Lewis, Joseph	October 1, 1906	Centerville
Shelley, John F.	September 3, 1905	San Francisco

COLORADO

Name	Birthdate	Birthplace
Mashburn, Lloyd A.	October 10, 1897	Greeley

CONNECTICUT

Name	Birthdate	Birthplace
Douglas, Charles	Na.	New London
Driscoll, John J.	December 11, 1911	Waterbury
Gibson, Everett G.	December 28, 1903	Wallingford
Skidmore, Thomas	August 13, 1790	Newton
Steward, Ira	March 10, 1831	New London

FLORIDA

Name	Birthdate	Birthplace
Azpeitia, Mario	November 22, 1899	Key West
Randolph, Asa P.	April 15, 1889	Crescent City

GEORGIA

Name	Birthdate	Birthplace
Dunwody, Thomas E.	August 1, 1887	Lafayette
Googe, George L.	July 25, 1900	Palaky
Griner, John F.	August 7, 1907	Camilla
Nance, Alexander S.	May 19, 1895	Bowman

ILLINOIS

Name	Birthdate	Birthplace
Barnum, Gertrude	September 29, 1866	Chester
Brown, Edward J.	November 20, 1893	Chicago
Bryson, Hugh	October 4, 1914	(rural)
Burke, Walter J.	September 14, 1911	Antioch
Christman, Elisabeth	Na.	Chicago
Crull, John L.	August 4, 1901	Geneosea
Davidson, Roy E.	July 4, 1901	Fairmount

Name	Birthdate	Birthplace
Durkin, Martin P.	March 18, 1894	Chicago
Farrington, Frank	1873	Fairburg
Germano, Joseph S.	February 12, 1904	Chicago
Gibson, John W.	August 23, 1910	Harrisburg
Goldberg, Arthur J.	August 8, 1908	Chicago
Haley, Margaret A.	November 15, 1861	Joliet
Hallbeck, Elroy C.	May 15, 1902	Chicago
Hapgood, Powers	December 28, 1899	Chicago
Horn, Roy	March 10, 1872	Warsaw
Howard, Charles P.	September 14, 1879	Harvel
Jimerson, Earl W.	September 2, 1889	East St. Louis
Kasten, Frank	January 13, 1878	Dolton
Keefe, Daniel J.	September 27, 1852	Willowsprings
Keenan, Joseph D.	November 5, 1896	Chicago
Kennedy, Thomas	November 2, 1887	Lansford
Lane, Dennis	1881	Chicago
Lawson, George W.	July 4, 1876	Chicago
Lee, William G.	November 29, 1859	La Prairie
Leighty, George E.	August 16, 1897	Phillips
Luhrsen, Julius G.	April 1, 1877	Des Plaines
McFetridge, William L.	November 28, 1893	Chicago
Mahoney, William	January 13, 1869	Chicago
Martin, Warren H.	August 16, 1902	Marion
Mitchell, John	February 4, 1870	Braidwood
Mooney, Thomas J.	December 8, 1882	Chicago
Nelson, Oscar F.	September 29, 1884	Chicago
Olander, Victor A.	November 28, 1873	Chicago
Petrillo, James C.	March 16, 1892	Chicago
Phillips, James A.	September 10, 1873	Clay County
Possehl, John	1886	Chicago
Reagan, Ronald	February 6, 1911	Tampico
Redmond, John P.	June 2, 1892	Chicago
Rickert, Thomas A.	April 24, 1876	Chicago
Shields, James P.	June 9, 1889	Neoga
Tahney, James P.	1897	Chicago
Tracy, Daniel W.	April 7, 1886	Bloomington
Werkau, Carlton W.	September 25, 1907	Clifton
White, John P.	February 28, 1870	Coal Valley

INDIANA

Name	Birthdate	Birthplace
Bacon, Emery F.	May 1, 1909	Indianapolis
Buckmaster, Leland S.	March 30, 1894	Geneva
Clark, Jesse	November 21, 1901	Terre Haute
Cope, Elmer F.	July 24, 1903	Elwood
Debs, Eugene V.	November 5, 1855	Terre Haute
Gainor, Edward J.	August 1, 1870	Greencastle
Givens, Paul A.	October 11, 1891	Indianapolis
Hoffa, James R.	February 14, 1913	Brazil
Kelsay, Ray	July 8, 1888	Marion
Megel, Carl J.	December 3, 1899	Hayden

IOWA

Name	Birthdate	Birthplace
Brown, Guy L.	August 22, 1893	Boone
Clark, Lewis J.	April 23, 1902	Centerville
Eklund, John M.	September 14, 1909	Burlington
Garretson, Austin B.	September 14, 1856	Winterset
Hayes, Frank J.	1882	What Cheer
Knight, Orie A.	September 24, 1902	New Hampton
Lewis, Alma D.	January 23, 1889	Colfax
Lewis, John L.	February 12, 1880	Lucas
Nockles, Edward N.	September 21, 1869	Dubuque
Stone, Warren S.	February 1, 1860	Ainsworth
Whitney, Alexander F.	April 12, 1873	Cedar Falls

KANSAS

Name	Birthdate	Birthplace
Dunne, Vincent R.	April 17, 1889	Kansas City
Fraser, Harry W.	June 7, 1884	Topeka
Keating, Edward	July 9, 1875	Kansas City

KENTUCKY

Name	Birthdate	Birthplace
Gorman, Patrick E.	November 27, 1892	Louisville
St. John, Vincent	July 16, 1876	Newport
Spradling, Abe L.	June 19, 1885	Woodford County

LOUISIANA

Name	Birthdate	Birthplace
Marciante, Louis P.	August 2, 1898	Lutcher
Williams, Elijah H.	August 16, 1895	Bienville Parish

MAINE

Name	Birthdate	Birthplace
Buckley, Leo J.	February 4, 1899	Lewiston
Williams, Benjamin H.	March 15, 1877	Monson

MARYLAND

Name	Birthdate	Birthplace
McCurdy, Joseph P.	March 20, 1892	Baltimore
Mathias, Charles G.	August 17, 1913	Baltimore County
Valentine, Joseph F.	May 13, 1857	Baltimore

MASSACHUSETTS

Name	Birthdate	Birthplace
Alpine, John P.	ca. 1868	Boston
Burns, Thomas F.	June 19, 1906	Holyoke
Dullzell, Paul	June 15, 1879	Boston
English, John F.	April 14, 1889	Boston

Name	Birthdate	Birthplace
Fenton, Francis P.	March 11, 1895	Boston
Fitzgerald, Albert J.	1906	Lynn
Foster, William Z.	February 25, 1881	Taunton
Haggerty, Cornelius J.	January 10, 1894	Boston
Huddell, Arthur M.	June 15, 1869	Danvers
Litchman, Charles H.	April 8, 1849	Marblehead
McNamara, Patrick V.	October 4, 1894	North Weymouth
McNeill, George E.	August 4, 1837	Amesbury
Sullivan, Jere L.	January 3, 1863	Willimansett

MICHIGAN

Name	Birthdate	Birthplace
Frankensteen, Richard T.	March 6, 1907	Detroit
Hutcheson, Maurice A.	May 7, 1897	Saginaw County
Hutcheson, William L.	February 7, 1874	Saginaw County
Kehrer, Elmer T.	January 11, 1921	Brighton
Labadie, Joseph A.	April 18, 1850	Paw Paw
Maloney, William E.	June 17, 1884	Detroit
Nestor, Agnes	June 24, 1880	Grand Rapids
Selden, David S.	June 5, 1914	Dearborn

MINNESOTA

Name	Birthdate	Birthplace
Frey, John P.	February 24, 1871	Mankato
Helstein, Ralph	December 11, 1908	Duluth
Mohn, Einar O.	August 27, 1906	Atwater
O'Connor, Harvey	March 29, 1898	Minneapolis
Powers, Frank B.	May 13, 1888	Clear Lake
Ruttenberg, Harold J.	May 22, 1914	St. Paul
Soderstrom, Reuben G.	March 10, 1888	Wright County

MISSISSIPPI

Name	Birthdate	Birthplace
Martin, Harry L. Jr.	October 28, 1908	Hollandale
Ramsay, Claude E.	December 18, 1916	Ocean Springs
Whitfield, Owen H.	1892	Jamestown

MISSOURI

Name	Birthdate	Birthplace
Baer, Fred W.	August 16, 1884	Kansas City
Buchanan, Joseph R.	December 6, 1851	Hannibal
Dobbs, Farrel	July 25, 1907	Queen City
Gilbert, Henry E.	October 5, 1906	Ethel
Haggerty, John B.	1884	St. Louis
Harrison, George M.	July 19, 1895	Lois
Johnson, William D.	October 18, 1881	Brookfield
Knight, Felix H.	December 10, 1876	Montgomery County
Livingston, John W.	August 17, 1908	Iberia
Miller, Edward S.	June 24, 1901	Cameron
Noonan, James P.	December 15, 1878	St. Louis
Ornburn, Ira M.	November 28, 1889	Moberly
Raftery, Lawrence M.	February 27, 1895	St. Louis
Randolph, Woodruff	January 31, 1892	Warrenton
Rollings, John I.	July 1, 1905	St. Charles County
Wood, Reuben T.	August 7, 1884	Springfield

MONTANA

Name	Birthdate	Birthplace
Boyle, William A.	December 1, 1904	Bald Butte
Graham, Sylvester	September 1, 1899	Sheridan
Robinson, Reid	June 7, 1908	Butte

NEBRASKA

Name	Birthdate	Birthplace
Brewer, Roy M.	August 9, 1909	Cairo
Jewell, Bert M.	February 5, 1881	Brock
Lyon, Arlon E.	October 15, 1899	Thedford
Siemiller, Paul L.	September 4, 1904	Gothenberg

NEW HAMPSHIRE

Name	Birthdate	Birthplace
Bagley, Sarah	Na.	Meredith
Collins, Jennie	1828	Amoskeag
Flynn, Elizabeth G.	August 7, 1890	Concord

NEW JERSEY

Name	Birthdate	Birthplace
Barkan, Alexander E.	August 8, 1909	Bayonne
Beirne, Joseph A.	February 16, 1911	Jersey City
Cosgrove, John T.	September 11, 1873	Elizabeth
Eames, Thomas B.	November 20, 1882	Williamstown
Grogan, John J.	March 26, 1914	Hoboken
Kavanagh, William F.	September 2, 1878	Jersey City
Kenin, Herman D.	October 26, 1901	Vineland
McGrady, Edward F.	January 29, 1872	Jersey City
Moore, Ely	July 4, 1798	Belvidere
Murphy, Vincent	August 1, 1893	Newark
Schnitzler, William F.	January 21, 1904	Newark
Scully, John J. J.	February 10, 1867	South Amboy
Stephens, Uriah S.	August 3, 1821	Cape May County
Tighe, Michael F.	March 10, 1858	Boonton

NEW MEXICO

Name	Birthdate	Birthplace
Huerta, Dolores	Na.	Na.

NEW YORK

Name	Birthdate	Birthplace
Barry, Thomas B.	July 17, 1852	Cohoes
Bloor, Ella R.	July 8, 1862	Staten Island
Bowen, William J.	1868	Albany
Brennan, Peter J.	May 24, 1918	New York City
Broun, Heywood C.	December 7, 1888	Brooklyn
Brown, Irving J.	November 20, 1911	New York City
Bugniazet, Gustave M.	1878	New York City
Commerford, John	Na.	Brooklyn
Conlon, Peter J.	September 23, 1869	Brooklyn
Curran, Joseph E.	March 1, 1906	New York City
Ettor, Joseph J.	October 6, 1885	Brooklyn
Feeney, Frank	April 22, 1870	New York City
Fisher, Joseph A.	May 1, 1896	New York City
Fitzgerald, Frank A.	September 5, 1885	New York City
Flore, Edward	December 5, 1877	Buffalo
Gillmore, Frank	May 14, 1867	New York City
Gleason, Thomas W.	November 8, 1900	New York City
Gray, Richard J.	December 6, 1887	Albany
Greenberg, Max	August 6, 1907	New York City
Helfgott, Simon	November 15, 1894	New York City
Heller, George	November 20, 1905	New York City
Henderson, Donald J.	February 4, 1902	New York City
Hickey, Thomas L.	1893	New York City
Holderman, Carl	January 15, 1894	Hornell
Jennings, Paul J.	March 19, 1918	Brooklyn
Jessup, William J.	February 7, 1827	New York City
Lynch, James M.	January 11, 1867	Manlius
McGuire, Peter J.	July 6, 1852	New York City
Maguire, Matthew	1850	New York City
Maso, Sal	July 25, 1900	New York City
Meany, George	August 16, 1894	New York City
Miller, Marvin J.	April 14, 1917	New York City
Milliman, Elmer E.	November 22, 1890	Mount Morris
Montgomery, Robert	May 21, 1904	Beacon
Morreale, Vincent F.	July 29, 1902	New York City
Mullaney, Joseph A.	June 11, 1872	New York City

Name	Birthdate	Birthplace
Murray, Thomas A.	1885	New York City
Oakes, Grant W.	April 18, 1905	Westfield
Pachler, William J.	August 20, 1904	Thornwood
Pressman, Lee	July 1, 1906	New York City
Robins, Margaret D.	September 6, 1868	Brooklyn
Rosenblum, Frank	May 15, 1888	New York City
Ryan, Joseph P.	May 11, 1884	Babylon
Shanker, Albert	September 14, 1928	New York City
Slamm, Levi D.	ca. 1800	New York City
Troup, Augusta L.	ca. 1848	New York City
Van Arsdale, Harry Jr.	November 23, 1905	New York City
Vorse, Mary H.	ca. 1882	New York City
Walsh, Richard F.	February 20, 1900	Brooklyn
Windt, John	Na.	New York City
Wurf, Jerry	April 18, 1919	New York City

NORTH CAROLINA

Name	Birthdate	Birthplace
Scott, Sam H.	March 1, 1901	Orange County

NORTH DAKOTA

Name	Birthdate	Birthplace
Hughes, Roy O.	September 24, 1887	Portland

OHIO

Name	Birthdate	Birthplace
Abel, Iorwith W.	August 11, 1908	Magnolia
Biemiller, Andrew J.	July 23, 1906	Sandusky
Cashen, Thomas C.	September 15, 1879	South Thompson
Doherty, William C.	February 23, 1902	Glendale
Feller, Karl F.	August 6, 1914	Dayton
Fox, Martin	August 22, 1848	Cincinnati

Name	Birthdate	Birthplace
Gosser, Richard T.	December 13, 1900	Toledo
Green, William	March 3, 1873	Coshocton
Hayes, Maximilian S.	May 25, 1866	Havana
Leonard, Richard	February 22, 1902	New Straitsville
Lyons, John H.	October 29, 1919	Cleveland
McBride, John	July 25, 1854	Wayne County
Mahon, William D.	August 12, 1861	Athens County
Mitch, William A.	April 10, 1881	Minersville
Robertson, David B.	May 13, 1876	West Austintown
Tetlow, Percy	December 16, 1875	Leetonia
Thimmes, James G.	October 4, 1896	Hemlock
Thomas, Norman M.	November 20, 1884	Marion
Thomas, Rolland J.	June 9, 1900	East Palestine
Townsend, Willard S.	December 4, 1895	Cincinnati
Travis, Robert C.	February 7, 1906	Toledo

OREGON

Name	Birthdate	Birthplace
McDonald, Joseph D.	July 10, 1895	Clatskanine

PENNSYLVANIA

Name	Birthdate	Birthplace
Baldanzi, George	January 23, 1907	Black Diamond
Barnes, John M.	June 22, 1866	Lancaster
Bittner, Van A.	March 20, 1885	Bridgeport
Bower, Andrew P.	May 14, 1869	Apollo
Brown, Harvey W.	October 28, 1883	Dow
Brown, Henry S.	October 24, 1920	Pittsburgh
Cannon, Joseph D.	October 26, 1871	Locust Gap
Carey, James B.	August 12, 1911	Philadelphia
Coefield, John	June 18, 1869	Petroleum Center
Coulter, Clarence C.	June 4, 1882	Venango County
Donnelly, Samuel B.	November 7, 1866	Concord

Name	Birthdate	Birthplace
Easton, John B.	September 26, 1880	Allegheny County
Ervin, Charles W.	November 22, 1865	Philadelphia
Fincher, Jonathan C.	1830	Philadelphia
Fitzsimmons, Frank E.	April 7, 1908	Jeannette
Foran, Martin A.	November 11, 1844	Choconut
Frayne, Hugh	November 8, 1869	Scranton
Gibbons, Harold J.	April 10, 1910	Taylor
Golden, Clinton S.	November 16, 1888	Pottsville
Helt, Daniel W.	September 24, 1883	Shamokin
Johns, John S.	March 4, 1915	Beaver Falls
Kennedy, Thomas	November 2, 1887	Lansford
Lewis, Thomas L.	1866	Locust Gap
McAvoy, Harold	November 5, 1904	Philadelphia
McDevitt, James L.	November 3, 1898	Philadelphia
McDonald, David J.	November 22, 1902	Pittsburgh
McSorley, William J.	December 13, 1876	Philadelphia
Maloney, James	September 11, 1870	Scranton
Maloy, Elmer J.	March 22, 1896	Pittsburgh
Marot, Helen	June 9, 1865	Philadelphia
Maurer, James H.	April 15, 1864	Reading
Minton, Lee W.	November 17, 1911	Washington
Moffett, Elwood S.	April 30, 1908	Williamstown
Moran, John J.	February 26, 1897	Cecil
Mortimer, Wyndham	March 11, 1884	Karthaus
O'Connell, James P.	August 22, 1858	Minersville
Pollock, William	November 12, 1899	Philadelphia
Powderly, Terence V.	January 22, 1849	Carbondale
Scholle, August	May 23, 1904	Creighton
Sullivan, James W.	March 9, 1848	Carlisle
Sweeney, Vincent D.	March 3, 1900	Pittsburgh
Sylvis, William H.	November 26, 1828	Armaugh
Weaver, George L. P.	May 18, 1912	Pittsburgh
Weihe, William	January 21, 1845	Baldwin
Wilson, James A.	April 23, 1876	Erie
Yablonski, Joseph A.	March 3, 1910	Pittsburgh

RHODE ISLAND

Name	Birthdate	Birthplace
Luther, Seth	Na.	Providence
Woodcock, Leonard F.	February 15, 1911	Providence

SOUTH CAROLINA

Name	Birthdate	Birthplace
Carroll, Thomas C.	May 22, 1894	Donalds
Christopher, Paul R.	February 14, 1910	Easley
Kirkland, Joseph L.	March 12, 1922	Camden
Talbot, Thomas W.	April 17, 1845	(rural)

SOUTH DAKOTA

Name	Birthdate	Birthplace
Kirwin, James	Na.	Terry

TENNESSEE

Name	Birthdate	Birthplace
Berry, George L.	September 12, 1882	Lee Valley
Mitchell, Harry L.	June 14, 1906	Halls
Suffridge, James A.	February 2, 1909	Knoxville

TEXAS

Name	Birthdate	Birthplace
Bates, Harry C.	November, 22, 1882	Denton
Carter, William S.	August 11, 1859	Austin
Luna, Charles	October 21, 1906	Celeste

UTAH

Name	Birthdate	Birthplace
Haywood, William D.	February 4, 1869	Salt Lake City
Lloyd, Thomas J.	November 13, 1895	Spanish Forks
Peterson, Esther	December 9, 1906	Provo

VERMONT

Name	Birthdate	Birthplace
Burke, John P.	January 21, 1884	North Duxbury
Sargent, Frank P.	November 18, 1854	East Orange

VIRGINIA

Name	Birthdate	Birthplace
Davis, Richard L.	December 24, 1864	Roanoke
Doak, William N.	December 12, 1882	Rural Retreat
Mason, Lucy R	July 26, 1882	Clarens

WASHINGTON

Name	Birthdate	Birthplace
Dennis, Eugene	August 10, 1905	Seattle
Travis, Maurice E.	April 24, 1910	Spokane

WEST VIRGINIA

Name	Birthdate	Birthplace
Cook, Harry H.	February 28, 1883	Wheeling
Dalrymple, Sherman H.	April 4, 1889	Walton
Duffy, James M.	June 28, 1889	Wheeling
Keeney, C. F.	Na.	Kanawha County
Reuther, Roy	August 29, 1909	Wheeling

Name	Birthdate	Birthplace
Reuther, Victor G.	January 1, 1912	Wheeling
Reuther, Walter P.	September 1, 1907	Wheeling
Ryan, Martin F.	October 23, 1874	Coldwater
Swisher, Elwood D.	March 24, 1913	Jenningston

WISCONSIN

Name	Birthdate	Birthplace
Addes, George P.	August 26, 1910	LaCrosse
Behncke, David L.	1897	(rural)
Burns, Matthew T.	November 6, 1887	Appleton
Chapman, Gordon W.	September 5, 1907	Tomah
George, Leo E.	January 3, 1888	Medford
Hartung, Albert F.	June 18, 1897	Catract
Hayes, Albert J.	February 14, 1900	Milwaukee
Krzycki, Leo	August 10, 1881	Milwaukee
Leighty, George E.	August 16, 1899	Phillips
Lennon, John B.	October 12, 1850	Lafayette County
Ohl, Henry Jr.	March 16, 1873	Milwaukee
Schoemann, Peter T.	October 26, 1893	Milwaukee
Weber, Frank J.	August 7, 1849	Milwaukee
Zander, Arnold S.	November 26, 1901	Two Rivers

DISTRICT OF COLUMBIA

Name	Birthdate	Birthplace
Borchardt, Selma M.	December 1, 1895	Washington
Delaney, George P.	February 20, 1909	Washington

VIRGIN ISLANDS

Name	Birthdate	Birthplace
Crosswaith, Frank R.	July 16, 1892	St. Croix
Totten, Ashley L.	October 11, 1884	St. Croix

COUNTRIES OTHER THAN THE UNITED STATES

AUSTRALIA

Name	Birthdate	Birthplace
Bridges, Harry A.	July 28, 1901	Melbourne
Henry, Alice	March 21, 1857	Richmond

AUSTRIA

Name	Birthdate	Birthplace
Berger, Victor L.	February 28, 1860	Nieder-Rehbach

(For individuals born between 1867-1919, see *Austria-Hungary*.)

AUSTRIA-HUNGARY

Name	Birthdate	Birthplace
Ernst, Hugo	December 11, 1876	Varasdin
Nagler, Isidore	February 25, 1895	Uscie Biscupie
Strasser, Adolph	Na.	Na.

(For individuals born before 1867, see *Austria* or *Hungary*.)

CANADA

Name	Birthdate	Birthplace
Allen, William L.	April 17, 1896	Comnock, Ontario
Calvin, William A.	February 5, 1898	St. John, New Brunswick
Cheyfitz, Edward T.	September 13, 1913	Montreal, Quebec
Johnston, Alvanley	May 12, 1875	Seeley's Bay, Ontario
Johnston, William H.	December 30, 1874	Westville, Nova Scotia
Kennedy, William P.	April 3, 1892	Huttonville, Ontario
Mazey, Emil	August 2, 1913	Regina, Saskatchewan
Merrill, Lewis R.	1908	Toronto, Ontario
Milne, J. Scott	January 21, 1898	Vancouver, British Columbia

Name	Birthdate	Birthplace
Morrison, Frank	November 23, 1859	Franktown, Ontario
O'Connor, Thomas V.	1870	Toronto, Ontario
Sefton, Lawrence F.	March 31, 1917	Iroquois Falls, Ontario

DENMARK

Name	Birthdate	Birthplace
Myrup, Andrew A.	March 13, 1880	Copenhagen

GERMANY

Name	Birthdate	Birthplace
Germer, Adolph F.	January 15, 1881	Welan
Obergfell, Joseph F.	July 26, 1881	Na.
Schoenberg, William	August, 1879	Na.

(See also *Saxony*.)

HUNGARY

Name	Birthdate	Birthplace
Weber, Joseph N.	June 21, 1866	Neu Beschenowa

(For individuals born between 1867-1919, see *Austria-Hungary*.)

ICELAND

Name	Birthdate	Birthplace
Fljozdal, Frederick H.	December 19, 1868	Na.

IRELAND

Name	Birthdate	Birthplace
Boyce, Edward	November 8, 1863	Na.

Name	Birthdate	Birthplace
Devyr, Thomas A.	1805	Donegal
Duffy, Frank	1861	County Montaghan
Fitzpatrick, John	April 21, 1871	Na.
Greene, Michael F.	January 1, 1884	Kilclohor, County Clare
Jones, Mary H.	May 1, 1830	Cork City
Lawrenson, Jack	October 22, 1906	Dublin
Lyden, Michael J.	1879	Barnikelle, County Mayo
McCarthy, Patrick H.	March 17, 1863	Killoughteen, County Limerick
McDonnell, J. P.	ca. 1840	Dublin
McMahon, Thomas F.	May 2, 1870	Ballybay, County Monaghan
McNulty, Frank J.	August 10, 1872	Londonderry
Molony, Joseph P.	November 6, 1906	Ennis, County Clare
Quill, Michael J.	September 18, 1905	Kilgarvan, County Kerry
Ratchford, Michael D.	August, 1860	County Clare
Roney, Frank	August 13, 1841	Belfast
Siney, John	July 31, 1831	Bornos, County Queens
Sullivan, David	May 7, 1904	Cork City
Swartz, Maud O.	May 3, 1879	County Kildare
Tobin, Daniel J.	April, 1875	County Clare
Wright, James L.	April 6, 1816	County Tyrone

ITALY

Name	Birthdate	Birthplace
Antonini, Luigi	September 11, 1883	Vallata Irpina, Avellino
Damino, Harry	1893	Na.
Giovannitti, Arturo	January 7, 1884	Campobasso
Hoffmann, Sal B.	April 5, 1899	Aversa
Moreschi, Joseph	1884	Na.
Ninfo, Salvatore	May 13, 1883	Santo Stefano
Romualdi, Serafino	November 18, 1900	Bastia Umbra

LATVIA. See *Russian Latvia*.

LITHUANIA. See *Russian Lithuania.*

LUXEMBOURG

Name	Birthdate	Birthplace
Woll, Matthew	January 25, 1880	Na.

MEXICO

Name	Birthdate	Birthplace
Galarza, Ernesto	August 15, 1905	Jalcocotan, Nayarit

THE NETHERLANDS

Name	Birthdate	Birthplace
Muste, Abraham J.	January 8, 1885	Zierikzee

NEW ZEALAND

Name	Birthdate	Birthplace
Trautmann, William E.	1869	Na.

NORWAY

Name	Birthdate	Birthplace
Furuseth, Andrew	March 12, 1854	Romedal
Lundeberg, Harry	March 25, 1901	Oslo

POLAND. See *Russian Poland.*

RUSSIA

Name	Birthdate	Birthplace
Barondess, Joseph	July 3, 1867	Kamenets-Podolsk, Ukraine
Baskin, Joseph	October 20, 1880	Minsk
Bisno, Abraham	1866	Belaya Tserkov
Breslaw, Joseph	April 18, 1887	Miskifky
Cohn, Fannia	April 5, 1888	Minsk
Feinberg, Israel	December 25, 1887	Berdichev, Ukraine
Gold, Ben	September 8, 1898	Bessarabia
Heller, Jacob J.	August 21, 1889	Na.
Hochman, Julius	January 12, 1892	Bessarabia
Hyman, Louis	June 17, 1884	Witebask
Kaufman, Morris	September, 1884	Minsk
Kazan, Abraham E.	December 15, 1888	Kiev, Ukraine
London, Meyer	December 29, 1871	Suwalki
Mendelowitz, Abraham	March 5, 1894	Nikolaev, Ukraine
Newman, Pauline	October 18, 1891	Na.
Perlstein, Meyer	September 15, 1884	Cartyz Bereza, Grodno
Pine, Max	1866	Liubavitch
Potofsky, Jacob S.	November 16, 1894	Radomisl, Ukraine
Price, George M.	May 21, 1864	Poltava, Ukraine
Rombro, Jacob	October 10, 1858	Zuphran, Wilna
Schlossberg, Joseph	May 1, 1875	Koidanovo, Belorussia
Schneiderman, Rose	April 6, 1884	Savin
Sigman, Morris	May 15, 1881	Costesh, Bessarabia
Stokes, Rose H. P.	July 18, 1879	Augustowo, Suwalki
Vladeck, Baruch C.	January, 1886	Dookorah, Minsk
Wolchok, Samuel	September 20, 1896	Bobruisk
Zaritsky, Max	April 15, 1885	Petrikov
Zimmerman, Charles S.	November 27, 1896	Kiev, Ukraine

RUSSIAN LATVIA

Name	Birthdate	Birthplace
Bellanca, Dorothy J.	August 10, 1894	Zemel
Hillquit, Morris	August 1, 1869	Riga

RUSSIAN LITHUANIA

Name	Birthdate	Birthplace
Blumberg, Hyman	November 25, 1885	Legum
Cahan, Abraham	July 7, 1860	Podberezye
Dyche, John A.	1867	Kovno
Hillman, Sidney	March 23, 1887	Zagare
Schlesinger, Benjamin	December 25, 1876	Krakai

RUSSIAN POLAND

Name	Birthdate	Birthplace
Dubinsky, David	February 22, 1892	Brest-Litovsk
Feinstone, Morris	1878	Warsaw
Hollander, Louis	February 5, 1893	Wadowice
Pizer, Morris	February 12, 1904	Na.
Rieve, Emil	June 8, 1892	Zyradow
Rose, Alex	October 15, 1898	Warsaw
Stulberg, Louis	April 14, 1901	Bogria

SAXONY

Name	Birthdate	Birthplace
Schilling, Robert	October 17, 1843	Osterburg
Sorge, Friedrich A.	November 9, 1828	Bethau bei Torgau

SPAIN

Name	Birthdate	Birthplace
Iglesias, Santiago	February 22, 1872	La Coruña

SWEDEN

Name	Birthdate	Birthplace
Anderson, Mary	August 27, 1872	Lidköping

Name	Birthdate	Birthplace
Hill, Joe	October 7, 1879	Gavle
Lindelof, Lawrence P.	May 18, 1875	Malmö, Skane
Peterson, Eric	September 3, 1894	Dalarne

UNION OF SOVIET SOCIALIST REPUBLICS. See *Russia, Russian Latvia, Russian Lithuania, Russian Poland.*

UNITED KINGDOM

Name	Birthdate	Birthplace
Arthur, Peter M.	1831	Paisley, Scotland
Brophy, John	November 6, 1883	St. Helens, England
Byron, Robert	ca. 1880	Lynwood, Scotland
Caddy, Samuel H.	December 9, 1883	Short Health, England
Cairns, Thomas F.	1875	Durhamshire, England
Cameron, Andrew C.	September 28, 1836	Berwick-on-Tweed, England
Clark, John	1888	Sheffield, England
Davis, James J.	October 27, 1873	Thedegar, South Wales
Derwent, Clarence	March 23, 1884	London, England
Duncan, James	May 5, 1857	Kincardine County, Scotland
Evans, George H.	March 25, 1805	Bromyard, England
Farquhar, John M.	April 17, 1832	Ayr, Scotland
Gompers, Samuel	January 27, 1850	London, England
Green, John	November 15, 1896	Clydebank, Scotland
Heighton, William	1800	Oundle, England
Hinchcliffe, John	1822	Bradford, England
Howat, Alexander	1876	Glasglow, Scotland
Irons, Martin	March 1, 1833	Dundee, Scotland
Jarrett, John	January 27, 1843	Elbow Vale, England
Kroll, John J.	June 10, 1885	London, England
Lawson, John C.	September 3, 1900	Aberdeen, Scotland
MacGowan, Charles J.	1887	Argyllshire, Scotland
Mitchell, James J.	November 25, 1896	Carfin, Scotland
Morgan, Thomas J.	October 27, 1847	Birmingham, England

Name	Birthdate	Birthplace
Murray, Philip	May 25, 1886	Blantyre, Scotland
O'Hare, John	June 14, 1904	Armadale, Scotland
Owen, Robert D.	November 9, 1801	Glasglow, Scotland
Padway, Joseph A.	July 25, 1891	Leeds, England
Phillips, Thomas	March 22, 1833	Whitson, England
Preston, George	November 3, 1864	Lincolnshire, England
Starr, Mark	April 27, 1894	Shoscombe, England
Swinton, John	December 12, 1829	Edinburgh, Scotland
Trevellick, Richard F.	May 20, 1830	St. Mary's, Scilly Isles
Turner, Frederick	1846	England
Walker, John H.	April 27, 1872	Binny Hill, Scotland
Watt, Robert J.	July 16, 1894	Scotland
Wilson, William B.	April 2, 1862	Blantyre, Scotland

VENEZUELA

Name	Birthdate	Birthplace
DeLeon, Daniel	December 14, 1852	Curaçao

YUGOSLAVIA. See *Austria-Hungary.*

NOT ASCERTAINED

Name	Birthdate	Birthplace
Donnelly, Michael	Na.	Na.
English, William	Na.	Na.
Ferral, John	Na.	Na.
Greene, Prince W.	Na.	Na.
Hagerty, Thomas J.	ca. 1862	Na.
Huber, William	Na.	Na.
Lewis, Thomas L.	1866	Na.
Little, Frank H.	1879	Na.
Mahoney, Charles E.	Na.	Na.
Moyer, Charles H.	Na.	Na.

Name	Birthdate	Birthplace
Nef, Walter T.	Na.	Na.
O'Neill, John M.	ca. 1857	Na.
Perkins, George W.	Na.	Na.
Rarick, Donald C.	1919	Na.
Sherman, Charles O.	Na.	Na.
Townsend, Robert Jr.	Na.	Na.
Wharton, Arthur O.	November 9, 1873	Na.
Wilson, D. Douglas	Na.	Na.

Appendix IV
Formal Education

Because it often was impossible to determine the exact extent of a person's education, especially at the lower levels, this Appendix is largely derived. In some cases, it was necessary to use yardsticks like the number of years of formal schooling or the age at which the individual became a full-time wage earner to determine the extent of his education. It was also difficult to determine the U.S. equivalent of a foreign education. Categories "1," "2," and "3" simply reflect attendence at a particular level and do not necessarily mean that the individual completed that level of education.

Key:

Category 1 - Grammar

2 - Secondary

3 - Special-Vocational (V), Night School (N), Business College (B), Labor College (L).

4 - College

5 - B.S. or M.A.

6 - M.A. or M.S.

7 - LLD or successfully passing bar exam

8 - PhD or M.D.

9 - Unknown

Category- Name	(1) Gra.	(2) Sec.	(3) Spc.	(4) Col.	(5) Bch.	(6) Mst.	(7) Law.	(8) Doc.	(9) Unk.
Abel, Iorwith W.	X	X	B						
Addes, George P.	X	X		X					
Allen, William L.	X								
Alpine, John P.	X								
Anderson, Mary	X								
Antonini, Luigi	X	X							
Arthur, Peter	X								
Azpeitia, Mario	X								
Bacon, Emery F.	X	X		X	X	X			
Baer, Fred W.	X								
Bagley, Sarah									X
Baldanzi, George	X								
Barkan, Alexander E.	X	X		X	X				
Barnes, John M.	X		C						
Barnum, Gertrude	X	X		X					
Barondess, Joseph	X	X		X					
Barry, Thomas B.	X								
Baskin, Joseph	X	X		X	X				
Bates, Harry C.	X	X							
Beck, Dave	X	X	C						
Behncke, David L.	X	X							
Beirne, Joseph A.	X	X		X					
Bellanca, Dorothy J.	X								
Berger, Victor L.	X	X							
Berry, George L.	X								
Biemiller, Andrew J.	X	X		X	X				
Birthright, William C.	X	X							
Bisno, Abraham	X								
Bittner, Van A.	X	X							
Bloor, Ella R.	X								
Blumberg, Hyman	X								
Borchardt, Selma M.	X	X		X	X	X	X		
Bowen, William J.	X								
Bower, Andrew P.	X		B						
Boyce, Edward	X								
Boyle, William A.	X								

Category- Name	(1) Gra.	(2) Sec.	(3) Spc.	(4) Col.	(5) Bc.	(6) Mst.	(7) Law.	(8) Doc.	(9) Unk.
Brennan, Peter J.	X	X		X	X				
Breslaw, Joseph	X								
Brewer, Roy M.	X	X							
Bridges, Harry A. R.	X	X							
Brophy, John	X		L						
Broun, Heywood C.	X	X		X					
Brown, Edward J.	X	X						X	
Brown Guy L.	X								
Brown, Harvey W.	X								
Brown, Henry S.	X	X		X					
Brown, Irving J.	X	X		X	X				
Bryson, Hugh	X	X	B						
Buchanan, Joseph R.	X								
Buckley, Leo J.	X								
Buckmaster, Leland S.	X	X		X					
Bugniazet, Gustave M.	X								
Burke, John P.	X	X		X					
Burke, Walter J.	X	X							
Burns, Matthew J.	X		C						
Burns, Thomas F.	X	X							
Byron, Robert	X								
Caddy, Samuel H.	X								
Cahan, Abraham	X	X		X	X				
Cairns, Thomas F.	X	X	C						
Calvin, William A.	X								
Cameron, Andrew C.	X								
Cannon, Joseph D.	X								
Carey, James B.	X	X		X					
Carroll, Thomas C.	X	X							
Carter, William S.	X	X		X					
Cashen, Thomas C.	X	X							
Chapman, Gordon W.	X	X		X	X				
Chavez, Cesar E.	X								
Cheyfitz, Edward T.	X	X		X	X				

Category- Name	(1) Gra.	(2) Sec.	(3) Spc.	(4) Col.	(5) Bch.	(6) Mst.	(7) Law.	(8) Doc.	(9) Unk.
Christman, Elisabeth	X								
Christopher, Paul R.	X	X		X					
Clark, Jesse	X		B						
Clark, John	X								
Clark, Lewis J.	X	X							
Coefield, John	X	X							
Cohn, Fannia	X								
Collins, Jennie									X
Commerford, John									X
Conlon, Peter J.	X		C						
Cook, Harry H.	X								
Cope, Elmer F.	X	X		X	X	X			
Cosgrove, John T.	X	X							
Coulter, Clarence C.	X	X							
Crosswaith, Frank R.	X		L						
Crull, John L.	X	X							
Curran, Joseph E.	X								
Dalrymple, Sherman H.	X								
Damino, Harry	X								
Davidson, Roy E.	X	X		X					
Davis, James J.	X	X	B						
Davis, Richard L.	X								
Debs, Eugene V.	X								
Delaney, George P.	X	X		X					
DeLeon, Daniel	X	X		X	X		X		
Dennis, Eugene	X	X		X					
Derwent, Clarence	X	X	V						
Devyr, Thomas A.	X								
Doak, William N.	X	X	B						
Dobbs, Farrel	X	X							
Doherty, William C.	X		V						
Donnelly, Michael									X
Donnelly, Samuel B.	X	X		X					
Douglas, Charles									X
Driscoll, John J.	X	X		X	X	X			

Category- Name	(1) Gra.	(2) Sec.	(3) Spc.	(4) Col.	(5) Bch	(6) Mst.	(7) Law.	(8) Doc.	(9) Unk.
Dubinsky, David	X								
Duffy, Frank	X								
Duffy, James M.	X								
Dullzell, Paul	X								
Duncan, James	X								
Dunne, Vincent R.	X								
Dunwody, Thomas E.	X	X		X					
Durkin, Martin P.	X		V						
Dyche, John A.									X
Eames, Thomas B.	X								
Easton, John B.	X		N						
Eklund, John M.	X	X		X	X	X			
English, John F.	X								
English, William									X
Ernst, Hugo	X	X							
Ervin, Charles W.	X		C						
Ettor, Joseph J.	X								
Evans, George H.	X								
Farquhar, John M.	X						X		
Farrington, Frank	None								
Feeney, Frank	X								
Feinberg, Israel	X	X							
Feinstone, Morris	X		V						
Feller, Karl F.	X	X							
Fenton, Francis, P.	X						X		
Ferral, John								X	
Fincher, Jonathan C.									X
Fisher, Joseph A.	X	X		X					
Fitzgerald, Albert J.	X	X							
Fitzgerald, Frank A.	X	X							
Fitzpatrick, John	X								
Fitzsimmons, Frank E.	X								
Fljozdal, Frederick H.	X		C						
Flore, Edward	X	X							
Flynn, Elizabeth G.	X	X							

Category- Name	(1) Gra.	(2) Sec.	(3) Spc.	(4) Col.	(5) Bch.	(6) Mst.	(7) Law.	(8) Doc.	(9) Unk.
Foran, Martin A.	X	X		X					
Foster, William Z.	X								
Fox, Martin	X								
Frankensteen, Richard T.	X	X		X	X				
Fraser, Harry W.	X								
Frayne, Hugh	X								
Frey, John P.	X	X							
Furuseth, Andrew	X								
Gainor, Edward J.	X	X							
Galarza, Ernesto	X	X		X	X	X		X	
Garretson, Austin B.	X	X							
George, Leo E.	X	X		X					
Germano, Joseph S.	X	X							
Germer, Adolph F.	X	X	C						
Gibbons, Harold J.	X	X	C						
Gibson, Everett G.	X								
Gibson, John W.	X	X		X					
Gilbert, Henry E.	X	X		X					
Gillmore, Frank	X	X							
Giovannitti, Arturo	X	X		X					
Givens, Paul A.	X	X							
Gleason, Thomas W.	X								
Gold, Ben	X								
Goldberg, Arthur J.	X	X		X	X	X	X		
Golden, Clinton S.	X								
Gompers, Samuel	X		N						
Googe, George L.	X	X	V						
Gorman, Patrick E.	X	X					X		
Gosser, Richard T.	X		V						
Graham, Sylvester	X	X							
Gray, Richard J.	X								
Green, John	X	X							
Green, William	X								
Greenberg, Max	X	X							
Greene, Michael F.	X								

Category- Name	(1) Gra.	(2) Sec.	(3) Spc.	(4) Col.	(5) Bch.	(6) Mst.	(7) Law.	(8) Doc.	(9) Unk.
Greene, Prince W.									X
Griner, John F.	X	X					X		
Grogan, John J.	X	X		X					
Hagerty, Thomas J.	X	X		X					
Haggerty, Cornelius J.	X								
Haggerty, John B.	X	X							
Haley, Margaret A.	X	X							
Hall, Paul	X								
Hallbeck, Elroy C.	X	X							
Hapgood, Powers	X	X		X	X				
Harrison, George M.	X								
Hartung, Albert F.	X								
Hayes, Albert J.	X								
Hayes, Frank J.	X								
Hayes, Maximilian S.	X								
Haywood, William D.	X								
Heighton, William	X								
Helfgott, Simon	X	X							
Heller, George	X	X		X					
Heller, Jacob J.	X	X		X					
Helstein, Ralph	X	X		X	X		X		
Helt, Daniel W.	X								
Henderson, Donald J.	X	X		X	X	X			
Henry, Alice	X	X							
Hickey, Thomas L.	X								
Hill, Joe	X								
Hillman, Sidney	X	X							
Hillquit, Morris	X	X					X		
Hinchcliffe, John									X
Hochman, Julius		X	C						
Hoffa, James R.	X								
Hoffmann, Sal B.	X	X							
Holderman, Carl	X	X							
Hollander, Louis	X	X							
Horn, Roy	X								
Howard, Charles P.	X								

Category- Name	(1) Gra.	(2) Sec.	(3) Spc.	(4) Col.	(5) Bch.	(6) Mst.	(7) Law.	(8) Doc.	(9) Unk.
Howat, Alexander									X
Huber, William									X
Huddell, Arthur M.	X								
Huerta, Dolores									X
Hughes, Roy A.	X	X							
Hutcheson, Maurice A.	X								
Hutcheson, William L.	X								
Hyman, Louis	X		N						
Iglesias, Santiago	X								
Irons, Martin	X								
Jarrett, John									X
Jennings, Paul J.	X	X							
Jessup, William J.	X								
Jewell, Bert M.	X								
Jimerson, Earl W.	X								
Johns, John S.	X	X							
Johnson, William D.	X								
Johnston, Alvanley	X		B						
Johnston, William H.	X								
Jones, Mary H.	X	X		X					
Kasten, Frank	X								
Kaufman, Morris	None								
Kavanagh, William F.	X								
Kazan, Abraham E.	X	X		X					
Keating, Edward	X								
Keefe, Daniel J.	X								
Keenan, Joseph D.	X	X							
Keeney, C. Frank									X
Kehrer, Elmer T.	X	X		X	X	X			
Kelsay, Ray	X								
Kenin, Herman D.	X	X		X	X		X		
Kennedy, Thomas	X								
Kennedy, William P.	X								
Kirkland, Joseph L.	X	X		X	X				

Category-	(1)	(2)	(3)	(4)	(5)	(6)	(7)	(8)	(9)
Name	Gra.	Sec.	Spc.	Col.	Bch.	Mst.	Law.	Doc.	Unk.
Kirwan, James									X
Knight, Felix H.	X	X							
Knight, Orie A.	X	X							
Kroll, John J.	X	X							
Krzycki, Leo	X								
Labadie, Joseph A.	X								
Lane, Dennis	X								
Lawrenson, Jack	X								
Lawson, George W.	X	X							
Lawson, John C.	X								
Lee, William G.	X								
Leighty, George E.	X	X							
Lennon, John B.	X								
Leonard, Richard	X								
Lewis, Alma D.	X								
Lewis, John L.	X	X							
Lewis, Joseph	X	X							
Lewis, Thomas L.									X
Lindelof, Lawrence P.	X	X		X					
Litchman, Charles H.	X	X							
Little, Frank H.									X
Livingston, John W.	X	X							
Lloyd, Thomas J.	X	X							
London, Meyer	X	X					X		
Luhrsen, Julius G.	X		V						
Luna, Charles	X	X							
Lundeberg, Harry	X								
Luther, Seth	X								
Lyden, Michael J.	X								
Lynch, James M.	X								
Lyon, Arlon E.	X	X							
Lyons, John H.	X	X		X	X				
McAvoy, Harold	X	X		X	X				
McBride, John	X								
McCarthy, Patrick H.	X								
McCurdy, Joseph P.	X	X		X	X				

Category- Name	(1) Gra.	(2) Sec.	(3) Sc.	(4) Col.	(5) Bch.	(6) Mst.	(7) Law.	(8) Doc.	(9) Unk.
McDevitt, James L.	X	X							
McDonald, David J.	X	X		X	X				
McDonald, Joseph D.	X	X							
McDonnell, J. P.									X
McFetridge, William L.	X	X					X		
McGowan, Charles J.	X								
McGrady, Edward F.	X	X	N						
McGuire, Peter J.	X		N						
McMahon, Thomas F.	X								
McNamara, Patrick V.	X	X	V						
McNeill, George E.	X								
McNulty, Frank J.	X								
McSorley, William J.	X								
Maguire, Matthew	X								
Mahon, William D.	X								
Mahoney, Charles E.									X
Mahoney, William	X						X		
Maloney, James	X								
Maloney, William E.	X								
Maloy, Elmer J.	X	X							
Marciante, Louis P.	X	X							
Marot, Helen	X	X		X					
Martin, Harry L.	X	X		X	X				
Martin, Warren H.	X	X		X	X				
Mashburn, Lloyd A.	X	X	V						
Maso, Sal	X	X		X					
Mason, Lucy R.	X	X							
Mathias, Charles G.	X	X	N						
Maurer, James H.	None								
Mazey, Emil	X	X							
Meany, George	X	X							
Megel, Carl J.	X	X		X	X				
Mendelowitz, Abraham	X								
Merrill, Lewis R.	X	X		X					

Category- Name	(1) Gra.	(2) Sec.	(3) Spc.	(4) Col.	(5) Bch.	(6) Mst.	(7) Law.	(8) Doc.	(9) Unk.
Miller, Edward S.	X	X							
Miller, Marvin J.	X	X		X	X				
Milliman, Elmer E.	X	X		X					
Milne, J. Scott	X	X							
Minton, Lee W.	X	X	B						
Mitch, William A.	X								
Mitchell, Harry L.	X	X							
Mitchell, James J.	X								
Mitchell, John	X		N	X					
Mitchell, Walter L.	X	X					X		
Moffett, Elwood S.	X	X							
Mohn, Einar O.	X	X		X					
Molony, Joseph P.	X								
Montgomery, Robert	X	X							
Mooney, Thomas J.	X								
Moore, Ely	X								
Moran, John J.	X	X							
Moreschi, Joseph									X
Morgan, Thomas J.	X	X					X		
Morreale, Vincent F.	X	X		X	X		X		
Morrison, Frank	X	X					X		
Mortimer, Wyndham	X								
Moyer, Charles H.									X
Mullaney, Joseph A.	X								
Murphy, Vincent	X	X	B						
Murray, Philip	X								
Murray, Thomas A.	X								
Muste, Abraham J.	X	X		X	X	X			
Myrup, Andrew A.	X								
Nagler, Isidore	X								
Nance, Alexander S.	X								
Nef, Walter T.									X
Nelson, Oscar F.	X	X					X		
Nestor, Agnes	X								
Newman, Pauline	X								
Ninfo, Salvatore	X								

Category- Name	(1) Gra.	(2) Sec.	(3) Spc.	(4) Col.	(5) Bch.	(6) Mst.	(7) Law.	(8) Doc.	(9) Unk.
Nockles, Edward N.	X								
Noonan, James P.	X								
Oakes, Grant W.	X	X	V						
Obergfell, Joseph F.	X	X							
O'Connell, James P.	X	X							
O'Connor, Harvey	X	X							
O'Connor, Thomas V.									X
O'Hare, John	X	X	N						
Ohl, Henry	X								
Olander, Victor A.	X								
O'Neill, John M.	X	X		X	X				
Ornburn, Ira M.	X								
Owen, Robert D.	X	X		X					
Pachler, William J.	X	X	B						
Padway, Joseph A.	X	X					X		
Parsons, Albert R.	X								
Perkins, George W.									X
Perlstein, Meyer	X		N						
Peterson, Eric	X								
Peterson, Esther	X	X		X	X	X			
Petrillo, James C.	X								
Phillips, James A.	X								
Phillips, Paul L.	X	X		X					
Phillips, Thomas	X								
Pine, Max	X								
Pizer, Morris	X	X		X					
Pollock, William	X	X							
Possehl, John	X								
Potofsky, Jacob S.	X	X							
Powderly, Terence V.	X						X		
Powers, Frank B.	X	X		X					
Pressman, Lee	X	X		X	X		X		
Preston, George	X								
Price, George M.	X	X		X				X	
Quill, Michael J.	X								
Raftery, Lawrence M.	X	X	V						

Category-	(1) Gra.	(2) Sec.	(3) Spc.	(4) Col.	(5) Bch.	(6) Mst.	(7) Law.	(8) Doc.	(9) Unk.
Name									
Ramsay, Claude	X	X		X					
Randolph, Asa P.	X	X		X					
Randolph, Woodruff	X	X					X		
Rarick, Donald C.	X	X							
Ratchford, Michael D.	X		N						
Reagan, Ronald	X	X		X	X				
Redmond, John P.	X	X		X					
Reuther, Roy	X	X		X					
Reuther, Victor	X	X		X					
Reuther, Walter P.	X	X		X					
Rickert, Thomas A.	X	X	B						
Rieve, Emil	X								
Robertson, David B.	X		N						
Robins, Margaret D.	X	X							
Robinson, Reid	X	X							
Rollings, John I.	X								
Rombro, Jacob	X	X		X					
Romualdi, Serafino	X	X		X					
Roney, Frank	X								
Rose, Alex	X	X							
Rosenblum, Frank	X								
Ruttenberg, Harold J.	X	X		X	X				
Ryan, Joseph P.	X								
Ryan, Martin F.	X	X							
St. John, Vincent									X
Sargent, Frank P.	X	X							
Schilling, Robert									X
Schlesinger, Benjamin	X								
Schlossberg, Joseph	X			X					
Schneiderman, Rose	X								
Schnitzler, William F.	X								
Schoemann, Peter T.	X								
Schoenberg, William	X								
Scholle, August	X	X							
Scott, Sam H.	X	X		X					
Scully, John J. J.	X	X	V						

Category- Name	(1) Gra.	(2) Sec.	(3) Spc.	(4) Col.	(5) Bch.	(6) Mst.	(7) Law.	(8) Doc.	(9) Unk.
Sefton, Lawrence F.	X	X							
Selden, David S.	X	X		X	X	X			
Shanker, Albert	X	X		X	X	X			
Shelley, John F.	X	X		X			X		
Sherman, Charles O.									X
Shields, James P.	X	X							
Siemiller, Paul L.	X								
Sigman, Morris	X								
Siney, John	None								
Skidmore, Thomas	X								
Slamm, Levi D.									X
Soderstrom, Reuben C.	X								
Sorge, Friedrick A.	X	X		X					
Spradling, Abe L.	X	X							
Starr, Mark	X	X		X					
Stephens, Uriah S.	X	X							
Steward, Ira	None								
Stokes, Rose H. P.	X								
Stone, Warren S.	X	X		X					
Strasser, Adolph									X
Stulberg, Louis	X	X		X					
Suffridge, James A.	X	X		X					
Sullivan, David	X	X							
Sullivan, James W.	X	X							
Sullivan, Jere L.	X								
Swartz, Maud O.	X	X							
Sweeney, Vincent D.	X	X		X	X				
Swinton, John	X			X					
Swisher, Elwood D.	X	X							
Sylvis, William H.	None								
Tahney, James P.	X	X							
Talbot, Thomas W.	X								
Tetlow, Percy	X		V						
Thimmes, James G.	X	X							
Thomas, Norman M.	X	X		X	X				

Category- Name	(1) Gra.	(2) Sec.	(3) Spc.	(4) Col.	(5) Bch.	(6) Mst.	(7) Law.	(8) Doc.	(9) Unk.
Thomas, Rolland J.	X	X		X					
Tighe, Michael F.	X								
Tobin, Daniel J.	X		N						
Totten, Ashley L.	X	X							
Townsend, Robert, Jr.									X
Townsend, Willard S.	X	X		X	X		X		
Tracy, Daniel W.	X	X							
Trautmann, William E.									X
Travis, Maurice E.	X								
Travis, Robert C.	X	X							
Trevellick, Richard F.									X
Troup, Augusta L.	X	X							
Turner, Frederick	X	X							
Valentine, Joseph F.	X								
Van Arsdale, Harry, Jr.		X	X						
Vladeck, Baruch C.	X			X					
Vorse, Mary H.	X	X							
Walker, John H.	X								
Walsh, Richard F.	X								
Watt, Robert J.	X		N						
Weaver, George L. P.	X	X		X					
Weber, Frank J.	X								
Weber, Joseph N.	X								
Weihe, William	X								
Werkau, Carlton W.	X	X							
Wharton, Arthur O.									X
White, John P.									X
Whitfield, Owen H.	X	X		X					
Whitney, Alexander F.	X	X							
Williams, Benjamin H.	X	X		X	X				
Williams, Elijah H.	X	X							
Wilson, D. Douglas									X
Wilson, James A.	X								

Category- Name	(1) Gra.	(2) Sec.	(3) Spc.	(4) Col.	(5) Bch.	(6) Mst.	(7) Law.	(8) Doc.	(9) Unk.
Wilson, William B.	X								
Windt, John									X
Wolchok, Samuel	X	X							
Woll, Matthew	X		N				X		
Wood, Reuben T.	X								
Woodcock, Leonard F.	X	X		X					
Wright, James L.	X	X							
Wurf, Jerry	X	X		X	X				
Yablonski, Joseph A.	X								
Zander, Arnold S.	X	X		X	X	X		X	
Zaritsky, Max	X	X							
Zimmerman, Charles S.	X	X							

Appendix V
Political Preference

Listings in this Appendix were determined not only by party membership but also by identification with or support of a political party. Because
party identification in some cases changed over time, some persons are
listed under more than one party. Category "3" includes a number of
different Socialist parties; the three major parties were the Socialist party of
America, the Socialist Labor party, and the Socialist Workers party. In
category "4" the American Labor party and the Liberal party are listed
together. When the American Labor party came increasingly under the
control of the Communists, most of its members transferred to the newly
organized Liberal party.

Key:

Category   1 - Democratic party
2 - Republican party
3 - Socialist parties
4 - American Labor party-Liberal party
5 - Self-identified nonpartisan
6 - Supporter of an independent labor party
7 - Communist party of America
8 - Not ascertained

Name	Category- (1) Dem.	(2) Rep.	(3) Soc.	(4) A/L	(5) N-P	(6) L-P	(7) CPA	(8) N/A
Abel, Iorwith W.	X							
Addes, George P.	X							
Allen, William L.								X
Alpine, John P.		X						
Anderson, Mary								X
Antonini, Luigi				X				
Arthur, Peter								X
Azpeitia, Mario								X
Bacon, Emery F.	X							
Baer, Fred W.	X							
Bagley, Sarah								X
Baldanzi, George								X
Barkan, Alexander E.	X							
Barnes, John M.			X					
Barnum, Gertrude								X
Barondess, Joseph			X					
Barry, Thomas B.								X
Baskin, Joseph			X					
Bates, Harry C.	X							
Beck, Dave		X						
Behncke, David L.	X							
Beirne, Joseph A.	X							
Bellanca, Dorothy J.				X				
Berger, Victor L.			X					
Berry, George L.	X							
Biemiller, Andrew J.	X		X					
Birthright, William C.	X							
Bisno, Abraham								X
Bittner, Van A.	X							
Bloor, Ella R.			X				X	
Blumberg, Hyman	X				X			
Borchardt, Selma M.								X
Bowen, William J.								X
Bower, Andrew P.			X					
Boyce, Edward			X					
Boyle, William A.								X

Name	Category- (1) Dem.	(2) Rep.	(3) Soc.	(4) A/L	(5) N-P	(6) L-P	(7) CPA	(8) N/A
Brennan, Peter J.	X							
Breslaw, Joseph								X
Brewer, Roy M.	X							
Bridges, Harry A. R.								X
Brophy, John					X			
Broun, Heywood C.			X					
Brown, Edward J.								X
Brown, Guy L.								X
Brown, Harvey W.					X			
Brown, Henry S.	X							
Brown, Irving J.								X
Bryson, Hugh	X					X		
Buchanan, Joseph R.			X					
Buckley, Leo J.								X
Buckmaster, Leland S.	X							
Bugniazet, Gustave M.								X
Burke, John P.								X
Burke, Walter J.	X							
Burns, Matthew J.	X							
Burns, Thomas F.								X
Byron, Robert								X
Caddy, Samuel H.	X							
Cahan, Abraham			X					
Cairns, Thomas F.					X			
Calvin, William A.								X
Cameron, Andrew C.						X		
Cannon, Joseph D.			X	X				
Carey, James B.	X							
Carroll, Thomas C.	X							
Carter, William S.	X							
Cashen, Thomas C.	X							
Chapman, Gordon W.	X							
Chavez, Cesar E.	X				X			
Cheyfitz, Edward T.								X
Christman, Elisabeth	X							
Christopher, Paul R.	X							

Name	(1) Dem.	(2) Rep.	(3) Soc.	(4) A/L	(5) N-P	(6) L-P	(7) CPA	(8) N/A
Clark, Jesse		X			X			
Clark, John								X
Clark, Lewis J.	X							
Coefield, John								X
Cohn, Fannia								X
Collins, Jennie								X
Commerford, John	X	X				X		
Conlon, Peter J.			X					
Cook, Harry H.					X			
Cope, Elmer F.	X							
Cosgrove, John T.	X							
Coulter, Clarence C.	X							
Crosswaith, Frank R.			X	X				
Crull, John L.		X						
Curran, Joseph E.				X				
Dalrymple, Sherman H.	X							
Damino, Harry								X
Davidson, Roy E.	X							
Davis, James J.		X						
Davis, Richard L.								X
Debs, Eugene, V.	X		X			X		
Delaney, George P.	X							
DeLeon, Daniel			X					
Dennis, Eugene							X	
Derwent, Clarence								X
Devyr, Thomas A.		X				X		
Doak, William N.		X						
Dobbs, Farrel			X					
Doherty, William C.	X							
Donnelly, Michael						X		
Donnelly, Samuel B.		X						
Douglas, Charles	X					X		
Driscoll, John J.	X							
Dubinsky, David				X	X			
Duffy, Frank		X						
Duffy, James M.								X

Name	(1) Dem.	(2) Rep.	(3) Soc.	(4) A/L	(5) N-P	(6) L-P	(7) CPA	(8) N/A
Dullzell, Paul								X
Duncan, James					X			
Dunne, Vincent R.			X			X		
Dunwody, Thomas E.	X							
Durkin, Martin P.	X							
Dyche, John A.								X
Eames, Thomas B.					X			
Easton, John B.		X						
Eklund, John M.	X							
English, John F.								X
English, William						X		
Ernst, Hugo	X							
Ervin, Charles W.			X					
Ettor, Joseph J.			X					
Evans, George H.						X		
Farquhar, John M.		X						
Farrington, Frank								X
Feeney, Frank		X						
Feinberg, Israel				X				
Feinstone, Morris			X	X		X		
Feller, Karl F.	X							
Fenton, Francis P.	X							
Ferral, John						X		
Fincher, Jonathan C.								X
Fisher, Joseph A.								X
Fitzgerald, Albert J.						X		
Fitzgerald, Frank A.								X
Fitzpatrick, John	X					X		
Fitzsimmons, Frank E.		X						
Fljozdal, Frederick H.					X			
Flore, Edward	X							
Flynn, Elizabeth G.							X	
Foran, Martin A.	X							
Foster, William Z.			X				X	
Fox, Martin								X
Frankensteen, Richard T.	X							

Name	(1) Dem.	(2) Rep.	(3) Soc.	(4) A/L	(5) N-P	(6) L-P	(7) CPA	(8) N/A
Fraser, Harry W.								X
Frayne, Hugh					X			
Frey, John P.		X						
Furuseth, Andrew					X			
Gainor, Edward J.	X							
Galarza, Ernesto								X
Garretson, Austin B.								X
George, Leo E.								X
Germano, Joseph S.	X							
Germer, Adolph F.			X					
Gibbons, Harold J.	X		X					
Gibson, Everett G.	X							
Gibson, John W.		X						
Gilbert, Henry E.								X
Gillmore, Frank	X							
Giovannitti, Arturo			X					
Givens, Paul A.								X
Gleason, Thomas W.	X							
Gold, Ben						X		
Goldberg, Arthur J.	X							
Golden, Clinton S.					X			
Gompers, Samuel	X				X			
Googe, George L.	X							
Gorman, Patrick E.					X			
Gosser, Richard T.								X
Graham, Sylvester	X							
Gray, Richard J.		X						
Green, John	X							
Green, William	X							
Greenberg, Max	X							
Greene, Michael F.								X
Greene, Prince W.								X
Griner, John F.	X							
Grogan, John J.	X							
Hagerty, Thomas J.			X					
Haggerty, Cornelius J.	X							

Name	(1) Dem.	(2) Rep.	(3) Soc.	(4) A/L	(5) N-P	(6) L-P	(7) CPA	(8) N/A
Haggerty, John B.	X							
Haley, Margaret A.						X		
Hall, Paul	X							
Hallbeck, Elroy C.	X							
Hapgood, Powers			X					
Harrison, George M.	X							
Hartung, Albert F.	X							
Hayes, Albert J.								X
Hayes, Frank J.	X							
Hayes, Maximilian S.			X			X		
Haywood, William D.			X					
Heighton, William						X		
Helfgott, Simon				X				
Heller, George	X							
Heller, Jacob J.				X				
Helstein, Ralph	X							
Helt, Daniel W.		X			X			
Henderson, Donald J.							X	
Henry, Alice								X
Hickey, Thomas L.								X
Hill, Joe			X					
Hillman, Sidney	X		X	X				
Hillquit, Morris			X					
Hinchcliffe, John	X					X		
Hochman, Julius				X				
Hoffa, James R.		X						
Hoffmann, Sal B.	X							
Holderman, Carl	X							
Hollander, Louis	X			X				
Horn, Roy					X			
Howard, Charles P.		X						
Howat, Alexander			X			X		
Huber, William								X
Huddell, Arthur M.								X
Huerta, Dolores								X
Hughes, Roy A.					X			

Name	(1) Dem.	(2) Rep.	(3) Soc.	(4) A/L	(5) N-P	(6) L-P	(7) CPA	(8) N/A
Hutcheson, Maurice A.		X						
Hutcheson, William L.		X						
Hyman, Louis				X		X		
Iglesias, Santiago			X					
Irons, Martin								X
Jarrett, John		X						
Jennings, Paul J.				X				
Jessup, William J.								X
Jewell, Bert M.								X
Jimerson, Earl W.	X							
Johns, John S.	X							
Johnson, William D.	X							
Johnston, Alvanley		X						
Johnston, William H.				X		X		
Jones, Mary H.	X			X		X		
Kasten, Frank		X						
Kaufman, Morris			X					
Kavanagh, William F.	X							
Kazan, Abraham E.								X
Keating, Edward	X							
Keefe, Daniel J.		X						
Keenan, Joseph D.	X							
Keeney, C. Frank								X
Kehrer, Elmer T.	X							
Kelsay, Ray								X
Kenin, Herman D.								X
Kennedy, Thomas	X							
Kennedy, William P.	X							
Kirkland, Joseph L.	X							
Kirwan, James								X
Knight, Felix H.								X
Knight, Orie A.	X							
Kroll, John J.	X							
Krzycki, Leo			X					
Labadie, Joseph A.			X			X		
Lane, Dennis								X

Name	(1) Dem.	(2) Rep.	(3) Soc.	(4) A/L	(5) N-P	(6) L-P	(7) CPA	(8) N/A
Lawrenson, Jack				X				
Lawson, George W.	X					X		
Lawson, John C.								X
Lee, William G.		X						
Leighty, George E.	X							
Lennon, John B.	X							
Leonard, Richard	X							
Lewis, Alma D.		X						
Lewis, John L.		X						
Lewis, Joseph	X							
Lewis, Thomas L.		X						
Lindelof, Lawrence P.		X						
Litchman, Charles H.		X						
Little, Frank H.			X					
Livingston, John W.	X							
Lloyd, Thomas J.								X
London, Meyer			X					
Luhrsen, Julius G.		X						
Luna, Charles								X
Lundeberg, Harry		X						
Luther, Seth								X
Lyden, Michael J.	X							
Lynch, James M.	X							
Lyon, Arlon E.								X
Lyons, John H.								X
McAvoy, Harold								X
McBride, John	X		X			X		
McCarthy, Patrick H.		X						
McCurdy, Joseph P.	X							
McDevitt, James L.	X							
McDonald, David J.	X							
McDonald, Joseph D.	X							
McDonnell, J. P.			X					
McFetridge, William L.		X						
McGowan, Charles J.	X							
McGrady, Edward F.	X							

Name	(1) Dem.	(2) Rep.	(3) Soc.	(4) A/L	(5) N-P	(6) L-P	(7) CPA	(8) N/A
McGuire, Peter J.			X					
McMahon, Thomas F.	X							
McNamara, Patrick V.	X							
NcNeill, George E.						X		
McNulty, Frank J.	X							
McSorley, William J.					X			
Maguire, Matthew			X					
Mahon, William D.	X							
Mahoney, Charles E.				X		X		
Mahoney, William								X
Maloney, James								X
Maloney, William E.								X
Maloy, Elmer J.	X							
Marciante, Louis P.	X							
Marot, Helen								X
Martin, Harry L.	X							
Martin, Warren H.	X							
Mashburn, Lloyd A.		X						
Maso, Sal					X			
Mason, Lucy R.								X
Mathias, Charles G.	X							
Maurer, James H.			X					
Mazey, Emil	X					X		
Meany, George	X							
Megel, Carl J.								X
Mendelowitz, Abraham				X				
Merrill, Lewis R.				X				
Miller, Edward S.	X							
Miller, Marvin J.	X							
Milliman, Elmer E.								X
Milne, J. Scott								X
Minton, Lee W.		X						
Mitch, William A.	X							
Mitchell, Harry L.	X		X					
Mitchell, James J.								X
Mitchell, John					X			

Name	(1) Dem.	(2) Rep.	(3) Soc.	(4) A/L	(5) N-P	(6) L-P	(7) CPA	(8) N/A
Mitchell, Walter L.	X							
Moffett, Elwood S.	X							
Mohn, Einar O.	X							
Molony, Joseph P.	X							
Montgomery, Robert	X	X						
Mooney, Thomas J.			X					
Moore, Ely	X							
Moran, John J.								X
Moreschi, Joseph								X
Morgan, Thomas J.			X					
Morreale, Vincent F.	X							
Morrison, Frank					X			
Mortimer, Wyndham			X					
Moyer, Charles H.			X			X		
Mullaney, Joseph A.	X							
Murphy, Vincent	X					X		
Murray, Philip	X							
Murray, Thomas A.	X							
Muste, Abraham J.			X					
Myrup, Andrew A.								X
Nagler, Isidore				X				
Nance, Alexander S.	X							
Nef, Walter T.			X					
Nelson, Oscar F.	X	X						
Nestor, Agnes	X							
Newman, Pauline			X	X				
Ninfo, Salvatore				X				
Nockles, Edward N.	X					X		
Noonan, James P.								X
Oakes, Grant W.	X					X		
Obergfell, Joseph F.								X
O'Connell, James P.	X							
O'Connor, Harvey			X					
O'Connor, Thomas V.		X						
O'Hare, John	X							
Ohl, Henry			X			X		

Name	(1) Dem.	(2) Rep.	(3) Soc.	(4) A/L	(5) N-P	(6) L-P	(7) CPA	(8) N/A
Olander, Victor A.								X
O'Neill, John M.			X					
Ornburn, Ira M.								X
Owen, Robert D.	X					X		
Pachler, William J.	X							
Padway, Joseph A.			X			X		
Parsons, Albert R.			X					
Perkins, George W.								X
Perlstein, Meyer	X							
Peterson, Eric					X			
Peterson, Esther	X							
Petrillo, James C.	X							
Phillips, James A.	X		X					
Phillips, Paul L.	X							
Phillips, Thomas						X		
Pine, Max			X					
Pizer, Morris				X				
Pollock, William								X
Possehl, John	X							
Potofsky, Jacob S.	X		X	X				
Powderly, Terence V.		X						
Powers, Frank B.	X							
Pressman, Lee	X			X		X	X	
Preston, George								X
Price, George M.								X
Quill, Michael J.				X				
Raftery, Lawrence M.	X							
Ramsay, Claude	X							
Randolph, Asa P.			X	X				
Randolph, Woodruff								X
Rarick, Donald C.	X							
Ratchford, Michael D.		X						
Reagan, Ronald	X	X						
Redmond, John P.								X
Reuther, Roy	X							
Reuther, Victor	X		X					

Name	(1) Dem.	(2) Rep.	(3) Soc.	(4) A/L	(5) N-P	(6) L-P	(7) CPA	(8) N/A
Reuther, Walter P.	X		X					
Rickert, Thomas A.					X			
Rieve, Emil	X			X				
Robertson, David B.					X			
Robins, Margaret D.	X	X				X		
Robinson, Reid						X		
Rollings, John I.	X							
Rombro, Jacob			X					
Romualdi, Serafino								X
Roney, Frank			X			X		
Rose, Alex			X	X				
Rosenblum, Frank								X
Ruttenberg, Harold J.								X
Ryan, Joseph P.	X							
Ryan, Martin F.								X
St. John, Vincent			X					
Sargent, Frank P.		X						
Schilling, Robert	X							
Schlesinger, Benjamin			X					
Schlossberg, Joseph			X					
Schneiderman, Rose	X		X	X		X		
Schnitzler, William F.	X							
Schoemann, Peter T.	X							
Schoenberg, William								X
Scholle, August	X							
Scott, Sam H.	X							
Scully, John J. J.	X							
Sefton, Lawrence F.			X					
Selden, David S.	X							
Shanker, Albert			X	X				
Shelley, John F.	X							
Sherman, Charles O.			X					
Shields, James P.								X
Siemiller, Paul L.	X							
Sigman, Morris			X					
Siney, John						X		

Name	(1) Dem.	(2) Rep.	(3) Soc.	(4) A/L	(5) N-P	(6) L-P	(7) CPA	(8) N/A
Skidmore, Thomas		X				X		
Slamm, Levi D.	X					X		
Soderstrom, Reuben C.		X						
Sorge, Friedrick A.		X	X					
Spradling, Abe L.								X
Starr, Mark				X				
Stephens, Uriah S.		X				X		
Steward, Ira						X		
Stokes, Rose H. P.			X				X	
Stone, Warren S.						X		
Strasser, Adolph			X					
Stulberg, Louis	X							
Suffridge, James A.		X						
Sullivan, David	X							
Sullivan, James W.								X
Sullivan, Jere L.								X
Swartz, Maud O.								X
Sweeney, Vincent D.								X
Swinton, John			X		X			
Swisher, Elwood D.								X
Sylvis, William H.	X					X		
Tahney, James P.								X
Talbot, Thomas W.								X
Tetlow, Percy		X						
Thimmes, James G.	X							
Thomas, Norman M.			X					
Thomas, Rolland J.	X							
Tighe, Michael F.	X							
Tobin, Daniel J.	X							
Totten, Ashley L.				X				
Townsend, Robert, Jr.						X		
Townsend, Willard S.								X
Tracy, Daniel W.	X							
Trautmann, William E.			X					
Travis, Maurice E.							X	
Travis, Robert C.	X							

Name	(1) Dem.	(2) Rep.	(3) Soc.	(4) A/L	(5) N-P	(6) L-P	(7) CPA	(8) N/A
Trevellick, Richard F.						X		
Troup, Augusta L.								X
Turner, Frederick								X
Valentine, Joseph F.								X
Van Arsdale, Harry, Jr.	X							
Vladeck, Baruch C.			X	X				
Vorse, Mary H.								X
Walker, John H.	X		X			X		
Walsh, Richard F.	X							
Watt, Robert J.					X			
Weaver, George L. P.	X							
Weber, Frank J.			X					
Weber, Joseph N.								X
Weihe, William	X	X						
Werkau, Carlton W.	X							
Wharton, Arthur O.								X
White, John P.								X
Whitfield, Owen H.								X
Whitney, Alexander F.	X							
Williams, Benjamin H.			X					
Williams, Elijah H.	X							
Wilson, D. Douglas			X					
Wilson, James A.								X
Wilson, William B.	X					X		
Windt, John	X					X		
Wolchok, Samuel	X			X				
Woll, Matthew		X						
Wood, Reuben T.	X		X					
Woodcock, Leonard F.	X							
Wright, James L.						X		
Wurf, Jerry	X							
Yablonski, Joseph A.	X							
Zander, Arnold S.	X							
Zaritsky, Max				X				
Zimmerman, Charles S.				X				

Appendix VI

Major Appointive and Elective Public Offices

This Appendix is divided into three major categories: U.S. government, state governments, and local governments. The year when the individual took office is listed.

UNITED STATES GOVERNMENT

Name	Year	Position
Alpine, John P.	1931	Assistant Secretary of Labor
Anderson, Mary	1920	Director of the Women's Bureau, Labor Dept.
Brennan, Peter J.	1972	Secretary of Labor
Chapman, Gordon W.	1961	Assistant to the Secretary of State
Davis, James J.	1921	Secretary of Labor
Delaney, George P.	1963	Director, Office of Labor Affairs, Agency for International Development
Doak, William N.	1930	Secretary of Labor
Doherty, William C.	1962	Ambassador to Jamaica
Donnelly, Samuel B.	1908	Public Printer
Durkin, Martin P.	1953	Secretary of Labor
Gibson, John W.	1945	Assistant Secretary of Labor
Goldberg, Arthur J.	1961	Secretary of Labor
Goldberg, Arthur J.	1962	Associate Justice, U.S. Supreme Court
Goldberg, Arthur J.	1965	Ambassador to the United Nations
Jarrett, John	1889	American Consul to Birmingham, England
Keefe, Daniel J.	1909	Commissioner General of Immigration
Litchman, Charles H.	1889	Special Agent, Treasury Department
McGrady, Edward F.	1933	Assistant Secretary of Labor
Mashburn, Lloyd A.	1953	Undersecretary of Labor
Moore, Ely	1845	U.S. Marshall
Nelson, Oscar F.	1917	Commissioner of Conciliation
O'Connor, Thomas V.	1921	Chairman, U.S. Shipping Board
Ornburn, Ira M.	1930	Member, U.S. Tariff Commission
Owen, Robert D.	1853	Charge d'Affairs to Naples
Owen, Robert D.	1854	Minister Resident, Naples
Peterson, Esther	1961	Assistant Secretary of Labor
Peterson, Esther	1964	Special Presidential Assistant on Consumer Affairs
Powderly, Terence V.	1897	Commissioner General of Immigration
Sargent, Frank P.	1902	Commissioner General of Immigration
Tracy, Daniel W.	1940	Assistant Secretary of Labor
Weaver, George L. P.	1961	Assistant Secretary of Labor for International Affairs

Weihe, William   1896 Deputy Immigration Inspector
Wilson, William V.   1913 Secretary of Labor

UNITED STATES CONGRESS

Name	Year	Position
Berger, Victor L.	1911	Representative
Berry, George L.	1937	Senator
Biemiller, Andrew J.	1945	Representative
Davis, James J.	1930	Senator
Farquhar, John M.	1885	Representative
Foran, Martin A.	1883	Representative
Iglesias, Santiago	1933	Representative (non-voting)
Keating, Edward	1913	Representative
London, Meyer	1915	Representative
McNamara, Patrick V.	1955	Senator
McNulty, Frank J.	1923	Representative
Owen, Robert D.	1843	Representative
Wilson, William B.	1907	Representative
Wood, Reuben T.	1933	Representative

STATE GOVERNMENTS

Name	Year	Position
Durkin, Martin P.	1933	Illinois State Director of Labor
Hayes, Frank J.	1937	Lieutenant Governor - Colorado
Holderman, Carl	1954	New Jersey Commissioner of Labor and Industry
Lynch, James M.	1914	New York Commissioner of Labor
Kennedy, Thomas	1935	Lieutenant Governor - Pennsylvania
Mahon, William D.	1898	Presiding Judge, Michigan State Court of Arbitration
Mashburn, Lloyd A.	1951	Labor Commissioner of California
Ratchford, Michael D.	1900	Ohio Commissioner of Labor Statistics
Schneiderman, Rose	1933	Secretary, New York State Department of Labor

Reagan, Ronald   1967 Governor - California
Swartz, Maud O.   1931 Secretary, New York State Department of Labor

STATE LEGISLATURES

Name	Year	Position
Barry, Thomas B.	1885	Representative - Michigan
Biemiller, Andrew J.	1937	Representative - Wisconsin
Boyce, Edward	1895	Representative - Idaho
Debs, Eugene V.	1885	Representative - Indiana
Easton, John B.	1927	Representative - West Virginia
English, William	1837	Representative - Pennsylvania
Fincher, Jonathan C.	1877	Representative - Pennsylvania
Green, William	1910	Senator - Ohio
Grogan, John J.	1943	Representative - New Jersey
Helt, Daniel W.	1917	Representative - Pennsylvania
Hinchcliffe, John	1873	Representative - Illinois
Iglesias, Santiago	1917	Senator - Puerto Rico
Litchman, Charles H.	1879	Representative - Massachusetts
McGrady, Edward F.		Representative - Massachusetts
Maurer, James H.	1911	Representative - Pennsylvania
Ohl, Henry	1917	Representative - Wisconsin
O'Neill, John M.		Representative - Colorado
Owen, Robert D.	1835	Representative - Indiana
Padway, Joseph A.	1925	Representative - Wisconsin
Shelley, John F.	1939	Senator - California
Soderstrom, Reuben G.	1917	Representative - Illinois
Tetlow, Percy	1913	Representative - Ohio
Weber, Frank J.	1907	Representative - Wisconsin
Weihe, William	1883	Representative - Pennsylvania

CITY GOVERNMENT

Name	Year	Position
Berger, Victor L.	1910	Alderman-at-Large-Milwaukee, Wis.

Foran, Martin A.	1911	Judge-Cleveland (Ohio) Court of Common Pleas
Grogan, John J.	1953	Mayor-Hoboken, N.J.
Kasten, Frank	1929	Mayor-Blue Island, Ill.
McCarthy, Patrick H.	1909	Mayor-San Francisco, Calif.
Mahoney, William	1933	Mayor-St. Paul, Minn.
Maloy, Elmer J.	1937	Mayor-Duquesne, Pa.
Moore, Ely	1839	Surveyor of the Port of New York City
Murphy, Vincent	1941	Mayor-Newark, N.J.
Nelson, Oscar F.	1923	Chicago City Council
Nelson, Oscar F.	1935	Judge-Chicago Superior Court
Ninfo, Salvatore	1937	City Council-New York City
Padway, Joseph A.	1925	Milwaukee (Wis.) County Civil Court
Powderly, Terence V.	1879	Mayor-Scranton, Pa.
Quill, Michael J.	1937	City Council-New York City
Shelley, John F.	1964	Mayor-San Francisco, Calif.
Vladeck, Baruch C.	1917	Board of Alderman-New York City
Vladeck, Baruch C.	1937	City Council-New York City

Index

About the Editors

Gary M Fink is an Associate Professor of History at Georgia State University, Atlanta. He has published *Labor's Search for Political Order* (1974) and numerous labor-related articles. Professor Fink is currently writing a history of the Congress of Industrial Organizations.

Milton Cantor is Professor of History at the University of Massachusetts, Amherst. He has published *Max Eastman* (1970) and currently is the managing editor of *Labor History.*

John Hevener is an Associate Professor of History at Mankato State College, Mankato, Minnesota. His recently completed study of the coal mining organizing wars of Harlan County, Kentucky, will be published by the University of Illinois Press.

Merl E. Reed is a Professor of History at Georgia State University, Atlanta. Besides numerous articles, he has written *New Orleans and the Railroads: The Struggle for Commercial Empire, 1830-1860* (1966). Professor Reed is the principal founder of the Southern Labor Archives at Georgia State University.

Donald G. Sofchalk is a Professor of History at Mankato State College, Mankato, Minnesota. A frequent contributor to scholarly journals, he is completing two mansucripts: a study of the Little Steel Strike of 1937 and a history of labor organizing on the Mesabi Iron Range.

Marie Tedesco is a graduate student at Georgia State University, Atlanta. She is writing her dissertation in the area of women's history.